LEX REX:

THE LAW IS KING

Published by Canon Press
P.O. Box 8729, Moscow, Idaho 83843
800.488.2034 | www.canonpress.com

Samuel Rutherford, *Lex Rex: The Law is King*
This Christian Heritage Series first edition copyright ©2020.
First published in 1644; modernized text.

Cover design by James Engerbretson
Cover illustration by Forrest Dickison
Interior design by Valerie Anne Bost and James Engerbretson

Printed in the United States of America.

Library of Congress Cataloging-in-Publication Data forthcoming

20 21 22 23 24 25   10 9 8 7 6 5 4 3 2 1

LEX REX:
THE LAW IS KING

BY SAMUEL RUTHERFORD

With an Introduction by Douglas Wilson

CONTENTS

INTRODUCTION

S amuel Rutherford was a great man of God. Not only so, but he was a man of God who exhibited great breadth of mind. This is simply another way of saying that he was not one who could be easily pigeon-holed.

If your only acquaintance with him came through his famous *Letters of Samuel Rutherford*, you would naturally conclude that he was a devotional writer of great piety, authority, and force. And someone once went through those *Letters* and pulled out a number of devotional gems, publishing them separately as *The Loveliness of Christ*. So if you read only *that*, you would conclude that Rutherford was a devotional writer of great genius.

And then if you picked up this book with that impression fixed in place, you would be startled to discover that you were also dealing with a tough-minded theologian and political theorist of the first rank. This might make you suspicious, and so you start to research some of his other activities, expecting to find out that he was also somehow an Olympic tri-athlete, and a world-class violinist. And a Navy SEAL. You know, *that* kind of person . . .

That is exaggeration. But it is true that Rutherford was a practical and pastoral theologian who could soar to great heights of glorious consolation. Rutherford was the one who said that when he was in the cellar of affliction, he would look for Christ's choicest wines. He also said that "dry wells send us to the fountain," and "if contentment were here, heaven were not heaven," and "there are many heads lying in Christ's bosom, but there is room for yours among the rest."

But Rutherford was also a bare-knuckle brawler who was clearly able to hold his own in the theological bar fight that was the seventeenth century. You are now holding in your hands the evidence of that.

Rutherford was one of the Scottish commissioners who attended the Westminster Assembly (1643-1649), and he was a major contributor to the famous Shorter Catechism. While serving as part of that Westminster Assembly, he also wrote this incendiary book. The title, as you no doubt noticed, is *Lex Rex*, which can be rendered as *The Law of the King*, or *The Law and the King*, or perhaps *The Law Is King*. Either way, the import of the book was that even the king must obey the law, because the king is also under the law. It is therefore not surprising that some who were in positions of authority took a dim view of his thesis.

After the interruption that was Cromwell, when Charles II returned to the throne in the Restoration, this book of Rutherford's was burned by the public hangman, indicating some marked level of official disapproval. Rutherford himself was summoned to appear before Parliament on the most serious charge of treason, but Rutherford was already on his deathbed when the summons came to him. This gave him the opportunity to deliver one of the best comebacks ever, at least if it was directed at political authorities who were intent on executing you.

> I have got a summons already before a superior judge and judicatory, and I behoove to answer my first summons, and ere your day come I will be where few kings and great folks come.

In the early 1980s, Francis Schaeffer wrote a book entitled *The Christian Manifesto*, and one of the points he made regarded the necessity of modern Christians coming to learn from the great Samuel Rutherford.

> Rutherford presents several arguments to establish the right and duty of resistance to unlawful government. First, since tyranny is satanic, not to resist it is to resist God— to resist tyranny is to honor God. Second, since the ruler is granted power conditionally, it follows that the people have the power to withdraw their sanction if the proper conditions are not fulfilled. The civil magistrate is a 'fiduciary figure'—that is, he holds his authority in trust for the people. Violation of the trust gives the people a legitimate base for resistance[1]

For Schaeffer, this was no academic question. What Rutherford was confronting and what we are dealing with today are the same. It is "exactly what we are facing today." And when we look at the issues that Schaeffer was considering the early eighties, and then consider *our* issues, we are brought to the point where we must say the root issues are exactly the same.

---

1. *The Complete Works of Francis Schaeffer, Vol. 5, A Christian Manifesto,* (Wheaton: Crossway, 1981), 474.

As preparations to bring this book back into print were being made, our nation was in a great deal of turmoil because of our presidential politics, because of impeachment, because of the coronavirus scare, because of the Black Lives Matter riots, and because of the feckless responses of many of our civil magistrates to all of this.

One of the most distressing things about all of it, however, was how much the political turmoil and overreach by authorities revealed about the ignorance of American Christians concerning their own political theology. Protestant Christians do have a long heritage when it comes to church/state relations (and this book is an essential part of that heritage), but we have been keeping this piece of legacy furniture in the attic for so long that it appears that most of us have forgotten completely about it.

For example, when governors and mayors ordered everyone to start wearing masks, numerous Christians simply assumed that the powers of an American governor were identical to those of an ancient Roman proconsul or worse, a Persian satrap. If someone who is in charge gives you what *looks* like a lawful order, then doesn't Romans 13 require us to obey that order, and with no backchat?

The answer is *no*. Not only is the answer *no*, but it is a thoroughly biblical *no*. It is an obedient *no*, not a disobedient *no*. But in order to be instructed in the reasons for such a response, you have to be prepared to work through books like this one.

Even a cursory acquaintance with Scripture should tell us that blind obedience must not be the whole story. It is true that the apostle Peter told us to submit ourselves to every ordinance of man for the Lord's sake, whether to the king or his governors (1 Pet. 2:13-14). But this was the same man

who escaped from jail with the help of an angel (Acts 12:7ff),
resulting in the execution of the guards, and who disappeared
from the book of Acts as a wanted man. According to church
history, he was finally executed by Rome. It is true that the
apostle Paul told us that God established our civic authorities (Rom. 13:1-7), and that trying to overthrow them was
rebellion against God. But this was the same man who evaded
being arrested by King Aretas (2 Cor. 11:32-33), and who also
was executed by Rome as a threat to their established order.

There was not a man in Saul's kingdom who had a higher
view of what it meant to be the Lord's anointed than David. When Saul came into the cave where David and his men
were hiding, David was urged to take Saul's life, which he
resolutely refused to do. But he did cut off a corner of Saul's
cloak, and his conscience even struck him for having done
that much. No one honored Saul more than David did (1 Sam.
24:5). And yet it has to be admitted that David spent quite
a bit of time running around the countryside with an armed
band (1 Sam. 23:26), resolutely not complying with Saul's ar-
dent wishes. Multiple examples of this sort are to be found in
the scriptural narrative.

But there is yet another layer to all of this. When Rutherford was presenting his arguments, they were straight from
the Bible and in his era they collided with a theology that was
ostensibly Christian, but alien to the Bible—that theology being called the "divine right of kings." We must be careful here
because Rutherford certainly believed that kings were established by God, and that they were accountable to Him. Rutherford's adversaries also believed the same, but they believed
that the king was accountable to God *and to no other*. Rutherford believed that the accountability of the king was not just
directly to God, but was also mediated by God through other

instruments, and the will of the people had to be included among those instruments.

And this brings us to the additional "layer" that I mentioned above. Although the contest was hot during the course of Rutherford's life, it has to be acknowledged that Rutherford's view *prevailed* in the development of the Western democracies. His teaching was later secularized (and thereby was corrupted), but the foundation of his political theory was resolutely biblical. As Douglas Kelly and others have capably demonstrated, the political thought of Calvin (and Knox, Rutherford, et al.) was instrumental in the formation of our political heritage.[1]

Rutherford held that the people were the "fountain-power" of political authority, and that they were the ones who delegated this authority to the magistrates. He also demonstrated that when such authority was abused, the people had the authority to rescind that delegation. This kind of thinking was evident in Book IV of Calvin's *Institutes*, in *Vindiciae Contra Tyrannos*, which was the work of "Junius Brutus" (a 16th century French Huguenot), John Knox and the Scottish Presbyterians, Oliver Cromwell and company, the English Puritans, and, of course, Samuel Rutherford.

This thinking shows up in phrases that we are very familiar with, phrases like "We the people . . ." Where did that come from? Among other places, it came from Samuel Rutherford.

Consider what is contained in the Idaho State Constitution:

> Political power inherent in the people. *All political power is inherent in the people.* Government is instituted for their equal protection and benefit, and *they have the right*

---

1. Douglas Kelly, *The Emergence of Liberty in the Modern World* (Phillipsburg, NJ: Presbyterian & Reformed, 1992).

to alter, reform or abolish the same whenever they may deem it necessary; and no special privileges or immunities shall ever be granted that may not be altered, revoked, or repealed by the legislature" (Article 1, Section 2, emphasis mine).

Thanks to Rutherford, and a long line of faithful Christians with him who made this same point time and again, this conviction is an essential part of our political legacy. More than that, it is embedded in our foundational *law*.

And this means that when modern Christians exhort us to do *"whatever* the governor says," and they do this in the name of obeying Romans 13, the irony is that they are violating Romans 13 as they do this. The duty of the people to resist unlawful encroachments of those who hold office is a duty that every citizen is a part of. To say that the people do *not* have the right to do this is to kick against our established constitutional authorities.

A lot of what is going on in the name of government today is actually nothing more than well-organized disobedience. This state of constitutional disarray did not happen overnight—many decades, many lies, many controversies, and many court decisions were involved in it. But one of the central reasons why this state of affairs has developed, and has gotten as bad as it has, has been the neglect of political theology by Christians.

Fortunately, we have older brothers who can encourage and teach us across the centuries. One blessing that we have been given in this generation has been the blessing of the digital revolution when it comes to publishing—and this has been a great blessing that has enabled us to reach back into the past in order to bring older encouragements back to life. If you are holding this book in hard copy, then that means that you have other resources available as well. *Vindiciae Contra Tyrannos*, mentioned earlier, has been republished by Canon Press as part of this same series, and *Calvin's Institutes, Book IV*, is also available.

It is hard to imagine anything more timely.

Douglas Wilson
Christ Church

THE AUTHOR'S PREFACE

Who doubts, Christian Reader, that innocence must be under the courtesy and mercy of malice, and that it is a real martyrdom to be brought under the lawless inquisition of the bloody tongue. Christ, the prophets, and apostles of our Lord went to heaven marked as traitors, seditious men, and such as turned the world upside down: accusations of treason to Caesar were an ingredient in Christ's cup, and therefore the author is the more willing to drink of that cup that touched his lip, who is our glorious Forerunner. What! If conscience toward God and credit with men cannot both go to heaven with the saints, the author is satisfied with the former companion and is willing to dismiss the other. Truth to Christ cannot be treason to Caesar, and for his choice he judges truth to have a nearer relation to Christ Jesus than the transcendent and boundless power of a mortal prince.

The author considered that popery and defection had made a large step in Britain, and that arbitrary government had over-swelled all banks of law, that it was now at the highest float, and that this sea approaching the farthest border of fancied absoluteness was at the point of ebbing, and the naked truth is that prelates, a wild and pushing cattle to the lambs and flock of Christ, had made a hideous noise, the wheels of their chariot did run an equal pace with the blood-thirsty mind of the daughter of Babel. Prelacy, the daughter planted in her mother's blood, must verify that word. As is the mother, so is the daughter. Why, do not the prelates now suffer? True, but their sufferings are not of blood, or kindred, to the calamities of these of whom Lactantius says "*O quam honesta voluntate miseri errant!*"[1] (*De Justitia*, 5.19) The causes of their suffering are hope of gain and glory, steering their helm to a shore they much desire, even to a church of gold, of purple, yet really of clay and earth; the lie is more active upon the spirits of men, not because of its own wickedness, but because men are more passive in receiving the impressions of error than truth; and opinions lying in the world's fat womb, or of a conquering nature; whatever notions side with the world, to prelates and men of their make are very efficacious.

There is another cause of the sickness of our time, God plagued heresy to beget Atheism and security, as atheism and security had begotten heresy; even as clouds through reciprocation of causes engender rain, rain begot vapors, vapors clouds, and clouds rain, so do sins overspread our sad times in a circular generation.

And now judgment presses the kingdoms, and of all the heaviest judgments the sword, and of swords the civil sword, threatens devastation, yet not, I hope, like the Roman civil sword, of which it was said,

Bella geri placuit nullos habitura triumphos.[2]

I hope this war shall be Christ's triumph, Babylon's ruin.

That which moved the author was not (as my excommunicate adversary like a Thraso says) the escapes of some pens,

---

1. All Latin and Greek translations which we have added in brackets.

2. Lucan, *The Civil War* 1.12.

which demanded that he write, for many before me have learnedly trodden in this path, but so that I might add a new testimony to the times.

I have not time to examine the Popish Prelate's[3] preface: I only give a taste of his gall in this preface, and of a virulent piece, of his *agnosco stylum et genium Thrasonis,*[4] in which he labors to prove how inconsistent presbyterian government is with monarchy, or any other government.

1. He denies that the crown and scepter is under any co-active power of pope or presbytery, or censurable, or dethronable; to which we say, presbyteries profess that kings are under the co-active power of Christ's keys of discipline, and that prophets and pastors, as ambassadors of Christ, have the keys of the kingdom of God, to open and let in believing princes, and also to shut them out, if they rebel against Christ; the law of Christ excepts none (Mat. 16:19; 18:15-16; 2 Cor. 10:6; Jer. 1:9) if the king's sins may be remitted in a ministerial way (as Job 20:23-24) as prelates and their priests absolve kings; we think they may be bound by the hand that loosed; presbyteries never dethroned kings, never usurped that power. Your father, Popish Prelate, has dethroned many kings; I mean the Pope, whose power by your own confession differs from yours by divine right only in extent (section 5).

2. When sacred hierarchy, the order instituted by Christ, is overthrown, what is the condition of sovereignty? Ans. Surer than before, when prelates deposed kings. 2. I fear Christ shall never own this order.

3. The miter cannot suffer, and the diadem be secured. Ans. Have kings no pillars to their thrones but antichristian

---

3. Archbishop John Maxwell of Tuam wrote *Sacro-Sancta Regum Majestas* in defense of royal absolutism.

4. Thraso was the God of over-boldness or insolence.

prelates? Prelates have trampled diadem and scepter under their feet, as histories teach us.

4. Do they not (puritans) magisterially determine that kings are not of God's creation by authoritative commission, but only by permission, extorted by importunity, and way given, that they may be a scourge to a sinful people? Ans. Any unclean spirit from hell could not speak a blacker lie. We hold that the king by office is the church's nurse father, a sacred ordinance, the deputed power of God, but by the Prelate's way all inferior judges and God's deputies on earth, who are also our fathers in the fifth commandment style are to be obeyed by no divine law; the king, misled by popish prelates, shall forbid to obey them, who is in downright truth, a mortal civil pope, may loose and liberate subjects from the tie of a divine law.

5. His inveighing against ruling elders, and the rooting out of antichristian prelacy without any word of Scripture on the contrary I pass as the extravagancy of a malcontent, because he is deservedly excommunicated for perjury, popery, Socinianism, tyranny over men's conscience, and invading places of civil dignity, and deserting his calling, and the camp of Christ, &c.

6. None were of old anointed but kings, priests, and prophets; who then is more obliged to maintain the Lord's anointed than priests and prophets? The church has never more beauty and plenty under any government than monarchy, which is most countenanced by God, and magnified by Scripture. Ans. Pastors are to maintain the rights of people and a true church no less than the right of kings; but prelates, the court parasites, and creatures of the king that are born for the glory of their king can do no less than profess this in words, yet it is true that Tacitus writes of such *Libentius cum fortuna principis, quam cum principe loquuntur*, and it is true that the church has had plenty under kings, not so much because they

were kings, as because they were godly and zealous, except the Popish Prelate says that the oppressing kings of Israel and Judah, and the bloody horns that made war with the lamb, are not kings. In the rest of the epistle he extols the Marquis of Ormond with base flattery, from his loyalty to the king and his more than admirable prudence in the treaty of cessation with the rebels; a woe is due to this false prophet, who calls darkness light, for the former was abominable and perfidious apostasy from the Lord's cause and people of God, whom he once defended, and the cessation was a selling of the blood of many hundred thousand Protestants, men, women, and sucking children.

This cursed Prelate has written of late a treatise against the presbyterian government of Scotland, in which there is a bundle of lies, hellish calumnies, and gross errors.

1. The first lie is that we have lay elders, but they are such as rule but labor not in the word and doctrine (1 Tim. 5:7).

2. The second lie is that deacons who only attend tables are joint rulers with pastors.

3. That we never, or rarely, use the lesser excommunication, that is, debarring from the Lord's Supper.

4. That any church judicature in Scotland exacts pecuniary mulcts, and threatens excommunication to the non-payers, and refuses to accept the repentance of any who are not able to pay: the civil magistrate only fines for drunkenness, and adultery, blaspheming of God, which are frequent sins in prelates.

5. A calumny it is to say that ruling elders are of equal authority to preach the word as pastors.

6. That laymen are members of presbyteries or general assemblies. Buchanan and Mr. Melvin were doctors of divinity; and could have taught such an ass as John Maxwell.

7. That expectants are intruders upon the sacred function, because, as sons of the prophets, they exercise their gifts for trial in preaching.

8. That the presbytery of Edinburgh has a superintending power, because they communicate the affairs of the church and write to the churches what they hear prelates and hell devise against Christ and his church.

9. That the king must submit his scepter to the presbytery; the king's scepter is his royal office, which is not subject to any judicature, no more than any lawful ordinance of Christ; but if the king as a man blaspheme God, murder the innocent, advance belly-gods (such as our prelates for the most part were) above the Lord's inheritance, the ministers of Christ are to say, "The king troubles Israel, and they have the keys to open and shut heaven to, and upon the king, if he can offend."

10. It is true that king James said a Scottish presbytery and a monarchy agree as well as God and the devil, but king James meant of a wicked king; else he spoke as a man.

11. That the presbytery out of pride refused to answer king James's honorable messengers is a lie; they could not in business of high concernment return a present answer to a prince, seeking still to abolish presbyteries.

12. It is a lie that all sins, even all civil business, come under the cognizance of the church, for only sins that are publicly scandalous fall under their power (Matt. 18:15-17, &c.; 2 Thess. 3:11; 1 Tim. 5:20). It is a calumny that they search out secret crimes or that they ever disgraced the innocent, or divided families; where there be flagrant scandals and pregnant suspicions of scandalous crimes, they search out these, as the incest of Spotswood, Popish Prelate of St Andrews, with his own daughter; the adulteries of Whiteford, Popish Prelate of Brichen, whose bastard came weeping to the assembly of

Glasgow in the arms of the prostitute: these they searched out, but not with the damnable oath, *ex officio* [in their office] that the high commission put upon innocents, to cause them accuse themselves against the law of nature.

13. The presbytery hinder not lawful merchandise; scandalous exhortation and unjust suits of law they may forbid; and so does the Scripture, as scandalous to Christians, 2 Cor. 6.

14. They repeal no civil laws; they preach against unjust and grievous laws, as, Isaiah does (10:1), and censure the violation of God's holy day, which prelates profaned.

15. We know no parochial popes, we turn out no holy ministers, but only dumb dogs, non-residents, scandalous, wretched, and apostate prelates.

16. Our moderator has no dominion, the Popish Prelate absolves him, while he says, "All is done in our church by common consent."

17. It is true, we have no popish consecration, such as Popish Prelate contends for in the mass, but we have such as Christ and his apostles used, in consecrating the elements.

18. If any sell the patrimony of the church, the presbytery censures him; if any take buds of malt, meal, beef, it is no law with us, no more than the bishop's five hundred marks or a year's stipend that the entrant gave to the Lord Bishop for a church. And whoever took buds in these days (as king James by the earl of Dunbar did buy episcopacy at a pretended assembly by foul budding) they were either men for the episcopal way, or perfidiously against their oath became bishops, all personal faults of this kind imputed to presbyteries agree to them under the reduplication of episcopal men.

19. The leading men that covered the sins of the dying man, and so lost his soul, were episcopal men, and though some men were presbyterians, the faults of men cannot prejudice the

truth of God, but the prelates always cry out against the rigor of presbyteries in censuring scandals; because they themselves do ill, they hate the light; now here the Prelate condemns them of remissness in discipline.

20. Satan, a liar from the beginning, says, The presbytery was a seminary and nursery of fiends, contentions, and bloods, because they excommunicated murderers against king James' will; which is all one to say, prophesying is a nurse of bloods, because the prophets cried out against king Ahab, and the murderers of innocent Naboth: the men of God must be either on the one side or the other, or then preach against reciprocation of injuries.

21. It is false that presbyteries usurp both swords because they censure sins which the civil magistrate should censure and punish. Elijah might be said then to mix himself with the civil business of the kingdom because be prophesied against idolaters' killing of the Lord's prophets, a crime which the civil magistrate was to punish. But the truth is the assembly of Glasgow, 1637, condemned the prelates, because they being pastors would also be lords of parliament, of session, of secret council, of exchequer, judges, barons, and in their lawless high commission would fine, imprison, and use the sword.

22. It is his ignorance that he says a provincial synod is an associate body chosen out of all judicial presbyteries, for all pastors and doctors without delegation by virtue of their place and office repair to the provincial synods and without any choice at all consult and voice there.

23. It is a lie that some leading men rule all here; indeed, episcopal men made factions to rent the synods, and though men abuse their power to factions, this cannot prove that presbyteries are inconsistent with monarchy; for then the Prelate,

the monarch of his diocesan rout, should be anti-monarchical in a higher manner, for he rules all at his will.

24. The prime men, such as Mr. R. Bruce, the faithful servant of Christ, were honored and attended by all, because of their suffering, zeal, holiness, their fruitful ministry in gaining many thousand souls to Christ. So, though king James cast him off, and did swear by God's name he intended to be king (the Prelate makes blasphemy a virtue in the king) yet king James swore he could not find an honest minister in Scotland to be a bishop, and therefore he was required to promote false knaves; but he said sometimes, and wrote it under his hand that Mr. R. Bruce was worthy of the half of his kingdom; but will this prove presbyteries inconsistent with monarchies? I should rather think that knave bishops by king James' judgment were inconsistent with monarchies.

25. His lies about Mr. R. Bruce, excerpted out of the lying manuscripts of apostate Spotswood, in that he would not but preach against the king's recalling from exile some bloody popish lords to undo all, are nothing comparable to the incests, adulteries, blasphemies, perjuries, Sabbath-breaches, drunkenness, profanity, &c., committed by prelates before the sun.

26. Our General Assembly is no other than Christ's court (Acts 15). made up of pastors, doctors, and brethren, or elders.

27. They ought to have no negative vote to impede the conclusions of Christ in his servants.

28. It is a lie that the king has no power to appoint time and place for the General Assembly, but his power is not privative to destroy the free courts of Christ, but accumulative to aid and assist them.

29. It is a lie that our General Assembly may repeal laws, command and expect performance of the king, or then

excommunicate, subject to them, force and compel king, judges, and all to submit to them. They may not force the conscience of the poorest beggar, nor is any Assembly infallible, nor can it lay bounds upon the souls of judges, which they are to obey with blind obedience; their power is ministerial, subordinate to Christ's law; and what civil laws parliaments make against God's word, they may authoritatively declare them to be unlawful, as though the emperor (Acts 15). had commanded fornication and eating of blood. Might not the Assembly forbid these in the synod? I conceive the prelates, if they had power, would repeal the act of parliament made, anno 1641, in Scotland, by his majesty personally present, and the three estates concerning the annulling of these acts of parliament and laws which established bishops in Scotland; therefore bishops set themselves as independent monarchs above kings and laws, and what they damn in presbyteries and assemblies that they practice themselves.

30. Commissioners from burghs, and two from Edinburgh, because of the largeness of that church, not for cathedral supereminence, sit in assemblies, not as sent from burghs, but as sent and authorized by the church session of the burgh, and so they sit there in a church capacity.

31. We desire doctors both in academies and in parishes, and our book of discipline holds forth such.

32. They hold (I believe with warrant of God's word) if the king refuse to reform religion, the inferior judges, and assembly of godly pastors, and other church-officers may reform; if the king will not kiss the Son and do his duty in purging the House of the Lord, may not Elijah and the people do their duty, and cast out Baal's priests? Reformation of religion is a personal act that belongs to all, even to anyone private person according to his place.

33. They may swear a covenant without the king, if he refuse, and build the Lord's house (2 Chron. 15:9) themselves, and relieve and defend one another when they are oppressed. For my acts and duties of defending myself and the oppressed do not tie my conscience conditionally, as long as the king consents, but absolutely, as all duties of the law of nature do (Jer. 22:3; Prov. 24:11; Isa. 18:6; 1:17).

34. The Popish Prelate condemns our reformation because it was done against the will of our popish queen. This shows what estimation he has of popery, and how he abhors protestant religion.

35. They deposed the queen for her tyranny, but crowned her son; all this is vindicated in the following treatise.

36. The killing of the monstrous and prodigious wicked cardinal in the Castle of St. Andrews and the violence done to the prelates who, against all law of God and man, obtruded a mass service upon their own private motion in Edinburgh anno 1637, can determine nothing against presbyterian government except our doctrine commend these acts as lawful.

37. What was preached by the servant of Christ, whom he calls the Scottish Pope,[1] is printed, and the Popish Prelate dared not, could not cite anything from it as popish or unsound; he knows that the man whom he so slanders knocked down the Pope and the prelates.

38. The making away the fat abbacies and bishoprics is a bloody heresy to the earthly-minded Prelate; the Confession of Faith commended by all the protestant churches as a strong bar against popery, and the book of discipline, in which the servants of God labored twenty years with fasting and praying and frequent advice and counsel from the whole reformed

---

1. Alexander Henderson, moderator of the General Assembly.

churches, are to the Popish Prelate a negative faith and devout imaginations; it is a lie that episcopacy by both sides was ever agreed on by law in Scotland.

39. And it was a heresy that Mr. Melvin taught, that presbyter and bishop are one function in Scripture, and that abbots and priors were not in God's books, *dic ubi legis* [speak where you read]; and is this a proof of inconsistency of presbyteries with a monarchy?

40. It is a heresy to the Popish Prelate that the church appoint a fast, when king James appointed an unseasonable feast, when God's wrath was upon the land, contrary to God's word (Isa. 22:12-14). And what! Will this prove presbyteries to be inconsistent with monarchies?

41. This assembly is to judge what doctrine is treasonable. What then? Surely the secret council and king in a constitute church is not synodically to determine what is true or false doctrine, more than the Roman emperor could make the church canon (Acts 15).

42. Mr. Gibson and Mr. Black preached against king James' maintaining the tyranny of bishops, his sympathizing with papists, and other notorious sins, and were absolved in a general Assembly; shall this make presbyteries inconsistent with monarchy? Nay, but it proves only that they are inconsistent with the wickedness of some monarchies, and that prelates have been like the four hundred false prophets that flattered king Ahab, and those men that preached against the sins of the king and court, by prelates in both kingdoms have been imprisoned, banished, their noses ripped, their cheeks burnt, their ears cut.

43. The godly men that kept the Assembly of Aberdeen, anno 1603, did stand for Christ's Prerogative, when king James took away all General Assemblies, as the event proved;

and the king may with as good warrant inhibit all Assemblies for word and sacrament, as much as for church discipline.

44. They excommunicate not for light faults and trifles, as the liar says: our discipline says the contrary.

45. This assembly never took on them to choose the king's counsellors, but those who were in authority took king James, when he was a child, out of the company of a corrupt and seducing papist Esme Duke of Lennox, whom the Popish Prelate names noble, worthy, of eminent endowments.

46. It is true Glasgow Assembly, 1637, voted down the high commission because it was not consented unto by the church, and yet was a church judicature, which took upon them to judge of the doctrine of ministers, and deprive them, and did encroach upon the liberties of the established lawful church judicatures.

47. This Assembly might well forbid Mr. John Graham, minister, to make use of an unjust decree, it being scandalous in a minister to oppress.

48. Though nobles, barons, and burgesses that profess the truth are elders, and thus members of the General Assembly, this is not to make the church the house and the commonwealth the hanging, for the constituent members, we are content to be examined by the pattern of synods (Acts 15:22-23). Is this inconsistent with monarchy?

49. The commissioners of the General Assembly are, 1. A mere occasional judicature. 2. Appointed by and subordinate to the General Assembly. 3. They have the same warrant of God's word that messengers of the synod (Acts. 15:22-27) have.

50. The historical calumny of the 17th day of December is known to all: 1. That the ministers had any purpose to dethrone king James, and that they wrote to John L. Marquis of Hamilton, to be king, because king James had made

defection from the true religion: Satan devised, Spotswood and this Popish Prelate vented this; I hope the true history of this is known to all. The holiest pastors and professors in the kingdom asserted this government, suffered for it, contended with authority only for sin, never for the power and office. These on the contrary side were men of another stamp, who minded earthly things, whose God was the world. 2. All the forged inconsistency between presbyteries and monarchies is an opposition with absolute monarchy and concluded with a like strength against parliaments, and all synods of either side, against the law and gospel preached, to which kings and kingdoms are subordinate. Lord establish peace and truth.

QUESTION 1.

WHETHER GOVERNMENT IS WARRANTED BY A DIVINE LAW.

How government is from God. Civil power, in the root, immediately from God.

I reduce all that I am to speak of the power of kings to the author or efficient, the matter or subject, the form or power, the end and fruit of their government, and to some cases of resistance. Thus, the question is either of government in general, or of particular kinds of government, such as government by one only, called monarchy, the government by some chief leading men, named aristocracy, the government by the people, going under the name of democracy. We cannot but put difference between the institution of the office, viz. government, and the designation of person or persons to the office. What is warranted by the direction of nature's light is warranted by the law of nature, and consequently by a divine law; for who can deny the law of nature to be a divine law?

That power of government in general must be from God, I make good, first, because "there is no power but of God; the powers that be are ordained of God" (Rom. 13:1). Second, God commands obedience, and so subjection of conscience to powers: "Therefore you must needs be subject, not only for wrath (or civil punishment) but also for conscience's sake." (Rom. 13:5); "Submit yourselves to every ordinance of man, for the Lord's sake, whether it be to the king as supreme," &c (1 Peter 2:13). Now God only by a divine law can lay a bond of subjection on the conscience, tying men to guilt and punishment if they transgress.

Conclusion. All civil power is immediately from God in its root; in that, first, God has made man a social creature, and one who inclines to be governed by man, then certainly he must have put this power in man's nature: so are we, by good reason, taught by Aristotle (*Politics* 1.2.). Second, since God and nature intend the policy and peace of mankind, then God and nature must have given to mankind a power to accomplish this end, and this must be a power of government. I see not then why John Prelate, Mr. Maxwell, the excommunicated prelate of Ross who speaks in the name of J. Armagh, had reason to say that he feared that we fancied that the government of superiors was only for the more perfect, but had no authority over or above the perfect, *nec rex, nec lex, justo posita*. He might have imputed this to the Brazilians, who teach that every single man has the power of the sword to revenge his own injuries, as Molina says (Tom. 1, *De justit. disp. 22*).

QUESTION 2.

WHETHER OR NOT GOVERNMENT IS WARRANTED BY THE LAW OF NATURE.

Civil society natural in radice, in the root, voluntary in modo, in the manner. Power of government and power of government by such and such magistrates are different. Civil subjection not formally from nature's laws. Our consent to laws is penal, not antecedently natural. Government by such rulers is a secondary law of nature. Family government and politic are different. Government by rulers is a secondary law of nature; family government and civil are different. Civil government by consequent is natural.

As domestic society is by nature's instinct, so is civil society natural *in radice*, in the root, and voluntary *in modo*, in the manner of coalescing. Politic power of government befits not man singly as one man, except in that root of reasonable nature; but supposing that men are combined in societies, or that one family cannot contain a society, it is natural that they join in a civil society, though the manner of union in a politic body, as Bodine says, is voluntary[1] (Gen. 10:10;

---

1. *De Republica* 1.6.

17

15:7); and Suarez says that a power of making laws is given by God as a property flowing from nature (tom. 1, *de legib. 3.3*). *Qui dat formam, dat consequentia ad formam;* not by any special action or grant, different from creation, nor will he have it to result from nature, while men be united into one politic body; which union being made, that power follows without any new action of the will.

We are to distinguish between a power of government and a power of government by magistracy. That we defend ourselves from violence by violence is a consequent of unbroken and sinless nature; but that we defend ourselves by devolving our power over in the hands of one or more rulers seems rather positively moral[1] than natural, except that it is natural for the child to expect help against violence from his father, for which cause I judge that learned senator Fernando Vazquez said well that princedom, empire, kingdom, or jurisdiction has its rise from a positive and secondary law of nations, and not from the law of pure nature.[2] First, the law says there is no law of nature agreeing to all living creatures for superiority;[3] for by no reason in nature has a boar dominion over a boar, a lion over a lion, a dragon over a dragon, a bull over a bull, and if all men be born equally free, as I hope to prove, there is no reason in nature why one man should be king and lord over another; therefore though I be otherwise taught by the aforesaid Prelate Maxwell, I conceive all jurisdiction of man over man to be as it were artificial and positive, and that it infers some servitude whereof nature from the womb has freed us, if you except the subjection of children to parents, and the wife to the husband; and the law says, *De jure gentium secundarius est omnis principatus* [All authority is

---

1. The term "positive" is key to Rutherford. It refers to something that is determined by human law, and varries from culture to culture. It is similar to the English term "posited." So when Rutherford says something is positively moral rather than natural, he is talking about things which are immoral because they go against custom, not because they are always evil in every time or age.

2. Vasquez *illust. quaest.* 1.41, num. 28-29.

3. Ib. 2, *in princ. F. de inst. et jur. et in princ.* in *Inst. Cod. tit., jus. nat. 1. disp.*

secondary to the law of the nations].[4] Second, this also the Scripture proves: the exalting of Saul or David above their brothers to be kings and captains of the Lord's people is ascribed not to nature (for king and beggar spring of one clay), but to an act of divine bounty and grace above nature (1 Sam. 13:13; Ps. 78:70-71).

1. There is no reason why royalists should deny government to be natural, but to be altogether from God, and that the kingly power is immediately and only from God, because it is not natural to us to be subject to government, but against nature for us to resign our liberty to a king, or any ruler or rulers; for this is much for us, and proves not but government is natural; it concludes that a power of government *tali modo* by magistracy, is not natural; but this is but a sophism, a κατα τι *ad illud quod est dictum* απλως [according to that which is said unadvisedly]. This special of government by resignation of our liberty is not natural, therefore, power of government is not natural; it follows not: *a negatione speciei non sequitur negatio generis, non est homo, ergo non est animal.* And by the same reason I may by an antecedent will agree to a magistrate and a law, that I may be ruled in a politic society, and by a consequent will only, yea, and conditionally only agree to the penalty and punishment of the law; and it is most true that no man by the instinct of nature gives consent to penal laws as penal, for nature does not teach a man, nor incline his spirit to yield that his life shall be taken away by the sword, and his blood shed, except on this remote ground. A man has a disposition that a vein be cut by the physician, or a member of his body cut off, rather than the whole body and life perish by some contagious disease; but here reason in cold blood, not a natural disposition, is the nearest prevalent cause and disposer of the business. When therefore a community by the instinct and guidance of nature incline to government and to defend themselves from violence, they do not by that instinct formally

---

4. Dominium est jus quoddam, *lib. fin. ad med., de long. temp. prest. 1, qui usum fert.*

agree to government by magistrates, and when a natural conscience gives a deliberate consent to good laws, as to this, "Whosoever sheds man's blood, by man shall his blood be shed" (Gen. 9:6), he tacitly consents that his own blood shall be shed, but this he consents unto consequently, tacitly, and conditionally if he shall do violence to the life of his brother, yet in such a way this consent proceeds not from a disposition every way purely natural. I grant reason may be required to assent to the conclusion, being, as it were, forced by the prevalent power of the evidence of an insuperable and invincible light in the premises, yet from natural affections there results an act of self-love for self-preservation. So David shall condemn another rich man, who has many lambs and robs his poor brother of his one lamb, and yet not condemn himself, though he be most deep in that fault (1 Sam. 12:5-6). Yet all this does not hinder, but government even by rulers has its ground in a secondary law of nature, which lawyers call *secundario jus naturale*, or *jus gentium secundarium*, a secondary law of nature, which is granted by Plato, and denied by none of sound judgment in a sound sense, and that is this, *Licet vim vi repellere*, it is lawful to repel violence by violence, and this is a special act of the magistrate.

2. But there is no reason why we may not defend by good reasons that political societies, rulers, cities, and incorporations have their rise and spring from the secondary law of nature. First, because by nature's law family government has its warrant, and Adam, even if there had never been any positive law, had a power of governing his own family and punishing evildoers; but as Tannerus says well[1] and as I shall prove, God willing, this was not properly a royal or monarchical power, and I judge by the reasoning of Sotus,[2] Molina,[3] and Victoria.[4] By what reason a family has a power of government and of punishing

---

1. *Ad Tannerus, m. 12, tom. 2, disp. 5. de peccatis, q. 5, dub. 1, num. 22.*
2. Soto, 4. de justit. q. 4, art. 1.
3. Tom. 1, *de just.* disp. 22.
4. In *Relect. de potest civil.* q. 4, art, 1.

malefactors, that same power must be in a society of men, supposing that society were not made up of families, but of single persons, for the power of punishing evildoers does not reside in one single man of a family or in them all, as they are single private persons, but as they are in a family. But this argument holds not but by proportion: for paternal government, or a fatherly power of parents over their families, and a politic power of a magistrate over many families are powers different in nature, the one being warranted by nature's law even in its species, the other being in its specie and kind warranted by a positive law and, in the general only, warranted by a law of nature. Second, if we once lay the supposition that God has immediately by the law of nature appointed there should be a government, and mediately defined by the dictate of natural light in a community that there shall be one or many rulers to govern a community, then the Scripture's arguments may well be drawn out of the school of nature: such as (1) the powers that be are of God (Rom. 12), therefore nature's light teaches that we should be subject to these powers; (2) it is against nature's light to resist the ordinance of God; (3) or not to fear him to whom God has committed the sword for the terror of evildoers; (4) or not to honor the public rewarder of well-doing; (5) or not to pay tribute to him for his work. Therefore I see that Govarruvias,[5] Soto,[6] and Suarez,[7] have rightly said, that power of government is immediately from God, and this or that definite power is mediately from God, proceeding from God by the mediation of the consent of a community, which resigns their power to one or more rulers, and to me, Barclay says the same,[8] *Quamvis populus potentiae largitor videatur*, &c.

---

5. Tr. 2, *pract.* quest. 1, n. 2-4.

6. *Loc. ett.*

7. *De Reg.* 3.4, n. 1-2.

8. *Contra Monarchomach.* 1.3.2.

QUESTION 3.

WHETHER ROYAL POWER AND DEFINITE FORMS OF GOVERNMENT ARE FROM GOD.

That kings are from God is understood in a fourfold sense. The royal power has warrant from divine institution. The three forms of government are not different in specie and nature. How every form is from God. How government is an ordinance of man, 1 Pet. 2:13.

The king may be said to be from God and His word in these several notions:

1. By way of permission, Jer. 42:10, "Say to them, Thus says the Lord of hosts, the God of Israel, Behold I will send and take Nebuchadnezzar the king of Babylon, my servant, and will set his throne upon these stones that I have hid, and he shall spread his royal pavilion over them." And thus God made him a catholic king, and gave him all nations to serve him (Jer. 27:6-8), though he was but an unjust tyrant, and his sword the best title to those crowns.

2. The king is said to be from God by way of naked approbation, God giving to a people power to appoint what

government they shall think good, but instituting none in particular in his word. This way some make kingly power to be from God in the general, but in the particular to be an invention of men, negatively lawful and not repugnant to the word, as the wretched popish ceremonies are from God. But we teach no such thing: let Maxwell[1] free his master Bellarmine (*De locis* 5.6, not. 5), and other Jesuits with whom he sides in Romish doctrine: we are free of this. Bellarmine says that political power in general is warranted by a divine law, but the particular forms of politic power (he means monarchy, with the first) is not by divine right, but *de jure gentium*, by the law of nations, and flows immediately from human election, as all things, says he, that appertain to the law of nations. So monarchy to Bellarmine is but an human invention, as Mr. Maxwell's surplice is, and Dr. Ferne says with Bellarmine (section 3).

3. A king is said to be from God by particular designation, as he appointed Saul by name for the crown of Israel. On this more hereafter.

4. The kingly or royal office is from God by divine institution, and not by naked approbation; for first we may well prove Aaron's priesthood to be of divine institution, because God does appoint the priest's qualification from his family, bodily perfections, and his charge. Second, we take the pastor to be by divine law and God's institution, because the Holy Ghost (1 Tim. 3:1-4) describes his qualifications; so may we say that the royal power is by divine institution, because God molds him: "You shall in any wise set him king over you, whom the Lord your God shall choose, one from among your brethren," &c. (Deut. 17:15); "There is no power but of God,

---

1. *The Sacred and Royal Pregative of Christian kings*, book 1, q. 1.

the powers that be are ordained of God" (Rom. 13:1). Third, that power must be ordained by God as his own ordinance, to which we owe subjection for conscience, and not for fear of punishment; but every power is such (Rom. 13). Fourth, to resist the kingly power is to resist God. Fifth, he is the minister of God for our good. Sixth, he bears the sword of God to take vengeance upon evil-doers. Seventh, the Lord expressly says, "Fear God, honor the king;" (1 Pet. 2:17) "Submit yourselves to every ordinance of man for the Lord's sake, whether it be to the king as supreme, or unto governors, as those that are sent by him,' &c. (v. 13-14); "Put them in mind to be subject to principalities and powers" (Tit. 3:1), and so the fifth commandment lays obedience to the king on us no less than to our parents; from which, I conceive that power to be of God, to which by the moral law of God we owe perpetual subjection and obedience. Eighth, kings and magistrates are God's, and God's deputies and lieutenants upon earth (Psalm 132:1, 6-7; Exod. 22:8; 4:16) and therefore their office must be a lawful ordinance of God. Ninth, by their office they are feeders of the Lord's people (Psalm 78:70–72), the shields of the earth (Ps. 47:9), nursing fathers of the church (Ps. 49:23), captains over the Lord's people (1 Sam. 9:19). Tenth, it is a great judgment of God when a land lacks the benefit of such ordinances of God (Isa. 3:1-3, 6-7, 11). The execution of their office is an act of the just Lord of heaven and earth, not only by permission, but according to God's revealed will in his word; their judgment is not the judgment of men, but of the Lord (2 Chron. 19:6), and their throne is the throne of God (1 Chron. 22:10). Jerome says to punish murderers and sacrilegious persons is not bloodshed, but the ministry and service of good

laws.[1] So if the king be a living law by office, and the law put
in execution which God has commanded, then as the moral
law is by divine institution, so must the officer of God be,
who is *custos et vindex legis divinae*, the keeper, preserver, and
avenger of God's law. Basilius says this is the prince's office,
Ut opem ferat virtuti, malitiam vero impugnet.[2]

When Paulinus Treverensis, Lucifer Metropolitane of Sar-
dinia, Dionysius Mediolanensis, and other bishops were commanded by Constantine to write against Athanasius, they
answered, *Regnum non ipsius esse, sed dei, a quo acceperit*, the
kingdom is God's, not his; as Athanasius says Optatus Mile-
vitanus helps us in the cause, where he says with Paul, "We
are to pray for heathen kings."[3] The genuine end of the magistrate, says Epiphanius, is *ut ad bonum ordinem universitatis
mundi omnia ex deo bene disponantur atque administrentur.*[4]

Objection. But some object that if the kingly power be of
divine institution, then any other government is unlawful and
contrary to a divine institution, and thus we condemn aristocracy and democracy as unlawful.

Answer. This consequence would follow if aristocracy and
democracy were not also of divine institution, as all my arguments prove; for I judge they are not governments different in
nature, if we speak morally and theologically, only they differ
politically and positively; nor is aristocracy anything but diffused and enlarged monarchy, and monarchy is nothing but
contracted aristocracy, even as it is the same hand when the
thumb and the four fingers are folded together and when all
the five fingers are dilated and stretched out; and wherever

---

1. Commentary on Jeremiah 1.4.
2. 125th Epistle.
3. *Epistula ad solita.*
4. Book 1, tom. 3, Heres. 40.

God appointed a king he never appointed him absolute and a sole independent angel, but joined always to him judges who were no less to judge according to the law of God (2 Chron. 19:6) than the king (Deut. 17:15). And in a moral obligation of judging righteously, the conscience of the monarch and the conscience of the inferior judges are equally under immediate subjection to the King of kings; for there is here a coordination of consciences, and no subordination, for it is not in the power of the inferior judge to judge, *quoad specificationem*, as the king commands him, because the judgment is neither the king's, nor any mortal man's, but the Lord's (2 Chron. 19:6-7).

Hence all the three forms are from God, but let no man say that if they are all indifferent and equally of God, societies and kingdoms are left in the dark, and know not which of the three they shall pitch upon, because God has given to them no special direction for one rather than for another. But this is easily answered. First, that a republic appoint rulers to govern them is not an indifferent, but a moral action, because to set no rulers over themselves I conceive would be a breach of the fifth commandment, which commands government to be one thing or another. Second, it is not in men's free will that they have government or no government, because it is not in their free will to obey or not to obey the acts of the court of nature, which is God's court, and this court enacts that societies suffer not mankind to perish, which must necessarily follow if they appoint no government; also it is proved elsewhere that no moral acts in their exercises and use are left indifferent to us; so then, the aptitude and temper of every commonwealth to monarchy rather than to democracy or aristocracy is God's warrant and nearest call to determine the wills and liberty of people to pitch upon a monarchy, *hic et nunc*, rather than any other form of government, though all the three are from God,

even as single life and marriage are both the lawful ordinances of God, and the constitution and temper of the body is a
calling to either of the two; nor are we to think that aristocracy and democracy are either unlawful ordinances, or men's
inventions, or that those societies which want monarchy do
therefore live in sins.

Obj. But some say that Peter calls any form of government
a human ordinance, (1 Pet. 2:13, ἀνθρωπίνη κτίσις); therefore
monarchy can be no ordinance of God.

Ans. Rivetus says, "It is called an ordinance of man, not because it is an invention of man, and not an ordinance of God,
but *respectu subjecti*" (*Decal. Mand.* 5); Piscator: "Not because
man is the efficient cause of magistracy, but because they are
men who are magistrates" (*in loc*); Diodatus: "Obey princes
and magistrates, or governors made by men, or among men"
(*annot.*); Oecumenius: "An human constitution, because it is
made by an human disposition, and created by human suffrages"; Dydimus: "Because over it presides presidents made
by men"; Cajetanus; Estius: "Every creature of God (as, preach
the gospel to every creature) in authority" (*in loc.*) But I take
the word, "every creature of man," to be put emphatically, to
commend the worth of obedience to magistrates, though but
men, when we do it for the Lord's sake; therefore Betrandus
Cardinalis Ednensis says, "He speaks so for the more necessity of merit" (Tom. 4, Bib.) and Glossa Ordinaria says, "Be
subject to all powers, *etiam ex infidelibus et incredulis,* even of
infidels and unbelievers." Lyranus: "For though they be men,
the image of God shines in them;" and the Syriac, as Lorinus says, leads us thereunto (*in loc.*), לבלזוח בני אנשא: Obey all
the children of men that are in authority. It is an ordinance
of men, not effectively, as though it were an invention and
a dream of men, but subjectively, because exercised by man.

Objectively, and τελικῶς, for the good of men, and for the external man's peace and safety especially, whereas church-officers are for the spiritual good of men's souls. And Durandus says well, "Civil power according to its institution is of God, and according to its acquisition and way of use is of man" (*de orig. juris.*) And we may thus far call the forms of magistrates a human ordinance; that some magistrates are ordained to care for men's lives and matters criminal, of life and death, and some for men's lands and estates; some for commodities by sea, and some by land; and are thus called magistrates according to these determinations or human ordinances.

QUESTION 4.

WHETHER THE KING IS ONLY AND IMMEDIATELY FROM GOD, AND NOT FROM THE PEOPLE.

How the king is from God, and how he is from the people. Royal power is three ways in the people. How royal power is radically in the people. The people makes the king. How any form of government is from God. How government is a human ordinance, 1 Pet. 2:3. The people create the king. Making a king and choosing a king not to be distinguished. David not a king formally, because anointed by God.

That this question may be the clearer we are to set down these considerations:

1. The question is whether the kingly office itself come from God. I conceive it is, and flows from the people, not by formal institution, as if the people had by an act of reason devised and excogitated such a power. God ordained the power; it is from the people only by a virtual emanation, in respect that a community having no government at all may ordain a king or appoint an aristocracy. But the question is concerning

the designation of the person: from where is it that this man
rather than that man is crowned king? And from where is it—
from God immediately and only—that this man rather than
that man, and this race or family rather than that race and
family is chosen for the crown? Or is it from the people also,
and their free choice? For the pastor's and the doctor's office
is from Christ only, but that John rather than Thomas is the
doctor or the pastor is from the will and choice of men—the
presbyters and people.

2. The royal power is in three ways in the people: first, radically and virtually, as in the first subject. Second, *Collative
vel communicative*, by way of free donation, they giving it to
this man, not to that man, that he may rule over them. Third,
limitate, they giving it so as these three acts remain with the
people (1) that they may measure out, by ounce weights, so
much royal power, and no more and no less; (2) so that they
may limit, moderate, and set banks and marches to the exercise (3); that they give it out, *conditionate*, upon this and that
condition, that they may take again to themselves what they
gave out, upon condition if the condition be violated. The
first I conceive is clear, first, because if all living creatures
have radically in them a power of self-preservation to defend
themselves from violence, as we see lions have paws, some
beasts have horns, some claws, men being reasonable creatures united in society must have power in a more reasonable
and honorable way to put this power of warding off violence
in the hands of one or more rulers, to defend themselves by
magistrates. Second, if all men are born, as far as civil power is
concerned, alike, since no man comes out of the womb with a
diadem on his head or a scepter in his hand, and yet men united in a society may give crown and scepter to this man and not
to that man, then this power was in this united society, but it

was not in them formally, for they should then all have been one king, and so both above and superior, and below and inferior to themselves, which we cannot say; therefore this power must have been virtually in them, because neither man nor community of men can give that which they neither have formally nor virtually in them. Third, royalists cannot deny that cities have power to choose and create inferior magistrates; therefore many cities united have power to create a higher ruler; for royal power is but the united and superlative power of inferior judges in one greater judge whom they call a king.

Conclus. The power of creating a man a king is from the people.

1. Because those who may create this man a king rather than that man have power to appoint a king; for a comparative action does positively infer an action. If a man have power to marry this woman and not that woman, we may strongly conclude that he has power to marry; now, the people made Omri king and not Zimri, and his son Ahab rather than Tibni the son of Sinath (1 Kings 16). Nor can it be replied that this was no lawful power that the people used, for that cannot elude the argument; for (1 Kings 1) the people made Solomon king and not Adonijah, though Adonijah was the elder brother.

Obj. They say, God did extraordinarily both make the office and designate Solomon to be king; the people had no hand in it, but approved God's act.

Ans. This is what we say: God by the people, by Nathan the prophet, and by the servants of David and the states crying, "God save king Solomon!" made Solomon king; and here is a real action of the people. God is the first agent in all acts of the creature. Where a people chooses a man to be their king, the states do no other thing under God but create this man rather than another; and we cannot here find two actions, one

of God, another of the people, but in one and the same action
God by the people's free suffrages and voices creates such a
man king, passing by many thousands; and the people are not
passive in the action, because by the authoritative choice of
the states the man is made from being a private man and no
king to a public person and a crowned king: "Hushai said to
Absalom, 'Nay, but whom the Lord and the people, and all the
men of Israel choose, his will I be, and with him will I abide'"
(2 Sam. 16:18); "The men of Israel said to Gideon, 'Rule you
over us'" (Judg. 8:22); "The men of Shechem made Abimelech king" (Judg. 9:6); "The people made Azariah king" (Judg.
11:8, 11; 2 Kings 14:21).

2. If God does regulate his people in making this man king,
not that man, then He thereby insinuates that the people have
a power to make this man king, and not that man. But God
does regulate His people in making a king; therefore the people have a power to make this man king, not that man king.
The proposition is clear, because God's law does not regulate a *non-ens*, a mere nothing, or an unlawful power; nor can
God's holy law regulate an unlawful power or an unlawful
action, but quite abolish and interdict it. The Lord sets not
down rules and ways for how men should not commit treason,
but the Lord commands loyalty and simply indicts treason. If
people have then more power to create a king over themselves
than they had to make prophets, then God forbidding them
to choose such a man for their king should say as much to his
people as if he would say, "I command you to make Isaiah and
Jeremiah prophets over you, but not these and those men."
This certainly should prove that not God only, but the people
also with God made prophets. I leave this to the consideration
of the godly. The prophets were immediately called of God to
be prophets, whether the people consented that they should

be prophets or not; therefore God immediately and only sent the prophets, not the people; but though God extraordinarily designated some men to be kings, and anointed them by his prophets, yet they were never actually installed kings till the people made them kings. I prove the assumption, "When you shall say, I will set a king over me, like all the nations that are about me, you shall set him king over you whom the Lord your God shall choose; one from among your brethren shall you set king over you: you may not set a stranger over you, which is not your brother" (Deut. 17:14-15). Should not this be an unjust charge to the people if God only without any action of the people should immediately set a king over them? Might not the people reply, we have no power at all to set a king over ourselves, more than we have power to make Isaiah a prophet, who saw the visions of God. To what end then should God mock us and say, "Make a brother and not a stranger king over you"?

3. Expressly Scripture says that the people made the king, though under God: "The men of Shechem made Abimelech king" (Judg. 9:6); "And all the people went to Gilgal, and there they made Saul king before the Lord" (1 Sam. 11:15); "We will not make any king" (2 King. 10:5). This would have been an irrational speech to Jehu if both Jehu and the people held the royalists' tenet, that the people had no power to make a king, nor any active or causative influence in it, but that God immediately made the king: "All these came with a perfect heart to make David king in Hebron" (1 Chron. 12:38) and all the rest were of one heart to make David king. On these words Lavater says the same way are magistrates now to be chosen, now this day God by an immediate oracle from heaven appoints the office of a king, but I am sure He does not immediately designate the man, but does only mark him out

to the people as one who has the most royal endowments, and the due qualifications required in a lawful magistrate by the word of God, "Men of truth, hating covetousness," &c. (Exod. 18:21); men who will judge causes between their brethren righteously, without respect of persons (Deut. 1:16-17);[1] Saul was chosen out of the tribes according to the law of God (1 Sam. 10:21); They might not choose a stranger (Deut. 17).

Abulensis, Serrarius, Cornelius a Lapide, Sancheiz, and other popish writers think that Saul was not only anointed with oil first privately by Samuel (1 Sam. 10:1-2) but also at two other times before the people, once at Mizpah, and another time at Gilgal, by a parliament and a convention of the states. And Samuel judged the voices of the people so essential to make a king that Samuel does not acknowledge him as formal king (1 Sam. 10:7-8, 17-19) though he honored him because he was to be king (1 Sam. 9:23-24) while the tribes of Israel and parliament were gathered together to make him king according to God's law (Deut. 17), as is evident.

First, since Samuel caused all the tribes of Israel to stand before the Lord, and the tribe of Benjamin was taken (1 Sam. 5:20). The law provided one of their own, not a stranger to reign over them, and, because some of the states of parliament did not choose him but, being children of Belial, despised him in their hearts (v. 27) therefore afterwards king Saul by his victory over the Ammonites had conquered the affections of all the people fully (v. 10-11). Samuel would have his coronation and election by the estates of parliament renewed at Gilgal by all the people (v. 14-15) to establish him king. Second, the Lord by lots found out the tribe of Benjamin. Third, the Lord found out the man, by name Saul the son of Kish, when

---

1. Com. in part 12, 38. *Hodie quoque in liberis urbibus, et gentibus, magistratus secundum dei verbum, Exod. 18, Deut. 1, eligendi sunt, non ex affectibus.*

he did hide himself among the stuff, that the people might do their part in creating the king, whereas Samuel had anointed him before. But the text says expressly that the people made Saul king, and Calvin, Martyr, Lavater, and popish writers, as Serrarius, Mendoza, Sancheiz, Cornelius a Lapide, Lyranus, Hugo Cardinalis, Carthusius, Sanctius do all from this conclude that the people, under God, make the king.

I see no reason why Barclay should here distinguish a power of choosing a king, which he grants the people has, and a power of making a king, which he says is only proper to God (*Contra Monarchomach.* 8.3).

Ans. Choosing of a king is either a comparative crowning of this man, not that man; and if the people have this it is a creating of a king under God, who principally disposes of kings and kingdoms; and this is enough for us. The want of this made Zimri no king, and those whom the rulers of Jezreel at Samaria (2 King. 10). refused to make kings, no kings.

This election of the people made Athaliah a princess; the removal of it, and transference of the crown by the people to Joash made her no princess; for, I ask you, what other calling of God has a race of a family and a person to the crown than the election of the states? There is now no voice from heaven, no immediately inspired prophets such as Samuel and Elisha, to anoint David, not Eliab; Solomon, not Adonijah. The δυναμις or the heroic spirit of a royal faculty of governing is, I grant, from God alone, not from the people; but I suppose that makes not a king, for then many sitting on the throne this day would not be kings, and many private persons would be kings. If they mean by the people's choosing nothing but the people's approbative consent, posterior to God's act of creating a king, let them show us an act of God making kings and establishing royal power in this family rather than in that family, which is prior to the people's consent: distinct from the people's consent I believe there is none at all.

Hence I argue if there be no calling or title on earth to tie the crown to such a family and person but the suffrages of the people, then the line of such a family, and the persons now, have no calling of God, no right to the crown, but only by the suffrages of the people, unless we say that there are no lawful kings on earth now that prophetic anointing and designation to crowns have ceased, contrary to express scripture (Rom. 13:1-3; 1 Pet. 2:13-17).

But there is no title on earth now to tie crowns to families, to persons, except the suffrages of the people; for first, conquest without the consent of the people is but royal robbery, as we shall see. Second, there is no prophetic and immediate calling to kingdoms now. Third, the Lord's giving of regal parts is somewhat, but I hope royalists will not deny that a child, young in years and judgment, may be a lawful king. Fourth, Mr. Maxwell's appointing of the kingly office does no more make one man a lawful king than another; for this would be a mistaken consequence. God has appointed that kings should be; therefore John a Stiles is a king; yea, therefore David is a king. It follows not. Therefore it remains only that the suffrages of the people of God is that just title and divine calling that kings have now to their crowns. I presuppose they have gifts to govern from God.

If the Lord's immediate designation of David and his anointing by the divine authority of Samuel had been that which alone without the election of the people made David formally king of Israel, then there were two kings in Israel at one time, for Samuel anointed David, and so he was formally king upon the ground laid by royalists: that the king has no royal power from the people; and David, after he himself was anointed by Samuel, various times calls Saul the Lord's anointed, and that by the inspiration of God's Spirit, as we and royalists do both agree. Now two lawful supreme monarchs in one kingdom I conceive to be most repugnant to God's truth and sound reason, for they are as repugnant as two most highs or as two infinities. It shall follow that David all the while between his anointing by Samuel and his coronation by the suffrages of all Israel at Hebron was lacking in discharging and acquitting himself of his royal duty, God having made him formally a king, and so laying upon him a charge to execute justice and judgment, and defend religion which he did not discharge.

All David's suffering, upon David's part, must be unjust, for as king he should have cut off the murderer Saul, who killed the priests of the Lord, especially seeing Saul by this ground must be a private murderer, and David the only lawful king. David, if he was formally king, deserted his calling in flying to the Philistines; for a king should not forsake his calling upon any hazard, even of his life, no more than a pilot should give over the helm in an extreme storm; but certainly God's dispensation in this warrants us to say no man can be formally a lawful king without the suffrages of the people: for Saul, after Samuel from the Lord anointed him, remained a private man and no king, till the people made him king and elected him, and David, anointed by that same divine authority, remained formally a subject, and not a king, till all Israel made him king at Hebron; and Solomon, though by God designated and ordained to be king, yet was never king until the people made him so (1 Kings 1); therefore there flows something from the power of the people by which he who is no king now becomes a king formally, and by God's lawful call; whereas before the man was no king, but with regard to royal power a mere private man. And I am sure birth must be less than God's designation to a crown, as is clear: Adonijah was older than Solomon, yet God will have Solomon, the younger by birth, to be king, and not Adonijah. And so Mr. Symons and other court prophets must prevaricate, who will have birth without the people's election to make a king, and the people's voices but a ceremony.

I think royalists cannot deny that a people ruled by aristocratic magistrates may elect a king, and a king so elected is formally made a lawful king by the people's election; for of six willing and gifted to reign, what makes one a king and not the other five? Certainly by God's disposing the people to choose this man, and not another man. It cannot but be said that God gives the kingly power immediately, and that by him kings reign is true. The office is immediately from God, but the question now is what is that which formally applies the office and royal power to this person rather than to the other five as fitting? Nothing can here be dreamed of but God's inclining the hearts of the states to choose this man and not that man.

QUESTION 5.

WHETHER OR NOT THE POPISH PRELATE,
THE AUHOR OF SACRO SANCTA REGUM
MAJESTAS, CALLED THE SACRED AND ROYAL
PREROGATIVE OF KINGS, PROVES THAT GOD IS
THE IMMEDIATE AUTHOR OF SOVEREIGNTY,
AND THAT THE KING IS NO CREATURE OF THE
PEOPLE'S MAKING.

*Kings made by the people, though the office in abstracto was
immediately from God. The people have a real action, more than
approbation, in making a king. Kinging of a person ascribed to the
people. Kings in a special manner are from God, but it follows not;
therefore, not from the people. The place Prov. 8:15 proves not but
kings are made by the people. Nebuchadnezzar and other heathen kings
had no just title before God to the kingdom of Judah, and various other
subdued kingdoms.*

Consider, 1. that the excommunicated prelate says, "Kings are not immediately from God as by any special ordinance sent from heaven by the ministry of angels and prophets; there were but some few such; as Moses, Saul, David, &c.,

yet something may immediately proceed from God, and be his special work, without a revelation or manifestation extraordinary from heaven; so the designation to a sacred function is from the church and from man, yet the power of word, sacraments, binding and loosing, is immediately from Jesus Christ. The apostle Matthias was from Christ's immediate constitution, and yet he was designated by men (Acts 1). The soul is by creation and infusion, without any special ordinance from heaven, though nature begets the body, and disposes the matter, and prepares it as fit to be conjoined with the soul, so as the father is said to beget the son" (section 2).

Ans. First, the unchurched Prelate strives to make us hateful by the title of the chapter: that God is by His title the immediate author of sovereignty, and who denies that? Not those who teach that the person who is king is created king by the people, no more than those who deny that men are now called to be pastors and deacons immediately, and by a voice from heaven, or by the ministry of angels and prophets, because the office of pastors and deacons is immediately from God. Second, when he has proved that God is the immediate author of sovereignty, what then? Shall it follow that the sovereign *in concreto* may not be resisted, and that he is above all law, and that there is no armor against his violence but prayers and tears? Because God is the immediate author of the pastor and of the apostle's office, does it therefore follow that it is unlawful to resist a pastor though he turn robber? If so, then the pastor is above all the king's laws. This is the Jesuit, ready made, and there is no armor against the robbing prelate but prayer and tears.

2. He says in his title, that "the king is no creature of the people's making." If he mean the king in the abstract, that is, the royal dignity, whom speaks he against? Not against us, but

against his own father, Bellarmine, who says that "sovereignty has no warrant by any divine law."[1] If he mean that the man who is king is not created and elected king by the people, he contradicts himself and all the court doctors.

3. It is false that Saul and David's call to royalty was only from God "by a special ordinance sent from heaven," for their office is from the written word of God (Deut. 17:14), such as the killing of idolaters (v. 3, 7) and the office of the priests and Levites (v. 8-10) and this is no extraordinary office from heaven, more than that is from heaven which is warranted by the word of God. If he mean that these men, Saul and David, were created kings only by the extraordinary revelation of God from heaven, it is a lie; for besides the prophetic anointing of them, they were made kings by the people, as the Word says expressly; unless we say that David sinned in not setting himself down on the throne, when Samuel first anointed him king, and so he should have made away with his master, king Saul, out of the world, and there were not a few called to the throne by the people, but many, yea, all the kings of Israel and of Judah.

4. The prelate contends that a king is designated to his royal dignity "immediately from God, without an extraordinary revelation from heaven," as the man is "designated to be a pastor by men, and yet the power of preaching is immediately from God," &c., but he proves nothing, unless he prove that all pastors are called to be pastors *immediately*, and that God calls and designates to the office such a person immediately as he has immediately instituted by the power of preaching and the apostleship, and has immediately infused the soul in the body by an act of creation; and we cannot conceive how

---

1. *De Laicis* 5.6, not 5.

God in our days, when there are no extraordinary revelations, does immediately create this man a king, and immediately tie the crown to this family rather than to that. This he does by the people now, without any prophetic anointing, and by this medium, viz., the free choice of the people. He need not bring the example of Matthias more than of any ordinary pastor, and yet an ordinary pastor is not immediately called of God, because the office is from God immediately, and also the man is made pastor by the church.

The Popish Prelate says a thing is immediately from God in three ways. First, when it is solely from God, and presupposes nothing ordinary or human antecedent to the obtaining of it. Such was the power of Moses, Saul, and David; such were the apostles. Second, when the collation of the power to each a person is immediately from God, though some act of man be antecedent, as Matthias was an apostle. A baptized man obtains remission and regeneration, yet aspersion of water cannot produce these excellent effects. A king gives power to a favorite to make a lord or a baron, yet who is so stupid as to aver that the honor of a lord comes immediately from the favorite and not from the king. Third, when a man has by some ordinary human right a full and just right, the approbation and confirmation of this right is immediately from God (section 2).

The first way, sovereignty is not from God. The second way, sovereignty is conferred on kings immediately: though some created act of election, succession or conquest intervene, the interposed act contains not in it power to confer sovereignty; as in baptism, regeneration, if there be nothing repugnant in the recipient, is conferred not by water, but immediately by God. In sacred orders, designation is from men, power to supernatural acts from God. Election, succession, conquests, remotely and improperly constitute a king. To say in the third sense, that sovereignty is immediately from God by approbation or confirmation only is against Scripture (Prov. 8:15; Ps. 88:8; John 19); then the people say "You are God's, your power is from below." And Paul's "ordained of God," is "approved and confirmed only of God." The power of designation or application of the person to royalty is from man; the power of conferring royal power or of applying the person to royal power is from God. A man's hand may apply a faggot to the fire; the fire alone makes the faggot to burn.

Ans. First, apostles, both according to their office and the designation of their person to the office, were immediately and only from God, without any act of the people, and therefore are badly coupled with the royal power of David and king Saul, who were not formally made kings but by the people at Mizpah and Hebron.

Second, the second way God gives royal power, by moving the people's hearts to confer royal power, and this is virtually in the people, formally from God. Water has no influence to produce grace: God's institution and promise does it; unless you dream with your Jesuits, of *opus operatum*, that water sprinkled by the doing of the deed confers grace, *nisi ponatur obex*, what can the child do, or one baptized child more than another, to hinder the flux of remission of sins, if you mean not that baptism works as physic on a sick man, unless strength of humors hinder? And therefore this comparison is not alike. The people cannot produce so noble an effect as royalty, a beam from God. True, formally they cannot, but virtually it is in a society of reasonable men, in whom are left beams of authoritative majesty, which by a divine institution they can give to this man, to David, not to Eliab (Deut. 17:14). And I could well say the favorite made the lord, and placed honor in the man whom he made lord, by a borrowed power from his prince, and yet the honor of a lord is principally from the king.

Third, it is true the election of the people contains not formally royal dignity, but the Word says they made Saul, they made David king; so virtually election must contain it. Samuel's oil makes not David king: he is a subject after he is anointed; the people's election at Hebron makes him king, differs him from his brethren, and puts him in royal state, yet God is the principal agent. What immediate action God has here, is said and dreamed of, no man can divine, except Prophet Popish Prelate. The εξουσια, royal authority, is given organically by that act by which he is made king; another act is a nightdream, but by the act of election, David is from being no king made king. The collation of δυναμις royal gifts is immediately from God, but that formally makes not a king, if Solomon saw right, "servants riding on horses, princes going on foot."

Fourth, judge of the Prelate's subtilty, I dare say not his own; he steals from Spalato, but tells it not: "The applying of the person to royal authority is from the people; but the applying of royal authority to the person of the king is immediately and only from God; as the hand puts the faggot to the fire, but the fire makes it burn." To apply the subject to the accident, is it anything else but to apply the accident to the subject? Royal authority is an accident, the person of the king the subject. The applying of the faggot to the fire and the applying of the fire to the faggot are all one to anyone not destitute of common sense. When the people applies the person to the royal authority, they but put the person in the state of royal authority; this is to make a union between the man and royal authority, and this is to apply royal authority to the person.

Fifth, the third sense is the Prelate's dream, not a tenet of ours. We never said that sovereignty in the king is immediately from God by approbation or confirmation only, as if the people first made the king, and God did only by a posterior and latter act say Amen to the deed done, and subscribe, as recorder, to what the people does; thus the people should deal crowns and kingdoms at their pleasure, and God be pleased to ratify and make good their act. When God does apply the person to royal power is this a different action from the people's applying the person to royal dignity? It is not imaginable. But the people by creating a king applies the person to royal dignity, and God by the people's act of constituting the man king does by the mediation of this act convey royal authority to the man, as the church by sending a man and ordaining him to be a pastor does not by that, as God's instruments, infuse supernatural powers of preaching; these supernatural powers may be, and often are in him before he be in orders. And sometimes God infuses a supernatural power of government in a man when he is not yet a king, as the Lord turned Saul into another man neither at that point of time when Samuel anointed him, but afterwards: "After you shall come to the hill of God, the Spirit of the Lord shall come upon you, and you shall prophesy with them, and shall be turned into another man" (1 Sam. 10:5-6) nor yet at that time when he is formally made king by the people; for Saul was not king formally because of Samuel's anointing, nor yet was he king because another spirit was infused into him, for he was yet a private man till the states of Israel chose him king at Mizpah. And the word of God used words of action to express the people's power: and all the men of Shechem gathered together, and all the men of Milo, וימל'כו *regnare fecerunt*, they caused him to be king (Judg. 9:6). The same is said in 1 Sam. 10:15: They caused Saul to reign; 2 Kings 10:15: לא נמלדיאיש. We shall not king any man; 1 Chron. 12:38: They came to Hebron תדרגיר לחמלידא to king David over all Israel; Deut. 17: Three times the making of a king is given to the people. When you shall say, אשימה עלי מלך I shall set a king over me. If it were not in their power to make a king no law could be imposed on them not to make a stranger their king; 1 Kings 12:20: All the congregation kinged Jeroboam, or made him king over all Israel; 2 Kings 11:12: They kinged Joash, or made Joash to reign.

Sixth, the people are to say, you are God's, and your power is below, says the Prelate: What then? Therefore their power is not from God also? It follows not *subordinata non pugnant*. The Scripture says both the Lord exalted David to be king, and all power is from God, and so the power of a lord mayor of a city: the people made David king, and the people makes such a man lord mayor. It is the Anabaptists' argument: God writes his law in our heart and teaches his own children; therefore books and the ministry of men are needless. So all sciences and lawful arts are from God; therefore sciences applied to men are not from men's free will, industry, and studies. The prelate extols the king when he will have his royalty from God, the way that John Stiles is the husband of such a woman.

Popish Prelate. Kings are of God, they are God's, children of the Most High, his servants, public ministers; their sword and judgment are God's. This he has said of their royalty *in abstracto* and *in concreto*; their power, person, charge are all of divine extract, and so their authority and person are both sacred and inviolable (section 24).

Ans. So are all the congregation of the judges (Ps. 82:1, 6). All of them are God's; for he speaks not there of a congregation of kings. So are apostles, their office and persons of God, and so the prelates (as they think), the successors of the apostles, are God's servants; their ministry, word, rod of discipline, not theirs, but of God. The judgment of judges, inferior to the king, is the Lord's judgment, not men's (Deut. 1:17; 2 Chron. 19:6). Thus by the Prelate's logic the persons of prelates, mayors, bailiff, constables, pastors, are sacred and inviolable above all laws as are kings. Is this an extolling of kings? But where are kings' persons as men said to be of God, as the royalty *in abstracto* is? The Prelate sees beside his book, "But You shall die like men" (Ps. 82:7).

Popish Prelate. We begin with the law, in which, as God by himself prescribed the essentials, substantials, and ceremonies of his piety and worship, gave order for piety and justice. In Deut. 17:14-15, the king is here originally and immediately from God and independent from all others "set over them." *Them* is collective, that is, all and everyone. Scripture knows not this state principle. *Rex est singulis major, universis minor.* The person is expressed *in concreto*, "Whom the Lord your God shall choose." This peremptory precept discharges the people, all and everyone, diffusively, representatively, or in any imaginable capacity to attempt the appointing of a king, but to leave it entirely and totally to God Almighty.

Ans. Begin with the law, but end not with traditions. If God by himself prescribed the essentials of piety and worship, the other part of your distinction is that God, not by himself, but by his prelates, appointed the whole Romish rites as accidentals of piety. This is the Jesuits' doctrine. This place is so far from proving the king to be independent, and that it totally is God's to appoint a king that it expressly gives the people power to appoint a king; for the setting of a king over themselves, this one and not that one, makes the people to appoint the king, and the king to be less and to be dependent on the people, seeing God intends the king for the people's good, and not the people for the king's good. This text shames the Prelate, who also confessed that remotely and improperly succession, election, and conquest make the king, and so it is lawful for men remotely and improperly to invade God's chair.

Popish Prelate. Jesuits and puritans say it was a privilege of the Jews that God chose their king. So Suarez, Soto, Navarra.

Ans. The Jesuits are the Prelate's brethren; they are under one banner; we are in contrary camps to Jesuits. The Prelate said himself Moses, Saul, and David were by extraordinary revelation from God. Sure I am kings are not so now. The Jews had this privilege that no nation had. God named some kings to them, such as Saul, David; he does not so now. God did tie royalty to David's house by a covenant till Christ should come; he does not so now; yet we stand to Deut. 17.

Popish Prelate. Prov. 8:15: "By me kings reign." If the people had right to constitute a king, it would not have been king Solomon, but king Adonijah. Solomon says not of himself, but indefinitely, "By me," as by the Author, Efficient and Constituent, kings reign. *Per* is by Christ, not by the people, not by the high priest, state or presbytery; not *per me iratum*, by me in my anger, as some sectaries say. Paul's διαταγη του θεου, an ordinance by high authority not revocable. Sinesius so uses the word, Aristotle, Lucilius, Appian, Plutarch, בי in me and by me, and also Dr. Andrews. Kings indefinitely, all kings: none may distinguish where the law distinguishes not; they reign *in concreto*. That same power that makes kings must unmake them.

Ans. 1. The prelate cannot restrict this to kings only; it extends to parliaments also. Solomon adds ורזנ׳ם, and consuls, שדים all the sirs, and princes, ונד׳ב׳ם and magnificents, and nobles, and more ארצ כל שבטי and all the judges of the earth, they reign, rule, and decree justice by Christ. Here, then, mayors, sheriffs, provosts, constables are by the Prelate extolled as persons sacred, irresistible. Then the judges of England rule not by the king of Britain, as their author, efficient, constituent, but by Jesus Christ immediately; nor does the commissary rule by the prelate. All these, and their power, and persons, rule independently, and immediately by Jesus Christ. All inferior judges are διαταγη του θεου, the ordinances of God not revocable. Therefore the king cannot deprive any judge under him; he cannot declare the parliament no parliament: once a judge, and always and irrevocably a judge. This Prelate's poor pleading for kings deserves no wages. *Lavater intelligit superiores et inferiores magistratus, non est potestas nisi a deo, Vatablus consiliarios.*

2. If the people had absolute right to choose kings by the law of Israel, they might have chosen another than either Adonijah or Solomon; but the Lord expressly put an express law on them that they should make no king but him whom the Lord should choose (Deut. 17:4). Now the Lord did either by his immediately inspired prophet anoint the man, as he anointed David, Saul, Jehu, &c., or then he restricted by a revealed promise the royal power to a family and to the eldest by birth, and therefore the Lord first chose the man and then the people made him king. Birth was not their rule, as is clear, in that they made Solomon their king, not Adonijah, the elder; and this proves that God did both ordain kingly government to the kingdom of Israel, and chose the man, either in his person, or tied it to the firstborn of the line. Now we have no Scripture nor law of God to tie royal dignity to one man or to one family; produce a warrant for it in the Word, for that must be a privilege of the Jews for which we have no word of God. We have no immediately inspired Samuels to say, "Make David, or this man king," and no word of God to say, "Let the firstborn of this family rather than another family sit upon the throne;" therefore the people must make such a man king, following the rule of God's word (Deut. 17:14) and other rules showing what sort of men judges must be, such as Deut. 1:16-18; 2 Chron. 19:6; 7:3. It is true, kings in a special manner reign by Christ; therefore not by the people's free election? The Popish Prelate argues like himself: by this text a mayor of a city by the Lord decrees justice; therefore he is not made a mayor of a city by the people of the city. It follows not. None of us teach that kings reign by God's anger. We judge a king a

great mercy of God to church or state; but the text says not 'By the Lord kings and judges do not only reign and decree justice, but also murder protestants, by raising against them an army of papists.' And the word διαταγαι, powers, does in no Greek author signify irrevocable powers; for Uzziah was a lawful king and yet lawfully put from the throne, and "cut off from the house of the Lord" (2 Chron. 26). And interpreters of this passage deny that it is to be understood of tyrants. So the Chaldee paraphrase turns it well, *Potentes virga justitiae*;[1] so Lavater, and Diodatus says this place does prove "that all kings, judges and laws, *derivari a lege aeterna*, are derived from the Eternal Law."

The prelate, eating his tongue for anger, strives to prove that all power, and so royal power, is of God; but what can he make of it? We believe it, though he say sectaries prove, by ιαν μη, "That a man is justified by faith only;" so there is no power but of God only, but feel the smell of a Jesuit. It is the sectaries' doctrine that we are justified by faith only, but the prelates and the Jesuits go another way; not by faith only, but by works also. And all power is from God only, as the first Author, and from no man. What then? Therefore men and people interpose no human act in making this man a king and not that man. It follows not. Let us with the Prelate join Paul and Solomon together, and say that "sovereignty is from God, of God, by God, as God's appointment irrevocable." Then shall it never follow: it is inseparable from the person unless you make the king a man immortal.

As God only can remove the crown, it is true God only can put an unworthy and an excommunicated prelate from office and benefice. But how? Does that prove that men and the church may not also in their place remove an unworthy churchman, when the church, following God's word, delivers to Satan? Christ only, as head of the church, excommunicates scandalous men; therefore the church cannot do it. And yet the argument is as good the one way as the other,

---

1. 12, q. 93, art. 3.

for all the churches on earth cannot make a minister properly: they but designate him to the ministry whom God has gifted and called. But shall we conclude that no church on earth, but God only by an immediate action from heaven can deprive a minister? How then dare prelates excommunicate, unmake, and imprison so many ministers in the three kingdoms? But the truth is, take this one argument from the Prelate, and all that is in his book falls to the ground, to wit, sovereignty is from God only. A king is a creature of God's making only, and what then? Therefore sovereignty cannot be taken from him; so God only made Aaron's house priests. Solomon had no law to depose Abiathar from the priesthood. Possibly the Prelate will grant all. The passage, Rom. 13, which he says has tortured us, I refer to a fitter place: it will be found to torture court parasites.

I go on with the Prelate: "Sacred sovereignty is to be preserved, and kings are to be prayed for, that we may lead a godly life" (section 3). What then? All in authority are to be prayed for, even parliaments; by that text pastors are to be prayed for, and without them sound religion cannot well subsist. Is this questioned: that kings should be prayed for, or are we wanting in this duty? But it follows not that all dignities to be prayed for are immediately from God, not from men.

Popish Prelate. Solomon speaks first of the establishment of government before he speaks of the works of creation (Prov. 8); therefore better not be at all as be without government. And God fixed government in the person of Adam before Eve or anyone else came into the world; and how shall government be, and we enjoy the fruits of it, unless we preserve the king's sacred authority inviolable?

Ans. 1. Moses speaks of creation before he speaks of kings (Gen. 1), and he speaks of Adam's sins before he speaks of redemption through the blessed Seed (Gen. 3); therefore it would be better never be redeemed at all than to be without sin.

2. If God made Adam a governor before he made Eve and any of mankind, he was made a father and a husband before he had either

son or wife. Is this the Prelate's logic? He may prove that two eggs on his father's table are three this way.

3. There is no government where sovereignty is not kept inviolable. It is true, where there is a king, sovereignty must be inviolable. What then? Arbitrary government is not sovereignty.

4. He intimates aristocracy, and democracy, and the power of parliaments, which makes kings, to be nothing but anarchy, for he speaks here of no government but monarchy.

Popish Prelate. There is need of grace to obey the king (Ps. 18:43; 144:2). It is God who subdues the people under David. Rebellion against the king is rebellion against God (1 Pet. 2:17; Prov. 24:12). Therefore kings have a near alliance with God.

Ans. 1. There is much grace in papists and prelates then, who are accustomed to write and preach against grace.

2. Lorinus your brother Jesuit will with good warrant of the texts infer that the king may make a conquest of his own kingdoms of Scotland and England by the sword, as David subdued the heathen.

3. Arbitrary governing has no alliance with God; a rebel to God and his country, and an apostate, has no reason to term lawful defense against cut-throat Irish rebellion.

4. There is need of much grace to obey pastors, inferior judges, masters (Col. 3:22-23); therefore their power is from God immediately, and no more from men than the king is created king by the people, according to the way of royalists.

Popish Prelate. God says of Pharaoh I have raised you up (Ex. 9:17). Elisha, directed by God, constituted the king of Syria (2 Kings 8:13). Pharaoh, Abimelech, Hiram, Hazael, Hadad, are no less honored with the appellation of kings than David, Saul, &c. Nebuchadnezzar is honored to be called, by way of excellency, God's servant (Jer. 29:9), which God gives to David, a king according to his own heart. And Isa. 45:1: "Thus says the Lord to his anointed, Cyrus," and God names him near a hundred years before he was born; Isa. 44:28:

"He is my shepherd"; Dan. 5:21: God gives kingdoms to whom he will; Dan. 5:21: empires, kingdoms, royalties, are not disposed of by the composed contracts of men, but by the immediate hand and work of God; Hos, 13:11: "I gave you a king in my anger, I took him away in my wrath;" Job 36:7: He places kings in the throne, &c.

Ans. Here is a whole chapter of seven pages for one raw argument ten times before repeated.

1. Exod. 9:7: I have raised up Pharaoh. Paul expounds it (Rom. 9) to prove that king Pharaoh was a vessel of wrath fitted for destruction by God's absolute will; and the Prelate following Arminius with treasonable charity applies this to our king. Can this man pray for the king?

2. Elisha anointed, but did not constitute Hazael king; he foretold he should be king, and if he be a king of God's making, who slew his sick prince and invaded the throne by innocent blood, judge you, I would not take kings of the Prelate's making.

3. If God give to Nebuchadnezzar the same title or the servant of God which is given to Daniel (Ps. 18:1, and 116:16) and to Moses (Jos. 1:2) all kings, because kings, are men according to God's heart. Why is not royalty then founded on grace? Nebuchadnezzar was not otherwise his servant than he was the hammer of the earth and a tyrannical conqueror of the Lord's people. All the heathen kings are called kings. But how came they to their thrones for the most part? Like David and Hezekiah? But God anointed them not by his prophets; they came to their kingdoms by the people's election, or by blood and rapine; the latter way is no ground to you to deny Athaliah to be a lawful princess: she and Abimelech were lawful princes, and their sovereignty as immediately and independently from God as the sovereignty of many heathen kings. See then how justly Athaliah was killed as a bloody usurper of the throne, and this would license your brethren, the Jesuits, to stab heathen kings, whom you will have as well kings as the Lord's anointed, though Nebuchadnezzar and many

of them made their way to the throne, against all law of God and man through a bloody patent.

4. Cyrus is God's anointed and his shepherd too; therefore his arbitrary government is a sovereignty immediately depending on God, and above all law; it is a wicked consequence.

5. God named Cyrus near a hundred years before he was born; God named and desired Judas very individually, and named the donkey that Christ should ride on to Jerusalem (Zech. 9:9) some more hundred years than one. What, will the Prelate make them independent kings for that?

6. God gives kingdoms to whom he will. What then? This will prove kingdoms to be as independent and immediately from God as kings are; for as God gives kings to kingdoms, so he gives kingdoms to kings, and no doubt he gives kingdoms to whom he will. So he gives prophets, apostles, pastors, to whom he will; and he gives tyrannical conquests to whom he will; and it is Nebuchadnezzar to whom Daniel speaks that from the Lord, and he had no just title to many kingdoms, especially to the kingdom of Judah, which yet God, the King of kings, gave to him because it was his good pleasure; and if God had not commanded them by the mouth of his prophet Jeremiah, might they not have risen and with the sword have vindicated themselves and their own liberty, no less than they lawfully by the sword vindicated themselves from under Moab (Judges 3). and from under Jabin, king of Canaan, who for twenty years mightily oppressed the children of Israel (Judges 4).

Now this Popish Prelate, by all these instances, making heathen kings to be kings by as good a title as David and Hezekiah, condemns the people of God as rebels, if being subdued and conquered by the Turk and Spanish king they should by the sword recover their own liberty; and that Israel and the saviors which God raised to them had not warrant from the law of nature to vindicate themselves to liberty, which was taken from them violently and unjustly by the sword. From all this it shall well follow that the tyranny of bloody conquerors is immediately and only dependent from God, no less than lawful sovereignty; for Nebuchadnezzar's sovereignty over the people of God, and many other kingdoms also, was avenged by God as tyranny (Jer. 1:6-7), and therefore the vengeance of the Lord, and the vengeance of his temple came upon him and his land (Jer. 1:16ff). It is true the people of God were commanded by God to submit to the king of Babylon, to serve him, and to pray for him, and to do the contrary was rebellion; but this was not because the king of Babylon was their king, and because the King of Babylon had a command of God to bring under his yoke the people of God. Thus Christ had a commandment to suffer the death of the cross (John 10:18), but had Herod and Pilate any warrant to crucify him? None at all.

7. He says royalties, even of heathen kings, are not disposed of by the composed contracts of men, but by the immediate hand and work of God. But the contracts of men to give a kingdom to a person, which a heathen community may lawfully do, and so by contract dispose of a kingdom, is not opposite to the immediate hand of God, appointing royalty and monarchy at His own blessed liberty. Lastly, he says, God took away Saul in his wrath; but I pray you, did God only do it? Then had Saul, because a king, a patent royal from God to kill himself, for so God took him away, and we are rebels by this if we suffer not the king to kill himself. Well pleaded.

QUESTION 6.

WHETHER OR NOT THE KING BE SO ALLENARLY[1] FROM BOTH, IN REGARD TO THE SOVEREIGNTY AND DESIGNATION OF HIS PERSON, AS HE IS NO WAY FROM THE PEOPLE, BUT ONLY BY MERE APPROBATION

The forms of government not from God by an act of naked providence, but by his approving will. Sovereignty not from the people by sole approbation. Though God has peculiar acts of providence in creating kings, it follows not from this that the people make not kings. The Popish Prelate exposits prophecies true only of David, Solomon, and Jesus Christ, as true of profane heathen kings. The Popish Prelate makes all the heathen kings to be princes, anointed with the holy oil of saving grace.

Dr. Ferne, a man much for monarchy, says, "Though monarchy has its excellency, being first set up by God in Moses, yet neither monarchy, aristocracy, nor any other form is *jure divino*, but we say," says he, "the power itself, or that sufficiency of authority to govern that is in a monarchy or

---

1. Solely.

aristocracy, abstractly considered from the qualification of other forms, is a flux and constitution subordinate to that providence; an ordinance of that *dixi* or silent word by which the world was made, and shall be governed under God."[2] This is a great debasing of the Lord's anointed, for so sovereignty has no warrant in God's word, formally as it is such a government, but is in the world by providence, as sin is, and as the falling of a sparrow to the ground, but God's word has not only commanded that government should be but that fathers and mothers should be, and not only that politic rulers should be, but also kings by name, and other aristocratic judges should be (Rom. 13:3; Deut. 17:14; 1 Pet. 2:17; Prov. 24:21; Prov. 15:16). If the power of monarchy and aristocracy, abstracted from the forms, is from God, then it is no more lawful to resist aristocratic government and our lords of parliament or judges than it is lawful to resist kings.

But hear the Prelate's reasons to prove that the king is from the people by approbation only, "The people are said to set a king over them only as the saints are said to judge the world (1 Cor. 6), that is, by consenting to Christ's judgment; so the people do not make a king by transferring on him sovereignty, but by accepting, acknowledging, and reverencing him as king, whom God has both constituted and designated king."

Ans. 1. This is said, but not a word proved, for the Queen of Sheba and Hiram acknowledged, reverenced, and obeyed Solomon as king, and yet they made him not king, as the princes of Israel did.

2. Reverence and obedience of the people is relative to the king's laws, but the people's making a king is not relative to the laws of a king; for then he should be a king giving laws

and commanding the people as king before the people make him king.

3. If the people's approving and consenting that an elected king be their king presupposes that he is a king, designated and constituted by God, before the people approve him as king, let the Popish Prelate give us an act of God now designating a man king, for there is no immediate voice from heaven saying to a people, 'This is your king,' before the people elect one of six to be their king. And this infallibly proves that God designates one of six to be a king, to a people who had no king before by no other act but by determining the hearts of the states to elect and designate this man king, and pass over any of the other five.

4. When God forbids them to choose a stranger (Deut. 17), he presupposes they may choose a stranger; for God's law now given to man in the state of sin presupposes he has corruption of nature to do contrary to God's law. Now if God did hold forth that their setting a king over them was but the people's approving the man whom God shall both constitute and designate to be king, then he should presuppose that God was to designate a stranger to be the lawful king of Israel, and the people should be interdicted to approve and consent that the man should be king whom God should choose; for it was impossible that the people should make a stranger king (God is the only immediate king-creator), the people should only approve and consent that a stranger should be king; yet upon supposition that God first constituted and designated the stranger king, it was not in the people's power that the king should be a brother rather than a stranger; for if the people have no power to make a king, but do only approve him or consent to him when he is both made and designed of God to be king, it is not in their power that he be either brother

or stranger, and so God commands what is simply impossible. Consider the sense of the command by the Prelate's vain logic: I, Jehovah, as I only create the world of nothing, so I only constitute and designate a man, whether a Jew or Nebuchadnezzar, a stranger, to be your king; yet I forbid you, under the pain of my curse, that you set any king over yourselves, but only a brother. What is this, but I forbid you to be creators by omnipotent power?

5. To these add the reasons I produced before, that the people by no shadow of reason can be commanded to make this man king, not that man, if they only consent to the manmade king, but have no action in the making of the king.

Popish Prelate. All the acts, real and imaginable, which are necessary for the making of kings, are ascribed to God. Take the first king as a ruling case, "Behold the king whom You have chosen, and whom You have desired; and, behold, the Lord has set a king over you!" (1 Sam. 12:13). This election of the people can be no other but their admittance or acceptance of the king whom God has chosen and constituted, as the words, "whom You have chosen," imply. 1 Sam. 9:17; 1 Sam. 10:1: You have Saul's election and constitution, where Samuel as priest and prophet anoints him, doing reverence and obeisance to him, and ascribing to God that he did appoint him supreme and sovereign over his inheritance. And the same expression is "The Lord has set a king over you;" (1 Sam. 12:13), which is, "I have set my king upon my holy hill of Zion" (Ps. 2:6). Neither man nor angel has any share in any act of constituting Christ king (Deut. 17). The Lord vindicates as proper and peculiar to Himself the designation of the person. It was not arbitrary to the people to admit or reject Saul so designated. It pleased God to consummate the work by the acceptance, consent, and approbation of the people, *ut suaviore modo*, that by a smoother way he might encourage Saul to undergo the hard charge, and make his people the more heartily, without grumbling and scruple, to reverence and obey him. The people's admittance possibly added something to the solemnity and to the pomp, but nothing to the essential and real constitution or necessity; it only puts the subjects *in mala fide*, if they should contravene, as the intimation of a law, the coronation of an hereditary king, the enthronement of a bishop. And 1 Kings, 3:7: "you have made your servant king;" 1 Sam. 16:1: "I have provided me a king;" Ps. 18:50: He is God's king; Ps. 89:19: "I have exalted one chosen out of the people;" ver. 20: He anoints them; ver. 27: adopts them: "I will make him my firstborn." The firstborn is above every brother individually, and above all, though a thousand, combined.

Ans. 1. By this reason, inferior judges are no less immediate deputies of God, and so irresistible, than the king, because God took off the spirit that was on Moses, and immediately poured it on the seventy elders, who were judges inferior to Moses (Num. 2:14-16)

2. This Popish Prelate cannot make a syllogism. If all the acts necessary to make a king are ascribed to God, none to the people, then God both constitutes and designates the king, but the former the Scripture says; therefore, if all the acts be ascribed to God, as though to the prime kingmaker and disposer of kings and kingdoms, and none to the people in that notion, then God both constitutes and designates a king. Both major and minor are false. The major is as false as the very Popish Prelate himself. All the acts necessary for war-making are in an eminent manner ascribed to God, such as (1). The Lord fights for his own people (2). The Lord scattered the enemies (3). The Lord slew Og, king of Bashan (4). The battle is the Lord's (5). The victory the Lord's; therefore Israel never

fought a battle. So Deut. 32: The Lord alone led his people; the Lord led them in the wilderness; their bow and their sword gave them not the land. God wrought all their works for them (Isa. 26:12); therefore Moses led them not; therefore the people went not on their own legs through the wilderness; therefore the people never shot an arrow, never drew a sword. It follows not. God did all these as the first, eminent, principal, and efficacious pre-determinator of the creature (though this Arminian and popish prelate heed not, to honor God). The assumption is also false, for the people made Saul and David kings, and it would be ridiculous that God should command them to make a brother, not a stranger, king, if it was not in their power whether he should be a Jew, a Scythian, an Ethiopian, who was their king, if God alone did without them choose, constitute, designate the person, and perform all acts essential to make a king; and the people had nothing more in them than to admit and consent, and that for the solemnity and pomp, not for the essential constitution of the king.

In 1 Sam. 9:17 and 10:1, we have not Saul elected and constituted king. Samuel did obeisance to him and kissed him because of the royal honor which God was to put upon him; for before this prophetic anointing he made him sit in the chief place, and honored him as king (1 Sam. 9:22), when Samuel was still materially king and the Lord's vicegerent in Israel. If then the Prelate conclude anything from Samuel's doing reverence and obeisance to him as king, it shall follow that Saul was formally king, before Samuel anointed him and kissed him (1 Sam. 10:1), and that must be before he was formally king; otherwise he was in God's appointment king, before ever he saw Samuel's face; and it is true he ascribes honor to him, as to one appointed by God to be supreme sovereign, for that which he should be, not for that which he was, since he

set him in the chief place (1 Sam. 9:22); and, therefore, it is
false that we have Saul's election and constitution to be king
(1 Sam. 10). For after that the people are rebuked for seeking
a king, with a purpose to dissuade them from it as a sinful
desire, and he is chosen by lots after that and made king, and
after Samuel's anointing of him he was a private man, and did
hide himself among the stuff (ver. 22).

3. The Prelate, from ignorance or willfully, I know not, says
the expression and phrase is the same, 1 Sam. 12:13, and Ps.
2:6, which is false; for 1 Sam. 12-13, it is ‫ח נתז יהוה עליבמ מלך‬
‫והו‬. Behold the Lord has given you a king, such is the expression (Hos. 13:11). I gave them a king in my wrath, but that
is not the expression in Psalm 2:6, but this, ‫סלכי ואני נסכחי‬
"But I have established him my king," and even if it were the
same expression, it follows not that the people have no hand
any other way in appointing Christ their head (though that
phrase also be in the Word, Hos. 1:11) than by consenting and
believing in him as king; but this proves not that the people
in appointing a king has no hand but naked approbation, for
the same phrase does not express the same action; nay, the
judges are to kiss Christ (Ps. 2:12) the same way, and by the
same action that Samuel kissed Saul (1 Sam. 10:1) and the
idolaters kissed the calves (Hos. 13:2), for the same Hebrew
word is used in all the three places, and yet it is certain the
first kissing is spiritual, the second a kiss of honor, and the
third an idolatrous kissing.

4. The anointing of Saul cannot be a leading rule to the
making of all kings to the world's end; for the Popish Prelate, forgetting himself, said that only some few, such as Moses, Saul, and David, &c. by extraordinary manifestation from
heaven were made kings.

5. He says it was not arbitrary for the people to admit or reject Saul so designated. What means he? It was not *morally* arbitrary, because they were under a law (Deut. 17:14-15) to make him king whom the Lord should choose. That is true. But was it not arbitrary to them to break a law *physically*? I think he, who is a professed Arminian, will not so side with Manicheans and fatalists. But the Popish Prelate must prove it was not arbitrary, either morally or physically, to them not to accept Saul as their king, because they had no action at all in the making of a king. God did it all, both by constituting and designating the king. Why then did God (Deut. 17) give a law to them to make this man king, not that man, if it was not in their free will to have any action or hand in the making of a king at all? But that some sons of Belial would not accept him as their king is expressly said (1 Sam. 10:27) and how did Israel conspire with Absalom to unking and dethrone David, whom the Lord had made king? If the Prelate mean it was not arbitrary to them physically to reject Saul, he speaks wonders; the sons of Belial did reject him, therefore they had physical power to do it. If he means it was not arbitrary, that is, it was not lawful to them to reject him, that is true, but does it follow they had no hand nor action in making Saul king, because it was not lawful for them to make a king in a sinful way, and to refuse him whom God choose to be king? Then see what I infer. (1). That they had no hand in obeying him as king, because they sinned in obeying unlawful commandments against God's law, and so they had no hand in approving and consenting he should be king; the contrary of which the Popish Prelate says. (2). So might the Popish Prelate prove men are passive and have no action in violating all the commandments of God, because it is not lawful to them to violate any one commandment.

6. The Lord (Deut. 17) vindicates this as proper and peculiar to himself: to choose the person, and to choose Saul. What then? Therefore now the people, choosing a king, have no power to choose or name a man, because God anointed Saul and David by immediate manifestation of his will to Samuel; this consequence is nothing, and also it follows in no manner that therefore the people made not Saul king.

7. That the people's approbation of a king is not necessary is the saying of Bellarmine and the papists, and that the people choose their ministers in the apostolic church, not by a necessity of a divine commandment, but to conciliate love between pastor and people. Papists hold that if the Pope make a popish king the head and king of Britain against the people's will, yet is he their king.

8. David was then king all the time Saul persecuted him. He sinned, truly, in not discharging the duty of a king, only because he lacked a ceremony, the people's approbation, which the Prelate says is required to the solemnity and pomp, not to the necessity, and truth, and essence of a formal king. So the king's coronation oath and the people's oath must be ceremonies; and because the Prelate is perjured himself, therefore perjury is but a ceremony also.

9. The enthronement of bishops is like the kinging of the Pope. The apostles must spare thrones when they come to heaven (Luke 22:29-30); the popish prelates, with their head the Pope, must be enthroned.

10. The hereditary king he makes a king before his coronation, and his acts are as valid before as after his coronation. It might cost him his head to say that the Prince of Wales is now king of Britain, and his acts, acts of kingly royalty, no less than our sovereign is king of Britain, if laws and parliaments had their own vigor from royal authority.

11. I allow that kings are as high as God has placed them, but God said of all kings, "I will make him my firstborn," &c. (Ps. 89:26-27), which is true of Solomon as the type (2 Sam. 7; 1 Chron. 17:22; 2 Sam. 7:12); and fulfilled by Christ, and by the Holy Ghost spoken of him is blasphemous (Heb. 1:5-6); for God said not to Nero, Julian, Dioclesian, Belshazzar, Evil-merodach, who were lawful kings, "I will make him my firstborn," and that any of these blasphemous idolatrous princes should cry to God, "He is my father, my God," &c. is divinity well-befitting an excommunicated prelate. Of the king's dignity above the kingdom I speak not now; the Prelate pulled it in by the hair, but hereafter we shall hear of it.

Popish Prelate: God only anointed David (1 Sam. 16:4) the men of Bethlehem, yea, Samuel knew it not before. God says, "With mine holy oil have I anointed him," (Ps. 89:91). 1. He is the Lord's anointed. 2. The oil is God's, not from the apothecary's shop, nor the priest's vial; this oil descended from the Holy Ghost, who is no less the true olive than Christ is the true vine, yet not the oil of saving grace, as some fantastics say, but holy (1.) from the author, God, (2.) from influence in the person it makes the person of the king sacred, (3.) from influence on his charge, his function and power is sacred.

Ans. 1. The Prelate said before, David's anointing was extraordinary; here he draws this anointing to all kings.

2. Let David be formally both constituted and designated king various years before the states made him king at Hebron, and then (1) Saul was not king; the Prelate will term that treason. (2) This was a dry oil. David's person was not made sacred, nor his authority sacred by it, for he remained a private man, and called Saul his king, his master, and himself a subject. (3) This oil was, no doubt, God's oil, and the Prelate will have it the Holy Ghost's, yet he denies that saving grace, yea,

he denies that any supernatural gift should be the foundation of royal dignity and that it is a pernicious tenet. So to me he would have the oil from heaven, and yet not from heaven. (4) This holy oil, wherewith David was anointed (Ps. 89:20) is the oil of saving grace; his own dear brethren, the papists, say so, and especially Lyranus, Glossa ordinaria, Hugo Cardinalis, his beloved Bellarmine, and Lorinus, Calvin, Musculus, Marloratus. If these be fanatics, if as I think they are to the Prelate, yet the text is evident that this oil of God was the oil of saving grace, bestowed on David as on a special type of Christ, who received the Spirit above measure and was the anointed of God (Ps. 45:7) whereby all his "garments smell of myrrh, aloes and cassia," (ver. 8) and "his name Messiah is as ointment poured out (Song. 1). This anointed shall be head of his enemies. "His dominion shall be from the sea to the rivers" (ver. 25). He is in the covenant of grace (ver. 26). He is "higher than the kings of the earth." The grace of perseverance is promised to his seed (ver. 28-30). His kingdom is eternal, "as the days of heaven" (ver. 35-36). If the Prelate will look under himself to Diodatus and Ainsworth, [1] this holy oil was poured on David by Samuel, and on Christ was poured the Holy Ghost, and that by warrant of Scripture (1 Sam. 16:1; 13:14; Luke 4:18, 21; John 3:34) and Junius and Mollerus says with them.[2] Now the Prelate takes the court way, to pour this oil of grace on many dry princes who without all doubt are kings essentially no less than David. He must see better than the man who, finding Pontius Pilate in the Creed, said he endeavored to be a good man; so, because he has found Nero the tyrant, Julian the apostate, Nebuchadnezzar, Evil-merodach, Hazael, Hagag, all the kings of Spain, and, I doubt not, the Great Turk in Ps. 89:19-20, so all these kings are anointed with the oil of grace, and

---

1. *Annot.*

2. *Annot. in loc; Com. ib.*

all these must make their enemies' necks their footstool. All these are higher than the kings of the earth and are hard and fast in the covenant of grace, &c.

Popish Prelate. All the royal ensigns and acts of kings are ascribed to God. The crown is of God (Isa. 62:3; Ps. 21:3). In the emperor's coin was a hand putting a crown on their head. The heathen said they were θεοστιφῦς, as though holding their crowns from God Ps. 18:39: you have girt me with strength (the sword is the emblem of strength) unto battle. See Judg. 7:17: their scepter is God's scepter. Exod. 4:20; 17:9: we read of two rods, Moses' and Aaron's. Aaron's rod budded: God made both the rods. Their judgment is the Lord's (2 Chron. 19:6). Their throne is God's (1 Chron. 19:21). The fathers called them, *sacra vestigia, sacra majestas*, their commandment, *divalis jussio*. The law says all their goods are *res sacras*. Therefore our new statists disgrace kings if they blaspheme not God, in making them the derivatives of the people: the basest extract of the basest of irrational creatures, the multitude, the commonalty.

Ans. This is all one argument from the Prelate's beginning of his book to the end: In a most special and eminent act of God's providence kings are from God, but therefore they are not from men and men's consent. It follows not. From a most special and eminent act of God's providence Christ came into the world and took on Him our nature; therefore He came not of David's loins. It is a vain consequence. There could not be a more eminent act than this. Ps. 40: "A body you have given me;" therefore he came not of David's house, and from Adam by natural generation, and was not a man like us in all things except sin. It is tyrannical and domineering logic. Many things are ascribed to God only by reason of a special and admirable act of providence, such as the saving of the world by Christ, the giving of Canaan to Israel, the bringing his people out from Egypt and from Chaldea, the sending of the gospel to both Jew and Gentile, &c.; but

say we that God did none of these things by the ministry of men, and
weak and frail men?

1. How proves the Prelate that all royal ensigns are ascribed to
God, because the church universal shall be as a crown of glory and
a royal diadem in the hand of the Lord (Isa. 62); therefore, *baecu-
lus in angulo*, the church shall be as a seal on the heart of Christ.
What then? Jerome, Procopius, Cyrillus, with good reason, render
the meaning thus: Thou, O Zion and church, shall be to me a royal
priesthood, and a holy people. For that he speaks of his own kingdom
and church is most evident (ver. 1-2): "For Zion's sake I will not hold
my peace," &c.

2. God put a crown of pure gold on David's head (Ps. 21:3); therefore Julian, Nero, and no elective kings are made and designated to
be kings by the people. He shall never prove this consequence. The
Chaldee paraphrase applies it to the reign of King Messiah; Diodatus speaks of the kingdom of Christ; Ainsworth makes this crown
a sign of Christ's victory; Athanasius, Eusebius, Origen, Augustine,
Dydimus expound it of Christ and his kingdom. The Prelate extends
it to all kings, as the blasphemous rabbis, especially Rabbi Solomon,
deny that he speaks of Christ here. But what more reason is there to
expound this of the crowns of all kings given by God (which I deny
not) to Nero, Julian, &c., than to expound the foregoing and following verses as applied to all kings? Did Julian rejoice in God's salvation? Did God grant Nero his heart's desire? Did God grant (as it is
in ver. 4) life eternal to heathen kings as kings? Which words all interpreters expound of the eternity of David's throne, till Christ come,
and of victory and life eternal purchased by Christ, as Ainsworth,
with good reason, expounds it. And what though God gave David
a crown, was it not by second causes and by bowing all Israel's heart
to come in sincerity to Hebron to make David king (1 Kings 12:38)?
God gave corn and wine to Israel (Hos. 2) and shall the prelate and

the anabaptist infer, therefore, he gives it not by ploughing, sowing, and the art of the husbandman?

3. The heathen acknowledges a divinity in kings, but he is blind who reads them and sees not in their writings that they teach that the people make kings.

4. God girt David with strength, while he was a private man, and persecuted by Saul, and fought with Goliath, as the title of the same bears; and he made him a valiant man of war, to break bows of steel; therefore he gives the sword to kings as kings, and they receive no sword from the people. This is poor logic.

5. The Popish Prelate sends us (Judg. 7:17) to the singular and extraordinary power of God with Gideon; and, I say, that same power behooved to be in Oreb and Zeeb (ver. 27) for they were שרי princes, and such as the Prelate, from Prov, 7:15, says have no power from the people.

6. Moses's and Aaron's rods were miraculous. This will prove that priests are also God's, and their persons sacred. I see not (except the Prelate would be at worshipping of relics) what more royal divinity is in Moses's rod, because he wrought miracles by his rod, than there is in Elijah's staff, in Peter's napkin, in Paul's shadow. This is like the strong symbolical theology of his fathers the Jesuits, which is not argumentative, unless he say that Moses, as king of Jeshurun, wrought miracles, and why should not Negro's, Caligula's, Pharaoh's, and all kings' rods then dry up the Red Sea and work miracles?

7. We give all the styles to kings that the fathers gave, and yet we think not when David commands to kill Uriah, and a king commands to murder his innocent subjects in England and Scotland, that that is *divalis jussio*, the command of a god; and that this is a good consequence. Whatever the king commands, though it were to kill his most loyal subjects, is the commandment of God; therefore the king is not made king by the people.

8. Therefore, says he, these new statists disgrace the king. If a new statist, sprung out of a poor pursuivant of Crail, from the dunghill to the court, could have made himself an old statist, and more expert in state affairs than all the nobles and soundest lawyers in Scotland and England, this might have more weight.

9. Therefore the king (says th Popish Prelate) is not "the extract of the basest of rational creatures." He means, *fex populi*, his own house and lineage; but God calls them his own people, "a royal priesthood, a chosen generation," and Ps. 78:71 will warrant us to say the people is much worthier before God than one man, seeing God chose David for "Jacob his people, and Israel his inheritance," that he might feed them. John Popish Prelate's father's suffrage in making a king will never be sought. We make not the multitude, but the three estates, including the nobles and gentry, to be as rational creatures as any apostate prelate in the three kingdoms.

QUESTION 7.

WHETHER THE POPISH PRELATE CONCLUDE THAT
NEITHER CONSTITUTION NOR DESIGNATION OF
KINGS IS FROM THE PEOPLE.

The excellency of kings makes them not of God's only constitution
and designation. How sovereignty is in the people, and how not. A
community does not surrender their right and liberty to their rulers, so
much as their power active to do, and passive to suffer, violence. God's
loosing of the bonds of kings by the mediation of the people's despising
him proves against the Popish Prelate that the Lord takes away and
gives royal majesty mediately, not immediately. The subordination
of people to kings and rulers is both natural and voluntary; the
subordination of beasts and creatures to man is merely natural. The
place, Gen. 9:5, "He that sheds man's blood," &c. discussed.

The Popish Prelate aims (but it is an empty aim) to prove that
the people are wholly excluded. I answer only arguments not
pitched on before, as the Prelate says.

Popish Prelate. 1. To whom can it be more proper to give the rule
over men than to Him who is the only king truly and properly of the
whole world? 2. God is the immediate author of all rule and power

that is among all his creatures, above or below. 3. Man before the fall received dominion and empire over all the creatures below immediately, such as Gen. 1:28 and 9:2; therefore we cannot deny that the most noble government (to wit monarchy) must be immediately from God, without any contract or compact of men.

Ans. 1. The first reason concludes not what is in question; for God only gives rule and power to one man over another; therefore he gives it immediately. It follows not.

2. It shall as well prove that God does immediately constitute all judges, and therefore it shall be unlawful for a city to appoint a mayor, or a shire a justice of peace.

3. The second argument is inconsequent also, because God in creation is the immediate author of all things, and, therefore, without consent of the creatures or any act of the creature, created an angel, a nobler creature than man, and a man than a woman, and men above beasts, because those that are not can exercise no act at all. But it follows not that all the works of providence, such as is the government of kingdoms, are done immediately by God; for in the works of providence for the most part in ordinary God works by *me*Ans. It is then as good a consequence as this: God immediately created man, therefore he keeps his life immediately also without food and sleep; God immediately created the sun, therefore God immediately without the mediation of the sun gives light to the world. The making of a king is an act of reason, and God has given a man reason to rule himself, and therefore has given to a society an instinct of reason to appoint a governor over themselves; but no act of reason goes before man be created, therefore it is not in his power whether he be created a creature of greater power than a beast or no.

4. God by creation gave power to a man over the creatures, and so immediately, but I hope men cannot say, God by creation has made a man king over men.

5. The excellency of monarchy (if it be more excellent than any other government, of which hereafter) is no ground for it being immediately from God as well as man's dominion over the creature; for then the work of man's redemption, being more excellent than the raising of Lazarus, should have been done immediately without the incarnation, death and satisfaction of Christ (for no act of God without himself is comparable to the work of redemption, 1 Pet. 1:11-12; Col. 1:18-22) and God's less excellent works, such as His creating of beasts and worms, should have been done mediately, and his creating of man immediately.

Popish Prelate. They who execute the judgment of God must needs have the power to judge from God; but kings are deputies in the exercise of the judgments of God, therefore the proposition is proved. How is it imaginable that God reconciles the world by ministers, and saves man by them (1 Cor. 5; 1 Tim. 4:16) unless they receive a power so to do from God? The assumption is let none say Moses and Jehoshaphat spoke of inferior judges (Deut. 1:17; 1 Chron, 19:6); for that which the king does to others he does by himself. Also, the execution of the kingly power is from God; for the king is the servant, angel, legate, minister of God (Rom. 13:6-7). God properly and primarily is King, and King of kings, and Lord of lords (1 Tim. 6:15; Rev. 1:5); all kings, related to him, are kings equivocally and in resemblance, and he the only King,

Ans. 1. That which is in question is never concluded, namely, that "the king is both immediately constituted and designated king by God only, and not by the mediation of the people;" for when God reconciles and saves men by pastors, he saves them by the intervening action of men; so he scourges his people by men as by his sword (Ps. 17:14) hand, staff, rod (Isa. 10:5) and his hammer. Does it follow that God only does immediately scourge his people, and that wicked men have no more hand and action in scourging his people than the

Prelate says the people has a hand in making a king? And that is no hand at all by the Prelate's way.

2. We may borrow the Prelate's argument: Inferior judges execute the judgment of the Lord, and not the judgment of the king; therefore, by the Prelate's argument God does only by immediate power execute judgment in them, and the inferior judges are not God's ministers, executing the judgment of the Lord. But the conclusion is against all truth, and so must the Prelate's argument be; and that inferior judges are the immediate substitutes and deputies of God is hence proved, and shall be hereafter made good, if God will.

3. God is properly King of kings, so He is God properly *causa causarum*, the Cause of causes, the Life of lives, the Joy of joys. What! Shall it then follow that he works nothing in the creatures by their mediation as causes? Because God is Light of lights, does He not enlighten the earth and air by the mediation of the sun? Then God communicates not life mediately by generation; He causes not his saints to rejoice with joy unspeakable and glorious by the intervening mediation of the Word. These are vain consequences. Sovereignty and all power and virtue is in God infinitely, and what virtue and power of action is in the creatures, as they are compared with God, are in the creatures equivocally and in resemblance, and χατὰ δοξὴν in opinion rather than really. Hence it must follow that second causes work none at all, no more than the people has a hand or action in making the king, and that is no hand at all, as the Prelate says. And God only and immediately works all works in the creatures, because both the power of working and actual working comes from God, and the creatures, in all their working, are God's instruments. And if the Prelate argue so frequently from power given by God, to prove that actual reigning is from God immediately, the Lord "gives the power to get wealth" (Deut. 8:18). Will it follow that Israel gets no riches at all, or that God does not mediately by them and their industry get them? I think not.

Popish Prelate. To whom can it be due to give the kingly office but to Him only who is able to give the endowment and ability for the office? Now God only and immediately gives ability to be a king, as the sacramental anointing proves (Josh. 3:10). Othniel is the first judge after Joshua, and it is said, "And the Spirit of the Lord came upon him, and he judged Israel." The like is said concerning Saul and David.

Ans. 1. God gave royal endowments immediately, therefore he immediately now makes the king. It follows not, for the species of government is not that which formally constitutes a king, for then Nero, Caligula, Julian, should not have been kings; and those who come to the crown by conquest and blood, are essentially kings, as the Prelate says. But be all these Othniels upon whom the Spirit of the Lord comes? Then they are not essentially kings who are babes and children, and foolish and destitute of the royal endowments; but it is one thing to have a royal gift, and another thing to be formally called to the kingdom. David had royal gifts after Samuel anointed him, but if you make him king before Saul's death, Saul was both a traitor all the time that he persecuted David, and so no king, and also king and God's anointed, as David acknowledges him, and, therefore that spirit that came on David and Saul makes nothing against the people's election of a king, as the Spirit of God is given to pastors under the New Testament, as Christ promised; but it will not follow that the designation of the man who is to be pastor should not be from the church and from men, as the Prelate denies that either the constitution or designation of the king is from the people, but from God only.

2. I believe the infusion of the Spirit of God upon the judges will not prove that kings are now both constituted and designated by God solely, only, and immediately; for the judges were indeed immediately, and for the most part extraordinarily, raised up by God; and God indeed in the time of the Jews was the King of Israel in another manner than he was the King of all the nations, and is the King of Christian realms now, and, therefore, the people's despising of Samuel was a

refusal that God should reign over them, because God in the judges revealed Himself even in matters of policy, as what should be done to the man that gathered sticks on the Sabbath day, and the like, as He does not now to kings.

Popish Prelate. Sovereignty is a ray of divine glory and majesty, but this cannot be found in people, whether you consider them jointly or singly; if you consider them singly, it cannot be in every individual man, for sectaries say that all are born equal with a like freedom, and if it be not in the people singly, it cannot be in them jointly, for all the contribution in this compact and contract, which they fancy to be human composition and voluntary constitution, is only by a surrender of the native right that everyone had in himself. From where, then, can this majesty and authority be derived? Again, where the obligation among equals is by contract and compact, violation of the faith plighted in the contract, cannot in proper terms be called disobedience or contempt of authority. It is no more but a receding from and a violation of that which was promised, as it may be in states or countries confederate. Nature, reason, conscience, Scripture, teach that disobedience to sovereign power is not only a violation of truth and breach of covenant, but also high disobedience and contempt, as is clear (1 Sam. 10:26). So when Saul (chap. 11) sent a yoke of oxen, hewed in pieces, to all the tribes, the fear of the Lord fell on the people, and they came out with one consent (1 Sam. 11:7); also He looses the bonds of kings (Job 11:18), that is, he looses their authority and brings them into contempt; and he girds their loins with a girdle, that is, he strengthens their authority and makes the people to reverence them. Heathens observe that there is θειον τι, some divine thing in kings. Profane histories say that this was so eminent in Alexander the Great that it was a terror to his enemies, and a powerful loadstone to draw men to compose the most seditious councils, and cause his most experienced commanders embrace and obey his counsel and command. Some stories write that, upon some great exigency, there was some resplendent majesty in the eyes of Scipio. This kept Pharaoh from lifting his hand against Moses, who charged him so boldly with his sins. When Moses did speak with God face to face in the mount, this resplendent glory of majesty so awed the people that they dared not behold his glory (Exod. 34); this repressed the fury of the people, enraged against Gideon from destroying their idol (Judg. 6); and the fear of man is naturally upon all living creatures below (Gen. 9). So what can this reverence, which is innate in the hearts of all subjects toward their sovereigns, be but the ordinance unrepealable of God and the natural effect of that majesty of princes with which they are endowed from above?

Ans. 1. I never heard any shadow of reason till now, and yet (because the lie has a latitude) here is but a shadow, which the Prelate stole from M. Anton, and I may say confidently this Plagiarius has not one line in his book which is not stolen, and for the present Spalato's argument is but spilt, and the nerves cut from it, while it is both bleeding and lamed. Let the reader compare them, and I pawn my credit he has ignorantly clipped Spalato. But I answer, "Sovereignty is a beam and ray" (as Spalato says) "of divine majesty, and is not either formally or virtually in the people." It is false that it is not virtually in the people; for there are two things in the judge, either inferior or supreme, for the argument holds in the majesty of a parliament, as we shall hear (1). The gift or grace of governing (the Arminian Prelate will be offended at this), (2). The authority of governing. The gift is supernatural, and is not in man naturally, and so not in the king; for he is physically but a mortal man, and this is a gift received, for Solomon asked it by prayer from God. There is a capacity passive in all individual men for it. As for the official authority itself, it is virtually in all in whom any of God's image is remaining since the fall, as is clear, as may be gathered from Gen. 1:28; yea, the father, the master, the judge, has it by God's institution, in some measure, over son, servant, and subject, though it be more in the supreme ruler; and for our purpose, it is not requisite that authoritative majesty should be in all (what is in the father and husband I hope to clear) I mean, it needs not to be formally in all, and so all are born alike and equal. But he who is a Papist, a Socinian, an Arminian, and therefore delivered to Satan by his mother church, must be the sectary, for we are where this Prelate left us, maintainers of the Protestant religion, contained in the Confession of Faith and National Covenant of Scotland, when this Demas forsook us and embraced the world.

2. Though not one single man in Israel be a judge or king by nature, nor have in them formally any ray of royalty or magistratical authority, yet it follows not that Israel, parliamentarily convened, has no such authority as to name Saul king in Mizpah and David king in Hebron (1 Sam. 10:24-25; 1 Chron. 11:12; 12:38-39). One man alone has not the keys of the kingdom of heaven (as the Prelate dreams), but it follows not that many convened in a church way has not this power (Matt. 18:17; 1 Cor. 5:1-4). One man has not strength to fight against an army of ten thousand; does it follow, therefore, that an army of twenty thousand has not strength to fight against these ten thousand? Though one Paul cannot synodically determine the question (Acts 15), it follows not that the apostles, and elders, and brethren, convened from various churches, has not power to determine it in a lawful synod; and, therefore, from a disjoined and scattered power, no man can argue to a united power. So no one man is an inferior ruler, nor has he the rays and beams of a number of aristocratical rulers; but it follows not that all these men, combined in a city or society have not power in a joint political body to choose inferior or aristocratic rulers.

3. The Popish Prelate's reason is nothing. All the contribution (says he) in the compact body to make a king is only by a surrender of the native right of every single man (the whole being only a voluntary contribution). How then can there be any majesty derived from them? I answer, very well, for the surrender is so voluntary that it is also natural and founded on the law of nature that men must have

governors, either many or one supreme ruler. And it is voluntary and depends on a positive institution of God whether the government be by one supreme ruler, as in a monarchy, or in many, as in an aristocracy, according as the necessity and temper of the commonwealth do most require. This constitution is so voluntary, as it has below it the law of nature for its general foundation, and above it, the supervenient institution of God, ordaining that there should be such magistrates, both kings and other judges, because without such all human societies should be dissolved.

4. Individual persons in creating a magistrate do not properly surrender their right, which can be called a right; for they do but surrender their power of doing violence to those of their fellows in that same community, so that they shall not now have moral power to do injuries without punishment; and this is not right or liberty properly, but servitude, for a power to do violence and injuries is not liberty, but servitude and bondage. But the Prelate talks of royalty as of mere tyranny, as if it were a proper dominion and servile empire that the prince has over his people, and not more paternal and fatherly than lordly or masterly.

5. He says, "Violation of faith, plighted in a contract among equals, cannot be called disobedience; but disobedience to the authority of the sovereign is not only breach of covenant, but high disobedience and contempt." But violation of faith among equals as equals is not properly disobedience; for disobedience is between a superior and an inferior, but violation of faith among equals, when they make one of their equals their judge and ruler is not only violation of truth, but also disobedience. All Israel and Saul, while he is a private man seeking his father's asses, are equals by covenant, obliged one to another; and so any injury done by Israel to Saul in that case is not disobedience, but only violation of faith. But when all Israel makes Saul their king, and swears to him obedience, he is not now their equal, and an injury done to him now is both a violation of their faith and

high disobedience also. Suppose a city of aldermen, all equal among themselves in dignity and place take one of their number and make him their mayor and provost: a wrong done to him now is not only against the rules of fraternity, but disobedience to one placed by God over them.

6. 1 Sam. 11:7: "The fear of the Lord fell on the people, and they came out with one consent to obey Saul," therefore God has placed authority in kings, which is not in people. It is true; because God has transferred the scattered authorities that are in all the people in one mass and, by virtue of his own ordinance has placed them in one man, who is king. What follows? That God confers this authority immediately upon the king without the mediation of any action of the people? Yea, the contrary rather follows.

7. God looses the bond of kings; that is, when God is to cast off kings, He causes them to loose all authority, and makes them come into contempt with the people. But what does this prove? That God takes away the majesty and authority of kings immediately, and therefore God gave to kings this authority immediately, without the people's conveyance? Yea, I take the Prelate's weapon from him. God does not take the authority of the king from him immediately, but mediately by the people's hating and despising him when they see his wickedness, as the people see Nero a monster-a prodigious blood-sucker. Upon this, all the people condemn him and despise him, and so the majesty is taken from Nero and all his mandates and laws, when they see him trample upon all laws, divine and human, and that mediately by the people's heart despising of his majesty; and so they repeat, and take again that awesome authority that they once gave him. And this proves that God gave him the authority mediately, by the consent of man.

8. Nor speaks he of kings only, but he pours contempt מל ברִיני ע super munificos (ver. 21). Pineda. Aria. Mont. super Principes, upon

nobles and great men; and this place may prove that no judges of the earth are made by men.

9. The heathen say that there is some divinity in princes, as in Alexander the Great and Scipio, toward their enemies, but this will prove that princes and kings have a superiority over those who are not their native subjects, for something of God is in them in relation to all men that are not their subjects. If this be a ground strong and good, because God only and independently from men takes away this majesty, as God only and independently gives it, then a king is sacred to all men, subjects or not subjects. Then it is unlawful to make war against any foreign king and prince, for in invading him or resisting him you resist that divine majesty of God that is in him; then you may not lawfully flee from a tyrant no more than you may lawfully flee from God.

10. Scipio was not a king; therefore this divine majesty is in all judges of the earth in a more or less measure; therefore God, only and immediately, may take this spark of divine majesty from inferior judges. It follows not. And kings, certainly, cannot infuse any spark of a divine majesty on any inferior judges, for God only immediately infuses it in men; therefore it is unlawful for kings to take this divinity from judges, for they resist God who resist parliaments, no less than those who resist kings. Scipio has divinity in him as well as Caesar, and that immediately from God, and not from any king.

11. Moses was not a king when he went to Pharaoh, for he had not as yet a people. Pharaoh was the king, and because Pharaoh was a king, the divines of Oxford must say his majesty must not in words of rebuke be resisted more than by deeds.

12. Moses's face did shine as a prophet receiving the law from God, not as a king. And is this sunshine from heaven upon the face of Nero and Julian? It must be, if it be a beam of royal majesty, if this prattler say right but this majesty was a type (2 Cor. 3:7), which did

adumbrate the glory of the law of God, and is far from being a royalty due to all heathen kings.

13. I would our king would show such a majesty in breaking the images and idols of his queen, and of papists about him.

14. The fear of Noah, and the regenerated who are in covenant with the beasts of the field (Job 5:23) is upon the beasts of the earth, not by approbation only, as the people make kings by the Prelate's way; nor yet by free consent, as the people freely transfer their power to him who is king. The creatures inferior to man have by no act of free will chosen man to be their ruler and transferred their power to him, because they are by nature inferior to man; and God by nature has subjected the creatures to man (Gen. 1:28) and so this proves not that the king by nature is above the people—I mean the man who is king, and therefore though God had planted in the hearts of all subjects a fear and reverence toward the king, upon supposition that they have made him king, it follows not that this authority and majesty is immediately given by God to the man who is king without the intervening consent of the people, for there is a native fear in the scholar to stand in awe of his teacher, and yet the scholar may willingly give himself to be a disciple to his teacher, and so give his teacher power over him. Citizens naturally fear their supreme governor of the city, yet they give to the man who is their supreme governor that power and authority which is the ground of awe and reverence. A servant naturally fears his master, yet often he gives his liberty and resigns it up voluntarily to his master, and this was not extraordinary among the Jews, where the servant did entirely love the master, and is now most ordinary when servants do for hire tie themselves to such a master. Soldiers naturally fear their commanders, yet they may and often do by voluntary consent make such men their commanders, and therefore from this it follows in no way that the governor of a city, the teacher, the master, the commander in war, has not his power and

authority only and immediately from God, but from his inferiors, who by their free consent appointed them for such places.

Popish Prelate (Arg. 7). This seems, or rather is, an unanswerable argument, No man has power of life and death but the Sovereign Power of life and death, namely, God (Gen. 9:5). God says thrice that He will require the blood of man at the hands of man, and this power God has committed to God's deputy: Whosoever sheds man's blood כאדם by man shall die, by the king, for the world knew not any kind of government at this time but monarchical, and this monarch was Noah, and if this power is from God, why not all sovereign power? Seeing it is homogeneous, and as jurists say *in indivisibili posita*, a thing in its nature indivisible, and that cannot be distracted or impaired, and if every man had the power of life and death, God should not be the God of order.

The Popish Prelate takes the pains to prove out of the text that a magistracy is established in the text.

Ans. 1. Let us consider this unanswerable argument (1). It is grounded upon a lie, and a conjecture never taught by any but himself, namely, that כאדם by, or in, or through man, must signify a magistrate, and a king only. This king was Noah. Never interpreter, nay, not commonsense can say that no magistrate is here understood but a king. The consequence is vain: His blood shall be shed by man; therefore by a magistrate? It follows not; therefore by a king? It follows not. There was not a king in the world as yet. Some make Belus, the father of Ninus, the first king and the builder of Babylon. This Ninus is thought the first builder of the city after called Nineveh, and the first king of the Assyrians. So says Quintus Curtius[1] and others, but grave authors believe that Nimrod was no other than Belus the father of Ninus. So

---

1. Book 5.

say Augustine,[1] Eusebius, Jerome;[2] and Eusebius[3] makes him the first
founder of Babylon; so say Clemens[4] and Pirerius,[5] and Josephus says
the same. Their times, their cruel natures are the same. Calvin says
Noah yet lived while Nimrod lived,[6] and the Scripture says, "Nimrod
began to reign, and be powerful on the earth." And Babel was לכחו
ראשיח ממ the beginning of his kingdom. No writer, Moses nor any
other, can show us a king before Nimrod. So Eusebius,[7] Paul Orosi-
us,[8] Jerome,[9] Josephus[10] say that he was the first king, and Tostatus
Abulens,[11] and our own Calvin, Luther,[12] Musculus on the place, and
Ainsworth make him the first king and the founder of Babylon. How
Noah was a king, or there was any monarchical government in the
world then, the Prelate has alone dreamed it. There was but fami-
ly-government before this.

2. And if there be magistracy here established by God, there is no
warrant to say it is only a monarchy; for if the Holy Ghost intends
a policy, it is a policy to be established to the world's end, and not to
be limited (as the Prelate does) to Noah's days. All interpreters upon
good ground establish the same policy that our Savior speaks of when
he says, "He shall perish by the sword who takes the sword" (Matt.
26:52). So the Netherlands have no lawful magistrate who has power
of life and death, because their government is aristocratic, and they

---

1. *De Civ. Dei* 16.17.
2. On Hosea 2.
3. *De prepar. Evan.* 9.3.
4. *Recog.* 4.
5. In Gen. 10:8-9, disp. 3, n. 67.
6. Commentary on Gen. 9.
7. Prologue on 1 Chron.
8. *De Ormesta mundi* 1.
9. *In traditio Hebrei in Gen.*
10. On Genesis 10.
11. On Gen. 10:9.
12. Com. ib.

have no king. So all acts of taking away the lives of evil-doers shall be acts of homicide in Holland. How absurd!

3. Nor do I see how the place in the native scope does establish a magistracy. Calvin says not so,[13] and interpreters deduce by consequence the power of the magistrate from this place. But the text is general: He who kills man shall be killed by man; either he shall fall into the magistrate's hand, or into the hand of some murderer; so Calvin,[14] Marlorat, &c. He speaks, says Pirerius, not of the fact and event itself, but of the deserving of murderers, and it is certain all murderers fall not into the magistrate's hands, but he says by God and man's laws they ought to die, though sometime one murderer kills another.[15]

4. The sovereign power is given to the king, therefore, it is given to him immediately without the consent of the people. It follows not.

5. Power of life and death is not given to the king only, but also to other magistrates, yea, and to a single private man in the just defense of his own life. Other arguments are but what the Prelate has said already.

---

13. Commentary.
14. *In lect.*
15. In Gen. 9:3-4, n. 37.

QUESTION 8.

WHETHER THE PRELATE PROVES BY FORCE OF
REASON THAT THE PEOPLE CANNOT BE CAPABLE OF
AN POWER OF GOVERNMENT.

In any community there is an active and passive power to government.
Popular government is not that by which the whole people are
governors. People by nature are equally indifferent to all the three
governments, and are not under anyone by nature. The Popish Prelate
denies the Pope his father to be the antichrist. The bad success of kings
chosen by people proves nothing against us, because kings chosen by
God had bad success through their own wickedness. The Popish Prelate
condemns King Charles's ratifying (Parl. 2, an. 1641) the whole
proceedings of Scotland in this present reformation. That there be any
supreme judges is an eminent act of divine providence, which hinders
not but that the king is made by the people. The people not patients in
making a king, as is water in the sacrament of baptism, in the act of
production of grace.

Popish Prelate. God and nature gives no power in vain, which may not be reduced into action; but an active power, or a power of actual governing, was never acted by the community; therefore this power cannot be seated in the community as in the prime and proper subject, and it cannot be in every individual person of a community, because government intrinsically and essentially includes a special distinction of governors, and some to be governed, and, to speak properly, there can no other power be conceived in the community, naturally and properly, but only *potestas passiva regiminis*, a capacity or susceptibility to be governed by one or by more, just as the first matter desires a form. This obliges all, by the dictate of nature's law, to submit to actual government, and as it is in every individual person, it is not merely and properly voluntary, because howsoever nature dictates that government is necessary for the safety of the society, yet every singular person by corruption and self-love has a natural aversion and repugnance to submit to any: every man would be a king himself. This universal desire, *appetitus universalis aut naturalis*, or universal propension to government, is like the act of the understanding assenting to the first principles of truth, and to the will's general propension to happiness in general, which propension is not a free act, except our new statists, as they have changed their faith, so they overturn true reason. It will puzzle them infinitely to make anything, in its kind passive, really active and collative of positive acts and effects. All know no man can give what he has not. An old philosopher would laugh at him who would say that a matter perfected and actuated by union with a form could at pleasure shake off its form and marry itself to another. They may as well say every wife has power to resume her freedom and marry another, as that any such power active is in the community, or any power to cast off monarchy.

Ans. 1. The Popish Prelate might have thanked Spalato for this argument, but he does not so much as cite him, for fear his theft be apprehended; but Spalato has it set down with stronger nerves than the Prelate's head was able to copy out of him. But Jac. de Almain,[1]

1. M. Anto. *De domini. Arch. Spalatens.* 6.2, n. 5-6.

and Navarrus,[1] with the Parisian doctors, said in the Council of Paris that political power is immediately from God, but first from the community; so that the community applies their power to this or that government—not of liberty, but by natural necessity—but Spalato and the plagiary Prelate do both look beside the book. The question does not now concern the *vis rectiva*, the power of governing in the people, but concerns the power government; for these two differ much. The former is a power of ruling and monarchical commanding of themselves. This power is not formally in the people, but only virtually, and no reason can say that a virtual power is idle because it cannot be actuated by that same subject that it is in; for then it should not be a virtual, but a formal power. Do not philosophers say such an herb virtually makes hot? And can the sottish Prelate say this virtual power is idle, and in vain given of God, because it does not formally heat your hand when you touch it.

2. The Popish Prelate, who is excommunicated for Popery, Socinianism, Arminianism, and is now turned apostate to Christ and his church must have changed his faith, not we, and be unreasonably ignorant, to press that axiom that "The power is idle that cannot be reduced to acts;"[2] for a generative power is given to living and sensitive creatures, this power is not idle though it be not reduced in act by all and every individual sensitive creature. A power of seeing is given to all who naturally do, or ought to see, yet it is not an idle power because many are blind, seeing it is put forth in action in many of that sort; so this power in the community is not idle because it is not put forth in acts in the people in which it is virtually, but is put forth in action in some of them whom they choose to be their governors; nor is it reasonable to say that it should be put forth in action by all the people, as if all should be kings and governors. But the question is not of the power of governing in the people, but of the power of

---

1. *De potest et La.* 1, q. 1.1, 6, et q. 2, 3, 5.

2. *Nem. don jud. not.* 3, n. 85.

government, that is, of the power of making governors and kings; and the community does put forth in act this power, as a free, voluntary, and active power; for (1.) a community transplanted to India, or any place of the world not before inhabited, has a perfect liberty to choose either a monarchy, or a democracy, or an aristocracy; for though nature may incline them to government in general, yet are they not naturally determined to anyone of those three more than another; (2.) Israel did of their own free will choose the change of government, and would have a king as the nations had; therefore they had free will, and thus an active power so to do, and not a passive inclination only to be governed, such as Spalato says agrees to the first matter; (3.) Royalists teach that a people under democracy or aristocracy have liberty to choose a king; and the Romans did this, therefore they had an active power to do it; therefore the Prelate's simile crooks: the matter at its pleasure cannot shake off its form, nor the wife cast off her husband being once married, but Barclay, Grotius, Amissens, Blackwood, and all the royalists teach that the people under any of these two forms of democracy or aristocracy may resume their power and cast off these forms and choose a monarch, and if monarchy be the best government, as royalists say, they may choose the best. And is this but a passive capacity to be governed? (4.) Of ten men fit for a kingdom they may designate one, and put the crown on his head, and refuse the other nine, as Israel crowned Solomon and refused Adonijah. Is this not a voluntary action, proceeding from a free, active, elective power? It will puzzle the pretended Prelate to deny this, that which the community does freely, they do not from such a passive capacity as is in the first matter in regard of the form. It is true that people, through corruption of nature, are averse to submit to governors "for conscience's sake, as unto the Lord," because the natural man, remaining in the state of nature, can do nothing that is truly good, but it is false that men have no active moral power to submit to superiors, but only a passive capacity to be governed.

He quite contradicts himself: for he said before that there is an "innate fear and reverence in the hearts of all men naturally, even in heathens, toward their sovereign" (section 4); yea, as we have a natural moral active power to love our parents and superiors (though it be not evangelically or legally in God's court, good) and so to obey their commandments, only we are averse to penal laws of superiors. But this proves in no way that we have only by nature a passive capacity to government; for heathens have by instinct of nature both made laws morally good, submitted to them, and set kings and judges over them, which clearly proves that men have an active power of government by nature. Yea, what difference makes the Prelate between men and beasts? For beasts have a capacity to be governed, even lions and tigers; but here is the matter, if men have any natural power of government, the Popish Prelate would have it, with his brethren the Jesuits and Arminians, to be not natural, but done by the help of universal grace; for so do they confound nature and grace. But it is certain our power to submit to rulers and kings, as to rectors, and guides, and fathers, is natural; to submit to tyrants in doing ills of sin is natural, but in suffering ills of punishment is not natural. "No man can give that which he has not" is true, but that people have no power to make their governors is that which is in question, and denied by us. This argument does prove that people have no power to appoint aristocratic rulers more than kings, and so the aristocratic and democratic rulers are all inviolable and sacred as the king. By this the people may not resume their freedom if they turn tyrants and oppressors. This the Prelate shall deny, for he asserts out of Augustine that the people may without sin change a corrupt democracy into a monarchy.

Popish Prelate. If sovereignty be originally inherent in the people, then democracy, or government by the people, would be the best government, because it comes nearest to the fountain and stream of the first and radical power in the people, yea, and all other forms of government would be unlawful; and if sovereignty is natively inherent in the multitude it must be proper to every individual of the community, which is against that false maxim of theirs, *Quisque nascitur liber.* Everyone by nature is born a free man, and the posterity of those who first contracted with their elected king are not bound to that covenant, but upon their native right and liberty may appoint another king without breach of covenant. The posterity of Joshua, and the elders in their time who contracted with the Gibeonites to incorporate them, though in a serving condition, might have made their fathers' government nothing.

Ans. 1. The Popish Prelate might thank Spalato for this argument also, for it is stolen; but he never once named him, lest his theft should be apprehended. So are his other arguments stolen from Spalato, but the Prelate weakens them, and it is seen stolen goods are not blessed. Spalato says, then, by the law of nature every commonwealth should be governed by the people, and by the law of nature the people should be under the worst government; but this consequence is nothing, for a community of many families is formally and of themselves under no government, but may choose any of the three; for popular government is not that wherein all the people are rulers, for this is confusion and not government, because all are rulers, and none are governed and ruled. But in popular government many are chosen out of the people to rule, and that this is the worst government is said gratis, without warrant; and if monarchy be the best of itself, yet when men are in the state of sin, in some other respects it has many inconveniences.

2. I see not how democracy is best because nearest to the multitude's power of making a king; for if all the three depend upon the free will of the people, all are alike afar off, and alike near hand to the people's free choice, according as they see most conducive to the safety and protection of the commonwealth, seeing the forms of government are not more natural than political incorporations of cities, yea, than of shires; but from a positive institution of God, who erects this rather than that, not immediately now, but mediately by the free

will of men; no one comes formally, and *ex natura rei*, nearer to the fountain than another, except that materially democracy may come nearer to the people's power than monarchy, but the excellency of it above monarchy is not from this concluded; for by this reason the number of four should be more excellent than the number of five, of ten, of a hundred, of a thousand, or of millions, because four comes near to the number of three, which Aristotle calls the first perfect number, *cui additur* το παν of which yet formally all do alike share in the nature and essence of number.

3. It is denied that it follows from this antecedent that the people have power to choose their own governors; therefore all governments except democracy, or government by the people, must be sinful and unlawful (1). Because government by kings is of divine institution, and of other judges also, as is evident from God's word (Rom. 13:1-3; Deut. 17:14; Prov. 8:15-16; 1 Pet. 2:13-14; Ps. 2:10-11, &c); (2.) Power of choosing any form of government is in the people; therefore there is no government lawful but popular government. It follows not at all, but presupposes that power to choose any form of government must be formally actual government; which is most false, yea, they are contrary, as the prevalence or power and the act are contrary; so these two are contrary or opposite. Neither is sovereignty, nor any government formally inherent in either the community by nature, nor in any one particular man by nature, and that every man is born free, so as no man, rather than his brother is born a king and a ruler, I hope, God willing, to make good, so long as the Prelate shall never answer on the contrary.

3. It follows not that the posterity living, when their fathers made a covenant with their first elected king, may without any breach of covenant on the king's part make void and null their fathers' election of a king, and choose another king, because the lawful covenant of the fathers, in point of government, if it be not broken, ties the children, but it cannot deprive them of their lawful liberty naturally inherent

in them to choose the fittest man to be king; but of this hereafter more fully.

4. Spalato adds (the Prelate is not a faithful thief): "If the community by the law of nature have power of all forms of government, and so should be by nature under popular government, and yet should refuse a monarchy and an aristocracy," yet, Augustine adds, "If the people should prefer their own private gain to the public good and sell the commonwealth, then some good man might take their liberty from them, and against their will erect a monarchy or an aristocracy."[1] But the Prelate and Augustine suppose the people to be under popular government. This is not our case; for Spalato and the Prelate presuppose by our grounds that the people by nature must be under popular government, Augustine dreams no such thing, and we deny that by nature they are under any form of government. Augustine, in a case most considerable thinks one good and potent man may take the corrupt people's power of giving honors, and making rulers from them, and give it to some good men, few or many, or to one; then Augustine lays down as a ground that which Spalato and the Prelate denies, that the people have power to appoint their own rulers; otherwise, how could one man take that power from them? The Prelate's fifth argument is but a branch of the fourth argument, and is answered already.

Popish Prelate would prove that kings of the people's making are not blessed by God. The first creature of the people's making was Abimelech (Judg. 9:22), who reigned only three years, well near Antichrist's time of endurance. He came to it by blood, and an evil spirit rose between him and the men of Shechem, and he made a miserable end. The next was Jeroboam, who had this motto: He made Israel to sin. The people made him king, and he made the same pretense of a glorious reformation that our reformers now make: new calves,

---

1. Augustine, *De lib. arb.* 1.6.

new altars, new feasts are erected; they banish the Levites and take
in the scum and dross of the vulgar, &c. Every action of Christ is our
instruction. Christ was truly born a king; notwithstanding, when the
people would make him a king, he disclaimed it—he would not be an
arbiter between two brethren differing (chap. 11).

Ans. I am not to follow the Prelate's order every way, though God
willing I shall reach him in the forthcoming chapters. Nor purpose I to
answer his treasonable railing against his own nation, and the judges of
the land, whom God has set over this seditious excommunicated apostate. He lays to us frequently the Jesuit's tenets, when as he is known
himself to be a papist. In this argument he says Abimelech did reign
only three years, well near Antichrist's reign. Is not this the basis and
the mother principle of popery: that the Pope is not the Antichrist, for
the Pope has continued many ages? He is not an individual man, but
a race of men; but the Antichrist, says Bellarmine, Stapleton, Becanus,
and the nation of Jesuits and poplings, shall be one individual man—a
born Jew, and shall reign only three years and a half.

But, 1. The argument from success proves nothing, unless the Prelate prove their bad success to be from this, because they were chosen by the people. When as Saul chosen of God, and most of the
kings of Israel and Judah, who undeniably had God's calling to the
crown, were not blessed by God; and their government was a ruin to
both people and religion, as the people were removed to all the kingdoms of the earth for the sins of Manasseh (Jer. 15:4). Was therefore
Manasseh not lawfully called to the crown?

2. For his instance of kings unlawfully called to the throne, he
brings us whole two, and tells us that he doubts, as many learned
men do, whether Jeroboam was a king by permission only, or by a
commission from God.

3. Abimelech was cursed, because he wanted God's calling to the
throne; for then Israel had no king, but judges, extraordinarily raised
up by God; and God did not raise him at all, only he came to the

throne by blood, and carnal reasons moving the men of Shechem to advance him. The argument presupposes that the whole lawful calling of a king is the voices of the people. This we never taught, though the Prelate make conquest a just title to a crown, and it is but a title of blood and rapine.

4. Abimelech was not the first king, but only a judge. All our divines, with the word of God, make Saul the first king.

5. For Jeroboam had God's word and promise to be king (1 Kings 11:34-38). But, in my weak judgment, he waited not God's time and way of coming to the crown; but that his coming to the throne was unlawful, because he came by the people's election is in question.

6. That the people's reformation, and their making a new king, was like the kingdom of Scotland's reformation, and the parliament of England's way now, is a traitorous calumny.

For, 1. It condemns the king, who has, in parliament, declared all their proceedings to be legal. Rehoboam never declared Jeroboam's coronation to be lawful, but contrary to God's word made war against Israel.

2. It is false that Israel pretended religion in that change. The cause was the rough answer given to the supplication of the estates, complaining of the oppression they were under in Solomon's reign.

3. Religion is still subjected to policy by prelates and cavaliers, not by us in Scotland, who sought nothing but reformation of religion and of laws so far as they serve religion, as our supplications, declarations, and the event proves.

4. We have no new calves, new altars, new feasts, but profess and really do hazard life and estate to put away the Prelate's calves, images, tree-worship, altar-worship, saints, feast-days, idolatry, masses; and nothing is said here but Jesuits, and Canaanites, and Baalites might say (though falsely) against the reformation of Josiah. Truth and purity of worship this year is new in relation to idolatry last year, but it is *simpliciter* older.

5. We have not put away the Lord's priests and Levites, and taken in the scum of the vulgar, but have put away Baal's priests, such as excommunicated Prelate Maxwell and other apostates, and resumed the faithful servants of God, who were deprived and banished for standing to the Protestant faith, sworn to by the prelates themselves.

6. Every action of Christ, such as his walking on the sea, is not our instruction in that sense that Christ's refusing a kingdom is directly our instruction. And did Christ refuse to be a king, because the people would have made him a king? That is, *non causa pro causa*, he refused it, because his kingdom was not in this world, and he came to suffer for men, not to reign over man.

7. The Prelate, and others who were lords of session, and would be judges of men's inheritances, and would usurp the sword by being lords of council and parliament, have refused to be instructed by every action of Christ, who would not judge between brother and brother.

Popish Prelate. Jephthah came to be judge by covenant between him and the Gileadites. Here you have an interposed act of man, yet the Lord himself, in authorizing him as judge, vindicates it no less to himself than when extraordinarily he authorized Gideon and Samuel (1 Sam. 12:11); therefore, whatsoever act of man intervenes, it contributes nothing to royal authority—it cannot weaken or repeal it.

Ans. It was as extraordinary that Jephthah, a bastard and the son of a harlot, should be judge as that Gideon should be judge. God vindicates to Himself, that He gives His people favor in the eyes of their enemies. But does it follow that the enemies are not agents, and to be commended for their humanity in favoring the people of God? So Ps. 65:9-10: God makes corn to grow; therefore clouds, and earth, and sun, and summer, and husbandry contributes nothing to the growing of corn. But this is that which he said before. We grant that this is an eminent and singular act of God's special providence: that He moves and bows the wills of a great multitude to promote such a man, who by nature comes no more out of the womb a crowned king than the poorest shepherd in the land, and it is an act of grace to endue him with heroic and royal parts for the government. But what is all this? Does it exclude the people's consent? In no ways. So the works of supernatural grace, as to love Christ above all things, to believe in Christ in a singular manner are ascribed to the rich grace of God. But can the Prelate say that the understanding and will in these acts are merely passive and contribute no more than the people contribute to royal authority in the king? And that is just nothing by the Prelate's way. And we utterly deny that as water in baptism has no action at all in the working of remission of sins, so the people has no influence in making a king; for the people are worthier and more excellent than the king, and they have an active power of ruling and directing themselves toward the intrinsic end of human policy, which is the external safety and peace of a society, insofar as there are moral principles of the second table, for this effect, written in their heart; and, therefore, that royal authority which, by God's special providence is united in one king and, as it were, over-gilded and lustered with princely grace and royal endowments, is diffused in the people, for the people have an after-approbative consent in making a king, as royalists confess water has no such action in producing grace.

QUESTION 9.

WHETHER OR NOT SOVEREIGNTY IS SO IN AND FROM THE PEOPLE, THAT THEY MAY RESUME THEIR POWER IN TIME OF EXTREME NECESSITY.

How the people is the subject of sovereignty. No tyrannical power is from God. People cannot alienate the natural power of self-defense. The power of parliaments. The Parliament has more power than the king. Judges and kings differ. People may resume their power, not because they are infallible, but because they cannot so readily destroy themselves as one man may do. That the Sanhedrin punished not David, Bathsheba, or Joab is but a fact, not a law. There is a subordination of creatures natural, government must be natural; and yet this or that form is voluntary.

The Prelate will have it a Babylonish confusion that we are divided in opinion. Jesuits (says he) place all sovereignty in the community. Of the sectaries, some warrant any one subject to make away his king, and such a work is no less to be rewarded than when one kills a wolf. Some say this power is in the whole community; some will have it in the collective body, not convened by warrant or writ of sovereignty, but when necessity (which is often fancied) of reforming state and church calls them together, some in the nobles and peers, some in the three estates assembled by the king's writ, some in the inferior judges.

I answer, if the Prelate were not a Jesuit himself, he would not bid his brethren take the mote out of their eye, but there is nothing here said but what Barclay said better before this plagiarius (*Contra Monarch.* 4.10). To which I answer: we teach that any private man may kill a tyrant, void of all title, and that great royalist says so also. And if he have not the consent of the people, he is an usurper, for we know no external lawful calling that kings have now, or their family, to the crown, but only the call of the people. All other calls to us are now invisible and unknown, and God would not command us to obey kings, and leave us in the dark, that we shall not know who is the king. The Prelate places his lawful calling to the crown in such an immediate, invisible, and subtle act of omnipotence as that by which God confers remission of sins by sprinkling with water in baptism, and that by which God directed Samuel to anoint Saul and David, not Eliab, nor any other brother. It is the devil in the Popish Prelate, not any of us, who teach that any private man may kill a lawful king, though tyrannical in his government. For the subject of royal power, we affirm, the first, and ultimate, and native subject of all power is the community, as reasonable men naturally inclining to a society, but the ethical and political subject, or the legal and positive receptacle of this power is various, according to the various constitutions of the policy. In Scotland and England it is the three estates of parliament; in other nations, some other judges or peers of the land. The Prelate had no more common sense for him to object a confusion of opinion to us, for this than to all the commonwealths on earth, because all have not parliaments, as Scotland has. All have not constables, and officials, and churchmen, and barons, lords of council, parliaments, &c., as England had, but the truth is the community, orderly convened, as it includes all the estates civil, have hand, and are to act in choosing their rulers. I see not what privilege nobles have above commons in a court of parliament by God's law; but as they are judges, all are equally judges, and all make up one congregation of God's. But the question now is if all power of governing (the Prelate, to make all the people kings, says, if all sovereignty) be so in the people that they retain power to guard themselves against tyranny, and if they retain some of it, *habitu*, in habit, and in their power. I am not now unseasonably, according to the Prelate's order, to dispute of the power of lawful defense against tyranny, but I lay down this maxim of divinity: Tyranny being a work of Satan is not from God, because sin, either habitual or actual, is not from God: the power that is, must be from God; the magistrate, as magistrate, is good in nature of office, and the intrinsic end of his office (Rom. 13:4) for he is the minister of God for your good, and therefore, a power ethical, political, or moral to oppress is not from God, and is not a power, but a licentious deviation of a power; and is no more from God but from sinful nature and the old serpent than a license to sin. God in Christ gives pardons of sin, but the Pope, not God, gives dispensations to sin. To this add, if for nature to defend itself be lawful, no community without sin has power to alienate and give away this power; for as no power given to man to murder his brother is of God, so no power to suffer his brother to be murdered is of God, and no power to suffer himself, *a fortiori*, far less can be from God. Here I speak not of physical power, for if free will be the creature of God, a physical power to acts which in relation to God's law are sinful must be from God.

But I now follow the Popish Prelate (section 9). Some of the adversaries, such as Buchanan, say that the parliament has no power to make a law, but only προσαυλευμα without the approbation of the community. Others, such as the Observator, say that the right of the gentry and commonalty is entirely in the knights and burgesses of the House of Commons, and will have their orders irrevocable. If then the common people cannot resume their power and oppose the parliament, how can tables and parliaments resume their power and resist the king?

Ans. The ignorant man should have thanked Barclay for this argument, and yet Barclay need not thank him, for it has not the nerves that Barclay gave it. But I answer, 1. If the parliament should have been corrupted by fair hopes (as in our age we have seen the like) the people did well to resist the Prelate's obtruding the Mass Book, when the lords of the council pressed it, against all law of God and man, upon the kingdom of Scotland, and therefore it is denied that the acts of parliament are irrevocable. The observator said they were irrevocable by the king, he being but one man; the Popish Prelate wrongs him, for he said only they have the power of a law, and the king is obliged to consent by his royal office to all good laws, and neither king nor people may oppose them. Buchanan said, acts of parliament are not laws, obliging the people, till they be promulgated, and the people's silence, when they are promulgated, is their approbation, and makes them obligatory laws to them, but if the people speak against unjust laws, they are not laws at all, and Buchanan knew the power of the Scottish parliament better than this ignorant statist.

2. There is not like reason to grant so much to the king, as to parliaments, because certainly parliaments who make kings under God, or above any one man, and they must have more authority and wisdom than anyone king, except Solomon (as base flatterers say) should return to the thrones of the earth. And as the power to make just laws is all in the parliament, only the people have power to resist tyrannical laws. The power of all the parliament was never given to the king by God. The parliament is as much essentially judges as the king, and therefore the king's deed may well be revoked, because he acts nothing as king, but united with his great or lesser council, no more than the eye can see, being separated from the body. The peers and members of parliament have more than the king, because they have both their own power, being parts and special members of the people,

and also they have their high places in parliament, either from the people's express or tacit consent.

3. We allow no arbitrary power to the parliament, because their just laws are irrevocable, for the irrevocable power of making just laws does argue a legal, not an irrevocable, arbitrary power; nor is there any arbitrary power in the people, or in any mortal man. But of the covenant between king and people hereafter.

Popish Prelate. If sovereign power be habitually in the community, so as they may resume it at their pleasure, then nothing is given to the king but an empty title; for, at the same instant, he receives empire and sovereignty, and lays down the power to rule or determine in matters which concern either private or public good, and so he is both a king and a subject (section 10).

Ans. This naked consequence the Prelate says and proves not, and we deny it, and give this reason: The king receives royal power with the states to make good laws, and power by his royalty to execute those laws, and this power the community has devolved in the hands of the king and states of parliament, but the community keeps to themselves a power to resist tyranny, and to coerce it, and *eatenus* insofar is Saul subject that David is not to compare before him, nor to lay down Goliath's sword, nor to disband his army of defense, though the king should command him so to do.

Popish Prelate. By all politicians, kings and inferior magistrates are distinguished by their different specific entity, but by this they are not distinguished; nay, a magistrate is in a better condition than a king, for the magistrate is to judge by a known statute and law, and cannot be censured and punished but by law. But the king is censurable, yea, disabled by the multitude; yea, the basest of subjects may cite and summon the king before the underived majesty of the community, and he may be judged by the arbitrary law that is in the closet of their hearts, not only for real misdemeanor, but for fancied jealousies. It will be said good kings are in danger; the contrary appears this day, and ordinarily the best are in greatest danger. No government, except Plato's republic, lacks incommodities: subtle spirits may make them apprehend them. The poor people, bewitched, follow Absalom in his treason; they strike not at royalty at first, but labor to make the prince naked of the good council of great statesmen, &c. (section 16).

Ans. Whether the king and the under magistrate differ essentially, we shall see.

1. The Popish Prelate says all politicians grant it, but he says untruth. He brings the power of Moses and the judges to prove the power of kings; and so either the judges of Israel and the kings differ not essentially, or then the Prelate must correct the spirit of God, terming one book of Scripture מלכים kings; and another שופטים Judges, and make the book of Kings the book of Judges.

2. The magistrate's condition is not better than the king's, because the magistrate is to judge by a known statute and law, and the king not so. God molded the first king when he sits judging on his throne, to look to a written copy of the law of God as his rule (Deut. 17:18). Now, a power to follow God's law is better than a power to follow man's sinful will; so the Prelate puts the king in a worse condition than the magistrate, not we, who will have the king to judge according to just statutes and laws.

3. Whether the king be censurable and deposable by the multitude, he cannot determine out of our writings.

4. The community's law is the law of nature, not their arbitrary lust.

5. The Prelate's treasonable railings I cannot follow. He says that we agree not ten of us to a positive faith, and that our faith is negative, but his faith is Privative, Popish, Socinian, Arminian, Pelagian, and worse, for he was one of that same faith that we are of. Our Confession of Faith is positive, as the confession of all the reformed churches; but I judge he thinks the Protestant faith of all the reformed churches but negative. The incommodities of government, before our reformation, were not fancied but printed by authority. All the body of popery was

printed and avowed as the doctrine of the Church of Scotland and England, as the learned author and my much respected brother shows in his *Ludensium,* αντι κατακρισις, the Canterburian Self-conviction.[1] The parliament of England was never yet found guilty of treason. The good counsellors of great statesmen, that parliaments of both kingdoms would take from the king's majesty, are a faction of perjured Papists, Prelates, Jesuits, Irish cut-throats, Straffords, and Apostates; subverters of all laws, divine, human, of God, of church, of state.

Popish Prelate. In whomsoever this power of government be it is the only remedy to supply all defects, and to set right whatever is disjointed in church and state, and the subject of this superintending power must be free from all error in judgment and practice, and so we have a pope *in temporalibus*; and if the parliament err the people must take order with them, else God has left church and state remediless (section 15).

Ans. 1. This is stolen from Barclay also, who says, *Si Rex regnum suum alienae ditioni manciparit, regno cadit*: "If the king shall sell his kingdom, or enslave it to a foreign power, he falls from all right to his kingdom."[2] But who shall execute any such law against him? Not the people, not the peers, not the parliament; for this *mancipium ventris et aulae*, this slave says, "I know no power in any to punish or curb sovereignty but in Almighty God."

2. We see no superintending power on earth, in king or people, which is infallible, nor is the last power of taking order with a prince who enslaves his kingdom to a foreign power placed by us in the people because they cannot err. Court flatterers, who teach that the will of the prince is the measure of all right and wrong, of law and no law, and above all law, must hold that the king is a temporal pope, both in ecclesiastical and civil matters, but because they cannot so readily destroy themselves (the law of nature having given to them a contrary

---

1. Robert Baillie's book against Arminiansim and popery.

2. *Contra Monarchum.* 5.12, idem. 3, last section.

internal principle of self-preservation) as a tyrant who does care for himself and not for the people.

3. And because *Extremis morbis extrema remedia*, in an extraordinary exigent, when Ahab and Jezebel did undo the church of God, and tyrannize over both the bodies and consciences of priest, prophet and people, Elijah procured the convention of the states, and Elijah, with the people's help, killed all Baal's priests, the king looking on, without question, against his heart. In this case I think it is more than evident that the people resumed their power.

4. We teach not that people should supply all defects in government, nor that they should use their power when anything is done amiss by the king, no more than we king is to cut off the whole people of God when they refuse an idolatrous service, obtruded upon them against all law. The people are to suffer much before they resume their power; but this court slave will have the people to do what he did not himself; for when king and parliament summoned him, was he not obliged to appear? Non-compearance when lawful, royal, and parliamentary power summons is no less resistance than taking of ports and castles.

Popish Prelate. Then this superintending power in people may call a king to account, and punish him for any misdemeanor or act of injustice. Why might not the people of Israel's peers, or Sanhedrin, have summoned David before them, judged and punished him for his adultery with Bathsheba, and his murder of Uriah. But it is held by all that tyranny should be an intended universal, total, manifest destruction of the whole commonwealth, which cannot fall in the thoughts of any but a madman. What is recorded in the story of Nero's wish in this kind, may be rather judged the expression of transported passion than a fixed resolution.

Ans. The Popish Prelate, contrary to the scope of his book, which is all for the subject and seat of sovereign power, against all order, has plunged himself in the deep of defensive arms, and yet has no new thing.

1. Our law of Scotland will warrant any subject, if the king take from him his heritage, or invade his possession against law, to resist the invaders, and to summon the king's intruders before the lords of session for that act of injustice. Is this against God's word, or conscience?

2. The Sanhedrin did not punish David; therefore, it is not lawful to challenge a king for anyone act of injustice: from the practice of the Sanhedrin to conclude a thing lawful or unlawful is logic we may resist.

3. By the Popish Prelate's doctrine, the law might not put Bathsheba to death, nor yet Joab, the nearest agent of the murdering of innocent Uriah, because Bathsheba's adultery was the king's adultery—she did it in obedience to king David; Joab's murder was royal murder, as the murder of all the cavaliers, for he had the king's handwriting for it. Murder is murder, and the murderer is to die, though the king by a secret *let-alone*, a private and illegal warrant, command it; therefore the Sanhedrin might have taken Bathsheba's life and Joab's head also; and, consequently, the parliament of England, if they be judges (as I conceive God and the law of that ancient and renowned kingdom makes them) may take the head of many Joabs and Jermines for murder; for the command of a king cannot legitimate murder.

4. David himself, as king, speaks more for us than for the Prelate. 2 Sam, 12:7: "And David's anger was greatly kindled against the man (the man was himself, ver. 7, 'You are the man,') and he said to Nathan, as the Lord lives, the man that has done this thing shall surely die."

5. Every act of injustice does not unking a prince before God, as every act of uncleanness does not make a wife no wife before God.

6. The Prelate excuses Nero, and would not have him resisted, if "all Rome were one neck that he might cut it off with one stroke." (I read it of Caligula; if the Prelate see more in history than I do, I yield.)

7. He says the thoughts of total overturning of a kingdom must only fall on a madman. The king of Britain was not mad when he declared the Scots traitors (because they resisted the service of the mass) and raised an army of prelatical cut-throats to destroy them, if all the kingdom should resist idolatry (as all are obliged). The king slept upon this prelatical resolution many months: passions in fervor have not a day's reign upon a man; and this was not so clear as the sun, but it was as clear as written, printed proclamations, and the pressing of soldiers, and the visible marching of cut-throats, and the blocking up of Scotland by sea and land could be visible to men having five senses.

Covarruvias, a great lawyer, says that all civil power is *penes remp.* in the hands of the commonwealth, because nature has given to man to be a social creature, and it is impossible he can preserve himself in a society unless he, being in community, transform his power to a head.[1] He says: *Hujus vero civilis societatis et resp. rector ab alio quam ab ipsamet repub. constitui non potest juste et absq. tyrannide. Siquidem ab ipso Deo constitatus non est, nec electus cuilibet civili societati immediate Rex aut Princeps.* Aristotle says, "It is better that kings be got by election than by birth; because kingdoms by succession are *vere regia*, truly kingly: these by birth are more tyrannical, masterly, and proper to barbarous nations" (*Polit.* 3.10). And Covarruvius says, "Hereditary kings are also made hereditary by the tacit consent of the people, and so by law and consuetude."[2]

Spalato says, "Let us grant that a society shall refuse to have a governor over them, shall they be for that free? In no way. But there be many ways by which a people may be compelled to admit a governor; for then no man might rule over a community against their will. But

---

1. Tom. 2, pract. quest. 1, n. 2-4.
2. Tom. 2, pract. quest. de jurisd, *Castellan. Reip.* 1, n. 4.

nature has otherwise disposed, *ut quod singuli nollent, universi vellent,* that which everyone will not have, a community naturally desires."[1] And the Prelate says, "God is no less the author of order than he is the author of being; for the Lord who creates all conserves all, and without government all human societies should be dissolved and go to ruin; then government must be natural, and not depend upon a voluntary and arbitrary constitution of men. In nature the inferior creatures give a tacit consent and silent obedience to their superior, and the superior has a powerful influence on the inferior. In the subordination of creatures we ascend from one superior to another, till at last we come to one supreme, which by the way pleads for the excellency of monarchy. Among angels there is an order; how can it then be supposed that God has left it to the simple consent of man to establish a heraldry of *sub et supra,* of one above another, which neither nature nor the gospel does warrant? To leave it thus arbitrary, that upon this supposed principle mankind may be without government at all is vain, which paradox cannot be maintained. In nature God has established a superiority inherent in superior creatures, which is in no way derived from the inferior by communication in what proportion it will, and resumable upon such demands as the inferior wishes; therefore neither has God left to the multitude, the community, the collective, the representative or virtual body, to derive from itself and communicate sovereignty, whether in one or few or more in what measure and proportion pleases them, which they resume at pleasure."

Ans. To answer Spalato: No society has liberty to be without all government, for "God has given to every society," says Covarruvias, "a faculty of preserving themselves, and warding off violence and injuries; and this they could not do except they gave their power to one or many rulers."[2] But all that the Prelate builds on this false supposition, which is his fiction and calumny, not our doctrine, namely, "that it is

---

1. *De rep. eccles.* 6.2, n. 32.

2. Tom. 4, pract. quest. section 1, n. 2.

voluntary to man to be without all government, because it is voluntary to them to give away their power to one or more rulers," is a mere non-consequence.

1. We teach that government is natural, not voluntary, but the way and manner of government is voluntary. All societies would be quickly ruined if there were no government; but it follows not, therefore, God has made some kings, and that immediately, without the intervening consent of the people, and, therefore, it is not arbitrary to the people to choose one supreme ruler, and to erect a monarchy, or to choose more rulers, and to erect an aristocracy. It follows in no way. It is natural to men to express their mind by human voices. Is not speaking of this or that language, Greek rather than Latin (as Aristotle says) κατα συνθηκην by human institution? It is natural for men to eat, therefore election of this or that meat is not in their choice. What reason is in this consequence? And so it is a poor consequence also. Power of sovereignty is in the people naturally; therefore it is not in their power to give it out in that measure that pleases them, and to resume it at pleasure. It follows in no way. Because the inherency of sovereignty is natural and not arbitrary, therefore, the alienation and giving out of the power to one, not to three, thus much, not thus much, conditionally, not absolutely and irrevocably, must be also arbitrary. It is as if you should say a father having six children naturally loves them all, therefore he has not freedom of will in expressing his affection to give so much of his goods to this son, and that conditionally, if he use these goods well, and not more or less of his goods at his pleasure.

2. There is a natural subordination in nature in creatures superior and inferior, without any freedom of election. The earth made not the heavens more excellent than the earth, and the earth by no freedom of will made the heavens superior in excellency to itself. Man gave no superiority of excellency to angels above himself. The Creator of all beings did both immediately, without freedom of election in the creature, create the being of all the creatures and their essential degrees of

superiority and inferiority, but God created not Saul by nature king over Israel; nor is David by the act of creation by which he is made a man created also king over Israel; for then David should from the womb and by nature be a king, and not by God's free gift. Here both the free gift of God, and the free consent of the people intervene. Indeed God made the office and royalty of a king above the dignity of the people, but he by the intervening consent of the people makes David a king, not Eliab; and the people makes a covenant at David's inauguration, that David shall have so much power, namely, power to be a father, not power to be a tyrant, power to fight for the people, not power to waste and destroy them. The inferior creatures in nature give no power to the superior, and therefore they cannot give in such a proportion power. The denial of the positive degree is a denial of the comparative and superlative, and so they cannot resume any power, but the designation of these men or those men to be kings or rulers is a rational, voluntary action, not an action of nature, such as is God's act of creating an angel a nobler creature than man, and the creating of man a more excellent creature than a beast; and, for this cause, the argument is vain and foolish, for inferior creatures are inferior to the more noble and superior by nature, not by voluntary designation, or, as royalists say, by naked approbation, which yet must be an arbitrary and voluntary action.

3. The Popish Prelate commends order while we come to the most supreme; thus he commends monarchy above all governments because it is God's government. I am not against it, that monarchy well-tempered is the best government, though the question to me is most problematic; but because God is a monarch who cannot err or deny Himself; therefore that sinful man be a monarch is miserable logic; and he must argue solidly, forsooth, by this, because there is order, as he says, among angels, will he make a monarch and a king-angel? His argument, if it have any weight at all in it, drives at that, even that there be crowned kings among the angels.

QUESTION 10.

WHETHER OR NOT ROYAL BIRTH BE EQUIVALENT TO DIVINE UNCTION.

Impugned by eight arguments. Royalty not transmitted from father to son. A family may be chosen to a crown as a single person is chosen, but the tie is conditional in both. The throne, by special promise, made to David and his seed by God (Ps. 139) no ground to make birth, in foro Dei, a just title to the crown. A title by conquest to a throne must be unlawful, if birth be God's lawful titles. Royalists who hold conquest to be a just title to the crown teach manifest treason against King Charles and his royal heirs. Only, bona fortunae, not honor or royalty, properly transmittable from father to son. violent conquest cannot regulate the consciences of people to submit to a conqueror as their lawful king. Naked birth is inferior to that very divine unction that made no man a king without the people's election. If a kingdom were by birth the king might sell it. The crown is the patrimony of the kingdom, not of him who is king or of his father. Birth is a typical designation to the crown in Israel. The choice of a family to the crown resolves upon the free election of the people as on the fountain cause. Election of a family to the crown is lawful.

Symmons holds that birth is as good a title to the crown, as any given of God.[1] How this question can be cleared I see not, unless we dispute whether or not kingdoms are proper patrimonies derived from the father to the son. I take there is a large difference between a thing transmittable by birth from the father to the son, and a thing not transmittable. I conceive, as a person is chosen to be a king over a people, so a family or house may be chosen, and a kingdom at first choosing a person to be their king may also tie themselves to choose the firstborn of his body, but as they transfer their power to the father, for their own safety and peace (not if he use the power they give him to their destruction) the same way they tie themselves to his firstborn, as to their king. As they choose the father not as a man, but a man gifted with royal grace and a princely faculty for government, so they can out-tie themselves to his firstborn, as to one graced with a faculty of governing, and if his firstborn shall be born an idiot and a fool, they are not obliged to make him king, for the obligation to the son can be no greater than the obligation to the father, which first obligation is the ground, measure, and cause of all posterior obligations. If tutors be appointed to govern such a one, the tutors have the royal power, not the idiot; nor can he govern others who cannot govern himself. That kings go not as heritage from the father to the son, I prove.

1. God could not command them to choose such a one for the king (Deut. 17), and such a one who, sitting on his throne, shall follow the direction of God, speaking in his word, if birth were that which gave him God's title and right to the crown; for that would be as much as such a man should be heir to his father's inheritance, and the son not heir to his

---

1. *Loyal Subjects' Belief,* sect. 3.

father's crown, unless he were such a man. But God, in all
the law moral or judicial, never required the heir should be
thus and thus qualified, otherwise he would not be heir; but
he requires that a man, and so that a family, should be thus
and thus qualified, otherwise they should not be kings. And
I confirm it thus: The first king of divine institution must be
the rule, pattern, and measure of all the rest of the kings, as
Christ makes the first marriage (Matt. 19:8) a pattern to all
others, and Paul reduces the right administration of the Supper to Christ's first institution (1 Cor. 11:23). Now, the first
king is not a man qualified by naked birth (Deut. 17:14-15),
for then the Lord in describing the manner of the king and
his due qualifications should seek no other but this. You shall
choose only the firstborn, or the lawful son of the former king.
But seeing the king of God's first molding is a king by election, and what God did after, by promises and free grace, give
to David and his seed, even a throne till the Messiah should
come, and did promise to some kings, if they would walk in
his commandments, that their sons, and sons' sons, should sit
upon the throne in my judgment is not an obliging law that
sole birth should be as just a title, *in foro Dei* (for now I dispute the question in point of conscience) as royal unction.

2. If by divine institution God has impawned in the people's hand a subordinate power to the Most High, who gives
kingdoms to whom he will to make and create kings, then is
not sole birth a just title to the crown. But the former is true.
By precept God expressly says, "you shall choose him king,
whom the Lord shall choose" (Deut. 17:15). And if it had not
been the people's power to create their own kings, how does
God, after he had designated Saul their king, yet expressly in-
spire Samuel to call the people before the Lord at Mizpah to
make Saul king (1 Sam. 10)? And how does the Lord (ver. 22)

expressly show to Samuel and the people, the man that they might make him king? And because all consented not that Saul should be king, God will have his coronation renewed. Ver. 14: "Then said Samuel to the people: come and let us go to Gilgal, and renew the kingdom there." Ver. 15: "And all the people went to Gilgal, and there they made Saul king before the Lord in Gilgal." And how is it that David, anointed by God, is yet no king but a private subject, while all Israel make him king at Hebron?

3. If royal birth be equivalent to royal anointing and the best title; if birth speak and declare to us the Lord's will and appointment, that the firstborn of a king should be king, as M. Symmons and others say, then is all title by conquest, where the former king stands in title to the crown and has an heir unlawful. But the latter is against all the nation of the royalists, for Arnisaeus, Barclay, Grotius, Jo. Rossensis Episco., the Bishop of Spalato, Dr Ferne, M. Symmons, the excommunicate Prelate, if his poor learning may bring him in the roll teach that conquest is a lawful title to a crown. I prove the proposition: (1.) Because if birth speak God's revealed will, that the heir of a king is the lawful king, then conquest cannot speak contrary to the will of God, that he is no lawful king, but the conqueror is the lawful king. God's revealed will should be contradictory to himself, and birth should speak, it is God's will that the heir of the former king be king, and the conquest being also God's revealed will, should also speak that that heir should not be king. (2) If birth speak and reveal God's will that the heir be king, it is unlawful for a conquered people to give their consent that a conqueror be their king, for their consent being contrary to God's revealed will (which is that birth is the just title) must be an unlawful concept. If royalists say God, the King of kings, who immediately makes

kings may and does transfer kingdoms to whom he will, and when he puts the sword in Nebuchadnezzar's hand to conquer the king and kingdom of Judah, then Zedekiah or his son is not king of Judah, but Nebuchadnezzar is king, and God, being above his law, speaks in that case His will by conquests, as before he spoke His will by birth. This is all that can be said.

Ans. They answer black treason in saying so, for if Jeremiah from the Lord had not commanded expressly that both the king and kingdom of Judah should submit to the king of Babylon, and serve him, and pray for him as their lawful king, it would have been as lawful for them to rebel against that tyrant as it was for them to fight against the Philistines and the king of Ammon; but if birth be the just and lawful title, *in foro Dei*, in God's court, and the only thing that evidences God's will, without any election of the people that the firstborn of such a king is their lawful king, then conquests cannot now speak a contradictory will of God; for the question is not whether or not God gives power to tyrants to conquer kingdoms from the just heirs of kings which did reign lawfully before their sword made an empty throne, but whether conquest now, when Jeremiahs are not sent immediately from God to command, for example, Britain to submit to a violent intruder, who has expelled the lawful heirs of the royal line of the king of Britain, whether, I say, does conquest, in a such a violent way, speak that it is God's revealed will, called *Voluntas signi*, the will that is to rule us in all our moral duties, to cast off the just heirs of the blood royal, and to swear homage to a conqueror, and so as that conqueror now has as just right as the king of Britain had by birth. This cannot be taken off by the wit of any who maintain that conquest is a lawful title to a crown, and that royal birth without the people's election speaks God's regulating will in His word, that the firstborn of a king is a lawful king by birth, for God nowadays does not say the contrary of what He revealed in His word. If birth be God's regulating will, that the heir of the king is in God's court a king, no act of the conqueror can annul that word of God to us, and the people may not lawfully, though they were ten times subdued, swear homage and allegiance to a conqueror against the due right of birth, which by royalists' doctrine reveals to us the plain contradictory will of God. It is, I grant, often God's decree revealed by the event that a conqueror be on the throne, but this will is not our rule, and the people are to swear no oath of allegiance contrary to God's *Voluntas signi*, which is His revealed will in His word regulating us.

4. Things transferable and communicable by birth from father to son are only in law those which heathens call *bona fortunae* riches, as lands, houses, monies and heritages, and so says the law also. These things which essentially include gifts of the mind, and honor properly so called—I mean honor founded on virtue—as Aristotle with good reason makes honor *praeminum virtutis,* cannot be communicated by birth from the father to the son; for royal dignity includes these three constituent parts essentially, of which none can be communicable by birth: (1) The royal faculty of governing, which is a special gift of God above nature is from God. Solomon asked it from God, and had it not by generation from his father David; (2) The royal honor to be set above the people because of this royal virtue is not from the womb, for then God's Spirit would not have said, "Blessed are you, O land, when your king is the son of nobles" (Eccl. 10:17); this honor, springing from virtue, is not born with any man, nor is any man born with either the gift or honor to be a judge; God makes high and low, not birth. Nobles are born to great estates. If judging be heritage to any, it is a municipal positive law; I now speak in point of

conscience. (3) The external lawful title, before men come to a crown, must be God's will, revealed by such an external sign as by God's appointment and warrant is to regulate our will; but according to Scripture nothing regulates our will, and leads the people now that they cannot err following God's rule in making a king, but the free suffrages of the states choosing a man whom they conceive God has endued with these royal gifts required in the king whom God holds forth to them in his word (Deut. 17). Now there are but these to regulate the people, or to be a rule to any man to ascend lawfully, *in foro Dei*, in God's court to the throne: (1) God's immediate designation of a man by prophetic and divinely-inspired anointing, as Samuel anointed Saul and David; this we are not to expect now, nor can royalists say it. (2) Conquest, seeing it is an act of violence and God's avenging justice for the sins of a people cannot give in God's court such a just title to the throne as the people are to submit their consciences unto, unless God reveal his regulating will by some immediate voice from heaven, as he commanded Judah to submit to Nebuchadnezzar as to their king by the mouth of Jeremiah. Now this is not a rule to us; for then, if the Spanish king should invade this land and, as Nebuchadnezzar did, deface the temple and instruments and means of God's worship, and abolish the true worship of God, it would be unlawful to resist him after he had once conquered the land; neither God's word, nor the law of nature could permit this, I suppose, even by grant of adversaries; now no act of violence done to a people, though in God's court they have deserved it, can be a testimony to us of God's regulating will, unless it have some warrant from the law and testimony, it is no rule to our conscience to acknowledge him a lawful magistrate, whose sole law to the throne is an act of the bloody instrument of divine wrath, I mean the sword. That, therefore,

Judah was to submit, according to God's word, to Nebuchadnezzar, whose conscience and best warranted calling to the
kingdom of Judah was his bloody sword, even if we suppose
Jeremiah had not commanded them to submit to the king of
Babylon, I think cannot be said. (3) Naked birth cannot be
this external signification of God's regulating will to warrant
the conscience of any to ascend to the throne, for the authors
of this opinion make royal birth equivalent to divine anointing, for David anointed by Samuel, and so anointed by God, is
not king: Saul remained the Lord's anointed many years, not
David, although anointed by God; the people's making him
king at Hebron, founded upon divine anointing, was not the
only external lawful calling that we read of that David had
to the throne; then royal birth, because it is but equivalent
only to divine anointing, not superior to divine anointing, it
cannot have more force to make a king than divine anointing.
And if birth was equivalent to divine anointing, what needed
Joash, who had royal birth, be made king by the people? And
what needed Saul and David, who had more than royal birth,
even divine anointing, be made kings by the people? And Saul,
having the vocal and infallible testimony of a prophet, needed
not the people's election—the one at Mizpah and Gilgal, and
the other at Hebron.

   5. If royal birth be as just a title to the crown as divine
anointing, and so as the people's election is no title at all, then
is it unlawful that there should be a king by election in the
world now; but the latter is absurd, so is the former. I prove
the proposition, because where conquerors are wanting, and
there is no king for the present, but the people governing, and
so much confusion abounds, they cannot lawfully appoint a
king, for his lawful title before God must either be conquest—
which to me is no title (and here, and in this case, there is no

conquest) or the title must be a prophetic word immediately inspired by God, but this is now ceased; or the title must be royal birth, but here there is no royal birth, because the government is popular, unless you imagine that the society is obliged in conscience to go and seek the son of a foreign king to be their king. But I hope that such a royal birth should not be a just title before God to make him king of that society to which He had no relation at all, but is a mere stranger. Thus in this case no title could be given to any man to make him king, but only the people's election, which is that which we say. And it is most unreasonable that a people under popular government cannot lawfully choose a king to themselves, seeing a king is a lawful magistrate, and warranted by God's word, because they have not a king of royal birth to sit upon the throne.

Mr. Symmons says that birth is the best title to the crown, because after the first of the family had been anointed, anointing was no more used in that family (unless there arose a strife about the kingdom, as between Solomon and Adonijah, Joash and Athaliah); the eldest son of the predecessor was afterward the chosen of the Lord, his birthright spoke the Lord's appointment as plainly as his father's anointing.[1]

Ans. 1. It is a conjecture that anointing was not used in the family after the first anointing, unless the contest was between two brethren; that is said, not proved, for 2 Kings 23:30, when good Josiah was killed, and there was no contest concerning the throne of that beloved prince, the people of the land took Jehoahaz his son, and anointed him, and made him king in his father's stead, and the priests were anointed (Lev. 6:22), yea,

---

1. *Loyal Subjects' Belief*, sect. 3.

all the priests were anointed (Numb. 3:3), yet read we not in the history, where this or that man was anointed.

2. In that Adonijah, Solomon's elder brother, was not king, it is clear that God's anointing and the people's electing made the right to the crown, and not birth.

3. Birth *de facto* did designate the man, because of God's special promises to David's house; but how does a typical descent made to David and some others by God's promise prove that birth is the birthright and lawful call of God to a crown in all after ages? For as gifts to reign goes not by birth, so neither does God's title to a crown go.

M. Symmons: A prince once possessed of a kingdom coming to him by inheritance can never by any upon any occasion be dispossessed of it without horrible impiety and injustice. Royal anointing was an indelible character of old: Saul remained the Lord's anointed till the last gasp. David dared not take the right of government actually unto him, although he had it in reversion, being already anointed to it, and had received the spirit of it.

Ans. 1. This is the question, if a prince, once a prince by inheritance, cannot be dispossessed of it without injustice; for if a kingdom be his by birth, as an inheritance transmitted from the father to the son, I see not but that any man upon necessary occasions may sell his inheritance; but if a prince sell his kingdom, a very Barclay and a Grotius with reason will say he may be dispossessed and dethroned, and take up his indelible character then. (2) A kingdom is not the prince's own, so as it is injustice to take it from him as to take a man's purse from him; the Lord's church in a Christian kingdom is God's heritage, and the king alone a shepherd, and the sheep in the court of conscience are not his. (3) Royal unction is not an indelible character: for neither Saul nor David were all their days kings by it, but lived many days private men after divine anointing, while the people anointed them kings, unless you say that there were two kings at once in Israel, and that Saul, killing David, should have killed his own lord and his anointed. (4) If David dared not take the right of government actually on him, then divine anointing made him not king, but only designated him to be king; the people's election must make the king.

M. Symmons adds, "He that is born a king and a prince can never be unborn, *Semel Augustus semper Augustus*; yea, I believe the eldest son of such a king is, in respect of birth, the Lord's anointed in his father's lifetime, even as David was before Saul's death, and to deprive him of his right of reversion is as true injustice as to dispossess him of it."[1]

Ans. It is proper only to Jesus Christ to be born a king. Sure I am no man brings out of the womb with him a scepter and a crown on his head. Divine anointing gives a right infallibly to a crown, but birth does not so; for one may be born heir to a crown, as was hopeful prince Henry, and yet never live to be king. The eldest son of a king, if he attempt to kill his father, as Absalom did, and raise forces against the lawful prince, I conceive he may be killed in battle without any injustice. If in his father's time he be the Lord's anointed, there are two kings, and the heir may have a son, and so there shall be three kings, possibly four, all kings by divine right.

The Prelate of Rochester says, "The people and nobles give no right to him who is born a king; they only declare his right."[2]

Ans. This is said, not proved. A man born for an inheritance is by birth an heir, because he is not born for these lands as a means for the end, but by the contrary these lands are for the heir as the means for the end; but the king is for his kingdom as a means for the end, as the watchman for the city, the living law for peace and safety to God's

---

1. *Loyal Subjects' Belief*, sect. 3.
2. *Joan. Episco. Roffens. de potest. Papae.* 2.5.

people, and therefore is not *heres hominum*, an heir of men, but men are rather *heredes regis*, heirs of the king.

Arnisaeus says, "Many kingdoms are purchased by just war, and transmitted by the law of heritage from the father to the son, besides the consent of the people, because the son receives right to the crown not from the people, but from his parents; nor does he possess the kingdom as the patrimony of the people keeping only to himself the burden of protecting and governing the people, but as a propriety given to him *lege regni*, by his parents, which he is obliged to defend and rule, as a father looks to the good and welfare of the family, yet so also as he may look to his own good."[1]

Ans. We read in the word of God that the people made Solomon king, not David or any king can leave in his testament a kingdom to his son. He says the son has not the right of reigning as the patrimony of the people, but as a propriety, given by the law of the kingdom by his parents. Now this is all one as if he said the son has not the right of the kingdom as the patrimony of the people, but as the patrimony of the people, which is good nonsense; for the propriety of reigning given from father to son by the law of the kingdom is nothing but a right to reign given by the law of the people, and the very gift and patrimony of the people, for *lex regni*, this law of the kingdom is the law of the people, tying the crown to such a royal family, and this law of the people is prior and more ancient than the king, or the right of reigning in the king, or which the king is supposed to have from his royal father, because it made the first father the first king of the royal line. For I demand how does the son succeed to his father's crown and throne? Not by any promise of a divine covenant that the Lord makes to the father, as he promised that David's seed should sit on his throne till the Messiah should come. This, as I conceive, is vanished with the commonwealth of the Jews; nor can we now find any

---

1. *Arnisaeus de authorit. princip.* 1, n. 13.

immediate divine constitution, tying the crown now to such a race, nor can we say this comes from the will of the father-king, making his son king.

For, 1. There is no Scripture can warrant us to say the king makes a king, but the Scripture holds forth that the people made Saul and David kings.

2. This may prove that the father is in some way a cause why this son succeeds king, but he is not the cause of the royalty conferred upon the whole line, because the question is, who made the first father a king? Not himself. Nor does God now immediately by prophets anoint men to be kings: then must the people choose the first man, then must the people's election of a king be prior and more ancient than the birth-law to a crown, and election must be a better right than birth. The question is from where comes it that not only the first father should be chosen king, but also from where is it that, whereas it is in the people's free will to make the succession of kings go by free election, as it is in Denmark and Poland, yet the people does freely choose, not only the first man to be king, but also the whole race of the firstborn of this man's family to be kings. All here must be resolved in the free will of the community. Now, since we have no immediate and prophetic enthroning of men, it is evident that the lineal deduction of the crown from father to son through the whole line is from the people, not from the parent.

3. Thus, I add this as my sixth argument: That which takes away that natural aptitude and nature's birthright in a community, given to them by God and nature, to provide the most efficacious and prevalent means for their own preservation and peace in the fittest government, that is not to be held; but to make birth the best title to the crown, and better than free election, takes away and impedes that natural aptitude and nature's birthright of choosing, not simply a governor, but the best, the justest, the more righteous, and ties and fetters their choice to one of a house, whether he be a wise man, and

just, or a fool and an unjust man; therefore to make birth the best title to the crown is not to be held.

It is objected that parents may bind their after-generations to choose one of such a line, but by this argument their natural birthright of a free choice to elect the best and fittest is abridged and clipped, and so the posterity shall not be tied to a king of the royal line to which the ancestors did swear. See for this the learned author of "Scripture and Reasons pleaded for Defensive Arms" (section 4).

Ans. Frequent elections of a king, at the death of every prince, may have by accident and through the corruption of our nature bloody and tragic consequences, and to eschew these, people may tie and oblige their children to choose one of the firstborn, male or female, as in Scotland and England, of such a line; but I have spoken of the excellency of the title by election above that of birth, as though comparing things according to their own nature together, but give me leave to say that the posterity are tied to that line, 1. Conditionally: so the firstborn, *ceteris paribus*, be qualified, and have an head to sit at the helm. 2. Elections of governors would be performed as in the sight of God and, in my weak apprehension, the person coming nearest to God's judge, fearing God, hating covetousness; and to Moses' king (Deut. 17) one who shall read in the book of the law; and it would seem now that gracious morals are to us instead of God's immediate designation. 3. The genuine and intrinsic end of making kings is not simply governing, but governing the best way, in peace, honesty, and godliness (1 Tim. 2); therefore, these are to be made kings who may most expeditely procure this end. Neither is it my purpose to make him no king who is not a gracious man, only here I compare title with title.

Arg. 7. Where God has not bound the conscience, men may not bind themselves, or the consciences of the posterity. But God has not bound any nation irrevocably and unalterably to a royal line, or to one kind of government; therefore, no nation can bind their conscience, and the conscience of the posterity, either to one royal line, or irrevocably and unalterably to monarchy. The proposition is clear. 1. No nation is tied, *jure divino,* by the tie of a divine law, to a monarchy, rather than to another government. The Parisian doctors prove that the precept of having a pope is affirmative, and so ties not the church, *ad semper,* forever; and so the church is the body of Christ without the Pope; and all oaths to things of their nature indifferent, and to things the contrary of which is lawful and may be expedient and necessary, lay on a tie only conditionally, insofar as they conduce to the end. If the Gibeonites had risen in Joshua's days to cut off the people of God, I think no wise man can think that Joshua and the people were tied by the oath of God, not to cut off the Gibeonites in that case; for to preserve them alive as enemies was against the intent of the oath, which was to preserve them alive, as friends demanding and supplicating peace and submitting. The assumption is clear. If a nation sees that aristocratic government is better than monarchy, *hic et nunc,* that the consequences of such a monarchy are bloody, destructive, tyrannical; that the monarchy compels the free subjects to Mahomedanism, to gross idolatry, they cannot by the divine bond of any oath bind their natural freedom, which is to choose a government and governors for their safety and for a peaceable and godly life, or fetter and chain the wisdom of the posterity unalterably to a government or a royal line, which, *hic et nunc,* contrary to the intention of their oath, proves destructive and bloody. And in this case, even the king, though tied by an oath to govern, is obliged to the practices of the Emperor Otho; and as Speed says of Richard II, to resign the crown for the eschewing of the effusion of blood. And who doubts but the second wits of the experienced posterity may correct the first wits of their fathers; nor shall I ever believe that the fathers can leave in legacy by oath any chains of the best gold to fetter the later wits of posterity to a choice destructive to peace and true godliness.

Arg. 8. An heritor may defraud his firstborn of his heritage, because of his dominion he has over his heritage: a king cannot defraud his firstborn of the crown. An heritor may divide his heritage equally among his twelve sons: a king cannot divide his royal dominions in twelve parts, and give a part to every son, for so he might turn a monarchy into an aristocracy, and put twelve men in the place of one king. Any heritor taken captive may lawfully pledge all, yea, and give all his inheritance as a ransom for his liberty, for a man is better than his inheritance, but no king may give his subjects as a price or ransom.

Yet I shall not be against the succession of kings by birth with good limitations, and shall agree, that through the corruption of man's nature it may be so far profitable as it is peaceable and prevents bloody tumults, which are the bane of human societies. Consider further for this.[1] Yet Aristotle, the flower of nature's wit prefers election to succession (*Politics* 3.10). He prefers Carthage to Sparta, though their kings came of Hercules. Plutarch in Scylla says he would have kings as dogs, that is, best hunters, not those who are born of best dogs. Tacitus: *Naci et generari a Principibus, fortuitum, nec ultra aestimantur* (*Histories* 1).

---

1. Aegid. Romanus, *De reg. princi.* 3.5, *Turrecremat. and Joan. de terrae Reubeae, 1 tract. contr. Rebelles,* ar. 1, con. 4.

QUESTION 11.

WHETHER OR NOT HE BE MORE PRINCIPALLY A KING WHO IS A KING BY BIRTH, OR HE WHO IS A KING BY THE FREE ELECTION OF THE PEOPLE.

The elective king comes nearer to the first king (Deut. 17). If the people may limit the king, they give him the power. A community have not power formally to punish themselves. The hereditary and the elective prince in various considerations is better or worse, each one than another.

Assert. 1. Without detaining the reader, I desire liberty to assert that, where God establishes a kingdom by birth, that government, *hic et nunc*, is best, and because God principally distributes crowns, when God establishes the royal line of David to reign, he is not principally a king who comes nearest and most immediately to the fountain of royalty, which is God's immediate will, but God established, *hic et nunc*, for reasons related to types (with reverence of the learned) a king by birth.

Assert. 2. But to speak of them, *ex natura rei*, and according to the first mold and pattern of a king by law, a king by election is more principally king (*magis univoce et per se*) than an hereditary prince. (1) Because in hereditary crowns, the first family being chosen by the free suffrages of the people, for that cause *ultimate*, the hereditary prince comes to the throne, because his first father, and in him the whole line of the family, was chosen to the crown, and *propter quod unumquodque tale, id ipsum magis tale*. (2). The first king ordained by God's positive law must be the measure of all kings, and more principally the king than he who is such by derivation. But the first king is a king by election, not by birth: you shall in any case set him king over you, whom the Lord your God shall choose; one from among your brethren shall you set over you (Deut. 17:15). (3). The law says, *Surrogatum fruitur privilegiis ejus, in cujus locum surrogatur*, he who is substituted in the place of another, enjoys the privileges of him in whose place he succeeds. But the hereditary king has royal privileges from him who is chosen king. Solomon has the royal privileges of David his father, and is therefore king by birth, because his father David was king by election, and this I say, not because I think sole birth is a just title to the crown, but because it designates him who indeed virtually was chosen, when the first king of the race was chosen (4). Because there is no dominion of either royalty, or any other way by nature, no more than an eagle is born king of eagles, a lion king of lions; neither is a man by nature born king of men; and, therefore, he who is made king by suffrages of the people must be more principally king than he who has no title but the womb of his mother.

Dr Ferne is so far with us to father royalty upon the people's free election as on the formal cause that he says if to designate the person and to procure limitation of the power in the exercise of it be to give the power, we grant the power is from the people, but (says he) you will have the power originally from themselves in another sense, for you say they reserve power to depose and displace the magistrate; sometimes they make the monarchy supreme, and then they divest themselves of all power, and keep none to themselves; but before established government they have no politic power by which they may lay a command on others, but only a natural power of private resistance, which they cannot use against the magistrate.[1]

Ans. But to take off those by the way.

1. If the king may choose A. B. an ambassador, and limit him in his power, and say, 'Do this, and say this to the foreign state you go to, but no more,' half a wit will say the king creates the ambassador, and the ambassador's power is originally from the king; and we prove the power of the lion is originally from God, and of the sea and the fire is originally from God, because God limits the lion in the exercises of its power, that it shall not devour Daniel, and limits the sea, as Jeremiah says, when as he will have its proud waves to come here and no farther, and will have the fire to burn those who threw the three children into the fiery furnace, and yet not to burn the three children; for this is as if Dr. Ferne said, The power of the king of six degrees, rather than his power of five, is from the people, therefore the power of the king is not from the people; yea, the contrary is true.

2. That the people can make a king supreme, that is, *absolute*, and so resign nature's birthright, that is, a power to defend themselves, is not lawful, for if the people have not absolute power to destroy themselves, they cannot resign such a power to their prince.

3. It is false that a community, before they be established with formal rulers, have no politic power; for consider them as men only, and not as associated, they have indeed no political power, but before magistrates be established, they may convene and associate themselves in a body, and appoint magistrates, and this they cannot do if they had no politic power at all.

4. They have virtually a power to lay on commandments, in that they have power to appoint to themselves rulers, who may lay commandments on others.

_____

1. Dr Fern, part 3, sect. 3.

5. A community has not formally power to punish themselves, for to punish is to inflict *malum disconveniens naturae*, an evil contrary to nature, but in appointing rulers and in agreeing to laws, they consent they shall be punished by another, upon supposition of transgression, as the child willingly going to school submits himself in that to school discipline, if he shall fail against any school law, and by all this it is clear, a king by election is principally a king. Barclay then fails, who says no man denies but succession to a crown by birth is agreeable to nature.[1] It is not against nature, but it is no more natural than for a lion to be born a king of lions.

Obj. Most of the best divines approves an hereditary monarch, rather than a monarch by election.

Ans. So do I in some cases. In respect of empire simply, it is not better; in respect of empire now, under man's fall in sin, I grant it to be better in some respects. So Salust in *Jugurtha*: *Natura mortalium imperii avida.* Tacitus, *Hist.* 2: *Minore discrimine princeps sumitur, quam queritu*; there is less danger to accept of a prince at hand than to seek one afar off. In a kingdom to be constituted, election is better; in a constituted kingdom, birth seems less evil. In respect of liberty, election is more convenient; in respect of safety and peace, birth is safer and the nearest way to the well.[2]

---

1. *Cont. Monarcham.* 2.
2. Bodin, *De Rep.* 6.4; *Thol. de Rep.* 7.4.

QUESTION 12.

WHETHER OR NOT A KINGDOM MAY LAWFULLY BE PURCHASED BY THE SOLE TITLE OF CONQUEST.

There is a twofold right of conquest: Conquest turned in an after-consent of the people becomes a just title. Conquest is not a signification to us of God's approving will. Mere violent domineering is contrary to the acts of governing. Violence has nothing in it of a king. A bloody conqueror is not a blessing, per se, as a king is. Strength as prevailing is not law or reason. Fathers cannot dispose of the liberty of posterity not born. A father, as a father, has not power of life and death. Israel and David's conquests of the Canaanites, Edomites, Ammonites was not lawful because of conquest, but upon a divine title of God's promise.

The Prelate asserts confidently that a title to a kingdom by conquest without the consent of a people is so just and evident by Scripture that it cannot be denied; but the man brings no Scripture to prove it (section 17). Mr. Marshall says a conquered kingdom is but *continuata injuria*, a continued robbery (Let. 7). A right of conquest is twofold. 1. When there is no just cause. 2. When there is just reason and ground of the war. In this latter case, if a prince subdue a whole land which justly deserves to die, yet, by his grace, who is so

131

mild a conqueror, they may be all preserved alive, now among those who have thus injured the conqueror, as they deserve death, we are to differentiate the persons offending, and the wives, children—especially those not born—and such as have not offended. The former sort may resign their personal liberty to the conqueror, that the sweet life may be saved. He cannot be their king properly; but I conceive that they are obliged to consent that he be their king upon this condition: that the conqueror put not upon them violent and tyrannical conditions that are harder than death. Now in reason we cannot think that a tyrannical and unjust domineering can be God's lawful means of translating kingdoms, and for the other part, the conqueror cannot domineer as king over the innocent, and especially the children not yet born.

Assert. 1. A people may be by God's special commandment subject to a conquering Nebuchadnezzar and a Caesar, as to their king, as Judah was commanded by the prophet Jeremiah to submit unto the yoke of the king of Babylon, and to pray for him, and the people of the Jews were to give to Caesar the things of Caesar, and yet both those were unjust conquerors; for those tyrants had no command of God to oppress and reign over the Lord's people, yet were they to obey those kings, so the passive subjection was just and commanded by God, and the active, unjust and tyrannical, and forbidden by God.

Assert. 2. This title by conquest, through the people's later consent, may be turned into a just title, as in the case of the Jews in Caesar's time, for which cause our Savior commanded to obey Caesar, and to pay tribute unto him, as Dr Ferne confesses (section 7). But two things are to be condemned in the Doctor. 1. That God manifests his will to us in this work of providence, by which he transfers kingdoms. 2. That this is an over-awed consent.

Now to the former I reply, 1. If the act of conquering be violent and unjust, it is no manifestation of God's regulating and approving will, and can no more prove a just title to a crown because it was an act of divine providence than Pilate and Herod's crucifying of the Lord of glory, which was an act of divine providence, flowing from the will and decree of divine providence (Acts 2:23; 4:28) is a manifestation that it was God's approving will that they should kill Jesus Christ.

2. Though the consent be some way over-awed, yet is it a sort of contract and covenant of loyal subjection made to the conqueror, and therefore sufficient to make the title just; otherwise, if the people never give their consent, the conqueror, domineering over them by violence, has no just title to the crown.

Assert. 3. Mere conquest by the sword, without the consent of the people, is no just title to the crown.

Arg. 1. Because the lawful title that God's word holds forth to us, besides the Lord's choosing and calling of a man to the crown is the people's election (Deut. 17:15), all that had any lawful calling to the crown in God's word, such as Saul, David, Solomon, &c., were called by the people; and the first lawful calling is to us a rule and pattern to all lawful callings.

Arg. 2. A king, as a king and by virtue of his royal office, is the father of the kingdom, a tutor, a defender, protector, a shield, a leader, a shepherd, a husband, a patron, a watchman, a keeper of the people over which he is king, and so the office essentially includes acts of fatherly affection, care, love, and kindness to those over whom he is set, so as he who is clothed with all these relations of love to the people cannot exercise those official acts on a people against their will and by mere violence. Can he be a father, a guide and a patron to us against our will, and by the sole power of the bloody sword? A benefit conferred on any against their will is no benefit. Will he by the awesome dominion of the sword be our farther, and we unwilling to be his sons, and head over such as will not be members? Will he guide me as a father, a husband, against my will? He cannot come by mere violence to be a patron, a shield, and a defender of me through violence.

Arg. 3. It is not to be thought that that is God's just title to a crown which has nothing in it of the essence of a king, but a violent and bloody purchase, which is in its prevalence in an oppressing Nimrod, and the crudest tyrant that is has nothing essential to that which constitutes a king; for it has nothing of heroic and royal wisdom and gifts to govern, and nothing of God's approving and regulating will, which must be manifested to any who would be a king, but by the contrary cruelty has rather baseness and witless fury, and a plain reluctance with God's revealed will, which forbids murder. God's law should say, "Murder you, and prosper and reign," and by the act of violating the sixth commandment, God should declare his approving will, namely, his lawful call to a throne.

Arg. 4. There are none under a law of God who may resist a lawful call to a lawful office, but men may resist any impulse of God stirring them up to murder the most numerous and strongest, and chief men of a kingdom that they may reign over the fewest, the weakest, and the young, and lowest of the people against their will; therefore this call by the sword is not lawful. If it be said that the divine impulse, stirring up a man to make a bloody conquest that the ire and just indignation of God in justice may be declared on a wicked nation, is an extraordinary impulse of God, who is above a law, and therefore no man may resist it, then all bloody conquerors must have some extraordinary revelation from heaven to warrant their yielding of obedience to such an extraordinary impulse. And if it be so, they must show a lawful and immediate extraordinary impulse now, but it is certain the sins of the people conquered, and their most equal and just demerit before God, cannot be a just plea to legitimate the conquest; for though the people of God deserved devastation and captivity by the heathen in regard of their sins before the throne of divine justice, yet the heathen grievously sinned in conquering them. Zech. 1:15: "And I am very greatly displeased with the heathen that are at ease; for I was but a little displeased, and they helped forward the affliction." So though Judah deserved to be made captives and a conquered people because of their idolatry and other sins, as Jeremiah had prophesied, yet God was highly displeased at Babylon for their unjust and bloody conquest (Jer. 1:17-18, 33-34; 51:35): "The violence done to me and to my flesh be upon Babylon, shall the inhabitants of Zion say; and my blood upon the inhabitants of Chaldea, shall Jerusalem say." And that any other extraordinary impulse to be as lawful a call to the throne as the people's free election, we know not from God's word, and we have but the naked word of our adversaries that William the Conqueror without the people's consent made himself by blood the lawful king of England, and also of all their posterity, and that king Fergus conquered Scotland.

Arg. 5. A king is a special gift from God, given to feed and defend the people of God that they may lead a godly and peaceable life under him (Ps. 78:71-72; 1 Tim. 2:2), as it is a judgment of God that Israel is without a king many days (Hos. 3:4) and that there is no judge, no king, to put evil-doers to shame (Judg. 19. l). But if a king be given by God as a king by the acts of a bloody conquest, to be avenged on the sinful land over which he is made a king, he cannot be given, *actu primo*, as a special gift and blessing by God to feed but to murder and to destroy; for the genuine end of a conqueror as a conqueror is not peace, but fire and sword. If God change his heart from being a bloody devastator to become a father, prince, and feeder of the people, *ex officio*, now he is not a violent conqueror, and he came to that meekness by contraries which is the proper work of the omnipotent God, and not proper to man who, as he cannot work miracles, so neither can he lawfully work by contraries. And so if conquest be a lawful title to a crown, and an ordinary calling, as the opponents presume, every bloody conqueror must be changed into a loving father, prince, and feeder, and if God call him, none should oppose him, but the whole land should dethrone their own native sovereign (whom they are obliged before the Lord to defend) and submit to the bloody invasion of a strange lord, presumed to be a just conqueror, as if he were lawfully called to the throne both by birth and the voices of the people. And truly they deserve no wages who thus defend the king's prerogative royal; for if the sword be a lawful title to the crown, suppose the two generals of both kingdoms should conquer the most and the chiefest of the kingdom now, when they have so many forces in the field, by this wicked reason the one should have a lawful call of God to be king of England and the other to be king of Scotland; which is absurd.

Arg. 6. Either conquest, as conquest, is a just title to the crown, or as a just conquest. If as a conquest, then all conquests are just titles to a crown; then the Ammonites, Sidonians, Canaanites, Edomites, &c., subduing God's people for a time, have just title to reign over them, and if Absalom had been stronger than David, he would then have had the just title to be the Lord's anointed and king of Israel, not David, and so strength actually prevailing should be God's lawful call to a crown. But strength, as strength victorious, is not law nor reason: it would then be reasonable that Herod behead John Baptist, and the Roman Emperors kill the witnesses of Christ Jesus. If conquest, as just, be the title and lawful claim before God's court to a crown, then certainly a stronger king for pregnant national injuries may lawfully subdue and reign over an innocent posterity not yet born. But what word of God can warrant a posterity not born and so accessory to no offense against the conqueror (but only sin original) to be under a conqueror against their will and who has no right to reign over them but the bloody sword? For so conquest, as conquest, not as just, makes him king over the posterity. If it be said: The fathers may engage the posterity by an oath to surrender themselves as loyal subjects to the man who justly and deservedly made the fathers vassals by the title of the sword of justice, I answer: The fathers may indeed dispose of the inheritance of their children, because that inheritance belongs to the father as well as to the son; but because the liberty of the son being born with the son (all men being born free from all civil subjection) the father has no more power to resign the liberty of his children than their lives, and the father as a father has not power of the life of his child; as a magistrate he may have power, and as something more than a father, he may have power of life and death. I hear not what Grotius says, "Those who are not born have no accidents, and so no rights, *Non entis nulla sunt accidentia*; then children not born have neither right nor liberty."[1] And so no injury (may some say) can be done to children not born, though the fathers should give away their liberty to the conquerors: those who are not capable of law are not capable of injury contrary to law.

Ans. There is a virtual alienation of rights and lives of children not born unlawful, because the children are not born. To say that children not born are not capable of law and injuries virtual, which become real in time, might say, Adam did not any injury to his posterity by his first sin, which is contrary to God's word: so those who vowed yearly to give seven innocent children to the Minotaur to be devoured, and to kill their children not born to bloody Moloch, did no acts of bloody injury to their children; nor can any say then that fathers cannot tie themselves and their posterity to a king by succession. But I say, to be tied to a lawful king is no making away of liberty, but a resigning of a power to be justly governed, protected and awed from active and passive violence.

Arg. 7. No lawful king may be dethroned, nor lawful kingdom dissolved; but law and reason both says, *Quod vi partum est imperium, vi dissolvi potest.* Every conquest made by violence may be dissolved by violence: *Censetur enim ipsa natura jus dare ad id omne, sine quo obtineri non potest quod ipsa imperat.*

Obj. It is objected that the people of God by their sword conquered seven nations of the Canaanites; David conquered the Ammonites

---

1. *De jure belli et pacis* 2.4, n. 10.

for the disgrace done to his ambassadors; so God gave Egypt to Nebuchadnezzar for his hire in his service done against Judah. Had David no right over the Ammonites and Moabites but by expecting their consent? You will say, 'A right to their lands, goods and lives, but not to challenge their moral subjection.' Well, we doubt not but such conquerors will challenge and obtain their moral consent. But if the people refuse their consent, is there no way, for providence gives no right? So Dr Ferne,[1] so Arnisaeus.[2]

Ans. *A facto ad jus non vales consequentia,* God, to whom belongs the world and its fullness, disposed to Abraham and his seed the land of Canaan for their inheritance, and ordained that they should use their bow and their sword for the actual possession of it, and the like divine right had David towards the Edomites and Ammonites, though the occasion of David's taking possession of these kingdoms by his sword did arise from particular and occasional demands and injuries; but it follows in no way that, therefore kings now wanting any word of promise, and so of divine right to any lands may ascend to the thrones of other kingdoms than their own, by no other title than the bloody sword. That God's will was the chief patent here is clear, in that God forbade his people to conquer Edom, or Esau's possession, when as he gave them command to conquer the Amorites. I doubt not to say, if Joshua and David had no better title than their bloody sword, though provoked by injuries, they could have had no right to any kingly power over these kingdoms, and if only success by the sword be a right of providence, it is no right of precept. God's providence, as providence without precept or promise can conclude a thing is done or may be done, but cannot conclude a thing is lawfully and warrantably done, otherwise you might say the selling of Joseph, the crucifying of Christ, the spoiling of Job, were lawfully done. Though conquerors extort consent and oath of loyalty, yet that makes not over

---

1. Dr Ferne part 3, sect. 3.

2. Arnisaeus, *De authoritat princip.* 1, n. 12.

a royal right to the conqueror to be king over their posterity without their consent. Though the children of Ammon did a high injury to David, yet no injury can be recompensed in justice with the pressure of the constrained subjection of loyalty to a violent lord. If David had not had an higher warrant from God than an injury done to his messengers, he could not nave conquered them. But the Ammonites were the declared enemies of the church of God, and raised forces against David when they themselves were the injurers and offenders. And if David's conquest will prove a lawful title by the sword to all conquerors, then may all conquerors lawfully do to the conquered people as David did; that is, they may "put them under saws, and under harrows of iron, and under axes of iron, and cause them pass through the brick-kiln." But, I beseech you, will royalists say, that conquerors, who make themselves kings by their sword, and so make themselves fathers, heads, defenders, and feeders of the people, may use the most extreme tyranny in the world, such as David used against the children of Ammon, which he could not have done by the naked title of sword-conquest, if God had not laid a commandment of an higher nature on him to serve God's enemies so? I shall then say, if a conquering king be a lawful king, because a conqueror, then has God made such a lawful king both a father, because a king, and a tyrant, and cruel and lion-hearted oppressor of those whom he has conquered; for God has given him royal power by this example to put these, to whom he is a father and defender by office, to torment, and also to be a torturer of them by office, by bringing their backs under such instruments of cruelty as "saws, and harrows of iron, and axes of iron" (2 Sam. 12:30-31).

QUESTION 13.

WHETHER OR NOT ROYAL DIGNITY HAS ITS SOURCE FROM NATURE, AND HOW IT IS TRUE, "EVERY MAN IS BORN FREE," AND HOW SERVITUDE IS CONTRARY TO NATURE

There are seven sorts of superiority and inferiority. Power of life and death is from a positive law. A dominion is antecedent and consequent. Kings and subjects have no natural order. A man is born, consequenter, in politic relation. Slavery is not natural because of four reasons. That every man is born free in regard of civil subjection, not in regard of natural subjection (such as of children and wife to parents and husband) is proved by seven arguments. How necessary and how natural political government is. That parents should enslave their children is not natural.

I conceive it to be evident that royal dignity is not immediately, and without the intervention of the people's consent, given by God to any one person, and that conquest and violence is no just title to a crown. Now the question is if royalty flow from nature, if royalty be not a thing merely natural, neither can subjection to royal power be merely natural; but the former is rather civil than natural, and the question of the same nature is whether subjection or servitude be natural.

I conceive that there be various subjections to these that are above us some way natural, and therefore I rank them in order, thus: 1. There is a subjection in respect of natural being, as the effect to the cause; therefore, though Adam had never sinned, this morality of the fifth command should have stood in vigor, that the son by nature without any positive law should have been subject to the father, because from him he has his being as from a second cause. But I doubt if the relation of a father as a father necessarily infers a royal or kingly authority of the father over the son, or by nature's law that the father has a power of life and death over or above his children, and the reasons I give are (1.) Because power of life and death is by a positive law, presupposing sin and the rail of man; and if Adam, standing in innocence, could lawfully kill his son, though the son should be a malefactor, without any positive law of God, I much doubt (2.) I judge that the power royal, and the fatherly power of a father over his children, shall be found to be different; and the one is founded on the law of nature, the other, namely, royal power, on a mere positive law.

2. The degree or order of subjection natural is a subjection in respect of gifts or age. So Aristotle says, "Some are by nature servants" (*Politics* 1.3). His meaning is good, that some gifts of nature, as wisdom natural, or aptitude to govern, has made some men of gold fitter to command, and some of iron and day fitter to be servants and slaves. But I judge this title to make a king by birth, seeing Saul, whom God by supervenient gifts made a king, seems to owe small thanks to the womb or nature, that he was a king, for his cruelty to the Lord's priests speaks nothing but natural baseness. It is possible Plato had a good meaning (*De legib.*) who made six orders here. "1. That fathers command their sons; 2. The noble the ignoble; 3. The elder the younger; 4. The masters the servants; 5. The stronger the weaker; 6.

The wise the ignorant." Aquinas,[1] Driedo,[2] following Aristotle[3] hold, though man had never sinned there should have been a sort of dominion of the more gifted and wiser above the less wise and weaker, not antecedent from nature properly, but consequent, for the utility and good of the weaker, insofar as it is good for the weaker to be guided by the stronger, which cannot be denied to have some ground in nature. But there is no ground for kings by nature here.

1. Because even those who plead that the mother's womb must be the best title for a crown, and make it equivalent to royal anointing are to be corrected in memory thus: That it is merely accidental, and not natural, for such a son to be born a king, because the free consent of the people making choice of the first father of that line to be their king, and in him making choice of the firstborn of the family is merely accidental to father and son, and so cannot be natural.

2. Because royal gifts to reign are not held by either us or our adversaries to be the specific essence of a king: for if the people crown a person their king, say we, if the womb bring him forth to be a king, say the opponents, he is essentially a king, and to be obeyed as the Lord's anointed, though nature be very *parce* sparing, and a niggard in bestowing royal gifts; yea, though he be an idiot, say some, if he be the firstborn of a king, he is by just title a king, but must have curators and tutors to guide him in the exercise of that royal right that he has from the womb. But Buchanan says well, "He who cannot govern himself shall never govern others."[4]

Assert. 1. As a man comes into the world a member of a politic society, he is by consequence born subject to the laws of that society, but this makes him not from the womb and by nature subject to a king, as by nature he is subject to his father who begot him, no more

1. 22, q. 57, art. 3.
2. *De libert. Christ.* Book 1.
3. *Polit.* 7.14.
4. *De jure Regni apud Scotos.*

than by nature a lion is born subject to another king-lion; for it is by accident that he is born of parents under subjection to a monarch, or to either democratic or aristocratic governors, for Cain and Abel were born under none of these forms of government properly, and if he had been born in a new planted colony in a wilderness, where no government were yet established, he should be under no such government.

Assert. 2. Slavery of servants to lords or masters, such as were of old among the Jews, is not natural, but against nature. 1. Because slavery is *malum naturae*, a penal evil and contrary to nature, and a punishment of sin. 2. Slavery should not have been in the world, if man had never sinned, no more than there could have been buying and selling of men, which is a miserable consequence of sin and a sort of death, when men are put to the toiling pains of the hireling, who longs for the shadow, and under iron harrows and saws, and to hew wood, and draw water continually. 3. The original of servitude was when men were taken in war, to eschew a greater evil, even death, the captives were willing to undergo a lesser evil, slavery (S. Servitus, *De jure. Pers.*). 4. A man being created according to God's image, he is *res sacra*, a sacred thing, and can no more by nature's law be sold and bought, than a religious and sacred thing dedicated to God.[5]

Assert. 3. Every man by nature is a freeman born, that is, by nature no man comes out of the womb under any civil subjection to king, prince, or judge, to master, captain, conqueror, teacher, &c.

Arg. 1. Because freedom is natural to all, except freedom from subjection to parents, and political subjection is merely accidental, coming from some positive laws of men, as they are in a political society; whereas they might have been born with all concomitants of nature, though born in a single family, the only natural and first society in the world.

---

5. S. 1. *Instit. de inutil. scrupl. l. inter Stipulantem. S. Sacram. F. de verber. Obligat.*

Arg. 2. Man is born by nature free from all subjection, except of that which is most kindly and natural, and that is fatherly or filial subjection, or matrimonial subjection of the wife to the husband, and especially he is free of subjection to a prince by nature, because to be under jurisdiction to a judge or king has a sort of jurisdiction (argument, *L. Si quis sit fugitivus. F. de edil. edict. in S. penult. vel fin*), especially to be under penal laws now in the state of sin. The learned senator Ferdinandus Vasquez says every subject is to lay down his life for the prince (2.82, n.15). Now no man is born under subjection to penal laws or dying for his prince.

Arg. 3. Man by nature is born free, and as free as beasts, but by nature no beast, no lion is born king of lions, no horse, no bullock, no eagle, king of horses, bullocks, or eagles. Nor is there any subjection here, except that the young lion is subject to the old, every foal to its dam; and by that same law of nature, no man is born king of men, nor any man subject to man in a civil subjection by nature (I speak not of natural subjection of children to parents) and therefore Ferdinandus Vasquez said that kingdoms and empires were brought in, not by nature's law, but by the law of nations. He expounds himself elsewhere to speak of the law of nature secondary; otherwise the primary law of nations is indeed the law of nature, as appropriated to man (illustr. quest, 2.82, n. 6). If any reply that the natural freedom of beasts and birds, who never sinned, cannot be one with the natural freedom of man who is now under sin, and so under bondage for sin, my answer is that the subjection of the misery of man by nature because of sin is more than the subjection of beasts, comparing species and kinds of beasts and birds with mankind, but comparing individuals of the same kind among themselves; as lion with lion, eagle with eagle, and so man with man; in which respect, because he who is supposed to be the man born free from political subjection, even the king born a king is under the same state of sin, and so by reason of sin, of which he has a share equally with all other men by nature, he must be by nature born under as great subjection penal for sin (except the king be born void of sin) as other men; therefore he is not born freer by nature than other men, unless he come out of the womb with a king's crown on his head.

Arg. 4. To be a king is a free gift of God, which God bestows on some men above others, as is evident (2 Sam. 12:7-8; Ps. 75:6; Dan. 4:32) and therefore all must be born kings, if any one man be by nature a king born, and another a born subject. But if some be by God's grace made kings above others, they are not so by nature; for things which befit man by nature, befit all men equally, but all men equally are not born kings, as is evident, and all men are not equally born by nature under political subjection to kings, as the adversaries grant, because those who are by nature kings cannot be also by nature subjects.

Arg. 5. If men be not by nature free from political subjection, then must some by the law of relation by nature be kings. But none are by nature kings, because none have by nature these things which essentially constitute kings, for they have neither by nature the calling of God, nor gifts for the throne, nor the free election of the people, nor conquest, and if there be none a king by nature, there can be none a subject by nature. And the law says, *Omnes sumus natura liberi, nullius ditioni subjecti. lib. Manumiss. F. de just. et jur. S. jus antem gentium, Jus. de jur. nat.* We are by nature free, and *D. L. ex hoc jure cum simil.*

Arg. 6. Politicians agree to this as an undeniable truth, that as domestic society is natural, being grounded upon nature's instinct, so political society is voluntary, being grounded on the consent of men; and so political society is natural, *in radice*, in the root, and voluntary and free, *in modo*, in the manner of their union, and the Scripture clears to us that a king is made by the free consent of the people (Deut. 17:15) and so not by nature.

Arg. 7. What is from the womb, and so natural, is eternal and agrees to all societies of men; but a monarchy befits not all societies of men; for many hundred years, *de facto*, there was not a king till Nimrod's time, the world being governed by families, and till Moses' time we find no institution for kings (Gen. 7), and the numerous multiplication of mankind did occasion monarchies, otherwise, fatherly government being the first and measure of the rest, must be the best; for it is better that my father govern me than that a stranger govern me, and therefore, the Lord forbid his people to set a stranger over themselves to be their king. The Popish Prelate contends for the contrary (section 12). "Every man," says he, "is born subject to his father, of whom immediately he has his existence in nature; and if his father be the subject of another, he is born the subject of his father's superior."

Ans. But the consequence is weak. Every man is born under natural subjection to his father, therefore he is born naturally under civil subjection to his father's superior or king. It follows not. Yea, because his father was born only by nature subject to his own father, therefore he was subject to a prince or king only by accident, and by the free constitution of men, who freely choose politic government, whereas there is no government natural, but fatherly or marital, and therefore the contradictory consequence is true.

Popish Prelate. Every man by nature has immunity and liberty from despotic and hierarchical empire, and so may dispose of his own at will, and cannot enslave himself without his own free will; but God has laid a necessity on all men to be under government, and nature also laid this necessity on him, therefore this sovereignty cannot protect us in righteousness and honesty, unless it be entirely endowed with sovereign power to preserve itself and protect us.

Ans. The Prelate here deserts his own consequence, which is strong against himself, for if a man be naturally subject to his father's superior, as he said before, why is not the son of a slave naturally subject to his father's superior and master?

2. As a man may not make away his liberty without his own consent, so can he not without his own consent give his liberty to be

subject to penal laws under a prince without his own consent, either in his father's or in the representative society in which he lives.

3. God and nature have laid a necessity on all men to be under government, a natural necessity from the womb to be under some government, namely, a paternal government, that is true, but under this government politic, and namely under sovereignty, it is false; and that is but said, for why is he naturally under sovereignty rather than aristocracy? I believe any of the three forms are freely chosen by any society.

4. It is false that one cannot defend the people, unless he have entire power, that is to say, he cannot do good unless he have a vast power to do both good and ill.

Popish Prelate. It is accidental to any to render himself a slave, being occasioned by force or extreme indigence, but to submit to government congruous to the condition of man, and is necessary for his happy being, and natural, and necessary, by the inviolable ordinance of God and nature.

Ans. 1. If the father be a slave, it is natural and not accidental by the Prelate's logic to be a slave. 2. It is also accidental to be under sovereignty, and sure not natural; for then aristocracy and democracy must be unnatural, and so unlawful governments. 3. If to be congruous to the condition of man be all one with natural man (which he must say if he speak sense) to believe in God, to be an excellent mathematician, to swim in deep waters, being congruous to the nature of man, must be natural. 4. Man by nature is under government paternal, not political properly, but by the free consent of his will.

Popish Prelate. Luke 11:5, Christ himself was ὑποτασσόμινος subject to his parents (the word which is used, Rom. 13), therefore none are exempted from subjection to lawful government.

Ans. We never said that any were exempted from lawful government. The Prelate and his fellow Jesuits teach that the clergy are exempted from the laws of the civil magistrate, not we; but because

Christ was subject to his parents, and the same word is used (Luke 11), which is in Rom. 13, it will not follow, therefore, men are by nature subject to kings, because they are by nature subject to parents.

Popish Prelate. The father had power over the children, by the law of God and nature, to redeem himself from debt, or any distressed condition by enslaving his children begotten of his own body; if this power was not by the right of nature and by the warrant of God, I can see no other, for it could not be by mutual and voluntary contract of children and fathers.

Ans. 1. Show a law of nature, that the father might enslave his children; by a divine positive law, presupposing sin, the father might do that, and yet I think that may be questioned whether it was not a permission rather than a law, as was the bill of divorce, but a law of nature it was not.

2. The Popish Prelate can see no law but the law of nature here; but it is because he is blind or will not see. His reason is: It was not by mutual and voluntary contract of children and fathers, therefore it was by the law of nature; so he that cursed his father was to die by God's law. This law was not made by mutual consent between the father and the son, therefore it was a law of nature: the Prelate will see no better. Nature will teach a man to enslave himself to redeem himself from death, but that it is a dictate of nature that a man should enslave his son, I conceive not.

3. What can this prove but that if the son may by the law of nature be enslaved for the father, but that the son of a slave is by nature under subjection to slavery, and that by nature's law; the contrary of which he spoke in the page preceding, and in this same page.

As for the argument of the Prelate to answer Suarez, who labors to prove monarchy not to be natural, but of free consent, because it is various in sundry nations, it is the Jesuits' argument, not ours. I own it not. Let Jesuits plead for Jesuits.

QUESTION 14.

WHETHER OR NOT THE PEOPLE MAKE A PERSON
THEIR KING CONDITIONALLY OR ABSOLUTELY; AND
WHETHER THE KING IS TIED BY ANY SUCH COVENANT.

The king is under a natural, but no civil obligation to the people, as royalists teach. That the covenant civilly ties the king is proved by Scriptures and reasons. If the condition without which one of the parties would never have entered into covenant be not performed, that party is loosed from the covenant. The people and princes are obliged in their places for justice and religion, no less than the king. Insofar as the king presses a false religion on the people, catenus, they are understood not to have a king. The covenant gives a mutual co-active power to king and people to compel each other, though there be not one on earth higher than both to compel each of them. The covenant binds the king as king, not as he is a man only. One or two tyrannical acts deprive not the king of his royal right. Though there were no positive written covenant (which still we grant not) yet there is a natural, tacit, implicit covenant tying the king, by the nature of his office. If the king be made king absolutely, it is contrary to Scripture and the nature of his office. The people given to the king as a pledge, not as if they became his own to dispose of at his absolute will. The king could not buy, sell, borrow, if no covenant should tie him to men. The covenant sworn by Judah (2 Chron. 15) tied the king.

There is a covenant natural, and a covenant political and civil. There is no political or civil covenant between the king and his subjects, because there is no such equality (say royalists) between the king and his people, such that the king can be brought under any civil or legal obligation in man's court, to either necessitate the king civilly to keep an oath to his people, or to tie him to any punishment, if he fail, yet (say they) he is under natural obligation in God's court to keep his oath, but he is accountable only to God if he violate his oath.

Assert. 1. There is an oath between the king and his people, laying on, by reciprocation of bonds, mutual civil obligation upon the king to the people and the people to the king. 2 Sam. 5:3: "So all the elders of Israel came to the king to Hebron, and king David made a covenant with them in Hebron before the Lord, and they anointed David king over Israel." 1 Chron. 11:3: "And David made a covenant with them before the Lord, and they anointed David king over Israel, according to the word of the Lord by Samuel." 2 Chron. 23:2-3: "And they went about in Judah, and gathered the Levites out of all the cities of Judah, and the chief of the fathers of Israel, and they came to Jerusalem. And all the congregation made a covenant with the king [Joash] in the house of God." 2 Kings 11:17: "Jehoiada made a covenant between the Lord and the king and the people, that they should be the Lord's people; between the king also and the people." Eccl. 8:2: "I counsel you to keep the king's commandment, and that in regard of the oath of God." Then it is evident there was a covenant between the king and the people. That was not a covenant that did tie the king to God only, and not to the people, 1. Because the covenant between the king and the people is clearly distinguished from the king's covenant with the Lord (2 Kings 11:17). There was no necessity that this covenant should be made publicly before the people, if the king did not in the covenant tie and oblige himself to the people; nor needed it be made solemnly before the Lord in the house of God. 3. It is expressly a covenant that was between Joash the king and his people; and David made a covenant at his coronation with the princes and elders of Israel, therefore the people gave the crown to David covenant-wise, and upon condition that he should perform such and such duties to them. And this is clear by all covenants in the word of God: even the covenant between God and man is in like manner mutual, "I will be your God, and You shall be my people." The covenant is so mutual, that if the people break the covenant, God is loosed from his part of the covenant (Zech. 11:10). The covenant gives to the believer a sort of action of law, and *jus quoddam*, to plead with God in respect of his fidelity to stand to that covenant that binds him by reason of his fidelity (Isa. 43:26; 63:16; Dan. 9:4, 5), and far more a covenant gives ground of a civil action and claim to a people and the free estates against a king, seduced by wicked counsel to make war against the land, even though he did swear by the most high God that he should be a father and protector of the church of God.

Assert. 2. All covenants and contracts between man and man, yea, all solemn promises bring the covenanters under a law and a claim before men, if the oath of God be broken, as the covenant between Abraham and Abimelech (Gen. 21:27), Jonathan and David (1 Sam. 18:3). The spies profess to Rahab in the covenant that they made with her (Josh. 2:20): "And if you utter this our business, we will be quit of your oath which you have made us to swear." There be no mutual contract made upon certain conditions, but if the conditions be not fulfilled, the party injured is loosed from the contract. Barclay says, "This covenant obliges the king to God, but not the king to the people."

Ans. It is a vain thing to say that the people and the king make a covenant, and that David made a covenant with the elders and princes of Israel, for if he be obliged to God only, and not to the people, by a covenant made with the people, it is not made with the people at all, nay, it is no more made with the people of Israel than with the Chaldeans, for it binds David no more to Israel than to Chaldea, as a covenant made with men. Arnisaeus says "When two parties contract, if one perform the duty, the other is acquitted" (*Sect. Oex hujus mod. ubi vult just. de duob. reis,* book 3). Dr Ferne says, "Because everyone of them are obliged fully (*Just. eod.,* section 1) to God, to whom the oath is made (for that is his meaning), and if either the people perform what is sworn to the Lord or the king, yet one of the parties remains still under obligation, and neither does the people's obedience exempt the king from punishment, if he fail, nor the king's obedience exempt the people, if they fail, but everyone bears the punishment of his own sin, and there is no mutual power in the parties to compel one another to perform the promised duty, because that belongs to the praetor or magistrate, before whom the contract is made. The king has jurisdiction over the people, if they violate their oath; but the people has no power over the prince, and the ground that Arnisaeus lays down is this,[1] 1. The king is not a party contracting with the people, as if there were mutual obligations between the king and the people, and a mutual co-active power on either side. 2. That the care of religion belongs not to the people, for that has no warrant in the Word (says he). 3. We read not that the people was to command and compel the priests and the king to reform religion and abolish idolatry, as it must follow, if the covenant be mutual. 4. Jehoiada obliges himself, and the king, and the people, by a like law, to serve God (2 Kings 11); and here are not two parties but three: the high priest, the king, and the people, if this example prove anything. 5. Both king and people shall find the avenging hand of God against them, if they fail in the breach of their oath; everyone, king and people, by the oath stand obliged to God, the king for himself, and the people for themselves, but with this difference, the king owes to God proper and due obedience as any of the

---

1. *Arnis. de authorit. prin.* 1, n. 6-7.

subjects, and also to govern the people according to God's true region (Deut. 17; 2 Chron. 29), and in this the king's obligation differs from the people's obligation; the people, as they would be saved, must serve God and the king, for the same cause (1 Sam. 12). But besides this, the king is obliged to rule and govern the people, and keep them in obedience to God, but the people is not obliged to govern the king, and keep him in obedience to God, for then the people should have as great power and jurisdiction over the king, as the king has over the people, which is against the word of God, and the examples of the kings of Judah, but this comes not from any promise or covenant that the king has made with the people, but from a peculiar obligation according to which he is obliged to God as a man, not as a king:

Arg. 1. This is the mystery of the business which I oppose in these assertions.

Assert. 1. As the king is obliged to God for the maintenance of true religion, so are the people and princes no less in their place obliged to maintain true religion; for the people are rebuked, because they burn incense in all high places (2 Kings 17:11; 2 Chron. 33:17; Hos. 4:13). And the reason why the high places are not taken away is given in 2 Chron. 20:33, for as yet the people "had not prepared their heart unto the God of their fathers," but, you will reply, elicit acts of maintenance of true religion are commanded to the people, and that the places prove; but the question is *de actibus imperatis,* of commanded acts of religion surely none but the magistrate is to command others to worship God according to his word. I answer, in ordinary only, magistrates (not the king only but all the princes of the land) and judges are to maintain religion by their commandments (Deut. 1:16; 2 Chron. 1:2; Deut. 16:19; Eccles. 5:8; Hab. 1:4; Mic. 3:9; Zech. 7, 9; Hos. 5:10-11) and to take care of religion, but when the judges decline from God's way and corrupt the law, we find the people punished and rebuked for it: Jer. 15:4: "And I will cause them to be removed to all kingdoms of the earth, because of Manasseh, the son of

Hezekiah king of Judah, for that which he did in Jerusalem;" 1 Sam. 12:24-25: "Only fear the Lord; but if you shall still do wickedly, you shall be consumed, both you and your king." And this case, I grant, is extraordinary, yet so, as Junius Brutus proves well and strongly that religion is not given only to the king, that he only should keep it, but to all the inferior judges and people also in their kind, but because the estates never gave the king power to corrupt religion and press a false and idolatrous worship upon them, therefore when the king defends not true religion, but presses upon the people a false and idolatrous religion, in that they are not under the king, but are presumed to have no king, *catenus*, so far, and are presumed to have the power in themselves, as if they had not appointed any king at all; as if we presume the body had given to the right hand a power to ward off strokes and to defend the body; if the right hand should by a palsy, or some other disease, become impotent, and be withered up, when ill is coming on the body, it is presumed that the power of defense is recurred to the left hand, and to the rest of the body to defend itself in this case as if the body had no right hand, and had never communicated any power to the right hand. So if an incorporation accused of treason and in danger of the sentence of death shall appoint a lawyer to advocate their cause, and to give in their just defenses to the judge, if their advocate be stricken with dumbness, because they have lost their legal and representative tongue, none can say that this incorporation has lost the tongues that nature has given them, so as by nature's law they may not plead in their own just and lawful defense, as if they had never appointed the foresaid lawyer to plead for them. The king, as a man, is not more obliged to the public and regal defense of the true religion than any other man of the land; but he is made by God and the people king, for the church and people of God's sake, that he may defend true religion for the behalf and salvation of all. If therefore he defend not religion for the salvation of the souls of all in his public and royal way, it is presumed as undeniable that the people of God, who by the law of nature are to care for their own souls, are to defend in their way true religion which so nearly concerns them and their eternal happiness.

Assert. 2. When the covenant is between God, on the one part, and the king, priests, and people on the other, it is true if the one perform for his part to God the whole duty, the other is acquitted: as if two men be indebted to one man ten thousand pounds, if the one pay the whole sum the other is acquitted. But the king and people are not so contracting parties in covenant with God as that they are both indebted to God for one and the same sum of complete obedience, so if the king pay the whole sum of obedience to God, the people are acquitted; and if the people pay the whole sum, the king is acquitted: for everyone stands obliged to God for himself; for the people must do all that is their part in acquitting the king from his royal duty that they may free him and themselves both from punishment, if he disobey the King of kings; nor does the king's obedience acquit the people from their duty. Arnisaeus dreamed if he believed that we make king and people this way party-contractors in covenant with God. Nor can two copartners in covenant with God so mutually compel one another to do their duty; for we hold that the covenant is made between the king and the people, between mortal men; but they both bind themselves before God to each other. But says Arnisaeus, "It belongs to a praetor or ruler, who is above both king and people, to compel each of them, the king to perform his part of the covenant to the people, and the people to perform their part of the covenant to the king. Now there is no ruler but God, above both king and people." But let me answer. The consequence is not needful, no more than when the king of Judah and the king of Israel make a covenant to perform mutual duties one to another, no more than it is necessary that there should be a king and superior ruler above the king of Israel and the king of Judah, who should compel each one to do a duty to his fellow king; for the king and people are each of them above and below others in various respects: the people, because they create the man king, they are so above the king, and have a virtual power to compel him to do his duty, and the king as king has an authoritative power above the people, because royalty is formally in him, and originally and virtually only in the people; therefore may he compel them to their duty, as we shall hear presently, and therefore there is no need of an earthly ruler higher than both, to compel both.

Assert. 3. We shall hereafter prove the power of the people above the king, God willing, and so it is false that there is not mutual coactive power on each side.

Assert. 4. The obligation of the king in this covenant flows from the peculiar national obligation between the king and the estates, and it binds the king as king, and not simply as he is a man. 1. Because it is a covenant between the people and David, not as he is the son of Jesse, for then it should oblige Eliab, or any other of David's brethren; yea, it should oblige any man if it oblige David as a man, but it obliges David as a king, or as he is to be their king, because it is the specific act of a king that he is obliged unto, namely, to govern the people in righteousness and religion with his royal power. And so it is false that Arnisaeus says that "the king, as a man, is obliged to God by this covenant, not as a king."

2, He says by covenant the king is bound to God as a man, not as a king, but so the man will have the king, as king, under no law of God, and so he must either be above God, as king, or co-equal with God, which are manifest blasphemies. For I thought always the royalists had not denied that the king, as king, was obliged to keep his oath to his subjects, in relation to God and in regard of natural obligation, so that he sins before God if he break his covenant with his people, though they deny that he is obliged to keep his covenant in relation to his subjects and in regard of politic or civil obligation to men. Sure I am this the royalists constantly teach.

3. He would have this covenant so made with men as it obliges not the king to men but to God. But the contrary is true. Besides the king and the people's covenant with the Lord, king Joash made another covenant with the people, and Jehoiada the priest was only a witness, or one who in God's name performed the rite of anointing; otherwise he was a subject on the people's side, obliged to keep allegiance to Joash as though to his sovereign and master. But certainly whoever makes a covenant with the people, promising to govern them according to God's word, and upon that condition and these terms receives a throne and crown from the people, he is obliged to what he promises to the people, *Omnis promittens, facit alteri, cui promissio facta est, jus in promittentem.* Whosoever makes a promise to another, gives to that other a sort of right or jurisdiction to challenge the promise. The covenant between David and Israel was a shadow, if it tie the people to allegiance to David as their king, and if it tie not David as king to govern them in righteousness, but leave David loose to the people, and only tie him to God, then it is a covenant between David and God only, but the text says it is a covenant between the king and the people (2 Kings 11:17; 2 Sam. 5:3).

Arg. 2. Hence our second argument. He who is made a minister of God, not simply, but for the good of the subject, and so he take heed to God's law as a king, and govern according to God's will, he is insofar only made king by God as he fulfills the condition and insofar as he is a minister for evil to the subject, and rules not according to that which the book of the law commands him as king, insofar he is not by God appointed king and ruler, and so must be made a king by God conditionally, but so has God made kings and rulers (Rom. 13:4; 2 Chron. 6:16; Ps. 89:30-31; 2 Sam. 7:12; 1 Chron. 28:7-9). This argument is not brought to prove that Jeroboam or Saul leave off to be kings when they fail in some part of the condition, or as if they were not God's vicegerents, to be obeyed in things lawful, after they have gone on in wicked courses, for the people consenting to make

Saul king, they give him the crown, *pro hac vice*, at his entry absolutely. There is no condition required in him before they make him king, but only that he covenant with them to rule according to God's law. The conditions to be performed are consequent and posterior to his actual coronation and his sitting on the throne. But the argument presupposes that which the Lord's word teaches, namely, that the Lord and the people give a crown by one and the same action: for God formally makes David a king by the princes and elders of Israel choosing of him to be their king at Hebron, and therefore, seeing the people make him a king covenant-wise and conditionally, as long as he rule according to God's law, and the people resigning their power to him for their safety and for a peaceable and godly life under him, and not to destroy them and tyrannize over them. It is certain God gives a king that same way by that very same act of the people, and if the king tyrannize, I cannot say it is beside the intention of God making a king, nor yet beside his intention as a just punisher of their transgressions; for to me, as I conceive, nothing either good or evil falls out beside the intention of Him who "does all things according to the pleasure of his will." If then the people make a king, as a king, conditionally, for their safety, and not for their destruction (for as a king he saves, as a man he destroys, and not as a king and father) and if God, by the people's free election, make a king, God makes him a king conditionally, and so by covenant, and therefore when God promises to David's seed and to Solomon a throne, he promises not a throne to them immediately, as he raised up prophets and apostles without any mediate action and consent of the people, but he promises a throne to them by the mediate consent, election, and covenant of the people (2 Sam. 7:12; 1 Chron. 28:7-9); which condition and covenant he expresses in the very words of the people's covenant with the king: "So they wait as kings in the law of the Lord, and take heed to God's commandment and statutes to do them."

Obj. 1. But then Solomon, falling in love with many outlandish women, and so not walking according to God's law, loses all royal dignity and kingly power, and the people is not to acknowledge him as king, since the kingly power was conferred upon him rather than Adonijah, upon such a condition, which condition not being performed by him, it is presumed that neither God, nor the people under God, as God's instruments in making king, conferred any royal power on him.

Ans. It does not follow that Solomon, falling in love with strange women, does lose royal dignity, either in the court of heaven or before men; because the conditions of the covenant upon which God by the people made him king must be exposited by the law (Deut. 17). Now that cannot bear that any one act contrary to the royal office, yea, that anyone or two acts of tyranny does deprive a man of the royal dignity that God and the people gave him; for so David, committing two acts of tyranny, one of taking his own faithful subject's wife from, and another in killing himself, should deprivee himself of all the kingly power that he had, and that therefore the people after his adultery and murder were not to acknowledge David as their king, which is most absurd; for as one single act of unchastity is indeed against the matrimonial covenant, and yet does not make the woman no wife at all, so it must be such a breach of the royal covenant as makes the king no king, that annuls the royal covenant, and deprives the prince of his royal authority and power, that must be interpreted a breach of the oath of God, because it must be such a breach upon supposition of which the people would not have given the crown, but upon supposition of his destructiveness to the commonwealth they would never have given to him the crown.

Obj. 2. Yet at least it will follow that Saul, after he is rejected by God for disobedience in not destroying the Amalekites, as Samuel speaks to him (1 Sam. 15) is no longer to be acknowledged king by the people, at least after he commits such acts of tyranny, as are 1 Sam. 18:12-15, &c.; and after he had killed the priests of the Lord and persecuted innocent David without cause he was no longer, either in the court of heaven or the court of men to be acknowledged as king, seeing he had manifestly violated the royal covenant made with the people (1 Sam. 11:14-15), and yet after those breaches, David acknowledges him to be his prince and the Lord's anointed.

Ans. 1. The prophet Samuel's threatening is not exposited of actual unkinging and rejecting of Saul at the present (1 Sam. 17); for after that, Samuel both honored him as king before the people and prayed for him, and mourned to God on his behalf as king (1 Sam. 16:1-2), but the threatening was to have effect in God's time, when he should bring David to the throne, as was prophesied, upon occasion of less sin, even his sacrificing and not waiting the time appointed, as God had commanded (1 Sam. 13:13; 14:2). The people and David's acknowledgment of Saul to be the Lord's anointed and a king, after he had committed such acts of tyranny as seem destructive of the royal covenant and inconsistent with it, cannot prove that Saul was not made king by the Lord and the people conditionally, and that for the people's good and safety, and not for their destruction, and it does well prove, (1) That those acts of blood and tyranny committed by Saul were not done by him as king, or from the principle of royal power given to him by God and the people; (2) That in these acts they were not to acknowledge him as king (3); That these acts of blood were contrary to the covenant that Saul did swear at his inauguration, and contrary to the conditions that Saul in the covenant took on himself to perform at the making of the royal covenant; (4) They prove not but the states who made Saul king might lawfully dethrone him, and anoint David their king. But David had reason to hold him for his prince and the Lord's anointed, so long as the people recalled not their grant of royal dignity, as David or any man is obliged to honor him as king whom the people makes king, though he were a bloodier and more tyrannical man than Saul. Any tyrant stands *in titulo* as long as the people and estates who made him king have not recalled their grant; so as neither David, nor any single man, though six hundred with him, may unking him or detract obedience from him as king; so many acts of disloyalty and breaches of laws in the subjects, though they are contrary to this covenant that the states make with their prince, does not make them to be no subjects, and the covenant mutual stands thus.

Arg. 3. 1. If the people as God's instruments bestow the benefit of a crown on their king upon condition that he will rule them according to God's word, then is the king made king by the people conditionally, but the former is true, therefore so is the latter. The assumption is proved thus: Because to be a king is to be an adopted father, tutor, a political servant and royal watchman of the state, and the royal honor and royal maintenance given to him is a reward of his labors and a kingly hire. And this is the apostle's argument: Rom. 13:6: "For this cause pay you tribute also, [there is the wages] for they are God's ministers, attending continually upon this very thing." There is the work. *Qui non implet conditionem a se promissam, cadit beneficio.* It is confirmed thus: The people either makes the man their prince conditionally (1) that he rule according to law or absolutely; (2) so that he rule according to will or lust; or (3) without any vocal transactions at all, but only *brevi manu,* say, "Reign you over us, and, God save the king," and so there be no conditions spoken on either side; or (4) the king is obliged to God for the condition which he promises by oath to perform toward the people, but he is to make no reckoning to the people whether he perform his promise or no, for the people being inferior to him, and he, *solo Deo minor,* only next and immediate to God, the people can have no *jus,* no law over him by virtue of any covenant. But the first standing, we have what we seek; the second is contrary to Scripture. He is not made absolutely a king to rule according to his will and lust (Deut. 17:15-16); for "reign you over us" should have this meaning: "Come you and play the tyrant over us, and let your lust and will be a law to us," which is against natural sense; nor can the sense and meaning be according to the third: That the people, without any express, vocal, and positive covenant give a throne to their king to rule as he pleases, because it is a vain thing for the Prelate and other *Mancipia Aulae*, court-bellies, to say Scotland and England must produce a written authentic covenant between the first king and their people, because, say they, it is the law's word. *Do non apparentibus et non existentibus eadem lex*, that covenant which appears not, it is not, for in positive covenants that is true, and in such contracts as are made according to the civil or municipal laws, or the secondary law of nature. But the general covenant of nature is presupposed in making a king, where there is no vocal or written covenant. If there be no conditions between a Christian king and his people, then those things which are just and right according to the law of God, and the rule of God in molding the first king are understood to rule both king and people as if they had been written, and here we produce our written covenant (Deut. 17:15; Josh. 1:8-9; 2 Chron. 31:32). Because this is as much against the king as the people, and more; for if the first king cannot bring forth his written and authentic tables to prove that the crown was given to him and his heirs and his successors, absolutely and without any conditions, so as his will shall be a law, *cadit causa*, he loses his cause (say they). The king is in possession of the royal power absolutely without any condition, and you must put him from his possession by a law. I answer this is most false: (1) Though he were in *mala fide*, and in unjust possession, the law of nature will warrant the people to repeal their right and plead for it, in a matter which concerns their heads, lives, and souls; (2) The parliaments of both kingdoms standing in possession of a legislative power to make laws proves clearly that the king is in no possession of any royal dignity conferred absolutely, and without any condition upon him, and, therefore, it is the king's part by law to put the estates out of possession, and though there were no written covenant, the standing law and practice of many hundred acts of parliament is equivalent to a written covenant.

2. When the people appointed any to be their king, the voice of nature exposits their deed, though there be no vocal or written covenant; for that fact-of making a king-is a moral lawful act warranted by the word of God (Deut. 17:15-16; Rom. 13:1-2) and the law of nature; and, therefore, they having made such a man their king, they have given him power to be their father, feeder, healer, and protector; and so must only have made him king conditionally, so he be a father, a feeder, and tutor. Now, if this deed of making a king must be exposited to be an investing with an absolute, and not a conditional power, this fact shall be contrary to Scripture and to the law of nature; for if they have given him royal power absolutely, and without any condition, they must have given to him power to be a father, protector, tutor, and to be a tyrant, a murderer, a bloody lion, to waste and destroy the people of God.

3. The law permits the bestower of a benefit to interpret his own mind in the bestowing of a benefit, even as a king and state must exposit their own commission given to their ambassador, so must the estates exposit whether they bestowed the crown upon the first king conditionally or absolutely.

4. If it stand, then must the people give to their first elected king a power to waste and destroy themselves, so as they may never control it, but only leave it to God and the king to reckon together, but so the condition is a chimera. "We give you a throne, upon condition you swear by Him who made heaven and earth, that you will govern us according to God's law, and you shall be answerable to God only, not to us, whether you keep the covenant you make with us, or violate it." But how a covenant can be made with the people, and the king obliged to God, not to the people, I conceive not. This presupposes that the king, as king, cannot do any sin, or commit any act of tyranny against the people, but against God only, because if he be obliged to

God only as a king by virtue of his Covenant, how can he fail against an obligation where there is no obligation? But as a king he owes no obligation of duty to the people, and indeed so do our good men expound Ps. 51, "Against you, you only have I sinned," not against Uriah; for if he sinned not as king against Uriah, whose life he was obliged to preserve as a king, he was not obliged as a king by any royal duty to preserve his life. Where there is no sin, there is no obligation not to sin, and where there is no obligation not to sin, there is no sin. By this the king as king is loosed from all duties of the second table, being once made a king he is above all obligation to love his neighbor as himself, for he is above all his neighbors, and above all mankind, and only less than God.

Arg. 4. If the people be so given to the king, that they are committed to him as a pledge, oppignerated in his hand as a pupil to a tutor, as a distressed man to a patron, as a flock to a shepherd; and so they remain the Lord's church, his people, his flock, his portion, his inheritance, his vineyard, his redeemed ones, then they cannot be given to the king as oxen and sheep, that are freely gifted to a man, or as a gift or sum of gold or silver that the man to whom they are given may use so that he cannot commit a fault against the oxen, sheep, gold, or money that is given to him, however he shall dispose of them. But the people are given to the king to be tutored and protected by him, so as they remain the people of God and in covenant with him, and if the people were the goods of fortune (as heathens say), he could no more sin against the people than a man can sin against his gold; now, though a man by adoring gold, or by lavish profusion and wasting of gold may sin against God, yet not against gold; nor can he be in any covenant with gold, or under any obligation of either duty or sin to gold, or to lifeless and reasonless creatures properly, therefore he may sin in the use of them, and yet not sin against them, but against God. Hence, of necessity, the king must be under obligation to the Lord's people in another manner than that he should only answer to God for the loss of men, as if men were worldly goods under his hand, and as if being a king he were now by this royal authority privileged from the best half of the law of nature, namely, from acts of mercy and truth, and covenant-keeping with his brethren.

Arg. 5. If a king, because a king, were privileged from all Covenant obligation to his subjects, then could no law of men lawfully reach him for any contract violated by him; then he could not be a debtor to his subjects if he borrowed money from them, and it would be utterly unlawful either to crave him money, or to sue him at law for debts, yet our civil laws of Scotland tie the king to pay his debts, as any other man, yea, and king Solomon trafficking, and buying, and telling between him and his own subjects would seem unlawful; for how can a king buy and sell with his subjects, if he be under no covenant obligation to men, but to God only. Yea, then, a king could not marry a wife, for he could not come under a covenant to keep his body to her only, nor if he committed adultery, could he sin against his wife, because being immediate unto God, and above all obligation to men, he could sin against no covenant made with men, but only against God.

Arg. 6. If that was a lawful covenant made by Asa, and the states of Judah, "That whosoever would not seek the Lord God of their fathers, should be put to death, whether small or great, whether man or woman," (2 Chron. 15:13) this obliges the king, for anything I see, and the princes, and the people, but it was a lawful covenant; therefore the king is under a covenant to the princes and judges, as they are to him; it is replied by Barclay: "If a master of a school should make a law, whosoever shall go out at the school doors without liberty obtained of the master, shall be whipped, it will not oblige the schoolmaster that he shall be whipped if he go out at the school doors without liberty; so neither does this law oblige the king, the supreme lawgiver."

Ans. 1. Suppose that the scholars have no less hand and authority magisterial in making the law than the schoolmaster, as the princes of

Judah had a collateral power with king Asa about that law, it would follow that the schoolmaster is under the same law.

2. Suppose going out at school doors were that way a moral neglect of studying in the master, as it is in the scholars, as the not seeking of God is as heinous a sin in king Asa, and no less deserving death, than it is in the people, then should the law oblige schoolmaster and scholar both without exception.

3. The schoolmaster is clearly above all laws of discipline which he imposes on his scholars, but none can say that king Asa was clearly above that law of seeking of the Lord God of his fathers. Diodorus Siculus says the kings of Persia were under an oath, and that they might not change the laws (1.17), and so were the kings of Egypt and Ethiopia. The kings of Sparta, which Aristotle calls just kings, renew their oath every month. Romulus so covenanted with the senate and people. Carolus V Austriacus swears he shall not change the laws without the consent of the electors, nor make new laws, nor dispose or pledge anything that belongs to the empire. So read we *Spec. Saxon,* book 3, act. 54, and Xenophon says there was a covenant between Cyrus and the Persians (*Cyroped.* book 8). The nobles are crowned when they crown their king, and exact a special oath of the king. So does England, Poland, Spain, Arragonia, &c. Alber. Gentlis[1] and Grotius[2] prove that kings are really bound to perform oaths and contracts to their people; but "notwithstanding there be such a covenant, it follows not from this (says Arnisaeus) that if the prince break his covenant and rule tyrannically, the people shall be free, and the contract or covenant nothing."[3]

Ans. The covenant may be materially broken, while the king remains king, and the subjects remain subjects; but when it is both

---

1. *Alber. Gentilis in disput. Regal.* 2.12, 3.14-16.

2. *De jure belli et poc.* 2.11-13.

3. *De authoritate princip.* 1, n. 7-8, 10.

materially and formally declared by the states to be broken, the people must be free from their allegiance, but of this more hereafter.

Arg. 7. If a master bind himself by an oath to his servant, he shall not receive such a benefit of such a point of service; if he violate the oath, his oath must give his servant law and right both to challenge his master, and to be free from that point of service; an army appoints such a one their leader and captain, but they revise to do it unless he swear he shall not betray them to the enemy. If he does betray them, then must the soldiers be loosed from that contract. If one be appointed pilot of a ship, and not but by an oath, if he sell the passengers to the Turks, they may challenge the pilot of his oath; and it is clear that (1) the estates should refuse the crown to him who would refuse to govern them according to God's law, but should profess that he would make his own will a law, therefore the intention of the oath is clearly conditional; (2) when the king swears the oath, he is but king *in fieri*, and so not as king above the states of kingdoms. Now his being king does not put him in a case above all civil obligation of a king to his subjects, because the matter of the oath is that he shall be under them so far in regard of the oath of God.

Arg. 8. If the oath of God made to the people do not bind him to the people to govern according to law, and not according to his will and lust, it should be unlawful for any to swear such an oath, for if a power above law befits, essentially, a king as a king, as royalists hold, he who swears such an oath should both swear to be a king to such a people, and should swear to be no king, in respect by his oath he should renounce that which is essential to a king,

Arnisaeus objects: *Ex particularibus non potest colligi conclusion universalis*, some few of the kings, as David and Joash, made a covenant with the people; it follows not that this was an universal law.

Ans. Yea, the covenant is (Deut. 17), and must be a rule to all; if so just a man as David was limited by a covenant, then all the rest also.

QUESTION 15.

*WHETHER THE KING BE UNIVOCALLY, OR ONLY
ANALOGICALLY, AND BY PROPORTION, A FATHER.*

*Adam not king of the whole earth because a father. That the king is a
father metaphorically and improperly is proved by eight arguments.*

It is true Aristotle says that the kingly power is a fatherly power
(Polit. 1.3.11); and Justin *Pater quamvis legum contemptor, quamvis
impius sit, tamen pater est* (*Novell.* 12.2). But I do not believe that, as
royalists say, the kingly power is essentially and univocally that same
with a paternal or fatherly power; or that Adam, as a father, was as a
father and king, and that suppose Adam should live in Noah's days
that by divine institution and without consent of the kingdoms and
communities on earth, Adam *hoc ipso*, and for no other reason but because he was a father, should also be the universal king and monarch
of the whole world; or suppose Adam was living to this day, that all
kings that has been since, and now are, held their crowns from him,
and had no more kingly power than inferior judges in Scotland have,
under our sovereign king Charles, for so all that have been and now
are lawful kings would be unjust usurpers; for if fatherly power be

the first and native power of commanding, it is against nature that a monarch who is not my father by generation should take that power from me, and be a king over me and my children.

1. But I assert, first, that though the Word warrant us to esteem kings fathers (Isa. 49:23; Jud. 5:7; Gen. 20:2), yet are not they essentially and formally fathers by generation. Num. 11:12: "Have I conceived all this people? Have I begotten them?" and yet are they but fathers metaphorically—by office, because they should care for them as fathers do for children, and so come under the name of fathers in the fifth commandment, and therefore rigorous and cruel rulers are leopards, and lions, and wolves (Ezek. 22:27; Zeph. 3:3). If then tyrannical judges be not essentially and formally leopards and lions, but only metaphorically, neither can kings be formally fathers.

2. Not only kings but all judges are fathers, in defending their subjects from violence and the sword, and fighting the Lord's battles for them, and counselling them. If therefore royalists argue rightly, a king is essentially a father, and fatherly power and royal power are of the same essence and nature. As, therefore, he who is once a father is ever a father, and his children cannot take up arms against him to resist him, for that is unnatural and repugnant to the fifth commandment, so he who is once a king is evermore a king, and it is repugnant to the fifth commandment to resist him with arms. It is answered that the argument presupposes that royal power and fatherly power is one and the same in nature, even though they differ in nature, and are only one by analogy and proportion; for so pastors of the Word are called fathers (1 Cor. 4:15), it will not follow that once a pastor, evermore a pastor, and that if therefore pastors turn wolves, and by heretical doctrine corrupt the flock, they cannot be cast out of the church.

3. A father as a father has not power of life and death over his sons, because by divine institution the sword is given by God to kings and judges (Rom. 13), and if Adam had had any such power to kill his son Cain for the killing of his brother Abel, it would been given to

him by God as a political power different from a fatherly power; for a fatherly power is such as formally to preserve the life of the children, and not to take away the life, yea, and Adam, though he had never sinned, nor any of his posterity, Adam should have been a perfect father, as he is now endued with all fatherly power that any father now has; yea, God should not have given the sword or power of punishing evil-doers, since that power should have been in vain, if there had been no violence, nor bloodshed, or sin on the earth; for the power of the sword and of lawful war is given to men now in the state of sin.

4. Fatherly government and power is from the bosom and marrow of that fountain law of nature, but royal power is not from the law of nature, more than is aristocratic or democratic power. Dr. Ferne says monarchy is not *jure divino* (I am not of his mind) nor yet from the law of nature, but *ductu naturae*, by the guidance of nature.[1] Sure it is from a supervenient commandment of God, added to the first law of nature, establishing fatherly power.

5. Children having their life and first breathings of nature from their parents must be in a more entire relation from their father than from their prince. Subjects have not their being natural, but their civil, political and peaceable well-being from their prince.

6. A father is a father by generation, and giving the being of nature to children, and is a natural head and root, without the free consent and suffrages of his children, and is essentially a father to one child, as Adam was to one Cain, but a prince is a prince by the free suffrages of a community, and cannot be a king to one only, and he is the political head of a civil corporation.

7. A father, so long as his children lives, can never leave off to be a father, though he were mad and furious—though he be me most wicked man on earth. *Qui genuit filium non potest non genuisse filium*, what is once past cannot by any power be not past; a father is a father

---

1. Part 1, section 3.

forever. But by confession of royalists, as Barclay, Hugo Grotius, and Arnisaeus, and others grant, if a king sell his subjects by sea or land to other nations, if he turn a furious Nero, he may be dethroned, and the power that created the king under such express conditions (such as if the king violate them by his own consent, he shall be put from the throne) may cease to hold him king; and if a stronger king conquer a king and his subjects, royalists say the conqueror is a lawful king, and so the conquered king must also lawfully come down from his throne and become a lawful captive sitting in the dust.

8. Learned politicians, as Bartholomeus Romulus (*Defens.* part 1, n. 153) and Joannes de Anania (*in c. fin. de his qui fil. occid*) teach that "the father is not obliged to reveal the conspiracy of his son against his prince; nor is he more to accuse his son than to accuse himself, because the father loves the son better than himself" (*D. Listi quidem. Sect. Fin. quod.met. caus. et D. L. fin. c. de cura furiosi*) and certainly a father had rather die in his own person than choose to die in his son's, in whom he affects a sort of immortality, *in specie, quando non potest in individuo*; but a king does not love his subjects with a natural or fatherly love thus; and if the affections differ, the power which seconds the affection for the conservation either of being or well-being must also differ proportionally.

The Popish Prelate objects against us thus, stealing word by word from Arnisaeus (section 7).[2] 1. When a king is elected sovereign to a multitude, he is surrogated in the place of a common father. Exod. 20:12: "Honor your father." Then, as a natural father receives not paternal right, power, or authority from his sons, but has this from God and the ordinance of nature, nor can the king have his right from the community. 2. The maxim of the law is, *Surrogatus gaudet privilegus ejus cui surrogatur, et qui succedit in locum, succedit in jus.* The person surrogated has all the privileges that he has in whose place

---

2. *De potest princip.* 3, n. 1-2.

he succeeds; he who succeeds to the place succeeds to the rights; the adopted son, or the bastard who is legitimated and comes in the place of the lawful born son, comes also in the privileges of the lawful born son. A prince elected comes to the full possession of the majesty of a natural prince and father, for *Modus acquirendi non tollit naturale jus possidendi* (says Arnisaeus, more fully than the poor Plagiarius), the manner of acquiring anything, takes not away the natural possession, for however things be acquired, if the title be just, possession is the law of nations. Then when the king is chosen in place of the father, as the father has a divine right by nature (so must the king have that same) and seeing the right proprietor (says the pamphleting Prelate) had his right by God by nature, then howsoever the designation of the person is from the disordered community, yet the collation of the power is from God immediately, and from his sacred and inviolable ordinance. And what can be said against the way by which anyone elected obtained his right, for seeing God does not now send Samuels or Elishas to anoint or declare kings, we are in His ordinary providence to conceive the designation of the person is the manifestation of God's will, called *voluntas signi*, as the schools speak, just so as when the church designates one to sacred orders.

Ans. 1. He that is surrogated in the place of another, due to him by a positive law of mart, he has law to all the privileges that he has in whose place he is surrogated, that is true. He who is made assignee to an obligation for a sum of money has all the rights that the principal party to whom the bond or obligation was made. He who comes in the place of a mayor of a city, of a captain in an army, of a pilot in a ship, or of a pope, has all the privileges and rights that his predecessors had by law. *Jus succedit juri, persona jure predita personae jure preditae.* So the law, so far as my reading can reach, who profess myself a divine, but that he who succeeds to the place of a father by nature should enjoy all the natural rights and privileges of the person to whom be succeeds, I believe the law never dreamed it; for then the adopted son, coming in place of the natural son, has right to the natural affection of the father. If any should adopt Maxwell the prelate, should he love him as the pursuivant of Crail (Maxwell's father) loved him, I conceive not, has the adopted son his life, his being, the figure bodily, the manners of the son in whose place he is adopted, or does he naturally resemble the father as the natural son does? The Prelate did not read this law in any approved jurist, though he did steal the argument from Arnisaeus, and stole the citations of Homer and Aristotle out of him, with a little metathesis. A natural son is not made a son by the consent of parents, but he is a son by generation; so must the adopted son be adopted without the free consent and grace of the father adopting; so here the king comes in the place of a natural father. But I conceive the law says not that the elected king is a king without consent of the objects, as a natural father is a father without the consent of his sons. Nor is it a law true, as "once a father always a father," so once an elected king always a king, though he sell his subjects, being induced to it by wicked counsellors. If the king have no privileges but what the natural father has, in whose place he comes, then as the natural father in a free kingdom has not power of life and death over his sons, neither has the king power of life and death over his subjects. This is no law. This maxim should prove good if the king were essentially a father by generation and natural propagation, but he is only a father metaphorically and by a borrowed speech. A father *non generando, sed politice alendo, tuendo, regendo*, therefore an elected prince comes not in the full possession of all the natural power and rights of a natural father.

2. The Popish Prelate speaks disgracefully of the church of God, calling it a disorderly community, as if he himself were born of kings, whereas God calls the king their shepherd, and the people, God's flock, inheritance and people; and they are not a disorderly body by nature, but by sin, in which sense the Prelate may call king, priest and people, a company of heirs of God's wrath, unless he be an Arminian

still, as once he was. If we are in ordinary providence now, because we have not Samuels and prophets to anoint kings, to hold the designation of a person to be king to be the manifestation of God's will, called *voluntas signi*, is treason, for if Scotland and England should designate Maxwell in the place of king Charles our native sovereign (an odious comparison) Maxwell should be lawful king; for what is done by God's will, called by our divines (they have it not from schoolmen, as the Prelate ignorantly says) his *signified will*, which is our rule, is done lawfully. There can be no greater treason put in print than this.

QUESTION 16.

WHETHER OR NOT A DESPOTIC AND MASTERLY DOMINION BEFITS THE KING BECAUSE HE IS KING.

That the king has no masterly dominion over the subjects as if they were his servants is proved by four arguments. The king cannot domineer over men since they are reasonable creatures. The king cannot give away his kingdom or his people as if they were his proper goods. A violent surrender of liberty does not bind. A surrender of ignorance is in so far involuntarily as it oblige not. That the goods of the subjects are not the king's is proved by eight arguments. All the goods of the subjects are the king's in a fourfold sense.

I may here dispute whether the king be lord, having a masterly dominion both over men and things. But I first discuss shortly his dominion over his subjects.

It is agreed on by divines that servitude is a penal fruit of sin and against nature. *Institutt. de jure personarum, Sect. 1, and F. de statu hominum. l. libertas*, because all men are born by nature of equal condition.

Assert. 1. The king has no proper, masterly, or lordly dominion over his subjects; his dominion is rather fiduciary and ministerial than masterly,

175

1. Because royal empire is essentially to feed, rule, defend, and to govern in peace and godliness as the father does his children (1 Tim, 2:2); Ps. 78:71: "He brought him to feed Jacob his people, and Israel his inheritance;" Isa,. 55:4: "I gave him for a leader and commander to the people;" 2 Sam. 5:2: "you shall feed my people Israel" (2 Sam. 5:2; 1 Chron. 11:2; 1 Chron. 17:6). And so it is for the good of the people, and to bring those over whom he is a feeder and ruler to such a happy end, and, as says Althusius (*Polit.* 1, n. 13) and Marius Salomonius it is to take care of the good of those over whom the ruler is set, and, *conservare est, rem illaesam servare*, to keep a thing safe (*De princ.* section 2). But to be a master, and to have a masterly and lordly power over slaves and servants is to make use of servants for the owner's benefit, not for the good of the slave,[1] therefore are servants bought and sold as goods.[2]

2. Not to be under governors and magistrates is a judgment of God (Isa. 3:6-7; 3:1; Hos. 3:4; Judg. 19:1-2) but not to be under a master as slaves are is a blessing, seeing freedom is a blessing of God (John 8:33; Exod. 21:2, 26-27; Deut. 15:12) so he that kills Goliath his father's house shall be free in Israel (1 Sam, 17:25, cf. Jer. 34:9; Acts 22:28; 1 Cor. 9:19; Gal. 4:26, 31). Therefore the power of a king cannot be a lordly and masterly power, for then to be under a kingly power should both be a blessing and a curse, and just punishment of sin.

3. Subjects are called the servants of the king (1 Sam. 15:2; 2 Chron. 13:7; 1 Kings 12:7; Exod. 10:1-2; Exod. 9:20) but they are not slaves, because they are his brethren: Deut. 17:20: "That the king's heart be not lifted up against his brethren;" and his sons (Isa. 49:23), and the Lord gave his people a king as a blessing (1 Kings 10:9; Hos. 1:11; Isa. 1:26; Jer. 17:25) "and brought them out of the house of bondage" (Exod. 20:2) as out of a place of misery. And therefore to

---

1. l.2, *De leg. l. Servus de servit. expert. Dance polit. l.1, Tolossan. De Rep. l.1.1, n. 15-16.*

2. *Jure belli. F. de statu hominum l. et servorum.*

be the king's servants in the place cited is some other thing than to be the king's slaves.

4. The master might in some cases sell the servant for money, yea for his own gain he might do it (Nehem. 5:8; Eccles. 2:7; 1 Kings 2:32; Gen. 9:25; Gen. 26:14; 2 Kings 4:1; Gen. 20:14, and might give away his servants; and the servants were the proper goods and riches of the master (Eccles. 2:7; Gen. 30:43; Gen. 20:14; Job 1:3, 15), but the king may not sell his kingdom or subjects, or give them away for money, or any other way; for royalists grant that king to be a tyrant, and worthy to be dethroned, who shall sell his people; for the king may not dilapidate the rents of the crown and give them away to the hurt and prejudice of his successors[3] and far less can he lawfully sell men and give away a whole kingdom to the hurt of his successors, for that would be to make merchandise of the living temples of the Holy Ghost; and Arnisaeus says, servitude is *praeter naturam*, beside nature (*De authorit. princip.* 3, n. 7); he might have said, contrary to nature (*De stat. homin.* 1.5.2, *Inst. de jur. perso.* 3, *et Novel. 89*); but the subjection of subjects is so consonant to nature, that it is seen in bees and cranes. Therefore a dominion is defined as a faculty of using of things to what uses you will. Now a man has not this way an absolute dominion over his beasts, to dispose of them at his will, for a good man has mercy on the life of his beast (Prov. 12:10), nor has he dominion over his goods to use them as he will, because he may not use them to the damage of the commonwealth, he may not use them to the dishonor of God, and so God and the magistrate have laid some bound on his dominion. And because the king being made a king leaves not off to be a reasonable creature, he must be under a law, and so his will and lust cannot be the rule of his power and dominion, but law and reason must regulate him. Now if God had given to the king a dominion over men as reasonable creatures, His power

---

3. *L. ult. Sect. sed nostr. c. Comment. de lege, l. peto, 69, Sect. fratrem de lege, 2, l. 32, ultimo, D. T.*

and dominion which by royalists is conceived to be above law should be a rule to men as reasonable men, which would make men under kings no better than brute beasts, for then should subjects exercise acts of reason, not because good and honest, but because their prince commands them so to do, and if this cannot be said, none can be at the disposing of kings in politic acts liable to royal government, that way that the slave is in his actions under the dominion of his master.

Obj. 1. The Prelate objects out of Spalato, Arnisaeus, and Hugo Grotius (for in his book there is not one line which is his own, except his railings): "All government and superiority in rulers is not primely and only for the subjects' good; for some are by God and nature appointed for the mutual and inseparable good of the superior and inferior, as in the government of husband and wife, or father and son; and in *herili dominio,* in the government of a lord and his servant, the good and benefit of the servant is but secondary and consecutively intended, it is not the principal end, but the external and adventitious, as the gain that comes to a physician is not the proper and internal end of his art, but follows only from his practice of medicine."

Ans. 1. The Prelate's logic tends to this: some government tends to the mutual good of the superior and inferior, but royal government is some government; therefore, nothing follows from a major proposition, *Ex particulari affirmante, in prima figura,* or of two particular propositions. 2. If it be thus formed, every marital government, and every government of the lord and servant is for the mutual good of the superior and inferior, but royal government is such, therefore the assumption is false, and cannot be proved, as I shall presently clear.

Obj. 2. Solomon disposed of Cabul and gave it to Hiram, therefore a conquered kingdom is for the good of the conqueror especially.

Ans. Solomon's special giving away some titles to the king of Tyre, being a special act of a prophet as well as a king, cannot warrant the king of England to sell England to a foreign prince, because William made England his own by conquest, which also is a most false supposition, and this he stole from Hugo Grotius, who condemns selling of kingdoms.

Obj. 3. A man may render himself totally under the power of a master without any conditions; and why may not the body of a people do the like? Even to have peace and safety, surrender themselves fully to the power of a king? A lord of great manors may admit no man to live in his lands but upon a condition of a full surrender of him and his posterity to that lord. Tacitus shows us it was so anciently among the Germans: those engaged in the campaigns surrendered themselves fully to the Romans.

Ans. What compelled people may do to redeem their lives, with loss of liberty, is nothing to the point; such a violent conqueror who will be a father and a husband to a people, against their will, is not their lawful king; and that they may sell the liberty of their posterity not yet born is utterly denied as unlawful; yea, a violent father to me is a father, and not a father, and the posterity may vindicate their own liberty given away unjustly before they were born, *Qua omne regnum vi partum potest vi dissolvi.*

Obj. 4. But (says Dr Ferne) these which are ours, and given away to another, in which there redounds to God by donation a special interest, as in things devoted to holy uses, though after they be abused, yet we cannot recal them; therefore, if the people be once forced to give away their liberty, they cannot recal it, far less if they willingly resign it to their prince.

Ans. 1. This is not true, when the power is given for the conservation of the kingdom, and is abused for its destruction; for a power to destruction was never given, nor can it by rational nature be given. Mortifications given to religious uses by a positive law may be recalled by a more divine and stronger law of nature, such as this, "I will have mercy and not sacrifice." Suppose David, of his own proper heritage, had given the showbread to the priests, yet, when David and his men are famishing, he may take it back from them against their will.

Suppose Christ had bought the ears of corn, and dedicated them to the altar, still he and his disciples might eat them in their hunger. The vessels of silver, dedicated to the church, may be taken and bestowed on wounded soldiers.

2. A people free may not and ought not to totally surrender their liberty to a prince, confiding on his goodness (1) Because liberty is a condition of nature that all men are born with, and they are not to give it away, no, not to a king, except in part and for the better that they may have peace and justice for it, which is better for them, *hic et nunc*; (2) If a people, trusting in the goodness of their prince, enslave themselves to him, and he shall afterwards turn tyrant, a rash and temerarious surrender obliges not, *Et ignorantia facit factum quasi involuntarium.* Ignorance makes the fact some way involuntary; for if the people had believed that a meek king would nave turned a roaring lion, they should not have resigned their liberty into his hand, and therefore the surrender was tacitly conditional to the king as meek, or whom they believed to be meek, and not to a tyrannical lord, and therefore, when the contract is made for the utility of the one party, the law says their place is for after wits, that men may change their mind and resume their liberty, though if they had given away their liberty for money, they cannot recall it; and if violence made the surrender of liberty, here is slavery, and slaves taken in war, so soon as they can escape and return to their own, they are free.[1] So the learned Ferdin. Vasquez says, "The bird that was taken, and has escaped, is free"(illust. 1.2.82, n. 15). Nature in a forced people, so soon as they can escape from a violent conqueror, makes them a free people, and *si solo tempore* (says Ferd. Vasquez) *justificatur subjectio, solo tempore facilius justificabitur liberatio* (1.2.82, n. 6).

Assert. 2. All the goods of the subjects belong not to the king. I presuppose that the division of goods does not necessarily flow from

---

1. *D. Sect. item. ea justit. de rerum divin. l. nihil. F. de capt.* 1.3.

the law of nature, for God made man before the fall lord of the creatures indefinitely; but what goods be Peter's, and not Paul's, we know not. But supposing man's sin, though the light of the sun and air be common to all and religious places be proper to none, yet it is morally impossible that there should not be a distinction of *meum et tuum*, mine and thine, and the decalogue forbidding theft and coveting the wife of another man (yet is she the wife of Peter, not of Thomas, by free election, not by an act of nature's law) does evidence to us that the division of things is so far forth (men now being in the state of sin) of the law of nature that it has evident ground in the law of nations; and thus far natural that the heat that I have from my own coat and cloak, and the nourishment from my own meat are physically incommunicable to any. But I hasten to prove the proposition: If, (1) I have leave to permit that in time of necessity all things are common by God's law: a man travelling might eat grapes in his neighbor's vineyard, though he was not licensed to carry any way. I doubt if David, wanting money, was required to pay money for the showbread, or for Goliath's sword, supposing these to be the very goods of private men, and ordinarily to be bought and sold. Nature's law in extremity for self-preservation has instead a royal prerogative above all laws of nations and all civil laws than any mortal king, and therefore, by the civil law all are the king's in case of extreme necessity. In this meaning, any one man is obliged to give all he has for the good of the commonwealth, and so far the good of the king, insofar as he is head and father of the commonwealth; (2) All things are the king's, in regard of his public power to defend all men and their goods from unjust violence; (3) All are the king's, in regard of his act of conservation of goods, for the use of the just owner; (4) All are the king's in regard of a legal limitation, in case of a damage offered to the commonwealth. Justice requires confiscation of goods for a fault, but confiscated goods are to help the interested commonwealth, and the king, not as a man (to bestow them on his children) but as a king.

To this we may refer these called *bona caduca et inventa*, things lost by shipwreck or any other providence.[1]

Arg. 1. And the reasons why private men are just lords and proprietors of their own goods are: because by order of nature division of goods comes nearer to nature's law and necessity than any king or magistrate in the world; and because it is agreeable to nature that every man be warmed by his own fleece, nourished by his own meat; therefore, to conserve every man's goods to the just owner and to preserve a community from the violence of rapine and theft, a magistrate and king was devised. So it is clear, men are just owners of their own goods by all good order, both of nature and time, before there be any such thing as a king or magistrate. Now, if it be good that every man enjoy his own goods, as just proprietor of them for his own use, before there be a king, who can be proprietor of his goods? And a king being given by God for a blessing, not for any man's hurt and loss, the king comes in to preserve a man's goods, but not to be their lord and owner himself, nor to take from any man God's right to his own goods.

Arg. 2. When God created man at the beginning, He made all the creatures for man, and made them by the law of nature the proper possession of man, but then there was not any king formally as king; for certainly Adam was a father before he was a king, and no man being either born or created a king over another man, no more than the first lion and the first eagle that God created, were by the birthright and first start of creation by nature the king of all lions and all eagles to be after created, no man can by nature's law be the owner of all goods of particular men. And because the law of nations, founded upon the law of nature, has brought in *meum et tuum*, mine and thine, as proper to every particular man, and the introduction of kings cannot overturn nature's foundation, neither civility nor grace destroys

---

1. *Ulpian, tit. 19, t. c. de bonis vacantibus. C. de Thesauro.*

but perfects nature, and if a man be not born a king, because he is a man, he cannot be born the possessor of my goods.

Arg. 3. What is a character and note of a tyrant, and an oppressing king as a tyrant, is not the just due of a king as a king, but to take the proper goods of subjects, and use them as his own is a proper character and note of a tyrant and oppressor; therefore the proposition is evident: A king and a tyrant are by way of contradiction contrary one to another. The assumption is proved thus: Ezek. 45:9-10: "Thus says the Lord, Let it suffice you, O princes of Israel: remove violence and spoil, and execute judgment and justice; take away your exactions from my people, says the Lord. You shall have just balances, and a just ephah, and a just bath." If all be the king's, he is not capable of extortion and rapine. God complains of the violence of kings: Micah 3:1, 3: "Is it not for you to know judgment who eat the flesh of my people, and flay their skins from off them? And they break their bones and chop them in pieces, as though for the pot, and as flesh within the caldron" (cf. Isa. 3:14; Zeph. 3:3). Was it not an act of tyranny in king Ahab to take the vineyard of Naboth? And in king Saul to take the people of God's "fields and vineyards, and olive yards, and give them to his servants (1 Sam. 8:14)?" Was it a just fault that Hybreas objected to Antonius, exacting two tributes in one year, that he said, "If you must have two tributes in one year, then make for us two summers and two harvests in one year?" This cannot be just. If all be the king's, the king takes but his own.

Arg. 4. Subjects under a monarch could not give alms, nor exercise works of charity; for charity must be my own: Isa. 18:7: "Is it not to deal your bread to the hungry," &c.; Eccles. 11:1: "Cast your bread upon the waters;" and the law says: "It is theft to give of another man's to the poor," yea, the distinction of poor and rich should have no place under a monarchy; he only should be rich.

Arg. 5. When Paul commands us to pay tribute to princes (Rom. 13:6) because they are the ministers of God, he lays this ground: that the king has not all, but that the subjects are to give to him from their goods.

Arg. 6. It is the king's place, by justice, to preserve every man in his own right and under his own fig tree; therefore, it is not the king's house.

Arg. 7. Even Pharaoh could not make all the victuals of the land his own, while he had bought it with money, and everything is presumed to be free (*allodialis*, free land) unless the king prove that it is bought or purchased.[1]

Arg. 8. If the subjects had no propriety in their own goods, but all were the prince's due, then the subject should not be able to make any contract of buying and selling without the king, and every subject were in the case of a slave. Now the law says when he makes any covenant, he is not obliged civilly to keep it,[2] because the condition of a servant, he not being *sui juris*, is compared to the state of a beast, though he be obliged by a natural obligation, being a rational creature, in regard of the law of nature.[3] The subject could not by Solomon be forbidden to be surety for his friend, as king Solomon does counsel (Prov. 6:1-3) he could not be condemned to bring on himself poverty by sluggishness (as in Prov. 6:6-10); nor were he to honor the Lord with his riches (as in Prov. 3:9), nor to keep his covenant, though to his loss (Ps. 15:14), nor could he be merciful and lend (Ps. 37:26), nor had he power to borrow, nor could he be guilty in not paying all again (Ps. 37:21). For subjects, under a monarchy, can neither perform a duty, nor fail in a duty in the matter of goods. If all be the king's, what power or dominion has the subject in disposing of his prince's goods? See more in *Petr. Rebuffus, tract. congruae portionis, n. 225. Sed quoad dominium rerum,* &c.

---

1. *L. actius, C. de servit, et aqua. et Joan. And. m. C. F. de ind. et hosti. in C. minus de jur.*

2. *L. 2. F. de Noxali. act. l. 2. F. ad legem aquil.*

3. *L. naturaliter, L. si id quod, L. interdum, F. de cond. indebit. cum aliis.*

QUESTION 17.

WHETHER OR NOT THE PRINCE HAVE PROPERLY THE FIDUCIARY OR MINISTERIAL POWER OF A TUTOR, HUSBAND, PATRON, MINISTER, HEAD, MASTER OF A FAMILY, NOT OF A LORD OR DOMINATOR.

The king is a tutor rather than a father as these are distinguished. A free community not properly and in all respects a minor and pupil. The king's power is not properly marital and husbandly. The king is a patron and servant. The royal power only from God, immediatione simplicis constitutionis et solum solitudine casae primae, but not immediatione applicationis dignitatis ad personam. The king is the servant of the people both objectively and subjectively. The Lord and the people by one and the same act according to the physical relation makes the king. The king is the head of the people only metaphorically, not essentially, not univocally, which is proved by six arguments. His power is fiduciary only.

That the power of the king is fiduciary, that is, given to him immediately by God in trust, royalists deny not, but we hold that the trust is put upon the king by the people. We deny that the people give themselves to the king as a gift, for what is freely given cannot be taken again, but they gave themselves to the king as a pawn, and if the pawn be abused or not used in that manner as it was conditioned to be used, the party in whose hand the pawn is entrusted fails in his trust.

Assert. 1. The king is more properly a tutor than a father.

1. Indigency is the cause of tutors: the parents die; what then shall become of the orphan and his inheritance? He cannot guide it himself, therefore nature devised a tutor to supply the place of a father, and to govern the tutor; but with this consideration: the father is lord of the inheritance, and if he be distressed may sell it, that it shall never come to the son, and the father for the bad deserving of his son may disinherit him; but the tutor, being but a borrowed father, cannot sell the inheritance of the pupil, nor can he for the pupil's bad deserving by any dominion of justice over the pupil take away the inheritance from him and give it to his own son. So a community of itself, because of sin, is a naked society that can but destroy itself, and everyone eat the flesh of his brother; therefore God has appointed a king or governor who shall take care of that community, rule them in peace, and save all from reciprocation of mutual acts of violence, yet so as because a trust is put on the ruler of a community which is not his heritage, he cannot dispose of it as he pleases, because he is not the proper owner of the inheritance.

2. The pupil, when he comes to age, may call his tutor to an account for his administration. I do not acknowledge that as a truth which Arnisaeus says, "The commonwealth is always minor and under tutory, because it always has need of a curator and governor, and can never put away its governor; but the pupil may grow to age and wisdom, so that he may be without all tutors and can guide himself, and so may call in question on his tutor, and the pupil cannot be his judge, but must stand

to the sentence of a superior judge, and so the people cannot judge or punish their prince: God must be judge between them both" (*De authoritate prin.* 3, n. 5).

But this is begging the question; every comparison halts. There is no community but is major in this: that it can appoint its own tutors, and though it cannot be without all rulers, yet it may well be without this or that prince and ruler, and therefore may resume its power, which it gave conditionally to the ruler for its own safety and good, and insofar as this condition is violated, and power turned to the destruction of the commonwealth, it is to be esteemed as not given, and though the people be not a politic judge in their own cause, yet in case of manifest oppression nature can teach them to oppose defensive violence against offensive. A community in its political body is also above any ruler and may judge what is manifestly destructive to itself.

Obj. The pupil has not power to appoint his own tutor, nor does he give power to him; so neither does the people give it to the king.

Ans. The pupil has not indeed a formal power to make a tutor, but he has virtually a legal power in his father, who appoints a tutor for his son; and the people has virtually all royal power in them, as in a sort of immortal and eternal fountain, and may create to themselves many kings.

Assert. 2. The king's power is not properly and univocally a marital and husbandly power, but only analogically.

1. The wife by nature is the weaker vessel, and inferior to the man, but the kingdom, as shall be demonstrated, is superior to the king.

2. The wife is given as an help to the man, but by the contrary, the father here is given as an help and rather to the commonwealth, which is presumed to be the wife.

3. Marital and husbandly power is natural, though it be not natural but from free election that Peter is Ana's husband, and should have been, though man had never sinned; but royal power is a politic constitution, and the world might have subsisted, even if aristocracy or democracy had been the only and perpetual governments. So let the Prelate glory in his borrowed logic; he had it from Barclay: "It is not in the power of the wife to repudiate her husband, though never so wicked. She is tied to him forever, and may not give to him a bill of divorcement, as by law the husband might give to her. If therefore the people swear loyalty to him, they keep it, though to their hurt" (Ps. 15).

Ans. There is nothing here said, unless Barclay and the Plagiary prove that the king's power is properly a husband's power, which they cannot prove but from a simile that crooks. But a king, elected upon conditions, that if he sell his people he shall lose his crown, is as essentially a king as Adam was Eve's husband, and yet by grant of parties the people may never divorce from such a king and dethrone him, if he sell his people, but a wife may divorce from her husband, as the argument says. And this poor argument the Prelate stole from Dr Ferne (part 2, sect. 3). The keeping of covenant, though to our hurt, is a penal hurt, and loss of goods, not a moral hurt and loss of religion.

Assert. 3. The king is more properly a sort of patron, to defend the people (and therefore has no power given either by God or man to hurt the people) and a minister, or public and honorable servant (Rom. 13:4), for he is the minister of God to you for good. 1. He is the commonwealth's servant objectively, because all the king's service, as he is king, is for the good, safety, peace, and salvation of the people, and in this he is a servant. 2. He is the servant of the people representatively, in that the people has impawned in his hand all their power to do royal service.

Obj. 1. He is the servant of God, therefore he is not the people's servant, but their sovereign lord.

Ans. It follows not: because all the services the king, as king, performs to God are acts of royalty, and acts of royal service, as terminated on the people, or acts of their sovereign lord, and this proves that to be their sovereign is to be their servant and watchman.

Obj. 2. God makes a king only, and the kingly power is in him only, not in the people.

Ans. 1. The royal power is only from God immediately, *immediatione simplicis constitutionis, et solum a Deo solitudine primae causae*, by the immediation of simple constitution, none but God appointed there should be kings.

But, 2. Royal power is not in God, nor only from God, *immediatione applicationis regiae dignitatis ad personam, nec a Deo solum, solitudine causae applicantis dignitatem, huic, non illi*, in respect of the applying of royal dignity to this person, not to that.

Obj. 3. Though royal power were given to the people, it is not given to the people as if it were the royal power of the people, and not the royal power of God; neither is it any otherwise bestowed on the people but as on a beam, a channel, an instrument by which it is derived to others, and so the king is not the minister or servant of the people.

Ans. It is not in the people as in the principal cause: true, all royal power that way is only in God, but it is in the people as in the instrument, and when the people make David their king at Hebron, in that same very act God by the people using their free suffrages and consent makes David king at Hebron; so God only gives rain, and none of the vanities and supposed gods of the Gentiles can give rain (Jer. 14:22), and yet the clouds also give rain, as nature, as an organ and vessel out of which God pours down rain upon the dry earth (Amos 9:6), and every instrument under God that is properly an instrument is a sort of vicarious cause in God's place, and so the people as in God's place apply royal power to David, not to any of Saul's sons, and appoint David to be their royal servant to govern, and in that to serve God, and to do that which a community now in the state of sin cannot formally do themselves, and so I see not how it is a service to the people, not only objectively, because the king's royal service tends to the good, and peace, and safety of the people, but also subjectively, in regard of his power and royal authority which he exercises as king from the people under God, as God's instruments, and therefore the king and parliament give out laws and statutes in the name of the whole people of the land, and they are but flatterers and belie the Holy Ghost who teach that the people do not make the king; for Israel made Saul king at Mizpah, and Israel made David king at Hebron.

Obj. 4. Israel made David king, that is, Israel designated David's person to be king, and Israel consented to God's act of making David king, but they did not make David king.

Ans. I say not that Israel made the royal dignity of kings: God instituted that himself (Deut. 17); but the royalist must give us an act of God going before an act of the people's making David king at Hebron, by which David of no king is made formally a king, and then another act of the people, approving only and consenting to that act of God, by which David is made formally from being no king to being a king. This royalists shall never instruct, for there are only two acts of God here: 1. God's act of anointing David by the hand of Samuel; and 2. God's act of making David king at Hebron; and a third they shall never give. But the former is not that by which

David was essentially and formally changed from the state of a private subject and no king into the state of a public judge and supreme lord and king, for (as I have proved) after this act of anointing of David king, he was designated only and set apart to be king in the Lord's fit time, and after this anointing, he was no more formally a king than Doeg or Nabal were kings, but a subject who called Saul the Lord's anointed and king, and obeyed him as another subject does his king; but it is certain God by no other act made David king at Hebron than by Israel's act of free electing him to be king and leader of the Lord's people, as God by no other act sends down rain on the earth, but by His melting the clouds and causing rain to fall on the earth; and therefore to say Israel made David king at Hebron, that is, Israel approved only and consented to a prior act of God's making David king is just to say Saul prophesied, that is, Saul consented to a prior act of the Spirit of God who prophesied, and Peter preached (Acts 2), that is, Peter approved and consented to the Holy Ghost's act of preaching, which to say is childish.

Assert. 4. The king is a head of the commonwealth only metaphorically, by a borrowed speech in a political sense, because he rules, commands, directs the whole political body in all its operations and functions. But he is not univocally and essentially the head of the commonwealth.

1. The very same life in number that is in the head is in the members; there are various distinct souls and lives in the king and in his subjects.

2. The head natural is not made a head by the free election and consent of arms, shoulders, legs, toes, fingers, &c. The king is made king only by the free election of his people.

3. The natural head, so long as the person lives, is ever the head, and cannot cease to be a head while it is seated on the

shoulders; the king, if he sell his people's persons and souls, may leave off to be a king and head.

4. The head and members live together and die together; the king and the people are not so; the king may die and the people live.

5. The natural head cannot destroy the members and preserve itself, but king Nero may waste and destroy his people. Dr Ferne, M. Symmons, the Popish Prelate, when they draw arguments from the head do but dream, as the members should not resist the head. Natural members should not or cannot resist the head, though the hand may pull a tooth out of the head, which is no small violence to the head, but the members of a political body may resist the political head. This or that king is not the adequate and total political head of the commonwealth, and therefore though you cut off a political head, there is nothing done against nature. If you cut off all kings of the royal line and all governors aristocratic, both king and parliament, this would be against nature, and a commonwealth which would cut off all governors and all heads should go against nature and run to ruin quickly. I conceive a society of reasonable men cannot lack governors.

6. The natural head communicates life, sense, and motion to the members, and is the seat of external and internal senses; the king is not so.

Assert. 5. Hence the king is not properly the head of a family, for as Tholossa says well nature has one intention in making the thumb, another intention in making the whole hand, another in forming the body; so there is one intention of the God of nature in governing of one man, another in governing a family, another in governing a city; nor is the thumb king of all the members; so domestic government is not monarchical properly (*De Rep.* 1.5.5). 1. The mother has a parental power as the father has (Prov. 4:5; 10:3; 31:17); so the fifth commandment says, "Honor your father and your mother." 2. Domestic government is natural, monarchical politic. 3. Domestic is necessary; monarchical is not necessary; other government may be as well as it. 4. Domestic is universal; monarchical not so. 5. Domestic has its rise from natural instinct without any farther instruction; a monarchical government is from election, choosing one government, not another. Hence that is a fiduciary power, or a power of trust, in which the thing put in trust is not either his own proper heritage or gift, so as he may dispose of it as he pleases, as men dispose of their goods or heritage. But the king may not dispose of men as men as he pleases; nor of laws as he pleases; nor of governing men, killing or keeping alive, punishing and rewarding, as he pleases. My life and religion, and so my soul in some cases are committed to the king as to a public watchman, even as the flock to the feeder, the city to the watchmen; and he may betray it to the enemy. Therefore, he has the trust of life and religion, and has both tables of the law in his custody, *ex officio*, to see that other men than himself keep the law. But the law is not the king's own, but given to him in trust. He who receives a kingdom conditionally and may be dethroned if he sell it or put it away to any other, is a fiduciary patron, and has it only in trust. So Hottoman (quest. ill. 1), Ferdinand. Vasquez (illust. quest. l.1.4), Althusius (*polit.* 24, n. 35); so says the law of every factor or deputy (1.40, 1.63, *procur.* 1.16, *dict.* 1). *Antigonus dixit regnum esse nobilem servitutem.* Tiberius Caesar called the senate, *dominum suum*, his lord (Suetonius *in vita Tiberii*, section 29).

QUESTION 18.

WHAT IS THE LAW OR MANNER OF THE KING IS (1 SAM. 8:9, 11) DISCUSSED FULLY

The power and the office badly differentiated by Barclay. What תפשט *מלך, the manner of the king is, by the harmony of interpreters, ancient and modern, protestants and papists. Crying out (1 Sam. 8) is not necessarily a remedy of tyranny, nor a praying with faith and patience. Resisting of kings that are tyrannical, and patience is not inconsistent. The law of the king is not a permissive law, as was the law of divorce. The law of the king (1 Sam. 12:23-24) is not a law of tyranny.*

1 Sam. 8:11. "This will be the manner of the king who
shall reign over you" &c.

This place (1 Sam. 8:11) the law or manner of the king is alleged to prove both the absolute power of kings and the unlawfulness of resistance; therefore I crave leave here to vindicate the place, and to make it evident to all that the place speaks for no such matter. Grotius argues thus: "that by this place, the people oppressed with injuries of a tyrannical king have nothing left them but prayers and cries to God, and

194

therefore there is no ground for violent resisting."[1] Barclay will have us to distinguish *inter officium regis, et potestatem*, between the king's office and the king's power, and he will have the Lord here speaking, not of the king's office, what he ought to do before God, but what power a king has beside and above the power of judges, to tyrannize over the people, so as the people has no power to resist it. He will have the office of the king spoken of (Deut. 17), and the power of the king (1 Sam. 8), and that power which the people was to obey and submit unto without resisting.[2]

But I answer, 1. It is a vain thing to distinguish between the office and the power; for the power is either a power to rule according to God's law, as he is commanded (Deut. 17) and this is the very office or official power which the King of kings has given to all kings under him, and this is a power of the royal office of a king, to govern for the Lord his Maker; or this is a power to do ill and tyrannize over God's people, but this is accidental to a king and the character of a tyrant, and is not from God, and so the law of the king in this place must be the tyranny of the king, which is our very mind.

2. "*Reges sine dominatione ne concipi quidem possunt; judices dominationem in populum minime habebant.*" Hence it is clear that Barclay says that the judges of Israel and the kings are different in essence and nature, so that domination is so essential to a king that you cannot conceive a king but he must have domination, whereas the judges of Israel had no domination over the people. Hence I argue that whereby a king is essentially distinguished from a judge that must be from God; but by domination, which is a power to oppress the subject, a king is essentially distinguished from a judge of Israel;

---

1. *De jure belli et pacis* 1.4, n. 3.
2. *Contra Monarchom* 2.

therefore, domination and a power to do acts of tyranny, as they are expressed (ver. 11-13) and to oppress a subject is from God, and so must be a lawful power. But the conclusion is absurd; the assumption is the doctrine of Barclay. The major proposition I prove.

1. Because both the judge and the king was from God: for God gave Moses a lawful calling to be a judge, so did he to Eli and to Samuel, and hence the king is a lawful ordinance of God (Deut. 17:15). If then the judge and the king be both lawful ordinances, and if they differ essentially, as Barclay says, then that specific form which distinguishes the one from the other, namely, domination and a power to destroy the subject, must be from God, which is blasphemous, for God can give no moral power to do wickedly, for that is license and a power to sin against a law of God, which is absolutely inconsistent with the holiness of God, for so the Lord might deny himself, and dispense with sin. God avert such blasphemies!

2. Now if the kingly power be from God, that which essentially and specifically constitutes a king must be from God, as the office itself is from God. Barclay says expressly that the kingly power is from God, and that same, which is the Specific form that constitutes a king, must be that which essentially separates the king from the judge, if they be essentially different, as Barclay dreams.[1] Hence have we this *jus regis*, this manner or law of the king to tyrannize and oppress, to be a power from God, and so a lawful power, by which you shall have this result of Barclay's interpretation, that God made a tyrant as well as a king.

3. By this difference that Barclay puts between the king and the judge, the judge might be resisted; for he had not this

---

1. *Contra Monarchom* 3.2.

power of domination that Saul has, contrary to Rom. 13:2;
Exod. 22:28; 20:12.

But let us try the text first, המלך משפט the word cannot
enforce us to exposit משפט a law, our English renders, Show
them the manner of the king. Arri. Montanus turns it *ratio
regis*. I grant the LXX render it, το δικαιαμα του βασιλεως
The Chaldee Paraphrase says, *Statutum regis.*[2] Jerome trans-
lates it *jus regis*, and also Calvin, but I am sure the Hebrew,
both in words and sense, bears a custom; yea, and the word
משפט signifies not always a law, as in Josh. 6:14: "They com-
passed the city כמשפט seven times;" the LXX. κατὰ τὸν κρῖμα
τουτό; 2 Kings 17:26: They "know not the manner of the God
of the land;" Ver. 33: "they served their own gods, after the
manner of the heathen." כמשפט הזיים cannot be according
to the law or right of the heathen, except משפט, be taken in
an evil part: the LXX. κατα τον κριμα των εθνων, ver. 34,
"Until this day they do after these manners;" 1 Kings 18:28:
Baal's priests "cut themselves with knives כמשפטם after their
manner:" The LXX: κατα τον εθισμον αυτων. Gen. 40:13: you
shall give the cup to Pharaoh, according as you were wont
to do; כמשפט. Exod. 21:9: "He shall deal with her after the
manner of daughters;" 1 Sam. 27:11: "And David saved neither man nor woman alive, to bring tidings to Gath, saying,
so did David, and so will his manner be," משפטו. It cannot
be they meant that it was David's law, right, or privilege, to
spare none alive. 1 Sam. 2:13: "And the priests' custom with
the people was," &c. ומשפט הכהגים. This was a wicked custom,
not a law, and the LXX turns it, και τον δικαιωμα του ιεριως,
and therefore δικαιωμα is not always taken in a good meaning; so P. Martyr, "He means here of an usurped law;"[3] Calvin,

Non jus a deo prescriptum, sed tyranidem, "He speaks not of God's law here, but of tyranny;"[1] and Rivetus, **משפט** signifies not ever *jus,* law. *Sed aliquando morem sive modum et rationem agendi,* "The custom and manner of doing:"[2] so Junius[3] and Tremellius. Diodatus exposits *jus,* This law, "namely (says he) that which is now grown to a common custom, by the consent of nations and God's toleration." [4] Glossa, (to speak of papists) *Exactionem et dominationem,* "The extortion and domination of king Saul is here meant."[5] Lyra exposits it *tyranny;* Tostatus Abulens, "He means here of kings indefinitely who oppressed the people with taxes and tributes, as Solomon and others."[6] Cornelius a Lapide, "This was an unjust law." Cajetanus calls it tyranny. Hugo Cardinal names them, *exactiones et servitutes,* "exactions and slaveries," and Serrarius speaks not here, *Quid Reges jure possint,* "What they may do by right and law," *Sed quid audeant,* "What they will be bold to do, and what they tyrannically decern against all laws of nature and humanity," and so speaks Thomas Aquinas;[7] so also Mendoza speaks of the "law of tyrants," and among the fathers Clemens Alexandrinus says on this place, *Non humanum pollicetur dominum, sed insolentem daturum minatur tyrannum,* "He promises not a humane prince, but threatens to give them an insolent tyrant," and the like also says Bede,[8] and an excellent lawyer Pet. Rebuffus says, *Etiam loquitur de tyranno qui non erat a Deo electus.*

---

1. Cone. 1 Sam. 8.
2. In *decal., Exod. 20, in 5, mundat.*
3. *Annot., in 1 Sam. 2:13.*
4. *Annot., 1 Sam. 8:3.*
5. Glossa interlinearis.
6. In 1 Reg. 8, q. 17, de q. 21.
7. Thomas Aquinas, *De Regni Princip.* 11.
8. Expo. in Samuel, 1.2.

And that he speaks of Saul's tyrannical usurpation, and not of the law prescribed by God, Deut. 17,[9] I prove. 1. He speaks of such a power as is answerable to the acts here spoken of, but the acts here spoken of are acts of mere tyranny; ver. 11: "And this will be the manner of your king that shall reign over you: he will take your sons, and appoint them for himself for his chariots, and to be his horsemen, and some shall run before his chariots." Now, to make slaves of their sons was an act of tyranny.

2. To take their fields, and vineyards, and olive-yards from them, and give them to his servants was no better than Ahab's taking Naboth's vineyard from him, which by God's law he might not lawfully sell, except in the case of extreme poverty, and then, in the year of jubilee, he might redeem his own inheritance.

3. Ver. 15-16: To put the people of God to bondage, and make them servants was to deal with them as the tyrant Pharaoh did.

4. He speaks of such a law, the execution whereof should "make them cry out to the Lord because of their king," but the execution of the just law of the King (Deut. 17) is a blessing, and not a bondage which should make the people cry out of the bitterness of their spirit.

5. It is clear here that God is by his prophet not instructing the king in his duty, but as Rabbi Levi Ben. Gersom says, "Terrifying them from their purpose of seeking a king, and foretelling the evil of punishment that they should differ under a tyrannical king,"[10] but he speaks not one word of these necessary and comfortable acts of favor that a good king by his good government was to do for his people (Deut. 17:15-16). But he speaks of contrary facts here, and that he is dissuading them from suiting a king is clear from the text. (1). Because he says, Give them their will, but yet protest against their

---

9. *Pet. Rebuffus tract. de incongrua. prert* 21.

10. Ben. Gersom. in 1 Sam. 8; *Pezelius in exp. leg. Mosai,* 1.4.8; *Tossan. in not. Bibl. Bosseus de Rep. Christ. potest, supra regem,* 2, n. 103. *Bodin. De Rep.* 1.1.19. *Brentius, homil.* 27, in 1 Sam. 8.

unlawful course. (2). He bids the prophet lay before them the tyranny and oppression of their king, which tyranny Saul exercised in his time, as the story shows. (3). Because how ineffectual Samuel's exhortation was is set down, ver. 19, "Nevertheless they would not obey the voice of Samuel, but said, nay, but we will have a king over us." If Samuel had not been dehorting them from a king, how could they be said in this to refuse to hear the voice of Samuel?

6. The ground of Barclay and royalists here is weak, for they say that the people sought a king like the nations, and the kings of the nations were all absolute, and thus tyrants, and God granted their unlawful desire, and gave them a tyrant to reign over them such as the nations had.[1] The plain contrary is true. They sought not a tyrant, but one of the special reasons why they sought a king was to be freed of tyranny, for 1 Sam. 8:3: "Because Samuel's sons turned aside after lucre, and took bribes, and perverted judgment; therefore all the elders of Israel gathered themselves together, and came to Samuel, to Ramah, and there they sought a king."

7. One could not more clearly speak with the mouth of a false prophet the author of "Active and Passive Obedience" does, while he will have Samuel here to describe a king, and to say, "Ye have formerly committed one error in shaking off the yoke of God and seeking a king; so now beware you fall not in the next error, in casting off the yoke of a king, which God, at your own desire, has laid on you, for God only has power to make and unmake kings; therefore prepare yourselves patiently to suffer and bear.

Ans. 1. For if he were exhorting to patient suffering of the yoke of a king, he should presume it was God's revealed and regulating will that they should have a king. But the scope of Samuel's sermon is to dissuade them from a king, and they by the contrary (ver. 19) say, "Nay, but we will have a king," and there is not one word in the text

---

1. Dr Ferne, sect. 2.

that may intimate patience under the yoke of a king. 2. There is here
the description of a tyrant, not of a king. 3. Here is a threatening and
a prediction, not anything that smells of an exhortation.

Obj. But it is evident that God, teaching the people how to behave
themselves under the unjust oppressions of their king, set down no
remedy but tears, crying to God, and patience; therefore resistance is
not lawful.[2]

Ans. Though this be not the place due to the doctrine of resistance,
yet, to vindicate the place,

1. I say, there is not one word of any lawful remedy in the text;
only it is said, **מלפני מלבבם וזעתם ביום ההוא**, *Et clamatis in ilia die a
faciebus regis vestri*. It is not necessarily to be exposited of praying to
God; Job 35:9: "By reason of the multitude of oppressions, they make
the oppressed to cry," **חעיקו** *clamare faciunt*; Isa. 15:4: "And Heshbon
shall cry: **קעזתו** the armed soldiers of Moab shall cry out." There is no
other word here than does express the idolatrous prayers of Moab.
Isa. 17:12; Hab. 2:11: "The stone shall cry out of the wall **קעזת**;" Deut.
22:24: "You shall stone the maid **לא־אשר על־דבר** because she cried not
צעקה," but she is not to be stoned because she prayed not to God; Ps.
18:4: "David's enemies cried, and there was none to save, even to the
Lord, and he heard not."

2. Even if it was the prophet's meaning, "they cried to the Lord,"
yet it is not the crying of a people humbled and in faith speaking
to God in their troubles; Zech. 7:13: "They cried, and I would not
hear." Therefore royalists must make crying to God out of the bitterness of affliction, without humiliation and faith, and such prayers
of sinners as God hears not (Ps. 18:41; John 9:31; Isa. 17:12) to be

---

2. Dr Ferne, part 3, sect. 2. Learned authors teach that God's law (Deut. 17).
and the משפט a manner of the king (1 Sam. 8:9) are opposite one to another, so
*Gersom. in trinprino. sac. adu. lat. par. 4, Alp. 06, lit. I. cons. 8, Buchan. de jure regni
apud Scot. Chasson. cat. glo. mundi cons, 24, n. 16, cons. 35. Tholoss. 1.9.1. Rossen. de
polus, Rep. 2, n. 10. Magdebnrg. in trac. de off. ma.*

the only remedy of a people oppressed by a tyrannical King. Now, it is certain God prescribes no unlawful means to an oppressed people under their affliction; therefore it is clear here that God speaks only of evils of punishment, such as is to cry in trouble and not be heard of God, and that he prescribes here no duty at all, nor any remedy. 3. All Protestant divines say, *Ex particulari non valet argumentum negative*, "From one particular place, a negative argument is not good." This remedy is not written in this particular place, therefore it is not written at all in other places of Scripture; so 1 Tim. 1:19, the end of excommunication is that the party excommunicated may learn not to blaspheme; therefore the end is not also that the church be not infected. It follows not. The contrary is clear (1 Cor. 5:6). Dr. Ferne and other royalists teach us that we may supplicate and make prayers to a tyrannical king. We may fly from a tyrannical king, but neither supplicating the king nor flying from his fury shall be lawful means left by this argument, because these means are no more in this text (where royalists say the Spirit of God speaks of purpose of the means to be used against tyranny) than violent resistance is in this text.

Barclay, Feme, Grotius, Arnisaeus, the Popish Prelate following them, say, "An ill king is a punishment of God for the sins of the people and there is no remedy but patient suffering."

Ans. Truly it is a silly argument. The Assyrians coming against the people of God for their sins, is a punishment of God (Is. 10:5; 12:13). But does it follow that it is unlawful for Israel to fight and resist the Assyrians, and that they had warrant to do no other thing but lay down arms and pray to God, and fight none at all? Is there no lawful resisting of ills of punishment, but mere prayers and patience? The Amalekites came out against Israel for their sins; Sennacherib against Hezekiah for the sins of the people; Asa's enemies fought against him for his sins and the people's sins. Shall Moses and the people, Hezekiah and Asa, do then nothing but pray and suffer? Is it unlawful with the sword to resist them? I believe not. Famine is often a punishment of God in a land (Amos 4:7-8). Is it therefore in famine unlawful to till the earth, and seek bread by our industry, and are we to do nothing but to pray for daily bread? It is a vain argument.

Observe, therefore, the wickedness of Barclay (*Contra monarch.* 1.2), for he would prove that "a power of doing ill, and that without any punishment to be inflicted by man is from God; because our laws punish not perjury, but leaves it to be punished of God (1.2.1, *de Reb, cred. Cujacius*, l.2, obs. section 19); and the husband in the law of Moses had power to give a bill of divorce to his wife and send her away, and the husband was not to be punished. And also stews and work-houses for harlots, and to take usury are tolerated in many Christian commonwealths, and yet these are all sorts of murders by the confession of heathen; therefore (says Barclay) God may give a power of tyrannical acts to kings, so that they shall be under no punishment to be inflicted by men.

Ans. All this is an argument from fact. 1. A wicked magistracy may permit perjury and lying in the commonwealth, and that without punishment, and some Christian commonwealths, he means his own synagogue of Rome, spiritual Sodom, a cage of unclean birds, suffers harlots by law, and the whores pay so many thousands yearly to the Pope and are free of all punishment by law, to eschew homicides, adulteries of Romish priests, and other greater sins; therefore God has given power to a king to play the tyrant without any fear of punishment to be inflicted by man. But if this be a good argument, the magistrate to whom God has committed the sword to take vengeance on evil doers (Rom. 13:3-6) such as are perjured persons, professed whores and harlots, has a lawful power from God to connive at sins and gross scandals in the commonwealth, as they dream that the king has power given from God to exercise all acts of tyranny without any resistance.

But, 1. This was a grievous sin in Eli, that he being a father and a judge punished not his sons for their uncleanness, and his house in

God's heavy displeasure was cut off from the priesthood for it. Then God has given no such power to the judge.

2. The contrary duty rests on the judge, to execute judgment for the oppressed (Job 29:12-17; Jer. 22:15-16), and perverting of judgment and conniving at the heinous sins of the wicked is condemned (Num. 5:31-32; 1 Sam. 15:23; 1 Kings 20:42-43; Isa. 1:17; 10:1; 5:23), and therefore God has given no power to a judge to permit wicked men to commit grievous crimes without any punishment. As for the law of divorce, it was indeed a permissive law, by which the husband might give the wife a bill of divorce, and be free of punishment before men, but not free of sin and guiltiness before God, for it was contrary to God's institution of marriage at the beginning, as Christ says; and the prophet says (Mal. 2) that the Lord hates putting away, but that God has given any such permissive power to the king, that he may do what he pleases, and cannot be resisted, this is in question.

3. The law spoken of in the text is by royalists called, not a consuetude of tyranny, but the divine law of God, whereby the king is formally and essentially distinguished from the judge in Israel; now if so, a power to sin and a power to commit acts of tyranny, yea, and a power in the king's sergeants and bloody emissaries to waste and destroy the people of God, must be a lawful power given of God; for a lawful power it must be if it comes from God, whether it be from the king in his own person, or from his servants at his commandment, and by either put forth in acts, as the power of a bill of divorce was a power from God, exempting either the husband from punishment before men, or freeing the servant, who at the husband's command should write it and put it in the hands of the woman. I cannot believe that God has given a power, and that by law, to one man to command twenty thousand cut-throats to kill and destroy all the children of God, and that he has commanded his children to give their necks and heads to Babel's sons without resistance. This I am sure is another matter than a law for a bill of divorce to one woman married

by free election of a changeable and inconstant man. But sure I am, God gave no permissive law from heaven like the law of divorce, for the hardness of the heart, not of the Jews only, but also of the whole Christian and heathen kingdoms under a monarch, that one emperor may, by such a law of God as the law of divorce. Kill, by bloody cut-throats, such as the Irish rebels are, all the nations that call on God's name, men, women, and sucking infants. And if Providence impede the catholic issue, and dry up the seas of blood, it is good; but God has given a law, such as the law of divorce, to the king, whereby he, and all his, may, without resistance, by a legal power given of God, who gives kings to be fathers, nurses, protectors, guides, yea the breath of nostrils of his church, as special mercies and blessings to his people, he may, I say, by a law of God, as it is 1 Sam. 8:9, 11, cut off nations, as that lion of the world, Nebuchadnezzar, did. So royalists teach us.

Barclay says the Lord spoke to Samuel the law of the king, and wrote it in a book, and laid it up before the Lord (*Contra Monarch.*, 1.2). But what law? That same law which he proposed to the people when they first sought a king. But that was the law contemning precepts, rather for the people's obeying than for the king's commanding; for the people was to be instructed with those precepts, not the king. Those things that concerned the king's duty (Deut. 17). Moses commanded to he put into the ark, but so if Samuel had commanded the king that which Moses (Deut. 17) commanded, he would have done no new thing, but would have done again what was once done *actum egisset*, but there was nothing before commanded the people concerning their obedience and patience under evil princes. Joseph. Lantiq wrote, το μελλοντα κατα, the evils that were to befall them (6.5).

Ans. 1. It was not that same law, for though this law was written to the people, yet it was the law of the king, and I pray you did Samuel write in a book all the rules of tyranny and teach Saul, and all the kings after him (for this book was put in the ark of the covenant, where also was the book of the law) how to play the tyrant? And what

instruction was it to king or people to write to them a book of the
wicked ways of a king, which nature teaches without a doctor? Sanctius says on the place. These things which by men's fraud and to the
hurt of the public may be corrupted were kept in the tabernacle, and
the book of the law was kept in the ark. Cornelius à Lapide says, It
was the law common to king and people, which was commonly kept
with the book of the law in the ark of the covenant. Lyra contradicts
Barclay. He exposits *Legem, legem regni non secundum, usurpationem
supra positam sed secundum ordinationem Dei positam* (Deut. 17). The-
odatius excellently exposits it the fundamental laws of the kingdom,
inspired by God to temper monarchy with a liberty befitting God's
people, and with equity toward a nation-to withstand the abuse of an
absolute power.

2. Can any believe Samuel would have written a law of tyranny, and
put that book in the ark of the covenant before the Lord, to be kept
to the posterity, seeing he was to teach both king and people the good
and the right way (1 Sam. 12:23-25).

3. Where is the law of the kingdom called a law of punishing innocent people?

4. To write the duty of the king in a book, and apply it to the king,
is no more superfluous than to teach the people the good and the
right way out of the law, and apply general laws to particular persons.

5. There is nothing in the law (1 Sam. 8:9-12) of the people's patience, but rather of their impatient crying out, God not hearing nor
helping, and nothing of that in this book, for anything that we know,
and Josephus speaks of the law in 1 Sam. 8, not of this law in 1 Sam. 12.

QUESTION 19.

WHETHER OR NOT THE KING BE IN DIGNITY AND POWER ABOVE THE PEOPLE.

In what consideration the king is above the people, and the people above the king. How it is true that a means, as a means, is inferior to the end. The king inferior to the people. The church, because it is the church, is of more excellency than the king, because he is king. The people being those to whom the king is given is worthier than the gift. And the people are immortal, the king mortal. The king is a means only, not both the efficient, or author of the kingdom, and a means; two necessary distinctions of a meAns. If sin had never been, there should have been no king. The king is to give his life for his people. The consistent cause more excellent than the effect and the people more excellent than the king. It is impossible that people can limit royal power, but they must give royal power also. That the people have an action in making a king is proved by four arguments. Though it were granted that God immediately made kings, yet it is no consequent: God only, and not the people, can unmake him. The people appointing a king over themselves retain the fountain-power of making a king. The means inferior to the end, and the king, as a king, is a meAns. The king as a means and also as a man is inferior to the people. To swear non-self-preservation, and to swear self-murder is all one. The people cannot make away their

power, 1. Their whole power, nor 2. Irrevocably to the king. The people
may resume the power they give to the commissioners of parliament,
when it is abused. The tables in Scotland are lawful, when the ordinary
judicatures are corrupt. Quod efficit tale id ipsum magis tale discussed,
and the fountain-power in the people is derived only in the king. The
king is a fiduciary, a life-renter, not a lord or heritor. How sovereignty
is in the people. How in a community there is power of life and death.
A community void of rulers is yet, and may be a politic body, and
judges gods analogically.

In this grave question, various considerations are to be pondered.
1. There is a dignity material in the people scattered, they being
many representations of God and his image, which is in the king also,
and formally more as king, he being endued with formal magisterial
and public royal authority. In the former regard, this or that man is
inferior to the king, because the king has that same remainder of the
image of God that any private man has, and something more: he has
a political resemblance to the King of heavens, being a little god, and
so is above any one man.

2. All these of the people taken collectively having more of God,
as being representations, are according to this material dignity more
excellent than the king, because many are more excellent than one,
and the king according to the magisterial and royal authority he has is
more excellent than they are, because he partakes formally of royalty
which they have not formally.

3. A means or medium, as it is such, is less than the end, though the
thing materially that is a means may be more excellent. Every means,
as a means, under that reduplication, has all its goodness and excel-
lence in relation to the end, yet an angel that is a means (or medium)
and a ministering spirit, ordained by God as an heir of life eternal
(Heb. 1:13), considered materially is more excellent than a man (Ps.
8:6; Heb. 2:6-8).

4. A king and leader, in a military consideration, and as a governor and conserver of the whole army, is more worth than ten thousand of the people (2 Sam. 18:13).

5. But simply and absolutely the people is above and more excellent than the king, and the king in dignity is inferior to the people; and that upon these reasons:

Arg. 1. Because he is the means ordained for the people, as for the end, that he may save them (2 Sam. 19:9) a public shepherd to feed them (Ps. 78:70-73) the captain and leader of the Lord's inheritance to defend them (1 Sam. 10:1) the minister of God for their good (Rom. 13:4).

Arg. 2. The pilot is less than the whole passengers; the general less than the whole army; the tutor less than all the children; the physician less than all the living men whose health he cares for; the master or teacher less than all the scholars, because the part is less than the whole; the king is but a part and member (though I grant a very eminent and noble member) of the kingdom.

Arg. 3. A Christian people, especially, is the portion of the Lord's inheritance (Deut. 32:9), the sheep of his pasture—his redeemed ones—for whom God gave his blood (Acts 21:28). And the killing of a man is to violate the image of God (Gen. 9:6), and therefore the death and destruction of a church, and of thousand thousands of men, is a sadder and a more heavy matter than the death of a king who is but one man.

Arg. 4. A king as a king, or because a king is not the inheritance of God, nor the chosen and called by God, nor the sheep or flock of the Lord's pasture, nor the redeemed of Christ, for those excellencies befit not kings because they are kings, for then all kings should be endued with those excellencies, and God should be an acceptor of persons if he put those excellencies of grace upon men for external respects of highness and kingly power, and worldly glory and splendor; for many living images and representations of God, as He is holy or more excellent than a political representation of God's greatness and majesty, such as the king is, because that which is the fruit of a love of God, which comes nearer to God's most special love, is more excellent than that which is farther removed from his special love. Now, though royalty be a beam of the majesty of the greatness of the King of kings and Lord of lords, yet is it such a fruit and beam of Gods greatness as may consist with the eternal reprobation of the party loved; so now God's love, from which he communicates his image representing his own holiness comes nearer to his most special love of election of men to glory.

Arg. 5. If God give kings to be a ransom for his church, and if He slay great kings for their sake, such as Pharaoh king of Egypt (Isa. 43:9) and Sihon king the Amorites, and Og king of Bashan (Ps. 136:18-20); if He plead with princes and kings for destroying His people (Isa. 3:12–14); if He make Babylon and her king a threshing-floor for the "violence done to the inhabitants of Zion," (Jer. 51:33–35) then His people as His people must be so much dearer and more precious in the Lord's eyes than kings, because they are king; by how much more His justice is active to destroy the one, and His mercy to save the other. Neither is the argument taken off by saying the king must in this question be compared with His own people; not a foreign king, with other foreign people, over whom He does not reign, for the argument proves that the people of God are of more worth than kings as kings; and Nebuchadnezzar and Pharaoh, for the time were kings to the people of God, and foreign kings are no less essentially kings than kings native are.

Arg. 6. Those who are given by God as gifts for the preservation of the people to be nurse-fathers to them, those must be of less worth before God than those to whom they are given since the gift, as the gift, is less than the party on whom the gift is bestowed. But the king is a gift for the good and preservation of we people, as is clear (Isa. 1:26); and from this that God gave his people a king in his wrath, we may conclude that a king of himself, unless God be angry with his people, must be a gift.

Arg. 7. That which is eternal and cannot politically die, yea, which must continue as the days of heaven, because of God's promise, is more excellent than that which is both accidental, temporary, and mortal. But the people are both eternal as people, because "one generation passes away, and another generation comes" (Eccles. 1:4) and as a people in covenant with God (Jer. 3:40-41) in respect that a people and church, though mortal in the individuals, yet the church, remaining the church, cannot die, but the king as king may and does die. It is true, where a kingdom goes by succession, the politicians say the man who is king dies, but the king never dies, because some other, either by birth or free election, succeeds in his room. But I answer, people by a sort of necessity of nature succeeds to people, generation to generation, unless God's judgment, contrary to nature, intervene to make Babylon no people, and a land that shall never be inhabited (which I both believe and hope for, according to God's word of prophecy). But a king by a sort of contingency succeeds to kings; for nature does not tell us there must be kings to the world's end, because the essence of governors is kept safe in aristocracy and democracy, though there were no kings; and that kings should necessarily have been in the world if man had never fallen in sin, I am not by any cogent argument induced to believe, I conceive there should have been no government but those of fathers and children, husband and wife, and (which is improperly government) some more gifted with supervenient additions to nature as gifts and excellencies of engines. Now on this point Althusius says the king in respect of office is worthier than the people (but this is but an accidental respect), but as the king is a man he is inferior to the people (*Polit.* 38, n. 114).

Arg. 8. He who by office is obliged to expend himself and to give his life for the safety of the people, must be inferior to the people. So Christ says the life is more than raiment or food, because both these

give themselves to corruption for man's life; so the beasts are inferior
to man, because they die for our life, that they may sustain our life.
And Caiaphas prophesied right that it was better that one man die
than the whole nation perish (John 11:50), and in nature, elements
against their particular inclination defraud themselves of their private
and particular ends, that the commonwealth of nature may stand; as
heavy elements ascend, light descend, lest nature should perish by
a vacuity. And the Good Shepherd (John 10) gives his life for his
sheep; so both Saul and David were made kings to fight the Lord's
battles, and to expose their lives to hazard for the safety of the church
and people of God. But the king by office is obliged to expand his life
for the safety of the people of God; he is obliged to fight the Lord's
battles for them, to go between the flock and death, as Paul was willing to be spent for the church.

It may be objected that Jesus Christ gave Himself a ransom for
His church, and His life for the life of the world, and was a gift given
to the world (John 3:16; 4:10), and He was a mean to save us, and
so what arguments we have before produced to prove that the king
must be inferior to the people, because he is a ransom, a means, a gift,
are not conclusive, I answer, 1. Consider a means reduplicatively, and
formaliter as a means; and secondly, as a means materially, that is, the
thing which is a means.

2. Consider that which is only a means, and ransom, and gift, and
no more, and that which, beside that it is a means, is of a higher nature also. So Christ formally as a means, giving His temporal life for
a time, according to the flesh, for the eternal life of all the catholic
church, to be glorified eternally (not His blessed Godhead and glory,
which as God He had with the Father from eternity) in that respect
Christ has the relation of a servant, ransom, gift, and some inferiority
in comparison of the church of God, and his Father's glory, as a means,
is inferior to the end, but Christ materially, *in concreto*, Christ is not
only a means to save his church, but as God (in which consideration

he was the immortal Lord of life) He was more than a means, even the Author, Efficient and Creator of heaven and earth, and so there is no ground to say that he is inferior to the church, but the absolute head, king, the chief of ten thousand; more in excellency and worth than ten thousand millions of possible worlds of men and angels. But such a consideration cannot befall any mortal king, because consider the king materially as a mortal man, he must be inferior to the whole church, for he is but one, and so of less worth than the whole church; as the thumb, though the strongest of the fingers, yet it is inferior to the hand, and far more to the whole body as any part is inferior to the whole. Consider the king reduplicative and formally as king, and by the official relation he has, he is no more than but a royal servant, an official means tending, *ex officio*, to this end: to preserve the people, to rule and govern them, and a gift of God, given by virtue of His office, to rule the people of God, and so in any way inferior to the people.

Arg. 9. Those who are before the people and may be a people without a king must be of more worth than that which is posterior and cannot be a king without them. For thus God's self-sufficiency is proved in that He might be and eternally was blessed forever without His creature, but His creature cannot subsist in being without Him. Now, the people were a people many years before there was a government (save domestic) and are a people where there is no king, but only an aristocracy or a democracy, but the king can be no king without a people. It is vain that some say the king and kingdoms are relatives, and not one is before another, for it is true in the naked relation; so are father and son, master and servant, *Relata simul natura*, but sure there is a priority of worth and independency, for all that, in the father above the son and in the master above the servant, and so in the people above the king; take away the people, and Dionysius is but a poor schoolmaster.

Arg. 10. The people in power are superior to the king, because every efficient and constituent cause is more excellent than the effect.

Every means is inferior in power to the end,[1] but the people is the efficient and constituent cause, the king is the effect; the people is the end; both intended by God to save the people to be a healer and a physician to them (Isa 3:7); and the people appoint and create the king out of their indigence to preserve themselves from mutual violence. Many things are objected against this. That the efficient and constituent cause is God, and the people are only the instrumental cause, and Spalato says that the people does indirectly only give kingly power, because God at their act of election ordinarily gives it.

Ans. 1. The Scripture says plainly, as we heard before, the people made kings, and if they do, as other second causes produce their effects, it is all one that God as the principal cause makes kings, else we should not argue from the cause to the effect among the creatures.

2. God by that same action that the people creates a king does also by them, as by His instruments create a king, and that God does not immediately at the naked presence of the act of popular election confer royal dignity on the man without any action of the people, as they say, by the church's act of conferring orders, God does immediately without any act of the church infuse from heaven supernatural liabilities on the man, without any active influence of the church, is evident by this.

1. The royal power to make laws with the king, and so a power eminent in their states representative to govern themselves is in the people; for if the most high acts of royalty be in them, why not the power also? And so, what need to fetch a royal power from heaven to be immediately infused in him, seeing the people have such a power in themselves at hand?

2. The people can and does limit and bind royal power in elected kings, therefore they have in them royal power to give to the king.

---

1. *Sa. Jun. Brutus*, q. 31; *Bucher* 1.1.16; *Author Lib. de office, Magistr*, q. 6; *Hencenius* disp. 2, n. 6; *Joan Roffensis Epist. de potest. Pap.* 1.2.5; *Spalato de Repu. Ecclesiast.* 1.6.2, n. 3.

Those who limit power can take away so many degrees of royal power, and those who can take away power can give power, and it is inconceivable to say that people can put restraint upon a power immediately coming from God. If Christ immediately infused an apostolic spirit into Paul, mortal men cannot take from him any degrees of that infused spirit; if Christ infuse a spirit of nine degrees, the church cannot limit it to six degrees only. But royalists consent that the people may choose a king upon such conditions to reign, as he has royal power of ten degrees, whereas his ancestor had by birth a power of fourteen degrees.

3. It is not intelligible that the Holy Ghost should give commandment unto the people to make this man king (Deut. 17:16), and forbid them to make that man king, if the people had no active influence in making a king at all; but God solely and immediately from heaven did infuse royalty in the king without any action of the people, save a naked consent only, and that after God had made the king, they should approve only with a later act of naked approbation.

4. If the people by other governors, as by heads of families and other choice men, govern themselves and produce these same formal effects of peace, justice, religion, on themselves, which the king does produce, then is there a power of the same kin, and as excellent as the royal power, in the people, and there is no reason but this power should be held to come immediately from God, as the royal power; for it is in every way of the same nature and kind, as I shall prove. Kings and judges differ not in nature and species, but it is experienced that people do by aristocratic guides govern themselves, &c.; so then, if God immediately infuse royalty when the people chooses a king, without action of the people, than must God immediately infuse a beam of governing on a provost and bailee when the people choose such, and that without any action of the people, because all powers are, *in abstractio*, from God (Rom. 13:2). And God as immediately makes inferior judges as superior (Prov. 8:16) and all promotion (even

to be a provost or mayor) comes from God only, as to be a king, unless
royalists say all promotion comes from the east and from the west,
and not from God, unless promotion to the royal throne; the contrary
of which is said (Psal, 75:6-7; 1 Sam. 2:7-8). Not only kings, but all
judges are gods (Ps. 82:1-2), and therefore all must be the same way
created and molded by God, unless by Scripture the royalist can show
us a difference. An English prelate gives reasons why people, who are
said to make kings as efficients and authors cannot unmake them:
the one is because God as chief and sole supreme moderator makes
kings,[1] but I say Christ as the chief moderator and head of the church
does immediately confer abilities upon a man to be a preacher, and
though by industry that man acquire abilities, yet in regard the church
does not so much as instrumentally confer those abilities, they may
be said to come from God immediately, in relation to the church who
calls the man to the ministry, yea, royalists as our excommunicated
Prelate learned from Spalato, say that God at the naked presence of
the church's call does immediately infuse that from heaven by which
the man is now in holy orders and a pastor, whereas he was not so before, and yet prelates cannot deny but they can unmake ministers, and
have practiced this in their unhallowed courts; and therefore, though
God immediately without any action of the people make kings, this is
a weak reason to prove they cannot unmake them. As for their indelible character, that prelates cannot take from a minister, it is nothing if
the church may unmake a minister, though his character go to prison
with him. We seek no more but to annul the reason. God immediately makes kings and pastors; therefore no power on earth can unmake
them. This consequence is as weak as water.

2. The other cause is because God has erected no tribunal on earth
higher than the king's tribunal, therefore no power on earth can unmake a king. The antecedent and consequence is both denied, and is a

---

1. *Joan. Roffens. de potest, pap.* 1.8.5.

begging of the question, for the tribunal that made the king is above the king. Though there be no tribunal formally regal and kingly above the king, yet is there a tribunal virtual eminently above him in the case of tyranny; for the states and princes have a tribunal above him.

Assert. To this the constituent cause is of more power and dignity than the effect, and so the people are above the king. The Popish Prelate borrowed an answer from Arnisaeus, and Barclay, and other royalists, and says, if we knew anything in law or were ruled by reason, "every constituent" (Arnisaeus[2] and Barclay, more accurately than the Popish Prelate had a head to transcribe their words) "where the constituent has resigned all his power in the hand of the prince whom he constitutes is of more worth and power than he in whose hand he resigns the power; so the proposition is false. The servant who has constituted his master lord of his liberty is not more worthy than his master whom he has made his lord and to whom he has given himself as a slave (for after he has resigned his liberty he cannot repent, he must keep covenant though to his hurt) yea, such a servant is not only not above his master, but he cannot move his foot without his master." "The governor of Britain" says Arnisaeus "being despised by king Philip, resigned himself as vassal to king Edward of England, but did not for that make himself superior to king Edward. Indeed, he who constitutes another under him as a legate is superior, but the people do constitute a king above themselves, not a king under themselves, and therefore the people are not by this made the king's superior, but his inferior."

Ans. 1. It is false that the people does or can by the law of nature resign their whole liberty in the hand of a king. 1. They cannot resign to others that which they have not in themselves. *Nemo potest dare quod non habet*, but the people have not an absolute power in themselves to destroy themselves or to exercise those tyrannical acts

---

2. *De authorit. princip.* 1, n. 1.

spoken of (1 Sam. 8:11-15, &c.), for neither God nor nature's law has given any such power.

2, He who constitutes himself a slave is supposed to be compelled to that unnatural act of alienation of that liberty which he has from his Maker from the womb, by violence, constraint, or extreme necessity, and so is inferior to all free men, but the people does not make themselves slaves when they constitute a king over themselves because God, giving to a people a king, the best and most excellent governor on earth, gives a blessing and special favor (Isa. 1:2; Hos. 1:1; Isa. 3:6-7; Ps. 79:70-72), but to lay upon his people the state of slavery, in which they renounce their whole liberty, is a curse of God (Gen. 9:25; 27:29; Deut. 28:32, 36). But the people, having their liberty to make any often, or twenty, their king, and to advance one from a private state to an honorable throne, whereas it was in their liberty to advance another and to give him royal power of ten degrees, whereas they might give him power of twelve degrees, of eight, or six, must be in excellency and worth above the man whom they constitute king and invest with such honor; as honor in the fountain, and *honos participans et originatus*, must be more excellent and pure than the derived honor in the king, which is *honos participatus et originatus*. If the servant give his liberty to his master, therefore he had that liberty in him, and in that act, liberty must be in a more excellent way in the servant as in the fountain than it is in the master, and so this liberty must be purer in the people than in the king, and therefore in it both the servant is above the master and the people worthier than the king. And when the people give themselves conditionally and covenant-wise to the king, as to a public servant, and patron, and tutor, as the governor of Britain out of his humor gave himself to king Edward, there is even here a note of superiority. Every giver of a benefit, as a giver, is superior to him to whom the gift is given, though after the servant has given away his gift of liberty by which he was superior he cannot be a superior, because by his gift he has made himself inferior. The people constitutes a king above themselves, I distinguish *supra se*, above themselves according to the fountain-power of royalty, that is false; for the fountain-power remains most eminently in the people, 1. Because they give it to the king, *ad modum recipientis*, and with limitations; therefore it is unlimited in the people, and bounded and limited in the king, and so less in the king than in the people. 2. If the king turn distracted, and an ill spirit from the Lord come upon Saul, so as reason be taken from a Nebuchadnezzar, it is certain the people may put curators and tutors over him who has the royal power. 3. If the king be absent and taken captive, the people may give the royal power to me, or to some few, to exercise it as *custodes regni*. And, 4. if he die, and the crown go by election, they may create another with more or less power, all of which shows that they never constituted over themselves a king in regard of fountain-power; for if they give away the fountain, as a slave sells his liberty, they could not make use of it. Indeed they set a king above them, *quoad potestatem legum executivam*, in regard of a power of executing laws and actual government for their good and safety, but this proves only that the king is above the people, κατα τι, in some respect. But the most eminent and fountain-power of royalty remains in the people as in an immortal spring, which they communicate by succession to this or that mortal man, in the manner and measure that they think good. Ulpian[1] and Bartolus[2] cited by our Prelate out of Barclay are only to be understood of the derived, secondary, and borrowed power of executing laws, and not of the fountain-power, which the people cannot give away, no more than they can give away their rational nature; for it is a power natural to conserve themselves, essentially adhering to every created being. For if the people give all their power away, what shall they reserve to make a new king, if this man die? What if the royal line should cease? There be no prophets immediately sent of God to make kings. What if he

---

1. Ulpian 1.1, *ad Sc. Tubil.*
2. *Bartolus ad l. hostos* 24.

turn tyrant, and destroy his subjects with the sword? The royalists say, they may fly, but when they made him king, they resigned all their power to him, even their power of flying; for they bound themselves by an oath (say royalists) to all passive and lawful active obedience, and, I suppose, to stand at his tribunal, if he summoned the three estates upon treason to come before him is contained in the oath that royalists say binds all, and is contradictory to flying. Arnisaeus, a more learned jurist and divine than the Popish Prelate, answers the other maxim, "The end is worthier than the means leading to the end, because it is ordained for the end. These means," says he "which refer their whole nature to the end, and have all their excellency from the end, and have excellency from no other thing but from the end, are less excellent than the end. That is true, such an end as medicine is for health." And Hugo Grotius: "Those means which are only for the end, and for the good of the end, and are not for their own good also are of less excellency and inferior to the end, but so the assumption is false. But these means which beside their relation to the end have an excellency of nature in themselves are not always inferior to the end. The disciple, as he is instituted, is inferior to the master, but as he is the son of a prince, he is above the master. But by this reason the shepherd should be inferior to brute beasts, to sheep, and the master of the family is for the family, and refers all that he has for the entertaining of the family, but it follows not therefore the family is above him. The form is for the action; is therefore the action more excellent than the form, and an accident than the subject or substance?" (1.1.3, n. 8). And Grotius says, "Every government is not for the good of another, but some for its own good, as the government of a master over the servant, and the husband over the wife."

Ans. I take the answer thus: Those who are mere means, and only means referred to the end, they are inferior to the end; but the king as king has all his official and relative goodness in the world, as relative to the end. All that you can imagine to be in a king as a king is all relative to the safety and good of the people (Rom. 13:4). "He is a minister for your good." He should not, as king, make himself, or his own gain and honor, his end. I grant the king as a man shall die as another man, and so he may secondarily intend his own good, and what excellency he has as a man is the excellency of one mortal man, and cannot make him amount in dignity, and in the absolute consideration of the excellency of a man to be above many men and a whole kingdom, for the more good things there be, the better they are, so the good things be multipliable, as a hundred men are better than one; otherwise if the good be such as cannot be multiplied, as one God, the multiplication makes them worse, as many gods are inferior to one God. Now if royalists can show us any more in the king than these two, we shall be obliged to them, and in both he is inferior to the whole.

The Prelate and his followers would have the maxim to lose credit; for then (say they) the shepherd should be inferior to the sheep; but in this the maxim fails indeed, because the shepherd is a reasonable man, and the sheep brute beasts, and so must be more excellent than all the flocks of the world. Now, as he is a reasonable man, he is not a shepherd, nor in that relation referred to the sheep and their preservation as a means to the end, but he is a shepherd by accident, for the unruliness of the creatures, for man's sin, withdrawing themselves from that natural dominion that man had over the creatures before the fall; in that relation of a means to the end, and so by accident is this official relation put on him, and according to that official relation, and by accident, man is put to be a servant to the brutish creature, and a means to so base an end. But all this proves him through man's sin and by accident to be under the official relation of a means to baser creatures than himself, as to the end, but not a reasonable man. But the king as king is an official and royal means to this end: that the people may lead a godly and peaceable life under him, and this official relation being an accident is of less worth than the whole people, as they are to be governed. And I grant the king's son in relation to blood and birth is more excellent than his teachers, but as he is taught, he is inferior to his teacher. But in both considerations the king is inferior to the people, or though he command the people, and so have an executive power of law above them, yet have they a fountain-power above him, because they made him king, and in God's intention He is given as king for their good, according to this: "you shall feed my people Israel," and that, "I gave him for a leader of my people."

The Popish Prelate says: "The constituent cause is more excellent than the effect constituted, where the constitution is voluntary and depends upon the free act of the will, such as when the king makes a viceroy or a judge, *durante beneplacito*, during his free will, but not when a man makes over his right to another; for then there should be neither faith nor truth in covenants, if people might make over their power to their king, and retract, and take back what they have once given.

Ans. This a begging of the question; for it is denied that the people can absolutely make away their whole power to the king. It depends on the people that they be not destroyed. They give to the king a political power for their own safety, and they keep a natural power to themselves which they must conserve, but cannot give away, and they do not break their covenant when they put in action that natural action to conserve themselves, for though the people should give away that power, and swear though the king should kill them all they should not resist nor defend their own lives, yet that being against the sixth commandment, which enjoins natural self-preservation, it should not oblige the conscience, for it should be intrinsically sinful; for it is all one to swear to non-self-preservation as to swear to self-murder.

If the people (says the Prelate, begging the answer from Barclay),[1] the constituent, be more excellent than the effect, and so the people

---

1. *Sac Sanc. Maj. Section 9 stolen from Barclay, 5.12.*

above the king, because they constitute him king, then the counties and corporations may make void all the commissions given to the knights and burgesses of the House of Commons, and send others in their place, and repeal their orders; therefore Buchanan says that orders and laws in parliament were but προσδυλιματα preparatory consultations, and had not the force of a law till the people give their consent and have their influence authoritative, upon the statutes and acts of parliament; but the observatory holds that the legislative power is whole and entire in the parliament. But when the Scots were preferring petitions and declarations they put all power in the collective body and kept their distinct tables.

Ans. *1.* There is no consequence here; the counties and incorporations that send commissioners to parliament may make void their commissions and annul their acts because they constitute them commissioners. If they are unjust acts, they may disobey them and so disannul them, but it is presumed God has given no moral power to do ill, nor can the counties and corporations give any such power to evil, for they have not any such from God. If they be just acts, they are to obey them, and cannot retract commissions to make just orders. *Illud tantum possumus quod jure possumus*, and therefore, as power to govern justly is irrevocably committed by the three estates who made the king to the king, so is that same power committed by the shires and corporations to their commissioners, to decree in parliament what is just and good irrevocably, and to take any just power from the king which is his due is a great sin. But when he abuses his power to the destruction if his subjects, it is lawful to throw a sword out of a madman's hand, though it be his own proper sword, and though he have due right to it, and a just power to use it for good; for all fiduciary power abused may be repealed. And if the knights and burgesses of the House of Commons abuse their fiduciary power to the destruction of these shires and corporations who put the trust on them, the observator did never say that parliamentary power was so entire and irrevocably in them that the people may not resist them, annul their commissions, rescind their acts, and deprive them of fiduciary power, even as the king may be deprived of that same power by the three estates, for particular corporations are no more to be deprived of that fountain-power of making commissioners, and of the self-preservation than the three estates are.

2. The Popish Prelate comes not home to the mind of Buchanan, who knew the fundamental laws of Scotland, and the power of Parliaments; for his meaning was not to deny a legislative power in the parliament, but when he calls their parliamentary declarations προσδυλιματα, his meaning is only that which lawyers and schoolmen both say, *Leges non promulgatae non habens vim legis actu completo obligatoriae*, "Laws not promulgated do not oblige the subject while they be promulgated," but he fulfills Buchanan when he says, "Parliamentary laws must have the authoritative influence of the people, before they can be formal laws, or any more than προσδυλιματα or preparatory notions. And it was no wonder when the king denied a parliament, and the supreme senate of the secret council was corrupted, that the people did then set up tables, and extraordinary judicatures of the three estates, seeing there could not be any other government for the time."

Barclay answers to this: "The means is inferior to the end; it holds not; the tutor and curator is for the minor, as for the end, and given for his good; but it follows not that therefore the tutor in the administration of the minor or pupil's inheritance is not superior to the minor."[1]

Ans. It follows well that the minor virtually, and in the intention of the law, is more excellent than the tutor, though the tutor can exercise more excellent acts than the pupil by accident for defect of age in the minor, yet he does exercise those acts with subordination to the minor

---

1. *Contra Monarch.*, 4.11.

and with correction, because he is to render an account of his doings to the pupil coming to age; so the tutor is only more excellent and superior in some respect, κατα τι but not simply, and so is the king in some respect above the people.

The Popish Prelate begs from the royalists another of our arguments, *Quod efficit tale, est magis tale*, "That which makes another such is far more such itself."[2] If the people give royal power to the king, then far more is the royal power in the people. By this (says the Prelate) it shall follow, if the observator give all his goods to me to make me rich, the observator is more rich: if the people give most part of their goods to foment the rebellion, then the people are more rich, having given all they have upon the public faith.

Ans. *1.* This greedy Prelate was made richer than ten poor pursuivants by a bishopric; it will follow well, therefore, the bishopric is richer than the bishop, whose goods the curse of God blasts. 2. It holds in efficient causes, so working in other things as the virtue of the effect remains in the cause, even after the production of the effect. As the sun makes all things light, the fire all things hot, therefore the sun is more light, the fire more hot; but where the cause does alienate and make over in a corporeal manner that which it has to another, as the hungry Prelate would have the observator's goods, it holds not; for the effect may exhaust the virtue of the cause, but the people does, as the fountain, derive a stream of royalty to Saul and make him king, and yet so as they keep fountain-power of making kings in themselves, yea, when Saul is dead to make David king at Hebron, and when he is dead to make Solomon king, and after him to make Rehoboam king, and therefore in the people there is more fountain-power of making kings than in David, in Saul, in any king of the world. As for the Prelate's scoff about the people's giving of their goods to the good cause, I hope it shall by the blessing of God enrich

---

2. *Sacr. Sanc. Mal.*, 13, *stolen out of Arnisaeus De jure Majest.* 3, n. 1.

them more, whereas prelates by the rebellion in Ireland (to which they assent, when they council his Majesty to sell the blood of some hundred thousands of innocents killed in Ireland) are brought from having thousands a year to begging a morsel of bread.

The Popish Prelate answers that maxim, Quod efficit tale, id ipsum est magis tale, "That which makes another such, it is itself more such." It is true, *de principio formali effectivo* (as I learned in the university) of such an agent as is formally such in itself as is the effect produced. Next, it is such as is effective and productive of itself, as when fire heats cold water, so the quality must be formally inherent in the agent; as wine makes drunk, it follows not, wine is more drunk, because drunkenness is not inherent in the wine, nor is it capable of drunkenness, and therefore Aristotle qualifies the maxim with this, *Quod efficit tale est magnis tale, modo utrique insit,* "and it holds not in agents, who operate by donation, if the right of the king be transferred from the people to the king." The donation divests the people totally of it, unless the king have it by way of loan, which to my thinking never yet any spoke. Sovereignty never was, never can be in the community. Sovereignty has power of life and death, which none has over himself, and the community conceived without government, all as equal, endowed with nature's and native liberty, of that community no one can have power over the life of another. And so the argument may be turned home if the people be not *tales*, such by nature (as has formally royal power, he should say) they cannot give the king royal power; also, none has power of life and death, either more eminently or formally, the people either singly or collectively have not power over their own life, much less over their neighbors.

Ans. 1. The Prelate would make the maxim true of a formal cause, and this he learned in the University of St. Andrews. He wrongs the university, he rather learned it while he kept the calves of Crail. The wall is white from whiteness; therefore, whiteness is more white by the Prelate's learning. Never such thing was taught in that learned university.

2. *Principium formale effectivum* is as good logic as *principium effectivum materiale formale, finale.* The Prelate is in his accuracy of logic now. He yet makes the causality of the formal cause all one with the causality of the efficient; but he is weak in his logic.

3. He confounds a cause equivocal and a cause equivocal, and in that case the maxim holds not. Nor is it necessary to make true the maxim, that the quality be inherent in the cause the same way; for a city makes a mayor, but to be a mayor is one way in the city, and another way in him who is created mayor. The Prelate's maxim would help him, if we reasoned thus: The people makes the king, therefore the people is more a king, and more formally a sovereign than the king. But that is no more our argument than the simile that Maxwell used, as near heart and mouth both. Wine makes drunk the Prelate, therefore wine is more drunk. But we reason thus: The fountain-power of making six kings is in the people, therefore there is more fountain-power of royalty in the people than in anyone king. For we read that Israel made Saul king, and made David king, and made Abimelech king; but never that king Saul made another king, or that an earthly king made another absolute king.

4. The Prelate will have the maxim false, where the agent works by donation, which yet holds true by his own grant (section 9). The king gives power to a deputy, therefore there is more power in the king.

5. He supposes that which is the basis and foundation of all the question, that people divests themselves totally of their fountain-power, which is most false.

6. Either they must divest themselves totally (says he) of their power, or the king has power from the people by way of loan, which to my thinking never any yet spoke. But the Popish Prelate's thinking is short, and no rule to divines and lawyers; for to the thinking of the learned jurists, this power of the king is but fiduciary, and that is

(whether the Prelate think it or think it not) a sort of power by trust, pawn or loan. *Rex director Regni, non proprietarius.*[1] "The king is a life-renter, not a lord, or proprietor of his kingdom." So Novel. 85, in *princip*, et section 18, *Quod magistratus sit nudus dispensator et defensor jurium regni, non proprietarius, constat ex eo quod non posset alienare imperium, oppida, urbes, regionsve, vel res subditorum bonave regni.* So Gregory (*De Repub.* 1.3.8, through section 1, Sect. *praeterea de propo. feud*), Hottoman (quest, illust. 1), Ferdinan. Vasquez (1.1.4); Bossius (*de princip. et privileg. Illius*, n. 290), "The king is only a steward, and a defender of the laws of the kingdom, not a proprietor, because he has not power to make away the empire, cities, towns, countries, and goods of the subjects," and, *bona commissa magistratui, sunt subjecta restitution, et in prejudicium successorum alienari non possunt,* (per 1 idt. sect, sed nost. *Comment, de leg.* 1. peto 69, *fratrem de leg.* 2.1.32, *ult. d. t.*). "All the goods committed to any magistrate are under restitution; for he has not power to make them away, to the prejudice of his successors." The Prelate's thoughts reach not the secrets of jurists, and therefore he speaks with a warrant; he will say no more than his short-travelled thoughts can reach, and that is but at the door.

7. Sovereignty is not in the community (says the Popish Prelate). Truly it neither is, nor can be more than ten, or a thousand, or a thousand thousands, or a whole kingdom, can be one man; for sovereignty is the abstract, the sovereign is the concrete. Many cannot be one king or one sovereign: a sovereign must be essentially one, and a multitude cannot be one. But what then? May not the sovereign power be eminently, *fontaliter*, originally and radically in the people? I think it may, and must be. A king is not an under judge: he is not a lord of council and session formally, because he is more. The people are not king formally, because the people are eminently more than the king,

---

1. *Molinae. in consuet. Parisi, Tit.* 1, 9; 1 *Gloss.* 7, n. 9.

for they make David king, and Saul king, and the power to make a lord of council and session is in the king (say royalists).

8. A community has not power of life and death; a king has power of life and death (says the Prelate). What then? Therefore a community is not king. I grant all. The power of making a king, who has power of life and death is not in the people. Poor man! It is like prelates' logic. Samuel is not a king; therefore he cannot make David a king. It follows not by the Prelate's ground. So the king is not an inferior judge. What! Therefore he cannot make an inferior judge?

9. The power of life and death is eminently and virtually in the people, collectively taken, though not formally. And though no man can take away his own life, or has power over his own life for ally, yet a man, and a body of men, has power over their own lives, radically and virtually, in respect they may render themselves to a magistrate, and to laws which if they violate, they must be in hazard of their lives, and so they virtually have power of their own lives by putting them under the power of good laws for the peace and safety of the whole.

10. This is a weak consequence. None has power of his own life; therefore, far less of his neighbor's (says the Prelate). I shall deny the consequence. The king has not power of his own life, that is, according to the Prelate's mind, he can neither by the law of nature, nor by any civil law kill himself; therefore, the king has far less power to kill another; it follows not, for the judge has more power over his neighbor's life than over his own.

11. But, says the Popish Prelate, the community conceived without government, all as equal, endowed with nature's and native liberty, has no power of life and death because all are born free, and so none is born with dominion and power over his neighbor's life. Yea, but so Mr. Popish Prelate, a king considered without government, and as born a free man has not power of any man's life more than a community has, for king and beggar are born both alike free. But a community in this consideration, as they come from the womb, has

no political consideration at all. If you consider them as without all policy, you cannot consider them as invested with policy, yea, if you consider them so as they are by nature, void of all policy, they cannot so much as add their after-consent and approbation to such a man to be their king, whom God immediately from heaven makes a king; for to add such an after-consent is an act of government. Now, as they are conceived to lack all government, they cannot perform any act of government. And this is as much against himself as against us.

2. The power of a part and the power of the whole is not alike. Royalty never advances the king above the place of a member; and lawyers say, the king is above the subjects, *in sensu diviso*, in a divisive sense, he is above this or that subject; but he is inferior to all the subjects collectively taken, because he is for the whole kingdom, as a means for the end.

Obj. If this be a good reason that he is a means for the whole kingdom as for the end; that he is therefore inferior to the whole kingdom, then is he also inferior to any one subject; for he is a means for the safety of every subject as for the whole kingdom.

Ans. Every means is inferior to its complete, adequate, and whole end; and such an end is the whole kingdom in relation to the king; but every means is not always inferior to its incomplete, inadequate, and partial end. This or that subject is not adequate, but the inadequate and incomplete end in relation to the King,

The Prelate says, Kings are *Dii Elohim*, gods, and the manner of their propagation is by filiation by adoption sons of the Most High, and God's firstborn. Now, the firstborn is not above every brother severally, but if there were thousands, millions, numberless numbers, he is above all in precedency and power.

Ans. Not only kings but all inferior judges are gods. Ps. 82: God stands in the congregation of the gods, that is not a congregation of kings. So the master of the house shall be brought אל־האלהים to the gods, or to the judges (Exod. 22:8). And that there were more judges than one is clear by ver. 9. And if they shall condemn **ירשיעו** *jarshignur, condemnarint.* John 10.85: ίθι θεοὖς He called them gods. Exod. 4:16: "you shall be to Aaron **לאלהים** as a god." They are gods analogically only. God is infinite, not so the king. God's will is a law, not so the king's, God is an end to himself, not so the king. The judge is but God by office, and representation, and conservation of the people. It is denied that the firstborn is in power before all his brethren, though there were millions. That is but said, one as one is inferior to a multitude. As the firstborn was a political ruler to his brethren, he was inferior to them politically.

Obj. The collective university of a kingdom are subjects, sons, and the king their father, no less than this or that subject is the king's subject. For the university of subjects are either the king, or the king's subjects; for all the kingdom must be one of these two, but they are not the king; therefore they are his subjects.

Ans. All the kingdom, in any consideration, is not either king or subjects. I give a third: The kingdom collective is neither properly king nor subject; but the kingdom embodied in a state, having collateral is a co-ordinate power with the king.

Obj. The university is ruled by laws; therefore they are inferior to the king who rules all by law.

Ans. The university properly is no otherwise ruled by laws than the king is ruled by laws. The university formally is the complete politic body, endued with a legislative faculty, which cannot use violence against itself, and so is not properly under a law.

QUESTION 20.

WHETHER INFERIOR JUDGES ARE ESSENTIALLY THE IMMEDIATE VICEREGENTS OF GOD, AS KINGS, NOT DIFFEREING IN ESSENCE AND NATURE FROM KINGS.

Inferior judges are the immediate vicars of God, no less than the king. The consciences of inferior judges, are immediately subordinate to God, not to the king, either mediately or immediately. How the inferior judge is the deputy of the king. He may put to death murderers, as having God's sword committed to him no less than the king, even though the king command the contrary, for he is not to execute judgment, and to relieve the oppressed conditionally if a mortal king give him leave; but whether the king will or no, he is to obey the King of kings. Inferior judges are ministri regni, non ministri regis. The king does not make judges as he is a man by an act of private good-will, but as he is a king by an act of royal justice and by a power that he has from the people, who made him a supreme judge. The king's making inferior judges hinders not, but they are as essentially judges as the king who makes them, not by his own power, but by power borrowed from the people. The judges in Israel and the kings differ not essentially. Aristocracy as natural as monarchy, and as warrantable. Inferior judges depend some way on the king in fieri, but not in facto esse. The parliament are not judges by derivation from the king. The king cannot

make or unmake judges. There can be no heritable judges. Inferior
judges are more necessary than a king.

I t is certain that in one and the same kingdom the power of the
king is more in extension than the power of any inferior judge, but
if these powers of the king and the inferior judges differ *intensive* and
in *specie*, and nature is the question, though it be not all the question.

Assert. Inferior judges are no less essentially judges, and the immediate vicars of God than the king. Those who judge in the place
of God and exercise the judgement of God are essentially judges and
deputies of God, as well as the king; but inferior judges are such;
therefore the proposition is clear. The formal reason why the king is
univocally and essentially a judge is because the king's throne is the
Lord's throne; 1 Chron. 29 23: "Then Solomon sat on the throne
of the Lord, asking, instead of David his father." 1 Kings 1:13: It is
called David's throne, because the king is the deputy of Jehovah; and
the judgment is the Lord's. I prove the assumption. Inferior judges
appointed by king Jehoshaphat have this place. 2 Chron. 19:6: "The
king said to the judges, Take heed what You do, לאדם תשפטו כי ליהוה
כי לא, for You judge not for man, but for the Lord." Then, they were
deputies in the place of the Lord, and not the king's deputies in the
formal and official acts of judging. Ver. 7: "Therefore, now let the fear
of the Lord be upon you, take heed and do it; for there is no iniquity
with the Lord our God, nor respect of persons, or taking of gifts."

Hence I argue, 1. If the Holy Ghost in this good king forbid inferior judges, wresting of judgment, respecting of persons, and taking
of gifts, because the judgment is the Lord's, and if the Lord Himself
were on the bench, He would not respect persons, nor take gifts; then
he presumes that inferior judges are in the stead and place of Jehovah,
and that when these inferior judges should take gifts, they make, as

it were, the Lord, whose place they represent, to take gifts, and to do iniquity, and to respect persons; but that the Holy Lord cannot do.

2. If the inferior judges in the act of judging were the vicars and deputies of king Jehoshaphat, he would have said, judge righteous judgment. Why? For the judgment is mine, and if I, the king, were on the bench, I would not respect persons, nor take gifts, and you judge for me, the Supreme Judge, as my deputies. But the king says they judge not for man, but for the Lord (2 Chron. 19:6).

3. If, by this, they were not God's immediate vicars, but the vicars and deputies of the king, then being mere servants the king might command them to pronounce such a sentence, and not such a sentence as I may command my servant and deputy, insofar as he is a servant and deputy, to say this, and say not that, but the king cannot limit the conscience of the inferior judge because the judgment is not the king's, but the Lord's.

4. The king cannot command any other to do that as king, for the doing of which he has no power from God Himself; but the king has no power from God to pronounce what sentence He pleases, because the judgment is not His own but God's. And though inferior judges be sent by the king, and appointed by him to be judges, and so have their external call from God's deputy the king, yet because judging is an act of conscience, as one man's, conscience cannot properly be a deputy for another man's conscience, so neither can an inferior judge, as a judge, be a deputy for a king. Therefore, the inferior judges have designation to their office from the king, but if they have from the king that they are judges, and be not God's deputies, but the king's, they could not be commanded to execute judgement for God, but for the king; (Deut. 1:17) Moses appointed judges, but not as his deputies to judge and give sentence, as subordinate to him; for the judgment (says he) is the Lord's, not mine.

5. If all the interior judges in Israel were but the deputies of the king, and not immediately subordinate to God as His deputies then

could neither inferior judges be admonished nor condemned in God's word for unjust judgment, because their sentence should be neither righteous nor unrighteous judgment, but insofar as the king should approve it or disapprove it, and indeed that royalist Hugo Grotius says so, that an inferior judge can do nothing against the will of the supreme magistrate if it be so. Whenever God commands inferior judges to execute righteous judgment, it must have this sense: "Respect not persons in judgment, unless the king command you; crush not the poor, oppress not the fatherless, unless the king command you."[1] I understand not such policy. Sure I am the Lord's commandments, rebukes, and threats oblige in conscience the inferior judge as the superior, as is manifest in these scriptures (Jer. 5:1; Isa, 1:17, 21; 5:7; 10:2; 59:14; Jer. 22:8; Ezek. 18:8; Amos 5:7; Mic. 3:9; Hab. 1:4; Lev. 19:15; Deut. 17:11; 1:17; Exod. 23:2).

Grotius says, "It is here as in a category: the middle specie is, in respect of the superior, a specie respect of the inferior, a genus; so inferior magistrates in relation to those who are inferior to them and under them are magistrates or public persons; but in relation to superior magistrates especially the king, they are private persons, and not magistrates."

Ans. Jehoshaphat esteemed not judges, appointed by himself, private men, "Ye judge not for men, but for the Lord" (2 Chron. 19:6-7). We shall prove that under-judges are powers ordained by God; in Scotland the king can take no man's inheritance from him because he is the king; but if any man possess lands belonging to the crown, the king by his advocate must stand before the lord, judges of the session, and submit the matter to the laws of the land; and if the king, for property of goods, were not under a law, and were not to acknowledge judges as judges, I see not how the subjects in either kingdoms have any property I judge it blasphemy to say, that a sentence of an inferior

---

1. *De jure belli et pacis* 1.4.

judge must be no sentence, though never so legal nor just, if it be contrary to the king's will, as Grotius says.

He cites that of Augustine: "If the consul command one thing, and the emperor another thing, you condemn not the power, but you choose to obey the highest." Peter says he will have us one way to be subject to the king, as to the supreme, *sine ulla exceptione*, without any exception; but to those who are sent by the king, as having their power from the king.

Arg. 1. When the consul commands a thing lawful, and the king that same thing lawful, or a thing not unlawful, we are to obey the king rather than the consul. So I exposit Augustine: We are not to obey the king and the consul the same way, that is, with the same degree of reverence and submission, for we owe more submission of spirit to the king than to the consul, but *magis et minus non variant speciem*, more or less varies not the nature of things. But if the meaning be that we are not to obey the inferior judge, commanding things lawful, if the king command the contrary, this is utterly denied. But says Grotius, "The inferior judge is but the deputy of the king, and has all his power from him; therefore we are to obey him for the king."

Ans. The inferior judge may be called the deputy of the king (where it is the king's place to make judges) because he has his external call from the king, and is judge *in foro soli*, in the name and authority of the king; but being once made a judge, *in foro poli*, before God, he is as essentially a judge, and in his official acts, no less immediately subjected to God than the king himself.

Arg. 2. These powers to whom we are to yield obedience, because they are ordained by God, these are as essentially judges as the supreme magistrate the king, but inferior judges are such; therefore inferior judges are as essentially judges as the supreme magistrate. The proposition is Rom. 13:1, for that is the apostle's arguments; from which we prove kings are to be obeyed, because they are powers from God. I prove the assumption: inferior magistrates are powers from

God (Deut. 1:17; 19:6-7; Exod. 22:7; Jer. 5:1), and the apostle says, "The powers that be are ordained by God."

Arg. 3. Christ testified that Pilate had power from God as a judge (say royalists) no less than Caesar the emperor (John 19:11; 1 Pet. 2:12). We are commanded to obey the king and those that are sent by him, and that for the Lord's sake, and for conscience to God; and we must be subject to all powers that are of God, not only for wrath, but for conscience (Rom. 13:5).

Arg. 4. Those who are rebuked because they execute not just judgment as well as the king are supposed to be essentially judges, as well as the king; but inferior judges are rebuked because of this (Jer. 22:15-17; Ezek. 45:9-12; Zeph. 3:3; Amos 5:6-7; Eccles. 3:16; Mic. 3:2-4; Jer. 5:1, 31).

Arg. 5. He is the minister of God for good, and has the sword not in vain, but to execute vengeance on the evil-doers, no less than the king (Rom. 13:2-4). He to whom agrees by an ordinance of God the specific acts of a magistrate is essentially a magistrate.

Arg. 6. The resisting of the inferior magistrate in his lawful commandments is the resisting of God's ordinance, and a breach of the fifth commandment, as is disobedience to parents, and not to give him tribute, and fear, and honor is the same transgression (Rom. 13:1-7).

Arg. 7. These styles, of gods, of heads of the people, of fathers, of physicians and healers of the sons of the Most High, of such as reign and decree by the wisdom of God, &c. that are given to kings, for the which royalists make kings only judges, and all inferior judges but deputed, and judges by participation, and at the second hand, or given to inferior judges (Exod. 22:8-9; John 10:35). Those who are appointed judges under Moses (Deut. 1:16) are called in Hebrew or Chaldean (1 Kings 8:1-2; 5:2; Mic. 3:1; Josh. 23:2; Num. 1:16) ראשי *rasce*, ראשי fathers (Acts 7:2; Josh. 14:1; 19:16; 1 Chron. 8:28), healers (Isa. 3:7), gods, and sons of the Most High (Ps. 82:1-2, 6-7; Prov. 8:16-17). I much doubt if kings can infuse godheads in their subjects. I conceive they have from the God of gods these gifts whereby they are enabled to be judges, and that kings may appoint them judges, but can do no more: they are no less essentially judges than themselves.

Arg. 8. If inferior judges be deputies of the king, not of God, and have all their authority from the king, then may the king limit the practice of these inferior judges. Say that an inferior judge has condemned to death a paricide, and he be conveying him to the place of execution, the king comes with a force to rescue him out of his hand; if this inferior magistrate bear God's sword for the terror of ill-doers, and to execute God's vengeance on murderers, he cannot but resist the king in this, which I judge to be his office; for the inferior judge is to take vengeance on evil-doers, and to use the co-active force of the sword by virtue of his office to take away this paricide. Now, if he be the deputy of the king, he is not to break the jaws of the wicked (Job 29:17); not to take vengeance on evil-doers (Rom. 13:4); nor to execute judgment on the wicked (Ps. 149:9); nor to execute judgment for the fatherless (Deut. 10:18), unless a mortal man's creator, the king, say Amen. Now, truly then, God in all Israel was to rebuke no inferior judge for perverting judgment, as he does (Exod. 23:26; Mic. 3:2-4; Zech. 3:3; Num. 25:5; Deut. 1:16); for the king only is lord of the conscience of the inferior judge who is to give sentence, and execute sentence righteously, upon condition that the king, the only univocal and proper judge, first decree the same, as royalists teach.

Hear our Prelate: How is it imaginable that kings can be said to judge in God's place, and not receive the power from God (section 4)? But kings judge in God's place (Deut. 1:17; 2 Chron. 19:6). Let no man stumble (this is his prolepsis) at this: that Moses in the one place, and Jehoshaphat in the other, spoke to subordinate judges under them. This weakens in no way our argument; for it is a ruled case in law, *Quod quis facit per alium, facit per se*, all judgments of interior judges are in name authority, and by the power of the supreme, and are but communicatively and derivatively from the sovereign power.

Ans. How is it possible that inferior judges can be said to judge in God's place (Deut. 1:17; 2 Chron. 19:6), and not receive the power from God immediately without any consent or covenant of men? So says the Popish Prelate. But inferior judges judge in the place of God, as both the Popish Prelate and Scripture teach (Deut. 1:17; 2 Chron. 19:6). Let the Prelate see to the stumbling conclusion, for so he fears it proves to his bad cause. He says the places Deut. 1:17 and 2 Chron. 19:6 prove that the king judges in the place of God, because his deputies judge in the place of God. The Prelate may know we would deny this stumbling and lame consequence; for 1. Moses and Jehoshaphat are not speaking to themselves, but to other inferior judges, and do publicly exhort them. Moses and Jehoshaphat are persuading the regulation of the personal actions of other men who might pervert judgment.

2. The Prelate is much upon his law, after he had foresworn the gospel and religion of the church where he was baptized. "What the king does by another, that he does by himself." But were Moses and Jehoshaphat afraid that they should pervert judgment in the unjust sentence pronounced by under judges, of which sentence they could not know anything? And do inferior judges so judge in the name, authority, and power of the king, as not in the name, authority, and power of the Lord of lords and King of kings? Or is the judgment the king's? No, the Spirit of God says no such matter. The judgment executed by those inferior judges is the Lord's, not a mortal king's; therefore, a mortal king may not hinder them to execute judgment.

Obj. He cannot suggest an unjust sentence, and command an inferior judge to give out a sentence absolvatory on cut-throats, but he may hinder the execution of any sentence against Irish cut-throats.

Ans. It is all one to hinder the execution of a just sentence and to suggest or command the inferior judge to pronounce an unjust one; for inferior judges by conscience of their office are both to judge righteously, and by force and power of the sword given to them by God

(Rom. 13:1-4) to execute the sentence, and so God has commanded inferior judges to execute judgment, and has forbidden them to wrest judgment, to take gifts, unless the king command them so to do.

The king is by the grace of God, the inferior judge is judge by the grace of the king, even as the man is the image of God, and the woman the man's image.[1]

Ans. 1. This distinction is neither true in law nor conscience. Not in law, for it distinguishes not between *ministros regis, et ministros regni.* The servants of the king are his domestics, the judges are *ministros regni, non regis*; the ministers and judges of the kingdom, not of the king. The king does not show grace, as he is a man, in making such a man a judge; but justice as a king, by a royal power received from the people, and by an act of justice he makes judges of deserving men; he should neither for favor nor bribes make anyone judge in the land.

2. It is by the grace of God that men are to be advanced from a private condition to be inferior judges, as royal dignity is a free gift of God. 1 Sam. 2:7: "The Lord brings low and lifts up;" Ps. 75:7: "God puts down one and sets up another." Court flatterers take from God and give to kings, but to be a judge inferior is no less an immediate favor of God than to be king, though the one be a greater favor than the other. *Magis honos* and *Major honos* are to be considered.

Argument 9. Those powers which differ gradually, and *per magis et minus*, by more and less only, differ not in nature and species, and constitute not kings and inferior judges different univocally. But the power of kings and inferior judges are such; therefore kings and inferior judges differ not univocally.

That the powers are the same in nature, I prove, 1. by the specific acts and formal object of the power of both; for both are powers ordained by God (Rom. 13:1). To resist either is to resist the ordinance of God.

---

1. Symmon's *Loyal Subjects' Belief*, sect 1.

2. Both are by office a terror to evil workers, ver. 3.

3. Both are the ministers of God for good. Though the king send and give a call to the inferior judge, that does no more make the inferior judge's powers in nature and specie different than ministers of the Word, called by ministers of the Word, have offices different in nature. Timothy's office to be preacher of the Word differs not in specie from the office of the presbytery which laid hands on him, though their office by extension be more than Timothy's office. The people's power is put forth in those same acts, when they choose one to be their king and supreme governor, and when they set up an aristocratic government, and choose many, or more than one, to be their governors; for the formal object of one or many governors is justice and religion, as they are to be advanced. The form and manner of their operation is *brachio seculari* by a co-active power and by the sword. The formal acts of king and many judges in aristocracy are these same: the defending of the poor and needy from violence, the conservation of a community in a peaceable and a godly life (1 Tim. 2:2; Job 29:12-13; Isa. 1:17). These same laws of God that regulate the king in all his acts of royal government, and ties and obliges his conscience, as the Lord's deputy, to execute judgment for God, and not in the stead of men, in God's court of heaven, does in like manner tie and oblige the conscience of aristocratic judges and all inferior judges, as is clear and evident by these places (1 Tim. 2:2), not only kings, but all in authority παντες ος εν υπεροχη οντες are obliged to procure that their subjects lead a quiet and peaceable life, in all godliness and honesty. All in conscience are obliged to judge righteously between every man and his brother, and the stranger that is with them (Deut. 1:16). Neither are they to respect persons in judgment, but are to hear the small as well as the great, nor to be afraid of the face of men. The judgment administered by all is God's (2 Chron. 19:6). All are obliged to fear God (Deut. 17:19-20), to keep the words of the law, not to be lifted up in heart above their brethren (Isa. 1:17; Jer. 22:2-3). Let any man show me a

difference, according to God's word, but in the extension that what the king is to do as a king in all the kingdom and whole dominions (if God give to him many, as he save to David, and Solomon, and Joshua) that the inferior judges are to do in such and such circuits, and limited places, and I quit the cause; so as the inferior judges are little kings, and the king a great and delated judge, as a compressed hand or fist, and the and stretched out in fingers and thumb, are one hand; so here.

4. God owns inferior judges as a congregation of gods (Ps. 82:1-2), for that God sits in a congregation or senate of kings or monarchs I shall not believe till I see royalists show to me a commonwealth of monarchs convening in one judicature. All are equally called gods (John 10:35; Exod. 22:8) if for any cause, but because all judges, even inferior, are the immediate deputies of the King of kings, and their sentence in judgment as the sentence of the Judge of all the earth, I shall be informed by the Popish Prelate, when he shall answer my reasons, if his interdicted lordship may cast an eye to a poor presbyter below; and as wisdom is that by which kings reign (Prov. 8:15-16) by which princes rule, and nobles, even all the judges of the earth, all that is said against this is that the king has a prerogative royal by which he is distinguished from all judges in Israel, called *jus regis* משפט for (says Barclay) the king, as king, essentially has a domination and power above all, so as none can censure him or punish him but God, because there are no thrones above his but the throne of God.[1] The judges of Israel, such as Samuel, Gideon, &c. had no domination, the dominion was in God's hand. "We may resist an inferior judge (says Arnisaeus)[2] "otherwise there were no appeal from him, and the wrong we suffer were irreparable," as says Marantius.[3] "And all the judges of the earth," says Edward Symmons, "are from God more remotely; namely, *mediante rege* by the mediation of the Supreme,

---

1. *Contra Monarch.* 1.2.

2. *De authoritate princip., section* 3, n. 9.

3. *Marant.* disp. 1, *Zoan. tract. 3, de defens. Mynsing,* obs, 18, cent. 5.

even as the lesser stars have their light from God by the mediation of the sun.[4] To the first I answer: There was a difference between the kings of Israel and their judges, no question; but if it be an essential difference, it is a question.

For, 1. The judges were raised up in an extraordinary manner, out of any tribe, to defend the people, and vindicate their liberty, God remaining their king; the king, by the Lord's appointment was tied after Saul to the royal tribe of Judah, till the Messiah's coming. God took his own blessed liberty to set up a succession in the ten tribes.

2. The judges were not by succession from father to son: the kings were, as I conceive, for the typical eternity of the Messiah's throne, presignified to stand from generation to generation.

3. Whether the judges were appointed by the election of the people, or no, some doubt; because Jephthah was so made judge, but I think it was not a law in Israel that it should be so. But the first mold of a king is by election (Deut. 17). But that God gave power of domineering, that is, of tyrannizing, to a king, so as he cannot be resisted, which he gave not to a judge, I think no scripture can make good. For by what scripture can royalists warrant to us that the people might rise in arms to defend themselves against Moses, Gideon, Eli, Samuel, and other judges, if they should have tyrannized over the people, and that it is unlawful to resist the most tyrannical king in Israel and Judah? Yet Barclay and others must say this, if they be true to that principle of tyranny, that the *jus regis*, the law or manner of the king (1 Sam. 8:9, 11; and 1 Sam. 10:25) does essentially differ between the kings of Israel and the judges of Israel. But we think God gave never any power of tyranny to either judge or king of Israel, and domination in that sense was by God given to none of them. Arniseaus has as little for him, to say the inferior magistrate may be resisted, because we may appeal from him, but the king cannot be resisted, *quia sancticas*

---

4. Section 1.

majestatis id non permittit, the sanctity of royal majesty will not permit us to resist the king.

Ans. That is not Paul's argument to prove it unlawful to resist kings, as kings, and doing their office, because of the sanctity of their majesty, that is, as the man intends, because of the supreme, absolute, and unlimited power that God has given him. But this is a begging of the question, and all one as, to say, the king may not be resisted, because he may not be resisted; for sanctity of majesty, if we believe royalists, endues essentially an absolute supremacy of power, by which they are above the reach of all thrones, laws, powers, or resistance on earth. But the argument is resist not, because the power is from God. But the inferior magistrate's power is of God. Resist not, because you resist God's ordinance in resisting the judge, but the inferior judge is God's ordinance (Rom. 13:1; Deut. 1:17; 2 Chron. 19:6). Mr. Symmons says, "All judges on earth are from the king, as stars have their light from the sun."

I answer, 1. Then aristocracy would be unlawful, for it has not its power from monarchy. Had the lords of the Philistines, have the states of Holland no power but from a monarchy? Name the monarch. Have the Venetians any power from a king? Indeed, our Prelate says from Augustine: *Generale pactum est societatis humanae, obedire Regibus suis*, it is a universal covenant of human society, and a dictate of nature, that men obey their kings. "I beg the favor of sectaries," says he, "to show as much for aristocracy and democracy" (*Confessions* 3.8). Now all other governments, to those born at court, are the inventions of men. But I can show that same warrant for the one as for the other, because it is as well the dictate of nature that people obey their judges and rulers as it is that they obey their kings. And Augustine speaks of all judges in that place, though he names kings; for kingly government is no more of the law of nature than aristocracy or democracy; nor are any born judges or subjects at all. There is a natural aptitude in all to either of these, for the conservation of nature, and that is all.

Let us see that men, naturally inclining to government, incline rather to royal government than to any other. That the Popish Prelate shall not be able to show: for fatherly government, being in two, is not kingly, but nearer to aristocracy, and when many families were on earth, every one independent within themselves, if a common enemy should invade a tract of land governed by families, I conceive by nature's light they should incline to defend themselves, and to join in one politic body for their own safety, as is most natural. But, in that case they, having no king, and there were no reason of many fathers all alike loving their own families and self-preservation why one should be king over all, rather than another, except by voluntary compact. So it is clear that nature is nearer to aristocracy before this contract than a monarchy. And let him show us in multitudes of families dwelling together, before there was a king, as clear a warrant for monarchy as here is for aristocracy, though to me both be laudable and lawful ordinances of God, and the difference merely accidental, being one and the same power from the Lord (Rom. 13:1) which is in various subjects; in one as a monarchy, in many as in aristocracy, and the one is as natural as the other, and the subjects are accidental to the nature of the power.

2. The stars have no light at all but in actual aspect toward the sun, and they are not lightsome bodies by the free will of the sun, and have no immediate light from God formally, but from the sun; so as if there were no sun, there should be no stars.

3. For actual shining and sending out of beams of light *actu secundo*, they depend upon the presence of the sun, but for inferior judges, though they have their call from the king, yet have they gifts to govern from no king on earth, but only from the King of kings.

4. When the king is dead, the judges are judges, and they depend not on the king for their second acts of judging, and for the actual emission and putting forth their beams and rays of justice upon the poor and needy, they depend on no voluntary aspect, information,

or commandment of the king, but on that immediate subjection of their conscience to the King of kings. And their judgment which they execute is the Lord's immediately, and not the king's; and so the comparison halts.

Arg. 10. If the king dying, the judges inferior remain powers from God, the deputies of the Lord of Hosts, having their power from God, then are they essentially judges; yea, and if the estates in their prime representators and leaders have power in the death of the king to choose and make another king, then are they not judges and rulers by derivation and participation, or improperly, but the king is rather the ruler by derivation and participation than those who are called inferior judges. Now if these judges depend in their sentences upon the immediate will of him who is supposed to be the only judge, when this only judge dies, they should cease to be judges, for *Expirante mandatore expirat mandatum*; because the fountain-judge drying up, the streams must dry up. Now, when Saul died, the princes of the tribes remain by God's institution princes, and they by God's law and warrant (Deut. 17) choose David their king.

Arg. 11. If the king, through absolute power, do not send inferior judges and constitute them, but only by a power from the people, and if the Lord have no less immediate influence in making inferior judges than in making kings, then there is no ground that the king should be sole judge, and the inferior judge only judge by derivation from him, and essentially his deputy, and not the immediate deputy of God. If the former is true, therefore, so is the latter.

And, 1. That the king's absolute will makes not inferior judges is clear from Deut. 1:15. Moses might not follow his own will in making inferior judges whom he pleased: God tied him to a law (ver. 13) that he should take wise men, known among the people and fearing God and hating covetousness. And these qualifications were not from Moses, but from God, and no less immediately from God than the inward qualification of a king (Deut. 17), and therefore it is not God s law that the king may make inferior judges only, *Durante beneplacito*, during his absolute will; for if these divine qualifications remain in the seventy elders, Moses at his will could not remove them from their places.

2. That the king can make heritable judges more than he can communicate faculties and parts of judging, I doubt. Riches are of fathers, but not promotion, which is from God, and neither from the east nor the west: that our nobles are born lords of parliament and judges by blood is a positive law.

3. It seems to me from Isa. 3:1-4 that the inferior judge is made by consent of the people; nor can it be called a wronging of the king that all cities and burghs of Scotland and England have power to choose their own provosts, rulers, and mayors.

4. If it be warranted by God that the lawful call of God to the throne be the election of the people, the call of inferior judges must also be from the people, mediately or immediately. So I see no ground to say that the inferior judge is the king's vicegerent, or that he is in respect of the king, or in relation to supreme authority only a private man.

Arg. 12. These judges cannot but be univocally and essentially judges no less than the king, without which in a kingdom justice is physically impossible; and anarchy, and violence, and confusion must follow if they be wanting in the kingdom. But without inferior judges, though there be a king, justice is physically impossible, and anarchy and confusion, &c. must follow.

Now this argument is more considerable, that without inferior judges, though there be a king in a kingdom, justice and safety are impossible, and if there be inferior judges, though there be no king, as in aristocracy, and when the king is dead, and another not crowned, or the king is minor or absent or a captive in the enemy's land, yet justice is possible, and the kingdom preserved; the medium of the argument is grounded upon God's word: Num. 11:14-15. When Moses is unable alone to judge the people, seventy elders are joined with him (ver. 16, 17); so were the elders adjoined to help him (Exod. 24:1; Deut. 5:23; 22:16; Josh, 23:2; Judg. 8:14; 40:5, 11; 1 Sam. 40; 1 Kings 20:7; 2 Kings 6:32; 2 Chron. 34:29; Ruth 4:4; Deut. 19:12; Ezek. 8:1; Lam. 1:19); then were the elders of Moab thought to have a king. The natural end of judges has been indigence and weakness, because men could not in a society defend themselves from violence; therefore, by the light of nature they gave their power to one or more, and made a judge or judges to obtain the end of self-preservation. But nature uses the most efficacious means to obtain its end, but in a great society and kingdom, the end is more easily attained by many governors than by one only; for where there is but one, he cannot minister justice to all, and the farther that the children are removed from their father and tutor, they are the nearer to violence and injustice. Justice should be at as easy a rate to the poor as a draught of water. Samuel went yearly through the land to Bethel, Gilgal, Mizpah (1 Sam. 7:16), and brought justice to the doors of the poor. So were our kings of Scotland obliged to do of old, but now justice is as dear as gold. It is not a good argument to prove inferior judges to be only vicars and deputies of the king, because the king may censure and punish them when they pervert judgment. 1. Because the king in that punishes them not as judges, but as men. 2. That might prove all the subjects to be vicars and deputies of the king, because he can punish them all in the case of their breach of laws.

QUESTION 21.

WHAT POWER THE PEOPLE AND STATES OF PARLIAMENT HAS OVER THE KING, AND IN THE STATE.

The elders are appointed by God to be judges. Parliaments may convene and judge without the king. Parliaments are essentially judges, and so their consciences neither depends on the king, quoad specificationem, that is, that they should give out this sentence, not that, nec quoad exercitium, that they should not in the morning execute judgment.

Unjust judging and no judging at all are sins in the states. The parliament co-ordinate judges with the king, not advisers only by eleven arguments. Inferior judges are not the king's messengers or legates, but public governors. The Jews' monarchy mixed. A power executive of laws is more in the king, and a power legislative is more in the parliament.

It is true the king is the head of the kingdom, but the states of the kingdom are as the temples of the head, and so as essentially parts of the head as the king is the crown of the head.

Assert. 1. These *ordines regni,* the states, have been in famous nations: so there were fathers of families and princes of

tribes among the Jews; the Ephori among the Lacedemonians
(Polybius, *Histories*, 1.6); the senate among the Romans; the
forum superbiense among the Arragonians; the parliaments in
Scotland, England, France, Spain. Abner communed with the
elders of Israel to bring the king home (2 Sam. 3:17), and
there were elders in Israel, both in the time of the judges, and
in the time of the kings, who did not only give advice and
counsel to the judges and kings, but also were judges no less
than the kings and judges, which I shall make good by these
places: Deut. 21:19: the rebellious son is brought to the elders
of the city, who had power of life and death, and were caused
to stone him; Deut. 22:18: "The elders of the city shall take
that man and chastise him;" Josh. 20:4: but beside the elders of
every city, there were the elders of Israel and the princes, who
had also judicial power of life and death, as the judges and
king had; Josh. 22:30: even when Joshua was judge in Israel,
the princes of the congregation and heads of the thousands of
Israel did judicially consider whether the children of Reuben,
of Gad, and of half the tribe of Manasseh were apostates from
God, and the religion of Israel; 2 Sam. 5:3: all the elders of
Israel made David king at Hebron; and Num. 12: they are appointed by God not to be the advisers only and helpers of Moses, but to bear a part of the burden of ruling and governing
the people (ver. 14-17), that Moses might be eased. Jeremiah
is accused upon his life before the princes (26:10); the princes sit in judgment with Joshua (Josh. 7:4); Joshua and the
princes of the congregation swear to the Gibeonites that they
would not kill them (Josh. 9:15). The princes of the house of
Israel could not be rebuked for oppression in judgment (Mic.
3:1-3) if they had not had power of judgment. So they are
expressly made judges in the place of God (Zeph. 3:3; Deut.
1:17; 2 Chron. 19:6-7); and without advice or knowledge of

Samuel, the supreme judge, they convene and ask a king (1 Sam. 8:2); and without any head or superior, when there is no king, they convene a parliament, and made David king at Hebron; and when David is banished, they convene to bring him home again; when tyrannical Athaliah reigns, they convene and make Joash king, and that without any king; and there is a parliament convened, and it says not that Joshua was there, to take notice of a new altar (Josh, 22). It would have been better for the parliaments both of Scotland and of England to convene, though the king had not indicted and summoned a parliament, without the king, to take order with the wicked clergy who had made many idolatrous altars; and the Popish Prelate should have brought an argument to prove it unlawful, in *foro Dei*, to set up the tables and conventions in our kingdom, when the prelates were bringing in the grossest idolatry into the church: a service for adoring of altars, of bread, the work of the hand of the baker, a god more corruptible than any god of silver and gold.

And against Ahab's will and mind (1 Kings 18:19) Elijah causes to kill the priests of Baal, according to God's express law. It is true it was extraordinary, but no no more extraordinary than it is at this day. When the supreme magistrate will not execute the judgment of the Lord, those who made him supreme magistrate under God, who have under God sovereign liberty to dispose of crowns and kingdoms are to execute the judgment of the Lord when wicked men make the law of God of no effect. So Samuel killed Agag (1 Sam. 15:32), whom the Lord expressly commanded to be killed, because Saul disobeyed the voice of the Lord. I deny not that there is necessity of a clear warrant that the magistrate neglect his duty, either in not convening the states, or not executing the judgment of the Lord. I see not how the convening of a

parliament is extraordinary to the states, for none has power
ordinary when the king is dead, or when he is distracted, or
captive in another land, to convene the estates and parliament,
but them alone, and in their defect by the law of nature the
people may convene. But if they be essentially judges no less
than the king, as I have demonstrated to the impartial reader
in the former chapter, I conceive, though the state make a
positive law, for order's cause, that the king ordinarily convene parliaments, yet, if we dispute the matter in the court of
conscience, the estates have intrinsically (because they are the
estates, and essentially judges of the land) ordinary power to
convene themselves. Because, when Moses by God's rule has
appointed seventy men to be catholic judges in the land, Moses, upon his sole pleasure and will, has not power to restrain
them in the exercise of judgment given them by God; for as
God has given to anyone judge power to judge righteous judgment, though the king command the contrary, so has He given
to him power to sit down in the gate or the bench, when and
where the necessity of the oppressed people calls for it. For
the express commandment of God, which says to all judges,
execute judgment in the morning, involves essentially a precept to all the physical actions, without which it is impossible
to execute judgment, as if by a divine precept the judge must
execute judgment, therefore he must come to some public
place and he must cause party and witnesses come before him,
and he must consider, note, examine, in the place of judgment,
things, persons, circumstances: and so God, who commands
positive acts of judging, commands the judge's locomotive
power, and his natural actions of compelling by the sword the
parties to come before him, even as Christ, who commands his
servants to preach, commands that the preacher and the people go to church, and that he stand or sit in a place where all

may hear, and that he give himself to reading and meditating before he come to preach. And if God command one judge to come to the place of judgment, so does He command seventy, and so all estates to convene in the place of judgment. It is objected that "the estates are not judges, ordinary and habitually, but only judges at some certain occasions, when the king, for cogent and weighty causes, calls them, and calls them not to judge, but to give him advice and counsel how to judge."

Arg. 1. They are no less judges habitually than the king, when the common affairs of the whole kingdom necessitates these public watchmen to come together; for even the king judges not actually, but upon occasion. This is to beg the question: to say that the estates are not judges but when the king calls them at such and such occasions; for the elders, princes, and heads of families and tribes were judges ordinary, because they made the king.

Arg. 2. The kingdom by God, yea, and church, justice, and religion, so far as they concern the whole kingdom are committed not to the keeping of the king only, but to all the judges, elders, and princes of the land: and they are rebuked as evening wolves, lions, oppressors (Ezek. 22:27; Zech. 3:3; Isa. 3:14-15; Mic. 3:1-3) when they oppress the people in judgment, so are they (Deut. 1:16-17; 2 Chron. 19:6-7) made judges, and therefore they are no more to be restrained not to convene by the king's power (which is in this accumulative and auxiliary, not privative) than they can be restrained in judgment, and in pronouncing such a sentence, as the king pleased, and not such a sentence; because, as they are to answer to God for unjust sentences, so also for no just sentences, and for not convening to judge, when religion and justice, which are fallen in the streets, calls for them.

Arg. 3. As God in a law of nature has given to every man the keeping and self-preservation of himself and of his brother, Cain ought in his place to be the keeper of Abel his brother; so has God committed the keeping of the commonwealth by a positive law, not to the king alone, because that is impossible (Num. 11:14, 17; 2 Chron. 19:1-6; 1 Chron. 27).[1]

Arg. 4. If the king had such a power as king, and so from God, he should have power to break up the meeting of all courts of parliament, secret councils, and all inferior judicatures, and when the congregation of gods, as in Ps. 82, in the midst of which the Lord stands, were about to pronounce just judgment for the oppressed and poor, they might be hindered by the king, and so they should be as just as the king makes them, and might pervert judgment, and take away the righteousness of the righteous from him (Isa. 5:23) because the king commands, and the cause of the poor should not come before the judge, when the king so commands. And shall it excuse the estates to say we could not judge the cause of the poor, nor crush the priests of Baal, and the idolatrous mass-prelates, because the king forbade us? So might the king break up the meeting of the lords of session, when they were to discern that Naboth's vineyard should be restored to him, and hinder the states to repress tyranny, and this would be as much as if the states should say, 'We made this man our king, and with our good-will we agree he shall be a tyrant. For if God gave it to him as a king, we are to consent that he enjoy it.'

Arg. 5. If Barclay and other flatterers have leave to make the parliament but counsellors and advisers of the king, and the king to be the only and sole judge, the king is by that same reason the sole judge in relation to all judges; the contrary of which is clear (Num. 11:16; Deut. 1:16-17; Chron. 19:8; Rom, 13:1-2; 1 Pet. 2:13-14). Yea, but (say they) the king, when he sends an ambassador, he may tie him

---

1. Junius Brutus, q. 2, *vind. contr. Tyran.*

to a written commission, and insofar as he exceeds that, he is not an ambassador, and clear it is that all inferior judges (1 Pet. 2:13-14) are but sent by the king; therefore, they are so judges as they are but messengers, and are to adhere to the royal pleasure of the prince that sent them.

Ans. (1) The ambassador is not to accept an unjust embassage that fights with the law of nature. (2) The ambassador and the judge differ: the ambassador is the king and states' deputy, both in his call to the embassy, and also in the matter of the embassy, for which cause he is not to transgress what is given to him in writ as a rule, but the inferior judges and the high court of parliament, even if they were the king's deputies (as the parliament is in no sort his deputy, but he their deputy royal) yet it is only in respect of their call, not in respect of the matter of their commission, for the king may send the judge to judge in general according to the law, justice, and religion, but he cannot depute the sentence, and command the conscience of the judge to pronounce such a sentence, not such. The inferior judge in the act of judging is as independent, and his conscience as immediately subject to God as the king; therefore, the king owes to every sentence his approbative suffrage as king, but not either his directive suffrage, or his imperative suffrage of absolute pleasure.

Arg. 6. If the king should sell his country and bring in a foreign army, the estates are to convene, to take course for the safety of the kingdom.

Arg. 7. If David exhort the princes of Israel to help king Solomon in governing the kingdom and in building the temple (2 Chron. 32:3): if Hezekiah took counsel with his princes and his mighty men in the matter of holding off the Assyrians who were to invade the land; if David consult with the captains of thousands and hundreds to bring the ark of God to Kirjath-jearim (1 Chron. 13:1-4); if Solomon "assemble the elders of Israel, and all the heads of the tribes, and the chief of the fathers, to bring the ark of the tabernacle to the congregation of the Lord" (1 Kings 8:1); if Ahab gathered together the states of Israel in a matter that nearly concerned religion; if the elders and people counsel and decree that king Ahab should hearken to Ben-hadad king of Syria (1 Kings 20:8), and if Ahasuerus make no decrees without consent of his princes (Esth. 1:21); nor Darius any act without his nobles and princes; if Hamor and Shechem would not make a covenant with Jacob's sons, without the consent of the men of the city (Gen. 34:20), and Ephron the Hittite would not sell Abraham a burial place in his land without the consent of the children of Heth (Gen. 23:10); then must the estates have a power of judging with the king or prince in matters of religion, justice, and government which concern the whole kingdom. But the former is true by the records of Scripture; therefore so is the latter.

Arg. 8. The men of Ephraim complain that Jephthah had gone to war against the children of Ammon without them, and thus rose war between the men of Ephraim and the men of Gilead (Judges 12:1-3) and the men of Israel fiercely contended with the men of Judah, because they brought king David home again without them, pleading that they were in it despised (2. Sam. 19:41-43) which shows that the whole states have hand in matters of public government that concern all the kingdom, and when there is no king the chief of the people, and of all the tribes, go out in battle against the children of Benjamin (Judg. 20).

Arg. 9. Those who make the king, and so have power to unmake him in the case of tyranny, must be above the king in power of government; but the elders and princes made both David and Saul kings.

Arg. 10. There is not any who say that the princes and people did not right in rescuing innocent Jonathan from death against the king's will and his law (1 Sam. 14).

Arg. 11. The special ground of royalists is to make the king the absolute supreme, giving all life and power to the parliament and states, and of mere grace convening them. So says Ferne, the author of *Ossorianum*, but this ground is fase, because the king's power is fiduciary and put in his hand upon trust, and must be ministerial and borrowed from those who put him in trust, and so his power must be less and derived from the parliament. But the parliament has no power in trust from the King, because the time was when the man who is the king had no power, and the parliament had the same power that they now have, and now when the king has received power from them, they have the whole power that they had before, that is, to make laws; and resigned no power to the king, but to execute laws; and his convening of them is an act of royal duty, which he owes to the parliament by virtue of his office, and is not an act of grace; for an act of grace is an act of free will, and what the king does of free will, he may not do, and so he may never convene a parliament. But when David, Solomon, Asa, Hezekiah, Jehoshaphat, Ahaz, convened parliaments, they convened parliaments as kings, and so *ex debito et virtute officii*, out of debt and royal obligation, and if the king as the king, be *lex ammata*, a breathing and living law, the king as king, must do by obligation of law what he does as king, and not from spontaneous and arbitrary grace. If the Scripture holds forth to us a king in Israel, and two princes and elders who made the king, and had power of life and death, as we have seen, then is there in Israel monarchy tempered with aristocracy, and if there were elders and rulers in every city, as the Scripture says, here was also aristocracy and democracy, and for the warrant of the power of the estates, I appeal to jurists and to approved authors Arg. l. aliud, 160, sect. 1; *De Jur. Reg.* 1.22; *Mortuo de fidei.* 1.11, 14; *ad Mum.* 1.3.1, 4; *Sigenius De Bep. Judaeor.* 1.6.7; *Corneliuss Bertramo,* section 12; Junius Brutus, *Vindic. Contra. Tyran.* sect, 2; *Author Libelli de jur Magistrat. in subd.* q, 6; Althus. *Politic,* section 18; Calvin *Institut.* 1.4.20; *Pareus Coment. in Rom. 13*; Pet. Martyr in *Lib. Judic.* Section 3; Joan Marianus *De rege* 1.7; Hottoman *de jure Antiq. Regni Gallici* 1.1.12; Buchanan *De jure Regni apud Scotos.*

Obj. The king after a more noble way represents the people than the estates does; for the princes and commissioners of parliament have all their power from the people, and the people's power is concentrated in the king.

Ans. The estates taken collectively do represent the people both in respect of office, and of persons, because they stand judges for them; for many represent many, *ratione numeri et officii* better than one does. The king does improperly represent the people, though the power for actual execution of laws be more in the king, yet a legislative power is more in the estates. Neither will it follow that if the estates of a kingdom do anything but counsel a king, they must then command him, for a legal and judicial advice has influence in the effect to make it a law, not on the king's will, to cause him give the being of a law to that which without his will is no law, for this supposes that he is only judge.

Obj. What power the people reserves, they reserve it to themselves in *unitate*, as united in a parliament, and therefore what they do out of a parliament is tumultuous.

Ans. I deny the consequence: they reserve the power of self-preservation out of a parliament, and a power of convening in parliament for that effect that they may by common counsel defend themselves.

QUESTION 22.

WHETHER THE POWER OF THE KING AS KING IS ABSOLUTE, OR DEPENDENT AND LIMITED BY GOD'S FIRST MOLD AND PATTERN OF A KING.

The royalists make the king as absolute as the great Turk. That the king is not absolute in his power is proved by nine arguments. Why the king is a living law. Power to do ill not from God. Royalists say power to do ill is not from God, but power to do ill, as punishable by man, is from God. A king, actu primo, is a plague, and the people slaves, if the king, by God's institution be absolute. Absoluteness of royalty is against justice, peace, reason, and law, and against the king's relation of a brother. A damsel forced may resist the king. The goodness of an absolute prince hinders not but he is actu primo a tyrant.

D r. Ferne shows us it was never his purpose to plead for absoluteness of an arbitrary commandment, free from all moral restraint laid on the power by God's law; but only he strives for a power in the king that cannot be resisted by the subject (section 3). But truly we never disputed with royalists of any absolute power in the king, free from moral subjection to God's law. 1. Because any bond that God's law imposes on the king comes wholly from God and the nature of a divine law, and not from any voluntary contract or covenant, either express or *tacito*, between the king and the people who made him king; for if he fail against such a covenant, though he should exceed the cruelty of a king or a man and become a lion, a Nero, and a mother-killer, he should in all his inhumanity and breach of covenant be accountable to God, not to any man on earth. 2. To dispute with royalists if God's law lay any moral restraint upon the king, would be to dispute whether the king be a rational man or no, and whether he can sin against God, and shall cry in the day of God's wrath (if he be a wicked prince) hills fall on us and cover us, as it is in Rev. 6:15-16, and whether Tophet be prepared for all workers of iniquity, and certainly I justify the schoolmen in that question whether or not God could have created a rational creature, such a one as by nature is impeccable, and not naturally capable of sin before God? If royalists dispute this question of their absolute monarch, they are wicked divines.

We plead not at this time (says the Prelate, section 14, stealing from Grotius, Barclay, Arnisaeus, who spoke it with more sinews of reason) for a masterly or despotic, or rather for a slavish sovereignty, which is *dominium herile*, an absolute power, such as the great Turk this day exercises over his subjects, and the king of Spain has over and in his territories outside Europe: we maintain only *regiam potestatem, quae fundatur in paterna*, such royal, fatherly sovereignty, as we live under, blessed be God and our predecessors. This (says he) as it has its royal prerogative inherent to the crown naturally, and inseparable from it, so it trenches not upon the liberty of the person, or the property of the goods of the subject, but in and by the lawful and just acts of jurisdiction.

Ans. 1. Here is another absolute power disclaimed to be in the king; he has not such a masterly and absolute liberty as the Turk has. Why? John Popish Prelate, in such a tender and high point as concerns soul and body of subjects in three Christian kingdoms, you should have taught us. What bonds and fetters any covenant or paction between the king and people lays upon the king, why he has not as king the power of the great Turk, I will tell you. The great Turk may command any of his subjects to leap into a mountain of fire and burn himself quick, in conscience of obedience to his law. And what if the subject disobeys the great Turk, if the great Turk be a lawful prince, as you will not deny, and if the King of Spain should command foreign conquered slaves to do the like? By your doctrine, neither the one nor the other were obliged to resist by violence but to pray or fly, which both were to speak to stones and were like the man who in case of shipwreck made his devotion of praying to the waves of the sea, not to enter the place of his bed and drown him. But a Christian king has not this power: why? And a Christian king (by royalist's doctrine) has a greater power than the Turk (if greater can be): he has power to command his subjects to cast themselves into hell-fire, that is, to press on them a service in which it is written, 'Adore the work of men's hands in the place of the living God,' and this is worse than the Turk's commandment of bodily burning quick. And what is left to the Christian subjects in this case is the very same, and no other than is left to the Turkish and foreign Spanish subjects: Either fly, or make prayers. There is no more left to us.

2. Many royalists maintain that England is a conquered nation. Why, then see what power, by law of conquest, the king of Spain has over his slaves; the same must the king of England have over his subjects. For, to royalists, a title by conquest to a crown is as lawful as a title by birth or election; for lawfulness, in relation to God's law, is placed in an indivisible point, if we regard the essence of lawfulness; and therefore there is nothing left to England, but that all protestants who take the oath of a protestant king, to defend the true protestant religion, should, after prayers conveyed to the king through the fingers of prelates and papists, leave the kingdom empty to papists, prelates, and atheists.

3. All power restrained that it cannot arise from ten degrees to fourteen from the kingly power of Saul (1 Sam. 8:9, 11) to the kingly power of the great Turk, to fourteen, must either be restrained by God's law, or by man's law, or by the innate goodness and grace of the prince, or by the providence of God. A restraint from God's law is vain; for it is no question between us and royalists but God has laid a moral restraint on kings, and all men, that they have not moral power to sin against God. Is the restraint laid on by man's law? What law of man? The royalist says the king as king is above all law of man. Then (say I) no law of man can hinder the king's power of ten, to arise to the Turkish power of fourteen. All law of man, as it is man's law, is seconded either with ecclesiastic and spiritual co-action, such as excommunication, or with civil and temporal co-action, such as is the sword, if it be violated. But royalists deny that either the sword of the church in excommunication, or the civil sword, should be drawn against the king. This law of man should be produced by this profound jurist, the Popish Prelate, who mocks at all the statists and lawyers of Scotland. It is not a covenant between the king and people at his coronation, for though there were any such covenant, yet the breach of it does bind before God, but not before man. Nor can I see, or any man else, how a law of man can lay a restraint on the king's power of two degrees, to cancel it within a law, more than on a power of ten or fourteen degrees. If the king of Spain, the lawful sovereign of those over-European people (as royalists say) have a power of fourteen degrees over those conquered subjects, as a king I see not how he has not the like power over his own subjects of Spain, namely, even of fourteen; for what befits a king as a king (and kingly power from God he has as king) he has it in relation to all subjects, unless it be taken from him in relation to some subjects, and given by some law of God, or in relation to some other subjects. Now no man can produce any such law. The nature of the goodness and grace of the prince cannot

lay bonds on the king to cancel his power, that he should not usurp the power of the king of Spain toward his over-Europe.

Ans. 1. Royalists plead for a power due to the king, as king, and that from God, such as Samuel had (1 Sam. 8:9, 11; 10:25), but this power should be a power of grace and goodness in the king as a good man, not in the king as a king, and due to him by law, and so the king should have his legal power from God to be a tyrant. But if he were not a tyrant, but should lay limits on his own power, through the goodness of his own nature, no thanks to royalists that he is not a tyrant, for *actu primo* and as he is a king (as they say) he is a tyrant, having from God a tyrannical power of ten degrees, as Saul had (1 Sam. 8), and why not of fourteen degrees as well as the great Turk, or the king of Spain? If he use it not, it is his own personal goodness, not his official and royal power. The restraint of providence laid by God upon any power to do ill hinders only the exercise of the power not to break forth in as tyrannical acts as ever the king of Spain or the great Turk can exercise toward any. Yea, providence lays physical restraint, and possibly moral sometimes, upon the exercise of that power that devils and the most wicked men of the world have. But royalists must show us that providence has laid bounds on the king's power and made it fatherly and not masterly, so that if the power exceed bounds of fatherly power, and pass over to the despotic and masterly power, it may be resisted by the subjects; but that they will not say.

4. This paternal and fatherly power that God has given to kings, as royalists teach, trenches not upon the liberty of the subjects and the property of their goods, but in and by lawful and just acts of jurisdiction, says the Popish Prelate. Well, then it may trench upon the liberty of soul and body of the subjects but in and by lawful and just acts of jurisdiction. But none are to judge of these acts of jurisdiction whether they be just or not just other than the king, the only judge of supreme and absolute authority and power. And if the king command the idolatrous service in the obtruded service-book, it is a lawful and

a just act of jurisdiction. For to royalists, who make the kind's power absolute, all acts are so just to the subject, though he command idolatry and Mahommedanism, that we are to suffer only, and not to resist.

5. The Prelate presumes that fatherly power is absolute, but so if a father murder his child, he is not accountable to the magistrate therefore, but being absolute over his children, only the Judge of the world, not any power on earth, can punish him.

6. We have proved that the king's power is paternal or fatherly only by analogy and improperly.

7. What is this prerogative royal we shall hear by and by.

8. There is no restraint on earth laid upon this fatherly power of the king but God's law, which is a moral restraint. If then the king challenge as great a power as the Turk has, he only sins against God, but no mortal man on earth may control him, as royalists teach. And who can know what power it is that royalists plead for, whether a despotic power of lordly power or a fatherly power? If it be a power above law, such as none on earth may resist it, it is no matter whether it be above law of two degrees, or of twenty, even to the great Turk's power.

These go for oracles at court: Tacitus, *Principi summum rerum arbitrium Dii dederunt subditis obsequii gloria relicta est*; Seneca, *Indigna digna habenda sunt, Rex qua facuit*; Salust, *Impune quidvis facere, id est Regem esse*, as if to be a king and to be a god who cannot err were all one. But certainly these authors are taxing the license of kings, and not commanding their power. But that God has given no absolute and unlimited power to a king above the law, is evident by this.

Arg. 1. He who in his first institution is appointed of God by office, even when he sits on the throne, to take heed to read on a written copy of God's law, that he may "learn to fear the Lord his God, and keep all the words of this law," &c., he is not of absolute power above law. But the king as king (Deut. 17:18-19), while he sits on the throne is to do this; therefore the assumption is clear, for this is the law of the king as king, and not of a man as a man. But as he sits on the throne, he is to read on the book of the law, and because he is king, "his heart is not to be lifted up above his brethren," (ver. 20) and as king "he is not to multiply horses," &c. (ver. 16). So politicians make this argument good: they say, *Rex est lex viva, animata, et loquens lex*, the king as king, is a living breathing and speaking law. And there are three reasons for this:

1. If all were innocent persons, and could do no violence one to another, the law would rule all, and all men would put the law in execution, *agendo sponte*, by doing right of their own accord, and there should be no need of a king to compel men to do right. But now, because men are by nature averse to good laws, therefore there was need of a ruler who by office should reduce the law into practice; and so is the king the law reduced in practice.

2. The law is *ratio sive mens*, the reason or mind, free from all perturbations of anger, lust, hatred, and cannot be tempted to ill; and the king, as a man, may be tempted by his own passions, and therefore as king, he comes by office out of himself to reason and law, and so much as he has of law, so much of a king, and in his remotest distance from law and reason he is a tyrant.

3. *Abstracta concretis sunt puriora et perfectiora.* Justice is more perfect than a just man, whiteness more perfect than the white wall; so the nearer the king comes to a law, for the which he is a king, the nearer to a king, *Propter quod unumquodque tale, id ipsum magis tale.* Therefore, kings throwing laws to themselves as men, whereas they should have conformed themselves to the law have erred. Cambyses, the son of Cyrus, because he loved his own sister, would have "the marriage of the brother with the sister lawful." Anaxarchus said to Alexander (grieved in mind that he had killed Cleitus) *Regi ac Jovi themin atque iustitiam cissidere:* Judgment and righteousness did always accompany God and the king in all they do, but some to this purpose say better: The law, rather than the king, has power of life and death.

Arg. 2. The power that the king has (I speak not of his gifts) he has it from the people who make him king, as I proved before; but the people have neither formally nor virtually any power absolute to give the king. All the power they have is a legal and natural power to guide themselves in peace and godliness, and to save themselves from unjust violence by the benefit of rulers. Now, an absolute power above a law is a power to do ill and to destroy the people, and this the people have not themselves, it being repugnant to nature that any should have a natural power in themselves to destroy themselves, or to inflict upon themselves an evil of punishment to destruction. Though therefore it were given, which yet is not granted, that the people had resigned all power that they have into their king, yet if he use a tyrannical power against the people for their hurt and destruction, he uses a power that the people never gave him, and against the intention of nature, for they invested a man with power to be their father and defender for their good, and he fails against the people's intention in usurping an over-power to himself, which they never gave, never had, never could give; for they cannot give what they never had, and power to destroy themselves they never had.

Arg. 3. All royal power, whereby a king is a king and distinguished from a private man, armed with no power of the sword, is from God. But absolute power to tyrannize over the people and to destroy them is not a power from God; therefore, there is not any such royal power absolute. The proposition is evident, because that God who makes kings and disposes of crowns (Prov. 8:15-16; 2 Sam. 12:7; Dan. 4:32) must also create and give that royal and official power by which a king is a king. 1. Because God created man, he must be the author of his reasonable soul. If God be the author of things, he must be the author of their forms by which they are that which they are. 2. All power is God's (1 Chron. 29:11; Matt. 6:13; Ps. 62:11; 68:3; Dan. 2:37), and that absolute power to tyrannize is not from God. 1. Because, if this moral power to sin be from God, it being formally wickedness, God must be the author of sin. 2. Whatever moral power is from God, the exercises of that power, and its acts, must be from God, and so these acts must be morally good and just; for if the moral power be of God, as the author, so must the acts be. Now, the acts of a tyrannical power are acts of sinful injustice and oppression, and cannot be from God. 3. Politicians say there is no power in rulers to do evil, but to help and defend the people, as the power of a physician to destroy, of a pilot to cast away the ship on the rock, the power of a tutor to waste the inheritance of the orphan, and the power of father and mother to kill their children, and of the mighty to defraud and oppress, are not powers from God. So Ferdinand, Vasquez, Illustr. Quest. l.l.26, 45; Prickman, section 3, sect. *Soluta potestas*; Althus, *Pol.* 9, n. 25.

Barclay,[1] Grotius, Dr. Ferne (the Popish Prelate's wit could come up to it) say, "That absolute power to do ill, so as no mortal man can lawfully resist it, is from God, and the king has in this way power from God as no subject can resist it, but he must resist the ordinance of God, and yet the power of tyranny is not simply from God."

Ans. The law says, *Ilud possumus quod jure possumus* (*Papinus F. fillius, D. de cond. Just*). It is no power which is not lawful power. The royalists say power of tyranny, insofar as it may be resisted and is punishable by men, is not from God. But what is the other part of the distinction? It must be that tyrannical power is *simpliciter* from God, or in itself it is from God, but as it is punishable or restrainable by subjects it is not from God. Now, to be punishable by subjects is but an accident, and tyrannical power is the subject, yea, and it is a separable accident; for many tyrants are never punished, and their power is never restrained: such a tyrant was Saul, and many persecuting emperors. Now if the tyrannical power itself was from God, the argument is yet valid, and remains unanswered. And shall not this fall to the ground as false which Arnisaeus says *Dum contra officium*

---

1. *Contra Monarch.* book 2.

facit, magistratus non est magistratus quippe a quo non injuria, sed jus nasci debeat. (de autho, princ. section 2, n. 10; *L. meminerint:* 6. *C. unde 6. din. in C. quod quis,* 24, n. 4-5) *Et de hoc neminem dubitare aut dissentire scribit (Marant.* disp. 1, num. 14). When the magistrate does anything by violence and without law, insofar doing against his office, he is not a magistrate. Then, say I, that power by which he does is not of God. None does then resist the ordinance of God who resist the king in tyrannical acts. If the power, as it cannot be punished by the subject nor restrained be from God, therefore the tyrannical power itself, and without this accident-that it can be punished by men; it must be from God also. But the conclusion is absurd and denied by royalists. I prove the connection: if the king have such a power above all restraint, the power itself, namely, king David's power to kill innocent Uriah, and deflower Bathsheba, without the accident of being restrained or punished by men, it is either from God or not from God. If it be from God, it must be a power against the sixth and seventh commandments, which God gave to David, and not to any subject, and so David lied when he confessed this sin, and this sin cannot be pardoned because it was no sin, and kings, because kings, are under no tie of duties of mercy, and truth, and justice to their subjects, contrary to that which God's law requires of all judges (Deut. 1:16-17; 17:16-20; 2 Chron. 19:6-7; Rom. 13:3-4): if this power be from God, as it is unrestrainable and unpunishable by the subject, it is not from God at all; for how can God give a power to do ill, that is unpunishable by men, and not give that power to do ill? It is inconceivable; for in this very thing that God gives to David—a power to murder the innocent—with this respect that it shall be punishable by God only, and not by men, God must give it as a sinful power to do ill, which must be a power of dispensation to sin, and so not to be punished by either God or man, which is contrary to his revealed will in his word. If such a power as not restrainable by man be from God by way of permission, as a power to sin in devils and men is, then it is no royal power, nor any ordinance of God, and to resist this power is not to resist the ordinance of God.

Arg. 4. That power which makes the benefit of a king to be no benefit but a judgment of God, for instance making all the people slaves, such as were slaves among the Romans and Jews, is not to be asserted by any Christian; but an absolute power to do ill, and to tyrannize, which is supposed to be an essential and constitutive of kings, to difference them from all judges, makes the benefit of a king no benefit, but a judgment of God, as making all the people slaves. That the major may be clear, it is evident, 1. To have a king is a blessing of God, because to have no king is a judgment: Judg. 17:6: "Every man does what seems good in his own eyes." (Judg. 18:1; 19:1; 21:26). 2. So it is a part of God's good providence to provide a king for his people (1 Sam, 16:1; 2 Sam. 5:12). And David perceived that the Lord had established him king over Israel, and that he had exalted his kingdom for his people Israel's sake (2 Sam. 15:2-3, 6; 18:3; Rom. 13:2-4). If the king be a thing good in itself, then can he not, *actu primo*, be a curse and a judgment, and essentially a bondage and slavery to the people; also the genuine and intrinsic end of a king is the good (Rom. 13:4) and the good of a quiet and peaceable life in all godliness and honesty (1. Tim. 2:2), and he is by office, *custos utriusque tabulae*, whose genuine end is to preserve the law from violence, and to defend the subject; he is the people's debtor for all happiness possible to be procured by God's sword, either in peace or war, at home or abroad. For the assumption is evident. An absolute and arbitrary power is a king-law, such as royalists say God gave to Saul (1 Sam. 8:9, 11; 10:25) to play the tyrant, and this power, arbitrary and unlimited, above all laws, is that which (1) is given to God; (2) distinguishes essentially the kings of Israel from the judge, says Barclary, Grotius, Arnisaeus; (3) a constitutive form of a king; therefore it must be *actu primo*, a benefit, and a blessing of God; but if God has given my such power absolute to a king: as, 1. His will must be a law, either to do or suffer all the tyranny and cruelty of a tiger, a leopard, a Nero, or a Julian; then has God given, *actu primo*, a power to a king, as king, to enslave the people and flock of God, redeemed by the blood of God, as the slaves among the Romans and Jews, who were so under their masters, as their bondage was a plague of God, and the lives of the people of God under Pharaoh, who compelled them to work in brick and clay. 2. Though he cut the throats of the people of God, as the lioness Queen Mary did, and command an army of soldiers to come and burn the cities of the land, and kill man, wife, and children, yet in so doing he does the part of a king, so as you cannot resist him as a man and obey him as a king, but must give your necks to him, upon this ground: because this absolute power of his is ordained of God, and there is no power even to kill and destroy the innocent, but it is of God. So says Paul (Rom. 13), if we believe court-prophets, or rather lying-spirits, who persuade the king of Britain to make war against his three dominions. Now, it is clear that the distinction of bound and free continued in Israel even under the most tyrannical kings (2 Kings 4:1), yea, even when the Jews were captives under Ahasuerus (Esth. 7:4). And what difference should there be between the people of God under their own kings and when they were captives under tyrants, serving wood and stone and false gods, as was threatened as a curse in the law? (Deut. 28:25, 36, 64, 68). If their own kings, by God's appointment, have the same absolute power over them, and if he be a tyrant, *actu primo*, that is, if he be endued with absolute power, and so have power to play the tyrant, then must the people of God be *actu primo*, slaves, and under absolute subjection, for they are relatives, as lord and servant, conqueror and captive. It is true, they say, kings by office are fathers: they cannot put forth in action their power to destroy. I answer, it is their goodness of nature that they put not forth in action all their absolute power to destroy, which God has given them as kings, and therefore thanks are due to their goodness, because they do not, *actu secondo*, play the tyrant; for royalists teach that by virtue of their office God has given to them a royal power to destroy; therefore, the Lord's people are slaves under them, though they deal not with them as slaves, but that hinders not but the people by condition are slaves. So many conquerors of old did deal kindly with their slaves whom they took in war, and dealt with them as sons, but as conquerors they had power to sell them, to kill them, to put them to work in brick and clay. So say I here, royal power and a king cannot be a blessing and *actu primo* a favor of God to the people, for the which they are to pray when they want a king that they may have one, or to praise God when they have one. But a king must be a curse and a judgment, if he be such a creature as essentially and in the intention and nature of the thing itself has by office a royal power to destroy, and that from God; for then the people praying, "Lord give us a king" should pray, "Make us slaves, Lord: take our liberty and power from us, and give a power unlimited and absolute to one man, by which he may if he please, waste and destroy us, as all the bloody emperors did the people of God." Surely, I see not but they should pray for a temptation, and to be led into temptation when they pray God to give them a king, and therefore such a power is a vain thing.

Arg. 5. A power contrary to justice, to peace and the good of the people, that looks to no law as a rule, and so is unreasonable and forbidden by the law of God and the civil law (L. 15. *filius de condit. Instit.*) cannot be lawful power, and cannot constitute a lawful judge, but an absolute and unlimited power is such. How can the judge be the minister of God for good to the people (Rom. 13:4) if he have such a power as a king, given him by God, to destroy and waste the people?

Arg. 6. An absolute power is contrary to nature, and so unlawful; for it makes the people give away the natural power of defending their life against illegal and cruel violence, and makes a man who has need to be ruled and lawed by nature above all rule and law, and one who by nature can sin against his brethren such a one as cannot sin against any but God only, and makes him a lion and an unsocial man.

What a man is Nero, whose life is poetry and painting! Domitian, only an archer; Valentinian, only a painter; Charles IX of France, only a hunter; Alphonsus Dux Ferrariensis, only an astronomer; Philip of Macedonia, a musician; and all because they are kings. This our king denies when he says (art. 13): "There is power legally placed in the parliament more than sufficient to prevent and restrain the power of tyranny." But if they had not power to play the lions, it is not much that kings are musicians, hunters, &c.

Arg. 7. God in making a king to preserve his people should give liberty without all political restrain, for one man to destroy many, which is contrary to God's end in the fifth commandment, if one have absolute power to destroy souls and bodies of many thousands.

Arg. 8. If the kings of Israel and Judah were under the censures and rebukes of the prophets, and sinned against God and the people in rejecting these rebukes and in persecuting the prophets, and were under this law not to take their neighbor's wife, or his vineyard from him against his will, and the inferior judges were to accept the persons of none in judgment, small or great, and if the king yet remain a brother, notwithstanding he be a king, then is his power not above any law, nor absolute. For what reason? 1. He should be under one law of God to be executed by men, and not under another law? Royalists are to show a difference from God's word. 2. His neighbors, brother, or subjects may by violence keep back their vineyards and chastity from the king. Naboth may by force keep his own vineyard from Ahab. By the laws of Scotland, if a subject obtain a decree from the king of violent possession of the heritages of a subject, he has by law power to cast out, force, apprehend, and deliver to prison those who are tenants, brooking these lands by the king's personal commandment. If a king should force a damsel, she may violently resist, and by violence, and bodily opposing of violence to violence, defend her own chastity. Now, that the prophets have rebuked kings is evident: Samuel rebuked Saul; Nathan, David, Elijah king Ahab; Jeremiah is commanded to prophesy against the kings of Judah (Jer. 50:18) and the prophets practiced it (Jer. 19:3; 21:2; 22:13-16; Hos. 5:1). Kings are guilty before God because they submitted not their royal power and greatness to the rebukes of the prophets, but persecuted them.

The king on the throne remains a brother (Deut. 17:20); and so the judges or three estates are not to accept of the person of the king for his greatness in judgment (Ps. 22:22); and the judge is to give out such a sentence in judgment as the Lord (Deut. 1:16-17), with whom there is no iniquity, would give out if the Lord Himself were sitting in judgment; because the judge is in the very stead of God, as his lieutenant; (2 Chron. 19:6-7; Ps. 82:1-2; Deut. 1:17) and with God there is no respect of persons (2 Chron. 19:7; 1 Pet. 1:17; Acts 10:34). I do not intend that any inferior judge sent by the king is to judge the king, but those who gave him the throne, and made him king are truly above him, and to judge him without respect of persons, as God himself would judge if He were sitting on the bench.

God is the author of civil laws and government, and His intention is the external peace, and quiet life, and godliness of his church and people, and that all judges, according to their places, be nurse-fathers to the church (Isa. 49:23). Now God must have appointed sufficient means for this end, but there is no sufficient means at all, but a mere anarchy and confusion if to one man an absolute and unlimited power be given by God, by which at his pleasure He may obstruct the fountains of justice, and command lawyers and laws to speak not God's mind, that is justice, righteousness, safety, true religion, but the sole lust and pleasure of one man. And this one having absolute and irresistible influence on all the inferior instruments of justice may by this power turn all into anarchy and put the people in a worse condition than if there were no judge at all in the land. For that of politicians, that tyranny is better than anarchy, is to be taken *cum grano salis*, but I shall never believe that absolute power of one man, which is *actu primo* tyranny, is God's sufficient way of peaceable government.

Therefore, Barclay says nothing for the contrary when he says, "The Athenians made Draco and Solon absolute lawgivers, for *a facto ad jus non valet consequentia.*"[1] What if a roving people, trusting Draco and Solon to be kings above mortal men and to be gods gave them power to make laws, written not with ink, but with blood, shall other kings have from God the like tyrannical and bloody power from that to make bloody laws? Chytreus I (book 2) and Sleidan cites it (1.1), Sueron, *Sub paena periurii non tenentur fidem sevare regi degeneri.*

Arg. 9. He who is regulated by law, and swears to the three estates to be regulated by law, and accepts the crown covenant-wise, and so as the estates would refuse to make him their king, if either he should refuse to swear, or if they did believe certainly that he would break his oath, has no unlimited and absolute power from God or the people, for *foedus conditionatum, aut promissio conditionalis mutua, faeit jus alteri in alterum,* a mutual conditional covenant gives law and power over one to another. But from that which has been said, the king swears to the three estates to be regulated by law: he accepts the crown upon the tenor of a mutual covenant, &c.; for if he should, as king, swear to be king, that is, one who has absolute power above a law, and also to be regulated by a law, he should swear things contradictory, that is, that he should be their king, having absolute power over them and according to that power to rule them, and he should swear not to be their king, and to rule them, not according to absolute power, but according to law. If therefore this absolute power be essential to a king as a king, no king can lawfully take the oath to govern according to law, for then he should swear not to reign as king, and not be their king, for how could he be their king, lacking that which God has made essential to a king as a king?

---

1. *Contra Monarch.* book 2.

QUESTION 23.

*Prerogative taken two ways. Prerogative above laws is a garland
proper to infinite majesty. A threefold dispensation of power, justice,
and grace. Acts of mere grace may be acts of blood. An oath to the king
of Babylon tied not the people of Judah to all that absolute power could
command. The absolute prince is as absolute in acts of cruelty as in acts
of grace. Servants are not (1 Pet. 2:18-19) interdicted of self-defense.
The parliament materially only, not formally, has the king for their
lord. Reason is not a sufficient restraint to keep a prince from acts of
tyranny. Princes have sufficient power to do good, though they have
not absolute power to do evil. A power to shed innocent blood can be no
part of any royal power given by God. The king, because he is a public
person, lacks many privileges that subjects have.*

A prerogative royal I take two ways: either to be an act of mere
will and pleasure above or beside reason or law, or an act of
dispensation beside or against the letter of the law.

Assert. 1. That which royalists call the prerogative royal of princes
is the salt of absolute power, and it is a supreme and highest power of

a king as a king, to do above, without or contrary to a law or reason which is unreasonable.

1. When God's word speaks of the power of kings and judges (Deut. 17:15-17; 1:15-17), and elsewhere there is not any footstep or any ground for such a power, and therefore (if we speak according to conscience) there is no such thing in the world; and because royalists cannot give us any warrant, it is to be rejected.

2. A royal prerogative must be a power of doing good to the people, and grounded upon some reason or law, but this is but a branch of an ordinary limited power, and no prerogative above or beside law, yea, any power not mounded on a reason different from mere will or absolute pleasure is an irrational and brutish power, and therefore it may well be *jus personae* the power of the man who is king; it cannot be *jus coronae*, any power annexed to the crown, for this holds true of all the actions of the king, as a king, *illud potest rex, et illud tantum quod jure potest.* The king as king can do no more than that which upon right and law he may do.

3. To dispute this question, whether such a prerogative befit any king, as king, is to dispute whether God has made all under a monarch slaves by their own consent, which is a vain question. Those who hold such a prerogative must say the king is so absolute and unlimited a god on earth that either by law, or his sole pleasure beside law, he may regularly and rationally move all wheels in policy, and his uncontrolled will shall be the axletree on which all the wheels are turned.

4. That which is the garland and proper flower of the King of kings, as He is absolute above His creatures, and not tied to any law outside Himself that regulates His will, that must be given to no mortal man or king, unless we were to communicate that which is God's proper due to a sinful man, which must be idolatry. But to do royal acts out of an absolute power above law and reason is such a power as befits God, as is evident in positive laws and in acts of God's mere pleasure, where we see no reason outside the Almighty for the one side rather

than for the other, such as how God's forbidding the eating of the tree of knowledge makes the eating sin and contrary to reason; but there is no reason in the object: for if God should command eating of that tree, not to eat should also be sin. So God's choosing Peter to glory and his refusing Judas is a good and a wise act, but not good or wise from the object of the act but from the sole wise pleasure of God, because if God had chosen Judas to glory and rejected Peter, that act would have been no less a good and a wise act than the former. For when there is no law in the object but only God's will, the act is good and wise, seeing infinite wisdom cannot be separated from the perfect will of God, but no act of a mortal king, having sole and only will, and neither law nor reason in it, can be a lawful, a wise, or a good act.

Assert. 2. There is something which may be called a prerogative by way of dispensation, There is a threefold dispensation, one of power, another of justice, and a third of grace: 1. A dispensation of power is when the will of the lawgiver makes that act to be no sin which without that will would have been sin, as if God's commanding will had not intervened, the Israelites borrowing the ear-rings and jewels of the Egyptians, and not restoring them, had been a breach of the eighth commandment, and in this sense no king has a prerogative to dispense with a law. 2. There is a dispensation of law and justice not flowing from any prerogative, but from the true intent of the law, and thus the king, yea, the inferior judge, is not to take the life of a man whom the letter of the law would condemn, because the justice of the law is the intent and life of the law, and where nothing is done against the intent of the law, there is no breach of any law. 3. The third is not unlike unto the second, when the king exposits the law by grace, and this is twofold: (1) Either when he exposits it of his wisdom and merciful nature, inclined to mercy and justice, yet, according to the just intent, native sense, and scope of the law, considering the occasion, circumstances of the fact, and comparing both with the law, and this dispensation of grace I grant to the king, as when the tribute is great and the man poor, the king may dispense with the custom.[1] (2). The law says in a doubtful case the prince may dispense, because it is presumed the law can have no sense against the principal sense and intent of the law. But there is another dispensation that royalists do plead for, and that is, a power in the king, *ex mera gratia absolutae potestatis regalis*, out of mere grace of absolute royal power to pardon crimes which God's law says should be punished by death. Now, this they call a power of grace, but it is not a power of mere grace.

1. Though princes may do some things of grace, yet not of mere grace, because what kings do as kings, and by virtue of their royal office, that they do *ex debito officii* by debt right of their office, and that they cannot but do, it not being arbitrary to them to do the obligatory acts of their office, but what they do of mere grace that they do as good men, and not as kings, and that they may not do, just as, for example, some kings out of their pretended prerogative have given four pardons to one man for four murders. Now this the king might have left undone without sin, but of mere grace he pardoned the murderer who killed four men. But the truth is, the king killed the three last, because he has no power in point of conscience to dispense with blood (Num. 35:31; Gen. 9:6). These pardons are acts of mere grace to one man, but acts of blood to the community.

2. Because the prince is the minister of God for the good of the subject, and therefore the law says, "He cannot pardon and free the guilty of the punishment due to him; (*Contra l. quod favore, F. de leg, l. non ideo minus, F. de proc, l. legata inutiliter F. de lega. 1)* and the reason is clear: He is but the minister of God, a revenger to execute wrath upon him that does evil. And if the judgment be the Lord's, not man's, not the king's, as it is indeed (Deut. 1:17; 2 Chron. 19:6) he cannot draw the sword against the innocent, nor absolve the guilty, unless he would take on himself to carve and dispose of that which

---

1. Book 1.

is proper to his master. Now certain it is God only, univocally and essentially as God is the judge (Ps. 75:7) and God only and essentially king (Ps. 97:1; 99:1) and all men in relation to him are mere ministers, servants, legates, deputies, and in relation to him, equivocally and improperly, judges or kings, and mere created and breathing shadows of the power of the King of kings. And look, as the scribe following his own device, and writing what sentence he pleases, is not an officer of the court in that point, nor the pen and servant of the judge, so are kings and all judges but forged intruders and bastard kings and judges, insofar as they give out the sentences of men, and are not the very months of the King of kings to pronounce such a sentence as the Almighty himself would do, if he were sitting on the throne or bench.

3. If the king from any supposed prerogative royal may do acts of mere grace without any warrant of law, because he is above law by office, then also may he do acts of mere rigorous justice, and kill and destroy the innocent out of the same supposed prerogative; for God's word equally ties him to the place of a mere minister in doing good, as in executing wrath on evil-doers (Rom. 13:3-4). And reason would say he must be as absolute in the one as in the other, seeing God ties him to the one as to the other by his office and place, yea, by this acts of justice to evil-doers and acts of reward to well-doers shall be arbitrary morally, and by virtue of office to the king, and the word prerogative royal says this; for the word prerogative is a supreme power absolute that is loosed from all law, and so from all reason of law, and depending on the king's mere and naked pleasure and will, and the word royal or kingly is an epithet of office and of a judge, a created and limited judge, and so it must tie this supposed prerogative to law, reason, and to that which is *debitum legale officii* and a legal duty of an office; and by this our masters the royalists make God to frame a rational creature, which they call a king, to frame acts of royalty, good and lawful, upon His own mere pleasure and the super-dominion of his will above a law and reason. And from this

it is that deluded counsellors made king James (a man not of shallow understanding) and king Charles to give pardons to such bloody murderers as James a Grant, and to go so far on by this supposed prerogative royal that king Charles in parliament at Edinburgh, 1633 did command an high point of religion: that ministers should use, in officiating in God's service, such habits and garments as he pleases, that is, all the attire and habits of the idolatrous mass-priests that the Romish priests of Baal uses in the oddest point of idolatry (the adoring of bread) that the earth has, and by this prerogative the king commanded the Service Book in Scotland, anno 1637, without or above law and reason. And I desire any man to satisfy me in this: if the king's prerogative royal may over-leap law and reason in two degrees, and if he may as king, by a prerogative royal, command the body of popery in a popish book; if he may not by the same reason over-leap law and reason by the elevation of twenty degrees; and if you make the king a Julian (God forbid, and may He give the spirit of revelation to our king) may he not command all the Koran and the religion of the heathen and Indians? Royalists say the prerogative of royalty excludes not reason, and makes not the king to do as a brute beast, without all reason, but it gives a power to a king to do by his royal pleasure, not fettered to the dictates of a law; for in things which the king does by his prerogative royal he is to follow the advice and counsel of his wise council, though their counsel and advice does not bind the royal will of the king.

Ans. 1. I answer, it is to me, and I am sure to many more learned, a great question if the will of any reasonable creature, even of the damned angels, can will or choose anything which their reason, corrupted as it is, does not dictate *hic et nunc* to be good? For the object of the will of all men is good, either truly or apparently good to the doer; for the devil could not suit in marriage souls unless he war in the clothes of an angel of light; sin, as sin, cannot sell, or obtrude itself upon any, but under the notion of good. I think it seems good to the great Turk to command innocent men to cast themselves over a precipice two hundred fathoms high into the sea, and drown themselves to pleasure him; so the Turk's reason (for he is rational, if he be a man) dictates to his vast pleasure that that is good which he commands.

2. Counsellors to the king, who will speak what will please the queen, are but naked empty titles, for they speak *que placent non que prosunt*, what may please the king whom they make glad with their lies, not what law and reason dictates.

3. Absoluteness and unreasonable prerogative do not deny counsel and law also, for none more absolute, *de facto* (I cannot say *de jure*) than the kings of Babylon and Persia; for Daniel says of one of them "Whom he would he slew, and whom he would he kept alive, and whom lie would he set up, and whom he would he put down," (Dan. 5:19) and yet these same kings did nothing but by advice of their princes and counsellors, yea, so as they could not alter a decree and law, as is clear (Esth. 1:14-17, 21), yea, Darius, *de facto*, an absolute prince, was not able to deliver Daniel, because the law was passed, that he should be cast into the lions' den (Dan. 6:14-16).

4. That which the Spirit of God condemns as a point of tyranny in Nebuchadnezzar is no lawful prerogative royal; but the Spirit of God condemns this as tyranny in Nebuchadnezzar, that he slew whom he would, he kept alive whom he would, he set up whom he would, he put down whom he would. This is too God-like (Deut. 32:39). So Polanus[1] and Rollocus[2] on the place say, he did these things *Ex abusu legitimae potestatis*; for Nebuchadnezzar's will, in matters of death and life, was his law, and he did what pleased himself, above all law, beside any contrary to it (ver. 19). And our flatterers of kings draw the king's prerogative out of Ulpian's words, who says, "That is a law which seems good to the prince" but Ulpian was far from making the

---

1. On Daniel, section 5, 19.

2. Com. 16, ib.

prince's will a rule of good and ill, for he says the contrary, "That the law rules the just prince."

5. It is considerable here, that Sanchez[1] defines the absolute power of kings to be a plenitude and fullness of power, subject to no necessity, and bounded with rules of no public law; and so did Baldus[2] before him. But all politicians condemn that of Caligula (as Suetonius says[3]) which he spoke to Alexander the Great, "Remember that you must do all things, and that you have a power to do to all men what you please." And lawyers say that this is tyranny. Chilon, one of the seven wise of Greece (as Rodigi[4]) says better, "Princes are like gods, because they only can do that which is just; and this power, being merely tyrannical, can be no ground of a royal prerogative. There is another power (says Sanches) absolute, by which a prince dispenses without a cause in a human law; and this power, says he, may be defended. But he says what the king does by this absolute power he does it *valide*, validly, but not *jure*, by law; but by valid acts the Jesuit must mean royal acts. But no acts void of law and reason (say we) can be royal acts; for royal acts are acts performed by a king, as a king, and by a law, and so cannot be acts above or beside a law. It is true a king may dispense with the breach of a human law, as a human law, that is, if the law be death to any who goes upon the walls of the city, the king may pardon any, who, going up, discovers the enemies approach and saves the city. But, 1. The inferior judge according to the επεικεια, that benign interpretation that the soul and intent of the law requires, may do this as well as the king. 2. All acts of independent prerogative are above a law, and acts of free will having no cause or ground in the law, otherwise it is not founded upon absolute power, but on power ruled by law and reason. But to pardon a breach of the letter of the law of man

---

1. *De matr.*, tom. 1, book 2, dig. 16, n. 3.

2. Book 2, n. 40.

3. *In Calign.* 29.

4. Book 8, *Lect. Antiq.* section 1.

by expositing it according to the true intent of the law, and benignly, is an act of legal obligation, and so of the ordinary power of all judges, and if either king or judge kill a man for the violation of the letter of the law, when the intent of the law contradicts the rigid sentence, he is guilty of innocent blood. If that learned Ferdinandus Vasquez be consulted, he is against this distinction of a power ordinary and extraordinary in men;[5] and certainly if you give to a king a prerogative above a law, it is a power to do evil as well as good, but there is no lawful power to do evil; and Dr. Ferne is plunged in a contradiction by this, for he says "I ask when these emperors took away lives and goods at pleasure? Was that power ordained by God? No, but an illegal will and tyranny; but the power, though abused to execute such a wicked commandment, is an ordinance of God" (sect. 9).

Obj. 1. For the lawfulness of an absolute monarchy, the Eastern, Persian, and Turkish monarchy make absolute monarchy lawful, for it is an oath to a lawful obligatory thing, and judgment is denounced against Judah for breaking the oath of the king of Babylon (Ezek. 17:16, 18), and it is called the oath of God, and doubtless was an oath of absolute subjection; and the power was absolute, and yet the apostle calls it an ordinance of God (Rom. 13). The sovereignty of masters over servants was absolute, and the apostle exhorts not to renounce that title as too rigid, but exhorts to moderation in the use of it.

Ans. 1. That the Persian monarchy was absolute is but a *facto ad jus*, and no rule of a lawful monarchy, but that it was absolute I believe not. Darius (who was an absolute prince, as many think, but I think not) would gladly have delivered Daniel from the power of a law "And he set his heart on Daniel to deliver him, and he labored till the going down of the sun to deliver him," (Dan. 6:14) and was so sorrowful that he could not break through a law that he interdicted himself of all pleasures of musician; and if ever he had used the

---

5. Illust. quest. book 1.26, n. 2.

absoluteness of a prerogative royal, I conceive he would have done it in this, yet he could not prevail. But in things not established by law I conceive Darius was absolute, as to me is clear (Dan 6:24) but absolute not by a divine law, but *de facto, quod transierat in jus humanum,* by fact, which was now become a law.

2. It was God's oath, and God tied Judah to absolute subjection; therefore, people may tie themselves. It follows not, unless you could make good this inference: 1. God is absolute; therefore the king of Babylon may lawfully be absolute. This is a blasphemous consequence. 2. That Judah was to swear the oath of absolute subjection in the latitude of the absoluteness of the kings of Chaldea, I would see proved. Their absoluteness by the Chaldean laws was to command murder, idolatry (Dan. 3:4-5) and to make wicked laws (Dan. 6:7-8). I believe Jeremiah commanded not absolute subjection in this sense, but the contrary (Jer. 10:11). They were to swear the oath in the point of suffering; but what if the king of Chaldea had commanded them all, the whole holy seed, men, women, and children, out of his royal power to give their necks all in one day to his sword, were they obliged by this oath to prayers and tears, and only to suffer? And was it against the oath of God to defend themselves by arms? I believe the oath did not oblige to such absolute subjection, and though they had taken arms in their own lawful defense, according to the law of nature they had not broken the oath of God. The oath was not a tie to an absolute subjection of all and everyone, either to worship idols, or then to fly or suffer death. Now, the Service Book commanded in the king's absolute authority all Scotland to commit grosser idolatry in the intention of the work, if not in the intention of the commander, than was in Babylon. We read not that the king of Babylon pressed the consciences of God's people to idolatry, or that all should either fly the kingdom, and leave their inheritances to papists and prelates, or then come under the mercy of the sword of papists and atheists by sea or land.

3. God may command against the law of nature, and God's commandment makes subjection lawful, so as men may not now, being under that law of God, defend themselves. What then? Therefore that we owe subjection to absolute princes and their power must be a lawful power in no way follows. God's commandment by Jeremiah made the subjection of Judah lawful, and without that commandment they might have taken arms against the king of Babylon, as they did against the Philistines, and God's commandment makes the oath lawful. Suppose Ireland would all rise in arms, and come and destroy Scotland, the king of Spain leading; then we would by this argument not resist.

4. It is denied that the power as absolute is God's ordinance. And I deny utterly that Christ and his apostles did swear non-resistance absolute to the Roman emperor.

Obj. 2. It seems if well-doing be mistaken by the reason and judgment of an absolute monarch for ill-doing (1 Pet. 2:18-19), and we punished, yet the magistrate's will is the command of a reasonable will, and so to be submitted unto, because such a one suffers by law, where the monarch's will is a law, and in this case some power must judge. Now in an absolute monarchy all judgment resolves in the will of the monarch, as the supreme law, and if ancestors have submitted themselves by oath there is no repeal or redressment.

Ans. Whoever was the author of this treatise he is a bad defender of the defensive wars in England, for all the lawfulness of wars then must depend on this: 1. Whether England be a conquered nation at the beginning? 2. If the law-will of an absolute monarch, or a Nero, be a reasonable will, to which we must submit in suffering evil, I see not but we must submit to a reasonable will, if it be reasonable will in doing evil, no less than in suffering evil. 3. Absolute will-in absolute monarchies is no judge de jure, but an unlawful and a usurping judge (1 Pet. 2:18-19). Servants are not commanded simply to suffer. (I can prove suffering formally not to fall under any law of God but only patient suffering. I except Christ, who was under a peculiar commandment to suffer.) But servants, upon supposition that they are servants and buffeted unjustly by their masters are by the apostle Peter commanded (ver. 20) to suffer patiently. But it does not bind up a servant's hand to defend his own life with weapons if his master invade him, without cause, to kill him; otherwise, if God call him to suffer, he is to suffer in the manner and way as Christ did, not reviling, not threatening. 4. To be a king and an absolute master to me are contradictory, A king essentially is a living law; an absolute man is a creature that they call a tyrant, and no lawful king. Yet do I not mean that any that is a king and usurps absoluteness leaves off to be a king; but insofar as he is absolute he is no more a king than insofar as he is a tyrant. But further, the king of England says in a declaration, 1. The law is the measure of the king's powers 2. Parliaments are essentially lord-judges, to make laws essentially, as the king is, therefore, the king is not above the law. 3. *Magna Charta*, says the king, can do nothing but by laws, and no obedience is due to him but by law. 4. Prescriptions takes away the title of conquests.

Obj. 3. The king, not the parliament, is the anointed of God.

Ans. The parliament is as good, even a congregation of gods (Ps. 82:6).

Obj. 4. The parliament in the court in their acts say 'with consent of our sovereign lord.'

Ans. They say not 'at the commandment and absolute pleasure of our sovereign lord'. He is their lord materially, not as they are formally a parliament, for the king made them not a parliament; but sure I am the parliament had power before he was king, and made him king (1 Sam. 10:17-18).

Obj. 5. In an absolute monarchy there is not a resignation of men to any will as will, but to the reasonable will of the monarch, which, having the law of reason to direct it, is kept from injurious acts.

Ans. If reason be a sufficient restraint, and if God has laid no other restraint upon some lawful king, then is magistracy a lame, a needless ordinance of God; for all mankind has reason to keep themselves from injuries, and so there is no need of judges or king to defend them from either doing or suffering injuries. But certainly this must be admirable, if God, as author of nature, should make the lion king of all beasts, the lion remaining a devouring beast, and should ordain by nature all the sheep and lambs to come and submit their bodies to him by instinct of nature, and to be eaten at his will, and then say the nature of a beast in a lion is a sufficient restraint to keep the lion from devouring lambs. Certainly, a king being a sinful man and having no restraint on his power but reason, he may think it reason to allow rebels to kill, drown, hang, torture to death, a hundred thousand protestants, men, women, infants in the womb, and sucking babes, as is clear in Pharaoh, Manasseh, and other princes.

Obj. 6. There is no court or judge above the king; therefore he is absolutely supreme.

Ans. The antecedent is false. 1. The court that made the king from being a private man is above him, and here are limitations laid on him at his coronation. 2. The states of parliament are above him to censure him. 3. In case of open tyranny, though the states had not time to convene in parliament, if he bring on his people a host of Spaniards or foreign rebels, his own conscience is above him, and the conscience of the people far more called *conscientia terra,* may judge him in so far as they may rise up and defend themselves.

Obj. 7. Here the Prelate borrowing from Grotius, Barclay, Arnisaeus (or it is possible he be not so far traveled, for Dr. Ferne has the same) "Sovereignty weakened in aristocracy cannot do its work, and is in the next place to anarchy and confusion. When Zedekiah was overlorded by his nobles, he could neither save himself nor the people, nor the prophet, the servant of God, Jeremiah; nor could David punish Joab when he was overawed by that power he himself had put in his head. To weaken the hand is to distemper the whole body; if any good prince, or his royal ancestors, be cheated of their sacred right by fraud or force, he may at his fittest opportunity resume it. What a sin it is to rob God or the king of their due!" (section 14).

Ans. Aristocracy is no less an ordinance of God than royalty, for 1. All in authority are to be acknowledged as God's viceregents the senate, the consuls, as well as the emperor (Rom. 13. 1, and 1 Tim. 2); and so one ordinance of God cannot weaken another, nor can any but a lawless animal say aristocracy borders with confusion; but he must say order and light are sisters to confusion and darkness. 2. Though Zedekiah, a man void of God, was over-awed by his nobles and so could not help Jeremiah, it follows not that because kings may not do this and this is good, therefore they are to be invested with power to do all ill: if they do all the good that they have power to do, they will find a way to help the oppressed Jeremiahs. And because power to do both good and evil is given by the devil to our Scottish witches, it is a poor consequent that the states should give to the king power absolute to be a tyrant. 3. A state must give a king more power than ordinary, especially to execute laws, which requires unique wisdom, when a prince cannot always have his great council about with him to advise him. 1. That is power borrowed, and by loan, and not properly his own, and therefore it is no sacrilege in the states to resume what the king has by a fiduciary title, and borrowed from them. 2. This power was given to do good, not evil. David had power over Joab to punish him for his murder, but he executed it not upon carnal fears, and abused his power to kill innocent Uriah, which power neither God nor the states gave him. But how proves he the states took power from David, or that Joab took power from David to put to death a murderer? That I see not. 3, If princes' power to do good be taken from them, they may resume it when God gives opportunity; but this is to the Prelate perjury, that the people by oath give away their power to their king and resume it when he abuses it to tyranny. But it is no perjury in the king to resume a taken-away power, which if it be his own is yet *lis sub judice*, a great controversy. *Quod in Cajo licet in Nevio non licet*. So he teaches the king that perjury and sacrilege is lawful to him. If princes' power to do ill and cut the whole land off as one neck (which was the wicked desire of Caligula) be taken from them by the states, I am sure this power was never theirs, and never the people's; and you cannot take the prince's power from him which was never his power; I am also sure the prince should never resume an unjust power, though he were cheated of it.

Popish Prelate. It is a poor shift to acknowledge no more for the royal prerogative than the municipal law has determined, as some smatterers in the law say. They cannot distinguish between a statute declarative and a statute constitutive; but the statutes of a kingdom do declare only what is the prerogative royal, but do not constitute or make it. God Almighty has by himself constituted it. It is laughter to say the decalogue was not a law till God wrote it.

Ans. Here a profound lawyer calls all smatterers in the law, who cannot say that *non ens*, a prerogative royal, that is, a power contrary to God and man's law to kill and destroy the innocent, came not immediately down from heaven. But I profess myself no lawyer; but do maintain against the Prelate that no municipal law can constitute a power to do ill, nor can any law either justly constitute or declare such a fancy as a prerogative royal. So far is it from being like the decalogue, that is, a law before it be written, that this prerogative is neither law before it be written, nor after court-hunters have written for it, for it must be eternal as the decalogue if it have any blood from so noble a house. In what scripture has God Almighty spoken of a fancied prerogative royal?

Popish Prelate: Prerogative rests not in its natural seat, but in the king. God says, *Reddite*, not *Date*, render to kings that which is kings, not give to kings; it shall never be well with us if his anointed and his church be wronged.

Ans. The Prelate may remember a country proverb: he and his prelates (called the church, the scum of men, not the church) are like the tinker's dogs, they like good company: they must be ranked with the king. And hear a false prophet: It shall never be well with the land while arbitrary power and popery be erected, says he, in good sense.

Popish Prelate: The king has his right from God, and cannot make it away to the people. Render to Caesar the things that are Caesar's. Kings' persons, their charge, their right, their authority, their prerogative, are by Scriptures, fathers, jurists, sacred, inseparable ordinances inherent in their crowns, they cannot be made away; and when they are given to inferior judges, it is not *ad minuendam majestatem, sed solicitudinem*, to lessen sovereign majesty, but to ease them (section 16).

Ans. The king has his right from God. What, then not from the people? I read in Scripture, the people made the king, never that the king made the people. All these are inseparably in the crown, but he steals in prerogative royal, in the clause which is now in question, "Render to Caesar all Caesar's;" and therefore, says he, render to him a prerogative, that is, an absolute power to pardon and sell the blood of thousands. Is power of blood either the king's, or inherent inseparably in his crown? Alas! I fear prelates have made blood an inseparable accident of his throne. When kings by that public power given to them at their coronation make inferior judges, they give them power to judge for the Lord, not for men (Deut. 1:17; 2 Chron. 19:6). Now, they cannot both make away a power and keep it also; for the inferior judge's conscience hangs not at the king's girdle. He has no less power to judge in his sphere than the king has in his sphere, though the orb and circle of motion be larger in compass in the one than in the other; and if the king cannot give himself royal power, but God and the people must do it, how can he communicate any part of that power to inferior judges except by trust? Yea, he has not that power that other men have in many respects:

1. He may not marry whom he pleases; for he might give his body to a leper woman, and so hurt the kingdom. 2. He may not do as Solomon and Ahab, marry the daughter of a strange god, to make her the mother of the heir of the crown. He must in this follow his great senate. He may not expose his person to hazard of wars. 3. He may not go over sea and leave his watch-tower without consent. 4. Many acts of parliament of both kingdoms discharge papists to come within ten miles of the king. 5. Some pernicious counsellors have been discharged his company by laws. 6. He may not eat what meats he pleases. 7. He may not make wasters his treasurers. 8. Nor dilapidate the rents of the crown. 9. He may not disinherit his eldest son of the crown at his own pleasure. 10. He is sworn to follow no false gods and false religions, nor is it in his power to go to mass. 11. If a priest say mass to the king, by the law he is hanged, drawn, and quartered. 12. He may not write letters to the Pope by law. 13. He may not by law pardon seducing priests and Jesuits. 14. He may not take medicine for his health unless from physicians, sworn to be true to him. 15. He may not educate his heir as he pleases. 16. He has not power over his children, nor has he that power that other fathers have, to marry his eldest son as he pleases. 17. He may not befriend a traitor. 18. It is high treason for any woman to give her body to the king, unless she is his married wife. 19. He ought not to build sumptuous houses without advice from his council. 20. He may not dwell constantly where he pleases. 21. Nor may he go to the country to hunt, far less to kill his subjects and desert the parliament. 22. He may not confer honors and high places without his council. 23. He may not deprive judges at his will. 24. Nor is it in his power to be buried where he pleases, but among the kings. Now in most of these twenty-four points private persons have their own liberty far less restricted than the king.

QUESTION 24.

WHAT RELATION THE KING HAS TO THE LAW.

Human laws considered as reasonable, or as penal. The king alone has not a legislative power. Subordination of the king to the parliament and co-ordination are both consistent. Each one of the three governments has somewhat from each other, and they cannot be in its prevalence conveniently without the mixture of the other two. The king as a king cannot err, insomuch as he errs, he is not the remedy of oppression intended by God and nature. In the court of necessity the people may judge the king. Human laws are not so obscure as tyranny is visible and discernible. It is more requisite that the whole people, church, and religion be secured than one man. If there be any restraint by law on the king it must be physical, for a moral restraint is upon all men. To swear to an absolute prince as absolute is an oath catenus, unlawful, and not obligatory.

Mr. Symmons says that authority is rooted rather in the prince than in the law; for as the king gives being to the inferior judge, so he does to the law itself, making it authorizable; for *propter quod unum-quodque tale, id ipsum magis tale*, and therefore the king is greater than the law; others say that the king is the fountain of the law, and the sole and only lawgiver (section 6).

Assertion 1. 1. The law has a twofold consideration, (1). *Secundum esse paenale*, in relation to the punishment to be inflicted by man.[1] (2). *Secundum esse legis*, as it is a thing legally good in itself. In the former notion it is this way true: human laws take life and being so as to be punished or rewarded by men, from the will of princes and lawgivers, and so Symmons says true, because men cannot punish or reward laws except where they are made, and the will of rulers puts a sort of stamp on a law: that it brings the commonwealth under guiltiness if they break this law. But this makes not the king greater than the law, for therefore do rulers put the stamp of relation to punishment on the law, because there is intrinsic worth in the law prior to the act of the will of lawgivers for which it merits to be enacted, and therefore because it is authorizable as good and just, the king puts on it this stamp of a political law. God forms being and moral aptitude to the end in all laws, namely, the safety of the people, and the king's will is neither the measure nor the cause of the goodness of kings.

2. If the king be he who makes the law good and just, because he is more such himself then as the law cannot crook, and err, nor sin, neither can the king sin, nor break a law. This is blasphemy; every man is a liar: a law which deserves the name of a law cannot lie.

3. His ground is that there is such majesty in kings that their will must be done either in us or on us. A great untruth: Ahab's will must neither be done by Elijah, for he commands things unjust, nor yet on Elijah, for Elijah fled, and lawfully we may fly tyrants, and so Ahab's will in killing Elijah was not done on him.

Assertion 2. 1. Nor can it be made good that the king alone has power of making laws, because his power would then be absolute to inflict penalties on subjects without any consent of theirs; and that

---

[1] 1. 4. 23.

would be a dominion of masters, who command what they please, and under what pain they please. And the people consenting to be ruled by such a man, they tacitly consent to penalty of laws, because natural reason says an evil-doer should be punished; (*Florianus in l. inde. Vasquez,* 1.2.55, n. 3) therefore they must have some power in making these laws.

2. It is clear the princes judge with the people (Jer. 26). A legistlative power differs gradually only from a judicial power, both being collateral means to the purpose of government: the people's safety. But parliaments judge, therefore they have a legislative power with the king.

3. The parliament gives all supremacy to the king; therefore to prevent tyranny, it must keep a co-ordinate power with the king in the highest acts.

4. If the kingly line be interrupted, if the king be a child or a captive, they make laws who make kings; therefore, this legislative power recurs into the states, as to the first subject.

Obj. The king is the fountain of the law, and subjects cannot make laws to themselves more than they can punish themselves. He is only the supreme.[1]

Ans. The people being the fountain of the king must rather be the fountain of laws. It is false that no man makes laws to himself. Those who teach others teach themselves also (1 Tim. 2:12; 1 Cor. 14:34) though teaching be an act of authority. But they agree to the penalty of the law secondarily only, and so does the king who as a father does not will evil of punishment to his children, but by a consequent will. The king is the only supreme in the power ministerial of executing laws, but this is a derived power, so as no one man is above him; but in the fountain-power of royalty the states are above him.

---

1. Symmons' *Loyal Subjects,* sect. 5.

5. The civil law is clear: that the laws of the emperor have force only from this fountain, because the people have transferred their power to the king (book 1. *digest, tit.* 4, *de constit. Princip. leg.* 1, *sic Ulpian. Quod principi placuit (loquitur de principe formaliter, qua princeps est, non qua est homo) legis habet vigorem, utpote cum legi regia, quce de imperio ejus lata est. populus ei, et in cum, omne suum imperium et potestatem confer-at*). Yea, the emperor himself may be convened before the prince elector (*Aurea Bulla Carol.* 4, *Imper.*). The king of France may be convened before the senate of Paris. The states may resist a tyrant, as Bossius says (*de principe, et privileg. ejus*, n. 65. *Paris de puteo, in tract, syno. tit. de excess. reg.* section 3). Divines acknowledge that Elijah rebuked the halting of Israel between God and Baal, that their princes permitted Baal's priests to converse with the king. And is not this the sin of the land, that they suffer their king to worship idols? And therefore the land is punished for the sins of Manasseh, as Knox observes in his dispute with Lethington, where he proves that the states of Scotland should not permit the queen of Scotland to have her abominable mass (*Hist. of Scotland*). Surely the power or the prerogative of a sleepy or mad pilot to split the ship on a rock, as I conceive, is limited by the passengers. Suppose a father in a distemper set his own house on fire, and burn himself and his ten sons, I conceive his fatherly prerogative, which neither God nor nature gave, should not be looked to in this, but may bind him. Yea, Althusius, answering this, "That in democracy the people cannot both command and obey," says, "It is true, *secundum idem ad idem et eodem tempore.* But the people may (says he) choose magistrates by succession" (*Polit.* 39). Yea, I say, 1. They may change rulers yearly to remove envy: a yearly king would be more dangerous, the king being almost above envy. Men incline more to flatter than to envy kings. 2. Aristotle says he people may give their judgment of the wisest (*Polit.* 1.4.4; 1.6.2).

Obj. 1. Williams, bishop of Ossory, *in vindic. Reg* (a looking-glass for rebels) says, "To say the king is better than anyone does not prove him to be better than two, and if his supremacy be no more, then any other may challenge as much, for the prince is *singulis major*. A lord is above all knights; a knight above all esquires; and so the people have placed a king under them, not above them.

Ans. The reason is not alike: 1. For all the knights united cannot make one lord, and all the esquires united cannot make one knight; but all the people united made David king at Hebron.

2. The king is above the people by eminence of derived authority as a watchman, and in actual supremacy; and he is inferior to them in fountain-power, as the effect to the cause.

Obj. 2. The parliament (says Williams) "may not command the king; why then make they supplication to him, if their vote be a law?

Ans. They supplicate, *ex decentia*, of decency and convenience for his place, as a city supplicate a lord mayor, but they supplicate not *ex debito* of obligation, as beggars seek alms, then should they be cyphers. When a subject oppressed supplicates his sovereign tor justice, the king is obliged by office to give justice; and to hear the oppressed is not an act of grace and mercy, as to give alms, though it should proceed from mercy in the prince (Ps. 72:13) but an act of royal debt.

Obj. 3. The Popish Prelate objects: The most you claim to parliament is a co-ordinate power, which in law and reason run in equal terms. In law, *par in parem non habet imperium*; an equal cannot judge an equal, much less may an inferior usurp to judge a superior. Our Lord knew, *gratia visionis* the woman taken in adultery to be guilty, but he would not sentence her; to teach us, not improbably, not to be both judge and witness. The parliament are judges, accusers, and witnesses against the king in their own cause, against the imperial laws (section 9).

Ans. 1. The parliament is co-ordinate ordinarily with the king in the power of making laws, but the co-ordination on the king's part is by derivation on the parliament's part, *originaliter et fontaliter*, as in the fountain.

2. In ordinary there is coordination, but if the king turn tyrant, the estates are to use their fountain-power. And that of the law, *par in parem*, &c. is no better from his pen, that steals all he has, than from Barclay, Grotius, Arnisaeus, Blackwood, &c.: it is cold and sour. We hold the parliament that made the king at Hebron to be above their own creature, the king. Barclay says more accurately, "It is absurd that the people should both be subject to the king, and command the king also (*Contra Monarch.* 1.6).

Ans. 1. It is not absurd that a father natural, as a private man, should be subject to his son: even that Jesse, and his elder brother, the lord of all the rest, be subject to David their king. Royalists say, Our late queen, being supreme magistrate, might by law have put to death her own husband for adultery or murder. 2. The parliament should not be both accuser, judge, and witness in their own cause. 1. It is the cause of religion, of God, of protestants, and of the whole people. 2. The oppressed accuse; there is no need of witnesses in raising arms against the subjects. 3. The Popish Prelate could not object this, if against the imperial laws the king were both party and judge in his own cause, and in these acts of arbitrary power, which he has done through bad counsel, in wronging fundamental laws, raising arms against his subjects, bringing in foreign enemies into both his king-doms, &c. Now this is properly the cause of the king, as he is a man, and his own cause, not the cause of God; and by no law of nature, rea-son, or imperial statutes can he be both judge and party. 4. If the kind be sole supreme judge without any fellow sharers in power. (1) He is not obliged by law to follow counsel or hold parliaments; for counsel is not command. (2) It is impossible to limit him even in the exercises of his power, which yet Dr. Ferne says cannot be said; for if any of his power be retrenched, God is robbed says Maxwell. (3) He may by law play the tyrant *gratis*. Ferne objects the king is a fundamental with the estates; now foundations are not to be stirred or removed (section 7).

Ans. The king as king, inspired with law, is a fundamental, and his power is not to be stirred, but as a man wasting his people, he is a destruction to the house and community, and not a fundamental in that notion.

Some object: The three estates, as men and looking to their own ends, not to law and the public good, are not fundamentals, and are to be judged by the king.

Ans. By the people, and the conscience of the people, they are to be judged.

Obj. But the people also do judge as corrupt men, and not as the people, and a political body providing for their own safety.

Ans. I grant all; when God will bring a vengeance on Jerusalem, prince and people both are hardened to their own destruction. Now God has made all three. In every government where there is democracy, there are some chosen ones resembling an aristocracy, and some one for order, presiding in democratic courts, resembling a king. In aristocracy, as in Holland, there is something of a democracy: the people have their commissioners, and one duke or general, as the prince of Orange is some shadow of royalty; and in monarchy there are the three estates of parliament, and these contain the three estates, and so are something of the three forms of government, and there is no one government just that has not some of all three. Power and absolute monarchy are tyranny; unmixed democracy is confusion; untempered aristocracy is factious dominion; and a limited monarchy has from democracy respect to public good without confusion. From aristocracy safety in multitude of counsels without factious emulation, and so a bar laid on tyranny by the joint powers of many, and from sovereignty union of many children in one father, and all the three thus contempered have their own sweet fruits through God's blessing, and their own diseases by accident, and through men's corruption, and neither reason nor Scripture shall warrant anyone in its rigid purity without mixture. And God having chosen the best government to

bring men fallen in sin to happiness must warrant in any one a mixture of all three, as in mixed bodies the four elements are reduced to a
fit temper resulting in all the four, where the acrimony of all the four
first qualities is broken and the good of all combined in one.

1. The king, as the king, is an unerring and living law, and by grant
of Barclay, of old, was one of excellent parts, and noble through virtue
and goodness; and the goodness of a father as a father, of a tutor as
a tutor, of a head as a head, of a husband as a husband, do befit the
king as a king; so as king, he is the law itself, commanding, governing,
saving.[1]

2. His will as king, or his royal will, is reason, conscience, law.

3. This will is politically present (when his person is absent) in all
parliaments, courts, and inferior judicatures.

4. The king, as king, cannot do wrong or violence to any.

5. Among the Romans the name king and tyrant were common
to one thing. (1) Because, *de facto* some of their kings were tyrants, in
respect of their dominion, rather than kings (2) Because he who was
a tyrant *de facto* should have been, and was a king too *de jure*.

6. It is not lawful either to disobey or resist a king as a king, no
more than it is lawful to disobey a good law.

7. What violence, what injustice and excess of passion the king
mixes in with his acts of government are merely accidental to a king
as king, for because men by their own innate goodness will not, yea,
morally cannot do that which is lawful and just one to another, and
do naturally, since the fall of man, violence one to another; therefore
if there had not been sin, there should not have been need of a king,
more than there should have been need of a tutor to defend the child
whose father is not dead, or of a physician to cure sickness where
there is health; for remove sin, and there is neither death nor sickness;
but because sin has entered into the world, God devised, as a remedy

---

1. Barclay, *Adversus Monarcho. book 1.*

of violence and injustice, a living, rational, breathing law, called a king, a judge, a father. Now the aberrations, violence, and oppression of this thing which is the living, rational, breathing law, is no medium, no means intended by God and nature to remove violence. How shall violence remove violence? Therefore an unjust king, as unjust, is not that genuine ordinance of God appointed to remove injustice, but accidental to a king. So we may resist the injustice of the king, and not resist the king.

8. If then any cast off the nature of a king and become habitually a tyrant, so far it is not from God, nor any ordinance which God does own. If the office of a tyrant (to speak so) be contrary to a king's offices, it is not from God, and so neither is the power from God.

9. Yea, laws (which are no less from God than the king's are) when they begin to be hurtful, *cessant materialiter* they leave off to be laws, because they oblige *non secundum vim verborum, sed in vim sensus*, not according to the force of words, but according to sense, l. *non figura literarum F. de actione et obligatione, l. ita stipulatus*. But who (says the royalists) shall be judge between the king and the people, when the people allege that the king is a tyrant.

Ans. There is a court of necessity no less than a court of justice, and the fundamental laws must then speak, and it is with the people in this extremity, as if they had no ruler.

Obj. 1. But if the law be doubtful, as all human, all civil, all municipal laws may endure great dispute, the peremptory person expositing the law must be the supreme judge. This cannot be the people; therefore it must be the king.

Ans. 1. As the Scriptures in all fundamentals are clear, and exposit themselves, and *actu primo* condemn heresies, so all laws of men in their fundamentals, which are the law of nature and of nations are clear, and, 2. Tyranny is more visible and intelligible than heresy, and is soon decerned. If a king bring in upon his native subjects twenty thousand Turks armed, and the king lead them, it is evident they come not to make a friendly visit to salute the kingdom and depart in peace. The people have a natural throne of policy in their conscience to give warning, and materially sentence against the king as a tyrant, and so by nature are to defend themselves. Where tyranny is more obscure and the thread small, that it escape the eye of men, the king keeps possession, but I deny that tyranny can be obscure long.

Obj. 2. Dr. Ferne: A king may not, or cannot easily alter the frame of fundamental laws, he may make some actual invasion in some transient and unfixed acts, and it is safer to bear these, than to raise a civil war of the body against the head (section 6).

Ans. 1. If the king, as king, may alter any one wholesome law, by that same reason he may alter all. 2. You give short wings to an arbitrary prince, if he cannot overfly all laws to the subversion of the fundamentals of a state, if you make him, as you do (1) one who has the sole legislative power who allenarly[1] by himself makes laws, and his parliament and council are only to give him advice, which by law he may as easily reject as they can speak words to him, he may in one transient act (and it is but one) cancel all laws made against idolatry and popery, and command, through bad counsel in all his dominions the Pope to be acknowledged as Christ's vicar, and all his doctrine to be established as the catholic true religion. It is but one transient act to seal a pardon to the shedding of the blood of two hundred thousand killed by papists. (2) If you make him a king, who may not be resisted in any case, and though he subvert all fundamental laws, he is accountable to God only: his people have no remedy but prayers or flight.

Obj. 3. Ferne: Limitations and mixtures in monarchies do not imply a forcible restraining power in subjects, for the prevention of the dissolution of the state, but only a legal restraining power, and if such a restraining power be in the subjects by reservation, then it must be

---

1. Solely

expressed in the constitution of the government, and in the covenant between the monarch and his people. But such a condition is unlawful, which will not have the sovereign power secured is unprofitable for king and people, a seminary for seditions and jealousies (section 6).

Ans. 1. I understand not a difference between forcible restraining and legal restraining: for he must mean by "legal," man's law, because he says it is a law in the covenant between the monarch and his people. Now, if this be not forcible and physical, it is only moral in the conscience of the king, and a cipher[1] and a mere vanity; for God, not the people, puts a restraint of conscience on the King, that he may not oppress his poor subjects; but he shall sin against God—that is a poor restraint: the goodness of the king, a sinful man, inclined from the womb to all sin, and so to tyranny, is no restraint.

2. There is no necessity that the reserve be expressed in the covenant between king and people, more than in contract of marriage between a husband and a wife; beside her jointure, you should set down this clause in the contract: that if the husband attempt to kill the wife, or the wife the husband, in that case it shall be lawful to either of them to part company. For Dr. Ferne says, "That personal defense is lawful in the people, if the king's assault be sudden, without pretense of law, or inevitable." Yet the reserve of this power of defense is not necessarily to be expressed in the contract between king and people. Demands of the law of nature cannot be set down in positive covenants; they are presupposed.

3. He says, "A reservation of power by which sovereignty is not secured is unlawful." Lend me this argument: the giving away of a power of defense, and a making the king absolute is unlawful, because by it the people are not secured, but one man has by it the sword of God put in his hand, by which *ex officio* he may as king cut the throats of thousands and be accountable to none for it, but to God

---

1. Zero.

only. Now if the non-securing of the king make a condition unlawful, the non-securing of a kingdom and church, yea, of the true region (which are infinitely in worth above one single man) may far more make the condition unlawful.

4. A legal restraint on a king is no more unprofitable, and a seminary of jealousies between king and people, than a legal restraint upon people; for the king, out of a non-restraint, as out of seed, may more easily introduce tyranny and subversion of religion. If outlandish women tempt even a Solomon to idolatry, as people may introduce sedition out of a legal restraint laid upon a king, to say nothing that tyranny is a more dangerous sin than sedition, by how much more the lives of many and true religion are to be preferred to the safety of one and a false peace.

Obj. 4. An absolute monarch is free from all forcible restraint, and so far as he is absolute from all legal restraints of positive laws. Now in a limited monarch, there is only sought a legal restraint, and limitation cannot infer a forcible restraint, for an absolute monarch is limited also, not by civil compact, but by the law of nature and nations, which he cannot justly transgress. If therefore an absolute monarch, being exorbitant, may not be resisted because he transgresses the law of nature, how shall we think a limited monarch may be resisted for transgressing the bounds set by civil agreement.

Ans. 1. A legal restraint on the people is a forcible restraint, for if law be not backed with force, it is only a law of rewarding well-doing, which is no restraint, but an encouragement to do evil. If, then, there be a legal restraint upon the king, without any force, it is no restraint, but only such a request as this: be a just prince, and we will give your majesty two subsidies in one year.

2. I utterly deny that God ever ordained such an irrational creature as an absolute monarch. If a people unjustly and against nature's dictates make away irrevocably their own liberty, and the liberty of their posterity, which is not theirs to dispose off, and set over themselves

as base slaves, a sinning creature with absolute power, he is their king, but not as he is absolute, and that he may not be forcibly resisted, notwithstanding the subjects did swear to his absolute power (which oath in the point of absoluteness is unlawful, and so not obligatory) I utterly deny.

3. An absolute monarch (says he) is limited, but by law of nature. That is, Master Doctor, he is not limited as a monarch, not as an absolute monarch, but as a son of Adam, he is under the limits of the law of nature, which he should have been under though he had never been a king all his days, but a slave. But what then? Therefore, he cannot be resisted. Yes, Doctor, by your own grant he can be resisted: if he invade an innocent subject (say you) suddenly, without pretense of law, or inevitably; and that because he transgresses the law of nature. You say a limited monarch can less be resisted for transgressing the bounds set by civil agreement. But what if the thus limited monarch transgress the law of nature, and subvert fundamental laws? He is then, you seem to say, to be resisted. It is not for simple transgression of a civil agreement that he is to be resisted. The limited monarch is as essentially the Lord's anointed, and the power ordained of God, as the absolute monarch. Now resistance by all your grounds is unlawful, because of God's power and place conferred upon him, not because of men's positive covenant made with him.

To find out the essential difference between a king and a tyrant, we are to observe that it is one thing to sin against a man, another thing against a state. David, killing Uriah, committed an act of murder. But upon this supposition that David is not punished for that murder, he did not so sin against the state, and catholic good of the state, that he turns tyrant and ceases to be a lawful king. A tyrant is he who habitually sins against the catholic good of the subjects and state, and subverts law. Such a one should not be, as Jason, of whom it is said by Aeneas Silvius, *Graviter ferebat si non regnaret, quasi nesciret esse privatus.* When such as are monstrous tyrants are not taken away by the estates, God pursues them in wrath. Domitian was killed by his own family, his wife knowing of it; Aurelianus was killed with a thunderbolt; Darius was drowned in a river; Dioclesian, fearing death, poisoned himself; Salerius died eaten with worms, the end also of Herod and Antiochus; Maxentius was swallowed up in a standing river; Julian died, being stricken through with a dart thrown at him, whether by a man or an angel it is not known; Valens, the Arian, was burnt with fire in a little village by the Goths; Anastasius, the Eutychian emperor, was stricken by God with thunder; Gundericus Vandalus, when he rose against the church of God, being apprehended by the devil, died. Sometime the state has taken order with tyrants: the empire was taken from Vitellius, Heliogabalus, Maximinus, Didius, Julianus; so was the two *Childerici* of France served; so were also Sigebertus, Dagabertus, and Luodovic II of France, Christiernus of Denmark, Mary of Scotland, who killed her husband and raised forces against the kingdom; so was Henricus Valesius of Poland for flying the kingdom; Sigismundus of Poland for violating his faith to the states.

QUESTION 25.

WHETHER THE SUPREME LAW, THE SAFETY OF THE PEOPLE, IS ABOVE THE KING

The safety of the people is to be preferred to the king, for the king is not to seek himself, but the good of the people. Royalists make no kings but tyrants. How the safety of the king is the safety of the people. A king, for the safety of the people, may break through the letter and paper of the law. The king's prerogative above law and reason is not comparable to the blood that has been shed in Ireland and England. The power of dictators proves not a prerogative above law.

The law of the twelve tables is, *salus populi, suprema lex.* The safety of the people is the supreme and cardinal law to which all laws are to stoop. And that from these reasons:

1. *Originally*: Because if the people be the first author, fountain, and efficient under God, of law and king, then their own safety must be principally sought, and their safety must be far above the king, as the safety of a cause, especially of a universal cause, such as is the people, must be more than the safety of one, as Aristotle says (*polit.*1.3, alias 1.5) ου μητι πεφυκε το μερος υπερεχειν του παντος: "The part cannot be more excellent than the whole," nor the effect above the cause.

2. *Finaliter.* This supreme law must stand; for if all law, policy, magistrates, and power be referred to the people's good as the end (Rom. 13:4) and to their quiet and peaceable life in godliness and honesty, then must this law stand as of more worth than the king, as the end is of more worth than the means leading to the end, for the end is the measure and rule of the goodness of the means, and, *finis ultimus in influxu est potentissimus,* the king is good, because he conduces much for the safety of the people; therefore, the safety of the people must be better.

3. By way of limitation: because no law in its letter has force where the safety of the subject is in hazard; and if law or king be destructive to the people, they are to be abolished. This is clear in a tyrant or a wicked man.

4. In the desires of the most holy: Moses, a prince, desired for the safety of God's people, and rather than God should destroy his people that his name should be razed out of the book of life; and David says "Let your hand, I pray you, Lord my God, be on me, and on my father's house; but not on your people, that they should be plagued" (1 Chron. 21:17). This being a holy desire of these two public spirits, the object must be in itself true, and the safety of God's people and their happiness must be of more worth than the salvation of Moses and the life of David and his father's house.

The Prelate borrows an answer to this (section 16)—for he has none of his own—from Dr. Ferne (sect. 7): The safety of the subjects is the prime end of the constitution of government, but it is not the sole and adequate end of government in monarchy: for that is the safety of both king and people. And it befits the king to proportion his laws for their good, and it becomes the people to proportion all their obedience, actions, and endeavors for the safety, honor, and happiness of the king. It is impossible the people can have safety when sovereignty is weakened.

Ans. The Prelate would have the other half of the end, why a king is set over a people, to be the safety and happiness of the king, as well as the safety of the people. This is new logic indeed: that one and the same thing should be the means and the end. The question is for what end is a king made so happy as to be exalted king? The Prelate answers, he is made happy that he may be happy, and made a king that he may be made a king. Now is the king as king, to intend this half end? That is, whether or not he accepts the burden of setting his head and shoulders under the crown, for this end: that he may not only make the people happy, but also that he may make himself rich and honorable above his brethren, and enrich himself? I believe not: but that he feed the people of God; for if he intend himself, and his own honor, it is the intention of the man who is king, and *intentio operantis*, but it is not the intention of the king, as the king, or *intentio operis*. The king, as a king, is formally and essentially the "minister of God for our good," (Rom. 13:4; 1 Tim. 2:2) and cannot come under any notion as a king, but as a means, not as an end, nor as that which he is, to seek himself. I conceive God did forbid this in the molding of the first king (Deut. 17:18-19, 26). He is a minister by office, and one who receives honor and wages for this work, that, *ex officio* he may feed his people. But the Prelate says the people are to intend his riches and honor. I cannot say but the people may intend to honor the king; but the question is not whether the people be to refer the king and his government as a means to honor the king? I conceive not. But that end which the people, in obeying the king, in being ruled by him, may intend, is "That under him they may lead a quiet and peaceable life, in all godliness and honesty" (1 Tim. 2:2). And God's end in giving a king is the good and safety of His people.

Popish Prelate: To reason from the one part and end of monarchical government, the safety of the subjects, to the destruction and weakening of the other part of the end, the power of sovereignty and the royal prerogative, is a caption *a divisis*. If the king be not happy, and invested with the full power of a head, the body cannot be well. By anti-monarchists, the people at the beginning were necessitated to commit themselves, lives and fortunes, to the government of a king, because of themselves they had not wisdom and power enough to do it, and therefore, they enabled him with honor and power, without which he could not do this, being assured that he could not choose, but most earnestly and carefully endeavor this end, namely, his own and the people's happiness; therefore, the safety of the people issues from the safety of the king, as the life of the natural body from the soul. Weak government is near to anarchy. Puritans will not say, *Quovis modo esse, etiam paenale* is better than *non esse*: the Scripture says the contrary; it were better for some never to have been born than to be. Tyranny is better than no government (section 16).

Ans. 1. He knows not sophisms of logic who calls this argument *a divisis*; for the king's honor is not the end of the king's government. He should seek the safety of state and church, not himself; he himself is a private end, and a step to tyranny.

2. The Prelate lies when he makes us to reason from the safety of the subject to the destruction of the king. Ferne, Barclay, Grotius taught the hungry scholar to reason so. Where read he this? The people must be saved, that is the supreme law, therefore, destroy the king. The devil and the Prelate both shall not fasten this on us. But thus we reason: when the man who is the king endeavors not the end of his royal place, but through bad counsel, the subversion of laws, religion, and bondage of the kingdom, the free elites are to join with him for that end of safety, according as God has made them heads of tribes and princes of the people, and if the king refuse to join with them, and will not do his duty, I see not how they are in conscience liberated before God from doing their part.

3. If the Popish Prelate call resisting the king by lawful defensive wars the destruction of the head, he speaks with the mouth of one excommunicated and delivered up to Satan.

4. We endeavor nothing more than the safety and happiness of the king as king; but his happiness is not to suffer him to destroy his subjects, subvert religion, arm papists who have slaughtered above two hundred thousand innocent protestants, only for the profession of that true religion which the king has sworn to maintain. Not to rise in arms to help the king against these were to gratify him as a man, but to be accessory to his soul's destruction as a king.

5. That the royal prerogative is the end of a monarchy ordained by God, neither Scripture, law, nor reason can admit.

6. The people are to intend the safety of other judges as well as the king's. If parliaments be destroyed, whose it is to make laws and kings, the people can neither be safe, free to serve Christ, nor happy.

7. It is a lie that people were required at the beginning to commit themselves to a king; for we read of no king while Nimrod arose: fathers of families (who were not kings), and others, did govern till then.

8. It was not want of wisdom (for in many, and in the people, there must be more wisdom than in one man) but rather corruption of nature and reciprocation of injuries that created kings and other judges.

9. The king shall better compass his end, namely, the safety of the people, with limited power (*placent mediocria*) and with other judges added to help him (Num. 11:14, 16; Deut. 1:12-15) than to put in one man's hand absolute power; for a sinful man's head cannot bear so much new wine, such as exorbitant power is.

10. He is a base flatterer who says the king cannot choose, but earnestly and carefully endeavor his own and the people's happiness; that is, the king is an angel, and cannot sin and decline from the duties of a king. Of the many kings of Judah and Israel, how many chose this? All the good kings that have been may be written in a gold ring.

11. The people's safety depends indeed on the king, as a king and a happy governor; but the people shall never be fattened to eat the wind of an imaginary prerogative royal.

12. Weak government, that is, a king with a limited power, who has more power about his head than within his head, is a strong king, and far from anarchy.

13. I know not what he means, but his master Arminius's way and words are here, for Arminians say, "Being in the damned, eternally tormented, is no benefit; it were better they never had being than to be eternally tormented;"[1] and this they say to the defiance of the doctrine of eternal reprobation, in which we teach that though by accident and because of the damned's abuse of being and life, it would to them be better not to be, as is said of Judas, yet simpliciter comparing being with non-being, and considering the eternity of miserable being in relation to the absolute liberty of the Former of all things, who makes use of the sinful being of clay-vessels for the illustration of the glory of his justice and power (Rom. 9:17, 22; 1 Pet. 2:8; Jude 5:4) it is a censuring of God and his unsearchable wisdom, and a condemning of the Almighty of cruelty (God avert blasphemy of the unspotted and holy Majesty) who by Arminian grounds keeps the damned in life and being to be fuel eternally for Tophet, to declare the glory of His justice. But the Prelate preferred to go out of his way to salute and gratify a proclaimed enemy of free grace, Arminius, and thus he would infer that the king, lacking his prerogative royal and fullness of absolute power to do wickedly, is in a penal and miserable condition, and that it would be better for the king to be a tyrant with absolute liberty to destroy and save alive at his pleasure, as is said of a tyrant (Dan. 5:19) than to be no king at all. And here consider a principle of royalists' court faith: 1. The king is no king, but a lame and miserable judge, if he have not irresistible power to waste and destroy. 2. The king cannot be happy, nor the people safe, nor can the king do good in saving the needy, unless he have the uncontrollable and unlimited power of a tyrant to crush the poor and needy and lay waste

---

1. *Jac. Armini. Declar. Remonstrant.*

the mountain of the Lord's inheritance. Such court-ravens who feed upon the souls of living kings are more cruel than ravens and vultures, who are but dead carcasses.

Williams, bishop of Ossory, answers to the maxim, *Salus populi*, &c. "No wise king but will carefully provide for the people's safety, because his safety and honor is included in theirs, his destruction in theirs." And it is, says Lipsius, *egri animi proprium nihil diu pati*, Absalom was persuaded there was no justice in the land when he intends rebellion; and the poor Prelate, following him, spends pages to prove that goods, life, chastity, and fame depend on the safety of the king, as the breath of our nostrils, our nurse-father, our head, corner-stone, and judge (section 17.6, 18.1). The reason why all disorder was in church and state was not because there was no judge, no government; none can be so stupid as to imagine that. But because, 1. They wanted the most excellent of governments. 2. Because aristocracy was weakened so that there was no right. No doubt priests there were, but either they would not serve, or were over-awed (Hos. 4). No doubt in those days they had judges, but priests and judges were stoned by a rascally multitude, and they were not able to rule; therefore it is most consonant to Scripture to say. *Salus regis suprema populi salus*, the safety of the king and his prerogative royal is the safest sanctuary for the people. So Hos. 3:4; Lament. 2:9.

Ans. 1. The question is not of the wisdom, but of the power of the king, if it should be bounded by no law.

2. The flatterer may know, there be more foolish kings in the world than wise, and that kings misled by idolatrous queens, and by name Ahab ruined himself, and his posterity and kingdom.

3. The salvation and happiness of men standing in the exalting of Christ's throne and the gospel; therefore every king and every man will exalt the throne, and so let them have an uncontrollable power without constraint of law to do what they list, and let no bounds be

set to kings over subjects. By this argument their own wisdom is a law
to lead them to heaven.

4. It is not Absalom's mad malcontents in Britain, but there was really no justice to protestants, all indulgence to papists, popery, Arminianism, idolatry printed, preached, professed, rewarded by authority,
parliaments and church assemblies; the bulwarks of justice and religion were denied, dissolved, crushed, &c.

5. That by a king he understands a monarch (Judg. 17!) and that
such a one as Saul, of absolute power, and not a judge, cannot be
proved, for there were no kings in Israel in the judges' days, the government not being changed till near the end of Samuel's government.

6. And that they had no judges, he says, it is not imaginable. But I
rather believe God than the Prelate. Everyone did what was right in
his own eyes, because there was none to put evil-doers to shame. Possibly the estates of Israel governed some way for mere necessity, but
wanting a supreme judge, which they should have, they were loose;
but this was not because where there is no king, as Popish Prelate
would insinuate, there was no government, as is clear.

7. Of tempered and limited monarchy I think as honorably as the
Prelate, but that absolute and unlimited monarchy is more excellent
than aristocracy, I shall then believe when royalists shall prove such a
government, insofar as it is absolute, to be of God.

8. That aristocracy was now weakened I believe not, seeing God
so highly commends it, and calls it his own reigning over his people
(1 Sam. 8:7). The weakening of it through abuse is not to a purpose,
more than the abuse of monarchy.

9. No doubt, says he (Hos. 4), they were priests and judges, but they
were over-awed, as they are now. I think he would say (Hos. 3:4) otherwise he cites Scripture sleeping, that the priests of Antichrist be not
only over-awed, but out of the earth. I yield that the king be limited,
not over-awed, I think God's law and man's law allows.

10. The safety of the king as king is not only safety, but a blessing to church and state, and therefore this Popish Prelate and his fellows deserve to be hanged before the sun, who have led him on a war to destroy him and his protestant subjects. But the safety and flourishing of a king in the exercises of an arbitrary unlimited power against law and religion and to the destruction of his subjects is not the safety of the people, nor the safety of the king's soul, which these men, if they be the priests of the Lord, should care for.

The Prelate comes to refute the learned and worthy Observator. The safety of the people is the supreme law; therefore the king is bound in duty to promote all and every one of his subjects to all happiness. The Observator has no such inference, the king is bound to promote some of his subjects, even as king, to a gallows, especially Irish rebels, and many bloody malignants. But the Prelate will needs have God rigorous (hallowed be his name) if it be so; for it is impossible to the tenderest-hearted father to do so. Actual promotion of all is impossible. That the king intend it of all his subjects, as good subjects, by a throne established on righteousness and judgment is that which the worthy Observator means. Other things here are answered. The sum of his second answer is a repetition of what he has said. I give my word, in a pamphlet of one hundred and ninety-four pages, I never saw more idle repetitions of one thing twenty times before said, but he says, "The safety of the king and his subjects, in the moral notion, may be esteemed morally the same, no less than the soul and the body make one personal subsistence."

Ans. This is strange logic. The king and his subjects are *ens per aggregationem*, and the king, as king, has one moral subsistence, and the people another. Has the father and the son, the master and the servant, one moral subsistence? But the man speaks of their well-being, and then he must mean that our king's government that was not long ago, and is yet, namely, the popery, Arminianism, idolatry, cutting off men's ears and noses, banishing, imprisonment for speaking against

popery, arming of papists to slay protestants, pardoning the blood of
Ireland, that I fear, shall not be soon taken away, &c., is identically the
same with the life, safety, and happiness of protestants. Then life and
death, justice and injustice, idolatry and sincere worship, are identically one, as the soul of the Prelate and his body are one.

The third is but a repetition. The acts of royalty (says the Observator) are acts of duty and obligation; therefore, not acts of grace properly so called; therefore we may not thank the king for a courtesy. This
is no consequence. What fathers do to children are acts of natural
duty and of natural grace, and yet children owe gratitude to parents,
and subjects to good kings, in a legal sense. No, but in way of courtesy
only. The observator said the king is not a father to the whole collective body, and it is well said he is son to them, and they his maker.
Who made the king? Policy answers the state made him, and divinity,
God made him.

The Observator said well, the people's weakness is not the king's
strength. The Prelate says. Amen. He said that that perishes not to
the king which is granted to the people. The Prelate denies, because
what the king has in trust from God the king cannot make away to
another, nor can any take it from him without sacrilege.

Ans. True indeed, if the king had royalty by immediate trust and
infusion by God, as Elijah had the spirit of prophecy, that he cannot make away. Royalists dream that God, immediately from heaven,
now infuses faculty and right to crowns without any word of God. It
is enough to make an enthusiast leap up to the throne and kill kings.
Judge if these fanatics be favorers of kings. But if the king have royalty
mediately by the people's free consent from God, there is no reason
but people give as much power, even by ounce weights (for power
is strong wine and a great mocker) as they know a weak man's head
will bear and no more. Power is not an immediate inheritance from
heaven, but a birthright of the people borrowed from them; they may
let it out for their good, and resume it when a man is drunk with it.

The man will have it conscience on the king to fight and destroy his three kingdoms for a dream, his prerogative above law. But the truth is prelates do engage the king, his house, honor, subjects, church, for their cursed miters.

The Prelate vexes the reader with repetitions, and says the king must proportion his government to the safety of the people on the one hand, and to his own safety and power on the other hand.

Ans. What the king does as king, he does it for the happiness of his people. The king is a relative; yea, even his own happiness that he seeks, he is to refer to the good of God's people. He says farther the safety of the people endues the safety of the king, because the word *populus* is so taken, which he proves by a raw, sickly rabble of words, stolen out of Passerat's dictionary. His father, the schoolmaster, may whip him for frivolous etymologies.

This supreme law, says the Prelate, is not above the law of prerogative royal, the highest law, nor is *rex* above *lex*. The democracy of Rome had a supremacy above laws, to make and unmake laws; and will they force this power on a monarch, to the destruction of sovereignty?

Ans. This, which is stolen from Spalato, Barclay, Grotius, and others is easily answered. The supremacy of people is a law of nature's self-preservation, above all positive laws, and above the king, and is to regulate sovereignty, not to destroy it. If this supremacy of majesty was in people before they have a king, then, 1. They lose it not by a voluntary choice of a king, for a king is chosen for good, and not for the people's loss; therefore, they must retain this power, in habit and potency, even when they have a king. 2. Then supremacy of majesty is not a beam of divinity proper to a king only. 3. Then the people, having royal sovereignty virtually in them, make and so unmade a king, all which the Prelate denies.

This supreme law (says the Prelate, begging it from Spalato, Amisaeus, Grotius) advances the king, not the people; and the sense is the kingdom is really some time in such a case that the sovereign must exercise an arbitrary power and not stand upon private men's interests, or transgressing of laws made for the private good of individuals, but for the preservation of itself and the public may break through all laws. This he may in the case when sudden foreign invasion threatens ruin inevitably to king and kingdom: a physician may rather cut a gangrened member than suffer the whole body to perish. The dictator in case of extreme dangers (as Livy and Dion. Halicarnast show us) had power according to his own arbitrament, had a sovereign commission in peace and war, of life, death, persons, &c., not co-ordinate, not subordinate to any.

Ans. 1. It is not an arbitrary power, but naturally tied and fettered to this same supreme law, *salus populi*, the safety of the people, that a king break: through not the law, but the letter of the law, for the safety of the people; as the surgeon, not by any prerogative that he has above the art of surgery, but by necessity cuts off a gangrened member. Thus it is not arbitrary to the king to save his people from ruin, but by the strong and imperious law of the people's safety he does it; for if he did it not, he would be a murderer of his people.

2. He is to stand upon transgression of laws according to their genuine sense of the people's safety; for good laws are not contrary one to another, though, when he breaks through the letter of the law, yet he breaks not the law; for if twenty thousand rebels invade Scotland, he is to command all to rise, though the formality of a parliament cannot be had to indict the war, as our law provides, but the king does not command all to rise and defend themselves by prerogative royal, proper to him as king, and incommunicable to any but to himself.

1. There is no such din and noise to be made for a king and his incommunicable prerogative; for though the king would not be at all, yea, though he command the contrary (as he did when he came against Scotland with an English army) the law of nature teaches all to rise without the king.

2. That the king command this as king is not a particular positive law; but he does it as a man and a member of the kingdom. The law of nature (which knows no dream of such a prerogative) forces him to it, as every member is, by nature's indictment, to care for the whole.

3. It is poor hungry skill in this new statist (for so he names all Scotland) to say that any laws are made for private interests, and the good of some individuals. Laws are not laws if they be not made for the safety of the people.

4. It is false that the king, in a public danger, is to care for himself as a man, with the ruin and loss of any; yea, in a public calamity, a good king, such as David, is to desire he may die that the public may be saved (2 Sam. 24:17; Exod. 32:32). It is commended of all that the emperor Otho, yea, and Richard II of England, as M. Speed says resigned their kingdoms to eschew the effusion of blood (*Hist. of England*.). The Prelate advises the king to pass over all laws of nature, and slay thousands of innocents, and destroy church and state of three kingdoms, for a straw and supposed prerogative royal.

1. Now, certainly prerogative and absoluteness to do good and evil must be inferior to a law, the end of which is the safety of the people. For David wills the pestilence may take him away, and so his prerogative, that the people may be saved (2. Sam. 24:17), for prerogative is cumulative to do good, not privative to do ill; and so is but a means to defend both the law and the people.

2. Prerogative is either a power to do good or evil, or both. If the first be said, it must be limited by the end and law for which it is ordained. A means is no farther a means, but insofar as it helps towards the end, the safety of all. If the second be admitted, it is license and tyranny, not power from God. If the third be said, both reasons plead against this: that prerogative should be the king's end in the present wars.

3. Prerogative being a power given by the mediation of the people; yea, suppose (which is false) that it was given immediately by God,

yet it is not a thing for which the king should raise war against his subjects; for God will ask no more of the king than He gives to him. The Lord reaps not where he sows not. If the militia and other things are ordered to this for the holding off Irish and Spanish invasion by sea, and so for the good of the land, seeing the king in his own person cannot make use of the militia, he is to rejoice that his subjects are defended. The king cannot answer to God for the justice of war on his part. It is not a case of conscience that the king should shed blood for, namely, because the under-officers are such men, and not others of his choosing, seeing the kingdom is defended sufficiently except where cavaliers destroy it. And to me this is an unanswerable argument: that the cavaliers destroy not the kingdoms for this prerogative royal, as the principal ground, but for a deeper design, even for that which was working by prelates and malignants before the late troubles in both kingdoms.

4. The king is to intend the safety of his people, and the safety of the king as a governor; but not as this king, and this man Charles, that is a selfish end. A king David is not to look to that; for when the people was seeking his life and crown, he says "your blessing upon your people" (Ps. 3:8). He may care for, and intend that the king and government be safe; for if the kingdom be destroyed, there cannot be a new kingdom and church on earth again to serve God in that generation (Ps. 89:47), but they may easily have a new king again, and so the safety of the one cannot in reason be intended as a collateral end with the safety of the other, for there is no imaginable comparison between one man, with all his accidents of prerogative and absoluteness, and three national churches and kingdoms. Better the king weep for a childish trifle of a prerogative than that popery be erected, and three kingdoms be destroyed by cavaliers for their own ends.

5. The dictator's power is, 1. A fact, and proves not a point of conscience. 2. His power was in an demand of extreme danger to the commonwealth. The Popish Prelate pleads for a constant absoluteness

above laws to the king at all times, and that *jure divino*. 3. The dictator was the people's creature; therefore the creator, the people, had that sovereignty over him. 4. The dictator was not above a king, but the Romans ejected kings. 5. The dictator's power was not to destroy a state: he might be, and was resisted; he might be deposed.

Popish Prelate: The safety of the people is pretended as a law, that the Jews must put Christ to death, and that Saul spared Agag.

Ans. 1. No shadow for either in the word of God. Caiaphas prophesied, and knew not what he said, but that the Jews intended the salvation of the elect, in killing Christ, or that Saul intended a public good in sparing Agag shall be the Prelate's divinity, not mine.

2. What! Though many should abuse this law of the people's safety to wrong good kings, it ceases not therefore to be a law, and licenses not ill kings to place a tyrannical prerogative above a just dictate of nature.

In the last chapter the Prelate has no reasons, only he would have kings holy, and this he proves from Apocryphal books, because he is ebb in Holy Scripture; but it is Romish holiness, as is clear (section 16). 1. He must preach something to himself, that the king adore a tree-altar. Thus kings must be most reverend in their gestures. 2. The king must hazard his sacred life and three kingdoms, his crown, royal posterity, to preserve sacred things, that is, anti-Christian Romish idols, images, altars, ceremonies, idolatry, popery. 4. He must upon the same pain maintain sacred persons, that is, greasy apostate prelates. The rest, I am weary to trouble the reader withal, but know *ex ungue leonem*.

QUESTION 26.

WHETHER THE KING IS ABOVE THE LAW.

*The law is above the king in four things, in constitution, direction,
limitation, and co-action. In what sense the king may do all things.
The king is under the morality of laws; under fundamental laws,
not under punishment to be inflicted by himself, nor because of the
eminence of his place, but because of its physical incongruity. That
the king transgressing in a heinous manner is under the co-action of
law is proved by seven arguments. The coronation of a king, who is
supposed to be a just prince, yet proves after a tyrant, is conditional
and from ignorance, and so involuntary, and thus not obligatory in
law. Royalists confess a tyrant in exercise may be dethroned. How the
people is the seat of the power of sovereignty. The place Ps. 51, "Against
you only have I sinned," &c. discussed. Israel's not rising in arms
against Pharaoh is examined, as well as Judah's not working their own
deliverance under Cyrus. A covenant without the king's concurrence is
lawful.*

We may consider the question of the law's supremacy
over the king, either in the supremacy of constitution
of the king, or of direction, or of limitation, or of co-action

and punishment. Those who maintain this, "The king is not subject to the law," if their meaning be, "The king as king is not subject to the law's direction," they say nothing; for the king as the king is a living law; then they say, "The law is not subject to the law's direction," a very improper speech; or, the king as king is not subject to the coaction in the law; that is true, for he who is a living law, as such, cannot punish himself, as the law says.

Assert. 1. The law has a supremacy of constitution above the king:

1. Because the king by nature is not king, as is proved; therefore, he must be king by a politic constitution and law; and so the law, in that consideration, is above the king, because it is from a civil law that there is a king rather than any other kind of governor. 2. It is by law that among many hundred men, this man is king, not that man, and because by the which a thing is constituted, by the same thing it is or may be dissolved; therefore, 3. As a community, finding such and such qualifications as the law requires to be in a king, in this man, not in that man, therefore upon law-ground they make him a king, and upon law-grounds and just demerit they may unmake him again; for what men voluntary do upon condition, the condition being removed, they may undo again.

Assert. 2. It is denied by none but the king is under the directive power of the law, though many liberate the king from the coactive power of a civil law. But I see not what direction a civil law can give to the king if he be above all obedience, or disobedience, to a law, seeing all law-direction is in *ordine ad obedientian* in order to obey, except thus far, that the light that is in the civil law is a moral or natural guide to conduct a king in his walking; but this is the morality of the law which enlightens and informs, not any obligation that awes the king, and so the king is under God's and nature's law. This is nothing to the purpose.

Assert. 3. The king is under the law in regard of some coercive limitation; because, 1. There is no absolute power given to him to do what he wishes, as a man. And because, 2. God, in making Saul a king, does not by any royal stamp give him a power to sin, or to play the tyrant; for which cause I exposit these of the law: *omnia sunt possibilia regi, imperator omnia potest* (*Baldus in sect. F. de no. for. fidel, in F. et in prima constitut, col.* 2. *Chassanaeus in catalog. gloriae mundi. par.* 5. *considerat.* 24. *et tanta est ejus celsitudo, ut non posset ei imponi lex in regno suo. Curt, in consol.* 66. *col.* 6. *ad. F. Petrus Rebuff. Notab.* 3. repet, l. unicae. *de sentent. quas pro eo quod n.* 17). All these go thus: The king can do all things which by a law he can do, and that holds him, *id possumus quod jure possumus,* and therefore the king cannot be above the covenant and law made between him and his people at his coronation-oath; for then the covenant and oath should bind him only by a natural obligation, as he is a man, not by a civil or political obligation, as he is a king. So then, 1. It would be sufficient that the king should swear that oath in his cabinet-chamber, and it is but a mocking of an oath that he swear it to the people. 2. That oath given by the representative-kingdom should also oblige the subjects naturally, *in foro Dei*, not politically, *in foro humano*, upon the same reason. 3. He may be resisted as a man.

Assert. 4. The fourth case is if the king be under the obliging political co-action of civil laws, for that he, *in foro Dei*, be under the morality of civil laws, so as he cannot contravene any law in that notion but he must sin against God is granted on all hands (Deut. 17:20; Josh. 1:8; 1 Sam. 12:15). That the king bind himself to the same law that he does bind others is decent and obliges the king as he is a man, because, 1 It is said to be the law and the prophets, "All things whatsoever You would men should do unto you, do You even so to them" (Matt, 7:12). 2. It is the law, *imperator l. 4. digna vox. C. de lege et tit. Quod quisque juris in alium statuit, eodem et ipse utatur.* Julius Caesar commanded the youth who had deflowered the emperor's daughter to be scourged above that which the law allowed. The youth said to the emperor, *Dixisti legem Caesar*, "You appointed the law, Caesar." The emperor was so offended with himself that he had failed against the law, that for the whole day he refused to taste meat.[1]

Assert. 5. The king cannot but be subject to the co-active power of fundamental laws. Because, 1. This is a fundamental law that the free estates lay upon the king, that all the power that they give to the king as king is for the good and safety of the people, and so what he does to the hurt of his subjects, he does it not as king.

2. The law says. *Qui habet potestatem constitituendi etiam et jus adimendi* (l. *nemo.* 37.l.21. *de reg. jure*). Those who have power to make have power to unmake kings.

3. Whatever the king does as king, that he does by a power borrowed from (or by a fiduciary power which is his by trust) the estates, who made him king. He must then be nothing but an eminent servant of the state in the punishing of others. If, therefore, he be unpunishable, it is not so much because his royal power is above all law coaction as because one and the same man cannot be both the punisher and the punished, and this is a physical incongruity rather than a moral absurdity. So the law of God lays a duty on the inferior magistrate to use the sword against the murderer, and that by virtue of his office, but I much doubt, if for that he is to use the sword against himself in the case of murder, for this is a truth I purpose to make good. That suffering, as suffering, according to the substance and

---

1. Plutarch in *Apotheg.* Book 4.

essence of passion is not commanded by any law of God or nature to the sufferer, but only the manner of suffering. I doubt if it be not by the law of nature lawful even to the evil-doer, who has deserved death by God's law, to fly from the sword of the lawful magistrate; only the manner of suffering with patience is commanded by God. I know the law says here that the magistrate is both judge and the executor of the sentence against himself, in his own cause, for the excellency of his office. Therefore these are to be distinguished, whether the king, *ratione demeriti et jure* by law be punishable, or if the king can actually be punished corporally by a law of man, he remaining king; and since he must be a punisher himself, and that by virtue of his office. In matters of goods the king may be both judge and punisher of himself, as our law provides that any subject may plead his own heritage from the king before the inferior judges, and if the king be a violent possessor, and in mala fide for many years by law he is obliged upon a decree of the lords to execute the sentence against himself, *ex officio*, and to restore the lands and repay the damage to the just owner; and this the king is to do against himself, *ex officio*. I grant here the king as king punishes himself as an unjust man, but because bodily suffering is mere violence to nature, I doubt if the king, *ex officio*, is to do or inflict any bodily punishment on himself. *Nemo potest a scipso cogi. l. ille a quo*, sect. 13.

Assert. 6. There be some laws made in favor of the king as king as to pay tribute. The king must be above this law as king. True, but if a nobleman of a great rent be elected king, I know not if he can be free from paying to himself, as king, tribute, seeing this is not allowed to the king by a divine law (Rom. 13:6) as a reward of his work, and Christ expressly makes tribute a thing due to Caesar as a king (Matt. 22:21). There are some solemnities of the law from which the king may be free; Prickman relates what they are; they are not laws, but some circumstances belonging to laws, and he answers to many places alleged out of the lawyers, to prove the king to be above the law (*D.*

section 3, n. 78). Malderus will have the prince under that law, which concerns all the commonwealth equally in regard of the matter, and that by the law of nature, but he will not have him subject to these laws which concerns the subjects as subjects, as to pay tribute (in 12. art. 4, 6, 9, 96). He cites Francisc. a vict., Covarruvias, and Turrecremata. He also will have the prince under positive laws such as not to transport victuals; not because the law binds him as a law, but because the making of the law binds him, *tanquam conditio sine qua non*, even "as he who teaches another that he should not steal, he should not steal himself" (Rom. 2). But the truth is this is but a branch of the law of nature, that I should not commit adultery, and theft, and sacrilege, and such sins as nature condemns, if I shall condemn them in others, and does not prove that the king is under the co-active power of civil laws. Ulpianus says, "The prince is loosed from laws."[1] Bodine, "*Nemo imperat sibi*," no man commands himself.[2] Tholosanus says, "*Ipsius est dare, non accipere leges*," the prince gives laws, but receives none.[3] Donellus distinguishes between a *law* and a *royal law* proper to the king.[4] Trentlerus says, "The prince is freed from laws," and that he obeys laws, *de honestate, non de necessitate*, upon honesty, not of necessity. Thomas P and with him *Soto Gregorius de Valentia*, and other schoolmen, subject the king to the directive power of the law and liberate him from the coactive power of the law.[5]

Assert. 7. If a king turn a parricide, a lion, and a waster and destroyer of the people, as a man he is subject to the coactive power of the laws of the land. If any law should hinder that a tyrant should not be punished by law, it must be because he has not a superior but God, for royalists build all upon this; but this ground is false.

1. l.31. F. *de regibus.*
2. *De Repub.* 1.7.8.
3. *De Rep.* 1.7.20
4. Comment., 1.7.
5. Thomas, 1, q. 96, art. 6.

Arg. 1. Because the estates of the kingdom, who gave him the crown, are above him, and they may take away what they gave him; as the law of nature and God says. If they had known he would turn tyrant, they would never have given him the sword, and so, how much ignorance is in the contract they made with the king, as little of will is in it, and so it is not every way willing, but being conditional is supposed to be against their will. They gave the power to him only for their good, and that they may make the king, is clear (2 Chron. 23:11; 1 Sam. 10:17, 24; Deut. 17:14-17; 2 Kings 11:12; 1 Kings 16:21; .2 Kings 10:5; Judg. 9:6). Fourscore valiant men of the priests withstood Uzziah with bodily violence, and thrust him out, and cut him off from the house of the Lord (2 Chron. 26:18).

Arg. 2. If the prince's place do not put him above the laws of church discipline (Matt. 18, for Christ excepts none, and how can men except?) and if the rod of Christ's "lips smite the earth, and slay the wicked," (Isa. 11:4) and the prophets Elijah, Nathan, Jeremiah, Isaiah, &c., and John Baptist, Jesus Christ, and his Apostles, have used this rod of censure and rebuke, as servants under God, against kings, this is a sort of spiritual co-action of laws put in execution by men, and by due proportion bodily co-action being the same ordinance of God, though of another nature, must have the like power over all, whom the law of God has not excepted, but God's law excepts none at all.

Arg. 3. It is presumed that God has not provided better for the safety of the part than of the whole, especially when He makes the part a means for the safety of the whole. But if God have provided that the king, who is a part of the commonwealth, shall be free of all punishment, though he be a habitual destroyer of the whole kingdom, seeing God has given him to be father, tutor, savior, defender of it, and destined him as a means for their safety, then must God have worse, not better, provided for the safety of the whole than of the part. The proposition is clear, in that God (Rom. 13:4; 1 Tim. 2:2) has ordained the ruler, and given to him the sword to defend the whole kingdom and city, but we read nowhere that the Lord has given the sword to the whole kingdom, to defend one man, a king, though a ruler, going on in a tyrannical way of destroying all his subjects. The assumption is evident: for then the king, turning tyrant, might set an army of Turks, Jews, or cruel Papists to destroy the church of God, without all fear of law or punishment. Yea, this contrary to the doctrine of royalists: for Winzetus (*adversus Buchananum*) says of Nero, that he, seeking to destroy the senate and people of Home, and seeking to make new laws for himself, *excidit jure regni*, lost right to the kingdom. And Barclay says a tyrant, such as Caligula, *spoliare se jure regni*, spoils himself of the right to the crown (*Monarch.* 1.3, last section). And in that same place, *regem, si regnum suum alienae ditioni manciparit, regno cadere*, if the king sell his kingdom, he loses the title to the crown. Grotius: *Si rex hostili animo in totius populi exitium feratur, amittit regnum*, if he turn enemy to the kingdom, for their destruction, he loses his kingdom, because (says he) *voluntas imperandi, et voluntas perdendi, simul consistere non possunt,* a will or mind to govern and to destroy cannot consist together in one (*De jure belli et pacis*, 1.1.4, n. 7).

Now, if this be true: that a king, turning tyrant, loses title to the crown, this is either a falling from his royal title only in God's court, or it is a losing of it before men, and in the court of his subjects. If the former be said, 1. He is no king, having before God lost his royal title, and yet the people is to obey him as "the minister of Ged," and a power from God, when as he is no such thing. 2. In vain do these authors provide remedies to save the people from a tyrannical waster of the people, if they speak of a tyrant who is no king in God's court only, and yet remains a king to the people in regard of the law, for "the places speak of remedies that God has provided against tyrants *cum titulo*, such as are lawful kings but turn tyrants. Now by this they provide no remedy at all, if only in God's court, and not in man's court also, a tyrant lose his title. As for tyrants *sine titulo*, such as usurp the throne, and have no just claim to it, Barclay says, "Any private man may kill him as a public enemy of the state," (*adver. Monarch.* 1.4.10) but if he lose his title to the crown in the court of men, then is there a court of men to judge the king, and so he is under the co-active power of a law; then a king may be resisted, and yet those who resist him do not incur damnation; the contrary of which royalists endeavor to prove from Rom. 13; then the people may un-king one who was a king. But I would know who takes that θειον τι from him, by which he is a king, that beam of divine majesty? Not the people, because royalists say they neither can give nor take away royal dignity, and so they cannot unking him.

Arg. 4. The more will be in the consent (says Ferd. Vasquez) the obligation is the stricter (1.1.41). So doubled words (says the law, 1.1, section 13, n. 13) oblige more strictly. And all laws of kings, who are rational fathers, and so lead us by laws, as by rational means to peace and external happiness, are contracts of king and people. *Omnis lex sponsio et contractus Reip. sect.* 1, *Inst. de ver. relig.* Now the king, at his coronation-covenant with the people, gives a most intense consent, an oath, to be a keeper and preserver of all good laws, and so hardly he can be freed from the strictest obligation that law can impose. And if he keep laws by office, he is a means to preserve laws, and no means can be superior and above the end, but inferior to it.

Arg. 5. Bodine proves that emperors at first were but princes of the commonwealth, and that sovereignty remained still in the senate and people.[1] Marius Salomonius, a learned Roman civilian, wrote six books *de principatu*, to refute the supremacy of emperors above the state. Ferd. Vasq. proves that the prince by royal dignity leaves not off being a citizen, a member of the political body, and not a king, but a keeper of laws.[2]

Arg. 6. Hence, the prince remains, even being a prince, a social creature, a man as well as a king, one who must buy, sell, promise,

---

1. *De Rep.* 1.2.5.
2. Illust. quest. part. 1.1.1, n. 21.

contract, dispose; therefore, he is not *regula regulans*, but under rule of law, for it is impossible if the king can in a political way live as a member of a society, and do and perform acts of policy, and so perform them, as he may, by his office, buy and not pay; promise, and vow, and swear to men, and not perform, nor be obliged to men to render a reckoning of his oath, and kill and destroy, and yet in *curia politicae societatis*, in the court of human policy, be free; and that he may give inheritances, as just rewards of virtue and well-doing, and take them away again. Yea, seeing these sins, that are not punishable before men, are not sins before men, if all the sins and oppressions of a prince be so above the punishment that men can inflict, they are not sins before men, by which means the king is loosed from all guiltiness of the sins against the second table, for the *ratio formalis*, the formal reason why the judge by warrant from God condemns in the court of men the guilty man is that he has sinned against human society through the scandal of blasphemy, or that through some other heinous sin he has defiled the land. Now this is incident to the king as well as to some other sinful man.

To these and the like, hear what the excommunicated Prelate has to say: "They say" he means the Jesuits "every society of men is a perfect republic, and so must have within itself a power to preserve itself from ruin, and by that to punish a tyrant." He answers, "A society without a head is a disorderly rout, not a political body, and so cannot have this power" (section 15).

Ans. 1. The Pope gives to every society political power to make away a tyrant, or heretical king, and to unking him by his brethren the Jesuits' way. And observe how papists (of which number I could easily prove the Popish Prelate to be, by the popish doctrine that he delivered, while the iniquity of time and dominion of prelates in Scotland advanced him, against all worth of true learning and holiness, to be a preacher in Edinburgh) and Jesuits agree, as the builders of Babylon. It is the purpose of God to destroy Babylon.

2. This answer shall infer that the aristocratic governors of any free state, and that the Duke of Venice, and the senate there, is above all law and cannot be resisted, because without their heads they are a disorderly rout.

3. A political society, just as by nature's instinct they may appoint a head or heads to themselves, so also if their head or heads become ravenous wolves, the God of nature has not left a perfect society remediless; but they may both resist and punish the head or heads to whom they gave all the power that they have for their good, not for their destruction.

4. They are as orderly a body politic to unmake a tyrannical commander as they were to make a just governor. The Prelate says, "It is alike to conceive a political body without a governor as to conceive the natural body without a head." He means none of them can be conceivable. I am not of his mind. When Saul was dead, Israel was a perfect political body, and the Prelate, if he be not very obtuse in his head (as this hungry piece, stolen from others, shows him to be) may conceive a visible political society performing a political action, 2 Sam. 5:1-3) making David king at a visible and conceivable place, at Hebron, and making a covenant with him. And that they lacked not all governors is nothing to make them chimeras inconceivable. For when so many families before Nimrod were governed only by fathers of families, and they agreed to make either a king, or other governors, a head, or heads, over themselves, though the several families had government, yet these associated families had no government, and yet so conceivable a political body as if Maxwell would have appeared among them and called them a disorderly rout or an unconceivable chimera, they should have made the Prelate know that chimeras can knock down prelates. Neither is a king the life of a political body, as the soul is of the natural body. The body creates not the soul, but Israel created Saul king, and when he was dead, they made David king, and thus under God they created many kings as they succeeded, till the

Messiah came. No natural body can make souls to itself by succession; nor can Sees create new prelates always.

Popish Prelate. Jesuits and puritans differ infinitely: we are hopeful God shall cast down this Babel. The Jesuits, for all I know, seat the superintendent power in the community. Some sectaries follow them, and warrant any individual person to make away a king in case of defects, and the work is to be rewarded as when one kills a ravenous wolf. Some will have it in a collective body, but how? Not met together by warrant or writ of sovereign authority, but when fancy of reforming church and state calls them. Some will have the power in the nobles and peers; some in the three estates assembled by the king's writ; some in the inferior judges. I know not where this power to curb sovereignty is, but in Almighty God.

Ans. 1. Jesuits and puritans differ infinitely; true. Jesuits deny the Pope to be antichrist, hold all Arminian doctrine, Christ's local descent to hell, all which the Prelate did preach. We deny all this.

2. We hope also the Lord shall destroy the Jesuits' Babel; the suburbs of which, and more, are the popish prelates in Scotland and England.

3. The Jesuits, for all he knows, place all superintendent power in the community. The Prelate knows not all his brethren the Jesuits' ways but it is ignorance, not lack of good-will. For Bellarmine, Beucanus, Suarez, Gregor. de Valentia, and others, his dear fellows, say that all super-intendent power of policy, *in ordine ad spiritualia* is in the man, whose foot Maxwell would kiss for a cardinal's hat.

4. If these be all the differences, it is not much. The community is the remote and last subject, the representative body the nearest subject, the nobles a partial subject; the judges, as judges sent by the king, are so in the game that when an arbitrary prince at his pleasure sets them up, and at command that they judge for men, and not for the Lord, and accordingly obey, they are by this power to be punished, and others put in their place.

5. A true cause of convening parliaments the Prelate makes a fancy at this time: it is as if the thieves and robbers should say a justice-court were a fancy, but if the Prelate might compear before the parliament of Scotland (to which he is an outlaw like his father, 2 Thess. 2:4) such a fancy, I conceive, should hang him, and that deservedly.

Popish Prelate: The subject of this superintending power must be secured from error in judgment and practice, and the community and states then should be infallible.

Ans. The consequence is nothing. No more than the king, the absolute independent, is infallible. It is sure the people are in less hazard of tyranny and self-destruction than the king is to subvert laws and make himself absolute, and for that cause there must be a superintendent power above the king, and God Almighty also must be above all.

Popish Prelate. The parliament may err, then God has left the state remediless, unless the king remedy it.

Ans. There is no consequence here, unless the king be impeccable. Posterior parliaments may correct the former. A state is not remediless, because God's remedies in sinful men's hands may miscarry. But the question is now whether God has given power to one man to destroy men, subvert laws and religion without any power above him to coerce, restrain, or punish?

Popish Prelate: If when the parliament errs the remedy is left to the wisdom of God, why not when the king errs (section 16)?

Ans. Neither is antecedent true, nor the consequence valid, for the sounder part may resist, and it is easier to one to destroy many, having a power absolute, which God never gave him, than for many to destroy themselves. Then if the king Uzziah intrude himself and sacrifice, the priests do sin in remedying it.

Popish Prelate. Why might not the people of Israel, peers, or Sanhedrin have convened before them, judged, and punished David for his adultery and murder? Romanists and new statists acknowledge no case lawful, but heresy, apostasy, or tyranny; and tyranny, they say, must be universal, manifest as the sun, and with obstinacy, and invincible by prayers, as is recorded of Nero, whose wish was rather a transported passion than a fixed resolution. This cannot fall in the attempts of any but a madman. Now this cannot be proved of our king, but though we grant in the foresaid case, that the community may resume their power and rectify what is amiss, which we cannot grant, but this will follow by their doctrine in every case of bad administration.[1]

Ans. The Prelate draws me to speak of the case of the king's unjust murder, confessed (Ps. 51), to which I answer: He takes it for confessed, that it had been treason in the Sanhedrin or states of Israel to have taken on them to judge and punish David for his adultery and his murder, but he gives no reason for this, nor any word of God, and truly though I will not presume to go before others in this, God's law (Gen. 9:6, compared with Num. 35:30-31) seems to say against them.

6. Nor can I think that God's law, or His deputy the judges, are to accept the persons of the great, because they are great; (Deut. 1:17; 2 Chron. 19:6-7) and we say, we cannot distinguish where the law distinguishes not. The Lord speaks to under judges "you shall not respect the person of the poor, nor honor the person of the mighty," (Lev. 19:15) or of the prince, for we know what these names נדיל and ברא mean. I grant it is not God's meaning that the king should draw the sword against himself, but yet it follows not that if we speak of the demerit of blood that the law of God accepts any judge, great or small; and if the estates be above the king, as I conceive they are, though it be a human political constitution, that the king be free of all co-action of law, because it conduces for the peace of the commonwealth, yet if we make a matter of conscience, for my part I see no exception that God makes it, if men make, I crave leave to say, *a facto ad jus non sequitur*; and I easily yield that in every case the estates may coerce the king, if we make it a case of conscience. And for the place,

---

1. Stolen from Arnisaeus, *De authorit. prin.* 4, n. 5.

Ps. 51:4: "Against you, you only, have I sinned," **לְךָ לְבַדְּךָ חָטָאתִי** flatterers allege it to be a place proving that the king is above all earthly tribunals, and all laws, and that there was not on earth any who might punish king David, and so they cite Clemens Alexandrin (*Strom.* 1.4) Amobi. (Ps. 1), Dydimus, Jeromeim., but Calvin on the place, gives the meaning that most of the fathers give, *Domine, etiam si me totus mundus absolvat mihi tamen plusquam satis est, quod te solum judicem sentio.* It is true Beda, Euthymius, Ambrosius (Apol. David, sections 4 and 10) do all acknowledge from the place, *de facto*, there was none above David to judge him, and so does Augustine, Basilius Theodoret, say, and Chrystomus, and Cyrillus, and Jeromeimus (Epist. 22). Ambrose (Sermon 16, in Ps. 118), Gregorius, and Augustine (Joan 8) says, he means no man dared judge or punish him, but God only. Lorinus, the Jesuit, observes eleven interpretations of the fathers all to this sense: "Since (Lyra says) he sinned only against God, because God only could pardon him;" Hugo Cardinalis, "Because God only could wash him," which he asks in the text. And Lorinus, *Solo Deo conscio peccavi.* But the simple meaning is, 1. Against you only have I sinned, as my eye-witness and immediate beholder, and, therefore, he adds "and have done this evil in your sight." 2. Against you only, as my judge, that you may be justified when you judge, as clear from all unrighteousness, when you shall send the sword on my house. 3. Against you, O Lord only, who can wash me and pardon me (ver. 1-2). And if this "you only" exclude altogether Uriah, Bathsheba, and the law of the judges, as if he had sinned against none of these in their kind, then is the king, because a king, free, not only from a punishing law of man, but from the duties of the second table simply, and so a king cannot be under the best and largest half of the law, you shall love your neighbor as thyself. He shall not need to say, Forgive us our sins, as we forgive them that sin against us; for there is no reason, from the nature of sin, and the nature of the law of God, why we can say more the subjects and sons sin against the king and father, than to say the father and king sin against the sons and subjects. By those the king killing his father Jesse should sin against God, but not break the fifth commandment, nor sin against his father. God should in vain forbid fathers to provoke their children to wrath.

1. And kings to do injustice to their subjects, because by this the superior cannot sin against the inferior, inasmuch as kings can sin against none but those who have power to judge and punish them, but God only, and no inferiors, and no subjects have power to punish the kings; therefore kings can sin against none of their subjects, and where there is no sin, how can there be a law? Neither major nor minor can be denied by royalists.

2. We acknowledge tyranny must only unking a prince. The Prelate denies it, but he is a green statist. Barclay, Grotius Winzetus, as I have proved, grant it.

3. He will excuse Nero, as of infirmity, wishing all Rome to have one neck, that he may cut it off. And is that charitable of kings, that they will not be so mad as to destroy their own kingdom? But when histories teach us there have been more tyrants than kings, the kings are more obliged to him for flattery than for state-wit, unless we say that all kings who eat the people of God as they do bread owe him little for making them all mad and frantic.

4. But let them be Neroes, and mad, and worse, there is no coercing of them, but all must give their necks to the sword, if the poor Prelate be heard, and yet kings cannot be so mad as to destroy their subjects. Mary of England was that mad. The Romish princes who have given their power and strength to the beast, and do make war with the Lamb (Rev. 17:13); and kings inspired with the spirit of the beast, and drunk with the wine or the cup of Babel's fornications, are so mad; and the ten emperors are so mad, who wasted their faithfulest subjects.

Popish Prelate. If there be such a power in the peers, resumable in the exigent of necessity, as the last necessary remedy for safety of

church and state, God and nature not being deficient in things necessary, it must be proved out of the Scripture, and not taken on trust,
for *affirmanti incumbit probation.*

Ans. Mr. Bishop, what better is your **affirmanti** *incumbit &c.*, than
mine? For you are the affirmer. 1. I can prove a power in the king,
limited only to feed, govern, and save the people, and you affirm that
God has given to the king, not only a power official and royal to save,
but also to destroy and cut off, so that no man may say, Why do you
this? Shall we take this upon the word of an excommunicated prelate?
Profer tabulas John Popish Prelate, I believe you not: royal power is
(Deut. 17 18; Rom. 3:14). I am sure there is there a power given to the
king to do good, and that from God. Let John Popish Prelate prove a
power to do ill, given by God to the king. 2. "We shall quickly prove
that the states may repress this power, and punish the tyrant not the
king, when he shall prove that a tyrannical power is an ordinance of
God, and so may not be resisted; for the law of nature teaches, if I give
my sword to my fellow to defend me from the murderer, if he shall
fall to and murder me with my own sword I may (if I have strength)
take my sword from him.

Popish Prelate. 1. It is infidelity to think that God cannot help us,
and impatience that we will not wait on God. When a king oppresses
us, it is against God's wisdom that he has not provided another means
for our safety than intrusion on God's right. 2. It is against God's
power, 3. His holiness, 4. Christian religion, that we necessitate God
to so weak a means as to make use of sin, and we cast the aspersion
of treason on religion, and deter kings to profess reformed Catholic
religion; 5. We are not to jostle God out of his right.

Ans. 1. I see nothing but what Dr. Ferne, Grotius, Barclay, Blackwood, have said before, with some pretense of proving the consequence. The Popish Prelate gives us other men's arguments, but without bones. All would be good, if the state's coercing and curbing a
power which God never gave to the king were a sin and an act of

impatience and unbelief; and if it were proper to God only by His immediate hand to coerce tyranny.

2. He calls it not protestant religion, either here or elsewhere, but cunningly gives a name that will agree to the Roman catholic religion. For the Dominicans, Franciscans, and the Parisian doctors and schoolmen, following Ockham, Gerson, Almain, and other papists, call themselves reformed catholics. He lays this for a ground, in three or four pages, where these same arguments are again and again repeated *in terminus*, as his second reason was handled *ad nauseam*; his third reason is repeated in his sixth reason. He lays down, I say, this ground, which is the begged conclusion, and makes the conclusion the assumption, in eight raw and often-repeated arguments, namely, that the parliament's coercing and restraining of arbitrary power is rebellion, and resisting the ordinance of God. But he dare not look the place Rom. 13 on the face. Other royalists have done it with bad success. This I desire to be weighed, and I retort the Prelate's argument. But it is indeed the trivial argument of all royalists, especially of Barclay, obvious in his third book. If arbitrary and tyrannical power, above any law that the lawful magistrate commands under the pain of death—you shall not murder one man, you shall not take away the vineyard of one Naboth violently—be lawful and warrantable by God's word, then an arbitrary power above all divine laws is given to the keeping of the civil magistrate. And it is no less lawful arbitrary, or rather tyrannical power, for David to kill all his subjects and to plunder all Jerusalem (as I believe prelates and malignants and papists would serve the three kingdoms, if the king should command them) than to kill one Uriah, or for Ahab to spoil one Naboth. The essence of sin most agree alike to all, though the degrees vary.

Of God's remedy against arbitrary power hereafter, in the question of resistance; but the confused engine of the Prelate brings it in here, where there is no place for it.

7. His seventh argument is: Before God would authorize rebellion and give a bad precedent for it forever, he would rather work extraordinary and wonderful miracles, and therefore would not authorize the people to deliver themselves from under Pharaoh, but made Moses a prince to bring them out of Egypt with a stretched out arm. Nor did the Lord deliver his people by the wisdom of Moses or strength of the people, or any act that way of theirs, but by His own immediate hand and power.

Ans. I reduce the Prelate's confused words to a few; for I speak not of his popish term of St. Steven, and others the like, because all that he has said in a book of 149 pages might have been said in three sheets of paper. But I pray you, what is this argument to the question in hand, which is whether the king be so above all laws as people and peers in the case of arbitrary power, may resume their power and punish a tyrant? The Popish Prelate draws in the question of resistance by the hair. Israel's not rising in arms against king Pharaoh proves nothing against the power of a free kingdom against a tyrant.

1. Moses, who wrought miracles destructive to Pharaoh, might pray for vengeance against Pharaoh, God having revealed to Moses that Pharaoh was a reprobate; but may ministers and nobles pray so against king Charles? God forbid.

2. Pharaoh had not his crown from Israel.

3. Pharaoh had not sworn to defend Israel, nor became he their king upon condition he should maintain and profess the religion of the God of Israel; therefore Israel could not, as free estates, challenge him in their supreme court of parliament of breach of oath, and upon no terms could they unking Pharaoh: he held not his crown from them.

4. Pharaoh was never circumcised, nor within the covenant of the God of Israel in profession.

5. Israel had their lands by the mere gift of the king. I hope the king of Britain stands to Scotland and England in a fourfold contrary relation.

All divines know that Pharaoh, his princes, and the Egyptians were his peers and people, and that Israel was not his native subjects, but a number of strangers who by the laws of the king and princes by the means of Joseph had gotten the land of Goshen for their dwelling and liberty to serve the God of Abraham, to whom they prayed in their bondage (Exod. 2:23-24), and they were not to serve the gods of Egypt, nor were they of the king's religion. And therefore, his argument is thus: A number of poor exiled strangers under king Pharaoh, who were not Pharaoh's princes and peers, could not restrain the tyranny of king Pharaoh; therefore the three estates in a free kingdom may not restrain the arbitrary power of a king.

1. The Prelate must prove that God save a royal and kingly power to king Pharaoh, due to him by virtue of his kingly calling (according as royalists explain 1 Sam. 8:9, 11) to kill all the male children of Israel, to make slaves of themselves, and compel them to work in brick and clay, while their lives were a burden to them, and that if a Roman catholic, Mary of England, should kill all the male children of protestants, by the hands of papists, at the queen's commandment, and make bond-slaves of all the peers, judges, and three estates, who made her a free princes, yet notwithstanding that Mary had sworn to maintain the protestant religion, they were to suffer and not to defend themselves. But if God give Pharaoh a power to kill all Israel, so that they could not control it, then God gives to a king a royal power by office to sin, only the royalist saves God from being the author of sin in this: that God gave the power to sin, but yet with this limitation, that the subjects should not resist this power.

2. He must prove that Israel was to give their male children to Pharaoh's butchers, for to hide them was to resist a royal power, and to disobey a royal power given by God is to disobey God.

3. The subjects may not resist the king's butchers coming to kill them and their male children; for to resist the servant of the king in that in which he is a servant is to resist the king (1 Sam. 8:7; 1 Pet. 2:14; Rom. 13:1).

4. He must prove that upon the supposition that Israel had been as strong as Pharaoh and his people; that without God's special commandment (they then wanting the written word) they should have fought with Pharaoh, and that we now, for all wars, must have a word from heaven, as if we had not God's perfect will in his word, as at that time Israel chose to have in all wars (Judg. 18:5; 1 Sam. 14:37; Isa. 3:2; Jer. 38:37; 1 Kings 22:6; 1 Sam. 3:5; Judg. 20:27; 1 Sam. 23:2; 2 Sam. 16:23; 1 Chron. 10:14). But because God gave not them an answer to fight against Pharaoh, therefore we have no warrant now to fight against a foreign nation invading us; the consequence is null, and therefore this is a vain argument. The prophets never reprove the people for not performing the duty of defensive war against tyrannical kings; therefore, there is no such duty enjoined by any law of God to us. For the prophets never rebuke the people for not performing the duty of offensive wars against their enemies, except where God gave a special command and response from his own oracle that they should fight. And if God was pleased never to command the people to rise against a tyrannical king, they did not sin where they had no commandment of God; but I hope we have now a more sure word of prophecy to inform us.

5. The Prelate conjectures Moses' miracles, and the deliverance of the people by dividing the Red Sea, was to forbid and condemn defensive wars of people against their king; but he has neither Scripture nor reasons to do it. The end of these miracles was to seal to Pharaoh the truth of God's calling of Moses and Aaron to deliver the people, as is clear (Exod. 4:1-4, compared with 7:8-10). And that the Lord might get to himself a name on all the earth (Rom. 9:17; Exod. 9:16; 13:13-14). But of the Prelate's conjectural end the Scripture is silent,

and we cannot take an excommunicated man's word. What I said of Pharaoh, who had not his crown from Israel, that I say of Nebuchadnezzar and the king of Persia, keeping the people of God captive.

Popish Prelate: So in the book of Judges, when the people were delivered over to the hand of their enemies, because of their sins, he never warranted the ordinary judges or community to be their own deliverers, but when they repented, God raised up a judge. The people had no hand in their own deliverance out of Babylon; God effected it by Cyrus, immediately and totally. Is not this a real proof God will not have inferior judges to rectify what is amiss, but we must wait in patience till God provide lawful means, some sovereign power immediately sent by himself, in which course of his ordinary providence he will not be deficient.

Ans. 1. All this is beside the question, and proves nothing less than that peers and community may not resume their power to curb an arbitrary power. For in the first case, there is neither arbitrary nor lawful supreme judge. 2. If the first prove anything, it proves that it was rebellion in the inferior judges and community of Israel to fight against foreign kings not set over them by God, and that offensive wars against any kings whatsoever, because they are kings, though strangers, are unlawful. Let Socinians and anabaptists consider if the Popish Prelate help not them in this, and may prove all wars to be unlawful. 3. He is so malignant to all inferior judges, as if they were not powers sent of God, and to all governors that are not kings, and so upholders of prelates, and of himself as he conceives, that by his arguing he will have all deliverance of kings only, the only lawful means in ordinary providence; and so aristocracy and democracy, except in God's extraordinary providence, and by some divine dispensation, must be extraordinary and ordinarily unlawful. 1. The acts of a state, when a king is dead and they choose another, shall be an anticipating of God's providence. 2. If the king be a child, a captive, or distracted, and the kingdom oppressed with malignants, they are to wait, while

God immediately from heaven create a king to them, as he did Saul long ago. But have we now kings immediately sent as Saul was? How is the spirit of prophecy and government infused in them, as in king Saul? or are they by prophetical inspiration anointed as David was? I conceive their calling to the throne on God's part differs as much from the calling of Saul and David in some respect, as the calling of ordinary pastors, who must be gifted by industry and learning and called by the church, and the calling of apostles. 3. God would deliver His people from Babylon by moving the heart of Cyrus immediately, the people having no hand in it, not so much as supplicating Cyrus; therefore, the people and peers who made the king cannot curb his tyrannical power if he make captives and slaves of them, as the kings of Chaldea made slaves of the people of Israel. What! Because God uses another means, therefore, this means is not lawful. It follows in no sort. If we must use no means but what the captive people did under Cyrus, we may not lawfully fly, nor supplicate, for the people did neither.

Popish Prelate. You read of no covenant in Scripture made without the king (Exod. 34). Moses king of Jeshurun: neither tables nor parliament framed it. Joshua another (Josh, 24) and Asa (2 Chron. 15.; 2 Chron. 34.; Ezra 10). The covenant of Jehoiada in the nonage of Joash was the high priest's act, as the king's governor. There is a covenant with hell made without the king and a false covenant (Hos. 10:3-4).

Ans. We argue this negatively. 1. This is neither commanded, nor practiced, nor warranted by promise; therefore, it is not lawful. But this is not practiced in Scripture; therefore, it is not lawful. It follows it. Show me in Scripture the killing of a goring ox who killed a man; the not making battlements on a house; the putting to death of a man lying with a beast; the killing of seducing prophets who tempted the people to go awhoring and serve another God than Jehovah: I mean, a god made by the hand of the baker, such a one as the excommunicated Prelate is known to be, who has preached this idolatry in three kingdoms (Deut. 13). This is written, and all the former laws are divine precepts. Shall the precept make them all unlawful, because they are not practiced by some in Scripture? By this? I ask where read you that the people entered in a covenant with God, not to worship the golden image, and the king; and those who pretended they are the priests of Jehovah, the churchmen and relates, refused to enter in covenant with God? By this argument, the king and prelates, in non-practicing with us, lacking the precedent of a like practiced in Scripture, are in the fault.

2. This is nothing to prove the conclusion in question.

3. All these places prove it is the king's duty, when the people under him and their fathers have corrupted the worship of God to renew a covenant with God and to cause the people to do the like, as Moses, Asa, and Jehoshaphat did.

4. If the king refuse to do his duty, where is it written that the people ought also to omit their duty, and to love to have it so, because the rulers corrupt their ways (Jer. 5:31)? To renew a covenant with God is a point of service due to God that the people are obliged unto, whether the king command it or no. What if the king commanded not his people to serve God, or what if he forbid Daniel to pray to God? Shall the people in that case serve the King of kings only at the nod and royal command of an earthly king? Clear this from Scripture.

5. Ezra (ch. 5) had no commandment in particular from Artaxerxes, king of Persia, or from Darius, but a general (Ezra 7.23). "Whatsoever is commanded by the God of heaven, let it be diligently done for the house of the God of heaven." But the tables in Scotland, and the two parliaments of England and Scotland, who renewed the covenant and entered in covenant not against the king (as the Popish Prelate says) but to restore religion to its ancient purity, have this express law both from king James and king Charles in many acts of parliament that religion be kept pure. Now, as Artaxerxes knew nothing of the covenant, and was unwilling to subscribe it, and yet

gave to Ezra and the princes a warrant in general to do all that the
God of heaven required to be done, for the religion and house of the
God of heaven, and so a general warrant for a covenant without the
king, and yet Ezra and the people in swearing that covenant failed in
no duty against their king, to whom by the fifth commandment they
were no less subject than we are to our king; just so we are, and so
have not failed. But they say the king has committed to no lieutenant
and deputy under him to do what they please in religion without his
royal consent in particular, and the direction of his clergy, seeing he
is of that same religion with his people; whereas Artaxerxes was of
another religion than were the Jews and their governor.

Ans. Nor can our king take on himself to do what he pleases and
what the prelates (among whom those who ruled all are known, before the world and the sun, to be of another religion than we are)
pleases in particular. But see what religion and worship the Lord our
God, and the law of the land (which is the king's revealed will) allows
to us, that we may swear, though the king should not swear it; otherwise, we are to be of no religion but of the king's, and to swear no covenant but the king's, which is to join with papists against protestants.

6. The strangers of Ephraim and Manasseh, and out of Simeon
fell out of Israel in abundance to Asa, when they saw that the Lord
his God was with him (2 Chron. 15:9-10) and swore that covenant
without their own king's consent, their own king being against it. If
a people swear a religious covenant without their King, who is averse
to it, far more may the nobles, peers, and estates of parliament do it
without their king, and here is an example of a practice, which the
Popish Prelate requires.

7. That Jehoiada was governor and viceroy during the nonage of
Joash, and that by this royal authority the covenant was sworn is a
dream, to the end he may make the Pope and the archprelate, now
viceroys and kings, when the throne varies. The nobles were authors
of the making of that covenant, no less than Jehoiada was, yea, and

the people of the land, when the king was but a child, went unto the house of Baal, and broke down his images, &c. Here is a reformation, made without the king by the people.

8. Grave expositors say that the covenant with death and hell (Isa. 28) was the king's covenant with Egypt.

9. And the covenant (Hos. 10) is by none exposited as a covenant made without the king. I have heard said this Prelate, preaching on this text before the king exposited it so, but he spoke words (as the text is) falsely. The Popish Prelate, to the end of the chapter, gives instance of the ill success of popular reformation, because the people caused Aaron to make a golden calf, and they revolted from Rehoboam to Jeroboam, and made two golden calves, and they conspired with Absalom against David.

Ans. If the first example make good anything, neither the high priest, as was Aaron, nor the Popish Prelate, who claims to be descended of Aaron's house, should have any hand in reformation at all; for Aaron erred in that. And to argue from the people's sins to deny their power is no better than to prove Ahab, Jeroboam, and many kings in Israel and Judah committed idolatry therefore they had no royal power at all. In the rest of the chapter, for a whole page, he sings over again his matins in a circle, and gives us the same arguments we heard before; of which you have these three notes: 1. They are stolen, and not his own. 2. Repeated again and again to fill the field. 3. All hang on a false supposition, and a begging of the question. That the people, without the king, have no power at all.

QUESTION 27.

WHETHER OR NOT THE KING IS THE SOLE, SUPREME
AND FINAL INTERPRETER OF THE LAW.

He is not the supreme and peremptory interpreter. Nor is his will the
sense of the law. Nor is he the sole and only judicial interpreter of the
law.

This question conduces not a little to the clearing of the doubts concerning the king's absolute power, and the supposed sole legislative power in the king. And I think it not unlike to the question whether the Pope and Romish church have a sole and peremptory power of expositing laws, and the word of God? We are to consider that there is twofold exposition of laws: 1. One speculative in a school way, so exquisite jurists have a power to exposit laws. 2. Practical, insofar as the sense of the law falls under our practice, and this is twofold, her private and common to all, or judicial and proper to judges, and of this last is the question.

For this public, the law has one fundamental rule, *salus populi*, like the king of planets, the sun, which lends starlight to all laws, and by which they are exposited; whatever interpretation swerves either from fundamental laws of policy, or from the law of nature, and the law of nations, and especially from the safety of the public is to be rejected as a perverting of the law, and therefore, *conscientia humani generis*, the natural conscience of all men, to which the oppressed people may appeal unto when the king exposits a law unjustly, at his own pleasure the last rule on earth for expositing of laws. Nor ought laws to be made so obscure, as an ordinary wit cannot see their connection with fundamental truths of policy, and the safety of the people; and therefore I see no inconvenience, to say, that the law itself is *norma et regula juduiciandi*, the rule and directory to square the judge, and that the judge is the public practical interpreter of the law.

Assert. 1. The king is not the sole and final interpreter of the law.

1. Because then inferior judges should not be interpreters of the law, but inferior judges are no less essentially judges than the king (Deut. 1:17; 2 Chron. 19:6; 1 Pet. 2:14; Rom. 13:1-2) and so by office must interpret the law, else they cannot give sentence according to their conscience and equity. Now, expositing of the law judicially is an act of judging, and so a personal and incommunicable act; so as I can no more judge and exposit the law according to another man's conscience than I can believe with another man's soul, understand with another man's understanding, or see with another man's eye. The king's pleasure, therefore, cannot be the rule of the inferior judge's conscience, for he gives an immediate account to God, the Judge of all, of a just or an unjust sentence. Suppose Caesar shall exposit the law to Pilate, that Christ deserves to die the death. yet Pilate is not in conscience to exposit the law so. If therefore inferior judges judge for the king, they judge only by power borrowed from the king, not by the pleasure, will, or command of the king thus and thus expositing the law; therefore the king cannot be the sole interpreter of the law.

2. If the Lord say not to the king only, but also to other inferior judges, "Be wise, understand, and the cause that you know not, search out," then the king is not the only interpreter of the law. But the Lord

says not to the king only, but to other judges also. Be wise, understand, and the cause that you know not, search out; therefore the king is not the sole lawgiver. The major is clear from Ps. 2:10, "Be wise now therefore, O You kings, be instructed, You judges of the earth." So are commands and rebukes for unjust judgment given to others than to kings (Ps. 132:1-5, 18:1-2; Isa. 1:17, 23, 25-26; 3:14; Job 29:12-15; 31:21-22).

3. The king is either your sole interpreter of law, in respect he is to follow the law as his rule, and so he is a ministerial interpreter of the law, or he is an interpreter of the law according to that super-dominion of absolute power that he has above the law. If the former be held, then it is clear that the king is not the only interpreter, for all judges, as they are judges, have a ministerial power to exposit the law by the law, but the second is the sense of royalists.

Assert. 2. Hence our second assertion is that the king's power of expositing the law is a mere ministerial power, and he has no dominion of any absolute royal power to exposit the law as he will, and to put such a sense and meaning of the law as he pleases.

1. Because Saul makes a law "Cursed be the man that tastes any food till night, that the king may be avenged on his enemies," (1 Sam. 14:24), the law, according to the letter, was bloody, but according to the intent of the lawgiver and substance of the law, profitable, for the end was that the enemies should be pursued with all speed. But king Saul's expositing the law after a tyrannical way against the intent of the law, which is the diamond and pearl of all laws: the safety of the innocent people was justly resisted by the innocent people, who violently hindered innocent Jonathan to be killed. From this it is clear that the people and princes put on the law its true sense and meaning; for Jonathan's tasting of a little honey though as it was against that sinful and precipitate circumstance, a rash oath, yet it was not against the substance and true intent of the law, which was the people's speedy pursuit of the enemy. From this it is clear that the

people, including the princes, has a ministerial power to exposit the law aright, and according to its genuine intent, and that the king as king has no absolute power to exposit the law as he pleases.

2. The king's absolute pleasure can no more be the genuine sense of a just law than his absolute pleasure can be a law, because the genuine sense of the law is the law itself, as the formal essence of a thing differs not really, but in respect of reason from the thing itself. The Pope and Romish church cannot put on the Scripture, *ex plenitudine potestatis*, whatever meaning they will, no more than they can out of absolute power make canonic scripture. Now so it is that the king by his absolute power cannot make law no law. 1. Because he is king by or according to law, but he is not king of law. *Rex est rex secundum legem, sed non est dominus et rex legis.*

2. Because, although it have a good meaning, which Ulpian says, "*Quod principi placet legis vigorem habet,*" the will of the prince is the law, yet the meaning is not that anything is a just law, because it is the prince's will, for its rule formally; for it must be good and just before the prince can will it, and then he finding it so, he puts the stamp of a human law on it.

3. This is the difference between God's will and the will of the king, or any mortal creature. Things are just and good, because God wills them, especially things positively good (though I conceive it hold in all things) and God does not will things, because they are good and just; but the creature, be he king or any never so eminent, do will things because they are good and just, and the king's willing of a thing makes it not good and just; for only God's will, not the creature's, can be the cause why things are good and just. If therefore it be so, it must undeniably thus follow, that the king's will makes not a just law to have an unjust and bloody sense, and he cannot as king by any absolute super-dominion over the law put a just sense on a bloody and unjust law.

4. The advancing of any man to the throne and royal dignity puts not the man above the number of rational men. No rational man can create by any act of power never so transcendent or boundless a sense to a law contrary to the law. Nay, give me leave to doubt if Omnipotence can make a just law to have an unjust and bloody sense, *aut contra*, because it involves a contradiction; the true meaning of a law being the essential form of the law. Thus judge what brutish, swinish flatterers they are who say, "It is the true meaning of the law which the king, the only supreme and independent expositor of the law, says is the true sense of the law." There was once an animal, a fool of the first magnitude, who said he could demonstrate by invincible reasons that the king's dung was more nourishing food than bread of the flour of the finest wheat. For my part I could wish it were the demonstrator's only food for seven days, and that should be the best demonstration he could make for his proof.

5. It must follow that there can be no necessity of written laws to the subjects, against Scripture and natural reason, and the law of nations in which all accord: that laws not promulgated and published cannot oblige as law, yea, Adam, in his innocence, was not obliged to obey a law not written in his heart by nature except that God had made known the law, as is clear, "Hast you eaten of the tree whereof I commanded you that you shouldest not eat?" (Gen. 3:11). But if the king's absolute will may put on the law what sense he pleases out of his independent and irresistible supremacy, the laws promulgated and written to the subjects can declare nothing concerning what is to be done by the subjects as just, and what is to be avoided as unjust, because the laws must signify to the subjects what is just and what is unjust, according to their genuine sense. Now, their genuine sense according to royalists is not only uncertain and impossible to be known, but also contradictory; for the king obliges us without gainsaying to believe that the just law has this unjust sense. Thus this of flattering royalists is more cruel to kings than ravens (for these eat but dead

men, while they devour living men). When there is a controversy between the king and the estates of parliament, who shall exposit the law and render its native meaning? Royalists say, "Not the estates of parliament, for they are subjects, not judges, to the king, and only counsellors and advisers of the king." The king, therefore, must be the only judicial and final expositor. "As for lawyers" said Strafford "the law is not enclosed in a lawyer's cap." But I remember this was one of the articles laid to the charge of Richard II, that he said, "The law was in his head and breast." And indeed it must follow, if the king by the plenitude of absolute power be the only supreme uncontrollable expositor of the law, that is not law which is written in the acts of parliament, but that is the law which is in the king's breast and head, which Josephus (*Antiquities* 19.2) objected to Caius. And all justice and injustice should be finally and peremptorily resolved on the king's will and absolute pleasure.

6. The king either is to exposit the law by the law itself, or by his absolute power, loosed from all law, he exposits it, or according to the advise of his great senate. If the first be said, he is nothing more than other judges. If the second be said, he must be omnipotent, and more. If the third be said, he is not absolute, if the senate be only advisers, and he yet the only judicial expositor. The king often professes his ignorance of the laws, and he must then both be absolute above the law, and ignorant of the law, and the sole and final judicial expositor of the law. And by this, all parliaments, and their power of making laws, and of judging are cried down.

Obj. 1. Prov. 16:10, "A divine sentence is in the lips of the king; his mouth transgresses not in judgment;" therefore he only can exposit the law.

Ans. Lavater says (and I see no reason on the contrary) "By a king he means all magistrates." Aben Ezra and Isidorus read the words imperatively. The Tigurine version, "They are oracles which proceed from his lips; let not therefore his mouth transgress in judgment."

Vatabulus, "When he is in his prophecies, he lies not." Jansenius, "*Non facile errabit in judicando.*" Mich. Jermine, "If he pray." Calvin, "If he read in the book of the law, as God commands him" (Deut. 17). But why stand we on the place? "He speaks of good kings," says Cornel. A Lapide, "otherwise Jeroboam, Ahab, and Manasseh, erred in judgment." "And except," as Mercerus exposits it, "we understand him to speak of kings according to their office, not their facts and practice, we make them popes, and men who cannot give out grievous and unjust sentences on the throne," against both the Word and experience.

Obj. 2. Sometimes all is cast upon one man's voice; why may not the king be this one man?

Ans. The antecedent is false; the last voter in a senate is not the sole judge, else why should others give suffrages with him? This would be to take away inferior judges, contrary to God's word (Deut. 1:17; 2 Chron. 19:6-7; Rom. 13:1-3).

QUESTION 28.

*WHETHER OR NOT WARS RAISED BY THE ESTATES AND
SUBJECTS, FOR THEIR OWN JUST DEFENSE AGAINST
THE KING'S BLOODY EMISSARIES ARE LAWFUL.*

*The state of the question. If kings are absolute, a superior judge may
punish an inferior judge, not as a judge but as an erring man. By
divine institution all covenants to restrain their power must be
unlawful. Resistance in some cases is lawful. Six arguments for the
lawfulness of defensive wars. Many others follow.*

Arnisaeus perverts the question; he says, "The question is whether or not the subjects may according to their power judge the
king and dethrone him; that is, whether or not it is lawful for the
subjects in any case to take arms against their lawful prince, if he
degenerate, and shall wickedly use his lawful power."

1. The state of the question is much perverted, for these be different
questions. Whether the kingdom may dethrone a wicked and tyrannical prince, and whether the kingdom may take up arms against the
man who is the king in their own innocent defense. For the former is
an act offensive, and of punishing; the latter is an act of defense.

2. The present question is not of subjects only, but of the estates and parliamentary lords of a kingdom. I utterly deny these, as they are judges, to be subjects to the king; for the question is whether is the king or the representative kingdom greatest, and which of them be subject one to another? I affirm among judges, as judges, not one is the commander or superior, and the other the commanded or subject. Indeed, one higher judge may correct and punish a judge, not as a judge, but as an erring man.

3. The question is not so much concerning the authoritative act of war, as concerning the power of natural defense, upon supposition that the king be not now turned an habitual tyrant, but that upon some acts of misinformation, he come in arms against his subjects.

Arnisaeus makes two sort of kings, "Some kings *integrae majestatis*, of entire power and sovereignty; some kings by pactions, or voluntary agreement between king and people." But I judge this a vain distinction; for the limited prince, if he be limited to a power only of doing just and right, by this is not a prince *integrae majestatis*, of entire royal majesty, by which he may both do good and also play the tyrant, but a power to do ill being no ways essential, yea, repugnant to the absolute majesty of the King of kings, cannot be an essential part of the majesty of a lawful king, and therefore the prince, limited by voluntary and positive paction only to rule according to law and equity, is the good, lawful, and entire prince only if he have not power to do every thing just and good; in that regard he is not an entire and complete prince. So the man will have it lawful to resist the limited prince, not the absolute prince; by the contrary, it is more lawful to me to resist the absolute prince than the limited, inasmuch as we may with safer consciences resist the tyrant and the lion than the just prince and lamb. Nor can I assent to Cunnerius who holds that "these voluntary pactions between king and people, in which the power of the prince is diminished, cannot stand, because their power is given to them by God's word, which cannot be taken from them by any voluntary paction, lawfully," (*De officio princip, Christia*. sections 5 and 17) and from the same ground, Winzetus "will have it unlawful to resist kings, because God has made them irresistible" (*in velix. contr. Buchan*). I answer, if God by a divine institution make kings absolute and above all laws (which is a blasphemous supposition-the holy Lord can give to no man a power to sin, for God has not himself any such power) then the covenant between the king and people cannot lawfully remove and take away what God by institution has given, but because God has limited the first lawful king (Deut. 17), the mold of all the rest, the people ought also to limit him by a voluntary covenant; and because the lawful power of a king to do good is not by divine institution placed in an indivisible point. It is not a sin for the people to take some power, even of doing good, from the king, that he solely and by himself shall not have power to pardon an involuntary homicide, without advice and the judicial suffrages of the council of the kingdom, lest he instead of this give pardons to robbers, to abominable murderers, and in so doing, the people robs not the king of the power that God gave him as king; nor ought the king to contend for a sole power in himself of ministering justice to all, for God lays not upon kings burdens impossible, and God by institution has denied to the king all power of doing all good, because it is his will that other judges be sharers with the king in that power (Num. 14:16; Duet 1:14-17; 1 Pet. 2:14; Rom. 13:1-4) and therefore the duke of Venice, to me, comes nearest to the king molded by God (Deut. 17) in respect of power, *de jure*, of any king I know in Europe. And in point of conscience the inferior judge discerning a murderer and bloody man to die may *in foro conscientiae* despise the king's unjust pardon, and resist the king's force by his co-active power that God has given him and put to death the bloody murderer, and he sins if he do not this; for to me it is clear that the king cannot judge so justly and understandingly of a murderer in Scotland, as a judge to whom God has committed the sword in Scotland. Nor has the Lord laid that impossible burden on a king to judge so of a murder four hundred miles removed from the king, as the judge nearer to him, as is clear in Num. 14:16; 1 Sam. 7:15-17. The king should go from place to place and judge, and whereas it is impossible to him to go through three kingdoms, he should appoint faithful judges, who may not be resisted, no, not by the king.

1. The question is if the king command A. B. to kill his father or his pastor, the man neither being cited nor convicted of any fault, he may lawfully be resisted.

2. *Queritur.* If in that case in which the king is captured, imprisoned, and not *sui juris*, and awed or overawed by bloody papists, and so is forced to command a barbarous and unjust war, and if, being distracted physically or morally through wicked counsel, he command that which no father in his sober wits would command, even against law and conscience, that the sons should yield obedience and subjection to him in maintaining with lives and goods, a bloody religion and bloody papists: if in that case the king may not be resisted in his person, because the power lawful and the sinful person cannot be separated. We hold that the king using, contrary to the oath of God and his royal office, violence in killing against law and conscience his subjects by bloody emissaries may be resisted by defensive wars at the commandment of the estates of the kingdom.

But before I produce arguments to prove the lawfulness of resistance, a little of the case of resistance. 1. Dr. Ferne grants resistance by force to the king to be lawful, when the assault is sudden, without pretense of a law or reason, and inevitable (part 3, section 6). But if Nero burn Rome, he has a pretense of law and reason, yea, though all Rome, and his mother, in whose womb he lay, were one neck. A man who will with reason go mad has pretense of reason, and so of law, to invade and kill the innocent.

2. Arnisaeuss says, "If the magistrate proceed *extra-judicialiter*, without order of law by violence, the laws gives every private man

power to resist, if the danger be irrecoverable; yea, though it be recoverable." (section 2, n. 10, *L. prohibitum, C. de jur, fisc. l. que madmodum,* sect. 39, *magistratus ad l. aquil, l. nec. magistratibus* 32, *de injur*). Because while the magistrate does against his office, he is not a magistrate; for law and right, not injury, should come from the magistrate (*L. meminerint.* 6, *unde* 6). Yea, if the magistrate proceed judicially, and the loss be irrecoverable, jurists say that a private man has the same law to resist (*Marantius.* dis. 1, n. 35). And in a recoverable loss they say, every man is held to resist, *si evidenter constet de iniquitate,* if the iniquity be known to all (*D. D. Jason,* n. 19, des. n. 26, *ad l. ut vim dejust. et jur).*

3. I would think it not fit easily to resist the king's unjust exactors of custom or tribute (1). Because Christ paid tribute to Tiberius Caesar, an unjust usurper, though he was free from that, by God's law, lest he should offend. (2) Because we have agreater dominion over goods than over our lives and bodies, and it is better to yield in a matter of goods than to come to arms, for of sinless evils we may choose the least.

4. A tyrant without a title may be resisted by any private man. *Quia licet vim vi repellere,* because we may repel violence by violence; yea, he may be filled, *Ut l. et vim. F. de instit. et jure, ubi plene per omnes.* Vasquez, 1.1.3, n. 33; Barclay (*Contra Monarch.* 1.4.10).

For the lawfulness of resistance in the matter of the king's unjust invasion of life and religion, we offer these arguments.

Arg. 1. That power which is obliged to command and rule justly and religiously for the good of the subjects and is only set over the people on these conditions, and not absolutely, cannot tie the people to subjection without resistance, when the power is abused to the destruction of laws, religion, and the subjects. But all power of the law is thus obliged (Rom. 13:4; Deut. 17:18-20; 2 Chron. 19:6; Ps. 132:11-12; 139:30-31; 2 Sam. 7:12; Jer. 17:24-25) and has, and may be, abused by kings to the destruction of laws, religion, and subjects.

The proposition is clear. 1. For the powers that tie us to subjection only are of God. 2. Because to resist them is to resist the ordinance of God. 3. Because they are not a terror to good works, but to evil. 4. Because they are God's ministers for our good, but abused powers are not of God, but of men, or not ordinances of God; they are a terror to good works, not to evil; they are not God's ministers for our good.

Arg. 2. That power which is contrary to law, and is evil and tyrannical, can tie none to subjection, but is a mere tyrannical power and unlawful, and if it tie not to subjection, it may lawfully be resisted. But the power of the king, abused to the destruction of laws, religion, and subjects, is a power contrary to law, evil, and tyrannical, and ties no man to subjection; wickedness by no imaginable reason can oblige any man. Obligation to suffer of wicked men falls under no commandment of God, except in our Savior. A passion, as such, is not formally commanded, I mean a physical passion, such as to be killed. God has not said to me in any moral law: Be you killed, tortured, beheaded, but only: Be you patient, if God deliver you to wicked men's hands, to suffer these things.

Arg. 3. There is not a stricter obligation moral between king and people than between parents and children, master and servant, patron and clients, husband and wife, the lord and the vassal, between the pilot of a ship and the passengers, the physician and the sick, the doctor and the scholars, but the law grants (*1. Minime* 35, *de Relig. et sumpt. funer*) if these betray their trust committed to them, they may be resisted: if the father turn distracted, and arise to kill his sons, his sons may violently apprehend him, and bind his hands, and spoil him of his weapons; for in that he is not a father. Vasquez: *Si dominius subditum enormiter et atrociter oneraret, princeps superior vassallum posset ex toto eximere a sua jurisdictione, et etiam tacente subdito et nihil petente. Quid papa in suis decis. parliam. grat. decis.* 62. *Si quis Baro. abutentes dominio privari possunt.* (1, *Ilustr.* quest. section 8, n. 18). The servant may resist the master if he attempts unjustly to kill him, so may the wife do to the husband; if the pilot should willfully run the ship on a rock to destroy himself and his passengers, they might violently thrust him from the helm. Every tyrant is a furious man, and is morally distracted, as Althusius says (*Polit.* section 28, n. 30, and seq.).

Arg. 4. That which is given as a blessing, and a favor, and a screen, between the people's liberty and their bondage, cannot be given of God as a bondage and slavery to the people. But the power of a king is given as a blessing and favor of God to defend the poor and needy, to preserve both tables of the law, and to keep the people in their liberties from oppressing and treading one upon another. But so it is that if such a power be given of God to a king, by which, *actu primo*, he is invested of God to do acts of tyranny, and so to do them, that to resist him in the most innocent way, which is self-defense, must be a resisting God, and rebellion against the king, His deputy; then has God given a royal power as uncontrollable by mortal men, by any violence, as if God Himself were immediately and personally resisted, when the king is resisted, and so this power shall be a power to waste and destroy irresistibly, and so in itself a plague and a curse; for it cannot be ordained both according to the intention and genuine formal effect and intrinsic operation of the power, to preserve the tables of the law, religion and liberty, subjects and laws, and able to destroy the same. But it is taught by royalists that this power is for tyranny, as well as for peaceable government, because to resist this royal power put forth in acts either ways, either in acts of tyranny or just government is to resist the ordinance of God, as royalists say, from Rom. 13:1-3. And we know, to resist God's ordinances' and God's deputy *formaliter*, as His deputy, is to resist God himself (1 Sam. 8:7; Matt 10:40) as if God were doing personally these acts that the king is doing, and it imports as much as the King of kings does these acts in and through the tyrant. Now, it is blasphemy to think or say that when a king is drinking the blood of innocents, and wasting the church of God, that God, if he were personally present, would commit these same acts of tyranny (God avert such blasphemy!) and that God in and through the king, as His lawful deputy and vicegerent in these acts of tyranny is wasting the poor church of God. If it be said, in these sinful acts of tyranny, he is not God's formal vicegerent, but only in good and lawful acts of government, yet he is not to be resisted in these acts, not because the acts are just and good, but because of the dignity of his royal person. Yet this must prove that those who resist the king in these acts of tyranny must resist no ordinance of God, but only resist him who is the Lord's deputy, though not as the Lord's deputy. What absurdity is there in that more than to disobey him, re-using active obedience to him who is the Lord's deputy, not as the Lord's deputy, but as a man commanding besides his master's warrant?

Arg. 6. That which is inconsistent with the care and providence of God in giving a king to His church is not to be taught. Now God's end in giving a king to his church is the feeding, safety, preservation, and the peaceable and quiet life of his church (1 Tim. 2:2; Isa. 49:23; Ps. 79:71). But God should cross His own end in the same act of giving a king, if He should provide a king who by office were to suppress robbers, murderers, and all oppressors and wasters in his holy mount, and yet should give an irresistible power to one crowned lion, a king who may kill ten hundred thousand protestants for their religion in an ordinary providence, and they are by an ordinary law of God to give their throats to his emissaries and bloody executioners. If any say the king will not be so cruel, I believe it, because *actu secundo* it is not possibly in his power to be so cruel. We owe thanks to his good will that he kills not so many, but no thanks to the nature and genuine intrinsic end of a king, who has power from God to kill all these and that without resistance made by any mortal man. Yea, no thanks (God avert blasphemy!) to God's ordinary providence, which (if royalists may be believed) puts no bar upon the unlimited power of a man inclined to sin, and abuse his power to so much cruelty. Some may say the same absurdity does follow if the king should turn papist, and the

parliament all were papists. In that case there might be so many martyrs for the truth put to death, and God should put no bar of providence upon this power then more than now, and yet in that case the
king and parliament should be judges given of God, *actu primo*, and
by virtue of their office obliged to preserve the people in peace and
godliness. But I answer if God gave a lawful official power to king and
parliament to work the same cruelty upon millions of martyrs, and it
should he unlawful for them by arms to defend themselves, I should
then think that king and parliament were both *ex offico* by virtue of
their office, and *actu primo,* judges and fathers, and also by that same
office, murderers and butchers, which would be a grievous aspersion
to the unspotted providence of God.

Arg. 6. If the estates of a kingdom give the power to a king, it is
their own power in the fountain; and if they give it for their own
good, they have power to judge when it is used against themselves,
and for their evil, and so power to limit and resist the power that they
gave. Now that they may take away this power is clear in Athaliah's
case. It is true she was a tyrant without a title, and had not the right
of heaven to the crown, yet she had in men's court a title. For supposing all the royal seed to be killed, and the people consent, we cannot
say that for these six years or thereabout she was no magistrate; that
there were none on the throne of David at this time; that she was not
to be obeyed as God's deputy. But grant that she was no magistrate;
yet when Jehoash is brought forth to be crowned, it was a controversy
to the states to whom the crown should belong. 1. Athaliah was in
possession. 2. Jehoash himself being but seven years old could not be
judge. 3. It might be doubted if Joash was the true son of Ahaziah,
and if he was not killed with the rest of the blood royal.

Two great adversaries say with us; Hugo Grotius says he dare not
condemn this, if the lesser part of the people, and every one of them
indifferently, should defend themselves against a tyrant, *ultimo neces-
sitatis praesidio* (*De jur. belli et pacis,* 1.1, section 4, n. 7). The case of

Scotland, when we were blocked up by sea and land with armies: the case of England, when the king, induced by prelates, first attempted to bring an army to cut off the parliament, and then gathered an army, and fortified York, and invaded Hull, to make the militia his own, sure is considerable. Barclay says the people has *jus se tuendi adversus immanem saevitiem* (*Advers. Monarch.* 1.3.8) a power to defend themselves against prodigious cruelty. The case of England and Ireland, now invaded by the bloody rebels of Ireland, is also worthy of consideration. I could cite hosts more.

QUESTION 29.

*WHETHER, IN THE CASE OF DEFENSIVE WARS, THE
DISTNCTION OF THE PERSON OF THE KING AS A
MAN, WHO CAN COMMIT HOSTILE ACTS OF TYRANNY
AGAINST HIS SUBJECTS, AND OF THE OFFICE AND
ROYAL POWER THAT HE HAS FROM GOD AND THE
PEOPLE, CAN HAVE PLACE.*

*The king's person in concreto, and his office in abstracto, or, which is all
one, the king using his power lawfully to be distinguished (Rom. 13).
To command unjustly makes not a higher power. That the person may
be resisted and yet the office cannot be resisted is proved by fourteen
arguments. Contrary objections of royalists and of the Popish Prelate
answered. What we mean by the person and office in abstracto in this
dispute; we do not exclude the person in concreto altogether, but only the
person as abusing his power; we may kill a person as a man, and love
him as a son, father, wife, according to Scripture. We obey the king for
the law, and not the law for the king. The losing of habitual and actual
royalty different. That Pilate's power of crucifying Christ no law-power
given to him by God is proved against royalists by six arguments.*

B efore I can proceed to other Scripture proofs for the lawfulness of resistance, this distinction, rejected by royalists, must be
cleared. This is an evident and sensible distinction: The king *in concreto*, the man who is king, and the king *in abstracto*, the royal office
of the king. The ground of this distinction we desire to be considered
from Rom. 13. We affirm with Buchanan that Paul here speaks of the
office and duty of good magistrates, and that the text speaks nothing
of an absolute king, nothing of a tyrant, and the royalists distinguish
where the law distinguishes not, against the law (1. pret. 10, *gl. Bart,
de pub. in Rem.*), and therefore we move the question here: whether
or not to resist the illegal and tyrannical will of the man who is king
be to resist the king and the ordinance of God; we say no. Nor do we
deny the king, abusing his power in unjust acts, to remain king and
the minister of God, whose person for his royal office and his royal office are both to be honored, reverenced, and obeyed. God forbid that
we should do so as the sons of Belial, imputing to us the doctrine of
anabaptists, and the doctrine falsely imputed to Wycliffe, that dominion is founded upon supernatural grace, and that a magistrate being
in the state of mortal sin cannot be a lawful magistrate: we teach no
such thing. The Popish Prelate shows us his sympathy with papists,
and that he builds the monuments and sepulchers of the slain and
murdered prophets, when he revising to open his mouth in the gates
for the righteous, professes he will not purge the witnesses of Christ,
the Waldenses, and Wycliffe, and Huss of these notes of disloyalty,
but that these acts proceeding from this root of bitterness, the abused
power of a king, should be acknowledged with obedience active or
passive in these unjust acts we deny.

Assert. 1. It is evident from Rom. 13 that all subjection and obedience to higher powers commanded there is subjection to the power
and office of the magistrate in abstractor or, which is all one, to the
person using the power lawfully, and that no subjection is due by that

text or any word of God, to the abused and tyrannical power of the king, which I show from the text, and from other Scriptures.

1. Because the text says, "Let every soul be subject to the higher powers." But no powers commanding things unlawful, and killing the innocent people of God, can be ιχυσιαι ὑπερεχυσαι higher powers, but in that lower powers. He that commands not what God commands, and punishes and kills where God, if personally and immediately present, would neither command nor punish, is not in these acts to be subjected unto and obeyed as a superior power, though in habit He may remain a superior power; for all habitual, all actual superiority is a formal participation of the power of the Most High. Arnisaeus well says, "That of Aristotle must be true. It is against nature, better and worthier men should be in subjection to unworthier and more wicked men" (section 4); but when magistrates command wickedness, and kill the innocent, the non-obeyers so far are worthier than the commanders (whatever they be in habit and in office) actually, or in these wicked acts are unworthier and inferior, and the non-obeyers are in that worthier as being zealous adherents to God's command and not to man's will. I desire not to be mistaken; if we speak of habitual excellency, godly and holy men, as the witnesses of Christ in things lawful, are to obey wicked and infidel kings and emperors, but in that these wicked kings have an excellency in respect of office above them; but when they command things unlawful, and kill the innocent, they do it not by virtue of any office, and so in that they are not higher powers, but lower and weak ones. Laertius does explain Aristotle well, who defines a tyrant by this, "That he commands his subjects by violence;" and Arnisaeus condemns Laertius for this, "Because one tyrannical action does no more constitute a tyrant than one unjust action does constitute an unjust man." But he may condemn, as he does indeed (Covarruvias, pract. quest, 1, and Vasquez Illustr., quest. 1.1.47, n. 1, 12) for this is essential to a tyrant: to command and rule by violence. If a lawful prince do one or more acts of a tyrant, he

is not a tyrant for that, yet his action in that is tyrannical, and he does not that as a king, but in that act as a sinful man, having something of tyranny in him.

2. The powers that be are ordained by God as their author and efficient, but kings commanding unjust things and killing the innocent in these acts are but men, and sinful men, and the power by which they do these acts, a sinful and an usurped power, and so far they are not powers ordained by God, according to His revealed will, which must rule us. Now the authority and official power, *in abstracto*, is ordained of God, as the text says, and other Scriptures do show. And this politicians do clear, while they distinguish between *jus personae*, and *jus coronae*, the power of the person, and the power of the crown and royal office. They must then be two different things.

3. He that resists the power, that is, the official power, and the king as king and commanding in the Lord, resists the ordinance of God, and God's lawful constitution. But he who resists the man who is the king, commanding that which is against God and killing the innocent, resists no ordinance of God, but an ordinance of sin and Satan; for a man commanding unjustly and ruling tyrannically has in that no power from God.

4. They that resist the power and royal office of the king in things just and right shall receive to themselves damnation, but they that resist, that is, refuse for conscience to obey the man who is the king and choose to obey God rather than man, as all the martyrs did, shall receive to themselves salvation. And the eighty valiant men, the priests, who used bodily violence against king Uzziah's person, "and thrust him out or the house of the Lord," from offering incense to the Lord, which belonged to the priest only, received not damnation to themselves, but salvation in doing God's will and in resisting the king's wicked will.

6. The lawful ruler, as a ruler and in respect of his office, is not to be resisted, because he is not a terror to good works, but to evil, and

no man who does good is to be afraid of the office or the power, but to expect praise and a reward of the same. But the man who is a king may command an idolatrous and superstitious worship, send an army of cut-throats against them, because they refuse that worship, and may reward papists, prelates, and other corrupt men, and may advance them to places of state and honor because they kneel to a tree altar, pray to the east, adore the letters and sound of the word *Jesus*, teach and write Arminianism, and may imprison, deprive, confine, cut the ears, and slit the noses, and burn the faces of those who speak and preach and write the truth of God; and may send armies of cut-throats, Irish rebels, and other papists and malignant atheists to destroy and murder the judges of the land, and innocent defenders of the reformed religion, &c., the man, I say, in these acts is a terror to good works, an encouragement to evil, and those that do good are to be afraid of the king, and to expect no praise but punishment and vexation from him; therefore, this reason in the text will prove that the man who is the king, insofar as he does those things that are against his office, may be resisted, and that in these we are not to be subject, but only we are to be subject to his power and royal authority, *in abstracto*, insofar as according to his office he is not a terror to good works, but to evil.

7. The lawful ruler is the minister of God, or the servant of God, for good to the commonwealth; and to resist the servant in that wherein he is a servant, and using the power that he has from his master, is to resist the Lord his master. But the man who is the king, commanding unjust things, and killing the innocent, in these acts is not the minister of God for the good of the commonwealth; he serves himself and papists and prelates for the destruction of religion, laws, and commonwealth; therefore the man may be resisted by this text when the office and power cannot be resisted.

7. The ruler as the ruler and the nature and intrinsic end of the office is that he bear God's sword as an avenger to execute wrath on him

that does evil, and so cannot be resisted without sin. But the man who is the ruler, and commands things unlawful, and kills the innocent, carries the papist's and prelate's sword to execute, not the righteous judgment of the Lord upon the evil-doer, but his own private revenge upon him that does well; therefore, the man may be resisted, the office may not be resisted; and they must be two different things.

8. We must needs be subject to the royal office for conscience, by reason of the fifth commandment; but we must not needs be subject to the man who is king if he command things unlawful, for Dr. Ferne warrants us to resist if the ruler invade us suddenly without pretense of law or reason, and unavoidably; and Winzetus, Barclay, and Grotius, as before I cited, give us leave to resist a king turning a cruel tyrant; but Paul forbids us to resist the power, *in abstracto* (Rom. 13); therefore, it must be the man, *in concreto*, that we must resist.

9. Those we may not resist to whom we owe tribute, as a reward of the onerous work on which they as ministers of God do attend continually. But we owe not tribute to the king as a man, for then should we be indebted tribute to all men, but as a king, to whom the wages of tribute is due, as to a princely workman, a king as a king; therefore, the man and the king are different.

10. We owe fear and honor as due to be rendered to the man who is king, because he is a king, not because he is a man, for it is the highest fear and honor due to any mortal man, which is due to the king as king.

11. The man and the inferior judge are different, and we cannot by this text resist the inferior judge as a judge, but we resist the ordinance of God, as the text proves. But cavaliers resist the inferior judges as men, and have killed various members of both houses of parliament; but they will not say that they killed them as judges, but as rebels. If therefore to be a rebel, as a wicked man, and to be a judge, are distinguished thus, then to be a man and commit some acts of tyranny and to be the supreme judge and king are two different things.

12. The congregation, in a letter to the nobility say, "There is great difference between the authority, which is God's ordinance, and the persons of those who are placed in authority. The authority and God's ordinance can never do wrong, for it commands that vice and wicked men be punished, and virtue, with virtuous men and just, be maintained; but the corrupt person placed in this authority may offend, and most commonly do contrary to this authority. And is then the corruption of man to be followed by reason that it is clothed with the name of authority?" (Knox, *Hist. of Scotland*, 1.2). And they give instance in Pharaoh and Saul, who were lawful kings and yet corrupt men. And certainly the man and the divine authority differ, as the subject and the accident, as that which is under a law and can offend God, and that which is neither capable of law nor sin.

13. The king as king is a just creature, and by office a living and breathing law. His will, as he is king, is nothing but a just law; but the king as a sinful man is not a just creature but one who can sin and play the tyrant; and his will, as a private sinful man, is a private will and may be resisted. So the law says, "The king as king can do no wrong," but the king as a man may do a wrong. While as then the parliaments of both kingdoms resist the king's private will as a man, and fight against his illegal cut-throats, sent out by him to destroy his native subjects, they fight for him as a king, and obey his public legal will, which is his royal will, *de jure*; and while he is absent from his parliaments as a man, he is legally and in his law-power present, and so the parliaments are as legal as if he were personally present with them.

Let me answer royalists. The Popish Prelate says it is Solomon's word, "By me kings reign," kings, *in concreto*, with their sovereignty. He says not, 'by me royalty or sovereignty reigns.' And elsewhere he says that Barclay says, "Paul, writing to the Romans, keeps the usual Roman diction in this, who express by powers, *in abstracto*, the persons authorized by power, and it is the Scripture's dialect: by him were created "thrones, dominions, principalities," that is, angels; to say angels, *in abstracto,* were created (2 Pet. 2:10). They "speak evil of dignities" (Jude 8), "despise dominion," that is, they speak ill of Cajus, Caligula, Nero. Our Levites rail against the Lord's anointed, the best of kings in the world. Nero *in concreto,* bears not the sword in vain (Rom. 12:4). Arnisaeus says it better than the Prelate, (he is a witless thief) Rom. 13:4, "The royal power, *in abstracto,* does not bear the sword, but the person; not the power, but the prince himself bears the sword."[1] And the Prelate, poor man, following Dr. Ferne, says, "It is absurd to pursue the king's person with a cannon bullet at Edgehill, and preserve his authority at London, or elsewhere." So says Ferne, "The concrete powers here are purposed as objects of our obedience, which cannot be directed but upon power in some person; for it is said, αι ουσαι εξουσιαι. The powers that be are of God" (section 10). Now power cannot be ούπα existent but in some person, and, says Ferne, "Can power in the abstract have praise? Or is tribute paid to the power in the abstract? Yea, the power is the reason why we yield obedience to the person," &c.

The Prelate has as much learning as to copy out of Ferne, Barclay, Arnisaeus, and others, these words and the like, but has not wit to add the sinews of these authors' reason, and with all this he can in his preface call it his own, and "provoke any to answer him if they dare," whereas, while I answer this excommunicated pamphleteer, I answer these learned authors from which he steals all he has; and yet he must persuade the king he is the only man who can defend his Majesty's cause, and "the importunity (forsooth) of friends extorted this piece," as if it were a fault that this Delphic oracle (giving out railings and lies for responses) should be silent.

1. Not we only, but the Holy Ghost, *in terminis,* has this distinction. Acts 4:19; 5:29: "We ought to obey God rather than men." Then rulers (for of rulers sitting in judgment is that speech uttered) commanding

---

1. *De potest. princip.* section 2.11, 17.

and tyrannizing over the apostles are men contradistinguished from God; and as they command and punish unjustly, they are but men; otherwise commanding for God, they are gods, and more than men.

2. From Theophylaot also, or from Chrysotom on Rom. 13 we have this, The apostle speaks not (say they) περι των καθ ετασον αρχοντων, αλλα περι αυτου του πραγματος.

3. Sovereignty or royalty does not properly reign or bear the sword, or receive praise, and this accident does not bear a sword; nor do we think (or Paul speak, Rom. 13) of the abstracted due of power and royalty, subsisting out of its subject, nor dream we that the naked accident of royal authority is to be feared and honored as the Lord's anointed; the person or man who is the king, and bears the crown on his head, and holds the scepter in his hand is to be obeyed. Accidents are not persons, but they speak nonsense and are like brute beasts who deny that all the kingly honor due to the king must be due to him as a king, and because of the royal dignity that God has given to him, and not because he is a man; for a pursuivant's son is a man, and if a pursuivant's son would usurp the throne and take the crown on his head, and the scepter in his hand, and command that all souls be subject to such a superior power, because he is a man, the laws of Scotland would hang a man for a less fault, we know; and the Popish Prelate was wont to edify women, and converted souls to Christ, with such a distinction as *objectum quod*, and *objectum quo*, in the pulpits of Edinburgh, and it has good use here; we never took abstract royalty to be the king. The king of Scotland of old were not second notions, and we exclude not the person of the king; yet we distinguish, with leave of the Popish Prelate, between the person *in linea physica* (we must take *physica* largely here) and *in linea morali*, obedience, fear, tribute, honor is due to the person of the king, and to the man who is king, not because of his person or because he is a man (the Popish Prelate may know in what notion we take the name person) but because God by the people's election has exalted him to royal dignity, and for this cause evil-doers are to subject their throats and necks to the sword of the Lord's anointed's executioner or hangman, with patience, and willingly; because in taking away the head of evil-doers, for evil-doing, he is acting the office of the Lord, by whom he reigns; but if he take away their heads, and send out the long-tusked vultures and boars of Babylon, the Irish rebels, to execute his wrath, as he is in that act a misinformed man, and lacks the authority of God's law and man's law, he may be resisted with arms. For, 1. If royalists say against this, this: if a king turn an habitual tyrant, and induce an hundred thousand Turks to destroy his subjects upon mere desire of revenge, they are not to resist, but to be subject, and suffer for conscience. I am sure Grotius says, "If a king sell his subjects, he loses all title to the crown, and so may be resisted;"[1] and Winzetus says, "A tyrant may be resisted;"[2] and Barclay, "It is lawful for the people, in case of tyranny, to defend themselves, *adversus immanem saevetiam*, against extreme cruelty."[3] And I desire the Prelate to answer how people are subject in suffering such cruelty of the higher power, because he is God's ordinance, and a power from God, unless he say, as he sells his people, and barbarously destroys by the cut-throat Irish-men, his whole subjects refusing to worship idols, he is a man and a sinful man, *eatenus*, and an inferior power inspired by wicked counsel, not a king, *eatenus*, not a higher power; and that in resisting him thus the subjects resist not the ordinance of God. Also suppose king David defend his kingdom and people against Jesse, his natural father, who we suppose comes in against his son and prince, king David, with a huge army of the Philistines to destroy him and his kingdom, if he shall kill his own native father in that war, at some Edgehill, how shall he preserve at Jerusalem that honor and love that he owes to his father by virtue of the fifth commandment, "Honor your father and your mother, &c.,"

---

1. *De jur. et pacis,* 1.1.4, n. 7.

2. *Velitat. adver. Buchanan.*

3. *Adv. Monarchom.* 3.8.

let them answer this; except king David consider Jesse in one relation, *in abstracto*, as his father, whom he is to obey, and as he is a wicked man, and a perfidious subject, in another relation; and except king David say, he is to subject himself to his father, as a father, according to the fifth commandment, and that in the act of his father's violent invasion, he is not to subject himself to him, as he is a violent invader, and as a man. Let the royalist see how he can answer the argument, and how Levi is not to know his father and mother, as they are sinful men (Deut. 33:9) and yet to know and honor them as parents, and how an Israelite is not to pity the wife that lies in his bosom, when she entices him "to go a whoring after strange gods," but is to kill her (Deut. 13:6-8) and yet the husband is to "love the wife, as Christ loved his church" (Eph. 5:25). If the husband take away his wife's life in some mountain in the Holy Land, as God's law commands, let the royalists answer us, where is then the marital love he owes to her, and that respect due to her as she is a wife and a helper?

2. But let not the royalist infer that I am from these examples pleading for the killing of kings; for lawful resistance is one thing, and killing of kings is another, the one defensive and lawful, the other offensive and unlawful so long as he remains a king and the Lord's anointed; but if he be a murderer of his father, who does counsel his father to come to a place of danger where he may be killed, and where the king ought not to be, as Abner was worthy of death, who watched not carefully king Saul, but slept when David came to his bedside, and had opportunity to kill the king; they are traitors and murderers of the king, who either counselled his Majesty to come to Edgehill, where the danger was so great, or did not violently restrain him from coming thither, seeing kings' safety and lives are as much, yea, more, in the disposing of the people than in their own private will (2 Sam. 18:2-3); for certainly the people might have violently restrained king Saul from killing himself, and the king is guilty of his own death, and sins against his office and subjects, who comes out in person to any

such battles where he may be killed, and the contrary party free of his blood. And here our Prelate is blind if he see not the clear difference between the king's person and his office as king, and between his private will and his public and royal will.

3. The angels may be named thrones and dominions *in abstracto*, and yet created *in concreto*, and we may say the angel and his power are both created at once; but David was not both born the son of Jesse and a king at once, and the Popish Prelate by this may prove it is not lawful to resist the devil (for he is of the number of these created angels, Col. 1) as he is a devil; because in resisting the devil as a devil, we must resist an angel of God and a principality.

4. To speak evil of dignities (2 Pet. 2; Jude 8) Piscator insinuates is to speak evil of the very office of rulers, as well as of their manners; and Theodat. says on 2 Pet. 2 that "these railers speak evil of the place of governors and masters as unbeseeming believers." All our interpreters, such as Beza, Calvin, Luther, Bucer, Marloratus, from the place say it is a special reproof of anabaptists and libertines, who in that time maintained that we are all free men in Christ, and that there should not be kings, masters, nor any magistrates. However the abstract is put for me concrete, it is true, and it says we are not to rail upon Nero; but to say Nero was a persecutor of Christians, and yet obey him commanding what is just are very consistent.

5. "The persons are proposed to be the object of our obedience, (Rom. 13)" says Dr. Ferne. This is very true: but he is ignorant of our mind in expositing the word *person*. We never meant that fear, honor, royalty, tribute, must be due to the abstracted accident of kingly authority, and not to the man who is king; nor is it our meaning that royalty, *in abstracto*, is crowned king, and is anointed, but that the person is crowned and anointed. But, again, by a person, we mean nothing less than the man Nero wasting Rome, burning, crucifying Paul, and torturing Christians; and that we owe subjection to Nero, and to his person *in concreto*, as to God's ordinance, God's minister,

God's sword-bearer, in that notion of a person, is that only which we deny. Nay, in that Nero, *in concreto*, to us is no power ordained of God, no minister of God, but a minister of the devil, and Satan's armor-bearer, and therefore we owe not fear, honor, subjection, or tribute to the person of Nero. But the person thus far is the object of our obedience, that fear, honor, subjection, and tribute must be due to the man *in concreto*, to his person who is prince, but not because he is a man, or a person simply, or a sword-bearer of papists, but for his office, for that eminent place of royal dignity that God has conferred on his person. We know the light of the sun, the heat of fire, *in abstracto*, do not properly give light and heat, but the sun and fire *in concreto*, yet the *principium quo, ratio qua*, the principles of these operations in sun and fire be light and heat, and we ascribe illuminating of dark bodies, heating of cold bodies to sun and fire *in concreto*, yet not to the subjects simply, but to them as affected with such accidents; so here we honor and submit to the man who is king, not because he is a man, that would be treason, not because he uses his sword against the church, that would be impiety, but because of his royal dignity, and because he uses it for the Lord. It is true, Arnisaeus, Barclay, and Ferne say, "That kings leave not off to be kings when they use their power and sword against the church and religion. And also it is considerable that when the worst of emperors, bloody Nero, did reign, the apostle presses the duty of subjection to him, as to a power appointed of God, and condemns the resisting of Nero as the resisting of an ordinance of God. And certainly, if the cause and reason, in point of duty moral, and of conscience before God remain in kings, namely, that while they are enemies and persecutors, as Nero was, their royal dignity, given them by God remains, then subjection upon that ground is lawful, and resistance unlawful."

Ans. It is true, so long as kings remain kings, subjection is due to them because kings; but that is not the question. The question is if subjection be due to them when they use their power unlawfully and tyrannically. Whatever David did, though he was a king, he did it not as king; he deflowered not Bathsheba as king, and Bathsheba might with bodily resistance and violence lawfully have resisted king David, though kingly power remained in him, while he should thus attempt to commit adultery; otherwise David might have said to Bathsheba, "Because I am the Lord's anointed it is rebellion in you, a subject, to oppose any bodily violence to my act of forcing of you; it is unlawful to you to cry for help, for if any shall offer violently to rescue you from me, he resists the ordinance of God." Subjection is due to Nero as an emperor, but not any subjection is due to him in the burning of Rome and torturing of Christians, unless you say that Nero's power abused in these acts of cruelty was, 1. A power from God. 2. An ordinance of God. 3. That in these he was the minister of God for the good of the commonwealth. Because some believed Christians were free from the yoke of magistracy, and that the dignity itself was unlawful; and because he had set down the lawful church rulers (section 12), and in this and the following chapter, the duties of brotherly love of one toward another; so here (section 13) he teaches that all magistrates, suppose heathen, are to be obeyed and submitted unto in all things, so far as they are ministers of God. Arnisaeus objects to Buchanan, "If we are by this place to subject ourselves to every power, *in abstracto*, then also to a power contrary to the truth, and to a power of a king exceeding the limits of a king; for such a power is a power, and we are not to distinguish where the law distinguishes not."

Ans. 1. The law clearly distinguishes that we are to obey parents in the Lord, and if Nero command idolatry, this is an excessive power. Are we obliged to obey because the law distinguishes not? 2. The text says we are to obey every power from God that is God's ordinance, by which the man is a minister of God for good, but an unjust and excessive power is none of these three. 3. The text in words distinguishes not obedience active in things wicked and lawful, yet we are to distinguish.

Symmons. Is authority subjected solely in the king's law, and not at ll in his person, though put upon him both by God and man? Or is authority only the subject, and the person exercising the authority a bare accident to that, being in it only more separably, as pride and folly are in a man. Then, if one in authority command out of his own will, and not by law, if I neither actively nor passively obey, I do not so much as resist abused authority, and then must the prince, by his disorderly will, have quite lost his authority and become like another man, and yet his authority has not fled from him.

Ans. 1. If we speak accurately, neither the man solely, nor his power only is resisted; but the man clothed with lawful habitual power is resisted in such and such acts flowing from an abused power.

2. It is an ignorant speech to ask. Is authority subjected solely in the king's law, and not at all in his person, for the authority has all its power by law, not from the man's person? The authority has nothing from the person but a naked inheritance in the person, as in the subject, and the person is to be honored for the authority, not the authority for the person.

3. Authority is not so separable from the person as that for every act of lawless will the king loses his royal authority and ceases to be king. No, but every act of a king so far can claim subjection of the interior as the act of commanding and ruling has law for it; and insofar as it is lawless, the person in that act repugnant to law loses all due claim of actual subjection in that act, and in that act power actual is lost, as is clear (Acts 4:19; 5:29). The apostles say to rulers, "It is safer to obey God than man." What! Were not these rulers lawful magistrates armed with power from God? I answer habitually they were rulers and more than men, and to obey them in things lawful is to obey God. But actually in these unlawful commandments, especially being commanded to speak no more in the name of Jesus, the apostles do acknowledge them to be no more but men, and so their actual authority is as separable from the person as pride and folly from men.

Symmons. The distinction holds good for inferior magistrates, that they may be considered as magistrates and as men, because their authority is only sacred, and adds veneration to their persons, and is separable from the person. The man may live when his authority is extinguished, but it holds not in kings. King Saul's person is venerable as his authority, and his authority comes by inheritance, and dies, and lives inseparably with his person; and authority and person add honor, each one to another.

Ans. 1. If this be true, Manasseh, a king, did not shed innocent blood and use sorcery. He did not these great wickednesses as a man, but as a king. Solomon played the apostate as a king, not as a man; if it were so, the man must make the king more infallible than the Pope, for the Pope as a man can err; as a pope he cannot err, say papists. But prophets in their persons were anointed by God as Saul and David were; then must we say Nathan and Samuel erred not as men, because their persons were sacred and anointed, and indeed they erred not as prophets; therefore they erred not all. A king as a king is a holy ordinance of God, and so cannot do injustice; therefore they must do acts of justice as men. 1. The inferior judge is a power from God. 2. To resist him is to resist an ordinance of God. 3. He is not a terror to good works, but to evil. 4. He is a minister of God for good. 5. He is God's sword-bearer. His official power to rule may by as good right come by birth as the crown, and the king's person is sacred only for his office, and is anointed only for his office. For then the Chaldeans dishonored not inferior judges (Lam. 5:12) when they "hanged the prince, and honored not the faces of elders." It is in question if the king's actual authority be not as separable from him as the actual authority of the judge.

Symmons. The king himself may use this distinction. As a Christian he may forgive any that offends against his person, but as a judge, he must punish, in regard of his office.

Ans. Well then, flatterers will grant the distinction: when the king does good and pardons the blood of protestants, dead by bloody rebels; but when the king does acts of injustice, he is neither man nor king, but some independent absolute god.

Symmons. God's word ties me to every one of His personal commandments, as well as His legal commandments. Nor do I obey the king's law because it is established, or because of its known penalty, nor yet the king himself, because he rules according to law, but I obey the king's law, because I obey the king; and I obey the king because I obey God; I obey the king and his law because I obey God and His law. Better obey the command for a reverent regard to the prince than for a penalty.

Ans. It is hard to answer a sick man. It is blasphemy to seek this distinction of person and office in the King of kings, because by person in a mortal king we understand a man that can sin. 1. I am not obliged to obey his personal commandment unless I were his domestic; nor his unlawful personal commandments because they are sinful. 2. It is false that you obey the king's law because you obey the king; for then you say but this: I obey the king because I obey the king. The truth is obedience is not formally terminated on the person of the king. Obedience is relative to a precept, and it is men-service to obey a law, not because it is good and just, but upon this formal motive: because it is the will of a mortal man to command it. And reverence, love, fear, being acts of the affection, are not terminated on a law, but properly on the person of the judge, and they are modifications, or laudable qualifications of acts of obedience, not motives, not the formal reason why I obey, but the manner how I obey. And the apostle makes expressly fear of punishment a motive of obedience, while he says, "He bears not the sword in vain," (Rom. 13:4), therefore be subject to the king; and this hinders not personal resistance to unjust commandments.

Symmons: "You say, 'To obey the prince's personal commandment against his legal will is to obey himself against himself.' So say I: 'To obey his legal will against his personal will is to obey himself against himself, for I take his person to be himself.'"

Ans. 1. To obey the king's personal will when it is sinful (as we now suppose) against his legal will is a sin, and a disobedience to God and the king also, seeing the law is the king's will as king, but to obey his legal will against his sinful personal will (as it must be sinful if contrary to a just law) is obedience to the king as king, and so obedience to God.

2. You take the king's person to be himself, but you take *quid pro quo*; for his person here you must not take physically, for his suppost of soul and body, but morally: it is the king, as a sinful man doing his worst will against the law, which is his just and best will, and the rule of the subjects. And the king's personal will is so far just, and to regulate the subjects, insofar as it agrees with his legal will or his law, and this will can sin, and therefore may be crossed without breach of the fifth commandment; but his legal will cannot be crossed without disobedience both to God and the king.

Symmons: The king's personal will does not always presuppose passion, and if it be attended with passion, yet we must bear it for conscience sake.

Ans. We are to obey the king's personal will when the thing commanded is not sin, but his subjects as subjects have little to do with his personal will in that notion. It concerns his domestic servant, and is the king's will as he is the master of servants, not as he is king in relation to subjects, but we speak of the king's personal will as repugnant to law and contrary to the king's will as king, and so contrary to the fifth commandment, and this is attended often not only with passion, but also with prejudice, and we owe no subjection to prejudice and passions, or to actions commanded by these disordered powers, because they are not from God, nor his ordinances, but from men and the flesh, and we owe no subjection to the flesh.

Dr. Ferne: The distinction of personal and legal will has place in evil actions, but not in resistance, where we cannot sever the person and the dignity, or authority, because we cannot resist the power but we must resist the person who has the power. Saul had lawfully the command of arms, but that power he uses unjustly, against innocent David. I ask, When these emperors took away lives and goods at their pleasure, was that a power, ordained of God? No, but an illegal will, a tyranny. But they might not resist; nay, but they cannot resist; for that power and sovereignty employed to accomplish these illegal commandments was ordained and settled in them. When Pilate condemned our Savior, it was an illegal will, yet our Savior acknowledges in it that Pilate's power was given him from above (section 9).

Ans. 1. Here we have the distinction denied by royalists, granted by Dr. Ferne. But if when the king commands us to do wickedness we may resist that personal will, and when he commands us to suffer unjustly we cannot resist his will but we must resist also his royal person, what! Is it not still the king, and his person sacred, as his power is sacred, when he commands the subjects to do unjustly, as when he commands them to suffer unjustly? It would be fearful to say that when kings command any one act of idolatry, they are no longer kings. If, for conscience, I am to suffer unjustly when Nero commands unjust punishment, because Nero commanding so remains God's minister, why, but when Nero commands me to worship a heathen god, I am upon the same ground to obey that unjust will in doing ill; for Nero in commanding idolatry remains the Lord's minister: his person is sacred in the one commandment of doing ill, as in inflicting ill of punishment. And do I not resist his person in the one as in the other? His power and his person are as inseparably conjoined by God in the one as in the other.

2. In bodily thrusting out of Uzziah from the temple, these fourscore valiant men did resist the king's person by bodily violence, as well as his power.

3. If the power of killing the martyrs in Nero was no power ordained by God, then the resisting of Nero in his taking away the lives of the martyrs was but the resisting of tyranny, and certainly, if that power in Nero was τεταγμενη, a power ordained by God, and not to be resisted, as the place (Rom. 13) is alleged by royalists, then it must be a lawful power and no tyranny; and if it cannot be resisted because it was a power ordained and settled in him it is either settled by God, and so not tyranny (unless God be the author of tyranny) or then settled by the devil, and so may well be resisted. But the text speaks of no power but of that which is of God.

4. We are not to be subject to all powers *in concreto*, by the text; for we are not to be subject to powers lawful, yet commanding active obedience to things unlawful. Now subjection includes active obedience of honor, love, fear, paying tribute, and therefore necessarily force: some powers must be excepted.

5. Pilate's power is merely a power by divine permission, not a power ordained by God, as are the powers spoken of (Rom. 13). Gregorius expressly says, "This was Satan's power given to Pilate against Christ. *Manibus Satanae pro nostra redemptione se tradidit*" (mor. 1.3.11). Lyra, "*A principibus Romanorum et ulterius permissuma deo, qui eat potestas, superior.*" Calvin, Beza and Diodatus say the same; and that he cannot mean of legal power from God's regulating will is evident, 1. Because Christ is answering Pilate "Knowest though not that I have power to crucify thee?" (John 19:10). This was an untruth. Pilate had a command to worship him and believe in him; and whereas Ferne says, "Pilate had power to judge any accused before him" (section 9), it is true, but he being obliged to believe in Christ, he was obliged to believe in Christ's innocence, and so neither to judge nor receive accusation against him; and the power he says he had to crucify was a law-power in Pilate's meaning, but not in very deed any law-power, because a law-power is from God's regulating will in the fifth commandment, but no creature has a lawful or a law-power to crucify

Christ. 2. A law-power is for good (Rom. 13:4); a power to crucify Christ is for ill. 3. A law-power is a terror to ill works, and a praise to good; Pilate's power to crucify Christ was the contrary. 4. A law-power is to execute wrath on ill-doing; a power to crucify Christ is no such. 5. A law-power conciliates honor, fear, and veneration to the person of the judge; a power to crucify Christ conciliates no such thing, but a disgrace to Pilate. 6. The genuine acts of a lawful power are lawful acts; for such as is the fountain-power, such are the acts flowing from it. Good acts flow not from bad powers, neither has God given a power to sin, except by way of permission.

QUESTION 30.

WHETHER OR NOT PASSIVE OBEDIENCE IS A MEANS TO WHICH WE ARE SUBJECTED IN CONSCIENCE, BY VIRTUE OF A DIVINE COMMANDMENT, AND WHAT A MEANS RESISTANCE IS; THAT FLYING IS RESISTANCE.

The place 1 Peter 2:18 discussed. Patient bearing of injuries and resistance of injuries compatible in one and the same subject. Christ's non-resistance has many things rare and extraordinary, and is no leading rule to us. Suffering is either commanded to us comparatively only, that we rather choose to suffer than deny the truth; or the manner only is commanded: that we suffer with patience. The physical act of taking away the life or of offending when commanded by the law of self-defense is no murder. We have a greater dominion over goods and members (except in case of mutilation, which is a little death) than over our life. To kill is not naturally self-defense, but accidental. Defensive war cannot be without offense. What the nature of defensive and offensive wars is. Flying is resistance.

M uch is built, to commend patient suffering of ill and to condemn all resistance of superiors, by royalists, on the place, 1 Pet. 2:18, where we are commanded, being servants, to suffer buffets not only for ill-doing of good masters, but also undeservedly; and when we do well, we are to suffer of those masters that are evil, and so much more are we patiently without resistance to suffer of kings. But it is clear, the place is nothing against resistance, as in these assertions I clear:

Assert. 1. Patient suffering of wicked men and violent resisting are not incompatible, but they may well stand together; so this consequence is the basis of the argument, and it is just nothing: to wit, servants are to suffer unjustly wounds and buffeting of their wicked masters, and they are to bear it patiently; therefore, servants are in conscience obliged to non-resistance.

Now, Scripture makes this clear, 1. The church of God is to bear with all patience the indignation of the Lord, because she has sinned, and to suffer under wicked enemies which were to be trodden as mire in the streets (Micah 7:9-12); but even so they were not obliged to non-resistance and not to fight against these enemies, yea, they were obliged to fight against them also. If such were Babylon, Judah might have resisted and fought if God had not given a special commandment of a positive law that they should not fight; if these were the Assyrians and other enemies, or rather both, the people were to resist by fighting, and yet to endure patiently the indignation of the Lord. David did bear most patiently the wrong that his own son Absalom, and Ahithophel, and the people inflicted on him in pursuing him to take his life and the kingdom from him, as is clear by his gracious expressions (2 Sam. 15:25-26; 16:10-12; Ps. 3:1-3), yea, he prays for a blessing on the people that conspired against him (Ps. 3:8), yet did he lawfully resist Absalom and the conspirators, and sent out Joab and a huge army in open battle against them (2 Sam, 18:1-4, &c). and fought against them. And was not the people of God patient to endure the violence done to them in the wilderness by Og, king of Bashan; Sihon, king of Heshbon; by the Amorites, Moabites, &c.? I think God's law ties all men, especially His people, to as patient a suffering in wars (Deut. 8:16). God then trying and humbling His people, as the servant is to endure patiently, unjustly inflicted buffets (1 Pet. 2:18), and yet God's people at God's command did resist these kings and people, and did fight and kill them, and possess their land, as the history is clear. See the like in Josh. 11:18-19.

2. One act of grace and virtue is not contrary to another; resistance is in the children of God an innocent act of self-preservation, as is patient suffering, and therefore they may well subsist in one. And so says Amasa by the Spirit of the Lord, "Peace, peace be unto you, and peace to your helpers, for God helps you" (1 Chron. 12:18). Now in this David and all his helpers were resisters of king Saul.

3. The scope of the place (1 Pet. 2). is not to forbid all violent resisting, as is clear he speaks nothing of violent resisting either one way or the other, but only he forbids revengeful roasting of repaying one wrong with another, from the example of Christ who, "when he was reviled, reviled not again; when he suffered, he threatened not;" therefore, the argument is a fallacy, *ab eo quod docitur* κατα τι, *ad illud quod dicitur* απλως. Though therefore the master should attempt to kill an innocent servant, and invade him with a weapon of death suddenly without all reason or cause, or unavoidably, Dr. Ferne in that case does free a subject from guiltiness if he violently resist his prince; therefore, the servant who should violently resist his master in the aforesaid case should and might patiently suffer and violently resist, notwithstanding anything that royalists can conclude on the contrary (section 2).

4. No prince has a masterly or lordly dominion over his subjects, but only a free, ingenuous, paternal and tutorly oversight for the good of the people (Rom. 13:4). The master, especially in the apostle Peter's time, had a dominion over servants as over their proper goods.

Assert 2. Neither suffering formally as suffering, and so neither can non-resisting passive fall under any moral law of God, except in two conditions: 1. In the point of Christ's passive obedience, He being the eternal God as well as man, and so lord of His own blood and life, by virtue of a special commandment imposed on Him by his Father, was commanded to lay down His life, yea, and to be an agent as well as a patient in dying (Job. 10:18), yea, and actively He was to contribute something for His own death and offer himself willingly to death (Matt. 28:20), and knowing the hour that he was to depart out of this world unto the Father (John 13:1) would not only not fly—which is to royalists lawful, to us a special point of resistance (John 14:81; 18:4-7)—but upbraided Peter as the agent of Satan, who would dissuade him to die (Matt. 16:22-23) and would fight for him. And he does not fetch any argument against Peter's drawing of his sword from the unlawfulness of self-defense and innocent resistance (which He should have done if royalists plead with any pretense of reason from his example, against the lawfulness of resistance and self-defense) but from the absolute power of God.

2. From God's positive will, who commanded Him to die (Matt. 26:63-64). If therefore royalists prove anything against the lawfulness of resisting kings when they offer (most unjustly) violence to the life of God's servants, from this one merely extraordinary and rare example of Christ, the like of which was never in the world, they may from the same example prove it unlawful to fly, for Christ would not fly (Ps. 40:6-7; Heb. 10:6-9; John 14:31; 18:4-7). 1. They may prove that people sought by a tyrant to be crucified for God's cause are to reveal and discover themselves to an army of men who come to seek them (John 13:1-2; 18:4-7). 2. That martyrs are of purpose to go to the place where they know they shall be apprehended and put to death, for this Christ did, and are willingly to offer themselves to the enemy's army, for so did Christ (John 14:3; Mark 14:41-42; Matt. 26:46-47); and so by His example, all the parliament, all the innocents of the city of London, and assembly of divines are obliged to lay down arms and to go to their own death to prince Rupert, and the bloody Irish rebels. 3. By this example it is unlawful to resist the cut-throats of a king, for

Caesar in his own royal person, the high priest in person, came not out against Christ; yea, it is not lawful for the parliament to resist a Judas, who has fled as a traitorous apostate from the truth and the temple of Christ. 4. It is not lawful for innocents to defend themselves by any violence against the invasion of superiors, in Dr. Ferne's three cases in which he allows resistance: (1) When the invasion is sudden, (2) unavoidable, (3) without all pretense of law and reason. In the two last cases, royalists defend the lawfulness of self-defense. 5. If the example be pressed, Christ did not this and that: He resisted not with violence to save his own life; therefore, we are to abstain from resistance and such and such means of self-preservation; then, because Christ appealed not from inferior judges to the emperor Caesar, who no doubt would have shown Him more favor than the scribes and Pharisees did, and because Christ conveyed not a humble supplication to his sovereign and father Caesar, then because He proffered not a humble petition to prince Pilate for his life, He being an innocent man and His cause just, because He neither procured an orator to plead His own just cause, nor did He so plead for Himself, and give in word and writ all lawful and possible defenses for his own safety, but answered many things with silence, to the admiration of the judge (Mark 15:3-5) and was thrice pronounced by the judge to be innocent (Luke 22:23), because, I say, Christ did not all these for his own life, therefore it is unlawful for Scotland and England to appeal to the king to supplicate, to give in apologies, &c. I think royalists dare not say so. But if they say He would not resist, and yet might have done all these lawfully, because these be lawful means, and resistance with the sword unlawful, because "He that takes the sword, shall perish by the sword," let me answer then, 1. They leave the argument from Christ's example, who was thus far subject to higher powers that he would not resist and plead from the unlawfulness of resistance; this is *petitio principii*. 2. He that takes the sword without God's warrant, which Peter had not, but the contrary, he was himself a Satan to Christ, who would but counsel Him not to die; but there is no shadow of a word to prove that violent resisting is unlawful, when the king and his Irish cut-throats pursue us unjustly; only Christ says when God may deliver extraordinarily by his angels, unless it be his absolute will that his Son should drink the cup of death, then to take the sword, when God has declared His will on the contrary is unlawful, and that is all, though I do not question that Christ's asking for swords, and His arresting all his enemies to the ground backward (John 18:6) is a justifying of self-defense. But hitherto it is clear by Christ's example that He only was commanded to suffer. Now the second case in which suffering falls under a commandment is indirectly and comparatively when it comes to the election of the witness of Jesus, that it is referred to them, either to deny the truth of Christ and His name, or then to suffer death. The choice is apparently evident, and this choice that persecutors refer us unto is to us a commandment of God that we must choose suffering for Christ, and refuse sinning against Christ. But the supposition must stand that this alternative is unavoidable, that is not in our power to decline either suffering for Christ, or denying of Christ before men; otherwise no man is to expect the reward of a witness of Jesus, who having a lawful possible means of eschewing suffering, does yet cast himself into suffering needlessly. But I prove that suffering by men of this world falls not formally and directly under any divine positive law; for the law of nature, whatever Arminians in their declaration, or this Arminian excommunicate think with them (for they teach that God gave a commandment to Adam to abstain from such and such fruit, with pain and trouble to sinless nature) does not command suffering, or anything contrary to nature, as nature is sinless; I prove it thus:

1. Whatever falls under a positive commandment of God, I may say here, under any commandment of God, is not a thing under the free will and power of others, from whom we are not descended necessarily by natural generation, but that men of the world kill me, even

these from whom I am not descended by natural generation (which I speak to exclude Adam, who killed all his posterity) is not in my free will, either as if they had my common nature in that act, or as if I were accessory by counsel, consent, or approbation to that act, for this is under the free will and power of others, not under my own free will; therefore, that I suffer by others is not under my free will, and cannot fall under a commandment of God, and certainly it is an irrational law (glorified be His name) that God should command Antipas either formally to suffer, or formally not to suffer death by these of the synagogue of Satan (Rev. 2:13) because if they be pleased not to kill him, it is not in his free will to be killed by them; and if they shall have him in their power (unless God extraordinarily deliver) it is not in his power in an ordinary providence not to be killed.

2. All these places of God's word that recommend suffering to the followers of Christ do not command formally that we suffer; therefore, suffering falls not formally under any commandment of God. I prove the antecedent, because if they be considered, they prove only that comparatively we are to choose rather to suffer than to deny Christ before men (Mat. 10:28, 32; Rev. 2:13; Mat. 10:37; 16:24; 19:29) or then they command not suffering according to the substance of the passion, but according to the manner that we suffer, willingly, cheerfully, and patiently. Hence Christ's word to take up His cross, which is not a mere passion, but commends an act of the virtue of patience. Now no Christian virtue consists in a mere passion, but in laudable habits, and good and gracious acts, and the text we are now on (1 Pet. 2:18-19) does not recommend suffering from the example of Christ, but patient suffering, and so the word ὑποτασσόμενου, not simply enjoined, but εν παντι το φοβω in all fear (ver. 18) and the words ὑποφίζυν and υποφερειν, to suffer with patience, as in 2 Tim. 3:11; 1 Cor. 10:13, and υπομενει is to suffer patiently, (1 Cor. 13:7); love πάντα ὑπομίνυ suffers all things (Heb. 12:17); if you suffer correction (1 Tim. 5:5); she continues patiently in prayers (Heb. 12:2); Christ

endures the cross *patiently* (Rom. 15:5; 8:25; Luke 8:16; 21:29). The derivations from this signify patience: so do all our interpreters, Beza, Calvin, Marloratus, and popish expositors, as Lorinus, Estius, Carthusian, Lyra, Hugo Cardinalis, expound it concerning patient suffering, and the text is clear: it is suffering like Christ, without rendering evil for evil and reviling for reviling.

3. Suffering simply, according to substance of the passion (I cannot say action) is common to good and evil, and to the wicked, yea to the damned in hell who suffer against their will, and that cannot be joined according to its substance as an act of formal obedience and subjection to higher powers, kings, fathers, masters, by force of the fifth commandment, and of the place Rom. 13:1-2, which according to its substance wicked men suffer and the damned in hell also against their will.

4. Passive obedience to wicked emperors can but be enjoined (Rom. 13), but only in the manner and upon supposition that we must be subject to them, and must suffer against our wills all the evil of punishment that they can inflict; we must suffer patiently, and because it is God's permissive will that they punish us unjustly; for it is not God's ruling and approving will (called *voluntas signi*) that they should against the law of God and man kill us, and persecute us, and therefore neither Rom. 13, nor 1 Pet. 2, nor any other place in God's word, any common divine, natural, national, or any municipal law commands formally obedience passive or subjection passive, or non-resistance under the notion of passive obedience, yea, to me, obedience passive (if we speak of obedience, properly called, as relative essentially to a law) is a chimera, a dream, and *repugnantia in adjecto*, and therefore I utterly deny that resistance passive or subjection passive does formally fall under either commandment of God affirmative or negative; only the unlawful manner of resistance by way of revenge, or for defense of popery and false religion, and out of impatient toleration of monarchy or any tyranny is forbidden in God's word; and

certainly all the words used in Rom. 13, as they fall under a formal commandment of God, are words of action, not of any chimerical passive obedience, as we are not to resist actively God's ordinance, as his ordinance (ver. 1-2) that is, to resist God actively. We are to do good works, not evil, if we would have the ruler no terrorize to us (ver. 3). We must not do ill if we would be free of vengeance's sword (ver. 7); we are to pay tribute and to give fear and honor to the ruler, all which are evidently actions, not passive subjection; and if any passive subjection be commanded, it is not here, nor in the first commandment commanded, but in the first commandment under the hand of patience and submission under God's hand in sufferings, or in the third commandment under the hand of rather dying for Christ than denying his truth before men. Thus I argue here (Rom. 13; 1 Pet. 2; Tit. 3) is nothing else but an exposition of the fifth commandment; but in the fifth commandment only active obedience is formally commanded, and the subordination of inferiors to superiors is ordained, and passive obedience is nowhere commanded, but only *modus rei*, the manner of suffering, and the occasion of the commandment; here it is thought that the Jews converted under this pretext, that they were God's people, believed that they should not be subject to the Romans. A certain Galilean made the Galileans believe that they should not pay tribute to strangers, and that they should call none lord, but the God of heaven, as Josephus says (*Antiq. Judaic.* 1.20.2, and *De bell. Judaic.* 1.7.29) yea and Jerome (*Com. in Tit.*) says, at this time the sect of the Galileans were on foot. It is like the Jews were thought to be Galileans, and that their liberty, purchased in Christ, could not consist with the order of master and servant, king and subject. And to remove this, Paul established magistracy, and commands obedience in the Lord, and he is more to prove the office of the magistrate to be of God than any other thing, and to show what is his due than to establish absoluteness in Nero to be of God, yea, to me every word in the text speaks limitedness of princes and cries down absoluteness:

(1) no power of God, (2) no ordinance of God, who is a terror to evil, but a praise to good works, (3) no minister of God for good, &c. can be a power to which we submit ourselves on earth, as next unto God, without control. That passive obedience falls formally under no commandment of God, I prove thus: All obedience liable to a divine commandment does commend morally the performer of obedience as having a will conformed to God's moral law, and deformity between the will of him who performs not obedience involves the non-obedient in wrath and guiltiness. But non-passive subjection to the sword of the judge does not morally commend him that suffers not punishment; for no man is formally a sinner against a moral law because he suffers not the ill of punishment, nor is he morally good or to be commended because he suffers ill of punishment, but because he does the ill of sin. And all evil of punishment unjustly inflicted has God's *voluntas beneplaciti*, the instrumental and hidden decree of God, which orders both good and ill (Ephes. 1:11) for its rule and cause, and has not God's will or approbation called, *voluntas signi*, for its rule, both is contrary to that will. I am sure Epiphanius (1.1, *tom.* 3, *heres.* 40) Basilius (in Ps. 32). Nazianzen Orat (*ad subd. et Imperat).*, Hilar (*li. ad Constant*). and Augustine all cite these words, and say the same. If then passive subjection be not commanded, non-subjection passive cannot be forbidden, and this text, Rom. 13, and 1 Pet. 2 cannot a whit help the bad cause of royalists. All then must be reduced to some action of resisting; arguments for passive subjection, though there were shipfuls of them, they cannot help us.

Assert. 3. By the place, 1 Pet, 2, the servant unjustly buffeted is not to buffet his master again, but to bear patiently as Christ did, who when He was reviled, did not revile again. Not because the place condemns resistance for self-defense, but because buffeting again is formally re-offending, not defending: defending is properly a warding off a blow or stroke. If my neighbor come to kill me, and I can by no means save my life by flight, I may defend myself, and all divines say

I may rather kill before I be killed, because I am nearer by the law of nature and dearer to myself and my own life than to my brother, but if I kill him out of malice or hatred the act of defending by the unlawful manner of doing becomes an act of offending and murder, from which the mind of the blood-shedder will vary the nature of the action from which this corollary does naturally issue, that the physical action of taking away the life makes not murder nor homicide, and so the physical action of offending my neighbor is not murder. 1. Abraham may kill his son, he for whom the cities of refuge were ordained, and did kill his brother, yet, not hating him, he was not, by God's law, judged a murderer; and, 2. It necessarily from this follows that an act which is physically an act of offending my brother, yea even to the taking away of his life, is often morally and legally an act of lawful self-defense: an offending of another, necessitated from the sole invention of self-defense is no more than an act of innocent self-defense. If David with his men had killed any of Saul's men in a set battle, David and his men only intending self-defense, the war on David's part was merely defensive, for physical actions of killing, indifferent in themselves, yet commanded by a principle of natural self-defense and clothed with this formal end of self-defense, or according to the substance of the action, the act is of self-defense. If, therefore, one shall wound me mortally, and I know it is my death, after that to kill the killer of myself, I being only a private man, must be no act of self-defense, but of homicide, because it cannot be commanded by a sinless dictate of a natural conscience, for this end of self-defense, after I know I am killed. Any means not used for preventing death must be an act of revenge, not of self-defense, for it is physically unsuitable for the intended end of self-defense. And so, for a servant buffeted to buffet again, is of the same nature; the second buffet not being a conducible means to ward the first buffet, but a means to procure heavier strokes, and, possibly killing, it cannot be an act of self-defense; for an act of self-defense must be an act destinated *ex natura rei*, only for defense, and if it be known to be an act of sole offending, without any known necessary relation of a means to self-defense as the end, it cannot be properly an act of self-defense.

Assert. 4. When the matter is lighter, as in paying tribute or suffering a buffet of a rough master, though unjustly, we are not to use any act of re-offending. For though I be not absolute lord of my own goods, and so may not at my sole pleasure give tribute and expend monies to the hurting of my children, where I am not, by God's law or man's law, obliged to pay tribute and though I be not an absolute lord of my members, to expose face, and cheeks, and back to stripes and whips at my own mere will, yet have we a comparative dominion given to us by God in matters of goods, and disposing of our members (I think I may except the case of mutilation, which is a little death) for buffets, because Christ, no doubt to teach us the like, would rather give of His goods, and pay tribute where it was not due, than that this scandal be in the way of Christ, that Christ was no loyal subject to lawful emperors and kings. And Paul would rather not take stipend (1 Cor. 9), though it was due to him, than hinder the course of the gospel. And the like in 1 Cor. 6, where the Corinthians were rather to suffer loss in their goods than to go to law before infidel judges, and by the like to prevent greater inconveniences, and mutilation, and death. The Christian servant has that dominion over his members, rather to suffer buffets than to ward off buffets with violent resistance. But it is no consequence that innocent subjects should suffer death of tyrants, and servants be killed by masters, and yet that they shall not be allowed by the law of nature to defend themselves by re-offending, when only self-defense is intended, because we have not that dominion over life and death. And therefore, as a man is his brother's murderer, who with froward Cain will not be his brother's keeper, and may preserve his brother's life without loss of his own life, when his brother is unjustly preserved; so, when he may preserve his own life, and does not that which nature's law allows him to do (rather to kill before he be killed) he is guilty of self-murder, because he is deficient in the duty of lawful self-defense. But I grant, to offend or kill is not of the nature of defensive war, but accidental to it, and yet killing of cut-throats sent forth by the illegal commandment of the king may be intended as a means, and a lawful means, of self-defense. Of two evils of punishment we have a comparative dominion over ourselves: a man may cast his goods into the sea to redeem his life; so, to redeem peace, we may suffer buffets, but because death is the greatest evil of punishment, God has not made it eligible to us when lawful self-defense is at hand. But in defending our own life against tyrannical power, though we do it by offending and killing, we resist no ordinance of God, only I judge killing of the king in self-defense not lawful, because self-defense must be national on just causes.

Let here the reader judge Barclay: "If the King" says he "shall vex the commonwealth, or one port of it, with great and intolerable cruelty, what shall the people do? They have," says he "in that case a power to resist and defend themselves from injury, but only to defend themselves, nor to invade the prince, nor to resist the injury, nor to recede from reverence due to the prince" (*con. Monar.* 1.3.8).

I answer, 1. Let Barclay or the Prelate (if he may carry Barclay's books) or any distinguish these two: the people may resist a tyrant, but they may not resist the injuries inflicted by a tyrant's officers and cutthroats. I cannot imagine how to conciliate these two, for to resist the cruelty of a king is but to hold off the injury by resistance.

2. If this Nero waste the commonwealth insufferably with his cruelty, and remain a lawful king, to be honored as a king, who may resist him, according to the royalists' way? But from Rom. 13 they resist the ordinance of God. Resisting is not a mere suffering, nor is it a moral resisting by alleging laws to be broken by him. We had never a question with royalists about such resisting. Nor is this resisting non-obedience to unjust commandments; that resisting was never yet

in question by any except the papists, who in good earnest by consequent say it is better to obey men than God.

3. It is then resisting by bodily violence. But if the king have such an absolute power given him by God, as royalists fancy, from Rom. 13:1-2; 1 Sam. 8:9-11. I know not how subjects have any power given them by God to resist the power from God, and God's ordinance. And if this resisting extend not itself to defensive wars, how shall the people defend themselves from injuries, and the greatest injuries imaginable, from an army of cut-throats and idolaters, in war coming to destroy region, set up idolatry, and root out the name of God's people, and lay waste the mountain of the Lord's house? And if they may defend themselves by defensive wars, how can wars be without offending?

4. The law of nature teaches to repel violence with violence, when one man is oppressed, no less than when the commonwealth is oppressed. Barclay should have given either Scripture or the law of nature for his warrant here.

5. Let us suppose a king can be perjured, how are the estates of the kingdom, who are his subjects according to Barclay not to challenge such a tyrant of his perjury? He did swear he should be meek and merciful, and he has now become a furious lion. Shall the flock of God be committed to the keeping of a furious lion?

Dr. Ferne adds, "Personal defense is lawful against sudden and illegal invasion, such as Elisha practiced, even if it were against the prince to ward blows, and to hold the prince's hand, but not to return blows; but general resistance by arms cannot be without many unjust violences, and does immediately strike at the order which is the life of the commonwealth" (section 2).

Ans. 1. If it be natural to one man to defend himself against the personal invasion of a prince, then is it natural and warrantable to ten thousand, and to a whole kingdom, and what reason to defraud a kingdom of the benefit of self-defense more than one man?

2. Neither grace nor policy destroys nature; and how shall ten or twenty thousand be defended against cannons and muskets that kill afar off, unless they keep towns against the king (which Dr. Ferne and others say would have been treason in David, if he had kept Keilah against king Saul) unless they be armed to offend, with weapons of the like nature to kill rather than be killed, as the law of nature teaches.

3. To hold the hands of the prince is no less resisting violence than to cut the skirt of his garment, which royalists think unlawful, and is an opposing of external force to the king's person.

4. It is true, wars merely defensive cannot be unless they are offensive; but they are offensive by accident, and intended for mere defense, and they must be sinfully offensive wars, nor can any wan be *in rerum natura* now (I except the wars commanded by God, which only must have been sinful in the manner of doing) without some innocent being killed; but wars cannot for that be condemned.

5. Neither are offensive wars against those who are no powers and no ordinances of God, such as are cut-throat Irish, condemned prelates and papists now in arms, more destructive to the order established by God than acts of lawful war are, or the punishing of robbers. And by all this, protestants in Scotland and England should remain in their houses unarmed, while the papists and Irish come on them armed, and cut their throats, and spoil and plunder at will.

Nor can we think that resistance to a king, in holding his hands, can be natural; if he be stronger, it is not a natural means of self-preservation. Nature has appointed innocent and offending violence against unjust violence as a means of self-preservation. Goliath's sword is no natural means to hold Saul's hands, for a sword has no fingers; and if king Saul suddenly, without pretense of law or reason, or inevitably, should make personal invasion on David to kill him, Dr. Ferne says he may resist, but resisting is essentially a reaction of violence. Show us Scripture or reason for violent holding a king's hands in an unjust personal invasion, without any other reaction of offence. Walter Tor-rils killed king William II Rufus as he was shooting at a deer; the Earl of Suffolk killed Henry VIII at tilting: there is no treasonable intent here, and so no homicide. Defensive wars are offensive, *ex eventu et effectus* not *ex causa* or *ex intentione*.

But it may be asked if no passive subjection at all be commanded as due to superiors.

Ans. None properly so called, that is, purely passive, only we are, for fear of the sword, to do our duty. We are to suffer ill of punishment of tyrants, *ex hypothesi* that they inflict that evil on us some other way, and in some other notion than we are to suffer evil from equals; for we are to suffer of equals not for any paternal authority that they have over us, as certainly we are to suffer evil inflicted by superiors. I demand of royalists if tyrants inflicting evil of punishment upon subjects unjustly be powers ordained of God: if to resist a power in tyrannical acts be to resist God. Since we are not to yield active obe-dience to all the commandments of superiors, whether they be good or ill, by virtue of this place, Rom. 13, how is it that we may not deny passive subjection to all the acts of violence exercised, whether of in-justice, whether in these acts of violence in which the prince in *actu exercito* and formally, punishes not in God's stead, or in these in which he punishes tyrannically, in no formal or actual subordination to God, we owe passive subjection? I desire an answer to these.

Assert. 5. Flying from the tyranny of abused authority is a plain resisting of rulers in their unlawful oppression and perverting of judgment.

All royalists grant it lawful, and ground it upon the law of nature, that those that are persecuted by tyrannical princes may flee, and it is evident from Christ's commandment, "If they persecute you in one city, flee to another" (Matt. 10:23, and by Matt, 23:34). Christ fled from the fury of the Jews till his hour was come; Elijah, Uriah (Jer. 26:20), and Joseph and Mary fled; the martyrs did hide themselves in caves and dens of the earth (Heb. 11:37-38); Paul was let down through a window in a basket at Damascus. This certainly is resistance; for look, what legal power God has given to a tyrannical ruler, remaining a power ordained by God, to summon legally and set before his tribunal the servants of God, that he may kill them, and murder them unjustly, that same legal power he has to murder them; for if it be a legal power to kill the innocent, and such a power as they are obliged in conscience to submit unto, they are obliged in conscience to submit to the legal power of citing; for it is one and the same power.

1. Now, if resistance to the one power be unlawful, resistance to the other must be unlawful also; and if the law of self-defense or command of Christ warrant me to disobey a tyrannical power commanding me to compear to receive the sentence of death, that same law far more shall warrant me to resist and deny passive subjection in submitting to the unjust sentence of death.

2. When a murderer, self-convicted, flees from the just power of a judge lawfully citing him, he resists the just power ordained of God (Rom. 3); therefore by the same reason if we flee from a tyrannical power, we resist that tyrannical power, and so by royalists' ground we resist the ordinance of God by flying. Now, to be disobedient to a just power summoning a malefactor is to hinder that lawful power to be put forth in lawful acts; for the judge cannot purge the land of blood if the murderer flee.

3. When the king of Israel sends a captain and fifty lictors to fetch Elisha, these come instructed with legal power from the king; if I may lay fetters on their power by night, upon the ground of self-preservation, the same warrant shall allow me to oppose harmless violence for my own safety.

4. Royalists hold it unlawful to keep a stronghold against the king, though the fort be not the king's house, and though David would not have offended if he had kept Keilah against Saul, Dr. Ferne and

royalists say it would have been unlawful resistance. What more re-sistance is made to royal power by walls interposed than by seas and miles of earth interposed? Both are physical resistance, and violent in their kind.

QUESTION 31.

WHETHER SELF-DEFENCE BY OPPOSING VIOLENCE TO UNJUST VIOLENCE, BY LAWFUL, BY THE LAW OF GOD AND NATURE.

Self-defense in man is natural, but the means must be rational and just. What the method of self-defense may be. Violent re-offending in self-defense is the last remedy. It is physically impossible for a nation to fly in the case of persecution for religion, and so they may resist in their own self-defense. Tutela vitae proxima and remota. In a remote posture of self-defense, we are not to take us to re-offending, as David was not to kill Saul when he was sleeping, or in the cave, for the same cause. David would not kill Saul because he was the Lord's anointed. The king is not lord of chastity, name, or conscience, and so may be resisted. By universal and particular nature, that self-defense is lawful is proved by various arguments, and made good by the testimony of jurists. The love of ourselves is the measure of the love of our neighbors, and it enforces self-defense. Nature makes a private man his own judge and magistrate, when the magistrate is absent and violence is offered to his life, as the law says. How lawful self-defense is. What presumption is from the king's carriage to the two kingdoms are in law sufficient grounds of defensive wars. Offensive and defensive wars differ in the event and intentions of men, but not in nature and specie, nor

physically. David's case in not killing Saul nor his men is no rule to us
so that we may not in our lawful defense kill the king's emissaries, since
the cases are far different.

S elf-preservation in all creatures in which is nature is in the creatures suitable to their nature. The bull defends itself by its horns, the eagle by her claws and bill; it will not follow that a lamb will defend itself against a wolf any other way than by flying. So men, and Christian men, do naturally defend themselves, but the manner of self-defense in a rational creature is rational, and not always merely natural; therefore, a political community, being a combination of many natures, as neither grace, far less can policy, destroy nature, then must these many natures be permitted by God to use a natural self-defense. If the king bring in an army of foreigners, then a political community must defend itself in a rational way. Why? Self-defense is natural to man, and natural to a lamb, but not in the same way. A lamb or a dove naturally defends itself against beasts of another kind only by flight, not by reaction and re-offending; but it follows not that a man defending himself from his enemy only by flight. If a robber invade me, to take away my life and my purse, I may defend myself by re-action; for reason and grace both may determine the way of self-preservation. Thus royalists say a private man against his prince has no way to defend himself but by flight; therefore, a community has no other way to defend themselves but by flight.

1. The antecedent is false. Dr. Ferne allows to a private man supplications and denial of subsidies and tribute to the prince when he employs tribute to the destruction of the commonwealth, which by the way sn a clear resistance and an active

resistance made against the king (Rom. 13:6-7) and against a commandment of God, unless royalists grant tyrannical powers may be resisted.

2. The consequence is nothing, for a private man may defend himself against unjust violence, but not in any way he pleases; the first way is by supplications and apologies, he may not presently use violence to the king's servants before he supplicate, nor may he use re-offending, if flight may save. David used all the three in order. He made his defense by words, by the mediation of Jonathan; when that prevailed not, he took himself to flight, as the next; but because he knew flight was not safe in every way, and nature taught him self-preservation, and reason and light of grace taught him the means and the religious order of these means for self-preservation, therefore he adds a third: "He took Goliath's sword, and gathered six hundred armed men," and after that made use of a host. Now a sword and armor are not horsing and shipping for flight, but contrary to flight; so re-offending is policy's last refuge. A godly magistrate takes not away the life of a subject if other means can accomplish the end of the law, and so he is compelled and required to take away the life; so the private man in his natural self-defense is not to use re-action or violent re-offending in his self-defense against any man, far less against the servants of a king, but in the exigence of the last and most inexorable necessity. And it is true that M. Symmons says, "Self-defense is not to be used where it cannot be without sin" (section 11). It is certain, necessity is but a hungry plea for sin (Luke 14:18) but it is also true, re-offending comparatively, that I kill rather than I be killed in the sinless court of nature's spotless and harmless necessity is lawful and necessary, unless I be guilty of self-murder in the culpable omission of self-defense. Now a private man may fly, and

that is his second necessity, and violent re-offending is the
third means of self-preservation, but with leave violent re-offending is necessary to a private man when his second mean,
namely, flight, is not possible and cannot attain the end, as in
the case of David: if flight do not prevail, Goliath's sword and
a host of armed men are lawful. So, to a church and a community of protestants, men, women, aged, sucking children, sick,
and diseased, who are pressed either to be killed or forsake
religion and Jesus Christ, flight is not the second means, nor
a means at all, because not possible, and therefore not a natural means of preservation; for the aged, the sick, the sucking
infants, and sound religion in the posterity cannot flee; flight
here is physically, and by nature's necessity, impossible, and
therefore no lawful means. What is to nature physically impossible is no lawful means. If Christ have a promise that the
ends of the earth (Ps. 2:8) and the isles shall be his possession
(Isa. 49:1) I see not how natural defense can put us to flee,
even all protestants and their seed, and the weak and sick,
whom we are obliged to defend as ourselves, both by the law
of nature and grace. I read that seven wicked and idolatrous
nations were cast out of their land to give place to the church
of God to dwell there, but show me a warrant in nature's law
and in God's word that three kingdoms of protestants, their
seed, aged, sick, sucking children, should flee out of England,
Scotland, Ireland, and leave religion and the land to a king
and to papists, prelates, and bloody Irish, and atheists; and
therefore to a church and community having God's right and
man's law to the land, violent re-offending is their second
means (next to supplications and declarations, &c) and flight
is not required of them as of a private man; yea flight is not
necessarily required of a private man, except where it is a possible means of self-preservation; violent and unjust invasion

of a private man, which is unavoidable, may be obstructed with violent re-offending. Now the unjust invasion made on Scotland in 1640 for refusing the service-book, or rather the idolatry of the mass by it intended, was unavoidable; it was impossible for the protestants, their old and sick, their women and sucking children to flee over sea or to have shipping between the king's bring an army on them at Dunse Law, and the prelates' charging of the ministers to receive the mass book. Althusius says well that though private men may flee, yet the estates, if they flee, they do not do their duty, to commit a country, religion and all to a lion (*Polit.* section 38, n. 78). Let not any object, we may not devise a way to fulfill the prophecy, Ps. 2:8-9; Isa. 49:1; it is true, if the way be our own sinful way; nor let any object, a colony went to New England and fled the persecution. Answer, True, but if fleeing be the only means after supplication, there was no more reason that one colony should go to New England than it is necessary and by a divine law obligatory that the whole protestants in in the three kingdoms according to royalists' doctrine are to leave their native country and religion to one man, and to popish idolaters and atheists, willing to worship idols with them, and whither then shall the gospel be, which we are obliged to defend with our lives?

There is *tutela vitae proxima, et remota,* a mere and immediate defense of our life, and a remote or mediate defense; when there is no actual invasion made by a man seeking our life, we are not to use violent re-offending. David might have killed Saul when he was sleeping, and when he cut off the lap of his garment, but it was unlawful for him to kill the Lord's anointed, because he is the Lord's anointed, as it is unlawful to kill a man because he is the image of God (Gen. 9:6) except in case of necessity. The magistrate in case of necessity may kill the malefactor, though his *maleficus* do not put him in that case, that he has not now the image of God; how prudence and light of grace determine when we are to use violent re-offending for self-preservation, it is not left to our pleasure. In a remote posture of self-defense, we are not to use violent re-offending: David having Saul in his hand was in a remote posture of defense, the unjust invasion then was not actual, not unavoidable, not a necessary means in human prudence for self-preservation, for king Saul was then in a habitual, not in an actual pursuit of all the princes, elders, and judges of Israel, or of a whole community and church; Saul did but seek the life of one man, David, and that not for religion or a national pretended offense, and therefore he could not in conscience put hands on the Lord's anointed; but if Saul had actually invaded David for his life, David might in that case make use of Goliath's sword (for he took not that weapon with him as a cipher to boast Saul: it is no less unlawful to threaten a king than to put hands on him) and rather kill or be killed by Saul's emissaries, because then he should have been in an immediate and nearest posture of actual self-defense. Now the case is far otherwise between the king and the two parliaments of England and Scotland, for the king is not sleeping in his emissaries, for he has armies in two kingdoms, and now in three kingdoms by sea and land, night and day, in actual pursuit, not of one David, but of the estates, and a Christian community in England and Scotland, and that for religions, laws, and liberties; for the question is now between papist and protestant, between arbitrary or tyrannical government and law government, and therefore by both the laws of the political societies of both kingdoms, and by the law of God and nature, we are to use violent re-offending for self-preservation and put to this necessity, when armies are in actual pursuit of all the protestant churches of the three kingdoms, to actual killing, rather than we be killed and suffer laws and religion to be undone.

But, says the royalist, David's argument, "God forbid that I stretch out my hand against the Lord's anointed, my master the king," concludes universally that the king in his most tyrannical acts, still remaining the Lord's anointed cannot be resisted.

Ans. 1. David speaks of stretching out his hand against the person of king Saul: no man in the three kingdoms did so much as attempt to do violence to the king's person. But this argument is inconsequential, for a king invading in his own royal person the innocent subject, suddenly, without pretense of law or reason, and unavoidably, may be personally resisted, and that with opposing a violence bodily, yet in that invasion he remains the Lord's anointed.

2. By this argument the life of a murderer cannot be taken away by a judge, for he remains one endued with God's image and keeps still the nature of a man under all the murders that he does, but it follows in no way that because God has endowed his person with a sort of royalty, of a divine image, that his life cannot be taken; and certainly, if to be a man endued with God's image (Gen. 6:9-10) and to be an evil-doer worthy of evil punishment are different, to be a king and an evil-doer may be distinguished.

1. The grounds of self-defense are these: A woman or a young man may violently oppose a king if he force the one to adultery and incest, and the other to sodomy, though court flatterers should say the king, in regard of his absoluteness, is lord of life and death, yet no man ever said that the king is lord of chastity, faith, and oath that the wife has made to her husband.

2. Particular nature yields to the good of universal nature, for which cause heavy bodies ascend, airy and light bodies descend. If then a wild bull or a goring ox may not be let loose in a great market-confluence of people, and if any man turn so distracted as he smite himself with stones and kill all that pass by him or come at him, in that case the man is to be bound and his hands fettered, and all whom he invades may resist him were they his own sons, and may save their own lives with weapons much more a king turning a Nero. King Saul, vexed with an evil spirit from the Lord, may be resisted, and far more if a king endued with use of reason shall put violent hands on all his subjects, kill his son and heir, yea, and violently invaded by nature's law may defend themselves, and the violent restraining of such a one is but the hurting of one man, who cannot be virtually the commonwealth, but his destroying of the community of men sent out in wars as his bloody emissaries, to the dissolution of the commonwealth.

3. The cutting off of a contagious member that by a gangrene would corrupt the whole body is well warranted by nature, because the safety of the whole is to be preferred to the safety of a part. Nor is it much that royalists say, the king being the head, destroy him, and the whole body of the commonwealth is dissolved, just as if you cut off a man's head, and the life of the whole man is taken away, because, 1. God cuts off the spirits of tyrannical kings, and yet the commonwealth is not dissolved, no more than when a leopard or a wild boar running through children is killed can be the destruction of all the children in the land.

2. A king indefinitely is referred to the commonwealth as an adequate head to a monarchical kingdom; and remove all kings and the political body, as monarchical, in its frame is not monarchical, but it leaves not off to be a political body,

seeing it has other judges; but the natural body without the head cannot live.

3. This or that tyrannical king, being a transient mortal thing, cannot be referred to the immortal commonwealth, as an adequate correlate. They say, "the king never dies," yet this king can die; an immortal political body, such as the commonwealth, must have an immortal head, and that is a king as a king, not this or that man, possibly a tyrant, who is for the time (and eternal things abstract from time) only a king.

4. The reason of Fortunius Garcias, a skillful lawyer in Spain is considerable (*Comment. in l. ut vim vi ff. de justit et jure*) God has implanted in every creature natural inclinations and motions to preserve itself, and we are to love ourselves for God, and have a love to preserve ourselves rather than our neighbor, and nature's law teaches every man to love God best of all, and next ourselves more than our neighbor; for the law says, "you shall love your neighbor as thyself." Then says Malderius, "The love of ourselves is the measure of the love of our neighbor" (com. in 12, q. 26, tom. 2, section 10, concl. 2). But the rule and the measure is more perfect, simple, and more principal than the thing that is measured. It is true I am to love the salvation of the church: it comes nearer to God's glory more than my own salvation, as the wishes of Moses and Paul do prove; and I am to love the salvation of my brother more than my own temporal life, but I am to love my own temporal life more than the life of any other, and therefore, I am rather to kill than to be killed, the exigence of necessity so requiring. Nature without sin owns this as a truth, in the case of loss of life, *Proximus sum egomet mihi*: "He that loves his wife, loves himself; for no man ever yet hated his own flesh, but nourishes it, and cherishes it, even as the Lord the church." (Ephes. 5:28-29). As then nature ties the dam to defend the

young birds, and the lion her whelps, and the husband the
wife, and that by a comparative re-offending, rather than the
wife or children should be killed; yea, he that his wanting to
his brother (if a robber unjustly invade his brother) and helps
him not is a murderer of his brother, so far God's spiritual
law requiring both conservation of it in our person, and preservation in others. The forced damsel was commanded to cry
for help, and not the magistrate only, but the nearest private
man or woman was to come, by an obligation of a divine law
of the seventh commandment, to rescue the damsel with violence, even as a man is to save his enemy's ox or his ass out of
a pit. And if a private man may inflict bodily punishment of
two degrees to preserve the life and chastity of his neighbor
far rather than suffer his life and chastity to be taken away,
then he may inflict violence of four degrees, even to killing,
for his life and much more for his own life. So when a robber,
with deadly weapons, invades an innocent traveler to kill him
for his goods, upon the supposition that if the robber be not
killed, the innocent shall be killed. Now the question is which
of the two by God's moral law and revealed will in point of
conscience ought to be killed by his fellow? For we speak not
now of God's eternal decree of permitting evil, according to
the which murderers may crucify the innocent Lord of glory.
By no moral law of God should the unjust robber kill the innocent traveler; therefore, in this demand of providence, the
traveler should rather kill the robber. If any say by God's moral law no one should kill his fellow, and it is a sin against the
moral law in either to kill the other, I answer, if a third shall
come in when the robber and the innocent are invading each
other for his life, all acknowledge by the sixth commandment
the third may cut off the robber's arm to save the innocent,
but by what law of God he may cut off his arm he may take

his life also to save the other; for it is murder to wound un-justly and to dismember a man by private authority, as it is to take away his life; if, therefore, the third may take away the robber's member, then also his life, so long as he do it without malice or appetite of revenge, and if he may do it out of this principle, "you shall love your neighbor as yourself," because a man is obliged more to love his own flesh than his neighbor's (Ephes. 5:28) and so more to defend himself than to defend his neighbor; then may he oppose violence to the robber. As two men drowning in a water, the one is not obliged by God s law to expose himself to drowning to save his neighbor, but by the contrary, he is obliged rather to save himself, though it were with the loss of his neighbor's life. As in war, if soldiers in a strait passage be pursued on their life, nature teaches them to flee; if one fall, his fellow in that exigence is not only not obliged to lift him up, but he and the rest flying, though they trample on him and kill him, they are not guilty of murder, seeing they hated him not before (Deut. 19:4, 6) so Chemnitz (*loc. com. de vindic*, q. 3) allows private defense. 1. When die violence is sudden. 2. And the violence manifestly inevitable. 3. When the magistrate is absent and cannot help. 4. When moderation is kept as lawyers require. 1. That it be done incontinent; if it be done after the injury, it is revenge, not defense. 2. Not of desire of revenge. 3. With proportion of armor. If the violent invader invade not with deadly weapons, you must not invade him with deadly weapons; and certainly the law (Exod. 22) of a man's defending his house is clear. 1. If he come in the night, it is presumed he is a robber. 2. If he be taken with a weapon breaking the house and he comes to kill, a man may defend himself, wife, and children, 3. But he is but to wound him, and if he die of the wound, the defender is free; so the defender is not to intend his death, but to save himself.

5. It would be a mighty defect in providence to man if dogs by nature may defend themselves against wolves, bulls against lions, doves against hawks, if man, in the absence of the lawful magistrate, should not defend himself against unjust violence; but one man might raise armies of papists, sick for blood, to destroy innocent men.

They object, "When the king is present in his person, and his invaders, he is not absent, and so though you may rather kill a private man than suffer yourself to be killed, yet, because prudence determines the means of self-defense, you are to expose your life to hazard for justice of your king, and therefore not to do violence to the life of your king; nor can the body in any self-defense fight against the head that must be the destruction of the whole."

Ans. 1. Though the king be present as an unjust invader in wars against his innocent subjects, he is absent as a king, and a father and defender, and present as an unjust conqueror, and therefore the innocent may defend themselves when the king neither can, nor will defend them. "Nature makes a man," says the law,[1] "even a private man, his own judge, magistrate, and defender, *quando copiam judicis qui sibi jus reddat, non habet,* when he has no judge to give him justice and law." The subjects are to give their lives for the king as the king, because the safety of the king as king is the safety of the commonwealth. But the king, as offering unjust violence to his innocent subjects, is not king. Zoannet: *Transgrediens notoris officium suum judex, agit velut privatus aliquis, non ut magistratus.*[2] 3. If the

---

1. *Gener. de decur. l. 10, l. si alius, sect. Bellissime ubique Gloss. in vers. ex magn. not. per. ilium. text. ff. quod vi aut clam. l. ait praetor. sect. si debitorem meum. ff. de hisqur in fraud. credito*

2. Part 3, defens. n. 44, *ff. de injur. est bonus in simili in, l. qui fundum, sect. si. tutor, ff. pro emptore.*

political body fight against this head in particular, not as head, but as an oppressor of the people, there is no fear of dissolution; if the body rise against all magistracy, as magistracy and laws, dissolution of all must follow. Parliaments and inferior judges are heads (Num. 1:16; 10:4; Deut. 1:15; Josh. 22:21; Mic. 3:1, 9, 11; 1 Kings 8:1; 1 Chron. 5:25; 2 Chron. 5:2) no less than the king, and it is unlawful to offer violence to them, though I shall rather think a private man is to suffer the king to kill him rather than he kill the king, because he is to prefer the life of a private man to the life of a public man.

6. By the law of nature a ruler is appointed to defend the innocent. Now,by nature an infant in the womb defends itself first, before the parents can defend it, then when parents and magistrates are not (and violent invading magistrates are not in that magistrates) nature has commended every man to self-defense.

7. The law of nature excepts no violence, whether inflicted by a magistrate or any other. Unjust violence from a ruler is double injustice. 1, He does unjustly as a man. 2. As a member of the commonwealth. 3. He commits a special kind of sin of injustice against his office, but it is absurd to say we may lawfully defend ourselves from smaller injuries by the law of nature, and not from the greater. "If the Pope, says Fer. Vasquez command to take away benefices from the just owner, those who are to execute his commandment are not to obey, but to write back that that mandate came not from his holiness, but from the avarice of his officers; but if the Pope still continue and press the same unjust mandate, the same should be written again to him: and though there be none above the Pope, yet there is natural self-defense patent for all"

(illust. quest. l. 1.24, n. 24-25).[1] *Defensio vitae necessaria est, et a jure naturali profluit. Nam quod quisque ob tutelam corporis sui fecerit, jure fecisse videatur.*" *Etiamsi sequatur homidicium.*" (*L. ut vim. ff. de just, et jure* 16). Vasquez "*Etiam occidere licet ob defensionem rerum. vim vi repellere omnia jura permittunt in C. significasti*" (l.1.17, n. 5). Garcias Fortunius: "Defendere *se est juris naturae et gentium. A jure civili fuit additum moderamen inculpatae tutelae*" (*Comment. in l. ut vim. ff. de instit. et jur, n.* 3). Novel "*Occidens principem vel alium tyrannidem exercentem a poena homicidii excusatur*" (*defens. n.* 101). Grotius: "*Si corpus impetatur vi presente, cum periculo vitae non aliter vitabili, tunc bellum est licitum etiam cum interfectione periculum inferentis, ratio, natura quemque sibi commendat*" (*de jure belli et pacis,* 1.2.1, n. 3). Barclay: "*Est jus cuilibet se tenendi adversus immanem sevitiam.*" (*Advers. Monar.* 1.3.8).

But what ground (says the royalist) is there to take arms against the king? Jealousies and suspicions are not enough.

Ans. 1. The king sent first an army to Scotland, and blocked us up by sea, before we took arms. 2. Papists were armed in England. They have professed themselves in their religion of Trent to be so much the holier that they root out protestants. 3. The king declared we had broken loyalty to him since the last parliament. 4. He declared both kingdoms rebels. 5. Attempted in his emissaries to destroy the parliament; 6. And to bring in a foreign enemy. And the law says, "An imminent danger, which is a sufficient warrant to take up arms is not strokes, but either the terror of arming or threatening." Glossator: "*Unde 6. ait non esse verbera expectanda, sed vel terrorem*

---

1. Section *jus natura l, 1 distinc,* l.1, *ff. de vi et vi armata, l. injuriarum, ff. de injuria: C. significasti. 2, de hom. l. scientiam, sect. qui non aliter ff. ad leg. Aquil;* section *si vero 1, de sent. excom. et l. sed etsi ff. ad leg. Aquil.*

armorum sufficere, vel minas, et hoc esse imminens periculum."[2]
In most heinous sins, *conatus* the endeavor and aim, *etiamsi effectus non sequatur, puniri debet*, is punishable. Bartol: *"Si quis non dicam rapere"* (*in l.*).

The king has aimed at the destruction of his subjects, through the power of wicked counsellors, and we are to consider not the intention of the workers, but the nature and intention of the work. Papists are in arms: their religion, the conspiracy of Trent, their conscience (if they have any) their malice against the covenant of Scotland, which abjures their religion to the full, their ceremonies, their prelates, lead and necessitate them to root out the name of protestant religion, yea, and to stab a king who is a protestant. Nor is our king, remaining a protestant and adhering to his oath made at the coronation in both kingdoms, lord of his own person, master of himself, nor able as king to be a king over protestant subjects, if the papists, now in arms under his standard, shall prevail.

The king has been compelled to go against his own oath, and the laws which he did swear to maintain; the Pope sends to his popish armies both dispensations, bulls, mandates, and encouragements; the king has made a cessation with the bloody Irish and has put arms in the hands of papists. Now he being under the oath of God, tied to maintain the protestant religion, he has a metaphysically subtle, piercing faith in miracles who believes armed papists and prelates shall defend the religion of protestants; and those who have abjured prelates as the lawful sons of the Pope, that ο αντιχριστος and as the law says, *Quilibet in dubio praesumitur* (*bonus. L. merito praesumi. L. non omnes, sect. a Barbaris de re milit*). Charity belies not

---

2. In *d. l.* 1, *C. L. sed et si quemcunqtue in princ. ff. ad leg, Aquil* l.3, *quod qui armati ff. de vi et vi armata is qui aggressorem C. ad legem Corneli.*

ill; so charity is not a fool to believe all things. So says the
law, *Semel malus, semper praesumitur malus, in eodem genere.*
(*C semel malus de jure gentium in* 6). Once wicked is always
wicked in that kind. Marius Salamonius: We are not to wait
on strokes, the terror of armor, *omnium consensu*, by consent
of all is sufficient (*l. C, in L. ut vim atque injuriam ff. de just
et jure*). "If I see," says he, "the enemy take an arrow out of
the quiver, before he bend the bow, it is lawful to prevent him
with a blow-*cunctatio est periculosa.*" The king's coming with
armed men into the House of Commons to demand the five
members is very symbolic, and war was printed on that fact:
"he that runs may read." His coming to Hull with an army
shows not he had no errand there but to ask what it was in the
dock. Novellus, that learned Venetian lawyer, in a treatise for
defense, makes *continuatam rixam*, a continued upbraiding, a
sufficient ground of violent defense. He cites Dr. Comniter
(*in L. ut vim, ff, de just et jure*). Yea, he says, drunkenness
(defens. n. 44), error (n. 46), madness (n. 40, 50), ignorance
(n. 51, 52), impudence (n. 54), necessity (n. 56), lascivious-
ness (n. 58), continual reproaches (n. 59), the fervor of anger
(n. 64), threatening (n. 66), fear of imminent danger (n, 67),
and just grief do excuse a man from homicide, and that in
these he ought to be more mildly punished, *quia obnubila-
tum et mancum est consilium*, reason in these being lame and
clogged (Ambros. 1.1. offic). *Qui non repellit injuriam a socio,
cum potest, tam est in vitio, quam ille quifacit.* And as nature,
so the law says, "When the losses are such as can never be
repaired, such as death, mutilation, loss of chastity, *quoniam
facta infecta fieri nequeunt*, things of that kind once done can
never be undone, we are to prevent the enemy."[1] If the king

---

1.1. *Zonat. tract. defens.* par. 3, *l. in bello sect, factae de carpit. notat. Gloss. in l. si quis
provocatione.*

send an Irish rebel to cast me over a bridge and drown me in a water, I am to do nothing, while the king's emissary first cast me over and then in the next place I am to defend myself; but nature and the law of self-defense warrants me (if I know certainly his aim) to horse him first over the bridge, and then consult how to defend myself at my own leisure.

Royalists object that David in his defense never invaded and persecuted Saul; yea, when he came upon Saul and his men sleeping, he would not kill any, but the Scottish and parliament's forces not only defend, but invade, offend, kill, and plunder, and this is clearly an offensive, not a defensive war.

Ans. 1. There is no defensive war different in specie and nature from an offensive war; if we speak physically, they differ only in the event and intention of the heart, and it is most clear that the affection and intention does make one and the same action of taking away the life, either homicide, or no homicide. 1. If a man, out of hatred, deliberately take away his brother's life, he is a murderer *eatenus*, but if that same man had taken away that same brother's life by the flying off of an axe-head off the staff, while he was hewing timber, neither hating him before, nor intending to hurt his brother, he is no murderer by God's express law (Deut. 4:42; 19:4; Joshua 20:5). 2. The cause between the king and the two parliaments and between Saul and David are so different in this, as it is much for us. Royalists say David might, if he had seen offending to aid in self-preservation, have invaded Saul's men, and, say they, the case was extraordinary and binds not us to self-defense, and thus they must say: for offensive weapons such as Goliath's sword and a host of armed men cannot by any rational man be assumed (and David had the wisdom of God) but to offend, if providence should so dispose, and so what was lawful to David is lawful to us in self-defense; he might offend lawfully, and so may we.

2. If Saul and the Philistines, aiming (as under an oath) to set up Dagon in the land of Israel, should invade David and the princes and elders of Israel who made him king; and if David, with an host of armed men, he and the princes of Israel, should come in that case upon Saul and the Philistines sleeping, if in that case David might not lawfully have cut off the Philistines, and as he defended in that case God's church and true religion, if he might not then have lawfully killed, I say, the Philistines, I remit to the conscience of the reader. Now to us, papists and prelates under the king's banner are Philistines, introducing the idolatry of bread-worship and popery, as hateful to God as Dagon-worship.

3. Saul intended no arbitrary government, nor to make Israel a conquered people, nor yet to cut off all that professed the true worship of God; nor came Saul against these princes, elders, and people who made him King, only David's head would have made Saul lay down arms, but prelates, and papists, and malignants under the king intend to make the king's sole will a law, to destroy the court of parliament, which puts laws in execution against their idolatry, and their aim is that protestants be a conquered people, and their attempt has been till now to blow up king and parliament, to cut off all protestants; and they are in arms in various parts of the kingdom against the princes of the land, who are no less judges and deputies of the Lord than the king himself, and would kill, and do kill, plunder, and spoil us if we kill not them. And the case is every way now between armies and armies, as between a single man unjustly invaded for his life and an unjust invader. Neither in a natural action, such as is self-defense, is that of policy to be urged, none can he judge in his own cause, when oppression

is manifest: one may be both agent and patient, as the fire and water conflicting; there is no need of a judge, a community casts not off nature; when the judge is wanting, nature is judge, actor, accused, and all. Lastly, no man is lord of the members of his own body (*m. l. liber homo ff. ad leg. Aqui*), nor lord of his own life, but is to be accountable to God for it.

QUESTION 32.

WHETHER OR NOT THE LAWFULNESS OP DEFENSIVE WARS CAN BE PROVED FROM THE SCRIPTURE FROM THE EXAMPLES OF DAVID, THE PEOPLE'S RESCUING JONATHAN, ELISHA, AND THE EIGHTY VALIANT PRIESTS WHO RESISTED UZZIAH.

David justifiably raised an army of men to defend himself against the unjust violence of his prince Saul. David did not invade Saul and his men, since they did not aim at arbitrary government, at subversion of laws, religion, and extirpation of those that worshipped the God of Israel and opposed idolatry, but only pursued one single person, far unlike to our case in Scotland and England now. David's example is not extraordinary. Elisha's resistance proves defensive wars to be warrantable. Resistance made to King Uzziah by eighty valiant priests proves the same. The people's rescuing Jonathan proves the same. Libnah's revolt proves this. The city of Abel defended themselves against Joab, King David's general, when he came to destroy a city for one wicked conspirator, Sheba's sake.

D avid defended himself against king Saul, 1. By taking Goliath's sword with him. 2. By being captain to six hundred men, yea, it is more than clear (1 Chron. 12:22-34) that there came to David a host like the host of God, to help against Saul, exceeding four thousand. Now that this host came warrantably to help him against Saul, I prove, 1. Because it is said, "Now these are they that came to David to Ziklag, while he kept himself close, because of Saul the son of Kish; and they were among the mighty men, helpers of the war," and then so many mighty captains are reckoned out. "There came of the children of Benjamin and Judah to the hold of David." And there fell some of Manasseh to David: "As he went to Ziklag there fell to him of Manasseh, Kenah and Jozahad, Jediel and Michael, and Jozahad and Elihu, and Zilthai, captains of the thousands that were of Manasseh." "And they helped David against the hand of the rovers." "At that time day by day there came to David, until it was a great host, like the host of God." Now the same expression that is in the first verse, where it is said they came to help David against Saul, is repeated in ver. 16, 19-23.

2. That they warrantably came, is evident; because (1) the Spirit of God commends them for their valor and skill in war (ver. 2ff), which the Spirit of God does not in unlawful wars, (2) because Amassai (ver. 18), the Spirit of the Lord coming on him, says, "yours are we, David, and on your side, you son of Jesse; peace, peace unto you, and peace to your helpers, for your God helps you." The Spirit of God inspires no man to pray peace to those who are in an unlawful war.

3. That they came to David's side only to be sufferers, and to flee with David, and not to pursue and offend, is ridiculous. 1. It is said, "They came to David to Ziklag, while he kept himself close, because of Saul the son of Kish. And they were

among the mighty men, helpers of the war" (ver. 1). It is a
scorn to say that their might and their helping in war consist-
ed in being mere patients with David, and such as fled from
Saul, for they had been on Saul's side before, and to come with
armor to flee is a mocking of the word of God. 2. It is clear the
scope of the Spirit of God is to show how God helped his innocent servant David against his persecuting prince and master, king Saul, in moving so many mighty men of war to come
in such multitudes, all in arms, to help him in war. Now to
what end would the Lord commend them as fit for war, "men
of might, fit to handle shield and buckler, whose faces are as
the faces of lions, as swift as the roes on the mountains," (ver.
8) and commend them as helpers of David, if it were unlawful
for David and all those mighty men to carry arms to pursue
Saul and his followers, and to do nothing with their armor but
flee? Judge if the Spirit of God in reason could say, "All these
men came armed with bows," (ver. 2) and could "handle both
the right hand and the left in flinging stones, and shooting
of arrows," and that (ver. 22) all these "came to David, being
mighty men of valor, and they came as captains over hundreds,
and thousands, and they put to flight all them of the valleys,
both toward the east and toward the west," (ver. 13, 15) and
that "David received them, and made them captains of the
band," if they did not come in a posture of war, and for hostile
invasion, if need were? For if they came only to suffer and to
flee, not to pursue, bowmen, captains, and captains of bands
made by David, and David's helpers in the war, came not to
help David by flying, that was a hurt to David, not a help. It
is true, Mr. Symmons says, "Those that came out to David
strengthened him, but he strengthened not them; and David
might easily have revenged himself on the Ziphites, who did

good will to betray him to the hands of Saul, if his conscience had served him."

Ans. 1. This would infer that these armed men came to help David against his conscience, and that David was a patient in the business. The contrary is in the text: "David became a captain over them," (1 Sam. 26:2) and "If You come peaceably to help me, my heart shall be knit to you. Then David received them, and made them captains of the band" (1 Chron. 12:17-18). 2. David might have avenged himself upon the Ziphites, true, but that conscience hindered him cannot be proved. To pursue an enemy is an act of a council of war, and he saw it would create more enemies, not help his cause. 3. To David to kill Saul sleeping and the people who, out of a misinformed conscience came out, many of them to help their lawful prince against a traitor (as was supposed) seeking to kill their king and to usurp the throne, would not have been wisdom or justice, because to kill the enemy in a just self-defense must be, when the enemy actually does invade, and the life of the defendant cannot be otherwise saved. A sleeping enemy is not in the act of unjust pursuit of the innocent, but if an army of papists, Philistines, were in the fields sleeping, pursuing not one single David only for a supposed personal wrong to the king, but lying in the fields and camp against the whole kingdom and religion, and laboring to introduce arbitrary government, popery, idolatry, and to destroy laws, and liberties, and parliaments, then David would be obliged to kill these murderers in their sleep.

If any say the case is all one in a natural self-defense, whatever be the cause, and whoever be the enemy, because the self-defender is not to offend, unless the unjust invader be in actual pursuit; now armies in their sleep are not in actual pursuit.

Ans. 1. When one man with a multitude invades one man, that one man may pursue, as he sees most conducible for self-defense. Now the law says, "Threatenings and terror of armor makes imminent danger," and the case of pursuit in self-defense lawful; if therefore an army of Irish rebels and Spaniards were sleeping in their camp, and our king in a deep sleep in the midst of them, and these rebels actually in the camp besieging the parliament, and the city of London, most unjustly to take away parliament, laws, and liberties of religion, it should follow that General Essex ought not to kill the king's majesty in his sleep, for he is the Lord's anointed; but will it follow that General Essex may not kill the Irish rebels sleeping about the king; and that he may not rescue the king's person out of the hands of the papists and rebels, ensnaring the king, and leading him on to popery, and to employ his authority to defend popery, and trample upon protestant parliaments and laws? Certainly from this example this cannot be concluded. For armies in actual pursuit of a whole parliament, kingdom, laws, and religion (though sleeping in the camp) because in actual pursuit, may be invaded, and killed, though sleeping. And David uses no argument from conscience why he might not kill Saul's army (I conceive he had not arms to do that) and should have created more enemies to himself, and hazard his own life, and the life of all his men, if he had on purpose killed so many sleeping men; yea, the inexpedience of that, for a private wrong to kill God's misled people, would have made all Israel enemies to David. But David uses an argument from conscience only to prove it was not lawful for him to stretch forth his hand against the king, and for my part, so long as he remains king, and is not dethroned by those who made him king at Hebron, to put hands on his person, I judge utterly unlawful. One man sleeping cannot be in actual pursuit of another man so that the self-defender may lawfully kill him in his sleep, but the case is far otherwise in lawful wars: the Israelites might lawfully kill the Philistines encamping about Jerusalem to destroy it, and religion, and the church of God, though they were all sleeping; even though we suppose king Saul had brought them in by his authority, and though he were sleeping in the midst of the uncircumcised armies, and it is evident that a host of armed enemies, though sleeping, by the law of self-defense may be killed, lest they awake and kill us, whereas one single man, and that a king, cannot be killed. 2. I think, certainly, David would have done unwisely and hazarded his own life and all his men's, if he, and Abimelech, and Abishai, should have killed a host of their enemies sleeping: that would have been a work as impossible to three, as hazardous to all his men.

Dr. Ferne, as Arnisaeus did before him, says, "The example of David was extraordinary, because he was anointed and designated by God as successor to Saul, and so he must use an extraordinary way of guarding himself." Arnisaeus cites Alberic. Gentilis, that David was now exempted from among the number of subjects (section 2, n. 15).

Ans. 1. There were not two kings in Israel now, both David and Saul. 1. David acknowledges his subjection in naming Saul the Lord's anointed, and his master, lord, and king; and, therefore, David was still a subject. 2. If David would have proved his title to the crown by extraordinary ways, he who killed Goliath extraordinarily might have killed Saul by a miracle; but David goes a most ordinary way to work for self-defense, and his coming to the kingdom was through persecution, want, eating showbread in case of necessity, defending himself with Goliath's sword. 3. How was anything extraordinary and above a law, seeing David might have killed his enemy Saul, and, according to God's law, he spared him? And he argues from a moral duty: He is the Lord's anointed, therefore I will not kill him. Was this extraordinary above a law? Then, according to God's law, he might have killed him. Royalists cannot say so. What ground to say one of David's acts in his deportment towards Saul was extraordinary, and not all? Was it extraordinary that David fled? No, or that David consulted the oracle of God what to do when Saul was coining against him? 4. In an ordinary fact something may be extraordinary, as the dead sleep from the Lord upon Saul and his men (1 Sam. 26) and yet the fact, according to its substance, ordinary. 6. Nor is this extraordinary, that a distressed man, being an excellent warrior, as David was, may use the help of six hundred men, who by the law of charity are to help to deliver the innocent from death, yea, all Israel were obliged to defend him who killed Goliath. 6. Royalists make David's act of not putting hands on the Lord's anointed an ordinary moral reason against resistance, but his putting on of armor they will have extraordinary, and this is, I confess, a short way to an adversary to cull out something that is for his cause and make it ordinary, and something that is against his cause must be extraordinary. 7. These men by the law of nature were obliged to join in arms with David; therefore, the non-helping of an oppressed man must be God's ordinary law, a blasphemous tenet. 8. If David, by an extraordinary spirit, killed not king Saul, then the Jesuits' way of killing must be God's ordinary law.

2. David certainly intended to keep Keilah against king Saul, for the Lord would not have answered David in an unlawful fact; for that would be the same as if God should teach David how to play the traitor to his king; for if God had answered, 'They will not deliver you up, but they shall save you

from the hand of Saul,' as David believed he might say this, as well as its contradiction, then David would have chosen to keep the city; for certainly David's question presupposes he was to keep the city.

The example of Elisha the prophet is considerable: "But Elisha sat in his house, and the elders with him; and the king sent a man before him; but, ere the messengers came to him, he said to the elders, See now, the son of a murderer has sent to take away mine head" (2 Kings 6:32). 1. Here is unjust violence offered by king Joram to an innocent man. Elisha keeps the house violently against the king's messenger, as we did keep castles against king Charles's unlawful messengers: "Look," says he, "when the messenger comes, shut the door." 2. There is violence also commanded, and resistance to be made, "Hold him fast at the door." In the Hebrew it is, **כדלת ולחצתם אתו הרלת מנדו**. Arias Montan.: *Claudite ostium, et oppremetis eumin ostio,* "Violently press him at the door." And so the Chaldee paraphrase, *Ne sinatis eum introire,* Jerome. The LXX Interpreters, εκθλιψατι αυτον εν τη θυρα, dite eum *in ostio,* "Press him between the door and the wall." It is a word of bodily violence, according to Vatablus; yea, Theodoret will have king Joram himself held at the door. And, 3. It is no answer that Dr. Ferne and other royalists give: that Elisha made no personal resistance to the king himself, but only to the king's cut-throat, sent to take away his head; yea, they say, it is lawful to resist the king's cut-throats. But the text is clear that the violent resistance is made to the king himself also, for he adds, "Is not the sound of his master's feet behind him?" And by this answer, it is lawful to keep towns with iron gates and bars, and violently to oppose the king's cut-throats coming to take away the heads of the parliaments of both kingdoms, and of protestants in the three kingdoms.

Some royalists are so impudent as to say that there was no violence here, and that Elisha was an extraordinary man, and that it is not lawful for us to call a king the son of a murderer, as the prophet Elisha did; but Ferne, forgetting himself, says from this, "It is lawful to resist the prince himself, so far as to ward his blows and hold his hands" (section 2). But let Ferne answer if the violent binding of the prince's hand, that he shall not be able to kill, be a greater violence done to his royal person than David's cutting off the skirt of Saul's garment; for certainly the royal body of a prince is of more worth than his clothes. Now it was a sin, I judge, that smote David's conscience, that he being a subject, and not in the act of natural self-defense, did cut the garment of the Lord's anointed. Let Ferne see then how he will save his own principles; for certainly he yields the cause for me. I judge that the person of the king, or any judge who is the Lord's deputy, as is the king, is sacred; and that remaining in that honorable case, no subject can without guiltiness before God put hands on his person, the case of natural self-defense being excepted; for because the royal dignity does not advance a king above the common condition of men, and the throne makes him not leave off to be a man, and a man that can do wrong; and therefore as one that does manifest violence to the life of a man, though his subject, he may be resisted with bodily resistance in the case of unjust and violent invasion. It is a vain thing to say, "Who shall be judge between the king and his subjects? The subject cannot judge the king, because none can be judge in his own cause, and an inferior or equal cannot judge a superior or equal." But I answer, 1. This is the king's own cause also, and he does unjust violence as a man, and not as a king, and so he cannot be judge more than the subject. 2. Everyone that does unjust violence, as he is such, is inferior to the innocent, and so ought to be judged by some. 3. There is no need of the formality of a judge in things evident to nature's eye, such as are manifestly unjust violences. Nature, in acts natural of self-defense, is judge, party, accuser, witness, and all; for it is supposed the judge is absent when the judge does wrong. And for the plea of Elisha's extraordinary spirit, it is nothing extraordinary to the prophet to call the king the son of a murderer, when he complains to the elders for justice of his oppression, no more than it is for a plaintiff to libel a true crime against a wicked person, and if Elisha's resistance came from an extraordinary spirit, then it is not natural for an oppressed man to close the door upon a murderer, then the taking away of the innocent prophet's head must be extraordinary, for this was but an ordinary and most natural remedy against this oppression; and though to name the king the son of a murderer be extraordinary (and I should grant it without any hurt to this cause) it follows in no way that the self-defense was extraordinary. 4 four score of priests, with Azariah, are commended as valiant men (2 Chron. 26:17). LXX: υιοι δυναμεως Heb. בני־היל. Arius Montan.: *Filii virtutis*, Men of courage and valor, for that they resisted Uzziah the king, who would take on him to burn incense to the Lord against the law. Mr. Symmons: They withstood him not with swords and weapons, but only by speaking, and one but spoke (section 10).

I answer, 1. It was a bodily resistance; for beside that, Jerome turns it, *viri fortistimi*, most violent men. And it is a speech in the Scriptures taken for men valorous for war, such as 1 Sam. 16:26; 2 Sam. 17:10; 1 Chron. 5:18; and so does the phrase גבור הול Potent in valor; and the phrase, איש־הול, 2 Sam. 24:9; 11:16; 1 Sam. 31:12; and therefore all the eighty, not only by words, but violently, expelled the king out of the temple. 2. ויעמדו על־עזווהו Ar. Mont: *Et seterunt contra Huzzi-Jahu*;

the LXX say, ηαι υπιτνοπταν they resisted the king. So Dan. 11:17. The armies of the south shall not stand, Dan. 8:26, it is a word of violence. 3. The text says (ver. 20) and they thrust him out. ויכהילוחו Arias Mont. *Et fecerunt eum festinare*; Jerome. *Festinato expulerent eum.* The LXX says, The priest κατεσπασεν αυτον εκειθεν; so Vatablus, they cast him out. 4. It is said, "He was cut off from the house of the Lord" (ver. 21). Dr. Ferne says, "They are valiant men who dare withstand a king in an evil way by a home reproof, and by withdrawing the holy things from him, especially since by the law the leper was to be put out of the congregation" (section 4).

Ans. 1. He contradicts the text. It was not a resistance by words, for the text says, "They withstood him, and they thrust him out violently." 2. He yields the cause, for to withdraw the holy things of God by corporeal violence, and violently to pull the censer out of his hand, that he should not provoke God's wrath by offering incense to the Lord is resistance; and the like violence may by this example be used when the king uses the sword and the militia to bring in an enemy to destroy the kingdom. It is no less injustice against the second table that the king uses the sword to destroy the innocent than to usurp the censer against the first table. But Dr. Ferne yields that the censer may be pulled out of his hand, lest he provoke God to wrath; therefore, by the same very reason *a fortiore* the sword, the castles, the seaports, the militia, may be violently pulled out of his hand; for if there was an express law that the leper should be put out of the congregation, and therefore the king also should be subject to his church-censor, then He subjects the king to a punishment to be inflicted by the subjects upon the king.

1. Therefore the king is obnoxious to the co-active power of the law.

2. Therefore subjects may judge him and punish him.

3. Therefore he is to be subject to all church-censors no less than the people.

4. There is an express law that the leper should be put out of the congregation. What then? Flattering court divines say, "The king is above all these laws," for there is an express law of God as express as that ceremonial law on touching lepers, and a more binding law that the murderer should die the death. Will royalists put no exception upon a ceremonial law of expelling the leper, and yet put an exception upon a divine moral law concerning the punishing of murderers given before the law on Mount Sinai (Gen, 6:9). They so declare that they accept the persons of men.

5. If a leper king could not actually sit upon the throne, but must be cut off from the house of the Lord, because of an express law of God, these being inconsistent, that a king remaining among God's people, ruling and reigning, should keep company with the church of God, and yet be a leper, who was to be cut off, by a divine law, from the church. Now, I persuade myself, that far less can he actually reign in the full use of the power of the sword, if he use the sword to cut off thousands of innocent people; because, murdering the innocent and the fatherless and royal governing in righteousness and godliness, are more inconsistent by God's law, being morally opposite, than remaining a governor of the people, and the disease of leprosy, are incompatible.

6. I think not much that Barclay says "Uzziah remained king, after he was removed from the congregation for leprosy" (*Contra Monar.* 1.5.11).

1. Because that touches the question of dethroning kings, this is an argument brought for violent resisting of kings, and that the people did resume all power from Uzziah, and put

it in the "hand of Jotham his son, who was over the king's house, judging the people of the land" (ver. 21). And by this same reason the parliaments of both kingdoms may resume the power once given to the king, when he has proved more unfit to govern morally than Uzziah was ceremonially, that he ought not to judge the people of the land in this case.

2. If the priests did execute a ceremonial law upon king Uzziah, far more may the three estates of Scotland and the two houses of parliament of England execute the moral law of God on their king.

If the people may covenant by oath to rescue the innocent and unjustly-condemned from the sentence of death, notoriously known to be tyrannical and cruel, then may the people resist the king in his unlawful practices; but this the people did in the matter of Jonathan. Mr. Symmons and Dr. Ferne say, "With no violence, but by prayers and tears, the people saved Jonathan; as Peter was rescued out of prison by the prayers of the church, king Saul might easily be entreated to break a rash vow to save the life of his eldest son."

Ans. 1. I say not the common people did it, but the people, including *proceres regni* the princes of the land, and captains of thousands. 2. The text has not one word or syllable of either prayers, supplications or tears, but by the contrary, they bound themselves by an oath, contrary to the oath of Saul and swore, "God forbid: as the Lord lives, there shall not one hair of his head fall to the ground. So the people rescued Jonathan" (1 Sam. 14:44, 46). The church prayed not to God for Peter's deliverance with an oath that they must have Peter saved, whether God will or no. Though we read of no violence used by the people, yet an oath upon so reasonable a ground, 1. Without the king's consent, 2. Contrary to a standing law that they had agreed unto (ver. 24), 3. Contradictory to the king's sentence and unjust oath, 4. Spoken to the king in his race, all these prove that the people meant, and that the oath *ex conditione operis* tended to a violent resisting of the king in a manifestly unjust sentence. Chrysostom accuses Saul as a murderer in this sentence, and praises the people (hom. 14, *ad Pop., Antioch*): so Junius, Peter Martyr (whom royalists impudently cite); so Cornelius à Lapide, Zanchius, Lyra, and Hugo Cardinalis say, "It was tyranny in Saul, and laudable that the people resisted Saul," and the same is asserted by Josephus (*Antiquities* 1.6.7); so Althusius (*Polit.* section 38, n. 109).

We see also that Libnah revolted from under Jehoram, because he had forsaken the Lord God of his fathers (2 Chron. 21:10). It has no ground in the text that royalists say that the defection of Libnah is not justified in the text, but the cause is from the demerit of wicked Jeboram, because he made defection from God. Libnah made defection from him, as the ten tribes revolted from Rehoboam for Solomon's idolatry which before the Lord procured this defection, yet the ten tribes make defection for oppression.

I answer. Where the literal meaning is simple and obvious, we are not to go from it. The text shows what cause moved Libnah to revolt:[1] it was a town of the Levites, and we know they were longer found in the truth than the ten tribes (2 Chron. 13:8-10; Hosea 11:12). Lavater says Jehoram had pressed them to idolatry, and therefore they revolted. Zanchius and Cornelius à Lapide say this was the cause that moved them to revolt, and it is clear he caused Judah and the inhabitants of Jerusalem to go awhoring from God (ver. 13), and no doubt tempted Libnah to the like."

---

1. P. Mar. Commentary on 2 Kings, section 8, says Libnah revolted.

Yea, the city of Abel did well to resist Joab, David's general (2 Sam. 20), for he came to destroy a whole city for a traitor's sake, for Sheba; they resisted and defended themselves. The wise woman calls the city a mother in Israel, and the inheritance of the Lord (ver. 19), and Joab professes far be it from him to swallow up and destroy Abel (ver. 20). The woman says, "They said of old, they shall surely ask counsel at Abel; and so they ended the matter" (ver. 18), that is, the city of Abel was a place of prophets and oracles of old, where they asked responses of their doubts, and therefore peace should be first offered to the city before Joab should destroy it, as the law says (Deut. 20:10). From all which it is evident that the city in defending itself did nothing against peace so they should deliver Sheba, the traitor, to Joab's hand, which they accordingly did, and Joab pursued them not as traitors for keeping the city against the king, but professes that in that they did no wrong.

QUESTION 33.

WHETHER OR NOT ROM. 13:1 ARGUES ANYTHING AGAINST THE LAWFULNESS OF DEFENSIVE WARS.

The king not only understood, Rom. 13. And the place, Rom. 13, discussed.

The special ground of royalists from Rom. 13 against the lawfulness of defensive wars, is to make Paul (Rom. 13) speak only of kings. Hugo Grotius (*De jure belli et pac.* 1.1.4, n. 6), and Barclay (*Cont. Monar.* 1.3.9) say, "Though Ambrose expound the place. Rom. 13, *de solis regibus*, of kings only (this is false of kings *only*, he does not, but of kings *principally*) yet it follows not that all magistrates, by this place, are freed from all laws, because," says he, "there is no judge above a king on earth, and therefore he cannot be punished; but there is a judge above all inferior judges, and therefore they must be subject to laws" (Grotius, *De jure belli et pac.* 1.1.4, n. 6; Barclay, *Cont. Monar.* 1.3.9). So Dr. Ferne follows him (section 2) and our poor Prelate must be an accident to them (*Sacr. San. Maj.* section 2), for his learning cannot subsist *per se*.

Assert. 1. In a free monarchy (such as Scotland is known to be) by the higher power (Rom. 13) is the king principally in respect of dignity understood, but not solely and only as if inferior judges were not higher powers. 1. I say in a free monarchy; for no man can say that where there is not a king but only aristocracy, and government by states, as in Holland, that there the people are obliged to obey the king; and yet this text, I hope, can reach the consciences of all Holland: that there every soul must be subject to the higher powers, and yet not a subject in Holland is to be subject to any king, for *non entis nulla sunt accidentia*, 2. I said the king in a free monarchy is here principally understood in regard of dignity, but not in regard of the essence of a magistrate, because the essence of a magistrate does equally belong to all inferior magistrates, as to the king, as is already proved (let the Prelate answer if he can); for though some judges be sent by the king and have from him authority to judge, yet this does no more prove that inferior judges are improperly judges, and only such by analogy, and not essentially, than it will prove a citizen is not essentially a citizen, nor a church-officer essentially a church-officer, nor a son not essentially a living creature, because the former have authority from the incorporation of citizens, and of church-officers, and the latter has his life by generation from his father as God's instrument. For though the citizen and the church-officers may be judged by their several incorporations that made them, yet are they also essentially citizens and church-officers, as those who made them such.

Assert. 2. There is no reason to restrain the higher powers to monarchs only, or yet principally, as if they alone were essentially powers ordained by God, 1. Because he calls them

εξουσιαι υπερχουσαι higher powers. Now this will include all
higher powers, as Piscator observes on the place, and certainly
Rome had never two or three kings to which every soul should
be subject. If Paul had intended that they should have given
obedience to one Nero as the only essential judge, he would
have designated him by the noun in the singular number.

2. All the reasons that the apostle brings to prove that subjection is due befits inferior judges as well as emperors, for
they are powers ordained by God, and they bear the sword,
and we must obey them for conscience sake, and they are
God's deputies, and their judgment is not the judgment of
men, but of the Lord (2 Chron. 19:6-7; Deut. 1:16; Numb.
11:16-17). Tribute and wages be no less due to them as ministers and servants for their work than to the king, &c.

3. The apostle could not omit obedience to the good civil
laws enacted by the senate, nor could he omit to command
subjection to rulers, if the Romans should change the government and abolish monarchy and erect their ancient form of
government before they had kings.

4. This is canonical Scripture, and a clear exposition of the
fifth commandment, and so must reach the consciences of all
Christian republics where there is no monarchy.

5. Parallel places of Scripture prove this. Paul will have
prayers made to God for kings, and for all that are in authority, and the intrinsic end of all is a godly, honest, and peaceable life (1 Tim. 2:1-2). And 1 Pet. 2:13: "Submit to every
ordinance of man for the Lord's sake;" also Tit. 3:1: it is true,
subjection to Nero, or whom Tertullian said *Nihil nisi grande
bonum a Nerone damnatum* is commanded here (Apol. 5), but
to Nero as such a one as he is obliged, *de jure*, to be (whether
you speak of the office *in abstracto* or of the emperor *in concreto* in this notion, to me it is all one) but that Paul commands

subjection to Nero, and that principally and solely, as he was such a man, *de facto*, I shall then believe when antichristian prelates turn Paul's bishops (1 Tim. 2), which is a miracle.

6. Inferior judges are not necessarily sent by the king by any divine law, but chosen by the people, as the king is; and *de facto* is the practice of creating all magistrates of cities in both kingdoms.

7. Augustine (*expos, prop.* 72 on epist. Rom.), Irenaeus (1.6.24), Chrysostom (in Ps. 148, and on the place), and Jerome (*Advers. Vigilant.* epist. 53) expound it concerning masters, magistrates; so do Calvin, Beza, Parous, Piscator, Rollocus, Marloratus; so do popish writers, Aquinas, Lyra, Hugo Cardinalis, Carthusius, Pirerius, Toletus, Cornelius à Lapide, Salmeron, Estius, expound the place; and therefore there is no argument that royalists from here draw against resisting of the king by the parliaments, but they do strongly conclude against the cavaliers' unlawful wars against the parliaments and estates of two kingdoms.

Here is what the Popish Prelate says to the contrary: 1. They are called eminent powers; therefore, kings only.

Ans. It follows not, for these can be no other than παντες οι εν υπεροχη οντες (1 Tim. 2:2). But these are not kings, but in the text distinguished from βατιλεις kings, and they can be no other than αρχαι και εξουσιας, principalities and powers.

2. The reason of the apostle proves clearly that εξουσιας cannot mean king's only, for Paul adds of that same εξουσια "For there is no power but of God." It must be there is no supereminent royal power, that is not of God, and the powers only (so he must mean) that be are ordained by God. Now the latter is manifestly false, for inferior powers are of God. The powers of the Roman senate, of a master, of a father, are of God.

Popish Prelate. "Peter must expound Paul, and Paul's higher powers must be (1 Pet. 2). βατιλεις υπερεχοντες More reason that Paul expound Paul. Now παντες εν υπεροχη εντες (1 Tim. 2:2). All in authority are not kings.

Popish Prelate. "Are of God," or "ordained of God," cannot so properly be understood of subordinate powers, for that is not by immediate derivation from God, but immediately from the higher power the king, and mediately from God.

Ans. 1. It is most false that king David is so immediately a king from God that he is not also by the mediation of the people, who made him king at Hebron.

2. The inferior magistrates are also immediate vicars and ministers of God as the king, for their throne and judgment is not the king's, but the Lord's (Deut. 1:16; 2 Chron. 21:6).

3. Though they were mediately from man, it follows not that they are not so properly from God, for wisdom (Prov. 8) says as properly: "By me princes rule, and nobles, even all the judges of the earth;" as "By me kings reign" (ver. 16) and promotion is as properly from God, and not from the east and the west (Ps. 75:6-7), though God promote Joseph by the thankful munificence of Pharaoh, and Mordecai by Ahasuerus, Daniel by Darius, as if he gave them power and honor immediately from heaven.

Popish Prelate. Learned interpreters expound it so.

Ans. It is an untruth, for none expound it only and principally of kings. Produce one interpreter for that conceit.

Popish Prelate. Paul wrote this when Nero was monarch.

Ans. 1. Then must the text be expounded of Nero only. 2. He wrote this when Nero played the tyrant and persecuted Christians, therefore we are not to obey Neroes *now*. 3. He wrote it when the senate of Rome had power to declare Nero an enemy, not a father, as they did.

Popish Prelate. αι must be referred to the antecedent εξουσια υπερχουσα and this, "There is no power ει μη but of God," must undeniably infer there is no supreme power but of God; and so sovereignty relates to God as his immediate author, so sectaries reason, "Not justified by works (ἰαν μὴ) but by faith only" (Gal. 2:16). Then ει μη απο τους θεους must be a perfect exclusive, else their stronghold for justification is overthrown.

Ans. αἱ has a nearer antecedent, which is εξσια, it is alone without υπερχουσαι. And this grammar is not so good as Beza's, which lie rejected.

2. εαν μη will refer to God alone as the only cause, *in genere causa primae*. God alone gives rain, but not for that immediately, but by the mediation of vapors and clouds. "God alone kills and makes alive" (Deut. 32:39), that is, excluding all strange gods, but not immediately; for, by His people's fighting, He slew Og, king of Bashan, and cast out seven nations, yet they used bow and sword, as it is used in the book of Joshua; and, therefore, God killed not Og immediately. God has an infinite, eminent, transcendent way of working, so that in His kind He only works His alone; *Deus solus operatur solitudine primae causae non solus solitudine onmis causae*, God only gives learning and wisdom, yet not immediately always—often He does it by teaching and industry. God only makes rich, yet the prelates make themselves rich also with the fat of the flock; and God only makes poor, yet the Popish Prelate's courts, mediately also under God, made many men poor.

3. εαν μη is not such an exclusive particle when we ascribe it to God as when we ascribe it to two created causes, works and faith; and the protestants' form of arguing (Gal. 2) to prove "we are justified by faith," he calls our stronghold; therefore it is not his stronghold. In this point then he must be a papist,

and so he refuses to own protestant strongholds for justification by faith alone.

Dr. Ferne: As many as have souls must be subject to the higher powers spoken of here, but all inferior judges have souls (section 2).

Ans. 1. If the word souls be thus pressed, none shall be understood by higher powers, but the king only.

2. Certainly he that commands as he commands must be excepted, except because the king has a soul, you must subject the king to himself and to his own commandments royal, and so to penal laws.

3. Inferior judges as judges by this text must either be subject to themselves as judges (and by the same reason the king must be subject to himself, as he is a judge) or judges, as men, or as erring men are to be subject, which I would grant, but they are not subject as judges, no more than one as he commands can also obey as he commands. These are contradictory. I am not put off that opinion since I was at school, species *subjicibilis qua subjicibilis non est praedicabilis.*

4. If Nero make fathers rulers over their mothers and children, and command them by this public sword of justice to kill their own children and mothers, if a senate of such fathers disobey, and if with the sword they defend their own children and mothers, which some other Doegs, as judges, are to kill in the name and commandment of Nero, then they, resisting Nero's bastard commandment by this doctrine, resist the ordinance of God and resist the minister of God. I have not a faith stretched out so far to the Prelate's court-divinity. Yet Ferne says, "There was never more cause to resist higher powers, for their wicked Nero was emperor, when he now forbids resistance (Rom. 13) under the pain of damnation." I desire to be informed whether to resist the king's servants be to resist the

king? Dr. Ferne allows us in unavoidable assaults where death is imminent personal defense without offending, as lawful, whether the king or his emissaries invade without law or reason (section 2; part 3, section 9). Well then the resisting of the king's cut-throats, though they have a personal command of the King to kill the innocent, yet if they lack a legal command is no resisting of the king as king, for the servant has no more than the master gives; but the king in lawless commandments gave nothing royal to his cut-throats, and so nothing legal.

QUESTION 34.

WHETHER ROYALISTS PROVE BY COGENT REASONS THE UNNLAWFULNESS OF DEFENSIVE WARS.

Objections of royalists answered. The place Exod. 12:28, "you shall not revile the gods," &c. is addressed, as well as Eccles. 10:20. The place Eccles. 8:3-4, "Where the word of a king is," &c. is answered. The place Job. 34:18 answered, as well as Acts 23:3, "God shall smite you, you whited wall," &c. The emperors in Paul's time not absolute by their law. That objection that we have no practice for defensive resistance and that the prophets never complain of the omission of the resistance of princes is answered. The prophets cry against the sin of non-resistance when they cry against the judges, because they execute not judgment for the oppressed. Judah's subjection to Nebuchadnezzar, a conquering tyrant, is no warrant to us to subject ourselves to tyrannical acts. Christ's subjection to Caesar is nothing against defensive wars.

What reasons have already been discussed, I touch not.
Obj. 1. Arnisaeuss: "If we are to obey our parents, not if they be good, but simply whether they be good or evil

(so Justin, says of the king, *Quamvis legum contemptor quamvis impius, tamen pater, sect, si vero in ff. vos.* 12) then must we submit to wicked kings" (*De authority princip,* 2, n. 2).

Ans. *Valeat totum,* we are to submit to wicked kings and wicked parents, because kings and parents; but when it comes to actual submission, we are to submit to neither but in the Lord. The question is not touching subjection to a prince, let him be Nero, but if in acts of tyranny we may not deny subjection. There be great differences between wicked rulers and rulers commanding or punishing unjustly.

Obj. 2. Arnisaeus: "We may resist an inferior magistrate; therefore we may resist the supreme. It follows not; for an inferior judge has a majesty in fiction only, not properly: treason is or can only be committed against the king; the obligation to inferior judges is only for the prince: the person of none is sacred and inviolable but the king's (section 3, n. 9).

Ans. We obey parents, masters, kings, upon this formal ground, because they are God's deputies, and set over us not by man but by God; so that not only are we to obey them because what they command is good and just (such a sort of obedience an equal owes to the counsel of either equal or inferior) but also by virtue of the fifth commandment, because of their place of dignity. Now this majesty, which is the formal reason of subjection, is one and the same in specie and nature in king and constable, and only different gradually in the king and in other judges, and it is denied that there is any incommunicable sanctity in the king's person which is not in some degree in the inferior judge. All proceeds from this false ground that the king and inferior judges differ in nature, which is denied, and treason inferior may be committed against an inferior judge, and it is a fiction that the inferior judge does not resemble God as the king does; yea, there is a sacred majesty in all inferior judges, in the aged, in every superior, from which they deserve honor, fear, and reverence. Suppose there were no king on earth, as is clear in Scripture (Exod. 20:12; Levit. 19:32; Esther, 1:20; Ps. 149:9; Prov. 3:16; Matt, 13:57; Heb. 5:4; Isa. 3:3; Lam. 5:12; Mal. 1:6; Ps. 8:5) and this honor is but united in a special manner in the king, because of his high place.

Obj. 3. A king elected upon conditions may be resisted.

Ans. He is as essentially a king as a hereditary, yea, as an absolute prince, and no less the Lord's anointed than another prince; if then one, also another may be resisted.

Obj. 4. The oath of God binds the subjects; therefore, they must obey, not resist.

Ans. Obedience and resistance are very consistent. No doubt the people gave their oath to Athaliah, but to her as the only heir of the crown, they not knowing that Joash, the lawful heir, was living; so may conditional oaths (all of this kind are conditional) in which there is interpretative and virtual ignorance, be broken; as the people swear loyalty to such a man conceived to be a father, he afterwards turns tyrant, may they not resist his tyranny? They may. Also, no doubt Israel gave their oath of loyalty to Jabin (for when Nebuchadnezzar subdued Judah, he took an oath of loyalty of their king) yet many of Zebulun, Naphtali, and Issachar, Barak leading them, conspired against Jabin.

Obj. 5. There is no law to take a king's life if he turn a Nero: we never read that subjects did it.

Ans. The treatise of unlimited prerogative says, "We read not that a father, killing his children, was killed by them; the fact being abominable." The law excepts none (Gen. 6:9; Levit. 24:16). See Deut. 13:6: the dearest that nature knows are not excepted.

Obj. 6. Vengeance pursued Korah, Dathan, and Abiram, who resisted Moses.

Ans. From resisting of a lawful magistrate in a thing lawful, it follows not it must be unlawful to resist kings in tyrannical acts.

Obj. 7. Exod. 22:28: "you shall not revile the gods, nor curse the Ruler of the people." Exod. 10:20: "Curse not the king, no not in your thought, nor the rich in your bed-chamber."

Ans. The word *elohim* signifies all judges, and נשיא *nasi* signifies one lifted up above the people, says Rivetus (*in loc*). whether a monarch or many rulers. All cursing of any is unlawful, even of a private man (Rom. 12:14); therefore we may not resist a private man by this; the other text reads: condemn not the king, במדעך *in scientia tua.* Aria Mon., or in your conscience or thought, and it may prove resisting any rich man to be unlawful. Nothing in word or deed tending to the dishonor of the king may be done; now to resist him in self-defense, being a commandment of God in the law of nature, cannot fight with another commandment to honor the king, no more than the fifth commandment can fight with the sixth; for all resistance is against the judge, as a man exceeding the limits of his office, in that in which he is resisted, not as a judge.

Obj. 8. Eccles. 8:3-4: "Where the word of a king is there is power, and who may say to him, What do you?" Therefore, the king cannot be resisted.

Ans. Tremelius says well that "the scope is that a man go not from the king's lawful command in passion and rebellion;" Vatab.: "If you go from the king in disgrace, strive to be reconciled to him quickly;" Cajetanus: "Use not kings too familiarly, by coming too quickly to them or going too hastily from them;" Plutarch, "*Cum rege agendum ut cum rogo,* neither too near this fire nor too far off." Those have smarted who

have been too great in their favor: Ahasuerus slew Haman,
Alexander so served Cleitus and Tiberius Sejaunus, and Nero
Seneca. But the sense is clear, rebellion is forbidden, not resistance, so the Hebrew אל־תעמד כרכר רע stand not in an evil
matter, or in a rebellion, and he exhorts contrary to rebellion
against the king, by an argument taken from his power for
he does whatsoever pleases him. Where the word of a king
is, there is power, and who may say unto him, what do you?
The meaning is, in way of justice, he is armed with power
that cannot be resisted; otherwise Samuel said to king Saul
"you have done foolishly" (1 Sam. 13:13). Elijah said more to
Ahab than What have you done? And the prophets were to
rebuke sin in kings (2 Kings 3:14; Jer. 1:28; 22:3; Hosea 5:1-
2), and though Solomon here give them a power, he speaks
of kings as they are *de facto*; but, *de jure*, they are under a law
(Deut. 17:18). If the meaning be, as royalists dream, he does
whatsoever he will or desires, as a prince, by his royal, that is,
his legal will, by which he is *lex animata*, a breathing law, we
shall own that as truth, and it is nothing against us; but if the
meaning be that *de jure*, as king, he does whatsoever he will, by
the absolute supremacy of royal will, above all law and reason,
then Joram should by law as king take Elisha's head away, and
Elisha resisted God in saying. What does the king? and he
sinned in commanding to deal roughly with the king's messenger and hold him at the door; then the fourscore valiant
priests who said to king Uzziah, "What do you?" and resisted
him in burning incense, which he desired to do, sinned; then
Pharaoh, who said "The river Nilus is mine, I have made it for
myself" (Ezek. 29:3), and the king of Tyrus "I am God, I sit in
the seat of God," (Ezek. 27:2) should not be controlled by the
prophets, and no man should say to them, What say you? Did
Cyrus, as a king with a royal power from God and *jure regio*,

be angry at the river Ganges, because it drowned one of his horses, and punish it by dividing it in one hundred and thirty channels (*Sen.* 1.3, *de ira,* section 21)? And did Xerxes, *jure regio,* by a royal power given of God, when Hellespontus had cast down his bridges, command that three hundred whips should be inflicted on that little sea, and that it should be cast in fetters? And our royalists will have these mad fools doing these acts of blasphemous insolence against heaven to be honored as kings, and to act those acts by a regal power. But hear flatterers: a royal power is the good gift of God, a lawful and just power. A king acting and speaking as a king, speaks and acts law and justice. A power to blaspheme is not a lawful power; they did and spoke these things with a human and a sinful will; if therefore this be the royalists' meaning, as kings, 1. They are absolute, and so the limited and elected king is no king. 2. The king as king is above God's law put on him by God, Deut. 17:3. His will is the measure of good and evil. 4. It would be unlawful to say to the king of Cyrus, What say you? You are not God, according to this vain sense of royalists.

Obj. 9. Elihu says, "Is it fit to say to a king, you are wicked, and to princes, You are ungodly?" (Job. 34:18). Therefore, you may not resist kings.

Ans. 1. This text no more proves that kings should not be resisted then it proves that rich men, or liberal men, or other judges inferior, should not be resisted, for נריבים signifies all that, and it signifies liberal (Isa. 32:6); and the same word is in ver. 8:2. Deodatus and Calvin say the meaning is, "Learn from the respect that is due to earthly princes the reverence due to the sovereign Lord" (Mal. 1:8); for it is not convenient to reproach earthly kings, and to say to a prince, בליעל Belial, a word of reproach, signifying extreme wickedness. And you may not say to a man of place, רשע an extremely wicked man;

so are the words taken as signifying most vile and wicked men
(1 Sam. 2:12; 10:27; 2 Sam. 25:6; Ps. 1:1, 6; 11:5; 12:8; Prov.
14:4; Ps. 146:9), and in infinite places. For בליעל is a word of
extreme reproach, coming from בלי *sine non*, and יעל *profuit*
(Jud. 19:22) a most naughty and a lewd man, or from עיל *jugum*, a lawless man, who has cast off all yokes of God's or man's
laws. So then the meaning is that it is unlawful to reproach
earthly princes and men of place; far more is it unlawful to
reproach the Judge of the whole earth with injustice. And
what then? We may not reproach the king, as Shimei cursed
king David; therefore it is unlawful to resist the king in any
tyrannical acts. I shall deny the consequence; nay, as Pineda
observes, if the royalist press the words literally, it shall not be
lawful for prophets to reprove kings of their sins. Christ called
Herod a fox; Elijah called Ahab one that troubled Israel.

Obj. 10. Paul excuses himself that he called Ananias, the
high-priest, a whited wall (Acts 23).

Ans. Rivetus (Exod. 22) learnedly discussing the place,
thinks Paul, professing he knew him not to be the high-priest,
speaks ironically that he could not acknowledge such a man
for a judge. Piscator answers he could not then cite Scripture,
"It is written," &c.

Ans. But they may well insist in that act of smiting Paul
unjustly, he might be reproached; otherwise it is not lawful to
reproach him, and surely it is not as though Paul was ignorant that he was a judge; yea, it is certain he knew him to be
a judge. 1. He appeared before him as a judge to answer for
himself. 2. Paul says expressly he was a judge: "Sit you to judge
me after the law," &c (ver. 3). And therefore the place is for
us, for even according to the mind of all the fault was (if there
were any) in calling him a whited wall; and he resisted him

in judgment when he said, "Command you me to be smitten against the law?"

3. Though royalists rather put a fault on the apostle Paul (now in the act of prophesying judgment against Ananias, which afterwards took place) than upon their god, the king, yet the consequence amounts but to this: We may not revile the high-priest; therefore we may not resist the king in his illegal commandments. It follows not; yea, it should prove if a prelate come in open war to kill the innocent apostle Paul, the apostle might fly or hold his hands, but might not re-offend. Now the prelate is the high priest's successor, and so his base person is as sacred as the person of the Lord's anointed, the king. Hence the cavaliers had in one of their colors, which was taken by the Scots at the battle of Marston, July 2, 1644, the crown and the Prelate's miter, painted with these words, "*Nolite tangere Christos meos*," as if the antichristian miter were as sacred as the lawful crown of the king of Britain.

Obj. 11. Ferne: "If the senate and people of Rome, who a little before had the supreme government over the then-emperors that had made them lords of subjects might not resist their emperors, much less can the people of England have power of resistance against the succession of this crown, descending from the conqueror, who by force of arms but in justice conquered the kingdom." (sect. 9, 56).

Ans. 1. Though the Roman emperors were absolute (of which I much doubt) and though the senate had made them absolute, I deny that therefore they cannot be resisted. The unlawful resistance condemned by Paul (Rom. 13) is not upon the ground of absoluteness, which is in the court of God nothing, being never ordained by God, but upon reasons of conscience, because the powers are of God, and ordained by God. But some may say, *Volenti non fit injuria*, If a people totally resign their power, and swear non-resistance to a conqueror by compact they cannot resist. I answer neither does this follow, because it is an unlawful compact, and none is obliged to what is unlawful. For (1) It is no more lawful for me to resign to another my power of natural self-defense than I can resign my power to defend the innocent drawn to death, and the wives, children, and posterity that God had tied me unto; (2) The people can no more resign power of self-defense, which nature has given them than they can be guilty of self-murder, and be lacking in the lawful defense of kingdom and religion, (3) Though you make one their king with absoluteness of power, yet when he use that transcendent power, not for the safety but for the destruction of the state, it is known they could not resign to another that power which neither God nor nature gave them, namely, a power to destroy themselves.

2. I much doubt if the Roman emperor was absolute when Paul wrote this. Justinian says so (*Digest.* l.2, tit. 2) but he is partial in this cause. Bodine proves that the Roman emperors were but princes of the commonwealth, and that the sovereignty remained still in the senate and people (*De repub.* 1.2.5). Marius Salamon writes six books (*De Principatu*) on the contrary. How could they make their emperors absolute? Livy says, "The name of a king was contrary to a senate liberty." *Florus, Nomen Regis invidiosum,* They instituted a yearly feast, Feb. 23, called *Regifugium.* Cicero, as Augustine observes, *Regem Romae posthaec nec Dii, ne homines esse patiantur.* The emperors might do something *de facto,* but *Lex Regia* was not before Vespasian's time. Augustus took on him to be tribune of the people from ten years to ten. Suetonius and Tacitus say, "The succeeding kings encroached by degrees upon the people's liberty." For speedier execution of law, the kings in time of war were forced to do many things without the

senate, and after the reign of emperors, though there was no *Plebiscita*, yet there was *Senatus-consulta* and one great one is that the senate declared Nero to be an enemy to the state. It is thought Julius Caesar in the war against Pompey subdued the Romans and the senate, and they were subdued again in the battle of Octavius against Cassius and Brutus. But Tacitus says that was *de facto*, not *de jure* (*Anal.* l.1, s. 2) *Romae ruere in servitium, Consules, Patres, Eques.* Caligula intended to assume *diadema*, the ensign of a king, but his friends dissuaded him.

3. England is obliged to Dr. Ferne, who makes them a subdued nation; the contrary of which is known to the world.

Symmons: God is not honored by being resisted, no more is the king (section 6).

Ans. 1. I deny the consequence. Those who resist the king's personal will, and will not suffer him to ruin his crown and posterity in following papists against his oath at the coronation do honor him, and his throne and race, as a king, though for the time they displease him. 2. Uzziah was not dishonored in that he was resisted. 3. Nor do we honor the king when we flee from him and his law, yet that resistance is lawful, according to the way of royalists, and in truth also.

Obj. 12. Supreme power is not to be resisted by subordinate powers because they are inferior to the supreme.

Ans. 1. The bloody Irish rebels, then, being inferior to the parliament, cannot resist the parliament. 2. Inferior judges, as judges are immediately subordinate to God as the king, and must be guilty of blood before God if they use not the sword against bloody cavaliers and Irish cut-throats, unless you say inferior judges are not obliged to execute judgment except at the king's commandment.

Obj. As the Irish rebels are armed with the king's power, they are superior to the parliament.

Ans. So an army of Turks and Spaniards, armed with the king's power and coming against the two kingdoms[1] at the king's commandment, though they are but lictors in a lawless cause, are superior to the highest courts of parliament in the two kingdoms. But the king and the law gave power to the parliament first to resist rebels; now he gives power to rebels to resist the parliament. Here must be contradictory wills and contradictory powers in the king. Which of them is the king's will and his power? The former is legal and parliamentary; then because law is not contrary to law, the latter cannot be legal also, nor can it be from God, and to resist it then is not to resist God.

Obj. 13. If resistance be restrained to legal commandments, what shall we say to these arguments that Paul forbids resistance under these tyrannical governors and that from the end of their government, which is for good, and which their subjects did in some sort enjoy under them?

Ans. This proves nothing but that we are to co-operate with these governors, though tyrannical, by subjecting to their laws, so far as they come up to this end, the moral good and peace of their government; but Paul nowhere commands absolute subjection to tyrannical governors in tyrannical acts, which is still the question.

Obj. 14. He that has the supreme trust next to God should have the greatest security to his person and power; but if resistance be lawful he has a poor security.

Ans. 1. He that has the greatest trust should have the greatest security to his person and power in the keeping his power, and using it according to his trust for its own native end—for justice, peace, and godliness. God allows security to no man,

---

1. The temporal and spiritual kingdoms, both under Jesus Christ.

nor that his angels shall guard them, but only when they are in their ways and the service of God; otherwise, "there is no peace to the wicked."

2. It is denied that one man, having the greatest trust, should have the greatest security; the church and people of God for whose safety he has the trust as a means for the end should have a greater security; the city ought to have greater security than the watchers, the army than the leaders, "The good shepherd gives his life for his sheep."

3. A power to do ill without resistance is not security.

Obj. 15. If God appoint ministers to preach, then the sheep cannot seek safety elsewhere.

Ans. The wife is obliged to bed and board with her husband, but not if she fear he will kill her in the bed. The obedience of positive duties that subjects owe to princes cannot loose them from nature's law of self-preservation, nor from God's law of defending religion against papists in arms, nor are the sheep obliged to entrust themselves but to a saving shepherd.

Obj. 16. If self-defense, and that by taking up arms against the king, be an unlawful duty, how is it that you have no practice, no precept, no promise for it in all the word of God? 1. You have no practice: Ahab sold himself to do evil, he was an idolater, and killed the prophets; and his queen, a bloody idolatress, stirred him up to great wickedness. Elijah had as great power with the people as you have, yet he never stirred up the people to take arms against the king. Why did God at this time rather use extraordinary means of saving his church? Arnisaeus: "Elias only fled. Nebuchadnezzar, Ahab, Manasseh, and Julian were tyrants and idolaters, yet the people never raised an army against them" (*De autho. princ.* section 8). Bishop Williams of Ossory: "If brother, son, daughter, wife, or friend entice you to follow strange gods, kill them; not a word of the father. Children are to love their fathers, not to kill them" (Deut. 14). "Christ," says John Popish Prelate, "in the cradle taught by practice to flee from Herod, and all Christ's acts and sufferings are full of mysteries and our instructions. He might have had legions of angels to defend him, but would rather work a miracle in curing Malchus' ear as use the sword against Caesar. If sectaries give us a new creed, it will concern them never with expunging Christ's descent into hell, and the communion of saints, to raze out this. He suffered under Pontius Pilate. My resolution is (for this sin of yours) to dissolve in tears and prayers, and with my master say daily and hourly, "Father, forgive them," &c. Christ thought it an uncouth spirit to call for fire from heaven to burn the Samaritans because they refused him lodging. The prophets cried out against idolatry, blasphemy, murder, adultery, &c., and all sins; never against the sin of neglect, and murderous omission to defend church and religion against a tyrannical king. No promise is made to such a rebellious insurrection in God's word."

Ans. It is a great non-consequence: this duty is not practiced by any examples in God's word; therefore it is no duty. Practice in Scripture is a narrow rule of faith. Show a practice when a husband stoned his wife because she enticed him to follow strange gods, yet it is commanded (Deut. 13:6); when a man lying with a beast is put to death, yet it is a law (Exod. 22:19). Infinite more laws are the practice of which we find not in Scripture.

2. Jehu and the elders of Israel rooted out Ahab's posterity for their idolatry, and if Jehu out of sincerity and for the zeal of God had done what God commanded, he should have been rewarded; for say that it was extraordinary to Jehu that he should kill Ahab, yet there was an express law for it that he that stirs up others to idolatry should die the death (Deut.

13:6), and there is no exception of king or father in the law, and to except father or mother in God's matter is expressly against the zeal of God (Deut. 32:9). And many grave divines think the people to be commended in making Jehu king, and in killing king Nabab, and smiting all the house of Jeroboam for his idolatry; they did that which was a part of their ordinary duty according to God's express law (Deut. 13:6-9), though the facts of these men be extraordinary.

3. Ahab and Jezebel raised not an army of idolaters and malignants, such as are papists, prelates, and cavaliers, against the three estates to destroy parliaments, laws, and religion—and the people conspired with Ahab in the persecution and idolatry, to forsake the covenant, throw down the altars of God, and slay his prophets—so as in the estimation of Elijah (1 King 19:9-11) there was not one man, but they were malignant cavaliers; and has any Elijah now power with the cavaliers to exhort them to rise in arms against themselves, and to show them it is their duty to make war against the king and themselves in the defense of religion? When the prophets had much ado to convince the people that they sinned in joining with the king, what place was there to show them their sin in not using their own lawful defense? And in reason any may judge it unreasonable for Elijah to exhort of thousands of thousands in Israel poor seven thousand (of which many no doubt were women, aged, weak, and young) to rise in arms against Ahab and all Israel, unless God had given a positive and extraordinary commandment, and with all miraculous courage and strength in war against the whole land. And God works not always by miracles to save his church, and therefore the natural mandate of self-preservation in that case does no more oblige a few weak ones to lawful resistance than it obliged one martyr to rise against a persecuting Nero and

all his forces. Arnisaeus should remember we are not to tie our Lord to miracles.

1. Elijah did not only flee, but denounced wrath against the king and cavaliers who joined with them in idolatry, and when God gave opportunity, He showed himself and stirred the people up to kill Baal's Jesuits and seducing idolaters when the idolatrous king refused to do it; and Elijah with his own hand took them not, but all Israel being gathered together (1 Kings 18:19) the princes and judges did apprehend them (ver. 40), which is a warrant, when the king refuses to draw the sword of justice against armed papists that other judges are to do it.

2. For Jeremiah by the Lord expressly forbidden to fight against Nebuchadnezzar shows us the like for not defending ourselves against bloody papists and Irish cut-throats; for that example may as well prove (if it be a binding law to us) that our king should not raise his subjects to fight against a Spanish armada and a foreign prince; for before ever Nebuchadnezzar subdued the kingdom of Judah (Jer. 27:1) in the beginning of the reign of Jehoiakim (Jer. 36. and 37) the king of Judah is from the Lord commanded not to draw a sword against the king of Babylon. I hope this will not tie us and our king not to fight against foreign princes, or against the great Turk if they shall unjustly invade us and our king, and this example is against the king's resisting of a foreign prince unjustly invading him, as much as against us, for Nebuchadnezzar was a tyrannical invader, and the king of Judah the Lord's anointed.

3. The people also conspired with Manasseh, as with Ahab (Jer. 15:4).

4. Of emperors persecuting Christians we shall hear anon.

5. In Deut. 13, none are excepted: by a synecdoche the dearest are expressed, "son, daughter, brother, the friend that is as

your own soul;" therefore fathers also: "and husbands are to love their wives" (Ephes. 5:26), yet to execute judgment on them without pity (Deut. 13:8-9); the father is to love the son, yet if the son prophecy falsely in the name of the Lord, to kill him (Zech. 13:3). Hence love, fear, reverence toward the king, may be commanded, and defensive wars also.

6. Christ fled from Herod, and all His actions and sufferings are mysteries and instructions, says the poor Prelate. Christ kissed the man that to his knowledge came to betray Him; Christ fled not, but knowing where and when his enemy should apprehend Him, came willingly to the place; therefore we should not flee. His actions are so mysterious that John Popish Prelate, in imitation of Christ's forty days' fast, will fast from flesh in Lent, and the Prelate must walk on the sea and work miracles, if all Christ's actions be our instructions.

7. He might with more than twelve legions of angels defend himself, but he would not, not because resistance was unlawful—no shadow for that in the text—but because it was God's will that He should drink the cup His Father gave Him, and because to take the sword without God's warrant subjects the usurper of God's place to perish with the sword. Peter had God's revealed will that Christ chose to suffer (Matt. 26:52-53; 16:21-23) and God's positive command that Christ should die for sinners (John 10:24) may well restrain an act of lawful self-preservation, *hic et nunc*, and such an act as Christ lawfully used at another time (Luke 4:29-30; John 11:7-8). We rive no new creed; but this apostate has forsaken his old creed, and the religion of the Church of Scotland in which he was baptized. Nor do we expunge out of the creed Christ's descent into hell and the communion of saints, as the apostate says, but the popish local descent of Christ, and the popish advancing of the church's power above the Scriptures, and the

intercession and prayers to the saints, or of the saints for us, we deny, and this Prelate, though he did swear the doctrine of the Church of Scotland, preached expressly all these, and many other points of popery in the pulpits of Edinburgh.

10. We believe that Christ suffered under Pontius Pilate, but that Pilate had any legal power to condemn Christ, but only a power by a permissive decree (Acts 4:27-28) such as devils had by God's permission (Luke 22:63) we utterly deny.

11. The Prelate says it is his resolution, for our sin of natural self-defense, to dissolve in tears; because his bishopric, I conceive, by which he was wont to dissolve in cups (being drunk on the Lord's day, after he with other prelates had been at the Lord's supper, while the chamber in which they were was dissolved in vomiting) was taken from him.

12. The prophets cry against all sins, but never against the sin of non-resistance; and yet they had very tyrannical and idolatrous kings. This is but a weak argument. 1. The prophets cry not out against all sins: they cry not out against men-stealers, and killers of father and mother in express terms, yet do they by consequence condemn all these sins, and so do they condemn non-resistance in wars by consequence when they cry out: "The prophets prophesy falsely, and the priests bear rule by their means, and my people love to have it so" (Jer. 5:31). And when they complain that "the prophets and priests violate the law, her princes are like wolves ravening the prey to shed blood, and the people use oppression, and exercise robbery, and vex the poor," (Ezek. 22:26-28), and when they say not to the king only, but also to his servants, and the people that enter in by the gates, "Execute judgment and righteousness, and deliver the spoiled out of the hand of the oppressor" (Jer. 22:2). I pray you, who are the oppressors? I answer. The murdering judges: "As for my people, children

are their oppressors, and women rule over them," (Isa. 1:21)
"the ancients of the people grind the faces of the poor;" (Isa.
3:12, 14, 16) and when they are not valiant for the truth upon
the earth, and the Lord shall render to these men according
to their works, who forbear to help men that are drawn to
death, and those that be ready to be slain (Prov. 24:11); if they
shift the business, and say, Behold, we know not, does not he
that ponders the heart consider it? When therefore the Lord's
prophets complain that the people execute not judgment, relieve not the oppressed, help not and rescue not those that are
drawn to death unjustly by the king, or his murdering judges,
they expressly cry out against the sin of non-resistance.

2. The prophets cannot expressly and formally cry out
against the judges for non-resisting the king, when they join,
as ravening wolves with the king in these same acts of oppression, even as the judge cannot formally impanel twenty-four
men, sent out to guard the travelers from an arch-robber,
if these men join with the robber and rob the travelers and
become cut-throats as the arch-robber is, he cannot accuse
them for their omission in not guarding the innocent travelers, but for a more heinous crime: that not only they omitted
what was their duty, in that they did not rescue the oppressed
out of the hands of the wicked, but because they did rob and
murder, and so the lesser sin is swallowed up in the greater.
The under-judges are watchmen, and a guard to the church of
God; if the king turn a bosom robber, their part is "to deliver
the spoiled out of the hand of the oppressor," (Jer. 22:3) to
watch against domestic and foreign enemies, and to defend
the flock from wolves: "To let the oppressed go free, and to
break every yoke (Isa. 18:6); "To break the jaws of the wicked,
and pluck the spoil out of his teeth" (Job. 29:17). Now if these
judges turn lions and ravening wolves to prey upon the flock

and join with the king, as always they did when the king was an oppressor, "his princes made him glad with their lies," and joined with him, and the people with both (Jer. 1:18; 5:1; 9:1; Mic. 7:1; Ezek. 22:24-31; Jer. 15:1-3) it is no wonder if the prophets condemn and cry out against the hugest and most bloody crime of positive oppression, formally and expressly, and in that their negative murders in not relieving the oppressed must also be cried out against.

13. The whole land cannot formally be accused for nonresistance when the whole land are oppressors, for then they should be accused for not resisting themselves.

14. The king ought to resist the inferior judges in their oppression of the people by the confession of royalists; then this argument comes with the like force of strength on themselves. Let them show us practice, precept, or promise in the Word, where the king raised an army for defense of religion against princes and people who were subverting religion, and we shall make use of that same place of Scripture to prove that the estates and people who are above the king (as I have proved) and made the king, may and ought to resist the king, with the like force of scriptural truth in the like case.

15. Royalists desire the like precedent of practice and precept for defensive wars, but I answer, let them show us a practice where any king of Israel or Judah raised an army of malignants, of Philistines, Sidonians, or Ammonites, against the princes of Israel and Judah, convened in an assembly to take course for bringing home the captured ark of God, and vindicating the laws of the land, and raised an army contrary to the knowledge of the elders, princes, and judges, to set up Dagon, or tolerate the worship of the Sidonian gods, and yet princes, elders, judges, and the whole people, were obliged all to flee out of God's land, or then only to weep and

request that the king would not destroy souls and bodies of them and their innocent posterities, because they could not in conscience embrace the worship of Dagon and the Sidonian gods. When the royalists can parallel this with a precedent, we can answer. There was as small apparency of precedency in Scripture (unless you flee to the law of nature) that eighty priests, the subjects of king Uzziah, should put in execution a penal law against the Lord's anointed, and that the inferiors and subjects should resist the superior, and that these priests with the princes of the land should remove the king from actual government, all his days, and crown his son. At least make the father, their prince and superior (as royalist say) as good as a cipher. Is not this a punishment inflicted by inferiors upon a superior, according to the way of royalists? Now it is clear, a worshipping of bread and the mass commanded, and against law obtruded upon Scotland by influence of the counsel of known papists is to us and in itself as abominable as the worshipping of Dagon or the Sidonian gods; and when the kingdom of Scotland did but convene, supplicate, and protest against that obtruded idolatry, they were first declared rebels by the king, and then an army raised against them by prelates and malignants, inspired by the spirit of antichrist to destroy the whole land, if they should not submit, soul and conscience, to that wicked service.

QUESTION 35.

WHETHER THE SUFFERINGS OF THE MARTYRS IN THE PRIMITIVE CHURCH MILITANT IS AGAINST THE LAWFULNESS OF DEFENSIVE WARS.

Tertullian neither ours nor theirs in the question of defensive wars.

Obj. 1. Royalists think they burden our cause much with hatred, when they bring the fathers and ancient martyrs against us; so the Popish Prelate extracted out of other authors testimonies for this, and from 1. Armagh, in a sermon on Rom. 13; so the doctors of Aberdeen. The Prelate proves from Clement of Alexandria that the king is constituted by the Lord (1.7); so Ignatius.

Ans. 1. Unless he prove from these fathers that the king is from God only and immediately, he proves nothing.

Obj. 2. Iren proves that God gives kingdoms, and that the devil lied, Luke 4 (*Adv. haer.* 1.5.20); and we make the people to make kings, and so to be the children of the devil.

Ans. If we denied God to dispose of kingdoms, this man might allege the church of God in England and Scotland to be the sons of Satan; but God's word in Deut. 17:18 and many other places makes the people to make kings, and yet not devils. But to say that prelates should crown kings, and with their foul fingers anoint him, and that as the Pope's substitute is to make him that is the son of perdition a donor of kingdoms; also to make a man with his bloody sword to ascend to a throne is to deny God to be the disposer of kingdoms, and prelates teach both these.

Obj. 3. Tertullian *Inde est imperator, unde et homo, antequam imperator, inde potestas illi, unde et spiritus*, God is no less the creator of sovereignty than of the soul of man (*Apol.* section 30).

Ans. God only makes kings by His absolute sovereignty, as He only makes high and low, and so only He makes mayors, provosts, bailiffs, for there is no power but of him (Rom 13); therefore provosts and bailiffs are not from men. The reader shall not be troubled with the rest of the testimonies of this poor plagiary, for they prove what never man denied but prelates and royalists, namely, that kings are not from God's approving and regulating will, which they oppose, when they say sole conquest is a just title to the crown.

But they deserve rather an answer which Grotius, Barclay, Arnisaeus, and Spalato, allege, such as,

Obj. 1. Cyprian: *Non est fas Christianis, armis, ac vi tueri se adversus impetum persecutorum*, Christians cannot, by violence, defend themselves against persecutors (epist. 1).

Ans. If these words be pressed literally, it would not be lawful to defend ourselves against murderers; but Cyprian is expressly condemning in that place the seditious tumults of people against the lawful magistrate.

Obj. 2. The ancients say he was justly punished who did rend and tear the edict of Dioclesian and Maximinus (Eusebius, *Hist. Eccles.* 1.7.5).

Ans. To rend an edict is no act of natural self-defense, but a breach of a positive commandment of the emperor's, and could not be lawfully done, especially by a private man.

Obj. 3. Cyprian *Incumbamus gemitibus assiduis et deprecationibus crebris haec enim sunt munimenta spiritualia et tela divina quae protegunt* (epist. 56); and Ruffinus, *Ambrosius adversus reginse (Justinae Arinae) furorrm non se manu defensabat aut telo, sed jejuniis contintuatisque vigiliis sub altari positus* (1.2.6).

Ans. It is true Cyprian reputed prayers his armor, but not his only armor. Though Ambrose *de facto* used no other against Justina, the places say nothing against the lawfulness of self-defense. Ambrose speaks of that armor and these means of defense that are proper to pastors, and these are prayers and tears, not the sword; because pastors carry the ark, that is their charge, not the sword; that is the magistrate's place.

Obj. 4. Tertullian says expressly, that the Christians might, for strength and number, have defended themselves against their persecutors, but thought it unlawful. *Quando vel una nox pauculis faculis largitatem ultionis poss et operari, si malum malo dispungi penes nos liceret, sed absit ut igni humano vindicetur divina secta, aut doleat pati, in quo probetur. Si enim hostes extraneos, non tantum vindices occultos agere vellemus, deesset nobis vis numerorum et copiarum?* (*Apolog.* section 37)

Ans. I will not go about to say that Tertullian thought it lawful to raise arms against the emperor: I ingenuously confess Tertullian was in that error. But here is something of the man, and of the Christians.

1. Of the man, Tertullian after this turned a Montanist.

2. Pamelius says of him, in *vit, Tertul. inter Apocrypha numeratur-excommunicatu*s.

3. It was Tertullian's error in a fact, not in a question, that he believed Christians were so numerous as that they might have fought with the emperors.

4. M. Pryn does judiciously observe he not only thought it unlawful to resist, but also to flee (part 3, Sovereign Power of Parl.), and therefore wrote a book *de fuga*; and therefore as some men are excessive in doing for Christ, so also in suffering for Christ. From this I infer that Tertullian is neither ours nor theirs in this point; and we can cite Tertullian against them also. *Jam sumus ergo pares*; yea, Fox in his *Monuments* says, "Christians ran to the stakes to be burnt, when they were neither condemned nor cited."

5. What if we cite Theodoret? "Who, about that time, say that evil men reign αρχομενων ανανδρια, through the cowardliness of the subjects" (fol. 98. *De provid*) as the Prelate says of Tertullian, I turn it: if Theodoret were now living he would go for a rebel.

1. About that time Christians sought help from Constantine the Great against Lycinius their emperor, and overthrew him in battle, and the Christians, being oppressed by the king of Persia their own king sent to Theodosius to help them against him.

2. For the man, Tertullian in the place cited says, "The Christians were strangers under the emperor," *externi sumus*, and therefore they had no laws of their own, but were under the civil laws of heathen till Constantine's time, and they had sworn to Julian as his soldiers, and therefore might have and no doubt had scruples of conscience to resist the emperor.

3. It is known Julian had huge numbers of heathen in his army, and to resist would have been a great danger.

4. Lacking leaders and commanders (many prime men doubting of the lawfulness of it) though they had been equal in number, yet number is not all in war: skill in valorous commanders is required.

5. What if all Christians were not of Tertullian's mind?

6. If I would go to human testimonies, which I judge not satisfactory to the conscience, I might cite many: the practice of France, of Holland; the divines in Luther's time resolved resistance to be lawful (Sleidan. 8.8.22); Calvin, Beza, Parous, the German divines, Buchanan, and a host might be produced.

QUESTION 36.

WHETHER THE KING HAS THE POWER OF WAR ONLY.

Inferior judges have the power of the sword no less than the king. The people tied to acts of charity, and to defend themselves, the church, and their posterity against a foreign enemy, though the king forbid. Flying unlawful to the states of Scotland and England now, God's law tying them to defend their country. Parliamentary power a natural power above the king.

It is not hard to determine this question. The sword in a constitute commonwealth is given to the judge supreme or subordinate, Rom. 13:4: "He bears not the sword in vain" in the empire. The use of armor is restricted to the emperor by a positive law; so the law says, *Arrmorum officia nisi jussu principis sunt interdicta* (*Lib, de Cod. de Lege.* 1). *Imperat Valentinian nulli, nobis inconsultis, usus armorum tributatur* (*ad* 1. *Jul. Mai. l.* 3). War is a species and a particular, the sword is a general.

Assert. 1. The power of the sword by God's law is not proper and peculiar to the king only, but given by God to the inferior judges. 1. Because the inferior judge is essentially a judge no less than the king, as is proved; therefore he must bear the sword (Rom. 13:4). 2. Not Moses only but the congregation of Israel had power of life and death, and so of the sword; Num. 35:12: the man-slayer shall not die, "until he stand before the congregation in judgment;" ver. 24: "Then the congregation shall judge between the slayer and the avenger of blood;" Deut. 22:18: "The elders of the city shall take that man and chastise him;" ver. 21: "The men of the city shall stone her with stones;" Deut. 17:5; 19:12-13, 5:18-21; 21:19: "Then shall his father and his mother bring him to the elders of his city;" ver. 21: "And the men of the city shall stone him with stones;" 1 Kings 21:11: The elders and nobles that were inhabitants in his city stoned Naboth. 3. Inferior judges are condemned as murderers, who have shed innocent blood (Isa. 1:12; Ps. 94:5-6; Jer. 22:3; Ezek. 22:12, 27; Hosea 6:8; Zeph. 3:1-3); therefore they must have the power of the sword, hence, upon the same grounds.

Assert. 2. That the king only has the power of war, and raising armies must be but a positive civil law. For, 1. By divine right, if the inferior judges have the sword given to them by God, then have they also power of war, and raising armies.

2. All power of war that the king has is cumulative, not privative, and not destructive, but given for the safety of the kingdom; as therefore the king cannot take from one particular man the power of the sword for natural self-preservation, because it is the birthright of life, neither can the king take from a community and kingdom a power of rising in arms for their own defense. If an army of Turks shall suddenly invade the land, and the king's express consent cannot be had (for it is essentially involved in the office of the king as king that all the power of the sword that he has be for their safety) or if the king should as a man revise his consent, and interdict

and discharge the land to rise in arms, yet they have his royal consent, though they lack his personal consent, in respect that his office obliges him to command than to rise in arms.

3. Because no king, no civil power can take away nature's birthright of self-defense from any man, or a community of men.

4. Because if a king should sell his kingdom and invite a bloody conqueror to come in with an army of men to destroy his people, impose upon their conscience an idolatrous religion, they may lawfully rise against that army without the king's consent; for though royalists say they need not come in asinine patience and offer their throats to cut-throats, but may flee, yet several things hinder a flight.

1. They are obliged by virtue of the fifth commandment to remain, and with their sword defend the cities of the Lord and the king (2 Sam. 10:12; 1 Chron. 19:13); for if to defend our country and children and the church of God from unjust invaders and cut-throats by the sword be an act of charity that God and the law of nature requires of a people, as is evident (Prov. 24:11) and if the fifth commandment oblige the land to defend their need parents and young children from those invaders, and if the sixth commandment lay on us the like bond, all the land are to act works of mercy and charity, though the king unjustly command the contrary, except, royalists say, that we are not to perform the duties of the second table commanded by God if an earthly king forbid us; and if we exercise not acts of mercy towards our brethren, when their life is in hazard to save them, we are murderers, and so men may murder their neighbor if the king command them so to do; this is like the court-faith.

2. The king's power of wars is for the safety of his people; if he deny his consent to their raising of arms till they be destroyed, he plays the tyrant, not the king, and the law of

nature will necessitate them either to defend themselves (seeing flight of all in that case is harder than death), otherwise
they must be guilty of self-murder. Now, the king's commandment of not rising in arms at best is positive and against the
nature of his office, and it flows then from him as from a man,
and so must be far inferior to the natural commandment of
God, which commands self-preservation, if we would not be
guilty of self-murder and of obeying men rather than God;
so Althusius (*Polit.* section 25, n. 9), Halicarnas (*Antiq. Rom.*
1.4)., Aristotle (*Polit.* 1.3.3).

3. David took Goliath's sword and became a captain, a captain to a host of armed men in the battle, and fought the
battles of the Lord (1 Sam. 25:28) and this Abigail by the
spirit of prophecy, as I take it, says (ver. 29-31; 1 Sam. 22:2; 1
Chron. 12:1-3; 17:18, 21-22) not only without Saul's consent,
but against king Saul, as he was a man, but not against him as
he was king of Israel.

4. If there be no king, or the king be minor or an usurper,
such as Athaliah, be on the throne, the kingdom may lawfully make war without the king, as the children of Israel, four
hundred thousand footmen that drew sword, went out to war
against the children of Benjamin (Judg. 20). Judah had the
power of the sword when Josiah was but eight years old in the
beginning of his reign (2 Kings 22:1-2) and before Jehoash
was crowned king, and while he was minor (2 Kings 21), there
were captains of hundreds in arms raised by Jehoiada, and the
people of Judah, to defend the young king. It cannot be said
that this is more extraordinary than that it is extraordinary
for kings to die, and in the *interregnum,* wars in an ordinary
providence may fall out in these kingdoms, where kings go by
election, and for kings to fall to be minors, captives, tyrannical. And I shall be of that opinion that Mr. Symmons, who

holds that royal birth is equivalent to divine anointing, must also hold that election is not equivalent to divine anointing; for both election and birth cannot be of the same validity, the one being natural, the other a matter of free choice, which shall infer that kings by election are less properly, and analogically only, kings; and so Saul was not properly a king, for he was king by election, but I conceive that rather kings by birth must be less properly kings because the first king by God's institution, being the mold of all the rest, was by election (Deut. 17:18-20).

5. If the estates create the king, and make this man king, not that man (as is clear from Deut. 17:18 and 2 Chron. 5:1-4) they give to him the power of the sword, and the power of war, and the militia, and I shall judge it strange and reasonless that the power given to the king, by the parliament or estate of a free kingdom (such as Scotland is acknowledged by all to be) should create, regulate, limit, abridge, yea, and annul that power that created itself has God ordained a parliamentary power to create a royal power of the sword and war to be placed in the king, the parliament's creature, for the safety of parliament and kingdom, which yet is destructive of itself? Dr. Ferne says that "the king summons a parliament, and gives them power to be a parliament, and to advise and counsel him," and, in the meantime, Scripture says that the parliament creates the king (Deut. 17:18-20; 1 Sam. 10:20-25; 2 Sam. 5:1-4). Here is admirable reciprocation of creation in policy! Shall God make the mother to destroy the daughter? The parliamentary power that gives crown, militia, sword, and all to the king, must give power to the king to use sword and war for the destruction of the kingdom, and to annul all the power of parliaments, to make, unmake parliaments, and all parliamentary power. What more absurd?

Obj. 1. Symmons: These phrases: 1 Sam. 9:1: "When kings go forth to war," and Luke 14:31: "What king going forth to war," speak to my conscience, that both offensive and defensive war are in the king's hand.

Ans. It is not much to other men what is spoken to any man's conscience by phrase and customs; for by this no states, where there be no kings, but government by the best, or the people, as in Holland, or in other nations, can have power of war; for what time of year shall kings go to war who are not kings? And because Christ says, "A certain householder delivered talents to his servants," will this infer to any conscience that none but a householder may take usury? And when he says, "If the good man of the house knew at what hour the thief would come, he would watch," shall it follow the son or servant may not watch the house, but only the good man?

Obj. 2. Ferne: The natural body cannot move but upon natural principles, and so neither can the politic body move in war, but upon politic reasons from the prince, which must direct by law.

Ans. 1. This may well be retorted: the politic head cannot then move but upon politic reasons, and so the king cannot move to wars but by the law, and that is by consent of Parliament, and no law can principle the head to destroy the members.

2. If an army of cut-throats rise to destroy the kingdom, because the king is behind in his place in doing his duty, how can the other judges, the states and parliament, be accessory to murder committed by them in not raising armies to suppress such robbers? Shall the inferior judges be guilty of innocent blood because the king will not do his duty?

3. The political body ceases no more to renounce the principles of sinless nature in self-defense, because it is a political

body and subject to a king, than it can leave off to sleep, eat, and drink; and there is more need of politic principles to the one than the other.

4. The parliaments and estates of both kingdoms move in these wars by the king's laws, and are a formal politic body in themselves.

Obj. 2. The ground of the present wars against the king, says Dr. Ferne, is false, namely, that the parliament is co-ordinate with the king (section 4); but so the king shall not be supreme, the parliament's consent is required to an act of supremacy, but not to a denial of that act. And there can no more be two equal and co-ordinate supreme powers than there can be two supreme Gods; and *multitudo deorum est nullitas deorum*, many gods infer no gods (Arnisaeus, *de jure majestatis*, section 3; *in quo consistat essen. majest,* section 3, n. 1; and in *jur, majest, separ.,* &c. section 2, n. 2).

Ans. 1. If we consider the fountain-power, the king is sub-ordinate to the parliament, and not co-ordinate; for the con-stituent is above that which is constituted. If we regard the derived and executive power in parliamentary acts, they make but a total and complete sovereign power; yet so as the sover-eign power of the parliament, being habitually and underived a prime and fountain-power (for I do not here separate people and parliament) is perfect without the king, for all parlia-mentary acts, as is clear, in that the parliament make kings, make laws, and raise armies, when either the king is minor, captured, tyrannical, or dead; but royal power parliamentary without the parliament is null because it is essentially but a part of the parliament, and can work nothing separated from the parliament, no more than a hand cut off from the body can write; and so here we see two supremes co-ordinate. Among infinite things there cannot be two, because it involves a contradiction: that an infinite thing can be created, for then it should it be finite; but a royal power is essentially a derived and created power and supreme, *secundum quid*, only in relation to single men, but not in relation to the community; it is always a creature of the community, with leave of the royalist.

2. It is false that to an act of parliamentary supremacy the consent of the king is required, for it is repugnant that there can be any parliamentary judicial act without the parliament, but there may be without the king.

3. More false it is that the king has a negative voice in parliament; then he shall be sole judge, and the parliament, the king's creator and constituent, shall be a cipher.

Obj. 3. *Arnisaeus:*[1] The people are mad and furious; therefore supreme majesty cannot be secured, and rebels suppressed, and public peace kept if the power of armor be not in the king's hand only.

Ans. 1. To deprive the people of armor, because they may abuse the prince, is to expose them to violence and oppression, unjustly; for one king may more easily abuse armor than all the people; one man may more easily fail than a community.

2. The safety of the people is far to be preferred before the safety of one man, though he were two emperors, one in the east, another in the west, because the emperor is ordained by God for the good and safety of the people (1 Tim. 2:2).

3. There can be no inferior judges to bear the sword, as God requires (Rom. 13:4; Deut. 1:15-16; 1 Chron. 29:6-7) and the king must be sole judge, if he only have the sword, and all armor monopolized to himself.

Obj. 4. The causes of war, says Mr. Symmons, should not be made known to the subjects, who are to look more to the

---

1. *De jur. maj. de potest, armorum,* section 5, n. 4

lawful call to war from the prince than to the cause of the war (section 4).

Ans. 1. The parliament and all the judges and nobles are subjects to royalists, if they should make war and shed blood upon blind obedience to the king, not inquiring either in causes of law or act, they must resign their consciences to the king.

2. The king cannot make unlawful war to be lawful by any authority royal, unless he could raze out the sixth commandment; therefore subjects must look more to the causes of war than to the authority of the king, and this would be a fair way to make parliaments of both kingdoms set up popery by the sword, and root out the reformed religion upon the king's authority, as the lawful call to war, not looking to the causes of war.

QUESTION 37.

WHETHER THE ESTATES OF SCOTLAND ARE TO HELP THEIR BRETHEREN, THE PROTESTANTS OF ENGLAND, AGAINST CAVALIERS IS PROVED BY ARGUMENT.

Helping of neighbor nations is lawful. The various opinions concerning the point are considered. The law of Egypt against those that helped not the oppressed is considered.

Marianus says one is obliged to help his brother, *non vinculo effiaci*, not with any efficacious band, because in these (says he) *non est actio aut poena*, one may not have action of law against his brother, who revised to help him; yet (says he) as man he is obliged to man, *nexus civilis societatis*, by the bond of human society.

2. Others say one nation may indirectly defend a neighbor nation against a common enemy because it is a self-defense; and it is presumed that a foreign enemy, having overcome the neighbor nation, shall invade that nation itself who denies help and succor to the neighbor nation. This is a self-opinion, and to me it looks not like the spiritual law of God.

3. Some say it is lawful, but not always expedient, in which opinion there is this much truth: that if the neighbor nation have an evil cause, *neque licet, neque expedit*, it is neither lawful nor expedient. But what is lawful in the case of necessity so extreme, as is the loss of a brother's life or of a nation, must be expedient, because necessity of non-sinning makes any lawful thing expedient. As to help my brother in fire or water, requiring my present and speedy help, though to the loss of my goods must be as expedient as a negative commandment: you shall not murder.

4. Others think it lawful in the case that my brother seek my help only; otherwise I have no calling to it, to which opinion I cannot universally subscribe, it is held, both by reason and the soundest divines that to rebuke my brother of sin is *actua misericordiae et charitatis*, an act of mercy and charity to his soul; yet I hold I am obliged to rebuke him by God's law (Levit. 19:17), otherwise I hate him (Thess. 5:14; Col. 4:17; Math, 18:15). Nor can I think in reason that my duty of love to my brother does not oblige me but upon dependency on his free consent; but as I am to help my neighbor's ox out of a ditch, though my neighbor know not, and so I have only his implicit and virtual consent, so is the case here. I go not farther in this case of conscience if a neighbor nation be jealous of our help, and in an hostile way should oppose us in helping (which, blessed be the Lord, the honorable houses of the parliament of England have not done, though malignant spirits tempted them to such a course). What in that case we should owe to the afflicted members of Christ's body is a case that may be determined easily.

5. The fifth and last opinion is of those who think, if the king command papists and prelates to rise against the parliament and our brethren in England in wars, that we are obliged

in conscience, and by our oath and covenant, to help our native prince against them, to which opinion, with hands and
feet I should accord if our kind's cause were just and lawful; but from this it follows that we must thus far judge of
the cause as concerns our consciences in the matter of our
necessary duty, leaving the judicial cognizance to the honorable parent of England. But because I cannot return to all
these opinions particularly, I see no reason but the civil law
of a kingdom does oblige any citizen to help an innocent man
against a murdering robber, and that he may be judicially accused as a murderer who fails in his duty, and that Solon said
well, *Beatam remp esse illam, in qua quisque injuriam alterius
suam estimet,* it is a blessed society in which every man is
to repute an injury done against a brother as an injury done
against himself. As the Egyptians had a good law, by which he
was accused upon his head who helped not one that suffered
wrong, and if he was not able to help, he was held to accuse
the injurer, if not, his punishment was whips or three days'
hunger; it may be upon this ground it was that Moses slew the
Egyptian. Ambrose commended him for so doing.

Assert. We are obliged by many bonds to expose our lives,
goods, children, &c. in this cause of religion and of the unjust oppression of enemies, for the safety and defense of our
dear brethren and true religion in England. 1 Prov. 24:11-12:
"If you forbear to deliver them that are drawn to death, למות
לקחים (taken as captives to be killed) and those that are ready
to be slain. If you say. Behold we knew it not, does not he
that ponders the heart consider it? And he that keeps your
soul, does he not know it? And shall he not render to every
man according to his work." Mr. Jermine is too narrow, who
commenting on the place restricts all to these two: that the
priest should deliver by interceding for the innocent, and the

king by pardoning only. But to deliver is a work of violence, as David by the sword rescued his wives (1 Sam. 3:18); Hos. 5:14: "I will take away, and none shall rescue;" 1 Sam. 17:35: "I rescued the lambs out of his mouth," out of the lion's mouth, which befitted to be done with great violence; 2 Kings 18:34: "They have not delivered כי הצילו Samaria out of my hand." So Cornel. à Lapide: *Charitas suadet ut vi et armis eruamus injuste ductos ad mortem.* Ambrose cites this same text and commends Moses who killed the Egyptian in defending a Hebrew man (*offic.* 1.36). To deliver is an act of charity, and so to be done, though the judge forbid it, when the innocent is unjustly put to death.

Obj. But in so doing private men may offer violence to the lawful magistrate when he unjustly puts an innocent man to death and rescue him out of the hands of the magistrate; and this would be to bring in anarchy and confusion; for if it be an act of charity to deliver the innocent out of the hands of the magistrate, it is homicide to a private man not to do it; for our obedience to the law of nature ties us absolutely, though the magistrate forbid these acts, for it is known that I must obey God rather than men.

Ans. 1. The law of nature ties us to obedience in acts of charity, yet not to perform these acts after any way and manner in a mere natural way, *impetu naturae*; but I am to perform acts of natural charity in a rational and prudent way, and in looking to God's law; otherwise if my brother or father were justly condemned to die, I might violently deliver him out of the magistrate's hand, but by the contrary my hand should be first on him without natural compassion. Such as, if my brother or my wife have been a blasphemer of God (Deut. 13:6-8); therefore, I am to do acts natural, as a wise man observing (as Solomon says, Eccles. 8:5) "both time and judgment." Now, it would be no wisdom for one private man to hazard his own life by attempting to rescue an innocent brother, because he has not strength to do it, and the law of nature obliges me not to acts of charity when I in all reason see them impossible; but a multitude who had strength did well to rescue innocent Jonathan out of the hands of the king, that he should not be put to death; yet one man was not tied by the law of nature to rescue Jonathan if the king and prince had condemned him, though unjustly.

2. The host of men that helped David against king Saul (1 Sam. 22:2) entered in a lawful war, and Amasa, by the Spirit of the Lord, blesses his helpers, "Peace, peace be unto you, and peace be to your helpers, for your God helps you" (1 Chron. 12:18). Therefore, peace must be to the parliament of England, and to their helpers, their brethren of Scotland.

3. Numb. 32:1-3, &c.; Josh. 1:12-14: the children of Gad, and of Reuben, and the half tribe of Manasseh, though their inheritance fell to be on this side of Jordan, yet they were to go over the river armed to fight for their brethren, while they had also possession of the land, at the commandment of Moses and Joshua.

4. So Saul and Israel helped the men of Jabesh-Gilead conjoined in blood with them against Nahash the Ammonite, and his unjust conditions in plucking out their right eyes, 1 Sam. 11.

5. Jephthah (Judg. 12:2) justly rebukes the men of Ephraim because they would not help him and his people against the Ammonites.

6. If the communion of saints be any bond that England and we have "one Lord, one faith, one baptism, one head and savior, Jesus Christ," then are we obliged to help our bleeding sister-church against these same common enemies, papists and prelates; but the former is undeniably true, for we send

help to the Rochelle, if there had not been a secret betraying of our brethren, we send help to the recovery of the palatinate, and the aid of the confederate princes against Babel's strength and power, and that lawfully, but we did it at great leisure and coldly. Queen Elizabeth helped Holland against the king of Spain, and besides the union in religion, we sail in one ship together, being in one island under one king; and now, by the mercy of God, have sworn one covenant, and so must stand or fall together.

7. We are obliged by the union between the kingdoms concluded to be by the Convention of the Estates of Scotland, anno 1585, at the desire of the General Assembly, 1583, to join forces together at home, and enter in league with protestant princes and estates abroad, to maintain the protestant religion against the bloody confederacy of Trent, and accordingly this league between the two crowns was subscribed at Berwick, 1586, and the same renewed, 1567-8, as also the Confession of Faith subscribed when the Spanish armada was on our coasts.

8. The law of God, commanding that we love our neighbor as ourselves, and therefore to defend one another against unjust violence (*l. ut vim, ff. de just. et jur*) obliges us to the same, unless we think God can be pleased with lip-love in word only, which the Spirit of God condemns (1 John 2:9-10; 3:16). And the sum of law and prophets is that as we desire not men should refuse to help us when we are unjustly oppressed, so neither would we so serve our afflicted brethren.[1]

9. Every man is a keeper of his brother's life. There is a voluntary homicide when a man refuses food or medicine necessary for his own life, and refuses food to his dying brother, and

---

1. *l. in facto ff. de cond. et demonstr. Sect. Si uxor. Justit. de nupt.*

men are not born for themselves, and when the king defends not subjects against their enemies, all fellow-subjects by the law of nature, of nations, the civil and common law, have a natural privilege to defend one another, and are mutual magistrates to one another when there be no other magistrates. If an army of Turks or pagans would come upon Britain, if the king were dead, as he is civilly dead in this juncture of time, when he refuses to help his subjects, one part of Britain would help another; as Jehoshaphat, king of Judah, did right in helping Ahab and Israel, if the Lord had approved of the war. If the left hand be wounded, and the left eye put out, nature teaches that the whole burden of natural acts is devolved on the other hand and eye, and so are they obliged to help one another.

10. As we are to bear one another's burdens and to help our enemies to compassionate strangers, so far more those who make one body of Christ with us.

11. Meroz is under a curse, who helps not the Lord, so one part of a church another. A woe lies on them that are at ease in Zion and help not afflicted Joseph so far as they are able.

12. The law of gratitude obliges us to this. England sent an army to free both our souls and bodies from the bondage of popery and the fury of the French, upon which occasion a parliament at Leith (anno 1560) established peace and religion, and then afterwards they helped us against a faction of papists in our own bosom, for which we take God's name in a prayer, seeking grace never to forget that kindness.

13. When papists in arms had undone England (if God give them victory) they would next fall on us, and it would not be in the king's power to resist them. When our enemies within two days' journey are in arms and have the person of our kind and his judgement, and so the breathing-law of the two

kingdoms under their power, we should but sleep to be killed in our nest if we did not arise and fight for king, church, country, and brethren.

Obj. By these and the like grounds, when the king's royal person and life is in danger, he may use papists as subjects, not as papists, in his own natural self-defense.

Ans. 1 Hell and the devil cannot say that a thought was in any heart against the king's person. He slept in Scotland safe, and at Westminster in his own palace when the estates of both kingdoms would not so much as take the water-pot from his bedside, and his spear, and Satan instilled this traitorous lie, first in prelates, then in papists.

2. The king professes his maintenance of the true protestant religion in his declarations since he took arms, but if Saul had put arms in the hands of Baal's priests, and in an army of Sidonians, Philistines, Ammonites, professing their quarrel against Israel was not to defend the king, but their Dagon and false gods, clear it would be Saul's army should not stand in relation of helpers of the king's, but of advancers of their own religion. Now, Irish papists and English in arms press the king to cancel all laws against popery, and make laws for the free liberty of mass, and the full power of papists; then the king must use papists as papists in these wars.

QUESTION 38.

WHETHER MONARCHY IS THE BEST OF GOVERNMENTS

Whether monarchy is the best of governments has various considerations, in which each one may be less or more convenient. Absolute monarchy is the worst of governments. It is better to lack power to do ill than to have it. A mixed government is sweetest of all. Neither king nor parliament has a voice against law and reason.

Nothing more unwillingly do I write about than one word of this question. It is a dark way; circumstances in fallen nature may make things best to be, *hic et nunc*, evil, though to me it is probable that monarchy in itself, monarchy *de jure*, that is, lawful and limited monarchy is best, even now in a kingdom under the fall of sin, if other circumstances be considered.

But observe, I pray you, that Mr. Symmons and this poor Prelate do so extol monarchy, that there is not government save monarchy only; all other governments are deviations; and therefore Mr. Symmons says, "If I should affect another government than monarchy, I should neither fear God nor the king, but associate myself with the seditious," and so the question of monarchy is,

1. Which is the choicest government in itself, or which is the choicest government in policy, and in the condition of man fallen in the state of sin?

2. Which is the best government, that is, the most profitable, or the most pleasant, or the most honest? For we know that there be these three kinds of good things: things useful and profitable, *bona utilia;* things pleasant, *jucunda;* things honest, *honesta;* and the question may be every one of the three.

3. The question may be, which of these governments be most agreeable to nature? That is, either to nature in itself, as it agrees, *communiter* to all natures of elements, birds, beasts, angels, men, to lead them as a governor does to their last end; or, which government is most agreeable to men, to sinful men, to sinful men of this or that nation? For some nations are more ambitious, some more factious; some are better ruled by one, some better ruled by many, some by most and by the people.

4. The question may be in regard of the facility or difficulty of loving, fearing, obeying, and serving; and so it may be thought easier to love, fear, and obey one monarch than many rulers, in respect that our Lord says it is difficult to serve two masters, and possibly more difficult to serve twenty or an hundred.

5. The question may be in regard of the power of commanding, or of the justice and equity of commanding; thus from this last I shall set down the first thesis.

Assert. 1. An absolute and unlimited monarchy is not only not the best form of government, but it is the worst, and this is against our petty Prelate and all royalists. My reasons are these: 1. Because it is an unlawful ordinance, and God never ordained it; and I cannot ascribe the superlative degree to anything of which I deny the positive. Absolute government in a sinful and peaceable man is a wicked government, and not a power from God, for God never gave a power to sin. *Plenitudo potestatis ad malum et injuriam non extenditur*, Sozenus Junior (cons. 65) in *causa occurrenti* (l. 2). Ferdinand. Loazes in *suo sons. pro March, de Velex*, and so that learned senator, Ferd. Vasquez (1.1.5, n. 17). 2. It was better for the state that Epiminondas could not sleep than that he could sleep when the people were dancing, because, said he, "I wake that you may have leave to sleep and be secure;" for he was upon deep cogitations how to do good to the commonwealth when the people were upon their pleasures; because all kings, since the fall of the father, king Adam, are inclined to sin and injustice, and so had need to be guided by a law, even because they are kings, so they remain men. Omnipotence in one that can sin is a cursed power. With reason all our divines say the state of saving grace in the second Adam, where there is *non posse deficere*, they cannot fall away from God, is better than the state of the first Adam, where there was *posse non deficere*, a power not to fall away and that our free will is better in our country in heaven, where we cannot sin, than in the way to our country, on earth, where we have a power to sin; and so God's people is in a better case "Where her power to overtake her lovers is closed up with an hedge of thorns that she cannot find her paths;" (Hosea 2:6-7) than the condition of Ephraim, of whom God says "Ephraim is joined to idols, let him alone" (Hosea 4:17). So cannot that be a good government when the supreme power is in a sinful man, as inclinable to injustice by nature as any man, and more inclinable to injustice by the condition of his place than any, and yet by office he is one that can do no injustice against his subjects; he is a king, and so may destroy Uriah, kill his subjects. but cannot sin; and this is to flattering royalists the best government in the world. As if an unchained lion were the best governor, because unchained, to all the beasts, sheep, and lambs, and all others, which with his teeth and paws he may reach, and that by virtue of an ordinance of God.

3. What is one man under no restraint, but made a god on earth, and so drunk with the grandeur of a sinning-god, here under the moon and clouds? Who may hear good counsel from men of his own choosing, yet is under no restraint of law to follow it, being the supreme power absolute, high, mighty, and an impeccable god on earth. Certainly this man may more easily err and break out in violent acts of injustice than a number of rulers, grave, wise under a law. One being a sinful man shall sooner sin and turn a Nero (when he may go to hell, and lead thousands to hell with him gratis) than a multitude of sinful men who have less power to do against law, and a tyrannical killing of innocents, and a subversion of laws, liberties, and religion, by one who may by office and without resistance of mortal men do all ill, is more dangerous and hurtful than division and faction incident to aristocracy.

4. Caesar is great, but law and reason are greater; by an absolute monarchy all things are ruled by will and pleasure above law; then this government cannot be so good as law and reason in a government by the best or by many.

5. Under absolute monarchy, a free people is, *actu primo*, and in themselves enslaved, because though the monarch, so absolute, should kill all, he cannot be controlled; there is no more but flight, prayers, and tears remaining; and what greater power has a tyrant? None at all, so may we say. An absolute monarch is, *actu primo*, a sleeping lion, and a tyrant is a waking and a devouring lion, and they differ in accidents only.

6. This is the papists' way. Bellarmine (*de pontif.* 1.1.1), and Sanderus (*de visibili Monarchia*, 1.3.3), Turrere (*in sum de Eccles.* 1.2.2) prove that the government of the church is by an absolute monarch and pope, because that is the best government which yet is in question. So royalists prove commonwealths must be best governed by absolute monarchs, because that is the best government; but the law says it is contrary to nature, even though people should paction to make a king absolute: *Conventio procuratoria ad dilapidandum et dissipandum juri naturali contraria nulla est.*[1]

Assert. 2. Monarchy in its latitude—as heaven, and earth, and all the host in them are citizens—is the best government absolutely, because God's immediate government must be best; but that other governments are good or best so far as they come near to this must prove that there is a monarchy in angels if there be a government and a monarchy among fishes, beasts, birds, &c.; and that if Adam had never sinned, there should be one monarchy among all mankind. I profess I have no eye to see what government could be in that state, but paternal, or marital; and by this reason there should be one catholic emperor over all the kings of the earth, a position held by some papists and interpreters of the cannon law, which makes all the princes of the earth to be usurpers except those who acknowledge a catholic dominion of the whole earth in the emperor, to whom they submit themselves as vassals. If kings were gods and could not sin, and just, as Solomon in the beginning of his. reign and as David, I could say monarchy so limited must be better than aristocracy or democracy, 1. Because it is farthest from injustice, nearest to peace and

---

1. *L filius* 15, *de cond. Just. l. Nepos. procul* 125, *de verb. signif.* l. 188, *ubi. de jure Regni* l. 85, *d. tit.*

godliness.[1] 2. Because God ordained this government in his people. 3. By experience it is known to be less obnoxious to change, except that some think the Venetian commonwealth best, but with reverence I see small difference between a king and the Duke of Venice.

Assert. 3. Every government has something wherein it is best; monarchy is honorable and glorious-like before men; aristocracy, for counsel, is surest; democracy for liberty, and possibly for riches and gain is best. Monarchy obtains its end with more convenience, because the ship is easier brought to land when one sits at the helm than when ten move the helm. We more easily fear, love, obey, and serve one than many. He can more easily execute the laws.

Assert. 4. A limited and mixed monarchy, such as is in Scotland and England, seems to me the best government, when parliaments, with the king have the good of all the three. This government has glory, order, unity, from a monarch; from the government of the most and wisest it has safety of counsel, stability, strength; from the influence of the commons, it has liberty, privileges, promptitude of obedience.

Obj. 1. There is more power, terror, and love in one than in many.

Ans. Not more power; terror comes from sin, and so to nature fallen in sin in circumstances a monarchy is best.

Obj. 2. It is more convenient to nature that one should be lord than many.

Ans. To sinless nature, true, as in a father to many children.

Obj. 3. Monarchy, for invention of counsels, execution, concealing of secrets, is above any other government.

---

1. *M.* 1.3, *sect. aparet. ff. de administrat. tutor.* 1.2, *sect. novissime, ff. de orig. jur.* Aristotle, *pol.* 1.8.10, Bodin, *de Rep.* 1.6.4.

Ans. That is in some particulars, because sin has brought darkness on us; so are we all dull of invention, slow in execution, and by reason of the falseness of men, silence is needful; but this is the accidental state of nature, and otherwise there is safety in a multitude of counsellors; one commanding all without following counsel trusts in his own heart and is a fool.

Obj. 4. A monarch is above envy because he has no equal.

Ans. Granted; in many things a monarchy is more excellent, but that is nothing to an absolute monarchy, for which royalists contend.

Obj. 5. In a multitude there be more fools than wise men, and a multitude of vices, and little virtue is in many.

Ans. Mere multitude cannot govern in either democracy of aristocracy, for then all should be rulers, and none ruled, but many eyes see more than one; by accident one may see more than hundreds, but accidents are not rules.

Obj. 6. Monarchy is most perfect, because most opposite to anarchy and most agreeable to nature, as is evident in plants, birds, bees.

Ans. Government of sinless nature void of reason, as in birds and bees, is weak to conclude political civil government among men in sin, and especially absolute government. A king-bee is not absolute, nor a king-eagle, if either destroy its fellows: by nature all rise and destroy their king. A king-bee does not act by counsel borrowed from fellow-bees, as a king must do, and communication of counsels lessens absoluteness of a man. I see not how a monarchy is more opposite to anarchy and confusion than other governments. A monarch as one is more opposite to a multitude as many, but there is no less order in aristocracy than in monarchy; for a government essentially includes order of commanding and subjection. Now, one is not for absoluteness more contrary to anarchy than many; for that one now who can easily slip from a king to a tyrant cannot have a negative voice in acts of justice, for then should he have a legal power to oppose justice, and so for his absoluteness, he should be most contrary to order of justice; and a monarch, because absolute, should be a door-neighbor to disorder and confusion.

Obj. But the parliament has no power to deny their voices to things just, or to cross the law of God, more than the king.

Ans. It is true neither of them has a negative voice against law and reason, but if the monarch by his exorbitant power, may deny justice, he may by that same legal power do all injustice, and so there is no absoluteness in either.

Obj. Who should then punish and coerce the parliament in the case of exorbitance?

Ans. Posterior parliaments.

Obj. Posterior parliaments and people may both err.

Ans. All is true; God must remedy that only.

QUESTION 39.

WHETHER OR NOT ANY PREROGATIVE AT ALL ABOVE THE LAW IS DUE TO THE KING, AND WHETHER JURA MAJESTATIS IS ANY SUCH PREROGATIVE.

There is a threefold supreme power. What jura regalia are. Kings confer not honors from their fullness of absolute power, but according to the straight line and rule of law, justice, and good observing. What the law of the king is (1 Sam. 8:9, 11). The difference between kings and judges. The law of the king (1 Sam. 8:9, 11) is no permissive law, such as the law of divorce. What dominion the king has over the goods of the subjects.

I conceive kings are conceived to have a threefold supreme power. 1. Strictly absolute to do what they please, their will being simply a law. This is tyrannical. Some kings have it, *de facto, ex consuetudine,* but by a divine law none have it. I doubt if any have it by a human positive law, except the great Turk and the king of Spain, over his conquest without the borders of Europe, and some few other conquerors. 2. There is another power limited to God's law, the due proper right of kings (Deut. 17:18-20). 3. There is, a *potestas intermedia*, a middle power, not so vast as that which is absolute and tyrannical, which yet is some way human. This I take what jurists call jus *regium, lex regia, jura regalia regis*; Cicero, *jura majestatis*; Livius, *jura imperii*, and these royal privileges are such common and high dignities as no one particular magistrate can have, seeing they are common to all the kingdom, as that Caesar only should coin money in his own name. Hence the penny given to Christ, because it had Caesar's image and superscription (Matt. 22:20-21) infers by way of argumentation, αποδοτι ουν, &c., give therefore tribute to Caesar as his due; so the magazine and armory for the safety of the kingdom is in the king's hand. The king has the like of these privileges, because he is the common, supreme, public officer and minister of God for the good of all the kingdom; and, among these royal privileges, I reckon that power that is given to the king, when he is made king, to do many things without warrant of the letter of the law, without the express consent of his council, which he cannot always carry about with him, as the law says. The king shall not raise armies without consent of the parliament; but if an army of Irish, or Danes, or Spaniards, should suddenly land in Scotland, he has a power, without a formally-convened parliament, to command them all to rise in arms against these invaders and defend themselves, this power no inferior magistrate has as he is, but such a magistrate. And in many such exigencies, when the necessity of justice or grace requires an extemporal exposition of laws, *pro re nata*, for present necessary execution, some say only the emperor, others, all kings have these pleasures. I am of the mind of Arnisaeus that these privileges are not rewards given to princes for their great pains;[1] for the king is not obliged to govern the commonwealth because he receives these royal privileges as his reward, but because by office he is obliged to govern the commonwealth; therefore these privileges are given to him, and without them he could not so easily govern. But I am utterly against Arnisaeus, who says, "These are not essential to a king, because" says he "he creates marquises, dukes, nobles, &c., and constitutes magistrates, not because of his royal dignity, but by reason of his absolute power; for many princes have supreme power and cannot make nobles, and therefore to him they are *jura majestatis, non jura potestatis.*"

Ans. 1. The king, suppose a limited king, may and ought to make nobles, for he may confer honors as a reward of virtue; none can say Pharaoh by his absolute authority and not as a king advanced Joseph to be a noble ruler. We cannot say that, for there was merit and worth in him deserving that honor; and Darius, not by absolute authority, but on the ground of well-deserving (the rule by which kings are obliged, in justice, to confer honors) promoted Daniel to be the first president of all his kingdoms, because "an excellent spirit was in him;" (Dan. 6:3) and in justice the king could ennoble none rather than Daniel, unless he should fail against the rule of conferring honors. It is acknowledged by all that *honos est proemium virtuis,* honor is founded upon virtue, and therefore Darius did not this out of his absolute majesty, but as king.

2. All kings as kings, and by a divine law of God, and so by no absoluteness of majesty, are to make men of wisdom, fearing God, hating covetousness, judges under them (Deut. 1:13; 2 Chron. 19:6-7; Ps. 101:6-8).

---

1. *De jure, vi maj.* section 1, n. 3.

3. If we suppose a king to be limited, as God's king is (Deut. 17:18-20) yet is it his part to confer honors upon the worthiest. Now, if he have no absoluteness of majesty, he cannot confer honors out of a principle that is none at all, *unum quodque sicut est, ita operatur*; and if the people confer honors, then must royalists grant that there is an absolute majesty in the people, why then may they not derive majesty to a king? And why then do royalists talk to us of God's immediate creating of kings, without any intervening action of the people?

4. By this absoluteness of majesty, kings may play the tyrant, as Samuel foretells Saul would do (1 Sam. 8:9-14). But I cannot believe that kings have the same very official absolute power, from which they do both acts of grace, goodness, and justice, such as are to exposit laws extemporally in extraordinary cases, to confer honors upon good and excellent men of grace, to pardon offenders upon good grounds, and also do acts of extreme tyranny; for out of the same fountain does not proceed both sweet water and bitter. Then by this absoluteness kings cannot do acts of goodness, justice, and grace, and so they must do good as kings, and they must do acts of tyranny as men, not from absoluteness of majesty.

5. Inferior magistrates, in whom there is no absoluteness of majesty according to royalists, may expound laws also extemporally, and do acts of justice, without formalities of civil or municipal laws, so they keep the genuine intent of the law, as they may pardon one that goes up to the wall of a city, and discovers the approach of the enemy, when the watchmen are sleeping, though the law be that any ascending to the wall of the city shall die. Also, the inferior judge may make judges and deputies under himself.

6. This distinction is neither grounded upon reason or laws, nor on any word of God. Not the former, as is proved before,

for there is no absolute power in a king to do above or against law; all the official power that a king has is a royal power to good for the safety and good of his subjects, and that according to law and reason, and there is no other power given to a king as a king; and for Scripture, Arnisaeus alleges 1 Sam. 8. the manner or law of the king, ver. 9, 11, and he says it cannot be the custom and manner of the king, but must be the law of absolute majesty, 1. Because it was the manner of inferior judges, as Tiberius said of his judges, to flay the people, when they were commanded to shear them only; 2. Samuel's sons, who wrested judgment and perverted the law, had this manner and custom to oppress the people, as did the sons of Eli, and, therefore, without reason it is called the law of kings, *jus regnum*, if it was the law of the judges; for if all this law be tyrannical and but an abuse of kingly power, the same law may agree to all other magistrates, who by the same unjust power may abuse their power; but Samuel (as Brentius observes, *homi*. 27, *in* 1 Sam. *in princ*) does mean here a greater license than kings can challenge, if at any time they would make use of their plentitude of absolute power; and therefore, *nomine juris*, by the word *law* here, he understands a power granted by law, *jure*, or right to the king, but pernicious to the people, which Gregory calls *jus regium tyrannorum*, the royal law of tyrants. So Seneca, *hoc interest inter regem et tyrannum, species ipsa fortunae ac licentiae par est, nisi quod tyranni ex voluntate saeviunt, reges non nisi ex causa et necessitate? quid ergo? non reges quoque occidere solent? sed quoties fieri publica utilitas persuadet, tyrannis saevitia cordi est* (1 *de clem*, section 11). A tyrant in this differs from a king, *Qui ne ea quidem vult, quae sibi licent,* that a king will not do these things which are lawful; a tyrant does *quae libet*, what he pleases to do.

Ans. 1. Arnisaeus betrays his ignorance in the Scriptures, for the word מִשְׁפָּט signifies a custom, and a wicked custom, as by many Scriptures I have proved already: his reasons are poor. It is the manner of inferior judges, as we see in the sons of Eli and Samuel, to pervert judgment, as well as king Saul did; but the king may more oppress, and his tyranny has more pretense, and is more catholic than the oppression of inferior judges. It is not Samuel's purpose thus to distinguish the judges of Israel and the kings, in that the judges had no power granted them of God to oppress, because the people might judge their judges and resist them; and there was power given by God to the king so far to play the tyrant that no man could resist him, or say, What do you? The text will not bear any such difference; for it was as unlawful to resist Moses, Joshua, Samuel (as royalists prove from the judgment of God that came upon Korah, Dathan, and Abiram) as to resist king Saul and king David: royalists doubt not to make Moses a king. It was also no less sin to resist Samuel's sons or to do violence to their persons, as judging for the Lord and sent by the supreme judge, their father Samuel, than it was sin to resist many inferior judges that were lions and even wolves under the kings of Israel and Judah, so they judged for the Lord, and as sent by the supreme magistrate. But the difference was in this: that judges were extraordinarily raised up by God out of any tribe He pleased, and were believers (Heb. 11. 32) saved by faith, and so used not their power to oppress the people, though inferior judges, as the sons of Eli and Samuel, perverted judgment; and therefore in the time of the judges, God, who gave them saviors and judges, was their king; but kings were tied to a certain tribe, especially the line of David, to the kingdom of Judah.

2. They were hereditary, but judges are not so.

3. They were made and chosen by the people (Deut. 17:14, 16; 1 Sam. 10:17-20; 2 Sam. 5:1-3) as were the kings of the nations; and the first king (though a king be the lawful ordinance of God) was sought from God in a sinful imitation of the nations (1 Sam. 8:19-20) and therefore were not of God's peculiar election as the judges, and so they were wicked men, and many of them, yea, all for the most part, did evil in the sight of the Lord and their law. מִשְׁפַּט their manner and custom, was to oppress the people, and so were their inferior judges little tyrants, and lesser lions, leopards, evening wolves (Ezek. 22:27; Mic. 3:1-3; Isa. 3:14, 16). And the kings and inferior judges are only distinguished, *de facto*, that the king was a more catholic oppressor, and the old lion, and so had more art and power to catch the prey than the inferior judges, who were but whelps and had less power, but all were oppressors (some few excepted, and Samuel speaks of that which Saul was to be, *de facto*, not *de jure*, and the most part of the kings after him) and this tyranny is well called *jus regis,* the manner of the king, and not the manner of the judges, because it had not been the practice, custom, and מִשְׁפַּט, of the believing judges before Saul's reign, and while God was his people's king (1 Sam, 8:7) to oppress. We grant that all other inferior judges, after the people cast off God's government and, in imitation of the nations would have a king were also lesser tyrants, as the king was a greater tyrant, and that was a punishment of their rejecting God and Samuel to be their King and judge. How shall Arnisaeus prove that this manner or מִשְׁפַּט of the king was, *potestas concessa*, a power granted, I hope, granted by God, and not an abuse of kingly power; for then he and royalists must say that all the acts of tyranny ascribed to king Saul (1 Sam. 8:11-14) by reason of which they did cry out, and complain to God because of their oppression, was no abuse of

power given to Saul; therefore it was a use, and a lawful use of power given of God to their king, for there is no medium between a lawful power used in moral acts, and a lawful power abused, and indeed, Arnisaeus so distinguishes a king and a tyrant that he makes them all one in nature and specie. He says, a tyrant does, *quod licet,* that which by law he may do, and a king does not these things, *quae licent* that which by law he may do; but so to me it is clear a tyrant, acting as a tyrant, must act according to this מַשְׁפַּט of the king, and that which is lawful, and a king, acting as a king, and not doing these things that are lawful, must sin against his office, and the power that God has given to him, which was to commend and praise the tyrant, and to condemn and dispraise the king. If this law of the king be a permissive law of God, which the King may, out of his absoluteness, put in execution to oppress the people, such as a law of a bill of divorcement, as Arnisaeus, Barclay, and other royalists say, then must God have given a law to every king to play the tyrant, because of the hardness of the king's heart; but we would gladly see some word of God for this. The law of a bill of divorcement is a mere positive law, permitted in a particular exigent, when a husband, out of levity of heart and affection, cannot love his wife; therefore God by a law permitted him out of indulgence to put her away that both might have a seed (the lack of which, because of the blessed Seed to be born of woman, was a reproach in Israel) and though this was an affliction to some particular women, yet the intent of the law and the soul of it was a public benefit to the commonwealth of Israel, of which sort of laws I judge the hard usage permitted by God to his people—in the master toward the servant—and the people of God toward the stranger, of whom they might exact usury, though not toward their brethren. But that God should make a permissive law,

that Jeroboam might press all Israel to sin and worship the
golden calves, and that a king by law may kill, as a bloody
Nero, all the people of God by a divine permissive law has no
warrant in God's word. Judge, reader, if royalists make God to
confer a benefit on a land, when he gives them a king, if by a
law of God, such as the law for a bill of divorcement, the king
may kill and devour, as a lawful absolute lion, six kingdoms of
nations that profess Christ and believe in his name. For if the
king have a divine law to kill an innocent Jonathan, so as it be
unlawful to resist him, he may by that same law turn bloodier
than either Nero, Julian, or any that ever sucked the paps of a
lioness, or of whom it may be said, *Quaeque dedit nutrix ubera,
tigris erat,* and he shall be given as a plague of God, *ex conditione doni,* to the people, and the people, inasmuch as they are
gifted by God with a king, to feed them in a peaceable and
godly life, must be made slaves; now, it lacks reason that God
will have a permissive law of murdering the church of Christ,
a law so contrary to the public good and intrinsic intention
of a king and to the immutable and eternal law of nature that
one man, because of his power, may by God's permissive law
murder millions of innocents. Some may say, "It is against the
duty of love that by nature and God's law the husband owes
to the wife (Ephes. 5:25) that the husband should put away
his wife; for God hates putting away, and yet God made a
law, that a husband might give his wife a bill of divorce, and
so put her away; and by the same reason, God may make a
law, though against nature, that a king should kill and murder
without all resistance."

Ans. 1. The question is not if God may make permissive
laws to oppress the innocent; I grant he may do it, as He may
command Abraham to kill his son Isaac; and Abraham by law
is obliged to kill him, unless God retract his commandment,

and whether God retract it or not, he may intend to kill his son, which is an act of love and obedience to God; but this would be more than a permissive law.

2. We have a clear Scripture for a permissive law of divorce, and it was not a law tending to the universal destruction of a whole kingdom, or many kingdoms, but only to the grievance of some particular wives; but the law of divorce gave not power to all husbands to put away their wives, but only to the husband who could not command his affection to love his wife. But this law of the king is a catholic law to all kings (for royalists will have all kings so absolute, as it is sin and disobedience to God to resist any) that all kings have a divine law to kill all their subjects; surely, then, it would be better for the church to want such nurse-fathers, as have absolute power to suck their blood; and for such a perpetual permissive law continuing to the end of the world, there is no word of God. Nor can we think that the hardness of one prince's heart can be a ground for God to make a law so destructive to His church and all mankind; such a permissive law, being a positive law of God, must have a word of Christ for it, otherwise we are not to receive it. Arnisaeus thinks a tyrant, *in exercitio*, becoming a notorious tyrant, when there is no other remedy, may be removed from government, *sine magno scelere*, without great sin (*distru, Tyran. et princ.* chapter 4, n.16). But, I ask, how men can annul any divine law of God, though but a permissive law. For if God's permissive law warrant a tyrant to kill two innocent men, it is tyranny more or less, and the law distinguishes not.

3. This permissive law is expressly contrary to God's law, limiting all kings (Deut. 17:16-18). How then are we to believe that God would make an universal law contrary to the law that He established before Israel had a king?

4. What Brentius says is much for us, for he calls this מששמ
law a license, and so to use it, must be licentiousness.

5. Amisaeus desires that kings may use sparingly the plenitude of their power for public good; there must be, says he,
necessity to make it lawful to use the plenitude of their power
justly; therefore Ahab sinned in that he unjustly possessed
Naboth's vineyard, though he sinned specially in this: that he
came to the possession by murder, and it was peculiar to the
Jews that they could not transfer their possessions from one
tribe to another. But if it be so, then this power of absoluteness is not given by permissive law, by which God permitted
putting away of wives, for the object of a permissive law is sin;
but this plenitude of power may be justly put forth in act, says
he, if the public good may be regarded. I would know what
public good can legitimate tyranny and killing of the innocent: the intentions of men can make nothing intrinsic evil to
become good.

6. How can that be a permissive law of God, and not His
approving law, by which kings create inferior judges? For this
is done by God's approving will.

7. It is evident that Arnisaeus' mind is that kings may take
their subjects' vineyards and their goods, so long as they err
not in the manner and way of the act; so it would have been
if there had not been a peculiar law that Naboth should not
sell his vineyard, and if the king had had any public use for it,
he might have taken Naboth's vineyard from him; but he specially sinned, says he, *in eo maxime culpatur,* &c., that he took
away the man's vineyard by murdering of him; therefore, says
Arnisaeus that by the king's law (1 Sam. 8). "There is given to
the king, a dominion over the people's sons, daughters, fields,
vineyards, olive-yards, servants, and flocks" (1. *de potest, maj,
in bona privato.* 2). So he cites that Daniel puts all places, the

rocks of the mountains, the birds of the heaven (Dan. 2) under the king's power. So all is the king's in dominion, and the subjects in use only.

But 1. This law of the king, then, can be no ground for the king's absoluteness above law, and there can be no permissive law of God here; for that which asserts the king's royal dominion over persons and things, that must be the law of God's approving, not his permitting evil; but this is such a law as Arnisaeus says.

2. The text speaks of no law or lawful power, or of any absoluteness of king Saul, but of his wicked custom, and his rapine and tyranny: "He will take your sons, your daughters, your fields, and your vineyards from you." Saul took not these through any power of dominion by law, but by mere tyranny.

3. I have before cleared that the subjects have a propriety, and a use also, otherwise how could we be obliged by virtue of the fifth commandment to pay tribute to the king (Rom. 13:7), for that which we pay was as much the king's before we paid as when we have paid it.

4. Arnisaeus says all are the king's in respect of the universal jurisdiction that the king has in governing and ordering all to the universal end, the good of the commonwealth; for as universal nature cares for the conservation of the specie and kind, so does particular nature care for the conservation of individuals, so do men care for their private goods, and the king is to refer every man's private goods to the good of the public. But the truth is this takes not away propriety of goods from private men, retaining only the use to private men, and giving the dominion to the king, because this power that the king has of men's goods is not power of dominion, that the king has over the goods of men, as if the king were *dominus*, lord and owner of the fields and monies of the private subject; but

it is a power to regulate the goods for a public use, and supposes the abuse of goods, when they are monopolized to and for private ends. The power that the king has over my bread is not a power of dominion, so that he may eat my bread as if it were his own bread, and he be lord of my bread as I was once myself, before I abused it, but it is a dominion improperly and abusively so called, and is a mere fiduciary and dispensatory power, because he is set over my bread not to eat it, nor over my houses to dwell in them, but only with a ministerial power, as a public though honorable servant and watchman, appointed by the community as a means for an end, to regulate my bread, houses, monies and fields for the good of the public. Dominion is defined "a faculty to use a thing as you please, except you be hindered by force or by law;" (*Justin. tit. c. de legibus in l. digna vox, &c*). so have I a dominion over my own garments, house, money, to use them for uses not forbidden by the law of God and man, but I may not lay my corn-field waste, that it shall neither bear grass nor corn, the king may hinder that, because it is a hurt to the public; but the king, as lord and sovereign, has no such dominion over Naboth's vineyard. How the king is lord of all goods, *ratione jurisdictionis, et tuitionia se.* (Anton. *De paudrill. in l.; Altius.* n. 6, section *de servit;* Hottom. illust. quest, q. 1, *ad fin., conc.* 2; Lod. Molin. *De just, et jur.* dis. 25; Soto. *De justitia et jur.* 1.4, q. 4, art. 1).

QUESTION 40.

WHETHER OR NOT THE PEOPLE HAVE ANY POWER OVER THE KING, EITHER BY HIS OATH, COVENANT, OR ANY OTHER WAY.

The people have power over the king by reason of his covenant and promise. Covenants and promises violated infer co-action, de jure, by law, though not de facto. Mutual punishments may be where there is no relation of superiority and inferiority. Three covenants made by Arnisaeus. The king is not king while he swears the oath and is accepted as king by the people. The oath of the kings of France is considered. Hugo Grotius sets down seven cases in which the people may accuse, punish, or dethrone the king. The prince is a noble vassal of the kingdom upon four grounds. The covenant had an oath annexed to it. The prince is but a private man in a contract. How the royal power is immediately from God, and yet conferred upon the king by the people.

Aristotle says Ὁ μεν γαρ τυραννος το ιαυτου συμφερον σκοπει, ο οι βασιλευς το των αρχιμενων, ου γαρ εστι βασιλευς, ο μη αιταρκης και τοις αγαιθοις υπερεχων, "Α tyrant seeks his own, a king the good of the subjects; for he is no king who is not content and excels in goodness" (*Ethic.* 8.12). The former part of these words distinguish essentially the king by his office from the tyrant. Now, every office requires essentially a duty to be performed by him that is in office, and, where there is a duty required, there is some obligation; if it be a politic duty, it is a political obligation.

1. Now, among politic duties between equal and equal, superior and inferior, that is not, *de facto*, required co-action for the performance of it, but, *de jure*, there is; for two neighbor kings and two neighbor nations, both being equal and independent the one toward the other, the one owes a duty to the other; and if the Ammonites do a wrong to David and Israel, as they are equal, *de facto*, the one cannot punish the other, though the Ammonites do a disgrace to David's messengers, yet, *de jure*, David and Israel may compel them to political duties of political consociation (for between independent kingdoms there must be some political government, and some political and civil laws, for two or three making a society cannot dwell together without some policy) and David and Israel, as by the law of nature they may repel violence with violence, so, if the laws or neighborhood and nations be broken the one may punish the other, though there be no relation of superiority and inferiority between them.

2. Wherever there is a covenant and oath between equals, yea, or superiors and inferiors, the one has some co-active power over the other; if the father give his bond to pay to his son ten thousand pounds, as his patrimony to him, though before the giving of the bond the father was not obliged but only by the law of nature to give a patrimony to his son; yet now by a political obligation of promise, covenant, and writ, he is obliged so to his son to pay ten thousand pounds, that by

the law of nations and the civil law, the son has now a co-active power by law to compel his father, though his superior, to pay him no less than ten thousand pounds of patrimony. Though, therefore, the king should stand simply superior to his kingdom and estates (which I shall never grant, yet if the king come under covenant with his kingdom, as I have proved at length (section 13) he must, by that same, come under some co-active power to fulfill his covenant; for *omne promissum* (says the law) *cadit in debitum;* what any does promise falls under debt. If the covenant be political and civil, as is the covenant between king David and all Israel (2 Sam. 5:1-3) and between king Jehoash and the people (2 Kings 11:17-18) then the king must come under a civil obligation to perform the covenant, and though there be none superior to king and the people on earth to compel them both to perform what they have promised, yet, *de jure*, by the law of nations, each may compel the other to mutual performance. This is evident,

1. By the law of nations, if one nation break covenant to another, though both be independent, yet has the wronged nation a co-active power, *de jure* (by accident, because they are weaker they want strength to compel, yet they have right to compel them) to force the other to keep covenant, or then to punish them, because nature teaches to repel violence by violence, so it be done without desire of revenge and malice.

2. This is proved from the nature of a promise or covenant, for Solomon says: "My son, if you be surety for your friend, if you have stricken your hand with a stranger, you are snared with the words of your mouth, and are taken with the words of your mouth." (Prov. 6:1-2). But from where is it that a man free is now snared as a beast in a gin or trap? Certainly Solomon says it is by a word and striking of hands, by a word of promise and covenant. Now, the creditor has co-active power,

though he be an equal or an inferior to the man who is surety, even by law to force him to pay, and the judge is obliged
to give his co-active power to the creditor that he may force
the surety to pay. From this it is clear that a covenant makes
a free man under the co-active power of law to an equal or a
weaker, and the stronger is by the law of fraternity to help the
weaker with his co-active power, to cause the superior fulfill
his covenant. If then the king (giving, and not granting, he
were superior to his whole kingdom) come under a covenant
to them to seek their good, not his own, to defend true protestant religion, they have power to compel him to keep his
covenant, and Scotland (if the king be stronger than England,
and break his covenant to them) is obliged by God's law (Prov.
24:11) to ask their forces and co-active power to help their
brethren of England.

3. The law shall warrant to loose the vassal from the lord
when the lord has broken his covenant.[1]

Arnisaeus (q. 6. *An princeps qui jurat subditis, etc.* n. 2) says,
"This occasions confusion and sedition." "The Egyptians cast
off Ptolemaeus because he affected too much the name of a
king of the Romans, his own friend;" Dion: "The States punished Archidanius because he married a wife of a low stature"
(1.9); Plutarch "The ancient Burgundians thought it cause
enough to expel their king, if matters went not well in the
state," (*in Ages. in pris*); Marcel: "The Goths in Spain gave no

---

1. Hippolytus (*in l., Si quis viduam col.* 5, *et dixit de* quest. *l. Si quis
major.* 41 *et* 161. *Bartol n.* 41); the Magdeburgens (*in libel, de of-
ficc, magistrate. Imperatores et reges esse primarios vassallos imperii, et regni,
et proinde si feloniam contra imperium aut regnum committant, feudo privari,
proinde ut alios vasallos.*)

other cause of expelling their king, *nisi quod sibi displiceret*, because he displeased them" (1:27); Aimon (1.2.20, 1.4.35).

Ans. All these are not to be excused in people, but neither every abuse of power in a king dethrones a king, nor every abuse in people can make null their power.

Arnisaeus makes three kinds of oaths: The first is when the king swears to defend true religion and the Pope; and he denies that this is an oath of fidelity, or by paction or covenant made to the Pope or clergy; he says it is only on oath of protection, nor does the king receive the crown from the Pope or clergy.

Ans. 1. Arnisaeus divides oaths that are to be conjoined. We do not read that kings swear to defend religion in one oath, and to administer judgment and justice in another; for David made not two covenants, but only one with all Israel.

2. The king was not king while he did swear this oath, and therefore is must be a pactional oath between him and the kingdom, and it is true the king receives not a crown from the church; yet David received a crown from the church, for this end, "to feed the Lord's people," and so conditionally. Papir. Masse says, the king was not a king before the oath, and that he swore to be a keeper not only of the first, but also of the second table of the law: *Ego N. Dei grattia, mox futurus rex Francorum, in die ordinationis meae coram Deo, et sanctis ejus polliceor, quod servabo privilegia canonica, justitiamque et jus unicuique Praelato debitum, vosque defendam, Deo juvante, quantum potero, quemadmodum rex ex officio in suo regno defendere debet, unumquemque episcopum ac ecclesiam, et administrabo populo justitiam et leges, uti jus postulat* (1.3, *Chron. Gal*). And so it is ordained in the council of Toledo: *Quisquis deinceps regni sortitus fuerit apicem, non ante conscendat regiam sedem, quam inter reliquas conditiones sacramento policitus fuerit, quod*

non sinet in regno suo degere eum qui non sit catholicus. All these by Scripture are oaths of covenant (Deut. 17:17-18; 2 Sam. 5:1-4; 2 Kings 11:17-18).

Arnisaeus makes a second oath of absolute kings, who swear they shall reign according to equity and justice; and he says. "There is no need of this oath, a promise is enough; for an oath increases not the obligation" (*L. fin, de non num. pec*), only it adds the bound of religion; for there is no use of an oath where there is no paction of law against him that swears; if he violate the oath, there follows only the punishment of perjury. And the word of a prince is as good as his oath, only he condescends to swear to please the people, out of indulgence, not out of necessity. And the king does not therefore swear because he is made king, but because he is made king he swears. And he is not king because he is crowned, but he is crowned because he is king. Where the crown goes by succession, the king never dies, and he is king by nature before he be crowned."

Ans. 1. This oath is the very first oath spoken of before, included in the covenant that the king makes with the people; (2 Sam. 5:2-4) for absolute powers, by Arnisaeus' grant, does swear to do the duties of a king, as Bodinus makes the oath of France *Juro ego, per deum, ac promitto me juste regnaturum judicium equitatem ac misericordiam facturum* (*De Rep.* 1.1.8); and Papir. Masse (1.3, Chron) has the same expressly in the particulars. And by this a king swears he shall not be absolute; and if he swear this oath, he binds himself not to govern by the law of the king, by which he may play the tyrant, as Saul did (1 Sam. 8:9-12, &c), as all royalists expound the place.

2. It is but a poor evasion to distinguish between the king's promise and his oath; for the promise and covenant of any man, and so of the king, does no less bring him under a civil

obligation and politic co-action to keep his promise than an oath; for he that becomes surety for his friend does by no civil law swear he shall be good for the son, or perform in lieu and place of the friend; what he is to perform he does only covenant and promise, and in law and politic obligation he is taken and snared by that promise no less than if he had sworn. Reuben offered to be caution to bring Benjamin safe home to his old father (Gen. 42:37) and Judah also (Gen. 43:9) but they do not swear any oath; and it is true that an oath adds nothing to a contract and promise, but only it lays on a religious tie before God, yet so as consequently, if the contractor violate both promise and oath, he comes under the guilt of perjury, which a law of men may punish. Now, that a covenant brings the king under a political obligation as well as an oath is already proved, and farther confirmed by Gal. 3:15: "Though it be a man's testament or covenant, no man disannuls and adds to it." No man, even by man's law, can annul a confirmed covenant; and therefore the man that made the covenant brings himself under law to fulfill his own covenant, and so must the king put himself under men's law by a covenant at his coronation; yea, and David is reputed by royalists an absolute prince, yet he comes under a covenant before he be made a king.

3. It is but a weak reason to say that an oath is needless where no action of law can be against the king who swears, if it have any strength of reason. I retort it: a legal and solemn promise then is needless also, for there is no action of law against a king (as royalists teach) if he violate his promise. So then king David needlessly made a covenant with the people at his coronation; for though David should turn as bloody an enemy to the church as Nero or Julian, the people have no law-action against David; and why then did Jeremiah seek an oath of the king of Judah, that he would not kill him nor

deliver him into the hands of his enemies? And why did David seek an oath of Jonathan? It is not like Jeremiah and David could have law-action against a king and a king's son, if they did violate the oath of God; and farther, it is a begging of the question to say that the states can nave no action against the king if he should violate his oath. Hugo Grotius puts seven cases in which the people may have real action against the king to accuse and punish. (1) They may punish the king to death for matters capital, if so it be agreed on between the king and the people, as in Lacedaemonia; (2) He may be punished as a private man; (3) If the king make away a kingdom given to him by succession, his act is null, and he may be resisted, because the kingdom is a life-rent only to him; yea, says Barclay, he loses the crown; (4) He loses his kingdom, if with a hostile mind he seek the destruction of the kingdom; (5) If such a clause be put in that if he commit felony, or do such oppressions, the subjects shall be loosed from the bonds of subjection; then the king, failing thus, turns a private man; (6) If the king have the one-half or part of the kingdom, and the people or senate the other half; if the king prey upon that half which is not his own, he may violently be resisted, for insofar he has not the empire; (7) If, when the crown was given, this be declared, that in some cases he may be resisted, then some natural liberty is free from the king's power, and reserved in the people's hand.

4. It is then reason that the king swear an oath, 1. That the king's oath is but a ceremony to please the people, and that because he is king, and king by birth; therefore he swears, and is crowned is in question, and denied. No man is born a king, as no man is born a subject; and because the people makes him king, therefore he is to swear. The council of Toledo says, *non antea conscendat regiam sedem quam juret*, 2. An oath is a

religious obligation, no arbitrary ceremony. 3, He may swear in his cabinet-chamber, not covenanting with the people, as David and Jehoash did. 4. So he makes promises that he may be king, not because he is king; it would be ridiculous he should promise or swear to be a just king, because he is a just king; and by the same reason the estates swear the oath of loyalty to the new king, not that they may be loyal in all time coming, but because they are loyal subjects already; for if the one-half of the covenant on the king's part be a ceremony of indulgence, not of necessity, by the same reason the other half of the covenant must be a ceremony of indulgence also to the people.

Obj.; Arnisaeus says a contract cannot be dissolved in law, but by consent of two parties contracting, because both are obliged; (*l. ab emptione 58, in pr. de pact. l. 3, de rescind, vend, l. 80, de solu*); therefore, if the subjects go from the covenant that they have made to be loyal to the king, they ought to be punished.

Ans. A contract, the conditions whereof are violated by neither side, cannot be dissolved but by the joint consent of both; and in buying and selling, and in all contracts unviolated, the sole will of neither side can violate the contract: of this speaks the law. But I ask the royalists, if the contract between the spies sent to view Jericho, and Rahab the harlot, had not been null, and the spies free from any obligation if Rahab had neglected to keep within doors when Jericho was taken, though Rahab and the spies had never consented expressly to break the covenant? We hold that the law says with us, that vassals loss their farm if they pay not what is due.[1] Now, what are

---

1. In l.1, n. 4.

kings but vassals to the state, who, if they turn tyrants, fall from their right?

Arnisaeus says in the council of Toledo the subjects ask from the king, that kings would be meek and just, not upon the ground of a voluntary contract and paction, but because God shall rejoice in king and people by so doing (4.47).[2]

Ans. These two do no more fight with one another than that two merchants should keep faith one to another, both because God has said he shall dwell in God's mountain who swears and covenants, and stands to his oath and covenant, though to his loss and hurt (Ps. 15). and also because they made their covenant and contract thus and thus.

Arnisaeus. Every prince is subject to God, but not as a vassal; for a master may commit felony, and lose the propriety of his farm. Can God do so? The master cannot take the farm from the vassal without an express cause legally deduced; but cannot God take what He has given but by a law process? A vassal can entitle to himself a farm against the master's will, as some jurists say, but can a prince entitle a kingdom to himself against the God of heaven's will? Though we grant the comparison, yet the subjects have no law over the kings, because the coercive power of the vassal is in the lord of the manor, the punishing of kings belongs to God.

Ans. 1. We compare not the lord of a manor and the Lord of heaven together; all these dissimilitudes we grant, but as the king is God's vassal, so is he a noble and princely vassal to the estates of a kingdom because they make him. 2. They make him rather than another their noble servant. 3. They make him for themselves and their own godly, quiet, and honest life. 4. They, in their first election, limit him to such a way, to govern by law, and give to him so much power for their good, no more; in these four acts they are above the prince, and so have a coercive power over him.

---

2. Section 6.

Arnisaeus. It is to make the prince's fidelity doubtful to put him to an oath. Lawyers say there is no need of an oath, when a person is of approved fidelity.

Ans. 1. Then we are not to seek an oath of an inferior magistrate, of a commander in wars, of a pastor, it is presumed these are of approved fidelity, and it makes their integrity obnoxious to slander to put them on an oath. 2. David was of more approved fidelity than any king nowadays, and to put him to a covenant seemed to call his fidelity in question; Jonathan sought an oath of David to deal kindly with his seed when he came to the throne; Jeremiah sought an oath of the king of Judah. Did they put any note of falsehood on them therefore?

Arnisaeus. You cannot prove that ever any king gave an oath to his subjects in Scripture.

Ans. 1. What more unbeseeming kings is it to swear to do their duty, than to promise covenant-wise to do the same? And a covenant you cannot deny. 2. In a covenant for religious duties there was always an oath (2 Chron. 15:12-14) hence the rite of cutting a calf, and swearing in a covenant (Jer. 34:18). 3. There is an oath that the people gives to the king to obey him (Eccles. 8:2) and a covenant (2 Sam. 5:1-3) mutual between the king and people; I leave it to the judicious, if the people swear to the king obedience in a covenant mutual, and he swear not to them.

Arnisaeus shows to us a third sort of oath that limited princes do swear. This oath in Denmark, Sweden, Poland, Hungary, is sworn by the kings, who may do nothing without consent of the senate, and according to order of law; this is but the other two oaths specified, and a prince cannot contravene his own contract; the law says, in that the prince is but as a private man (*in l. digna vox C. de ll. Rom. cons.* 426, n. 17); and it is known that the emperor is constituted and created by the prince's electors, subject to them, and by law may be dethroned by them.

The Bishop of Rochester says from Barclay, "None can deprive a king of his power, but he that gave him the power, or has an express commandment so to do, from him that gave the power. But God only, and the people, gave the king his power; therefore God, with the people, having an express commandment from God, must deprive the king of power" (*De potest*, 2.20).

Ans. 1. This shall prove that God only, by an immediate action, or some having an express commandment from him, can deprive a preacher for scandals; Christ only, or those who have an express commandment from him, can excommunicate; God only, or the magistrate with him, can take, away the life of man (Numb. 11:14-16); and no inferior magistrates, who also have their power from God immediately (Rom. 13:1) if we speak of the immediation of the office, can deprive inferior judges of their power. God only by the husbandman's pains makes a fruitful vineyard; therefore, the husbandman cannot make his vineyard grow over with nettles and briers.

2. The argument must run thus, else the assumption shall be false. God only by the action of the people as His instrument, and by no other action, makes a lawful king; God only by the action of the people, as His instrument, can make a king; God only by the action of the people, as His instrument, can dethrone a king; for as the people, making a king, are in that doing what God does before them, and what God does by them in that very act, so the people unmaking a king does that which God does before we people; both the one and the other according to God's rule obliges (Deut. 17:14-20).

The Prelate, whose tribe seldom says truth, adds, "As a fatherly power, by God and nature's law over a family was in the father of a family before the children could either transfer their power or consent to the translation of that power to him, so a kingly power (which succeeds to a paternal or fatherly power) to govern many families, yea, and a kingdom, was in that same father, in relation to many families, before these many families can transfer their power. The kingly power flows immediately from God, and the people does not transfer that power, but does only consent to the person of the king, or does only choose his person at some tune. And though this power was principally given to the people, it is not so given to the people as if it were the people's power, and not God's, for it is God's power; neither is it any otherwise given to the people but as to a stream, a beam, and an instrument which may confer it to another." M. Antonius does more subtly illustrate the matter: "If the king should confer honor on a subject, by the hand of a servant who had not power or freedom to confer that honor, or not to confer it, but by necessity of the king's commandment must confer it, nothing should hinder us to say that such a subject had his honor immediately from the king: so the earth is immediately illuminated by the sun, although light be received on the earth, but by the intervening mediation of many inferior bodies and elements, because by no other thing but by the sun only is the light as an efficient cause in a nearest capacity to give light; so the royal power in whomsoever it be is immediately from God only, though it be applied by men to this or that person, because from God only, and from no other the kingly power is formally and effectively that which it is, and works that which it works; and if you ask by what cause is the tree immediately turned into fire, none sound in reason would say, it is made fire, not by the fire, but by him that laid the tree on the fire" (*De domini.* 1.6.2, n. 22-23). John Popish Prelate would have stolen this argument also, if he had been capable of it.

Ans. 1. A fatherly power is in a father, not before he has a child, but indeed before his children by an act of their free-will consent that he be their father; yea, and whether the children consent or no, from a physical act of generation, he must be the father; and let the father be the most wicked man, and let him be made by no moral requisite, yet is he made a father, nor can he ever leave off physically to be a father: he may leave off morally to do the duty of a father, and so be *non pater officio* but he cannot but be *pater naturae generantis*

6. So there never is, nor can be, any need that children's free consent intervene to make Kish the father of Saul, because he is by nature a father. To make Saul a king and a moral father by analogy and improperly, a father by ruling, governing, guiding, defending Israel by good laws, in peace and godliness, I hope there is some act of the people's free-will required even by Spalato's way; the people must approve him to be king, yea, they must king him, or constitute him king, say we. No such act is required of natural sons to make a physical father, and so here is a great halt in the comparison, and it is most false that there is a kingly power to govern many families in the same father before these many families can transfer their power to make him king. Put royalists to their logic, they have not found out a medium to make good that there is a formal kingly power by which Saul is king and father morally over all Israel before Israel chose him and made him, as Kish was Saul's father formally, and had a fatherly power to be his father, before Saul had the use of free-will to consent that he should be his father. Royalists are here at a stand. The man may have royal gifts before the people make him king, but this is not *regia potestas*, a royal power, by which the man is formally king. Many have more royal gifts than the man that bears the crown, yet are never kings, nor is there formally *regia potestas*, kingly power, in them. In this meaning Petrarch said, *Plures sunt reges quam regna,*

2. He says, "The people does not confer royal power, but only consent to the person of the man, or choice of his person." This is nonsense, for the people's choosing of David at Hebron to be king, and their refusing of Saul's seed to be king, what was it but an act of God by the free suffrages of the people conferring royal power on David, and making him king? Whereas in former times, David even anointed by Samuel at Bethlehem (1 Sam. 16) was only a private man, the subject of king Saul, and never termed by the Spirit of God a king; nor was he king till God, by the people's consent made him king at Hebron; for Samuel neither honored him as king, nor bowed to him

as king, nor did the people say, God save king David; but after this David acknowledged Saul as his master and king. Let royalists show us any act of God making David king, save this act of the people making him formally king at Hebron, and therefore the people, as God's instrument, transferred the power, and God by them in the same act transferred the power, and in the same they chose the person; the royalists affirm these to be different actions, *affirmanti incumbit probatio.*

3. This power is the people's radically, naturally, as the bees (as some think) have a power natural to choose a king-bee, so has a community a power naturally to defend and protect themselves; and God has revealed in Deut. 17:14-15 the way of regulating the act of choosing governors and kings, which is a special means of defending and protecting themselves; and the people is as principally the subject and fountain of royal power as a fountain is of water. I shall not contend, if you call a fountain God's instrument to give water, as all creatures are his instruments.

4. For Spalato's comparison, he is far out: for the people choosing one of ten to be their king have free will to choose any, and are under a law (Deut. 17:14-15) in the manner of their choosing, and though they err and make a sinful choice, yet the man is king, and God's king, whom they make king; but if the king command a servant to make A. B. a knight, if the servant make C. D. a knight, I shall not think C. D. is a valid knight at all; and indeed the honor is immediately here from the king, because the king's servant by no innate power makes the knight, but nations makes this man a king, not that man; and I conceive the man chosen by the people owes thanks and grateful service to the people, who rejected others, that they had power to choose, and made him king.

5. The light immediately and formally is light from the sun, and so is the office of a King immediately instituted of God (Deut. 17: 14). Whether the institution be natural or positive, it is no matter. 2. The man is not king, because of royal endowment, though we should

say these were immediately from God, to which instruction and education may also confer not a little; but he is formally king, *ratione* εξουσιας βασιλικης in regard of the formal essence of a king, not immediately from God, as the light is from the sun, but by the mediation of the free consent of the people (2 Sam. 5:1-3); nor is the people in making a king as the man who only casts wood in the fire; the wood is not made fire formally, but by the fire, not by the approach of fire to wood, or of wood to fire; for the people do not apply the royalty which is immediately in and from God to the person. Explicate such an application; for to me it is a fiction inconceivable, because the people has the royalty radically in themselves, as in the fountain and cause, and confers it on the man who is made king; yea, the people, by making David king confer the royal power on the king. This is so true that royalists, forgetting themselves, inculcate frequently in asserting their absolute monarch from Ulpian, but misunderstood that the people have resigned all their power, liberty, right of life, death, goods, chastity, a potency of rapine, homicides, unjust wars, &c., upon a creature called an absolute prince; even, says Grotius, as a man may make himself a slave, by selling his liberty to a master. Now if the people make away this power to the king, and this be nothing but the transcendent absoluteness of a king, certainly this power was in the people; for how can they give to a king that which they have not themselves? As a man cannot make away his liberty to a master by becoming a slave to him, if his liberty were immediately in God, as royalists say, sovereignty is immediately in God, and people can exercise no act about sovereignty, to make it over to one man rather than to another. People only have an after-approbation, that this man to whom God has given it immediately shall have it. Furthermore, they say, people in making a king may make such conditions as in seven cases a king may be dethroned, at least resisted, says Hugo Grotius: therefore people may give more or less, half or whole, limited or absolute royal power to the prince; but if this power were immediately in

God and from God, how could the people have the husbanding of it, at their need to expend it out in ounce weights, or pound weights, as they please? And that the people may be purveyors of it to sell or give it is taught by Grotius (*de jur. bel et pac.* 1.1.4); Barclay (*advers, monarch,* 1.4.6); Arnisaeus (section 6, *de majest. an princeps qui jurat subditis, &c.* n. 10, *n. se Aventium Anal. l.* 3); Chytreus (1.23, 28); Saxon Sleidan (book 1, *in fi*); yet Arnisaeus is not ashamed to cite Aristotle (*Polit.* 1.3) that he is not a true and absolute king who rules by laws, the point blank contrary of what Aristotle says.

QUESTION 41.

WHETHER THE POPISH PRELATE WITH REASON ASCRIBES TO US DOCTRINE OF JESUITS IN THE QUESTIONS OF LAWFUL DEFENSE.

That sovereignty is originally and radically in the people, as in the fountain, was taught by fathers, ancient doctors, sound divines, lawyers, before there was a Jesuit or a prelate whelped, in rerum natura. The Popish Prelate holds the Pope to be the vicar of Christ. Jesuits' tenets concerning kings are considered. The king is not the people's deputy by our doctrine; it is only the calumny of the Popish Prelate. The Popish Prelate will have power to act the bloodiest tyrannies on earth upon the church of Christ, the essential power of a king.

The Popish Prelate, without all ground, will have us all Jesuits in this point, but if we make good that this truth was in Scripture before a Jesuit was in the earth, he falls from his cause.

Popish Prelate: The Begardi says there was no government, no law given to the just. It fears me this age fancies to itself some such thing, and have learned of Korah, Dathan, &c. (section 1).

Ans. This calumniator, in the next words, belies himself when he says, we presuppose that those with whom we are to enter in lists do willingly grant that government is not only lawful and just, but necessary both for church and commonwealth: then we fancy no such thing as he imputes to us.

Popish Prelate. Some said that the right of dominion is founded on grace, whether the Waldensians and Huss held any such tenet, I cannot now insist to prove or disprove. Gerson and others held that there must be a new title and right to what men possess. Too many too confidently hold these or the like.

Ans. 1. That dominion is founded upon grace as its essential pillar, so as wicked men be no magistrates, because they are in mortal sin, was falsely imputed to ancient protestants, the Waldensians, Wycliff, and Huss, by papists; and this day by Jesuits, Suarez, Bellarmine, Becanus. The Popish Prelate will leave them under this calumny, that he may offend papists and Jesuits as little as he can, but he would lay it on us; but if the Popish Prelate think that dominion is not founded on grace, *de jure*, that rulers should have that spirit that God put on the seventy elders for their calling, and that they ought not to be "men fearing God and hating covetousness," as Grerson and others did, he belies the Scripture.

2. It is no error of Gerson that believers have a spiritual right to their civil possessions, but by Scripture (1 Cor. 4:21; Rev. 21:7).

Popish Prelate. The Jesuits are ashamed of the error of casuists, who hold that, *directum Imperium*, the direct and primary power, supreme, civil, and ecclesiastical, is in the Pope; and, therefore they give an indirect directive and coercive power to him over kings and states, *in ordine ad spiritualia,* so may he king and unking princes at his pleasure. Our presbyterians, if they run not fully this way, are very near to it.

Ans. 1. The windy man would seem versed in schoolmen. He should have named some casuists who hold any like thing.

2. The presbyterians must be popes, because they subject kings to the gospel, and Christ's scepter in church censures, and think Christian kings may be rebuked for blasphemy, bloodshed, &c., whereas prelates, *in ordine ad diabolica,* murder souls of kings.

3. Prelates do king princes. A popish archprelate, when our king was crowned, put the crown on king Charles' head, the sword and scepter in his hand, anointed him in his hands, crown, shoulders, arms, with sacred oil. The king must kiss the archbishop and bishops. Is not this to king princes *in ordine ad spiritualia?* And those that kings may unking, and judge what relation the popish archbishop Spotswood had when he proffered to the king the oath that the popish kings swears to maintain the professed religion (not one word of the true protestant religion) and will carefully root out all heretics and enemies (that is protestants as they exposit it) to the true worship of God, that shall be convicted by the church of God of the foresaid crimes. And when the prelates professed they held not their prelacies of the king, but of the Pope indeed, who are then nearest to the Pope's power, *in ordine ad spirititalia?*

4. How will this black-mouthed calumniator make presbyterians to dethrone kings? He has written a pamphlet of the inconsistency of monarchy and presbyterian government, consisting of lies, invented calumnies of his church in which he was baptized. But the truth is all his arguments prove the inconsistency of monarchs and parliaments, and transform

any king into a most absolute tyrant; for which treason he deserves to suffer as a traitor.

Popish Prelate. The puritan says that all power civil is radically and originally seated in the community; he here joins hands with the Jesuit (q. 1, section 1).

Ans. In six pages he repeats the same things, 1. Is this such a heresy that a colony cast into America by the tyranny of popish prelates, has power to choose their own government? All Israel was heretical in this; for David could not be their king, though designated and anointed by God (1 Sam. 16) till the people (2 Sam. 5) put forth in act this power, and made David king in Hebron.

2. Let the Prelate make a syllogism, it is but *ex utraque affirmante in secunda figura*, logic like the bellies of the court, in which men of their own way is disgraced and cast out of grace and court; because in this controversy of the king with his two parliaments, they are like Erasmus in God's matters, who said, *Lutherum nec accuso nec defendo.* He is discourted, whoever he be, who is in shape like a puritan, and not fire and sword against religion and his country, and oath and covenant with God; and so it is this: The Jesuit teaches that power of government is in the community originally. The puritan teaches that power of government is in the community originally; therefore, the puritan is a Jesuit. But so the puritan is a Jesuit, because he and the Jesuit teaches that there is one God and three persons. And if the Prelate like this reasoning, we shall make himself and the prelates, and court-divines, Jesuits upon surer grounds.

1. Jesuits teach (1) The Pope is not the antichrist; (2) Christ locally descended to hell to free some out of that prison; (3) It was sin to separate from Babylonish Home; (4) We are justified by works; (6) The merit of fasting is not to be condemned;

(6) The mass is no idolatry; (7) The Church is the judge of controversies; (8) All the Arminian points are safer to be believed than the contrary; yea, and all the substantials of popery are true, and catholic doctrine to be preached and printed.

2. The prelates and court-divines, and this Prelate, conspires in all these with the Jesuits, as is learnedly and invincibly proved in the treatise, called αυτοκαταχρισις, the Canterburian self-conviction; to which no man of the prelatical and Romish faction dared ever make answer for their hearts; and see then who are Jesuits.

3. This doctrine was taught by lawyers, protestants, yielded to by papists, before any Jesuit was whelped *in rerum natura*, Never learned man wrote of policy, till of late, but he held power of government by the light of nature must be radically and originally in a community. The Popish Prelate says Jesuits are not the fathers of this opinion (section 1). How then can the liar say, that the puritan conspires with the Jesuit? Suarez, the Jesuit *Non est novum, aut a Cardinali Bellarmino inventum* (*De primat. sum. pontifi.* 1.3.2, n. 10). The Jesuit Tannerus, will not have their family the mother of this opinion *Sine dubio communis omnium Theologorum et Jurisperitorum sententia, &c.*[1] The Jesuit Tolet (in Rom. 13) takes it for a ground, that the civil powers are from God, by the natural mediation of men, and civil societies.

4. Jesuits teach that there is no lawful Christian society, truly political that has a near and formal power to choose and ordain their own magistrates, but that which acknowledges subjection, and the due regulation of their creating of magistrates, to be due and proper to the Pope of Rome. We acknowledge in no way the bishop of Rome for a lawful bishop

---

1. Tom 2, disp. 5, de leg, q. 5, in 12, q. 95, 96; Dubi. 1, n. 7

and pastor at all. But this popish Prelate does acknowledge him, for he has these words: "It is high presumption in the Pope to challenge to himself the title or right of Christ's universal vicar on earth, by divine right. The Pope, the bishop of Rome, has no more by divine right (what he may have by positive ecclesiastical right is not pertinent for us now to examine and discuss) no higher privilege (unless it be in extent) than the meanest bishop of the world in his diocese" (section 6). And among all proofs, he passing by Scriptures, which should prove or improve a divine right, he will content himself with one proof of Cyprian and ends with these words, "Would God, both sides in this, and other controversies, would submit to the judgment of the holy fathers" (*de unitat. Eccles*).

1. Thus the Popish Prelate, in his fourth article (the other two I shall touch anon) makes puritans grosser than Jesuits, in dethroning kings; because if the king be deficient, the people may resume their power, and govern for him, and so dethrone the king. But Bellarmine holds the people cannot dethrone the king, but, *in certis casibus*, in some cases, that is (as Suarez says) *si Rex sua potestate in manifestam (Civatatis ceu Regni) perniciem abutatur* (*l.* 3, *q. de laic*). But I will demonstrate that if papists hold that the Pope may dethrone kings, this Prelate is of their mind; for, 1. The words I cited make good that he is for the Pope's supremacy; now it is a joint or part of his supremacy, to king and unking princes; 2. They make good that he is a papist; for, 1. It is presumption in the Pope to challenge to himself that he is Christ's universal vicar on earth, by divine right. Why says he not, by no right at all, but only he is not Christ's vicar by divine right? For it is evident that papists make him Christ's vicar only by ecclesiastical right; for they profess succession of popes to this day cannot be proved but by tradition, not by Scripture.

2. The Pope's supremacy, by papists, is expressly reckoned among unwritten traditions, and so there is no necessity that the right of it be proved from Scripture.

3. The Prelate expressly says, "He will not discuss the ecclesiastical right that the Pope has to be Christ's vicar;" and by that he clearly insinuates that he has a right to be Christ's vicar, besides a scriptural and divine right; only, for offending papists, he will not discuss it.

4. He has no higher privilege, says he, than other bishops, except in extent, by divine right. Now other bishops, as officers, in nature different from presbyters (for of such the Popish Prelate must speak in his own dialect) have their office by divine right; and this the Prelate's word must include, else he says nonsense to the matter in hand. And in extent the Pope has by divine right more than other bishops have. Now what is the Pope of Rome's extent? All know it is the whole catholic visible church on earth. If then all bishops be particular ambassadors in Christ's stead (2 Cor. 5:20) and so legates and deputies of Christ, he who by divine right is a bishop in extent over the whole world is as like one that calls himself the universal vicar of Christ as one egg is like another. The doctrine taught by this Prelate, so popish, and hints, yea, are more than evidences, of gross popery in this book, and his other pamphlet against presbyteries. And his desire that the controversy, concerning the Pope's supremacy and others, might be determined with submission to the judgment of the fathers, do cry that he is but a rotten papist. For why will he submit all other controversies to the judgment of the fathers? Why not to the prophets and apostles? Can fathers decide controversies better than the Word of God? A reason cannot be dreamed of why the fathers should be judges, and not the Scriptures, except that the Scriptures are obscure. Their authority and

light cannot determine and judge controversies, except insofar as they have authority from fathers and the church; and we know this to be *proprium quarto modo*, proper to Jesuits and papists, to cry, Fathers, fathers, in all controversies, though the fathers be more for us than for them, except two things: 1. What fathers speak for us, are corrupted by them. 2. What were but errors in fathers, when children add contumacy to error, becomes the heresies of the sons.

And it is most false that we join with Jesuits. 1. We teach no more against tyrants, *in exercitio*, than Grotius, Barclay, and Winzetus, in the matter of deposing kings; and in this, royalists conspire with Jesuits.

2. We deny that the Pope may loose subjects from the oath of fidelity when a king turns heretical.

3. That people, at the Pope's commandment, are to dethrone kings for heresy; so do the prelates, and their fellows, the papists, teach; so Gregory VII, practiced; so Aquinas taught (22 q. 12. ar. 2). Antonin (*sum. par.* 3.1.22.3, sect. 7) "you have put all things under the Pope's feet," *oves, id est, Christianos; boves. Judaeos et hereticos; pecora, Paganos;* so Navar (1.1.13) Pagans have no jurisdiction. Jaco. Symanca (*De Catho. Instit. tit.* 45, n. 25) "*Catholica uxor heretico viro debitum reddere non tenetur.*" *Item, Constat. haereticum privatum esse omni do minio naturali civili, politico, naturali quod habet in filios, nam propter haeresin patris efficiuntur filii sui juris, civili, quod habet in servos, ab eo enim servi liberantur, politico, quod rerum domini habent in subditos, ita Bannes* (22. q. 12, art. 10). Gregory (*de valent.* 22. dis. 1, q. 12, lod, Mol. to. 1, *de just. et jur. tract.* 2, dis. 29, 5.3). Papists hold that *generatio clerici est corruptio subditi,* churchmen are not subjects under the king's law. It is a canonical privilege of the clergy that they are not subject to the king's civil laws. Now this Prelate and his follows made the king

swear, at his coronation, to maintain all canonical privileges of the prelatical clergy, the very oath and words sworn by all the popish kings.

Popish Prelate. Power is given by the multitude to the king immediately, and by God mediately, not so much by collation, as by approbation; how the Jesuit and puritan walk all along in equal pace. See Bellarmine, 1.1, *de liac.* section 6. Suarez *Cont. sect. Angl.* 1.2.3.

Ans. It is a calumny that we teach that the power of the king is from God mediately, by mere approbation; indeed, a fellow of his, a papist, writing against the king's supremacy, Anthony Capel, says Saul was made king, and others also, by God's permission,[1] and *Deo invito et irato*, God being angry, that is not our doctrine; but with what real efficiency God has made men and communities rational and social men with the same has he made them by instinct of nature, by the mediation of reason, to create a king; and Bellarmine and Suarez say not God makes kings by approbation only.

Popish Prelate. The people may change monarchy into aristocracy or democracy, or aristocracy into monarchy; for all I know, they differ not in this neither.

Ans. 1. The Popish Prelate knows not all things: the two Jesuits, Bellarmine and Suarez are produced only, as if they were all Jesuits; and Suarez says (*De prim, po.* 1. 3, *n.* 4) *"Donationem absolutam semel validefactam revocari non posse, neque in totum, neque ex parce, maxime quando onerosa fuit,"* If the people once give their power to the king, they cannot resume it without cause; and laying down the grounds of Suarez and other Jesuits that our religion is heresy, they do soundly collect this consequence: that no king can be lord of the consciences of

---

1. *Tract, contra primatum Regis Angliae.*

their subjects, to compel them to an heretical religion." We teach that the king of Spain has no power over the consciences of protestant subjects to force them to idolatry, and that their souls are not his subjects, but only their persons, and in the Lord.

2. It is no great crime that if a king degenerate in a tyranny, or if the royal line fail, that we think the people have liberty to change monarchy into aristocracy, *aut contra*, Jesuits deny that the people can make this change without the rope's consent. We judge neither the great bishop, the Pope, nor the little popes, ought to have hand in making kings.

Popish Prelate. They say the power is derived to the king from the people, *comulative or communicative, non privative,* by way of communication, not by way of privation, so as the people deprive not themselves of this sovereignty. As the king makes a lieutenant in Ireland, not to deprive himself of his royal power, but to put him in trust for his service. If this be their mind, the king is in a poor case. The principal authority is in the delegate, and so the people is still judge, and the king their deputy.

Ans. The Popish Prelate takes on him to write, he knows not what; this is not our opinion. The king is king, and has the people's power, not as their deputy.

1. Because the people is not principal judge, and the king subordinate. The king, in the executive power of laws, is reality a sovereign above the people; a deputy is not so.

2. The people have irrevocably made over to the king their power of governing, defending, and protecting themselves, I exclude the power of self-preservation, which people can no more make away, it being sinless nature's birthright, than the liberty of eating, drinking, sleeping; and this the people cannot resume, except in case of the king's tyranny; there is no

power by the king so irrevocably resigned to his servant or deputy, but he may use it himself.

3. A delegate is accountable for all he does to those that put him in trust, whether he do ill or well. The king, in acts of justice, is not accountable to any; for if his acts be not liable to high suspicions of tyranny, no man may say to him, what do you? Only in acts of injustice; and those so tyrannical, that they be inconsistent with the habitual fiduciary repose and trust put on him, he is to render accounts to the parliament, which represents the people.

4. A delegate *in esse, in fieri,* both that he may be a delegate, and that he may continue a delegate, whether he do ill or well, depends on his pleasure who delegates him; but though a king depend *in fieri,* in regard of his call to the crown, upon the suffrages of his people, yet that he may be continued king, he depends not on the people simply, but only in case of tyrannical administration, and in this sense Suarez and Bellarmine spoke with no more honesty than we do, but with more than prelates do, for they profess any emissary of hell may stab a protestant king. We know the prelates profess the contrary, but their judgment is the same with Jesuits in all points; and since they will have the Pope Christ's vicar, by such a divine right as they themselves are bishops, and have the king under oath to maintain the clergy, bishops, and all their canonical privileges (amongst which the bishops of Rome's indirect power *in ordine ad spiritualia,* and to dethrone kings who turn heretics, is one principal right) I see not how prelates are not as deep in treason against kings as the Pope himself, and therefore, Popish Prelate, take the beam out of your own eye.

The Popish Prelate takes unlearned pains to prove that Gerson, Occam, Jac. de Almaine, and the Parisian doctors, maintained these same grounds anent the people's power over

kings in the case of tyranny, and that before Luther and Calvin were in the world; and this is to give himself the lie, that
Luther, Calvin, and we, have not this doctrine from Jesuits;
and what is Calvin's mind is evident (*Instit.* 1.4.4): all that
the estates may coerce and reduce in order a tyrant, otherwise they are deficient in their trust that God has given them
over the commonwealth and church; and this is the doctrine
for which royalists cry out against Knox of blessed memory,
Buchanan, Junius Brutus, Bouchier, Rossaeus, and Althusius.
Luther, *in scripto ad pastorem* (tom. 7, German, fol. 386) brings
two examples for resistance: the people resisted Saul when he
was willing to kill Jonathan his son, and Ahikam and other princes rescued Jeremiah out of the hands of the king of
Judah; and Gerardus cites many divines who second Luther
in this, as Bugenliagius, Justus Jonas, Nicholas Ambsderffius,
George Spalatinus, Justus Menius, Christopher Hofmanus.
It is known what is the mind of protestant divines, as Beza,
Parous, Melanchthon, Bucanus, Polanus, Chamer, and all the
divines of France, of Germany, and of Holland. No wonder
than prelates were upon the plot of betraying the city of Rochelle, and of the protestant church there, when they then will
have the protestants of France, for their defensive wars, to be
rebels, and siders with Jesuits, when, in these wars, Jesuits
sought their blood and ruin.

The Popish Prelate having shown his mind concerning the
deposing of Childerick by the Pope (of which I say nothing,
but the Pope was an antichristian usurper, and the poor man
never fit to bear a crown) he goes on to set down an opinion of some mute authors; he might devise a thousand opinions that way to make men believe he had been in a world of
learned men's secrets, and that never man saw the bottom of
the controversy while he, seeing the escapes of many pens (as

supercilious Bubo praises) was forced to appear a stair new risen in the firmament of pursuivants, and reveal all dreams, and teach all the new statists, the Gamaliels, Buchanan, Junius Brutus, and a world who were all sleeping, while this Lucifer, the son of the night, did appear, this new way of laws, divinity, and casuists' theology.

Popish Prelate. They hold sovereign power is primarily and naturally in the multitude, from it derived to the king, immediately from God. The reason of which order is because we cannot reap the fruits of government unless by compact we submit to some possible and accidental inconveniences.

Ans. 1. Who says so the Popish Prelate cannot name, that sovereign power is primarily and naturally in the multitude. Virtually (it may be) sovereignty is in the multitude, but primarily and naturally, as heat is in the fire, light in the sun, I think the Popish Prelate dreamed it; no man said it but himself; for what attribute is naturally in a subject, I conceive may directly and naturally be predicated of it. Now the Popish Prelate has taught us this very natural predication: "Our dreadful and sovereign lord, the multitude, commands this and that."

2. This is no more reason for a monarchy than for a democracy, for we can reap the fruits of no government except we submit to it.

3. We must submit in monarchy (says he) to some possible and accidental inconveniences. Here be soft words, but is subversion of religion, laws, and liberties of church and state. Introducing of popery, Arminianism, of idolatry, altar-worship, the mass (proved by a learned treatise, "the Canterburian self-conviction," printed 1641, third ed., never answered, couched under the name of inconveniency) the pardoning of the innocent blood of hundreds of thousand protestants in

Ireland, the killing of many thousand nobles, barons, commons, by the hands of papists in arms against the law of the land, the making of England a field of blood, the obtruding of an idolatrous service-book, with armies of men, by sea and land, to block up the kingdom of Scotland, are all these inconveniences only?

4. Are they only possible and accidental? But make a monarch absolute, as the Popish Prelate does, and tyranny is as necessary and as much intended by a sinful man, inclined to make a god of himself, as it is natural to men to sin, when they are tempted, and to be drunken and giddy with honor and greatness. Witness the kings of Israel and Judah, though *de jure* they were not absolute. Is it accidental to Nero, Julian, to the ten horns that grew out of the woman's head, who sat upon the scarlet colored beast, to make war against the Lamb and his followers, especially the spirit of Satan being in them?

Popish Prelate. They infer, 1. They cannot, without violation of a divine ordinance and breach of faith, resume the authority they have placed in the king. 2. It were high sin to rob authority of its essentials. 3. This ordinance is not αλογος but ευδοκια and has urgent reasons.

Ans. 1. These nameless authors cannot infer that an oath is broken which is made conditionally; all authority given by the people to the king is condition, that he use it for the safety of the people; if it be used for their destruction, they break no faith to resume it, for they never made faith to give up their power to the king upon such terms, and so they cannot be said to resume what they never gave.

2. So the Popish Prelate makes power to act all the former mischiefs, the essentials of a king. Balaam is not worthy his wages for prophesying thus, that the king's essentials is a power of blood, and destructive to people, law, religion, and

liberties of church and state, for otherwise we teach not, that people may resume from the king authority and power to disarm papists, to root out the bloody Irish, and in justice serve them as they have served us.

3. This ordinance of the people, giving lawful power to a king for the governing of the people in peace and godliness is God's good pleasure, and has just reasons and causes. But that the people make over a power to one man, to act all the inconveniences above named, I mean the bloody and destructive inconveniences, has nothing of God or reason in it.

Popish Prelate. The reasons of this opinion are: 1. If power sovereign were not in one, he could not have strength enough to act all necessary parts and acts of government. 2. Nor to prevent divisions which attend multitudes, or many endowed with equal power; and the authors say they must part with their native right entirely for a greater good, and to prevent greater evils. 3. To resume any part of this power, of which the people have totally divested themselves, or to limit it, is to disable sovereignty from government, loose the sinews of all society, &c.

Ans. 1. I know none for this opinion, but the Popish Prelate himself. The first reason may be made rhyme, but never reason: for though there be not absolute power to good and evil, there may be strength of limited power in abundance in the king, and sufficient for all acts of just government, and the adequate end of government, which is, *salus populi*, the safety of the people. But the royalist will have strength to be a tyrant, and act all the tyrannical and bloody inconveniences of which we spoke, an essential part of the power of a king; as if weakness were essential to strength, and a king could not be powerful as a king to do good, and save and protect, unless he had power also as a tyrant to do evil, and to destroy and waste his people. This power is weakness, and no part of the image of the greatness of the King of kings, whom a king represents.

2. The second reason condemns democracy and aristocracy as unlawful, and makes monarchy the only medicine to cure these; as if there were no government an ordinance of God save only absolute monarchy, which indeed is no ordinance of God at all, but contrary to the nature of a lawful king (Deut. 17:3).

3. That people must part with their native right totally to make an absolute monarch is as if the whole members of the body would part with their whole nutritive power, to cause the milt to swell, which would be the destruction of the body.

4. The people cannot divest themselves of power of defensive wars more than they can part with nature, and put themselves in a condition inferior to a slave, who, if his master, who has power to sell him, invade him unjustly, to take away his life, may oppose violence to unjust violence. And the other consequences are null.

QUESTION 42.

WHETHER ALL CHRISTIAN KINGS ARE DEPENDENT FROM CHRIST, AND MAY BE CALLED HIS VICEREGENTS.

Why God as God has a man as vicegerent under him, but not as mediator. The king is not head of the church. The king is a sub-mediator, and an under-redeemer, and a sub-priest to offer sacrifices to God for us if he be a vicegerent. The king is no mixed person. Prelates deny kings to be subject to the gospel. By no prerogative royal may the king prescribe religious observances and human ceremonies in God's worship. The Popish Prelate gives to the king a power arbitrary, supreme, and independent, to govern the church. Reciprocation of subjections of the king to the church, and of the church to the king, in various kinds, namely, of ecclesiastical and civil subjection, are no more absurd than for Aaron's priest to teach, instruct, and rebuke Moses, if he turn a tyrannical Ahab, and Moses to punish Aaron if he turn an obstinate idolater.

The Popish Prelate takes on him to prove the truth of this; but the question is not pertinent: it belongs to another head, to the king's power in church matters. I therefore only examine what he says, and follow him.

Popish Prelate. Sectaries have found a query of late that kings are God's, not Christ's lieutenants on earth. Romanists and puritans erect two sovereigns in every state, the Jesuit in the Pope, the puritan in the presbytery.

Ans. 1. We give a reason why God has a lieutenant, as God; because kings are gods, bearing the sword of vengeance against seditious and bloody prelates, and other evil doers. But Christ, God-man, the Mediator and head of the body, the church, has neither pope nor king to be head under him. The sword is communicable to men; but the headship of Christ is communicable to no king, nor to any created shoulders.

2. The Jesuit makes the Pope a king; and so this Popish Prelate makes him, in extent, the bishop of bishops, and so king, as I have proved. But we place no sovereignty in presbyteries, but a mere ministerial power of servants, who do not take on them to make laws and religious ceremonies, as prelates do, who indeed make themselves kings and lawgivers in God's house.

Popish Prelate. We speak of Christ as head of the church. Some think that Christ was king by his resurrection, *jure acquisito*, by a new title, right of merit. I think he was a king from his conception.

Ans. 1. You declare hereby that the king is a ministerial head of the church, under the head Christ. All our divines, disputing against the Pope's headship, say no mortal man has shoulders for so glorious a head. You give the king such shoulders. But why are not the kings, even Nero, Julian, Nebuchadnezzar, and Belshazzar, vicegerents of Christ, as mediator, as priest, as redeemer, as prophet, as advocate, presenting our prayers to God his father? What action, I pray you, have Christian kings, by office, under Christ, in dying and rising from the dead for us, in sending down the Holy Ghost, preparing mansions for us? Now, it is as proper and incommunicably reciprocal with the mediator to be the only head of the body, the church (Col. 1:18) as to be the only redeemer and advocate of his church.

2. That Christ was king from his conception, as man born of the virgin Mary, suits well with papists, who will have Christ, as man, the visible head of the church; that so as Christ-man is now in heaven, he may have a visible pope to be head in all ecclesiastical matters. And that is the reason why this Popish Prelate makes him head of the church by an ecclesiastical right, as we heard; and so he follows Becanus the Jesuit in this, and others of his fellows.

Popish Prelate. 1. Proof. If kings reign by בי per, in and through Christ, as the wisdom of God and the mediator, then are kings the vicegerents of Christ as mediator; but the former is said (Prov. 8:15-16); so Dr. Andrews, of blessed memory.

Ans. 1. I deny the major. All believers living the life of God, engrafted in Christ as branches in the tree (John 15:1-2) should, by the same reason, be vicegerents of the Mediator; so should the angels to whom Christ is a head (Col. 2:10) be his vicegerents; and all the judges and constables on earth should be under-mediators, for they live and act in Christ; yea, all the creatures in the Mediator are made new (Rev. 21:6; Rom. 8:20-22). 2. Dr. Andrew's name is a curse on the earth, his writings prove him to be a popish apostate.

Popish Prelate. 2. Christ is not only king of his church, but in order to his church, King over the kings and kingdoms of the earth (Ps. 2:5, 8). 3. Matt. 21:18, "To him is given all power in heaven and earth;" therefore, all sovereignty over kings.

Ans. 1. If all these be Christ's vicegerents, over whom He has obtained power, then, because the Father has given Him power over all flesh, to give them life eternal (John 17:1-2) then are all believers his vicegerents, yea, and all the damned men and devils, and death and hell, are His vicegerents; for Christ, as mediator, has all power given to Him as king of the church, and so power kingly over all His enemies, "to reign until He make them His foot-stool," (Ps. 110:1-2) "to break them with a rod of iron" (Ps. 2:9; 1 Cor. 15:24-27; Rev. 1:18, 20; 5:10-15). And by that same reason the Popish Prelate's fourth and fifth arguments fall to the ground. He is heir of all things; therefore, all things are His vicegerents. What more vain? He is Prince of the kings of the earth, and King of Ogs, of kings, of his enemies; therefore, sea and land are His vicegerents.

Popish Prelate: Kings are nurse-fathers of the church, therefore they hold their crowns of Christ. Divines say that by men in sacred orders Christ does rule His church mediately in those things which primely concern salvation, and that by kings' scepters and power He does protect his church, and what concerns external pomp, order, and decency. Then, in this latter sense, kings are no less the immediate vicegerents of Christ than bishops, priests, and deacons, in the former.

Ans. 1. Because kings hold their crowns of Christ as mediator and redeemer, it follows, by as good consequence, kings are sub-mediators, and under-priests, and redeemers, as vicegerents. Christ, as king, has no visible royal vicegerents under him.

2. Men in holy orders, sprinkled with one of the papists' five blessed sacraments such as antichristian prelates, unwashed priests to offer sacrifices, and popish deacons, are no more admitted by Christ to enter into His sanctuary as governors, than the leper into the camp of old, and the Moabite and Ammonite were to enter into the congregation of the Lord (Deut. 23:3); therefore, we have excommunicated this Popish Prelate and such Moabites out of the Lord's house. What be

the things that do not primely concern salvation, the Popish Prelate knows, namely, images in the church, altar-worship, antichristian ceremonies, which primely concern damnation.

3. I understand not what the Popish Prelate means. That the king preserves external government in order and decency. In Scotland, in our parliament, 1633, he prescribed the surplice, and he commanded the service-book, and the mass-worship. The Prelate degrades the king here, to make him only keep or preserve the prelates' mass-clothes; they intended, indeed, to make the king but the Pope's servant, for all they say and do for him now.

4. If the king be vicegerent of Christ in prescribing laws for the external ordering of the worship, and all their decent symbolical ceremonies, what more does the Pope and the prelate in that kind? He may, with as good warrant, preach and administer the sacraments.

Popish Prelate. Kings have the sign of the cross on their crowns.

Ans. Therefore, *baculus est in angulo*, prelates have put a cross in the king's heart, and crossed crown and throne too. Some knights, some ships, some cities and boroughs do carry a cross; are they made Christ's vicegerents of late? By what antiquity does the cross signify Christ? Of old it was a badge of Christians, no religious ceremony. And is this all? The king is the vicegerent of Christians. The prelates, we know, adore the cross with religious worship; so must they adore the crown.

Popish Prelate. Grant that the Pope is the vicar of Christ in spiritual things, it follows not, therefore, kings' crowns are subject to the Pope; for papists teach that all power that was in Christ, as man, as power to work miracles, to institute sacraments, was not transmitted to Peter and his successors.

Ans. This is a base consequence; make the Pope head of the church, the king, if he be a mixed person, that is, half a churchman and Christ's vicegerent, both He and prelates must be members of the head. Papists teach that all in Christ, as man, cannot be transmitted to Peter; but a ministerial catholic headship (say Bucanus and his fellows) was transmitted from Christ, as man and visible head, to Peter and the Pope.

Popish Prelate, I wish the Pope, who claims so near alliance with Christ, would learn of Him to be meek and humble in heart, so should he find rest to his own soul, to church and state.

Ans. 1. The same was the wish of Gerson, Occam, the doctors of Paris, the fathers of the councils of Constance and Basil yet all make him head of the church.

2. The excommunicate Prelate is turned chaplain to preach to the Pope; the soul-rest that protestants wish to the Pope is, "That the Lord would destroy him by the Spirit of his month" (2 Thess. 2:8). But to popish prelates this wish is a reformation of accidents, with the safety of the subject, the Pope, and is as good as a wish that the devil, remaining a devil, may find rest for his soul: all we are to pray for as having place in the church are supposed members of the church. The Prelate would not pray so for the presbytery by which he was ordained a pastor (1 Tim. 4:14) though he be now an apostate; it is gratitude to pray for his lucky father, the Pope. Whatever the Prelate wish, we pray for and believe that desolation shall be his soul-rest, and that the vengeance of the Lord and of His temple shall fall upon him and the prelates, his sons.

Popish Prelate. That which they purpose, by denying kings to be Christ's vicegerents is to set up a sovereignty ecclesiastical in presbyteries, to constrain kings, repeal his laws, correct his statutes, reverse his judgments, to cite, convent, and censure kings; and, if there be not power to execute what presbyteries decide, they may call and command the help of the people, in whom is the underived majesty and promise, and swear and covenant to defend their fancies against all mortal men, with their goods, lands, fortunes, to admit no decisive motion; and this sovereign association makes every private man an armed magistrate.

Ans. You see the excommunicate apostate strives against the presbytery of a reformed church, from which he had his baptism, faith, and ministry.

1. We deny the king to be the head of the church.

2. We assert, that in the pastors, doctors, and elders of the church, there is a ministerial power, as servants under Christ, in His authority and name to rebuke and censure kings; that there is revenge in the gospel against all disobedience (2 Cor. 2:6; 10:6); the rod of God (1 Cor. 4:21); the rod of Christ's lips (Isa. 11:4); the scepter and sword of Christ (Rev. 1:16; 19:15); the keys of his kingdom, to bind and loose, open and shut (Matt, 18:17-18; 16:19; 1 Cor. 5:1-3; 2 Thess. 3:14-15; 1 Tim. 1:19; 5:22; 5:17); and that this power is committed to the officers of Christ's house, call them as you will.

3. For reversing of laws made for the establishing of popery, we think the church of Christ did well to declare all these unjust, grievous decrees, and that woe is due to the judges, even the queen, if they should not repent (Isa. 10:1). And this Prelate must show his teeth in this against our reformation in Scotland, which he once commended in pulpit as a glorious work of God's right arm; and the Assembly of Glasgow, 1638, declared, that bishops, though established by acts of parliament, procured by prelates only, commissioners and agents for the churchy who betrayed their trust, were unlawful; and did supplicate that the ensuing parliament would annul these wicked acts. They think God privileges neither king nor others from church-censures. The popish prelates imprisoned and silenced the ministers of Christ, who preached against the public sins, the blood, oppressions, injustice, open swearing,

and blasphemy of the holy name of God, the countenancing of idolaters, &c, in king and court.

4. They never sought the help of the people against the most unjust standing law of authority.

5.. They did never swear and covenant to defend their own fancies; for the confession and covenant of the protestant religion, translated in Latin to all the protestants in Europe and America, being termed a fancy, is a clear evidence that this Popish Prelate was justly excommunicated for popery.

6. This covenant was sworn by king James and his house, by the whole land, by the prelates themselves; and to this fancy this Popish Prelate, by the law of our land, was obliged to swear when he received degrees in the university.

7. There is reason our covenant should provide against divisive motions. The prelates moved the king to command all the land to swear our covenant, in the prelatical sense, against the intent hereof, and only to divide and so command. Judge what religion prelates are of who will have the name of God profaned by a whole nation by swearing fancies.

8. Of making private men magistrates in defending themselves against cut-throats, enough already. Let the Popish Prelate answer if he can.

Popish Prelate. Let no man imagine me to privilege a king from the direction and just power of the church, or that, like Uzziah, should intrude upon sacred actions, *ea vi ordinis, in foro interno conscientiae,* to preach or administrate sacraments, &c.

Ans. Uzziah did not burn incense, *ex vi ordinis,* as if he had been a priest, but because he was a king and God's anointed. Prelates sit not in council and parliament, *ex vi ordinis,* as temporal lords. The pope is no temporal monarch, *ex vi ordinis,* yet all are intruders. So the Popish Prelate will license kings to administer sacraments, so they do it not *ex vi ordinis,*

Popish Prelate. Men in sacred orders, in things intrinsically spiritual, have immediately a directive and authoritative power, in order, to all whatsoever, although ministerial only as related to Christ; but that gives them no coercive civil power over the prince, *per se*, or *per accidens*, directly or indirectly, that either the one way or the other, any or many in sacred order, pope or presbytery, can cite and censure kings, associate, covenant, or swear to resist him, and force him to submit to the scepter of Christ. This power over man God Almighty uses not, much less has he given it to man (Ps. 110). His people are a willing people. *Suadenda non cogenda religio.*

Ans. 1. Pastors have a ministerial power, says he, in spiritual things, but in order to Christ; therefore, in order to others it is not ministerial, but lordly. So here a lordly power pastors have over kings, by the Popish Prelate's way. We teach it is ministerial in relation to all, because ministers can make no laws as kings can do, but only, as heralds, declare Christ's laws.

2. None of us give any coercive civil power to the church over either kings or any other—it is ecclesiastical; a power to rebuke and censure was never civil.

3. A religious covenant to swear to resist, that is, to defend ourselves, is one thing, and a lawful oath, as is clear in those of Israel that did swear Asa's covenant, without the authority of their own king (2 Chron. 15:9-12) and to swear to force the king to submit to Christ's scepter, is another thing. The presbytery never did swear or covenant any such thing; nor do we take sacrament upon it, to force the king. Prelates have made the king swear, and take his sacrament upon it, that he shall root out puritans, that is, protestants, whereas he did swear at his coronation to root out heretics, that is (if prelates were not traitorous in administering the oath) Arminians and papists, such as this Popish Prelate is known to be; but I hold that the

estates of Scotland have power to punish the king, if he labor to subvert religion and laws.

4. If this argument, that religion is to be persuaded, not forced, which the Popish Prelate uses, be good, it will make much against the king; for the king, then, can force no man to the external profession and use of the ordinances of God, and not only kings, but all the people should be willing.

Popish Prelate. Though the king may not preach, &c., yet the exercise of these things freely within his kingdom, what concerns the decent and orderly doing of all, and the external man, in the external government of the church, in appointing things arbitrary and indifferent, and what else is of this strain, are so due to the prerogative of the crown, as that the priests, without highest rebellion, may not usurp upon him; a king in the state and church is a mixed person, not simply civil, but sacred too. They are not only professors of truth, that they have in the capacity of Christians, but they are defenders of the faith as kings; they are not sons only, but nurse-fathers; they serve God, as Augustine says, as men, and as kings also.

Ans. 1. If you give the king power of the exercises of word and sacraments in his kingdom, this is deprivation of ministers in his kingdom (for he sure cannot hinder them in another kingdom) you may make him to give a ministerial calling, if he may take it away. By what word of God can the king close the mouth of the man of God, whom Christ has commanded to speak in his name?

2. If the king may externally govern the church, why may he not excommunicate; for this is one of the special acts of church government, especially seeing he is a mixed person, that is, half a churchman, and if he may prescribe arbitrary-teaching ceremonies, and instruct men in the duties of holiness required of pastors, I see not but he may teach the Word.

3. Dr. Ferne and other royalists deny arbitrary government to the king in the state, and with reason, because it is tyranny over the people; but prelates are not ashamed of commanding a thing arbitrary and indifferent in God's worship; shall not arbitrary government in the church be tyranny over the conscience. But, say they, "Churchmen teaches the king what is decent and orderly in God's worship, and he commands it."

Ans. 1. Solomon by no teaching of churchmen deposed Abiathar; David by no teaching of churchmen appointed the form of the temple.

2. has God given a prerogative royal to kings, by which they may govern the church, and as kings, they shall not know how to use it, but insofar as they are taught by churchmen?

3. Certainly, we shall once be informed by God's word what is this prerogative, if according to it, all the external worship of God may be ordered. Lawyers and royalists teach, that it is an absoluteness of power to do above or against a law, as they say from 1 Sam. 8:9-11, and by which the king may oppress, and, no man may say, what do you? Now, good Popish Prelate, if, by a plenitude of tyranny, the king prescribe what he will in the external worship and government of God's house, who can rebuke the king though he command all the antichristian ceremonies of Home, and of Turkey, yea, and the sacrificing of children to Moloch, for absoluteness royal will amount to shedding of innocent blood? For, if any oppose the king, or say, sir, what do you? He opposes the prerogative royal, and that is highest rebellion, says our Popish Prelate.

4. I see not how the king is a mixed person, because he is defender of the faith, as the Pope named the king of England, Henry VIII; he defends it by his sword, as he is a nurse-father, not by the sword that comes out of his mouth.

5. I would know how Julian, Nebuchadnezzar, Og, and Si-hon, were mixed persons, and did all in the external government of the church, and that by their office, as they were kings.

6. All the instances that Augustine brings to prove that the king is a mixed person proves nothing but civil acts in kings; as Hezekiah cast down the high places, the king of Nineveh compelled to obey the prophet Jonah, Darius cast Daniel's enemies to the lions.

Popish Prelate. If you make two sovereigns and two independents, there is no more peace in the state, than in Rebecca's womb while Jacob and Esau strove for the prerogative.

Ans. 1. What need Israel strive, when Moses and Aaron are two independents? If Aaron make a golden calf, may not Moses punish him? It Moses turn an Ahab, and sell himself to do wickedly, ought not eighty valiant priests and Aarons both rebuke, censure, and resist?

2. The Popish Prelate said, "Let no man imagine we privilege the king from the direction and power of the church, so he be no intruding Uzziah." I ask, Popish Prelate, what is this church power? Is it not supreme in its kind of church power? Or is it subordinate to the king? If it be supreme, see how Popish Prelate makes two supremes, and two sovereigns. If it be subordinate to the king, as he is a mixed person, the king is privileged from this power, and he may intrude as Uzziah; and by his prerogative, as a mixed person, he may say mass, and offer a sacrifice, if there be no power above his prerogative to curb him. If there be none, the Popish Prelate's imagination is real; the king is privileged from all church power. Let the Popish Prelate see to it. I see no inconvenience for reciprocations of subjections in two supremes; and that they may mutually censure and judge one another.

Obj. Not in the same cause: that is impossible. If the king say mass, shall the church judge and censure the king for intrusion? And because the king is also sovereign and supreme in his kind, he may judge and punish the church for their act of judging and censuring the king, it being an intrusion on his prerogative that any should judge the highest judge.

Ans. The one is not subject to the other, but in the case of mal-administration; the innocent as innocent, is subject to no higher punishing; he may be subject to a higher, as accusing, citing, &c. Now, the royalist must give instance in the same cause, where the church fails against the king and his civil law; and the king, in the same cause, fails against the church canon; and then it shall be easy to answer.

Popish Prelate. Religion is the bottom of all happiness, if you make the king only to execute what a presbytery commands, he is in a hard case, and you take from him the chiefest in government. Ecclesiastical power has the soul in subjection; the civil sovereignty holds a dead dominion over the body. Then the Pope and presbytery shall be in a better condition than the king. *Cic. in ver. omnes religione moventur:* superstition is furious, and maddens people, that they spare neither crown nor miter.

Ans. Cold and dry is the Popish Prelate when he spends four pages in declamation for the excellency of religion: the madness of superstition is nothing to the purpose.

1. The king has a chief hand in church affairs, when he is a nurse-father, and bears the royal sword to defend both the tables of the law, though he do not spin and weave surplices, and other base mass-clothes to prelates, and such priests of Baal: they dishonor his majesty, who bring his prerogative so low.

2. The king does not execute with blind obedience with us what the Pope commands, and the prelates, but with height of knowledge what synods discern; and he is no more made

the servant of the church by this, than the king of Judah and Nebuchadnezzar are servants to Jeremiah and Daniel, because they are to obey the word of the Lord in their mouth. Let them show a reason of this, why they are servants in executing God's will in discipline, and in punishing what the Holy Ghost, by his apostles and elders, decree, when any condemn the decree concerning the abstinence from blood, things strangled, &c (Acts 15), rather than when they punish murder, idolatry, blasphemy, which are condemned in the Word, preached by pastors of Christ; and farther, this objection would have some more color (in reality it has not) if kings were only to execute what the church ministerially, in Christ's name, commands to be done in synods; but kings may, and do command synods to convene, and do their duty, and command many duties, never synodically decreed; as they are to cast out of their court apostate prelates, sleeping many years in the devil's arms, and are to command trencher-divines, neglecting their flock, and lying at court attending the filing of a dead bishop, as ravens do an old dying horse, to go and attend the flock, and not the court, as this Popish Prelate did.

3. A king has greater outward glory, and may do much more service to Christ, in respect of extension, and is more excellent than the pastor, who yet, in regard of intention, is busied about nobler things, namely, the soul, the gospel, and eternity, than the king.

4. Superstition maddens men; but it follows not that true religion may not set them on work to defend soul and body against tyranny of the crown, and antichristian miters.

Popish Prelate. The kingdom had peace and plenty in the prelates' time.

Ans. 1. A belly-argument. We had plenty, when we sacrificed to the queen of heaven. If the traveler contend to have his purse again, shall the robber say, robbery was blessed with peace? The rest, to the end, are lies, and answered already. Only his invectives against ruling elders, falsely called lay-elders, are not to purpose. Parliament-priests, and lay and court-pastors, are lay-prophets.

2. That presbyteries meddle with civil business, is a slander. They meddle with public scandals that offends in Christ's kingdom. But the prelates by office were more in two elements, in church and state, than any frogs, even in the king's leaven-tubs, ordinarily.

3. Something he says of popes usurping over kings, but only of one of his fathers, a great unclean spirit, Gregory the Great. But if he had refuted him by God's word, he should have thrown stones at his own tribe; for prelates, like him, do *ex officio* trample upon the neck of kings,

4. His testimonies of one council and one father for all antiquity proves nothing. Athanasius said, "God has given David's throne to kings." What, to be heard by the church? No; to be minister of God, without, εξω, to tutor the church. And, because "kings reign by Christ," as the council of Armin says; therefore, it may follow, a bailee is also head of the church. It is taken from Prov. 8, and answered.

5. That presbyteries have usurped over kings more than popes, since Hildebrand, is a lie. All stories are full of the usurpation of prelates, his own tribe. The Pope is but a swelled fat prelate; and what he says of popes, he says of his own house.

6. The ministers of Christ in Scotland had never a contest with king James but for his sins, and his conniving with papists, and his introducing bishops, the ushers of the Pope.

QUESTION 43.

WHETHER THE KING OF SCOTLAND IS AN ABSOLUTE PRINCE, HAVING A PREROGATIVE ABOVE LAWS AND PARLIAMENTS.

The king of Scotland is subject to parliaments by the fundamental laws, acts, and constant practices of parliaments, ancient and late in Scotland. The king of Scotland's oath at his coronation is considered. A pretended absolute power given to James VI due to personal endowments; there is no ground of absoluteness to the king of Scotland. That the kings of Scotland are subject to laws and parliaments is proved by the fundamental law of elective princes, and out of the most partial historians, and our acts of parliament of Scotland. The coronation oath, sworn again at the coronation of James VI, and again, 1 Parl. James VI ibid. and seq. How the king is supreme judge in all causes. The power of the parliaments of Scotland is considered. The Confession of the faith of the church of Scotland, authorized by various acts of parliament, does evidently hold forth to all the reformed churches the lawfulness of defensive wars, when the supreme magistrate is misled by wicked counsel. The same proved from the confessions of faith in other reformed churches. The place, Rom. 13, exposited in our Confession of

> *faith. The confession, not only Saxonic, exhibited to the Council*
> *of Trent, but also of Helvetia, France, England, Bohemia,*
> *prove the same. William Laud and other prelates enemies to*
> *parliaments, to states, and to the fundamental laws of the three*
> *kingdoms of England, Scotland, and Ireland. The parliament of*
> *Scotland regulates, limits, and sets bounds to the king's power.*
> *Fergus the first king was not a conqueror. The king of Scotland*
> *below parliaments, considerable by them, has no negative voice.*

The negative part of this I hold in these assertions.

Assert. 1. The kings of Scotland have not any prerogative distinct from supremacy above the laws. If the people must be governed by no laws but by the king's own laws, that is, the laws and statutes of the realm, acted in parliament under pain of disobedience, then must the king govern by no other laws, and so by no prerogative above law. But the former is an evident truth by our acts of parliament; therefore, so is the latter. The proposition is confirmed, 1. Because whatever law enjoins passive obedience no way but by laws that must enjoin also the king actively to command no other way but by law; for to be governed by law essentially includes to be governed by the supreme governor only by law.

2. An act of regal governing is an act of law, and essentially an act of law; an act of absolute prerogative is no act of law, but an act above law, or of pleasure loosed from law; and so they are opposed as acts of law, and non-acts of law. If the subjects, by command of the king and parliament, cannot be governed but by law how can the king but be under his own and the parliament's law, to govern only by law? I prove the assumption from Parl. 3, of king James I, act 48, which ordains that "all and sundry the king's lieges be governed under the king's laws and statutes of the realm allenarly, and under

no particular laws or special privileges, nor by any laws of other countries or realms." Privileges do exclude laws. Absolute pleasure of the king as a man, and the law of the king as king, are opposed by way of contradiction; and so in Parl. 6, James IV, act 79, ratified Parl. 8, James VI, act 131.

2. The king, at his coronation (Parl. 1, James VI, act 8) swears "to maintain the true kirk of God, and religion now presently professed, in purity, and to rule the people according to the lawn and constitutions received in the realm, causing justice and equity to be ministered without partiality." This did king Charles swear at his coronation, and was ratified, Parl. 7, James VI, act 99. Hence he who, by the oath of God, is limited to govern by law, can have no prerogative above the law. If, then, the king change the religion and confession of faith, authorized by many parliaments (especially by Parl. 1, Charles, 1633) he goes against his oath. The king's royal prerogative, or rather supremacy (enacted Parl. 8, James VI, act 129; Parl. 18, act 1; Parl. 21, act 1, James; and Parl. 1, Charles, act 3) cannot be contrary to the oath that king Charles did swear at his coronation, which brings down the prerogative to governing according to the standing laws of the realm." It cannot be contrary to these former parliaments and acts, declaring that "the lieges are to be governed by the laws of the realm, and by no particular laws and special privileges" (but absolute prerogative is a special privilege above, or without law) which acts stand unrepealed to this day; and these acts of parliaments stand ratified by Parl. 1, Charles, 1633.

3. Parl. 8, James VI in the first three acts of it, the king's supremacy, and the power and authority of parliaments are equally ratified under the same pain: "Their jurisdictions, power, and judgments in spiritual or temporal causes, not ratified by his Majesty, and the three estates convened in

parliament, are discharged." But the absolute prerogative of the king above law, equity, and justice, was never ratified in any parliament of Scotland to this day.

4. By Parl. 12, James VI, act 114, all former acts in favor of the true church and religion being ratified, their power of making constitutions concerning το πριπου order and decency, the privileges that God has given to spiritual office-bearers, as well of doctrine and discipline, in matters of heresy, excommunication, collation, deprivation, and such like, warranted by the word of God, and also to assemblies and presbyteries, are ratified. Now in that parliament, in acts so contiguous, we are not to think that the king and three estates would make acts for establishing the church's power in all the former heads of government, in which royalists say, "the soul of the king's absolute prerogative does consist;" and therefore it must be the true intent of our parliament to give the king a supremacy and a prerogative royal (which we also give) but without any absoluteness of boundless and transcendent power above law, and not to obtrude a service-book, and all the superstitious rites of the church of Rome, without God's word, upon us.

5. The former act of parliament ratifies the true religion, according to the word of God, then could it never have been the intent of our parliament to ratify an absolute supremacy, according to which a king might govern his people, as a tyrannical lion, contrary to Deut. 17:18-20. And it is true, Parl. 18, James VI, acts 1 and 2, upon personal qualifications, gives a royal prerogative to king James over all causes, persons, and estates within his Majesty's dominion, whom they humbly acknowledge to be "sovereign monarch, absolute prince, judge and governor over all estates, persons, and causes."

These two acts, for my part I acknowledge, are spoken rather in court expressions than in law terms.

1. Because personal virtues cannot advance a limited prince (such as the kings of Scotland, *post hominum memoriam,* ever were) to be an absolute prince. "Personal graces make not David absolutely supreme judge over all persons and causes; nor can king James, advanced to be king of England, be for that made more king of Scotland, and more supreme judge than he was while he was only king of Scotland. A wicked prince is as essentially supreme judge as a godly king.

2. If this parliamentary figure of speech, which is to be imputed to the times, exalted king James to be absolute in Scotland, for his personal endowments, there was no ground to put the same on king Charles. Personal virtues are not always hereditary, though to me the present king be the best.

3. There is not any absoluteness above law in act 1, the parliament must be more absolute in themselves. King James VI had been various years, before this 18th parliament, king of Scotland; then, if they gave him by law an absoluteness, which he had not before, then they were more absolute. Those who can add absoluteness must have it in themselves. *Nemo dat quod non habet.* If it be said king James had that before the act; the parliament legally declared it to be his power, which, before the declaration, was his power; I answer, all he had before this declaration was, to govern the people according to law and conscience, and no more; and if they declare no other prerogative royal to be due to him, there is an end: we grant all. But, then, this which they call prerogative royal, is no more than a power to govern according to law, and so you had nothing to add to king James upon the ground of his personal virtues, only you make an oration to his praise in the acts of parliament.

4. If this absoluteness of prerogative be given to the king, the subjects, swearing obedience, swear that he has power

from themselves to destroy themselves: this is neither a lawful oath, nor though they should swear it, does it oblige them.

5. A supreme judge is a supreme father of all his children and all their causes; and to be a supreme father cannot be contrary to a supreme judge; but contrary it must be, if this supremacy make over to the prince a power of devouring as a lion, and that by a regal privilege, and by office, whereas he should be a father to save; or if a judge kill an evil-doer, though that be an act destructive to one man, yet is it an act of a father to the commonwealth. An act of supreme and absolute royalty is often an act of destruction to one particular man, and to the whole commonwealth. For example, when the king, out of his absolute prerogative, pardons a murderer, and he kills another innocent man, and out of the same ground the king pardons him again, and so till he kill twenty (for by what reason the prerogative gives one pardon, he may give twenty, there is a like reason above law for all) this act of absolute royalty is such an act of murder, as if a shepherd would keep a wolf in the fold with the sheep, he were guilty of the loss of these sheep. Now an act of destroying cannot be an act of judging far less of a supreme judge, but of a supreme murderer.

6. Whereas he is called "absolute prince and supreme judge, in all causes, ecclesiastical and civil," it is to be considered, 1. That the estates profess not in these acts to give any new prerogative, but only to continue the old power, and that only with that amplitude and freedom which the king and his predecessors did enjoy and exercise before: the extent of which is best known from the acts of parliament, histories of the time, and the oaths of the kings of Scotland.

2. That he is called absolute prince, not in any relation of freedom from law, or prerogative above law, to which, as unto the *norma regula ac mensura potestatis suae ac subjectionis meae,*

he is tied by the fundamental law and his own oath, but in opposition to all foreign jurisdiction or principality above him, as is evident by the oath of supremacy set down for acknowledging of his power in the first act of parliament 21, king James VI.

3. They are but the same expression, giving only the same power before acknowledged in the 129th act, Parl. 8, king James VI, and that only over persons or estates, considered *separatim*, and over causes; but neither at all over the laws nor over the estates, taken *conjunctim*, and as convened in parliament, as is clear, both by the two immediately subsequent acts of that parliament 8, James VI, establishing the authority of parliaments equally with the kings, and discharging all jurisdictions (albeit granted by the king) without their warrant, as also by the narrative depositive words and certification of the act itself; otherwise the estates convened in parliament might by virtue of that act be summoned before and censured by the king's majesty or his council, a judicatory substitute, be subordinate to and censured by themselves, which would be contrary to sense and reason.

4. The very terms of supreme judge, and in all causes, according to the nature of correlates, presupposes courts and judicial proceedings and laws, as the ground-work and rule of all, not a freedom from them.

5. Act 6, Parl. 20, James VI clearly interprets what is meant by the king's jurisdiction in all spiritual and ecclesiastical causes; to wit, to be only in the consistorial causes of matrimony, testaments, bastardy, adulteries, abusively called spiritual causes, because handled in commissary courts, in which the king appoints the commissary, his deputies, and makes the lords of the session his great consistory in all ecclesiastical causes, with reservation of his supremacy and prerogative in it.

7. Supreme judge in all causes, cannot be taken *quoad actus elicitos*, as if the king were to judge between two seamen, or two husbandmen, or two tradesmen, in that which is proper to their art; or between two painters. Certainly the king is not to judge which of the two draws the fairest picture, but which of the two wastes most gold on his picture, and so does interest most of the commonwealth. So the king cannot judge in all ecclesiastical causes, that is, he cannot, *quoad actos elicitos*, prescribe this worship, for example, the mass, not the sacrament of the Lord's supper. Therefore the king has but *actos imperatores* some royal political acts about the worship of God, to command God to be worshipped according to his word, to punish the superstitions or neglecters of divine worship; therefore, cannot the king be sole judge in matters that belong to the college of judges by the laws of Scotland, the lords of session only may judge these matters (Parl. 2, James I, act 45; Parl. 8, James III, act 62; Parl. 4, James III, act 105; Parl. 6, James I, act 83; Parl. 6, James I, act 86; Parl. 7, James V, act 104) and that only according to law, without any remedy of appellation to king or the parliament (Parl. 14, James II, act 62 and 63). And the king is by act of parliament inhibited to send any private letter to stay the acts of justice; or if any such letter be procured, the judges are not to acknowledge it as the king's will, for they are to proceed impartially according to justice, and are to make the law, which is the king and parliament's public revealed will, their rule (Parl. 5, James V, act 68; Parl. 8, James VI, act 139; Parl. 6, James VI, act 92). Nor may the lords suspend the course of justice, or the sentence or execution of decrees upon the king's private letter (Parl. 11, James VI, act 79, and Parl. 11, James VI, act 47). And so, if the king's will or desire, as he is a man, be opposite to his law and his will as king, it is not to be regarded. This is

a strong argument that the parliaments never made the king supreme judge, *quoad actus elicitos,* in all causes, nay not if the king have a cause of his own that concerns lands of the crown, far less can the king have a will of prerogative above the law by our laws of Scotland. And, therefore, when in Parl. 8, James VI, the king's royal power is established in the first act, the very next act immediately subjoined to it declares the authority of the supreme court of parliament continued past all memory of man unto this day, and constitute of the free voices of the three estates of this ancient kingdom, which in the parliament 1606 is called, "the ancient and fundamental policy of this kingdom;" and so fundamental, as if it should be innovated, such confusion would ensue as it could no more be a free monarchy as is expressed in the parliament's printed commission, 1604, by whom the same, under God, has been upheld, rebellious and traitorous subjects punished, the good and faithful preserved and maintained, and the laws and acts of parliament (by which all men are governed) made and established, and appoints the honor, authority, and dignity of the estates of parliament to stand in their own integrity, according to the ancient and laudable custom by-past, without alteration or diminution, and therefore discharges any to presume or take in hand, to impugn the dignity and the authority of the said estates, of to seek or procure the innovation or diminution of their power or authority, under the pain of treason," and, therefore, in the next act, they discharge all jurisdictions, or judicatories (albeit appointed by the king's majesty, as the high commission was) without their warrant and approbation; and that, as contrary to the fundamental laws above titled (Parl. 3, James I, act 48 and Parl. 6, James IV, act 79) by which the lieges should only be ruled by laws or acts passed in the parliament of this kingdom. Now, what was the ancient dignity, authority, and power of the parliaments of Scotland, which is to stand without diminution, that will be easily and best known from the subsequent passages, or historians, which can also be very easily verified by the old registers, whenever they should be produced. In the meantime, remember that in parliament and by act of Parl. James VI, for observing the due order of parliament, promises never to do or command anything which may directly or indirectly prejudge the liberty of free reasoning or voting of parliament (Parl. 11, James VI, act 40). And withal, to show the freedom of the parliament of Scotland from that absolute unlimited prerogative of the prince, and their liberty to resist his breaking of covenant with them, or treaties with foreign nations, You shall consider,

1. That the kings of Scotland are obliged, before they be inaugurated, to swear and make their faithful covenant to the true kirk of God, that they shall maintain, defend, and set forward the true religion confessed and established within this realm; even as they are obliged and restricted by the law of God, as well in Deuteronomy as in 2 Kings 11, and as they crave obedience of their subjects. So that the bond and contract shall be mutual and reciprocal, in all time coming, between the prince and the people, according to the word of God, as is fully expressed in the register of the convention of estates, July 1567.

2. That important acts and sentences at home (of which one is printed, Parl. 14, James III, act 112) and in treaties with foreign princes, the estates of parliament did append their several seals with the king's great seal (which to Grotius, Barclay, and Arnisaeus, is an undeniable argument of a limited prince, as well as the style of our parliament, that the estates, with the king, ordain, ratify, rescind, &c). as also they were

obliged, in case of the king's breaking these treaties, to resist him in them, even by arms, and that without any breach of their allegiance, or of his prerogative, as is yet extant in the records of our old treaties with England and France, &c. But to go on, and leave some high mysteries unto a rejoinder.

And to the end I may make good, 1. That nothing is here taught in this treatise but the very doctrine of the Church of Scotland, I desire that the reader may take notice of the larger Confession of the Church of Scotland, printed with the body of the confessions at Geneva, anno 1612, and authorized by James VI and the three estates in parliament, and printed in our acts of parliament (Parl. 16, James VI, anno 1567) among good works of the second table, says our Confession (art, 14) are these: To honor father, mother, princes, rulers, and superior powers. To love them, to support them, yea, to obey their charge (not repugning to the commandment of God) to save the lives of innocents, to repress tyranny, to defend the oppressed, to keep our bodies clean and holy, &c. The contrary of which is to disobey or resist any that God has placed in authority (while they pass not over the bounds of their office) to murder, or to consent to it, to bear hatred, or to let innocent blood be shed, if we may withstand it, &c. Now the Confession cites in the margin, Eph. 1:1, 7 and Ezek. 22:1-4, &c., where it is evident by the name of father and mother all inferior judges as well as the king, and especially the princes, rulers, and lords of parliament are understood.

2. The bloody city is to be judged, because they relieved not the oppressed out of the hand of the bloody princes (v. 6) who everyone of them did to their power shed innocent blood (Ezek. 22:6).

3. To resist superior powers, and so the estates of parliament, as the cavaliers of Scotland do, is resistance forbidden

(Rom. 13:1). The place is also cited in the Confession, and the Confession exposits the place (Rom. 13) according to the interpretation of all sound expositors, as is evident in these words, art. 24: "And therefore we confess and avouch, that such as resist the supreme power, doing that thing which appertains to his charge, do resist God's ordinance, and therefore cannot be guiltless. And farther, we affirm, that whosoever denies unto them aid, their counsel and support, while as the princes and rulers vigilantly travel in execution of their office, that the same men deny their help, support, and counsel to God, who, by the presence of his lieutenant, craves it of them." From which words we have clear:

1. That to resist the king or parliament is to resist them while as they are doing the thing that appertains to their charge, and while they vigilantly travel in the execution of their once. But while king and Parliament do acts of tyranny against God's law, and all good laws of men, they do not the things that appertain to their charge and the execution of their office; therefore, by our Confession, to resist them in tyrannical acts is not to resist the ordinance of God.

2. To resist princes and rulers, and so inferior judges, and to deny them counsel and comfort, is to deny help, counsel, and comfort to God. Let then cavaliers, and such as refuse to help the princes of the land against papists, prelates and malignants, know that they resist God's ordinance, which rebellion they unjustly impute to us.

3. Since it is added in our Confession, that God, by the presence of his lieutenant, craves support and counsel of the people, it is not so to be taken, as if then only we are to aid and help inferior judges and parliaments, when the king personally requires it, and not otherwise.

1. Because the king requires help, when, by his office, he is obliged to require our help and counsel against papists and malignants, though as misled, he should command the contrary: so if the law require our help, the king requires it *ex officio*.

2. This should expressly contradict our Confession, if none were obliged to give help and counsel to the parliaments and estates, unless the king in his own person were to require it, because (art. 14) it is expressly said that to save the lives of innocents, or repress tyranny, to defend the oppressed, not to suffer innocent blood to be shed, are works pleasing to God, which He rewards. Now we are not to think in reason, if the king shall be induced by wicked counsel to do tyrannical works, and to raise papists in arms against protestants, that God does by him, as by His lieutenant, require our help, comfort, and counsel in assisting the king in acts of tyranny, and in oppression, and in shedding innocent blood; yea, our Confession ties us to deny help and comfort to the king in these wicked acts, and therefore our help must be in the things that pertains to his royal office and duty only, otherwise we are to repress all tyranny (art. 14).

4. To save the lives of innocents, to repress tyranny, to defend the oppressed, are, by our Confession, good works, well pleasing to God, and so is this a good work, not to suffer innocent blood to be shed, if we may withstand it. Thus it is clear as the sun, that our Confession, according to the word of God, to which king Charles did swear at his coronation, does oblige and tie us in the presence of God and His holy angels, to rise in arms to save the innocent, to repress tyranny, to defend the oppressed. When the king, by ill counsel, sent armies by sea and land to kill and destroy the whole kingdom who should refuse such a service-book as they could not in conscience receive, unless they would disobey God, renounce

the Confession of Faith, which the king and they had sworn unto, and prove perfidious apostates to Christ and His church, what could we do, and that the same Confession, considering our bonds to our dear brethren in England, lays bonds on us to this, as a good work also, not to suffer their innocent blood to be shed, but to defend them, when they, against all law of God, of men, of state, of nations, are destroyed and killed. For my part, I judge it would have been a guiltiness of blood upon Scotland, if we had not helped them, and risen in arms to defend ourselves and our innocent brethren against bloody cavaliers. Add to this what is in the 24th article of the same Confession: "We confess, whosoever goes about to take away, or to confound the whole state of civil polity, now long established, we affirm the same men not only to be enemies to mankind, but also wickedly to fight against God's will." But those who have taken arms against the estates of Scotland, and the princes and rulers of the land, have labored to take away parliaments, and the fundamental laws of this kingdom, therefore, the Confession adds (art. 16): "We farther confess and acknowledge, that such persons as are placed in authority are to be loved, honored, feared, and held in most reverent estimation, because that they are lieutenants of God, in whose sessions God Himself does sit and judge; yea, even the judges and princes themselves, to whom, by God, is given the sword, to the praise and defense of good men, and to revenge and punish all open malefactors." Therefore, the parliament, and princes, and rulers of the land, are God's lieutenants on earth no less than the king, by our Confession of Faith; and those who resist them, resist the ordinance of God. Royalists say, they are but the deputies of the king, and when they do contrary to his royal will, they may be resisted, yea, and be killed, for insofar they are private men, though they are to be honored as judges when they act according to the king's will, whose deputies they are. But, I answer:

1. It is a wonder that inferior judges should be formally judges, insofar as they act conform to the will of a mortal king, and not insofar as they act conform to the will of the King of kings, seeing the judgment they execute is the King of kings', and not the judgment of a mortal king (2 Chron. 19:6).

2. Royalists cannot endure the former distinction as it is applied to the king, but they receive it with both hands as it is applied to inferior judges; and yet, certain it is, that it is as ordinary for a king, being a sinful man, to act sometimes as the lieutenant of God, and sometimes as an erring and mis-informed man, no less than the inferior judge acts sometimes according to the king's will and law, and sometimes according to his own private way; and if we are to obey the inferior judge as the deputy of the king, what shall become of his person, when cavaliers may kill him at some Edge-hill? For so they mock this distinction, as applied to the king in regard of his person and of his royal office; and for this point our Confession cites in the margin (Rom. 13:7; 1 Pet. 2:17; Ps. 82:1), which places do clearly prove that inferior magistrates are, 1. God's ordinances; 2. Gods on earth (Ps. 82:6); 3. Such as bear the Lord's sword; 4, "That they are not only (as the Confession says) appointed for civil policy, but also for main-tenance of true religion, and for suppressing of idolatry and superstition." Then, it is evident, to resist inferior magistrates is to resist God himself, and to labor to throw the sword out of God's hand. 6. Our Confession uses the same Scriptures cited by Junius Brutus, namely, Ezek. 22:1-7; Jer. 22:3, where we are no less than the Jews commanded to "execute judgment and righteousness, and deliver the spoiled out of the hands of the oppressor," for both the law of God and the civil law says,

Qui non impedit homicidium, quum potest is homicidii reus est.
I will cast in a word of other Confessions, lest we seem to be
Jesuits alone.

The Confession of Helvetia says *de Magistratu. viduas, pu-
pillos, afflictos asserat*, every magistrate is to defend the widow,
the orphan, and the oppressed (section 30). The French Confession says *Afirmamus ergo parendumesse legibus et statutis,
solvenda tribute, subjectiones denique jugum voluntarie toleran-
du, etiamsi infideles fuerint magistratus, dummodo Dei summum
imperium integrum et illibatum maneat* (art. 40), so clear it is
that all active obedience is due to all magistrates, and that
that yoke of passive obedience is to be tolerated but conditionally, with a *dummodo*, so long as the magistrate violate
not the supreme commandment of the King of kings; and we
know, accordingly, protestants of that church have taken defensive arms against their king. But our Popish Prelate can say
the Confessions of Scotland, Helvetia, France, and all the reformed churches, are Jesuitical, when as it was the doctrine of
the Waldensians, the protestants, Luther, Calvin, and others,
while as there was no Jesuit on earth.

The thirty-seventh article of the Church of England's Confession (article 37) is so far from erecting an absolute power in
the king, that they expressly bring down the royal prerogative
from the high seat and transcendent superlative power above
the law, and exposit the prerogative to be nothing but mere
law-power. "We only" say they "ascribe that prerogative to the
king which the Scripture does ascribe to all godly princes; that
is, that they cause all committed to their trust, whether ecclesiastical or civil persons, to do their duty, and punish with the
civil sword all disobedient offenders." In *Syntag. Confess.* "And
this they say in answer to some who believed the Church of

England made the king the head of the church." The Prelates" Convocation must be Jesuits to this Popish Prelate also.

So the thirty-sixth article of the Belgic Confession says of all magistrates, no less than of a king (we know, for tyranny of soul and body, they justly revolted from their king) *Idcirco magistratus ipsos gladio armavit, ut malos quidem plecant poenis probos vero tueantur, Horum porro esty non modo de civili politia conservanda esse solictoits, verum etiam dare operam ut sacrum ministerium conservetur, omnis idololatria et adulterinus Dei cultus e medio tollatyr, regnum antichristi diruatur* &c. Then, all magistrates, though inferior, must do their duty that the law of God has laid on them, though the king forbid them; but, by the Belgic Confession and the Scripture, it is their duty to relieve the oppressed, to use the sword against murdering papists and Irish rebels and destroying cavaliers; for, shall it be a good plea in the day of Christ to say, "Lord Jesus, we would have used your sword against bloody murderers if your anointed, the king, had not commanded us to obey a mortal king rather than the King of ages, and to execute no judgment for the oppressed, because He judged them faithful catholic subjects." Let all Oxford and cavalier doctors in the three kingdoms satisfy the consciences of men in this: that inferior judges are to obey a divine law, with a proviso that the king command them so to do, and otherwise they are to obey men rather than God. This is evidently held forth in the Argentine Confession, exhibited by four cities to the emperor Charles V, 1530, in the very same cause of innocent defense that we are now in in the three kingdoms of Scotland, England, and Ireland.

The Saxon Confession, exhibited to the Council of Trent (1661, art. 23) makes the magistrate's office essentially to consist in keeping of the two tables of God's law; and so, what can follow from this, but insofar as he defends murderers, or,

if he be a king, and shall with the sword or arms impede inferior magistrates (for the Confession speaks of all) to defend
God's law and true religion against papists, murderers, and
bloody cavaliers and hinder them to execute the judgment of
the Lord against evil doers, he is not, in that, a magistrate;
and the denying of obedience, active or passive, to him in that,
is no resistance to the ordinance of God; but, by the contrary,
the king himself must resist the ordinance of God.

The Confession of Bohemia is clear (art. 16) *Qui publico
munere magistratuque funguntur, quemcunque, gradum teneant,
se non suum, sed Dei opus agere sciant.* Hence all inferior or the
supreme magistrate, whatever be their place, they do not their
own work, nor the work of the king, but the work of God,
in the use of the sword; therefore, they are to use the sword
against bloody cavaliers, as doing God's work. Suppose the
king should forbid them to do God's work; and it says of all
magistrates: *Sunt autem magistratuum partes ac munus, omnibus
ex aequo jus dicere, in communem omnium usum, sine per sonarum
acceptatione, pacem ac tranquilitatem publicam tueri ac procura-
re de malis ac facinorosis, hanc inter turbantibus paenas sumere,
aliosque, omnes ab eorum vi et injuria vindicare.* Now, this confession was the faith of the barons and nobles of Bohemia who
were magistrates, and exhibited to the emperor, anno 1635, in
the cause not unlike unto ours now, and the emperor was their
sovereign; yet they profess they are obliged, in conscience, to
defend all under them from all violence and injuries, that the
emperor, or any other, could bring on them; and that this is
their office before God, which they are obliged to perform as
a work of God, and the Christian magistrate is not to do that
work which is not his own but God's, upon condition that
the king shall not inhibit him. What if the king shall inhibit
parliaments, princes, and rulers, to relieve the oppressed, to

defend the orphan, the widow, the stranger, from unjust violence? Shall they obey man rather than God?

To say no more of this: prelates in Scotland did what they could, 1. To hinder his Majesty to indict a parliament. 2. When it was indicted, to have its freedom destroyed by pre-limitations. 3. When it was sitting, their care was to divide, impede, and annul the course of justice. 4. All in the Popish Prelate's book tends to abolish parliaments, and to enervate their power. 5. There were many ways used to break up parliaments in England, and to command judges not to judge at all, but to interrupt the course of justice, is all one as to command unrighteous judgment (Jer. 22:3). 6. Many ways have been used by cavaliers to cut off parliaments, and the present parliament in England.

The paper found in William Laud's study, touching fears and hopes of the parliament of England, shows that cavaliers hate the supreme seat of justice, and wish it were not in the world, which is the highest rebellion and resistance made against superior powers.

1. He fears this parliament shall begin where the last left.

Ans. Whatever ungrateful courtier had hand in the death of king James deserved to come under trials

2. He fears they sacrifice some man.

Ans. 1. If parliaments have not power to cut off rebels, and corrupt judges, the root of their being is undone. 2. If they be lawful courts, none need fear them but the guilty.

3. He fears their consultations be long, and the supply must be present.

Ans. 1. Then cavaliers intend parliaments for subsidies to the king, to foment and promote the war against Scotland, not for justice. 2. He that fears long and serious consultations, to rip up and lance the wounds of church and state, is afraid that the wounds be cured.

4. He fears they deny subsidies, which are due by the law of God, nature, and nations, while parliaments have but their deliberation and consent for the manner of giving, otherwise this is to sell subsidies, not to give them.

Ans. Tribute, and the standing revenues of the king, are due by the law of God and nations; but subsidies are occasional rents given upon occasion of war, or some extraordinary necessity; and they are not given to the king as tribute and standing revenues, which the king may bestow for his house, family, and royal honor, but they are given by the kingdom, rather to the kingdom than to the king, for the present war, or some other necessity of the kingdom, and therefore are not due to the king as king, by any law of nature or nations, and so should not be given but by deliberation and judicial sentence of the states; and they are not sold to the king, but given out by the kingdom by statute of parliament, to be bestowed on the kingdom, and the king should sell no acts of justice for subsidies.

5. He dare not speak of the consequences, if the king grant bills of grace, and part with the flowrets of the crown.

Ans. He dare not say the people shall vindicate their liberty by selling subsidies to buy branches of the prerogative royal, and diminishing the king's fancied absoluteness; so would prelates have the king absolute, that they may ride over the souls, purses, persons, estates, and religion of men, upon the horse of pretended absoluteness.

6. He fears the parliament fall upon church business; but, 1. The church is too weak already; if it had more power, the king might have more both of obedience and service. 2. The houses can be no competent judges in point of doctrine. 3.

For the King, clergy, and convocation are judges in all causes ecclesiastical.

Ans. 1. This strikes at the root of all parliamentary power. 1. The Popish Prelate gives them but a poor deliberative power in subsidies; and that is, to make the king's will a law, in taking all the subjects' goods from them, to foment war against the subjects. 2, He takes all jurisdiction from them over persons, though they were as black traitors as breathe. 3. And spoils them of all power in church matters; to make all judges, yea, and the king himself yield blind obedience to the Pope and Prelate, and their illuminated clergy. Sure I am, Prelate Maxwell imputes this, but most unjustly, to presbyteries. What essential and fundamental privileges are left to parliaments? David and the parliament of Israel are impertinent judges in the matter of bringing home the ark of God. And for the church's weakness, that is, the weakness of the damned prelates, shall this be the king's weakness? Yes; the Popish Prelate must make it true, no bishop, no king.

7. He fears factious spirits will take heart to themselves, if the king yield to them without any submission of theirs.

Ans. The princes and judges of the land are a company of factious men, and so no parliament, no court, but at best some good advisers of a king to break up the parliament, because they refuse subsidies, that he may by a lawless way extort subsidies.

8. He desires the parliament may sit a short time, that they may not well understand one another.

Ans. He loveth short or no justice from the parliament; he fears they reform God's house, and execute justice on men like himself. But I return to the Scottish parliament.

Assert. 2. The parliament is to regulate the power of the king. The heritable sheriffs complain that the king grants commissions to others in cases pertaining to their office; upon which the estates (Parl. 6, James VI, act 82) discharge all such commissions, as also appoint that all murderers be judged by the justice general only. And in several acts the king is inhibited to grant pardons to malefactors, Parl. 11, James VI, act 75.

It is to be considered that king James, in his *Basilikon Doron*, lays down an unsound ground, that Fergus the first, father of one hundred and seven kings of Scotland, conquered this kingdom. The contrary whereof is asserted by Fordome, Major, Boethius, Buchanan, Holinshed, who run all upon this principle, that the estates of the kingdom did, 1. Choose a monarchy, and freely, and no other government. 2. That they freely elected Fergus to be their king. 3. King Fergus frequently convened the parliament called *Insulanorum duces, tribuum rectores, majorum consessus, conventus ordinum, conventus statuum, communitatum regni, phylarchi, primores, prindpes, patres*; and, as Holinshed says, they made Fergus king; therefore a parliament must be before the king; yea, and after the death of king Fergus, *philarehi coeunt concione advocata*, the estates convened without any king, and made that fundamental law *regni elective*, that when the king's children were minors, any of the Fergusian race might be chosen to reign, and this endured to the days of Kenneth; and Redotha, the seventh king, resigned and makes over the government into the hands of the parliament, and *Philarehi Tribuum Gubematores* ordained Thereus the eighth king. Buchanan (*l. 4, Rer. Scot)* calls him Reutha, and said he did this, *populo egre permittente*, then the royal power recurred to the fountain. Thereus, the eighth king, a wicked man, filled the kingdom with robbers, and fearing the parliament should punish him, fled to the Britons, and thereupon the parliament choose Connanus to be prorex and protector of the kingdom.

Finnanus, the tenth king, decreed, *Ne quid reges, quod majoris esse momenti, nisi de publici consilii authoritate juberent, et ne domestico consilio remp, administrarent, regia publicaque negotia non sine patrum consultatione ductuque tractarentur, nec bellum pacem aut faedera reges per se patrum, tribuumve, rectorum injussu facerent, demrentue;* then it is clear that parliaments were *consortes imperii,* and had the authority with and above the king. When a law is made that the kings should do nothing *injussu rectorum tribuum,* without commandment of the parliament, a cabinet-council was not lawful to the kings of Scotland. So Durstus, the eleventh king, swears to the parliament, *Se nihil nisi de primorum consilio acturum,* that he shall do nothing but by counsel of the rulers and heads of the kingdom.

The parliament, rejecting the lawful son of Corbredus, the nineteenth king, because he was young, created Dardanus, the nephew of Metellanus, king, which is a great argument of the power of the Scottish parliament of old for elective rather than hereditary kings.

Corbredus II, called Galdus, the twenty-first king, at his coronation, renouncing all negative voices, did swear, *Se majorum consiliis acquieturum,* that he should be ruled by the parliament; and it is said, *Leges quasdam tollere non potuit, adversante multitudine.*

Luctatus, the twenty-second king, is censured by a parliament, "*Quod spreto majorum consilio,*" he appointed base men to public offices.

Mogaldus, the twenty-third king, "*Ad consilia seniorum omnia ex prisco more revocavit,*" did all by the parliament, as the ancient custom was.

Conarus, the twenty-fourth king, was cast into prison by the parliament, "*Quod non expectato decreto patrum, quod summae erat potestatis, privatis consiliis administrasset*" because he did these weightiest business that concerned the kingdom, by private advice, without the judicial ordinance of parliament, that was of greatest authority. Where is the negative voice of the king here?

Ethodius II (son of Ethodius I) the twenty-eighth king (the parliament passing him by on account of his age, and electing Satrael, his father's brother, king before him) was a simple ignorant man; yet for reverence to the race of Fergus, kept the name of a king, but the estates appointed tutors to him.

Nathalocus, the thirtieth king, corrupting the nobles with buds and fair promises, obtained the crown.

Romachus, Fethelmachus, and Angusianus, or as Buchanan calls him, Aeneanus, contended for the crown, the parliament convened to judge the matter was dissolved by tumult, and Romachus chosen king, doing all, *non adhibito de more, consilio majorum*, was censured by the parliament.

Fergus II was created king by the states, *de more*.

Constantino, the forty-third king, a most wicked man, was punished by the states.

Aidanus, the forty-ninth king, by the counsel of St. Columba, governed all in peace, by three parliaments every year.

Ferchard I, the fifty-second king, and Ferchard II, the fifty-fourth king, were both censured by parliaments.

Eugenius VII, the fifty-ninth king, was judicially accused, and absolved by the states, of killing his wife Spondana.

Eugenius VIII, the sixty-second king, a wicked prince, was put to death by the parliament, *omnibus in ejus exitium, consentientibus*.

Donaldus, the seventieth king, is censured by a parliament, which convened, *pro salute reipublicae*, for the good of the land. So Ethus, the seventy-second king, *Ne unius culpa, regnum periret*.

Gregory, the seventy-third king, swears to maintain kirk and state in their liberties; the oath is ordained to be sworn by all kings at their coronation.

The estates complain of Duff, the seventy-eighth king, because contemning the counsel of the nobles, *Sacrificulorum consiliis abduceretur*, and that either the nobility must depart the kingdom, or another king must be made.

Culen, the seventy-ninth king, was summoned before the estates; so before him, Constantine III, the seventy-fifth king, did, by oath, resign the kingdom to the states, and entered in a monastery at St Andrews.

Kenneth III, the eightieth king, procured almost, *per vim*, says Buchanan, that the parliament should change the elective kings into hereditary; observe the power of parliaments.

After this Grim, and then Macbeth, the eighty-fifth king, is rebuked for governing by private counsel; in his time, the king is ordained by the states to swear to maintain the community of the kingdom.

When Malcom IV, the ninety-second king, would have admitted a treaty to the hurt of the kingdom, the nobles said, *Non jus esse regi*, the king had no right to take anything from the kingdom. *Nisi omnibus ordinibus consentientibus.*

In the time of Alexander, the ninety-fourth king, is ordained, *Acta regis oparteri confirmari decreto ordinum regni, quia ordinibus regni non consultis, aut adversantibus, nihil quod ad totius regni statum attinet, regi agere liceret*; so all our historians observe; by which it is clear, that the parliament, not the king, has a negative voice.

The states' answer to king Edward's legates, concerning Balzee's conditions in his contest with Bruce is that these conditions were made *a solo rege*, by the king only, without the estates of the kingdom, and therefore they did not oblige the kingdom.

In Robert the Bruce's reign, the ninety-seventh king, the succession to the crown is appointed by act of parliament, and twice changed; and in the league with France, *Quod quando de successuro rege ambigeretur apud Scotos, ea controtversia ab ordinum de creto decideretur.*

Robert, the hundredth king, in a parliament at Scoon, moved the states to appoint the earl of Carrick, his eldest son of the second marriage, to the crown, passing his children of the first marriage; and when he would have made a treaty, he was told, that he could not *inducias facere nisi ex sententia conventus publici*, he could not make truces but with the consent of the estates of parliament.

James I could not do anything in his oath in England. The parliament's approbation of the battle at Stirling against king James III is set down in the printed acts, because he had not the consent of the states.

To come to our first reformation, the queen regent, breaking her promise to the states, said, "Faith of promise should not be sought from princes;" the states answered that they then were not obliged to obey, and suspended her government as inconsistent with the duty of princes, by the articles of pacification at Leith, June 16, 1560. No peace or war can be without the states.

In the parliament thereafter (1560) the nobility say frequently to the queen. *Regum Scotorum limitatum esse imperium, nec unquam ad unius libidinem, sed ad legum praescriptum et nobilitatis consensum regi solitum.*

So it is declared, parliament at Stirling, 1578, and par;. 1567, concerning queen Mary, I need not insist here. James VI, July 21, 1567 was crowned, the earl of Morton and Hume, *jurarunt pro eo, et ejus nomine, in lege, eum doctrinam et ritus religionis, quae tum docebantur, publice quoad posset, servaturum, et contrarios oppugnaturum* (*Buch. Rer. Scot. Hist.* 1.18). The three estates revoke all alienations made by the king without consent of the parliament. Parl. 2, James VI, sections 2, 4-6.

Three parliaments of James II are held without any mention of the king, as 1437, 1438, and 1440, and acts 5 and 6 of Parl. 1440, the estates ordain the king to do such and such things, to ride through the country for doing of justice; and Parl. 1, James I. act 23, the estates ordained the king to mend his money; but show any parliament wherever the king does prescribe laws to the states, or censure the states.

In Parl. 1, James VI, the Confession of Faith being ratified, in acts made by the three estates, that the kings must swear at their coronation, "In the presence of the eternal God, that they shall maintain the true religion, right preaching, and administration of the sacraments now received and preached within this realm, and shall abolish and gain-stand all false religions contrary to the same, and shall rule the people committed to their charge, according to the will of God, laudable laws, and constitutions of the realm," &c.

The Parl. 1, James VI, 1567, approves the acts of parliament 1560, conceived only in name of the states, without the king and queen, who had deserted the same; so says the act (2, 4, 5, 20, 28). And so this parliament, wanting the king and queen's authority, is confirmed. Parl. 1572, act 51, king James VI; Parl. 1581, act 1; and Parl. 1581, act 115, in which it is declared that "They have been common laws from their first date," and are all ratified. Parl. 1587, and 1592, act 1; and stand ratified to this day by king Charles' parliament, 1633. The act of the Assembly, 1666, commends that parliament,

1560, as the "most lawful and free parliament that ever was in the kingdom."

Yea, even Parl. 1641, king Charles himself being present, an act was passed upon the occasion of the king's illegal imprisoning of the laird of Langton: that the king has no power to imprison any member of the parliament without consent of the parliament, which act, to the great prejudice of the liberty of the subject, would not have been left unprinted; for, by what law the king may imprison one member of the parliament, by that same reason he may imprison two, twenty, and a hundred; and so may he clap up the whole free estates, and where shall then the highest court of the kingdom be?

All politicians say the king is a limited prince, not absolute; where the king gives out laws, not in his own name, but in the name of himself and the estates judicially convened.

In p. 33 of the old acts of parliament, members are summoned to treat and conclude.

The duty of parliaments, and their power, according to the laws of Scotland, may be seen in the history of Knox, now printed at London (an. 1643), in the nobles proceeding with the queen, who killed her husband and married Bothwell, and was arraigned in parliament, and by a great part condemned to death; by many, to perpetual imprisonment.

After king Charles received not crown, sword, and scepter, until first he did swear the oath that king James his father did swear. He was not crowned till one of every one of the three estates came and offered to him the crown, with an express condition of his duty, before he be crowned.

After king Charles said, "I will by God's assistance bestow my life for your defense, wishing to live no longer than that I may see this kingdom flourish in happiness;" thereafter, the king showing himself on a stage to the people, the popish

LEX REX: THE LAW IS KING

archbishop said; "Sirs, I do present unto you king Charles, the right descended inheritor, the crown and dignity of this realm, appointed by the peers of the kingdom. And are you vailing to have him for your king, and become subject to him?" The king turning himself on the stage, to be seen by the people, they declared willingness, by crying, God save king Charles! Let the king live!

QUESTION 44.

GENERAL RESULTS OF THE FORMER DOCTRINE, IN SOME FEW COROLLARIES, IN TWENTY-TWO QUESTIONS.

Monarchy compared with other forms. How royalty is an issue of nature, and how magistrates as magistrates are natural. How absoluteness is not a ray of God's majesty, and resistance is not unlawful, because Christ and His apostles did not use it in some cases. Coronation is no ceremony. Men may limit the power that they gave not. The commonwealth is not a pupil or minor properly. Subjects are not more obnoxious to a king than clients, vassals, or children to their superiors. Whether subjection passive is natural. Whether king Uzziah was dethroned. Idiots and children are not complete kings. Children are kings in destination only. Denial of passive subjection in things is unlawful, not dishonorable to the king, more than denial of active obedience in the same things. The king may not make away or sell any part of his dominions. People may in some cases convene without the king. How, and in what way subjects are to pay the king's debts. Subsidies are the kingdom's due, rather than the king's. How the seas, ports, forts, castles, militia, magazine, are the king's, and how they are the kingdom's.

Quest. 1. Whether all governments be but broken governments and deviations from monarchy.

Ans. 1. It is denied: there is no less some of God's authority
in government by many, or some of the choicest of the people,
than in monarchy; nor can we judge any ordinance of man
unlawful, for we are to be subject to all for the Lord's sake (1
Pet. 2:13; Tit. 3:1; 1 Tim. 2:1-3). 2. Though monarchy should
seem the rule of all other governments, in regard of resemblance of the Supreme Monarch of all, yet it is not the moral
rule from which, if other governments shall err, they are to be
judged sinful deviations.

Quest. 2. Whether royalty is an immediate issue and spring
of nature.

Ans. No; for a man, fallen in sin, knowing naturally he has
need of a law and a government, could have, by reason, devised
governors, one or more; and the supervenient institution of
God, coming upon this ordinance, does more fully assure us,
that God, for man's good, has appointed governors; but, if
we consult with nature, many judges and governors, to fallen
nature, seem nearer of blood to nature than one only; for two,
because of man's weakness, are better than one. Now, nature
seems to me not to teach that only one sinful man should be
the sole and only ruler of a whole kingdom; God, in His word,
ever joined with the supreme ruler many rulers, who, as touching the essence of a judge (which is, to rule for God) were all
equally judges: some reserved acts, or a longer cubit of power
in regard of extent, being due to the king.

Quest. 3. Whether magistrates, as magistrates, be natural.

Ans. Nature is considered as whole and sinless, or as fall-
en and broken. In the former consideration, that man should
stand in need of some one to compel him with the sword to
do his duty, and not oppress, was no more natural to man than

to stand in need of lictors and hangmen, or physicians for the body, which in this state was not in a capacity of sickness or death; and so government by parents and husbands was only natural in the latter consideration. Magistrates, as magistrates, are two ways considered, 1. According to the knowledge of such an ordinance; 2. According to the actual erection of the practice of the office of magistrates. In the former notion, I humbly conceive that by nature's light, man now fallen and broken, even under all the fractions of the powers and faculties of the soul, does know that promises of reward, fear of punishment, and the co-active power of the sword, as Plato said, are natural means to move us, and wings to promote obedience and to do our duty; and that government by magistrates is natural. But, in the second relation, it is hard to determine that kings, rather than other governors, are more natural.

Quest. 4. Whether nature has determined that there should be one supreme ruler, a king, or many rulers, in a free community.

Ans. It is denied.

Quest. 5. Whether every free commonwealth has not in it a supremacy of majesty, which it may formally place in one or many.

Ans. It is affirmed.

Quest. 6. Whether absolute and unlimited power of royalty be a ray and beam of divine majesty immediately derived from God?

Ans. Not at all. Such a creature is not in the world of God's creation. Royalists and flatterers of kings are parents to this prodigious birth. There is no shadow of power to do ill in God. An absolute power is essentially a power to do without or above law, and a power to do ill, to destroy; and so it cannot come from God as a moral power by institution, though it come from God by a flux of permissive providence; but so things unlawful and sinful come from God.

Quest. 7. Whether the king may in his actions intend his own prerogative and absoluteness.

Ans. He can neither intend it as his nearest end, nor as his remote end. Not the former, for if he fight and destroy his people for a prerogative, he destroys his people that he may have a power to destroy them, which must be mere tyranny, nor can it be his remote end; for, granting that his supposed absolute prerogative were lawful he is to refer all lawful power and all his actions to a more noble end, namely, to the safety and good of the people.

Quest. 8. Do not they that resist the parliament's power, resist the parliament; and they that resist the king's power, resist the king; God has joined king and power: who dare separate them?

Ans. 1. If the parliament abuse their power, we may resist their abused power, and not their power parliamentary. Mr. Bridges does well distinguish (in his Annotations on the "Loyal Convert ") between the king's power, and the king's will. 2. The resistors do not separate king and power, but the king himself does separate his lawful power from his will, if he would and act tyranny out of this principle, will, passion, lust; not out of the royal principle of kingly power. So far we may resist the one, and not the other.

Quest. 9. Why, if God might work a miracle in the three children's resistance active, why does he evidence omnipotence in the passive obedience of these witnesses? The kingdom of Judah was Christ's birth-right, as man and David's son. Why did he not, by legions of men and angels, rather vindicate his own flesh and blood, than triumph by non-resistance, and the omnipotence of glory to shine in his mere suffering?

Ans. Who are you that dispute with God? He that kills with the jaw-bone of an ass, thousands, and he that destroyed the numberless Midianites by only three hundred, should no more put the three children to an unlawful act in the one, if they had by three men killed Nebuchadnezzar and all his subjects, than in the other. But nothing is said against us in a sophism a *non causa pro causa;* unless it be proved, God would neither deliver his three children, nor Christ from death, and the Jews from bondage, by miraculous resistance, because resistance is unlawful. And if patient suffering is lawful, therefore, is resistance unlawful? It is a poor consequent, and a begging of the question: both must be lawful to us; and so we hold, of ten lawful means, fit to accomplish God's blessed end, He may choose one and let go nine. Shall any infer, therefore, these other nine means are unlawful, because God chose a means different from those nine, and refused them? So may I answer by retortion. The three hundred sinned in resisting Midian, and defeating them. Why? Because it should be more honor to God, if they had, by suffering patiently the sword of Midian, glorified God in martyrdom. So Christ and the apostles, who could have wrought miracles, might have wrought reformation by the sword, and destroyed kings and emperors, the opposers of the Lamb; and they did reform by suffering; therefore, the sword is unlawful in reformation. It follows not. The means Christ used, is lawful; therefore, all other means that he used not, are unlawful. It is vain logic.

Quest. 10. Whether the coronation of a king is any other thing but a ceremony.

Ans. In the coronation there is, and may be, the ceremony of a shout and an acclamation, and the placing of a scepter in his right hand who is made king, and the like; but the coronation, *in concreto,* according to the substance of the act, is no

ceremony, nor any accidental ingredient in the constitution of
a king. 1. Because Israel should have performed a mere ceremonial action on Saul when they made him king, which we
cannot say; for as the people's act of coronation is distinctive,
so is it constitutive: it distinguished Saul from all Israel, and
did constitute him in a new relation, that he was changed
from no king to be a king. 2. The people cannot, by a ceremony, make a king; they must really put some honor on him, that
was not put on him before. Now this ceremony, which royalists do fancy coronation to be, is only symbolic and declarative, not really creative. It places nothing in the king.

Quest. 11. Whether subjects may limit the power that they
gave not to the king, it being the immediate result (without
intervening of law or any act of man) issuing from God only.

Ans. 1. Though we should allow (which in reason we cannot grant) that royal power were a result of the immediate
bounty of God, without any act of man, yet it may be limited
by men that it over-swell not its banks. Though God immediately make Peter an apostle, without any act of men, yet Paul,
by a sharp rebuke (Gal. 2) curbs and limits his power, that he
abuse it not to Judaizing. Royalists deny not, but they teach,
that the eighty priests that restrained Uzziah's power "from
burning incense to the Lord," gave no royal power to Uzziah.
Do not subjects, by flight, lay restraint upon a king's power,
that he kill not the subjects without cause? Yet they teach
that subjects gave no power to the king. Certainly this is a
proof of the immediate power of the King of kings that none
can fly from his pursuing hand (Ps. 139:1-3; Amos 9:1-4)
whereas men may fly from earthly kings. Nebuchadnezzar, as
royalists teach, might justly conquer some kingdoms, for conquest is a just title to the crown, say they. Now, the conqueror
then justly not only limits the royal power of the conquered,

king, but wholly removes his royalty and unkings him; yet, we know, the conqueror gave no royal power to the conquered king. Joshua and David took away royal power which they never gave, and therefore this is no good reason, the people gave not to the king royal power; therefore they could not lawfully limit it and take it away. 2. We cannot admit that God gives royal power immediately, without the intervention of any act of law; for it is an act of law, that the people chooses such a king, not such a king (Deut. 17); that the people, by a legal covenant, make Saul, David, and Joash, kings, and that God exercises any political action of making a king over such subjects, upon such a condition is absurd and inconceivable; for how can God make Saul and David kings of Israel upon this political and legal condition that they rule in justice and judgment, but there must intervene a political action? And so they are not made kings immediately. If God feed Moses by bread and manna, the Lord's act of feeding is mediate, by the mediation of second causes; if he feed Moses forty days without eating anything, the act of feeding is immediate; if God made David king, as he made him a prophet, I should think God immediately made him king; for God asked consent of no man, of no people, no, not of David himself, before he infused in him the spirit of prophecy; but he made him formally king, by the political and legal covenant between him and the people. I shall not think that a covenant and oath of God is a ceremony, especially a law-covenant, or a political paction between David and the people, the contents of which were fitly *de materia gravi et onerosa*, concerning a great part of obedience to the fifth commandment of God's moral law, the duties moral concerning religion, and mercy, and justice, to be performed reciprocally between king and people. Oaths, I hope, are more than ceremonies.

Quest. 12. Whether or not the commonwealth is not ever a pupil, never growing to age, as a minor under nonage does come not to need a tutor, but the commonwealth being still in need of a tutor, a governor, or king, must always be a tutor, and so the kingdom can never come to that condition as to accuse the king, it always being minor.

Ans. 1. Then can they never accuse inferior judges, for a kingdom is perpetually in such a nonage, as it cannot want them, when sometimes it wants a king. 2. Can the commonwealth, under democracy and aristocracy, being perpetually under nonage, ever then quarrel at these governments and never seek a king? By this reason they cannot. 3. The king, in all respects, is not a tutor-every comparison in something bears a leg; for the commonwealth, in their own persons, do choose a king, complain of a king, and resist an Uzziah, and tie their elective prince to a law. A pupil cannot choose his tutor, either his dying father, or the living law does that service for him; he cannot resist his tutor, he cannot tie his tutor to a law, nor limit him, when first he chooses him. *Pupillo non licet postulare tutorem suspecti, quamdiu sub tutela est, et manet impubes.*[1]

Quest. 13. Whether or not subjects are more obnoxious to a king than clients to patrons, and servants to masters, because the patron cannot be the client's judge, but some superior magistrate must judge both, and the slave had no refuge against his master, but only flight; and the king does confer infinite greater benefits on the subjects, than the master does on the slave, because he exposes his life, pleasure, ease, credit, and all for the safety of his subjects.[2]

---

1. *l. Pietatis 6, in sin.* section *de susp. Tutor. L. impuberem,* 7, and section *impuberes. Just. eod*
2. *De authorit. princip.,* section 3, n. 6.

Ans. 1. It is denied, for to draw the case to fathers and lords, in respect of children and vassals, the reason why sons, clients, vassals, can neither formally judge, nor judicially punish, fathers, patrons, lords, and masters, though never so tyrannical, is a moral impotence, or a political incongruity, because these relations of patron and client, fathers and children, are supposed to be in a community, in which are rulers and judges above the father and son, the patron and the client; but there is no physical incongruity that the political inferior punish the superior, if we suppose there were no judges on the earth, and no relation but patron and client; and, because, for the father to destroy the children is a troubling of the harmony of nature, and the highest degree of violence, therefore one violence of self-defense, and that most just, though contrary to nature, must be a remedy against another violence; but in a kingdom there is no political ruler above both king and people, and therefore, though nature have not formally appointed the political relation of a king rather than many governors and subjects, yet has nature appointed a court and tribunal of necessity, in which the people may, by innocent violence, repress the unjust violence of an injuring prince, so as the people injured in the matter of self-defense may be their own judge.

2. I wonder that any should teach that oppressed slaves had of old no refuge against the tyranny of masters, but only flight; for (1) the law expressly says that they might not only fly but also change masters, which we all know was a great damage to the master, to whom the servant was as good as money in the purse; (2) I have demonstrated before, by the law of nature, and out of various learned jurists, that all inferiors may defend themselves by opposing violence against unjust violence; to say nothing that unanswerably I have proved that the kingdom is superior to the king.

3. It is true. *Qui plus dat, plus obligat,* as the Scripture says (Luke 7) he that gives a greater benefit lays a foundation of a greater obligation. But, 1. If benefit be compared with benefit, it is disputable if

a king give a greater benefit than an earthly father, to whom, under God, the son is debtor for life and being, if we regard the compensation of eminency of honor and riches, that the people puts upon the king; but I utterly deny that a power to act tyrannical acts, is any benefit or obligation, that the people in reason can lay upon their prince, as a compensation or hire for his great pains he takes in his royal watch-tower. I judge it no benefit, but a great hurt, damage, and an ill of nature, both to king and people, that the people should give to their prince any power to destroy themselves, and therefore that people do reverence and honor the prince most, who lay strongest chains and iron fetters on him, that he cannot tyrannize.

Quest. 14. But are not subjects more subject to their prince (seeing the subjection is natural, as we see bees and cranes) to obey him, than servants to their Lord?[1] For jurists teach, that servitude is beside or against nature.[2]

Ans. There is no question, in active subjection to princes and fathers commanding in the Lord, we shall grant as high a measure as you desire. But the question is, if either active subjection to ill and unjust mandates, or passive subjection to penal inflictions of tyranny and abused power, be natural or most natural; or if subjects do renounce natural subjection to their prince, when they oppose violence to unjust violence. This is to beg the question. And for the commonwealth of bees and cranes, and crown and scepter among them, give me leave to doubt of it. To be subject to kings is a divine moral law of God; but not properly natural to be subject to co-action of the sword. Government and subjection to parents, is natural; but that a king is *juris naturae strictim*, I must crave leave to doubt. I hold him to be a divine moral ordinance, to which, in conscience, we are to submit in the Lord.

---

1. *De anthorit. princip. in popul.*, section 3, n. 7; *C. in Apib*, 7, 9, 1, *ex Hiero.* 4, *ad Rusic. Monach, Plin*, n. 17.
2. *l. 5, de stat. homi. sect*, 2, *just. et jur. pers.* section 3, *sect, et sicut Nov.* 89, *quib. med. nat. eff. sui*

Quest. 15. Whether king Uzziah was dethroned by the people?

Ans. Though we should say he was not formally unkinged and de-throned, yet if the royal power consist in an indivisible point, as some royalists say, and if Uzziah was removed to a private house, and could not reign, being a leper; certainly much royal power was taken from. It is true, Arnisaeus says he neither could be compelled to resign his power, nor was he compelled to resign his royal authority but he will-ingly resigned actual government, and remained king, as tutors and curators are put upon kings that are mad or stupid, and children, who yet govern all by the authority of lawful kings.[3] But that Uzziah did not deprive himself of the royal power voluntarily is clear. The reason why he dwelt in a house apart, and did not actually reign, is, because he was a leper; for, "He was cut off (says the text) from the house of the Lord; and Jotham, his son, was over the king's house, judging the people of the land" (2 Chron. 26:21), by which it is clear, by the express law of God, he being a leper, and so not by law to enter into the congregation, he was cut off from the house of the Lord; and he being passive is said to be cut off from the Lord's house. Whether, then, Uzziah turned necessity to a virtue, I know not: it is evident, that God's law removed the actual exercise of his power. If we obtain this, which God's word does give us, we have enough for our purpose, though Uzziah kept the naked title of a king, as indeed he took but up room in the catalogue of kings. Now, if by law he was cut off from actual governing, whether he was willing or not willing to deprive himself of reigning, is all one. And to say that furious men, idiots, stupid men, and children, who must do all royal acts by curators and tutors, are kings *jure*, with correction, is *petitio principii;* for then has God infused immediately from heaven (as royalists teach us) a royal power to govern a kingdom on those who are as capable of royalty as blocks. I conceive that the Lord (Deut. 17:14-17) commands the

---

3. *De jure Pontif. Rom. in Regna et Princ.,* section 5, n. 30.

people to make no blocks kings; and that the Lord has not done that himself in a binding law to us, which we have no commandment from him to do. I conceive that God made Josiah and Joash kings typical, and in destination, for His promise sake to David, while they were children, as well as he made them kings; but not *actu completo raitione officii* to be a rule to us now, to make a child of six years of age a king by office. I conceive children are to us only kings in destination and appointment; and for idiots and fools, I shall not believe (let royalists break their faith upon so rocky and stony a point, at their pleasure) that God has made them governors of others, by royal office, who can scarce number their own fingers; or that God ties a people to acknowledge stupid blocks for royal governors of a kingdom, who cannot govern themselves. But far be it from me to argue with Bellarmine (*de paenit.* 1.3.2) from Uzziah's bodily leprosy to infer that any prince who is spiritually leprous and turned heretical is presently to be dethroned. Nothing can dethrone a king but such tyranny as is inconsistent with his royal office. Nor dared I infer that kings, nowadays, may be removed from actual government for one single transgression. It is true, eighty priests, and the whole kingdom, so serving king Uzziah (their motives, I know, were divine) proves well that the subjects may punish the transgression of God's express law in the king, in some cases even to remove him from the throne; but as from God's commanding to stone the man that gathered sticks on the Sabbath day, we cannot infer that Sabbath-breakers are now to be punished with death; yet we may well argue, Sabbath-breakers may be punished, and Sabbath-breakers are not unpunishable, and above all law; so may we argue here, Uzziah, though a king, was punished; therefore kings are punishable by subjects.

Quest. 16. Whether or no, as the denial of active obedience in things unlawful is not dishonorable to the king, as king, he being obliged to command in the Lord only, so the denial of passive subjection to the king using unjust violence, be also no dishonoring of the king.

Ans. As the king is under God's law both in commanding and in exacting active obedience, so is he under the same regulating law of God, in punishing or demanding of us passive subjection, and as he may not command what he will, but what the King of kings warrants him to command, so may he not punish as he will, but by warrant also of the Supreme Judge of all the earth; and therefore it is not dishonorable to the majesty of the ruler, that we deny passive subjection to him when he punishes beside his warrant, more than it is against his majesty and honor that we deny active obedience when he commands illegally; else I see not how it is lawful to fly from a tyrannical king, as Elijah, Christ, and other of the witnesses of our Lord have done; and, therefore, what royalists say here is a great untruth, namely, that in things lawful we must be subject actively, in things unlawful, passively. For as we are in things lawful to be subject actively, so there is no duty in point of conscience, laying on us to be subject passively, because I may lawfully fly, and so lawfully deny passive subjection to the king's will, punishing unjustly.

Quest. 17. Whether the prince may make away any part of his dominions, as an island, or a kingdom, for the safety of the whole kingdoms he has; as if goods be like to sink an over-burdened ship, the seamen cast away a part of the goods in the sea, to save the lives of the whole passengers; and if three thousand passengers being in one ship, and the ship in a storm like to be lost, it would seem that a thousand may be cast over board, to save the lives of the whole passengers.

Ans. The kingdom being not the king's proper heritage, it would seem he cannot make away any part of his kingdom to save the whole, without the express consent of that part, though they be made away to save the whole. In things of this kind, men are not as the commodities of merchants, nor is the case alike; as when one thousand, of three thousand are to be cast into the sea to save all the rest, and that either by common consent, or by lots, or some other way; for it is one thing, when destruction is evidently inevitable, as in the casting so many men into the sea to save the whole and many passengers, and when a king for peace, or for help from another king, makes away part of his dominion. The Lord is here to be waited on in his good providence, and events are to be committed to him; but far less, can it be imaginably lawful for a king to make away a part of his dominions without their consent, that he may have help from a foreign prince to destroy the rest: this were to make merchandise of the lives of men.[1]

Quest. 18. Whether or not the convening of the subjects, without the king's will, be unlawful.

Ans. The convention of men, of itself, is an indifferent thing, and takes its specification from its causes, and manner of convening, though some convention of the subjects without the king, be forbidden; yet *ratio legis est anima legis*, the reason and intent of the law, is the soul of the law. Convention of the subjects, in a tumultuary way, for a seditious end, to make war without warrant of law is forbidden; but not when religion, laws, liberties, invasion of foreign enemies necessitate the subjects to convene, though the king and ordinary judicatures, going a corrupt way to pervert judgment, shall refuse to consent to their conventions. Upon which ground, no convention of tables at Edinburgh, or any other place (an. 1637, 1638, 1639) can be judged there unlawful; for if these be unlawful, because they are conventions of the leagues, without express act of parliament, then the convention of the leagues to quench a house on fire, and the convention of a country to pursue a wolf entered in the land to destroy women and children, which are warranted by the law of nature, should be lawless, or against acts of parliament.

Quest. 19. Whether the subjects be obliged to pay the debts of the king.

Ans. These debts which the king contracts as king, *in throno regali*, the people are to pay. For the law of nature and the divine law does

---

1. Illust. quest. 1.1, section 8, n. 8.

prove, that to every servant and minister wages is due (Rom. 13:5-6, compared with verse 4, and 1 Cor. 9:9-12; 1 Tim. 5:18). If the prince be taken in a war, for the defense of the people, it is just that he be redeemed by them: so the law says (*it. F. et C. de negotiis getis, et F. et C. Manda*) But, Ferdinandus Vasquez says, if the prince was not doing the business of the public, and did make war without advice and consent of the people, then are they not to redeem him.[2] Now certain it is, when the king raises war, and says, "God do so to me and mine, if I intend anything but peace," yet makes war not only against his oath, but also without consent of the parliament, and a parliament at that time convocated by his own royal writ, and not raised, and dissolved at all, but still sitting formally a parliament; if he borrow money from his own subjects, and from foreign princes, to raise war against his subjects and parliament, then the people are not obliged to pay his debts, 1. Because they are obliged to the king only as a king, and not as an enemy; but in so raising war he cannot he considered as a king. 2. Though if the people agree with him, and still acknowledge him king; it is impossible, *physice*, he can be their king, and they not pay his debts; yet they sin not, but may, *ex decentia, non ex debito legali*, pay his debts, yet are they not obliged by any law of God or man to pay his debts. But though it be true, by all law the king is obliged to pay his debt (unless we say, that all the people's goods are the king's: a compendious way, I confess, to pay all that any voluptuous Heliogabolus shall contract) yet it may easily be proved that what his subjects and foreign princes lent him to the raising of an unjust war are not properly debts, but expenses unjustly given out under the reduplication of formal enemies to the country, and so not payable by the subjects; and this is evident by law, because one may give most unjustly monies to his neighbor, under the notion of loan, which yet has nothing of the essence of loan and debt, but is mere delapidation,

---

2. Illust, quest. l.1.7, n. 6, *vicesimo tertio apparet*, &c

and cannot properly be debt by God's law; for the law regulates a man in borrowing and lending, as in other politic actions. If I, out of desire of revenge, should lend monies to a robber to buy powder and fuel to burn an innocent city, or to buy armor to kill innocent men, I deny that that is legally debt. I dispute not whether A. B., borrowing money formally, that thereby he may waste it on debauchery, shall be obliged to repay it to C. D. under the reduplication of debt; or if the borrower be obliged to pay what the lender has unjustly lent. I care not pray to God that all our king's debts may be paid; I have scarce faith so to do.

Quest. 20. Whether subsidies be due to the king as king.

Ans. There is a twofold subsidy; one *debitum*, of debt; another, *charitativum,* by way of charity. A subsidy of debt is rather the kingdom's due for their necessity than the king's due, as a part of his rent. We read of customs due to the king as king, and for conscience sake (Rom. 13:6) never of a subsidy or taxation to the kings of Israel and Judah, at any convention of the states. Augustus Caesar's taxing of all the world (Luke 2) for the maintenance of wars, cannot be the proper rent of Augustus, as emperor, but the rent of the Roman empire; and it is but the act of a man. Charitative subsidies to the king, of indulgence, because, through bad husbanding of the king's rents, he has contracted debts, I judge no better than royal and princely begging. Yet lawful they are, as owe charity to my brother, so to my father, so to my politic father the king. See Ferd. Vasq who desires that superiors, under the name of charity, hide not rapine (illust. quest. 1.1.8), and cites Cicero, gravely saying (*offic.* l.1) "*Nulla generi humano et justitios major pestis est, quam eorum, qui dum maxime fallunt, id agunt ut boni viri esse videantur,*" &c.

Quest. 21. Whether the seas, floods, roadways, castles, ports, public magazine, militia, armor, forts, and strongholds be the king's.

Ans. All these may be understood to be the king's in various notions. 1. The are the king's, *quoad custodiam, et publicam possessionem*, as
a pawn is the man's in whose hand the pawn is laid down.

2. They are the king's, *quoad jurisdictionem cumulativam, non priva-
tivam*. The king is to direct, and royally to command, that the castles,
forts, ports, strongholds, armor, marine, militia, be employed for the
safety of we kingdom. All the ways, bridges, and public roadways, are
the king's, insofar as he, as a public and royal watchman, is to secure
the subject from robbers, and to cognosce of unknown murders, by
himself and the inferior judges; yet may not the king employ any of
these against the kingdom. 3. They are the king's, as he is king, *quoad
offcallem, et regale, et publicam proprietatem*; for he has a royal and
princely propriety to all these, as his own, insofar as he uses them
according to law. 4. And thus they are the king's also, *quoad usum*, in
regard of official use. But, 1. They are the kingdom's, *quoad fructum*, in
regard of the effect and fruit. 2. They are the kingdom's, *finaliter*, being
destined for the safety and security of the kingdom.

3. They are the kingdom's, *quoad proprietotem propriam, et legalem
stricte sumptam*, according to the proper and legal propriety; and are
not the king's proper heritage as he is a man: 1. Because he may not
sell these forts, strongholds, ports, magazine, bridges, &c. to a stranger, or a foreign prince. 2. When the king is dead, and his heirs and
royal line interrupted, these all remain proper to the kingdom; yet so
as the state cannot, as they are men, make them away, or sell them,
more than the king; for no public persons, yea the multitude cannot
make away the security, safety, and that which necessarily conduces
to the security of the posterity. "The Lord build his own Zion, and
appoint salvation for walls and bulwarks!"

Made in the USA
Coppell, TX
10 October 2021

63810863R00341